THE PRACTICE OF COGNITIVE-BEHAVIOURAL HYPNOTHERAPY

THE PRACTICE OF COGNITIVE-BEHAVIOURAL HYPNOTHERAPY
A Manual for Evidence-Based Clinical Hypnosis

Donald J. Robertson

Routledge
Taylor & Francis Group
LONDON AND NEW YORK

First published 2013 by Karnac Books Ltd.

Published 2018 by Routledge
2 Park Square, Milton Park, Abingdon, Oxon OX14 4RN
711 Third Avenue, New York, NY 10017, USA

Routledge is an imprint of the Taylor & Francis Group, an informa business

Copyright © 2013 by Donald J. Robertson

The right of Donald J. Robertson to be identified as the author of this work has been asserted in accordance with §§ 77 and 78 of the Copyright Design and Patents Act 1988.

All rights reserved. No part of this book may be reprinted or reproduced or utilised in any form or by any electronic, mechanical, or other means, now known or hereafter invented, including photocopying and recording, or in any information storage or retrieval system, without permission in writing from the publishers.

Notice:
Product or corporate names may be trademarks or registered trademarks, and are used only for identification and explanation without intent to infringe.

British Library Cataloguing in Publication Data

A C.I.P. for this book is available from the British Library

ISBN-13: 9781855755307 (pbk)

Typeset by V Publishing Solutions Pvt Ltd., Chennai, India

CONTENTS

ACKNOWLEDGEMENTS   *vii*

ABOUT THE AUTHOR   *ix*

FOREWORD   *xi*

NOTE ON TERMINOLOGY AND CITATIONS   *xiii*

PART I: THE COGNITIVE-BEHAVIOURAL APPROACH TO HYPNOSIS

CHAPTER ONE
Introduction to cognitive-behavioural hypnotherapy   3

CHAPTER TWO
James Braid and the original hypnotherapy   31

CHAPTER THREE
Cognitive-behavioural theories of hypnosis   81

PART II: ASSESSMENT, CONCEPTUALISATION, AND HYPNOTIC SKILLS

CHAPTER FOUR
Assessment in cognitive-behavioural hypnotherapy   119

CHAPTER FIVE
Case formulation in cognitive-behavioural hypnotherapy — 141

CHAPTER SIX
Socialisation and hypnotic skills training — 183

PART III: COGNITIVE-BEHAVIOURAL HYPNOTHERAPY

CHAPTER SEVEN
Applied self-hypnosis and coping skills — 215

CHAPTER EIGHT
Affect: hypnotic exposure therapy — 275

CHAPTER NINE
Behaviour: Problem-Solving Hypnotherapy (PSH) — 311

CHAPTER TEN
Cognition: cognitive hypnotherapy — 355

CHAPTER ELEVEN
Conclusion and summary — 415

REFERENCES — 419

INDEX — 431

ACKNOWLEDGEMENTS

I would like to thank my fellow countryman James Braid for allowing me to benefit, over 150 years on, from his perseverance in the face of opposition, and his vigorous "common sense" philosophy of hypnotic therapeutics. Braid was a man of integrity who offered free treatment to many patients in his region and never sought to profit from his discovery. He continued to test and revise his views throughout his career and to share his knowledge and skills generously with others.

I thank my loving wife, Mandy, for her patience, help, and support. Thanks are also due to Daisy Robertson for her professional advice on the fine nuances of that difficult subject, the psycho-physiology of hypnotic catalepsy. I'd like to dedicate this book to my daughter, Poppy Louise Robertson, who was born when I was in the middle of writing it. I love you, Poppy. (Please stop trying to playing drums on my laptop's keyboard, though!)

ABOUT THE AUTHOR

Donald Robertson is a registered psychotherapist (UKCP/EAP) in private practice, specialising in clinical hypnosis and cognitive-behavioural therapy (CBT). He has been working as a therapist since 1996, and is currently the principal of the UK College of Hypnosis & Hypnotherapy, a private training provider.

Donald has published dozens of articles on hypnosis, philosophy, and psychotherapy in professional journals and periodicals. He is the author of *Build your Resilience* (Hodder), *The Philosophy of Cognitive-Behavioural Therapy* (Karnac), and the editor of *The Discovery of Hypnosis: The Complete Writings of James Braid, the Father of Hypnotherapy* (NCH). He regularly speaks at conferences and other events on issues such as hypnosis and philosophy in psychotherapy.

Donald originally comes from Ayr, on the West coast of Scotland. He previously worked as a counsellor with young offenders, drug users, and schoolchildren, before opening his private practice in Harley Street, London. He studied Mental Philosophy at Aberdeen University before completing his Masters degree in Psychoanalytic Studies at the Centre for Psychotherapeutic Studies, Sheffield University. He holds a number of qualifications in different therapeutic approaches, including two practitioner diplomas in CBT, one from the Centre for Stress Management and the other from Kings College, London.

FOREWORD

Over the last thirty years, the most significant development in the field of psychotherapy has been cognitive behavioural therapy (CBT). In terms of the standards and criteria under which any system of psychotherapy is nowadays evaluated, CBT ticks all of the boxes: a clear rationale with a solid grounding in mainstream psychology and its related disciplines; a rational and informed understanding of the problems and disorders that come within its scope; a coherent, and structured, approach to treatment that is informed by rigorous assessment, formulation, and clear goals; a commitment to continuous research into theory, process, and outcome; and many more. This is not to say that CBT is uncontroversial and without critics, but over the years it has proved flexible and able to incorporate new ideas and variations, thus extending the legitimate scope of its application over an astonishingly wide range. This progress continues unabated.

What about hypnotherapy? It may be argued that hypnotherapy as it is practiced today has been with us for much longer than CBT. Yet it has struggled to establish itself with anything like the same success as CBT. One reason may be that, over the years, many publications concerning hypnosis and hypnotherapy—articles and, particularly, books—have often been of poor or indifferent quality, their authors frequently failing to acknowledge the importance of the above standards and criteria for developing a psychological therapy. But there is another likely reason. It is often said that hypnosis is, for most purposes, not a therapy in itself; it is an *adjunct* to therapy, whether that therapy be psychodynamic, humanistic, behavioural, cognitive, and so on. And now that hypnosis is well-established as a real psychological phenomenon with a sound evidence base, we can make that statement with due confidence.

It is natural therefore that psychotherapists should look to ways of integrating hypnosis with CBT that enhance the scope and effectiveness of the latter, and thus establish what may be justifiably called 'cognitive-behavioural hypnotherapy'. And in this book, Donald Robertson proves that he is the right person for this task. First and foremost he approaches the subject matter with the same high standard of scholarship that is evident in his previous publication *The Discovery of Hypnosis*, and this includes careful attention to the historical context and to theoretical matters that inform the rationale of his approach. Readers who are already practitioners of CBT will appreciate the author's emphasis on therapy as a collaborative process and the importance of a thorough assessment and a careful formulation, without which therapy lacks a firm anchor. Due regard is also paid to preparing the patient for therapy. The author describes in detail how hypnotic procedures may be integrated with CBT, demonstrating this with a range of cognitive and behavioural methods such as exposure, reality testing, cognitive restructuring, and covert behavioural methods. His approach is well structured but flexible, and he demonstrates a firm grasp of his subject matter, which is considerable in scope. In particular, I believe he will convince readers who are already CBT therapists that learning how to include hypnosis in their repertoire of skills will pay them and their clients significant dividends. And those hypnotherapists wishing to incorporate CBT into their practice will be amply rewarded.

With *The Practice of Cognitive-Behavioural Hypnotherapy* the author has demonstrated the exacting standards by which all books on therapeutic hypnosis should be judged. I commend it to the reader.

Dr. Michael Heap
Author (with H. B. Gibson) of *Hypnosis in Therapy* (1991) and (with K. K. Aravind)
of *Hartland's Medical and Dental Hypnosis*, 4th Edition (2002).

NOTE ON TERMINOLOGY AND CITATIONS

There is some disagreement over the terminology in relation to hypnosis. I have preferred to use the term "hypnotism" to refer to the *practice* or *method* of the operator, and "hypnosis" for the *condition* of the hypnotic subject, although Braid used "hypnotism" for both and others use "hypnosis" for both. Some authors spurn the term "hypnotherapy" because they object to the connotation that hypnotism alone can constitute a therapy, and prefer to use the term "clinical hypnosis" to refer to the technique used as an adjunct to other psychological therapies such as cognitive-behavioural therapy (CBT). Likewise, the term "hypno-psychotherapy" is sometimes used by others to denote the incorporation of hypnosis within an integrative approach to psychotherapy. I will use the term "hypnotherapy", however, as it's so commonly employed and tends to make things slightly clearer to understand and easier to read at times. I do not believe that hypnosis constitutes a therapy in itself, though, but agree that it must generally be integrated with elements of other psychological therapies, such as CBT.

I've generally referred throughout to the hypnotist as "he" and his therapy client or hypnotic subject as "she" to help distinguish the two roles and because I am male and the majority of my own clients are female.

Unless otherwise stated, all quotations from James Braid are from *The Discovery of Hypnosis: The Complete Writings of James Braid* (2009), edited by Donald Robertson.

PART I

THE COGNITIVE-BEHAVIOURAL APPROACH TO HYPNOSIS

CHAPTER ONE

Introduction to cognitive-behavioural hypnotherapy

What do we mean by "cognitive-behavioural hypnotherapy" (CBH)? This term is sometimes used to refer to the integration of hypnosis with cognitive-behavioural therapy (CBT). However, as we shall see, it may also denote the adoption of a cognitive-behavioural reconceptualisation of hypnosis, which replaces the notion of "hypnotic trance" with an explanation based upon more ordinary psychological processes. In a sense, though, the practice of cognitive-behavioural hypnotherapy actually *predates* modern cognitive-behavioural therapy, although they are intimately connected. As we shall see in later chapters, the founder of hypnotism, James Braid, adopted an approach based on the Victorian philosophical psychology known as Scottish "common sense" realism, which arguably contains concepts that prefigure those of later cognitive-behavioural theorists. Hypnotism was discovered by Braid in 1841, and entailed a more common sense psychological explanation of the apparent effects of Mesmerism. Braid defined hypnotism as focused attention upon an expectant dominant idea or image (Braid, 2009). Later, Hippolyte Bernheim, perhaps the second most important figure in the history of hypnotism, said that there was no such thing as "hypnosis" other than heightened suggestibility, and named his approach "suggestive therapeutics" (Bernheim, 1887). Indeed, hypnotism is essentially the art and science of suggestion, and *not* that of inducing "trances" or altered states of consciousness. Hypnotherapy is therefore the therapy of "imaginative suggestion", of words that are used to stimulate the conscious imagination profoundly enough to bring about genuine therapeutic change.

Much of what we now know about the subject was first expressed in the original writings of Braid, who coined the term "hypnotism". He developed his theory and practice of hypnotism through constant experimentation and by carrying out public demonstrations in front of some of the leading scientists and academics of his day, one of whom, Prof. William B. Carpenter, became his ally and provided the original "ideo-motor reflex" conceptualisation of hypnotism, which we shall explore in more detail shortly. However, psychologists up to the present day have continued to carry out important research on hypnosis and its clinical applications. Some of the main researchers in the history of hypnotism were also key figures in the field of behavioural psychology, most notably Ivan Pavlov, Clark Hull, and Hans Eysenck. Their contributions influenced the theory and practice of hypnotism and, subsequently, the development of behaviour therapy in the 1950s, the precursor of modern cognitive-behavioural therapy. By providing a brief outline of the history of cognitive-behavioural hypnotherapy, then, we may come to a better understanding of its nature and its relationship with behaviour therapy and CBT.

The first point worth noting is perhaps that the cardinal technique of early behaviour therapy, systematic desensitisation, both greatly resembles behavioural hypnotherapy and was apparently derived from it. In fact, Joseph Wolpe, the developer of systematic desensitisation and arguably the founder of behaviour therapy, originally described his technique as "*hypnotic desensitisation*" (Wolpe, 1958, p. 203; Wolpe, 1954). As we shall discuss in more detail later, Wolpe based his own hypnotic induction technique on the earlier writings of Lewis Wolberg, whose well-known and influential textbook *Medical Hypnosis* described a similar *hypnotherapeutic* technique explained in terms of the same conditioning principles derived from behavioural psychology (Wolberg, 1948a). Likewise, Andrew Salter, one of the co-founders of behaviour therapy and the main pioneer of assertiveness training, was a hypnotist and one of the first authors to describe hypnotic skills training. Salter closely based both his approach to hypnotism and his behaviour therapy, called "conditioned reflex therapy", on the theories of Pavlov and Hull (Salter, 1949). Hypnotists can therefore plausibly argue that desensitisation, and many other, early behaviour therapy techniques, were already part of the armamentarium of behavioural hypnotherapy, and based on similar conceptualisations of the problem and treatment. Other early behaviour therapy techniques such as covert sensitisation (called "hypnotic aversion therapy" by hypnotists), covert (mental) rehearsal of behaviour, thought-stopping, relaxation training, meditation, etc., were also apparently derived from behavioural approaches to hypnotherapy, or at least preceded by them. Indeed, in the 1970s, Andre Weitzenhoffer, one of the leading researchers in the field of hypnosis, published a literature review illustrating the extent to which, for many decades, hypnotherapists had employed behavioural psychology concepts, derived from Hull and Pavlov, and used techniques overlapping behaviour therapy, forming an approach sometimes called "behavioural hypnotherapy" (Weitzenhoffer A. M., 1972). More recently, the hypnosis researcher Irving Kirsch has emphasised that, in particular, many imagery-based techniques found in behaviour therapy and CBT, such as systematic desensitisation, covert sensitisation, and covert modelling basically resemble typical hypnotic interventions, "minus the *hypnosis* label" (Kirsch, 1999, p. 217).

In addition to the long-standing and important links between behaviour therapy and hypnosis in the West, an early relationship developed between hypnosis and conditioning theories in Russia. Under the Soviet Union, hypnotism and psychotherapy developed in a direction sharply contrasting with the widespread adoption of psychoanalysis in America and Western Europe. Early Soviet psychotherapy was prominently based upon Pavlov's "cortical inhibition" theory of hypnosis and conditioning model of suggestion. In the heyday of Freudian psychoanalysis, which lacked any real empirical support, Soviet researchers were promoting a brief hypnotic conditioning therapy supported by relatively extensive clinical and experimental evidence (Platonov, 1959). In the 1940s and 1950s, when Pavlovian hypnotic psychotherapy became better known in the West, as Freudian psychoanalysis declined in popularity, it also became one of the inspirations for early behaviour therapy. As well as contributing to, or mirroring, the development of early behaviour therapy, these historical influences continued to shape the development of hypnotherapy throughout the latter part of the twentieth century and beyond, although their importance was, for a time, eclipsed by the influence of Milton Erickson, who adopted a more idiosyncratic and less empirical approach.

Of course, hypnotism is essentially a cognitive procedure: hypnotic suggestions are intended to evoke ideas (cognitions) that lead to certain desired hypnotic responses. Hence, behaviour therapists in the 1960s and early 1970s saw hypnosis as an obvious means of addressing cognitive factors and initially turned to the research on hypnosis for information and techniques until Beck's cognitive therapy gained more popularity (Clarke & Jackson, 1983, p. xiv). With the gradual advent of cognitive-behavioural therapy (CBT), in the 1960s and 1970s, inspired mainly by the work of Albert Ellis and Aaron T. Beck, an emphasis on the role of cognitions, particularly specific thoughts and underlying beliefs, was assimilated into much behaviour therapy. Ellis had, as a teenager, studied the autosuggestion techniques of Émile Coué, which had some influence over his later ideas about therapy (Ellis, 2004). As we shall see, both Beck and Ellis initially made explicit analogies between their own emphasis on dysfunctional thoughts, and irrational beliefs, and the notion of morbid autosuggestion as a cause of hysteria in Victorian hypnotism (Beck A. T., 1976; Ellis, 1962). The two main pioneers of cognitive therapy therefore explicitly acknowledged a fundamental historical link and similarity between cognitive theories of psychopathology and the basic concepts of early hypnotism. Moreover, although hypnotherapy has placed little emphasis on the disputation of faulty thinking, some cognitive therapy techniques resemble much older techniques of hypnotherapy, such as the use of mental imagery to modify beliefs (Beck, Emery & Greenberg, 2005) or coping statements to deal with stressful situations (Meichenbaum, 1977).

Cognitive-behavioural theories of hypnosis

The first major systematic programme of experimental research on hypnosis was conducted by the eminent American behavioural psychologist Clark L. Hull and summarised in his *Hypnosis & Suggestibility: An Experimental Approach* (1933). Hull concluded, after many studies, that nothing distinguished "hypnotism" from ordinary suggestion except the fact that hypnotic inductions appeared to be followed, fairly consistently, by a relative increase in ordinary suggestibility. Hull was particularly struck by the normality of hypnotic responses, specifically the fact that they appeared to follow several generic "laws of learning". He also found a high level of correlation between responsiveness to ordinary, direct verbal suggestions and responsiveness to hypnotic suggestions. These findings helped to inspire the subsequent development of a skeptical cognitive-behavioural tradition in hypnosis research and they have been replicated independently by several different groups of researchers (Lynn, Kirsch & Hallquist, 2008, p. 111; Sutcliffe, 1960). Anything that can be done in hypnosis can also be done without hypnosis, albeit to a lesser extent in some cases. Regression, amnesia, anaesthesia, hallucinations, etc., all typical "hypnotic phenomena", have consistently been replicated in non-hypnotised control groups (Barber, Spanos & Chaves, 1974). In other words, hypnosis does *something* but hypnotic responses don't seem to be anywhere near as "special", dramatic, or abnormal, as is popularly assumed. When the relative "ordinariness" of hypnotic responding is properly understood, the need for an *extraordinary* mechanism of action, such as "hypnotic trance", is rapidly undermined.

Hence, independent of developments in cognitive-behavioural therapy, hypnotism was also reconceptualised through the "cognitive-behavioural" theory of hypnosis, a term introduced by T. X. Barber and his colleagues, some of the leading psychological researchers in the field, in their seminal 1974 book on the scientific study of hypnosis (Barber, Spanos & Chaves, 1974). The cognitive-behavioural approach to hypnosis was itself much older than the use of this label, though. Barber himself began research in this area around 1955 (Barber, 1969, p. 179), following earlier work in a similar vein by the social psychologist Theodore Sarbin who also rejected the concept of "hypnotic trance", and reconceptualised hypnosis as a form of active imaginative identification with the socially-constructed role of the hypnotic subject (Sarbin, 1950; Sarbin & Coe, 1972). However, the personality theorist Robert White's aptly-named 1941 article "A preface to the theory of hypnotism" is usually cited as the origin of the social-psychological and cognitive-behavioural tradition in hypnosis. Research cited by White suggested that hypnotic responses were primarily due to the conscious attitudes and voluntary efforts of the subject. In an oft-quoted passage, he therefore redefined hypnosis as follows:

> Hypnotic behaviour is meaningful, goal-directed striving, its most general goal being to behave like a hypnotised person as this is continuously defined by the operator and understood by the client. (White, 1941)

From White's perspective "hypnosis" becomes essentially a verb rather than a noun, a skill rather than a passive state, something the subject actively "does" rather than something that automatically "happens" to her as a result of "mechanical" induction rituals and suggestions. All hypnosis is, to some extent, self-hypnosis—or rather "self-hypnotising". This early socio-cognitive perspective set the agenda for subsequent social psychologists and later cognitive-behavioural researchers to develop a nonstate theory of hypnosis, based on ordinary psychological processes rather than the hypothetical construct "hypnotic trance", and thereby to integrate the study of hypnosis within the wider field of general psychology.

However, as we have seen, the first explicit use of the term "cognitive-behavioural" in relation to the nonstate theory of hypnosis occurred in Barber's landmark 1974 publication. Cognitive-behavioural theorists basically reject the concept of "hypnotic trance", a special or abnormal state, as an explanation of hypnosis. Instead, based on extensive scientific research, they reconceptualise hypnosis in terms of a hypnotic "cognitive set" (or "mind set") and ordinary cognitive and behavioural processes. These consist of factors such as belief, imagination, expectation, attitudes toward hypnosis, motivation, depth of role-involvement, goal-directed fantasies, "coupling" suggestions with physical sensations, etc. Sometimes they have even rejected the term "hypnosis" itself as implying a special "trance" state but in this text we will retain that terminology with the caveat that by "hypnosis" is simply meant a set of attitudes and behaviours that mediate hypnotic responses, rather than an "altered state of consciousness" or "hypnotic trance".

Hence, the terms "nonstate", "socio-cognitive", "cognitive-behavioural", and even "skeptical", are sometimes used as synonyms for the same tradition in the field of hypnosis, which developed out of the seminal research of Sarbin and Barber in the 1950s and 1960s respectively, just prior to the cognitive revolution in behaviour therapy that started in the 1960s and 1970s and led to the composite term "cognitive-behavioural therapy" being widely adopted in the 1980s.

> The defining feature of the social cognitive view of hypnosis is a rejection of the traditional view that hypnotic experiences require the presence of an altered state of consciousness. (Lynn, Kirsch & Hallquist, 2008, p. 132)

This conclusion is supported by a large volume of converging scientific research findings. In particular numerous studies suggest that hypnotic inductions only tend to increase responsiveness to suggestions by a small margin and that the same increase can generally be achieved by cognitive-behavioural strategies designed to enhance motivation and expectation, or encourage active imagination in response to suggestions (Barber, Spanos & Chaves, 1974). Moreover, the way in which hypnotic subjects respond is largely determined by socially-learned expectations concerning their role in the procedure and the anticipated outcome. Finally, decades of brain-imaging research on hypnosis, despite some interesting findings, have signally failed to produce consistent evidence of a uniform alteration in brain functioning ("altered state") being experienced by typical hypnotic subjects. Although psychologists are now able to observe the brains of hypnotic subjects, through imaging technology, the fabled "hypnotic trance" simply isn't there to be seen (Lynn, Kirsch & Hallquist, 2008, p. 130). Hypnosis is *not* a "unitary state" and different patterns of neurological activity are observed when different types of suggestion are given (Horton & Crawford, 2004, p. 140). Hence, research findings from brain-imaging fundamentally conflict with the assumption that responses are mediated by a specific neurological state or "hypnotic trance".

People do report a variety of subjective feelings during hypnosis, although these are less dramatic and less frequent than is probably assumed. They tend to be correlates of the suggestions being given. To a lesser extent, but nevertheless to a surprising degree, control group subjects who are simply asked to sit with their eyes shut for a similar period of time without being hypnotised, also tend to report unusual feelings. Nonstate theorists, of course, accept the fact that many people report that they "feel hypnotised", "in a trance", etc. However, these sensations are neither uniform nor necessary to hypnosis, they do not normally appear to contribute to suggestibility, and they are better understood as side-effects of suggestion rather than evidence of a "hypnotic trance", which somehow causes suggestibility. They are often just the effect of sitting immobile with one's eyes shut in a strange environment for a prolonged period or the ordinary effects of relaxation or suggested imagery. Labelling feelings of being "spaced out", for example, as evidence of hypnotic trance is an example of the fallacy of confusing cause and effect. These are typically *consequences* of responding to suggestion rather than evidence of a special altered state of consciousness.

Nicholas Spanos, one of the most prolific researchers in the field of hypnosis, neatly summed up the socio-cognitive perspective as follows:

> Criticism of the traditional notion that hypnosis involves special psychological processes has a long history. During the latter half of the 20th century, this critical tradition culminated in modern formulations that view hypnotic phenomena without recourse to special psychological processes. Common to these formulations is the idea that the term *hypnosis* refers not to a state or condition of the person but to the historically rooted conceptions of hypnosis and hypnotic responding that are held by the participants in the mini-drama that is labelled the hypnotic situation. According to this perspective, hypnotic responding is context dependent; it is determined by the willingness of subjects to adopt the hypnotic role, by their understandings of what is expected of them in that role, by their understandings of how role requirements change as the situation unfolds, by how they interpret the complex and sometimes ambiguous communications that constitute hypnotic suggestions, by their willingness and ability to use their imaginal and other cognitive skills to create the subjective experiences called for by suggestions, and by how feedback from the hypnotist and from their own responding influences the definitions they hold of themselves as hypnotic subjects and the interpretations they apply to their hypnotic experiences. Taken together, these ideas constitute a socio-cognitive perspective toward hypnotic phenomena that challenges the traditional ideas that hypnosis is a special state and that hypnotic responding involves special processes. (Spanos, 1996, pp. 19–20)

As Spanos put it elsewhere, the concept of an abnormal "altered state of consciousness", or special "hypnotic trance", is no mere relevant to understanding what happens during hypnotic behaviour than it would be to understanding what happens during any other social behaviour, such as watching a play or being told a joke (Spanos, 1996, p. 39). In fact, hypothesising an unobservable "special state" is something of a pseudo-explanation: we don't say that jokes work by inducing a special "humorous state" in the mind or that compassionate behaviour is the consequence of someone entering a "compassionate trance-state". Even if these terms corresponded to specific neurological states, unique to them, there would still be something odd about these explanations because they completely ignore the social context and meaning of the behaviour. Perhaps the most important point to emphasise is that, according to the cognitive-behavioural theory of hypnosis, the concept of "hypnotic trance" is no more relevant to the interpretation of hypnotherapy than it would be to CBT or any other form of psychological therapy. Over fifty years ago, hypnotists could more easily claim that there was something special about hypnotism because there were few other psychological approaches competing with it by producing similar therapeutic results. However, modern CBT practitioners employ many of the same techniques as hypnotists, particularly mental imagery techniques, without any reference to the concept of "hypnotic trance" and they often do so with broadly comparable therapeutic results (Kirsch, Montgomery & Sapirstein, 1995).

There are, however, reasons for continuing to employ hypnosis. Indeed, despite his skeptical conclusions, Barber himself continued to use hypnotic induction techniques in his clinical practice, as do most other nonstate researchers. Even if we reject the concept of hypnotic trance, we are still left with a potentially useful armamentarium of suggestive strategies and techniques, involving verbal suggestions and mental imagery, etc. Hypnosis also seems to be associated with certain types of beneficial client expectations concerning therapeutic responses, related to the socially-learned perception of the hypnotic subject's role in the procedure. Clients often believe that hypnosis is a powerful way of suggesting responses such as anxiety-reduction, relaxation, and pain reduction, etc., and these expectations can become self-fulfilling prophecies or enhance self-confidence in their ability to make therapeutic changes. Moreover, hypnosis does typically entail the adoption of what has been termed a favourable "cognitive set" to suggestions, consisting of positive attitudes which can potentially facilitate and enhance certain therapy strategies and deep imaginal absorption and engagement with suggestions and instructions. Although this cannot be equated with "hypnotic trance", because it is typically within the range of normal experience, it does appear to have the potential to enhance relaxation and mental imagery techniques of the sort commonly used in other cognitive and behavioural therapies. Indeed, as we shall see, there is good empirical evidence supporting the effectiveness of hypnosis in addition to behaviour therapy and CBT (Kirsch, Montgomery & Sapirstein, 1995).

A cognitive reconceptualisation of hypnosis

In this text, the basic schema below is adopted, loosely based on Barber's "cognitive set" conceptualisation of hypnosis, and other work in this area, but organised in terms of the elements of problem-orientation derived from cognitive-behavioural research on problem-solving (D'Zurilla & Nezu, 2007). Following Barber, with some modification, hypnosis can be understood in terms of the following simple experimental (or antecedents-beliefs/behaviour-consequences) model, which replaces the mediating role of "hypnotic trance" with the concept of a hypnotic mind-set, or cognitive schemas:

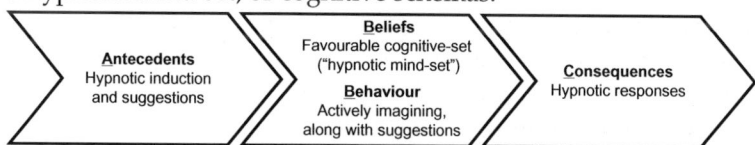

Antecedents	Beliefs	Consequences
Hypnotic induction and suggestions	Favourable cognitive-set ("hypnotic mind-set")	Hypnotic responses
	Behaviour	
	Actively imagining, along with suggestions	

According to cognitive-behavioural *theorists*, the hypnotic subject does not respond mechanically to suggestions but rather in an active, goal-directed manner, as a creative *problem-solver* (Lynn & Sivec, 1992). Likewise, cognitive-behavioural *therapists* have defined hypnosis as a coping strategy that clients can learn to apply across a variety of problematic situations (Golden, Dowd & Freidberg, 1987, p. xi). The former problem can be defined, in general terms, as how one is to fulfil the role of a "good hypnotic subject" or, more specifically, how to respond "automatically" to hypnotic suggestions. Indeed, the "positive cognitive set" in hypnosis can be seen as analogous to the modern concept of "problem orientation" from research on problem-solving (see later chapter on *Problem-Solving Therapy*). Subjects who are motivated to be hypnotised, confident in their ability to respond, optimistic about the process, and who expect to automatically experience the responses being suggested, will tend to respond better because they are "in the right mind-set" for hypnosis. Likewise, these components of the "hypnotic orientation" or "cognitive set" for hypnosis elaborate upon Braid's original psychological conceptualisation of hypnosis as selective attention ("mental abstraction") focused on an expectant dominant idea, that is, the idea of some suggested response being about to happen, and occurring in a seemingly automatic manner.

Hence, to be more specific, in this text, the hypnotic cognitive-set described by Barber will be reconceptualised in terms of the following five attitudes, derived from research on problem-solving orientation:

1. *Recognition.* Registering the hypnotic induction as a cue to activate a favourable mind-set and actively imagine the things suggested, but also interpreting hypnotic suggestions *as* hypnotic suggestions, that is,, as cues to respond hypnotically, and paying selective attention to them by focusing on their meaning, on the suggested theme or train of ideas, to the exclusion of task-irrelevant or competing thoughts ("distractions").
2. *Attribution.* Accurately attributing hypnotic responses to their specific cause, that is, to specific acts of imagination and relevant expectations, etc., rather than misattributing them to the mere voluntary compliance of the subject, to the words and actions of an external hypnotist, or the "unconscious mind", etc.
3. *Appraisal.* Estimating the demands of the situation or task favourably, seeing hypnotic suggestions as serving relevant goals, consistent with personal values, and as safe, an "opportunity rather than a threat", for example, such that misconceptions about the "danger of hypnosis" do not inhibit responses.
4. *Control.* First, estimating control over one's own contribution favourably, that is, being self-confident in one's ability to fulfil the role of hypnotic subject and perform associated tasks, adopting the right attitudes, imagining relevant things, etc ("self-efficacy"). Second, estimating the outcome of suggestions favourably by expecting that they will occur automatically in response to suggestions, if one adopts the appropriate mind-set and imaginative strategies ("response expectancy").
5. *Commitment.* Accurately estimating the time and effort required to respond hypnotically, neither procrastinating nor rushing. Also, being motivated and committing the time and effort required to respond, neither "trying too hard" nor adopting a too passive "wait and see" attitude.

The diagram below is intended to illustrate the convergence of these five elements in the hypnotic mind-set:

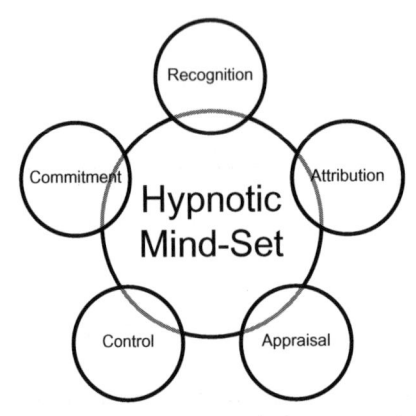

We'll be discussing existing cognitive-behavioural theories of hypnosis in more detail in a later chapter, along with this simple reconceptualisation based on problem orientation. CBT practitioners should immediately be able to recognise most of this terminology and relate it to wider issues in the field of therapy. For example, appraisals of threat and coping (control) may partially define the favourable hypnotic mind-set but, as we shall see, they are also integral to Beck's theory of anxiety.

One further point worth making at the outset is that as hypnotic suggestions or autosuggestions evoke ideas and it's the relationship with those ideas that matters most, any cognitive theory of hypnosis is arguably best understood as a "metacognitive" theory, a theory concerning cognitions *about* cognitions, beliefs about beliefs, etc. Hypnosis depends upon the hypnotic subject's expectation that suggested ideas will evoke the desired responses, or belief in "the power of suggestion", to put it very crudely. These are essentially beliefs about the nature and function of specific thoughts, and therefore can be described as "metacognitive" in nature. Metacognitive models of the role of beliefs about worry, rumination, and obsessions in emotional disorders may provide a useful comparison (Wells, 2009). These can arguably be interpreted as conceptualising worry, rumination, etc., in a way that makes them appear analogous to negative self-hypnosis (NSH), a subject we shall return to shortly.

The cognitive (or metacognitive) set for hypnotic responding, which broadly-speaking comes and goes with hypnotic induction and emerging, can be viewed as being based upon more enduring, superordinate cognitive structures. These can be conceptualised simply in terms of the subject's underlying "schema of hypnosis", which gives the procedure its personal meaning for each individual, derived from his prior history of social learning. "Schemas" (or "schemata") are "basic structures that integrate and attach meaning to events" and "mediate strategies for adaptation" (Alford & Beck, 1997, p. 36). Alford & Beck employ the definition given by English and English of a schema as, "the complex pattern, inferred as having been imprinted in the organismic structure by experience, that combines with the properties of the presented stimulus object or the presented idea to determine how the object or idea is to be perceived or conceptualized" (quoted in Alford & Beck, 1997, p. 43).

In other words, individuals have acquired some general background preconceptions relating to hypnotism from society that manifest in more specific attitudes, which come to the fore when they are actually about to be hypnotised. Social psychologists have also conceptualised hypnosis in terms of "role theory", where the central cognitive structure is the relatively high-level notion of a socially-constructed role-definition (Sarbin & Coe, 1972). From this wider or high-level perspective, probably the most important cognitive structure in relation to the hypnotic situation is the individual's personal schema relating to the socially-constructed role of the hypnotic subject. Hence, the "role" concept central to Sarbin's early socio-cognitive theory of hypnosis can be combined with the related concept of a "schema" in Beck's cognitive model of psychological functioning to provide a schema-based conceptualisation of hypnosis. In other words, loosely following Sarbin, hypnotism might be defined as a set of conventional rituals not for "inducing a trance" but rather for activating socially-learned cognitive schemas of what it means to behave like a hypnotic subject. The "hypnotic schema", once activated, is associated with specific "role expectations" or rules and assumptions about how to respond. In the same way, Beck defines anxiety as consisting in the activation of underlying schemas of "threat and vulnerability", which constitute a primal "anxious mode" of functioning. Writing more informally in his self-help workbook for the public, Beck refers to the anxiety mode, in which schemas are activated, as the "anxious mind-set" (Clark & Beck, 2012, p. 34), just as I have suggested referring to the "hypnotic mind-set", instead of "hypnotic trance", in this volume as a way of communicating these ideas to the client.

A genuinely "cognitive-behavioural" approach to hypnotherapy should therefore involve three distinct but complementary levels of conceptualisation:

1. Psychopathology. Cognitive-behavioural conceptualisation of the client's problems.
2. Treatment rationale. Cognitive-behavioural conceptualisation of the therapeutic process.
3. Hypnosis. Cognitive-behavioural reconceptualisation of hypnosis itself and hypnotic suggestions, in general, as well as in relation to therapeutic procedures.

The practical importance of adopting a cognitive-behavioural reconceptualisation of hypnosis will hopefully become apparent in the subsequent chapters. However, the most obvious consequence is that the role of the hypnotic subject is demystified and made more easily learnable. Hence, cognitive-behavioural theories of hypnosis have already led to the development of experimentally-supported procedures for "hypnotic skills training". Although there are several such approaches, the most extensively-researched is undoubtedly Nicholas Spanos' Carleton skills training program (CSTP) (Gorassini & Spanos, 1999). Hypnotic skills training involves socialising the subject to the role of hypnotic subject and collaboratively training her in specific cognitive and behavioural strategies, using models, coaching, and trial-and-error learning opportunities, etc. This approach has been repeatedly shown to increase hypnotic responsiveness among initially poorly-responding subjects. From a clinical perspective, the potential significance of being able to turn "bad" hypnotic subjects into "good" ones should be strikingly obvious.

Cognitive-behavioural case conceptualisation, or conceptualisation of clients' problems, can be easily integrated with the cognitive-behavioural theory of hypnotism, to which it is historically related. The role of dysfunctional cognitions, negative automatic thoughts, can simply be compared to that of what hypnotists originally termed negative "autosuggestion", or morbid "fixed ideas", but has more recently been dubbed "negative self-hypnosis" (NSH) by authors who integrate CBT and hypnotherapy (Golden, Dowd & Freidberg, 1987, p. 6). Lynn and Kirsch state of the link between hysteria and hypnosis: "Both may be seen as suggestive phenomena, one pathological and the other curative."

> The linkage is further strengthened by current research indicating that conversion and hypnotic responding share common neurological processes, that patients with conversion disorder have higher suggestibility scores than do patients in a control group, and that hypnotic suggestibility is related to the success of hypnosis-based treatment of [hysterical] conversion disorders. (Lynn & Kirsch, 2006, p. 37)

A simple ABC conceptualisation diagram based on this terminology might look as follows:

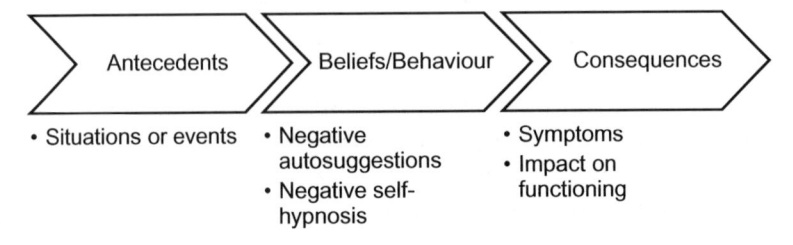

Antecedents	Beliefs/Behaviour	Consequences
• Situations or events	• Negative autosuggestions • Negative self-hypnosis	• Symptoms • Impact on functioning

Indeed, the concept of negative self-hypnosis, insofar as it refers to a mind-set that is particularly receptive to certain ideas, can be used to help explain metacognitive beliefs and processes that may also contribute to the effect of specific negative automatic thoughts. For example, selective and prolonged focus of attention on chains of negative thoughts, as in worry or rumination, may contribute to symptoms in a manner analogous to the role of focused attention in formal self-hypnosis. Likewise the expectation that certain thoughts are harmful ("Worry might give me a heart attack or make me lose my mind!") may contribute to pathological problems, such as anxiety, in a manner resembling negative self-hypnosis. Although, it appears extremely unlikely that such expectations could actually cause serious harm such as a real heart attack, they may nevertheless induce anxiety or panic attacks (Wells, 2009). By contrast, belief in the power of suggestion, combined with prolonged focused attention upon the idea "my body is relaxed and my heart is slowing down", may be capable of inducing relaxation and even lowering heart rate. Indeed, worry and rumination may provide particularly good examples of negative self-hypnosis, research on which may help to illuminate our understanding of deliberate therapeutic hypnosis.

Typically, cognitive models emphasise the central role of factors such as rigid demands (Ellis) or schemas and automatic thoughts (Beck) in the aetiology and maintenance of psychological problems. However, Braid repeatedly emphasised the role of negative automatic thoughts ("involuntary dominant ideas") in various psychological conditions especially so-called "conversion hysteria". He therefore employed hypnotherapy to "break down the pre-existing, involuntary fixed, dominant idea in the patient's mind, and its consequences" (Braid, 1853).

> The most striking cases of all, however, for illustrating the value of the hypnotic mode of treatment, are cases of hysterical paralysis, in which, without organic lesion, the patient may have remained for a considerable length of time perfectly powerless of a part, or of a whole body, from a dominant idea which has paralysed or misdirected his volition. (Braid, 1853)

Indeed, this concept of suggestion as both cause and cure of "hysteria" was central to Victorian hypnotherapy especially Bernheim's Nancy School, the most influential Victorian school of hypnotic psychotherapy, whose members, for example, attributed stuttering, blushing, and agoraphobia to irrational autosuggestion (Moll, 1889, p. 58). Hence, the attribution of various problems to involuntary "autosuggestion" was also taken over by the *New* Nancy School of Émile Coué (1923).

The founder of rational-emotive behaviour therapy (REBT), Albert Ellis, studied the writings of Coué as a young man (Ellis, 2004, p. 19) and, as noted earlier, negative cognition is repeatedly described in Ellis' early writings as a form of "negative autosuggestion." Musing over the therapeutic power of hypnotic suggestion, for example, he wrote:

> The answer to this riddle, in the light of the theory of rational-emotive psychotherapy, is simply that suggestion and autosuggestion are effective in removing neurotic and psychotic symptoms because *they are the very instruments which caused or helped produce these symptoms in the first place*. Virtually all complex and sustained adult human emotions are caused by ideas

or attitudes; and these ideas or attitudes are, first, suggested by persons and things outside the individual (especially by his parents, teachers, books, etc.); and they are, second, continually *auto-suggested* by himself. (Ellis, 1962, p. 277)

Ellis' early study of Couéism and autosuggestion seems therefore to have inspired the REBT theory of irrational beliefs. Likewise, in his earliest book on cognitive therapy, Beck compares his cognitive theory of psychopathology to the Victorian hypnotists' theory of "hysterical" autosuggestion which he dubs the "illustration *par excellence*" of cognitive distortion in psychiatric disorders. Beck draws direct analogies between the mechanism underlying hypnotherapy and his own approach, concluding that the Victorian hypnotherapists' autosuggestion theory is more consistent with cognitive therapy than Freud's psychoanalytic theory (Beck A. T., 1976, pp. 207–208). Although he didn't further develop this analogy between automatic negative thoughts and morbid autosuggestions it also featured, to some extent, in various aspects of Beck's later writings. For example, in discussing the threat appraisal model of anxiety, he and his colleagues write:

> The anxious patient gives himself a suggestion ("What if") and then acts on it as if it were true. (Beck, Emery & Greenberg, 2005, p. 281)

Automatic anxious thoughts, with which we shall primarily be concerned, typically take the form of "What if?" questions about feared catastrophes. If these do function in a manner analogous to autosuggestions then it becomes relatively easy to develop a conceptualisation of both the client's problems and the treatment ("cause and cure") based on cognitive-behavioural theories of hypnosis.

The parallel between Beck's concept of negative automatic thoughts and the Victorian hypnotists' notion of morbid or negative autosuggestion is therefore bound to be a central theme in any attempt to integrate hypnosis and cognitive therapy. Indeed, this way of looking at self-hypnosis and autosuggestion as both cause and cure inevitably influenced previous literature on cognitive-behavioural hypnotherapy.

> *Cognitive-behavioural Hypnotherapy (CBH)* [...] is a generic term for cognitive-behavioural approaches to hypnotherapy. CBH methods are based on the premise that most psychological disturbance results from a destructive type of self-hypnosis that has been termed *negative self-hypnosis* by Araoz. He explained that negative thinking and imagining are hypnoticlike when they are accepted without critical evaluation. The CBH client is shown how the content of negative self-hypnosis, self-defeating thoughts and images, can be changed through the corrective process of positive self-hypnosis. The client thus learns how to control the self-hypnotic process. (Golden, Dowd & Freidberg, 1987, p. 3)

There is a historical and theoretical basis, therefore, for integrating hypnosis and CBT. Moreover, there are further theoretical and empirical reasons to believe that there are advantages in doing so. Mental imagery has always been an important part of both behaviour therapy (Wolpe, 1990) and cognitive therapy (Beck A. T., 1970; Beck, Emery & Greenberg, 2005). However, the sense that the use of these techniques in CBT has yet to be fully explored has led to a recent growth of interest in mental imagery techniques (Hackmann, Bennett-Levy & Holmes, 2011).

Hypnotherapy is a rich source of many long-established imagery techniques, often already linked to cognitive-behavioural processes—a topic that later chapters will explore in detail. Hypnotists have long studied the nature and function of mental imagery and hypnosis is widely believed to provide a means of enhancing the subjective quality of mental imagery and responses to it. Hypnosis appears to offer methods of influencing attention, similar to meditation training, which may complement existing cognitive-behavioural therapy strategies for attention training or enhance other techniques. It also appears to be capable of influencing expectations in ways that can be used to evoke specific therapeutic responses, sometimes responses that do not appear to be easily brought under direct voluntary control, such as heart rate, circulation, digestion, etc. Hypnosis also provides us with a means of inducing relaxation in ways that can be flexibly adapted to suit different clients' needs, and which often seem to be particularly profound.

Clinical research on cognitive-behavioural hypnotherapy

Hypnotherapy probably has a stronger scientific evidence-base than most people realise. For example, a recent meta-analysis identified 57 good quality randomised controlled trials (RCTs), involving 1,829 participants, from a total of 444 studies examining the clinical efficacy of hypnosis, excluding "analogue" studies (Flammer & Bongartz, 2003). These researchers found that hypnosis had a "medium" (d = 0.56) effect size overall, compared to control groups. The effect size was greatest (d = 0.69) for those RCTs (n = 8) that involved treatment of anxiety. The authors note that these calculations must be considered conservative because they included all reported measures, even those close inspection suggested were probably not very sensitive to the effects of treatment. The range of conditions treated by these studies was very broad and included the following:

Tinnitus	Postoperative vomiting (following breast surgery)	Analgesia in interventional radiological procedures
Insomnia	Blood loss/pressure in maxillofacial surgery	Analgesia for invasive medical procedures
Duodenal ulceration	Analgesia during labour	Distress/pain in breast biopsy patients
Enuresis	Osteoarthritic pain	Treatment of burn pain
Asthma	Care of third molar surgery patients	Procedural pain during burn care
Warts	Healing process in bone fractures	Chemotherapy-related nausea/vomiting in children
Irritable bowel syndrome (IBS)	Local anaesthesia	Pain, distress, and anxiety in children undergoing bone marrow aspiration
Chronic and recurrent headaches	Postoperative recovery (open heart surgery)	Pain/nausea during cancer treatment
Hypertension	Analgesia/reducing unnecessary movement in ophthalmic surgery	Chemotherapy distress in children with cancer
Smoking	Improvement of postoperative course in children	
Test anxiety		
Posttraumatic Stress Disorder (PTSD)		
Anxiety		
Anxiety, quality of life and care following bypass surgery		

These researchers also found six studies reporting data on hypnotic susceptibility scale ratings, which together demonstrated a positive correlation (r = 0.44) between the patient's susceptibility to hypnotic suggestions in general and the outcome of treatment.

The precise nature of any interaction between hypnosis and specific cognitive-behavioural interventions, however, has not been extensively studied under controlled conditions. Nevertheless, modern research on hypnotherapy increasingly focuses upon integrating hypnotherapy and CBT since publication of Kirsch et al.'s influential meta-analysis which pooled data from eighteen separate controlled studies, including 577 participants, comparing the efficacy of "cognitive-behavioural hypnotherapy" to CBT alone. They concluded that for seventy per cent of patients (or ninety per cent if a possible statistical outlier is not excluded from the calculation) CBT was more effective when integrated with hypnosis, that is., that for the vast majority of clients cognitive-behavioural hypnotherapy is superior to CBT alone (Kirsch, Montgomery & Sapirstein, 1995, p. 214). Put differently, this review of the research provided statistical evidence of a mean "additive" effect of hypnosis when combined with standard behaviour therapy or CBT, across a variety of issues.

More recent studies have continued to identify an additive effect of hypnosis when incorporated into conventional CBT. For example, one piece of research found that the addition of hypnosis made standard CBT using cognitive restructuring and *in vivo* exposure for public speaking anxiety more effective (Schoenberger, Kirsch, Gearan, Montgomery & Pastyrnak, 1997). Likewise, a recent randomised controlled trial (RCT) comparing cognitive-behavioural hypnotherapy to standard CBT in the treatment of acute stress disorder (ASD), involved eighty-nine civilian survivors of trauma (Bryant, Moulds, Guthrie & Nixon, 2005). The researchers found both CBT and CBT+hypnosis to be equally effective, in terms of patients no longer meeting diagnostic criteria at six-month follow-up, and both cognitive-behavioural approaches to be about twice as effective as supportive counselling. However, CBT+hypnosis clients reported greater reduction of re-experiencing symptoms at post-treatment than the CBT group, which the researchers interpreted as evidence for their hypothesis that hypnosis was capable of enhancing the efficacy of imaginal exposure in the treatment of trauma, by increasing reliving, and thereby enhancing, emotional processing of traumatic memories. The approach adopted in this manual integrates hypnosis with standard CBT techniques such as coping skills training, exposure therapy, problem-solving and cognitive restructuring. The evidence from the studies above suggests that this may often be more effective than standard nonhypnotic CBT. For example, hypnotic induction and suggestions may enhance the use of imaginal exposure techniques of the kind discussed in later chapters.

Indeed, hypnotherapy may be particularly indicated in the treatment of anxiety symptoms. Although there has been some disagreement about this in the past, as Bryant observes, on the basis of a number of studies that report findings in this area, research increasingly suggests that anxious clients tend to be more responsive to hypnosis than average. Elevated levels of hypnotic responsiveness have been found in PTSD, acute stress disorder, phobias, and other disorders involving anxiety symptoms, and patients with multiple anxieties have been found more hypnotisable than those with single specific phobias (Bryant R. A., 2008, pp. 535–536).

> There is no doubt that hypnosis can facilitate established means of treating anxiety disorders. Fear conditioning and extinction models have led to [cognitive-behavioural] treatments that

involve new learning, and there is convergent evidence that this learning can be enhanced by hypnosis in numerous ways. The greater ability of hypnotized individuals to engage in imagery, focused attention, motivation to comply with instructions and imaginal rehearsal of mastery of fear all combines to potentiate the treatment gains for anxiety patients. (Bryant R. A., 2008, p. 545)

Moreover, hypnotherapy has typically performed well in the treatment of anxiety symptoms in controlled clinical outcome studies.

In addition to the treatment of anxiety, recent research has also supported the efficacy of hypnotherapy as a treatment for clinical depression. In particular, Assen Alladin, the author of a recent clinical manual for evidence-based *Cognitive Hypnotherapy* (Alladin, 2008) has employed hypnosis to induce positive imagery and feelings in depressed clients, in order, he postulates, to directly condition the formation of "anti-depressive pathways" in the brain. Good evidence in support of the efficacy of his cognitive hypnotherapy has already been produced by Alladin from a clinical trial, using eighty-four chronic depressives, in which cognitive hypnotherapy was compared head-to-head against the use of orthodox cognitive therapy in the treatment of depression. This study is particularly significant because it appears to meet the stringent research design criteria set down by the American Psychological Association for an empirically-supported treatment (EST) rated "probably efficacious" (Alladin & Alibhai, 2007).

The hypnotic cart before the horse

So how might skeptical or cognitive-behavioural theories of hypnosis influence things at a *practical* level? Most cognitive-behavioural theorists and therapists have adopted the view, as did Braid, that "hetero-hypnosis", being hypnotised by another person, is essentially guided *self-hypnosis* (Golden, Dowd & Freidberg, 1987, p. 119). Once we cease to view hypnosis in terms of relatively "mechanical" procedures for inducing an "altered state of consciousness" and more as a complex social interaction, comprising multiple cognitive and behavioural skills, operating at different levels, it becomes possible to radically reconsider the function of techniques such as the standard hypnotic induction. Indeed, the traditional view of hypnotic induction arguably puts the cart before the horse. It is often assumed, in loosely stimulus-response terms, that the hypnotist performs an induction that subsequently, a moment later, causes the subject to enter a hypnotic state, in a vaguely "mechanical" way. In other words, the technique appears to do most of the work and to "make" the passive client go into a "hypnotic trance", so-called. However, this may be fundamentally the wrong way round. Barber concluded from his extensive research on hypnosis that suggestions of sleep and relaxation were effective in bringing about a small but significant increment in hypnotic responsiveness. However, he also concluded that they probably did so by defining the situation in the mind of the subject as "hypnosis" rather than through any innate properties of relaxation or any sort of "hypnotic trance" (Barber, Spanos & Chaves, 1974, p. 25). He went on to hypothesise that standard induction suggestions of sleep and relaxation could be viewed as merely another set of test suggestions (Barber, Spanos & Chaves, 1974, p. 128).

Hence, an alternative to the conventional "trance-induction" hypothesis would be that the hypnotic induction acts as a cue or signal for the client to prepare herself, in anticipation, to respond to hypnotic suggestions by voluntarily adopting a favourable mind-set. Most hypnotic inductions, particularly the standard eye-fixation induction used in most research, involve a simple physical ("ideo-motor reflex") suggestion test. Knowing that they are, in a few seconds, going to be asked to imagine their eyes growing so heavy that they close automatically, good hypnotic subjects prepare themselves to respond. They "rearrange themselves" to get into the right mind-set and orientation, and shift their focus of attention on to the most relevant cues, probably the voice of the hypnotist and the location of the sensations being suggested. They adopt the appropriate mind-set in order to be able to pass the first test, that is, to respond to the hypnotic induction technique. It's important to realise that means hypnotic subjects enter hypnosis, at least to an initial extent, just *before* the hypnotic induction rather than *after* it; that is, in preparation rather than as a consequence.

Two key observations support this view. First, when subjects are asked to self-rate their level of hypnosis (on a subjective scale from zero to ten) at different stages during the procedure, in the author's experience the mean rating is about three immediately before the eye-fixation induction, rather than zero as one might expect, and about five-and-a-half immediately following it. This simple observation has been made literally hundreds of times by asking different subjects "From zero to ten, how hypnotised do you feel right now?" just before performing the eye-fixation induction or similar procedures. A second observation is that a number of researchers, and many clinicians, have found that simply asking subjects to "put yourself into hypnosis" is generally about as effective as performing the standard eye-fixation induction, or probably any other induction technique (Barber, Spanos & Chaves, 1974). Indeed, many hypnotherapists abbreviate induction and deepening techniques or dispense with them entirely after several sessions, especially with very responsive hypnotic subjects, who soon get beyond the stage of needing a formal induction to enter hypnosis. Even Braid made this observation on the basis of his initial experience with patients, many of whom could subsequently place themselves in hypnosis through "habit" and "imagination", as he put it, without a formal induction technique. This becomes much easier to understand if, following the cognitive-behavioural reconceptualisation of hypnosis, we try to dispense entirely with the concept of "hypnotic trance" and conclude instead, to put it crudely, that hypnotism is basically about inducing a set of attitudes or mind-set. The subject soon learns to adopt a favourable attitude, to "get into the right mind-set", in anticipation of the hypnotic induction and the demands it places upon her to respond to suggestion. However, she can also learn to adopt the right anticipatory attitude by being told about it, observing others being hypnotised and talking about it, or being progressively trained to respond to individual suggestion tests in a graduated manner.

A note on "Ericksonian" hypnosis

It is important to spell out the fact that these principles conflict with certain key aspects of one of the most popular approaches to hypnotherapy, the so-called "Ericksonian" approach, derived from the work of the late Dr. Milton Erickson. Erickson's approach is best-known for its emphasis on "indirect" forms of suggestion. However, these constitute a radical departure from traditional forms of hypnosis, which emphasise more direct methods. This has led to some disagreement over the extent to which Erickson's approach can be compared to previous forms of hypnotism, or even whether it might be better called something else, other than "hypnotism", to avoid confusion. One of the key difficulties here is that indirect suggestions appear to function by means of a fundamentally different mechanism from traditional hypnotic suggestion, meaning that conclusions derived from research on hypnosis do not necessarily relate to what Erickson's followers actually do under that name. For example, Lynn et al. define hypnotic suggestion as follows:

> Unlike placebos, misleading questions and other forms of indirect suggestion, hypnotic suggestions are requests for imaginative experiences, and for that reason they can also be termed imaginative suggestions. (Lynn, Kirsch & Hallquist, 2008, p. 112)

By that definition, much of "Ericksonian hypnotherapy" is clearly *not* employing hypnosis at all and would perhaps be better labelled "indirect suggestion therapy", which may or may not turn out to be a useful therapy approach in its own right but cannot claim to do so on the back of research on traditional direct-suggestion hypnotherapy. For example, in the meta-analytic study mentioned above, out of fifty-seven randomised controlled trials reviewed, only nineteen per cent were found to have employed predominantly indirect techniques (Flammer & Bongartz, 2003). Overall conclusions about the efficacy of hypnotherapy therefore relate mainly to the use of more traditional-style techniques.

Moreover, although it is often claimed by people promoting commercial workshops on "Ericksonian hypnosis" that the indirect approach is dramatically more effective than direct suggestion, especially with "resistant" clients, this appears to be little more than marketing hype. Indeed, a review of twenty-nine independent studies comparing direct and indirect suggestion styles was conducted by Lynn and his colleagues, which found both styles broadly equivalent in terms of their effectiveness (Lynn, Neufeld & Maré, 1993). They found no evidence across these studies that indirect suggestions improved responses to test items on hypnotic susceptibility scales, as Ericksonians had predicted, or that they somehow bypassed the subject's resistance.

> We believe it is fair to conclude that the best controlled studies provide no support for the superiority of indirect suggestions, and there are indications that direct suggestions are superior to indirect suggestions in terms of modifying subjects' experience of hypnosis. (Lynn, Neufeld & Maré, 1993, pp. 138–139)

Unfortunately, the Ericksonian approach also has the disadvantage of being more complex, time-consuming, and less consistent with general principles of evidence-based psychotherapy. Moreover, Lynn and Kirsch observe that many popular workshops that teach indirect hypnosis, loosely based on the Ericksonian approach, make absurdly extravagant claims for their methods.

> However, research indicates that many of these specialised techniques provide no benefit whatsoever, and some may even decrease the effectiveness of a hypnotic intervention. In general people who receive traditional authoritative and direct suggestions pass as many

> suggestions as do people who receive more permissive and indirect suggestions. Although direct or authoritative suggestions may engender feelings of suggestion-related involuntariness more so than would indirect or permissively worded suggestions, these differences are small in magnitude. (Lynn & Kirsch, 2006, p. 42)

It has also been the author's experience that many popular books and workshops tend to confuse students and to mislead them about the nature of hypnosis and its role in psychological therapy, often making claims that are completely inconsistent with research in the field of hypnotism.

Moreover, Erickson's approach emphasised the notion that the therapist should try to circumvent clients' "resistance" by influencing them outside of their awareness, using indirect means. This "pulling the wool over their eyes" approach to suggestion, which typically emphasises the need to deceive the client about the content of suggestions supposedly given, fundamentally clashes with some of the basic professional values of modern therapy, which emphasise "informed consent", collaboration, and education, etc. Likewise, Erickson is associated with the deceptive use of "paradoxical" therapy techniques, which run counter to the expectations of the client rather than being based upon a shared treatment rationale. Hence, regarding the cognitive therapy of anxiety, Beck and his colleagues write:

> Although some techniques may appear paradoxical (for example, if someone is afraid of anxiety, he is asked to experience it), cognitive therapy avoids paradoxical techniques in the usual [e.g., Ericksonian] sense. The therapist does not prescribe symptoms or use restraint-from-change procedures unless in a straightforward way with the rationale clearly spelled out. We have, for example, had patients purposefully try to make themselves more anxious as a way to counteract their anxiety. This is presented as a coping technique that the patient can choose to use, and is not a strategy the therapist is covertly [i.e., indirectly and surreptitiously] using to combat the patient's anxiety. (Beck, Emery & Greenberg, 2005, p. 176)

Likewise, Curwen, Palmer, and Ruddell, although including a chapter dedicated to hypnosis in their book on brief CBT, make a point of specifying that the Ericksonian "indirect suggestion" approach potentially conflicts with the basic collaborative stance in CBT.

> Because in cognitive behaviour therapy an open, collaborative approach is used in which the theory and practice of each intervention are explained to the client, direct suggestion explicitly focusing on the particular problem concerned is employed in the hypnosis script and indirect suggestion is avoided. (Curwen, Palmer & Ruddell, 2000, p. 132)

Arguably, therefore, the "indirect" approach characteristic of the followers of Erickson, insofar as it involves an element of deception, is inherently antagonistic to the basic CBT principle of collaboration. However, traditional hypnosis, which employs direct (conscious) suggestions to which the client gives her attention and her voluntary consent, is a different matter entirely, and completely consistent with CBT and the principle of collaborative therapy. Direct suggestions are sometimes termed "imaginative suggestions" to highlight the fact that they are intended as explicit invitations for the client to actively imagine the things being described and are therefore addressed primarily to her conscious mind, to put it crudely. As we shall see, Braid's original definition of hypnotism was in terms of focused (conscious) attention on a particular idea or mental image accompanied by the (conscious) expectation that some response would happen as a result. Only later, did certain authors seek to portray hypnotism, in more obfuscating and mystifying terms, as something to do with "talking to the unconscious mind" of the client.

Consequently, sometimes CBT practitioners are quite concerned that hypnotists encourage "magical thinking" or surround themselves with mystique. This is true of some approaches to hypnotherapy but not others. It was, in particular, a criticism levelled against Erickson by Barber. In a symposium discussion of one of Erickson's papers summarising some aspects of hypnosis research, Barber said:

> It seemed to me that half of Dr. Erickson's presentation was from the position of a natural scientist, psychologist, and psychiatrist trying to understand what hypnosis is; the other half of the time the presentation seemed to be from the position of someone of many years ago who really thought hypnosis was a mysterious, magical thing. [...] the subject goes into a trance, and when he is in a trance, magiclike things happen. It is implied that a kind of mysterious thing happens because of trance. (Barber, quoted in Erickson, 1980, pp. 333–334)

This quotation is important because it highlights very clearly the fundamental difference in outlook between the Ericksonian tradition in hypnotism and the cognitive-behavioural approach, represented by Barber. The more "common sense" and skeptical cognitive-behavioural perspective is fairly dominant in the current research literature, although many hypnotherapists are still drawn to the Ericksonian approach despite the lack of evidence supporting it.

Rationale for cognitive-behavioural hypnotherapy

So how do hypnotism and CBT relate *therapeutically*? Although the term CBT is often used as though it referred to a specific therapy, it's actually a diverse tradition comprising a wide range of approaches with different theoretical and practical assumptions.

> Talking about CBT as if it were a single therapy is misleading. Modern CBT is not a monolithic structure, but a broad movement that is still developing, and full of controversies. (Westbrook, Kennerley & Kirk, 2007, p. 1)

Among these approaches, in recent decades, Beck's cognitive theory of emotion had provided, to some degree, a common framework. Indeed, in *The Integrative Power of Cognitive Therapy*, Alford and Beck have argued at length in favour of the view that "cognitive therapy and theory not only constitute an effective, coherent approach, but also may serve as a unifying or 'integrative' paradigm for psychopathology and effective psychotherapy" (Alford & Beck, 1997). That argument clearly encompasses the possibility of integrating hypnotic techniques and concepts within the scope of the broad cognitive model of theory and practice. Indeed, Beck has explicitly set out a formal statement of cognitive therapy as a "technically eclectic" framework, and specified the following four criteria for assimilating other psychological therapy techniques, which might be taken to include hypnosis (Alford & Beck, 1997, p. 91).

1. The technique must be consistent with the principles of cognitive therapy and its theory of therapeutic change.
2. The treatment interventions must be derived from an adequate cognitive case conceptualisation, which should normally be shared with the client.
3. Treatment occurs within a framework of collaborative empiricism and guided discovery.
4. The standard interview structure is followed in each session, insofar as appropriate.

The cognitive therapy interview structure, or standard session agenda, consists of updates on progress, agenda setting, homework review, cognitive-behavioural interventions addressing one or two main agenda items, further homework planning, and feedback and summary, etc. Cognitive-behavioural hypnotherapy, as presented in this text, definitely meets Beck's specified criteria as it is designed to be consistent with the theoretical principles of cognitive therapy, based upon a cognitive-behavioural case conceptualisation, involves collaborative empiricism, and is structured around a standard CBT session format.

We've already noted some reasons for integrating hypnosis with CBT. From the birth of behaviour therapy in the 1950s and throughout the evolution of modern CBT, clinicians and researchers have observed that hypnosis appears to have "additive" value when combined with standard cognitive and behavioural therapies. Typically cited advantages include:

1. Many clients attribute a heightened expectation to the treatment, because of the perceived "power" of hypnosis.
2. Hypnosis seems capable of inducing and managing deep relaxation in a particularly effective and convenient manner and relaxation is of central importance to certain types of therapy, although not *essential* to hypnotism itself.
3. Hypnosis seems to facilitate a sense of benign dissociation or detachment especially useful in the management of pain.
4. By deliberately doing the contrary of what we know makes hypnotic suggestions work, we can develop "dehypnosis" strategies, resembling "distancing" in cognitive therapy and various more recent mindfulness and acceptance-based approaches.
5. Hypnosis frequently seems to enhance the vividness, detail, and perseverance of mental imagery in a way that can enhance many visualisation techniques, including imaginal exposure.
6. Hypnosis seems to facilitate enhanced experiencing of emotional states, such as during regression and abreaction, in a way which could potentially enhance exposure-based therapeutic interventions.
7. Hypnotherapy has evolved sophisticated methods of verbal and nonverbal suggestion which can potentially be used to supplement the benefits of other therapy interventions in many ways.

8. Training in autosuggestion and self-hypnosis offers clients a flexible coping skill that can be applied to a wide variety of situations.
9. Hypnotherapy has traditionally been a "creative melting pot" of ideas within which many different therapeutic techniques and strategies have evolved, that is, it has a vast toolbox of documented interventions.
10. Hypnotherapists, with their complex range of imagery and verbal techniques, have been especially good at developing recordings (self-hypnosis tapes and CDs) which conveniently and effectively supplement the use of face-to-face treatment sessions.

More recently, Assen Alladin's excellent book *Cognitive Hypnotherapy* has reviewed at length *nineteen* apparent strengths of hypnosis which he claims justify its assimilation within a CBT framework (Alladin, 2008, pp. 10–16). There are, in fact, a growing number of clinical textbooks which attempt to integrate techniques from hypnotherapy with CBT and *vice versa*. However, theory and practice are not totally correlated and some hypnotherapists employ CBT-related techniques without embracing the cognitive-behavioural *theory* of hypnosis. Alladin's approach to cognitive hypnotherapy, for example, employs Hilgard's "neo-dissociationist" theory in which hypnotic trance, rather than ordinary cognition, mediates behaviour (2008, p. 37). By contrast, explicitly "cognitive-behavioural" (nonstate) *theories* of hypnosis are, of course, especially well-suited to integration with CBT *techniques*. Integral to Barber's original cognitive-behavioural theory of hypnosis was the discovery that once the notion of "hypnotic trance" is set aside it becomes apparent that hypnotism functions by means of similar antecedents and mediating (cognitive and behavioural) factors to other psychological procedures, including cognitive and behavioural therapies such as systematic desensitisation (Barber, Spanos & Chaves, 1974, pp. 140–144).

> Hypnosis and cognitive-behavioural psychotherapy are well suited to each other because of the historical connection between them and their procedural similarities. The use of hypnosis in cognitive-behavioural therapy is as old as behaviour therapy itself. […] Cognitive and behavioural therapies are especially compatible with the cognitive-behavioural approach to hypnosis. (Kirsch, Capafons, Cardeña-Buelna & Amigó, 1999, pp. 4–5)

There are many similarities between hypnotherapy and CBT that become more apparent when hypnosis is reconceptualised in cognitive-behavioural terms. Undoubtedly, there is negligible reference to Socratic disputation, of the kind employed by cognitive therapists, in the history of hypnotherapy and therefore limited overlap with Beck and Ellis' approaches in that respect. (Although some early twentieth century hypnotists like Morton Prince and Platonov did assimilate Paul Dubois' "rational persuasion" method into hypnotherapy, which *is* a primitive cognitive disputation approach, this faded into obscurity.) However, "covert" behaviour therapy techniques like desensitisation, behaviour rehearsal, exposure, modelling, reinforcement, and sensitisation, and cognitive rehearsal techniques like Meichenbaum's "self-instruction training" (1977) bear considerable resemblance to hypnotherapy techniques. Moreover, one of the most obvious areas of overlap is in the application of mental imagery techniques in hypnotherapy and CBT.

Mental imagery in cognitive-behavioural hypnotherapy

Michael Yapko, a renowned authority on the treatment of depression using hypnosis, recently recounted the following story. Yapko observed Beck demonstrating his cognitive therapy with a young man suffering from anxiety and depression, who was helped to identify and dispute his unhealthy automatic thoughts.

> Then, Dr. Beck did something particularly interesting: He instructed the man to close his eyes and engage in an exercise in imagination. The man was told to visualise himself in a variety of situations that had previously been stressful. Dr. Beck suggested that he see himself in these familiar situations thinking and doing things differently, focusing on how his newly corrected thoughts and revised self-talk would lead him to handle the previously troublesome situations skilfully and successfully. The young man absorbed Dr. Beck's suggestions to associate new thoughts and feelings to those situations, and reported feeling that he could now handle those situations in much improved ways. His broad smile and apparent comfort suggested he was sincere in saying this. (Yapko in Alladin, 2008, p. ix)

Beck stated that this was an example of the cognitive therapy technique he called "success imagery". However, Yapko felt he was witnessing something virtually indistinguishable from the much older technique of hypnotic "age progression" and which could equally well be classified under a plethora of other names such as "mental rehearsal", etc.

Beck has repeatedly described the role of mental imagery techniques, similar to those used in hypnosis, in his early writings (Beck A. T., 1970). Indeed, his original textbook on cognitive therapy for anxiety includes a whole chapter on mental imagery techniques some of which are explicitly derived from hypnotherapy (Beck, Emery & Greenberg, 2005). Likewise, in her cognitive therapy manual, Judith Beck dedicated a chapter to "imagery" techniques, which clearly lend themselves to incorporation within the framework of cognitive-behavioural hypnotherapy (Beck J. S., 1995, pp. 229–247). Cognitive therapy has always recognised that automatic thoughts may take the form of mental images, which hypnotherapists would naturally conceptualise as a form of negative autosuggestion. Hence, Judith Beck emphasises techniques meant to identify and cope with spontaneous (automatic) mental imagery that causes distress. These include following images to completion, jumping ahead in time, coping in the image, changing the image, reality-testing, simply repeating, and substituting, stopping, or distracting oneself from automatic negative images (Beck J. S., 1995, pp. 232–243). She also refers to three imagery methods employed within the therapy session: rehearsal of coping strategies in imagination, "distancing" imagery (time projection), and "reduction of perceived threat" (Beck J. S., 1995, pp. 243–247). These and other imagery techniques commonly used in cognitive and behavioural therapies can be easily adapted for use in hypnotherapy, or self-hypnosis, and very often resemble widespread hypnotherapy techniques, which in some cases predate the development of CBT. Hence, we shall return to this subject to discuss them in more detail in later chapters.

It's almost a truism that people who vividly *imagine* something tend to respond somewhat as if it were actually happening, especially if they expect to do so. This simple, common sense observation constitutes part of the justification and rationale for combining hypnosis and

CBT. Behaviour therapists such as Joseph Wolpe and Arnold Lazarus made extensive use of imaginative techniques, and relaxation and fantasy scene presentation were integral to systematic desensitisation, the dominant technique of early behaviour therapy for anxiety (Wolpe & Lazarus, 1966; Wolpe, 1958). Beck refers to the power of the imagination and the use of such techniques in natural childbirth and hypnotherapy as a precedent for their own use of mental imagery in cognitive therapy for anxiety. Indeed a whole chapter of the original treatment manual for cognitive therapy of anxiety is dedicated to "modifying imagery" through induced fantasy, etc. (Beck, Emery & Greenberg, 2005, pp. 211–231). Likewise, Meichenbaum identified the following potential benefits of mental imagery in early cognitive-behavioural therapy (Meichenbaum, 1977, pp. 137–138).

1. The implicit stimuli that trigger maladaptive behaviour are better represented and identified in vivid imagery.
2. The client can be exposed to, and rehearse coping with, a wider range of situational cues.
3. There is greater emotional activation and involvement.
4. Imagery may permit the learning of an initial "outline" of a complex behavioural response, which facilitates subsequent learning.
5. With practice, once competence begins to develop, imagery rehearsal allows selective attention to the most important details of a target behaviour.

All of these benefits appear to be potentially enhanced in hypnosis, where subjects are encouraged to become more imaginatively involved and an attitude of positive expectation and self-confidence is deliberately cultivated in relation to imaginal rehearsal.

Meditation as dehypnosis

Perhaps one of the most important observations to make at the outset is that hypnotherapists drawing on CBT have naturally identified Beck's concept of "negative automatic thoughts" with the Victorian hypnotists' notion of negative autosuggestion and attempted to help clients develop more rational and helpful alternative cognitions to rehearse in the form of coping statements or autosuggestions.

> Cognitive-behavioural hypnotherapy is particularly useful for overcoming negative self-hypnosis because the positive internal dialogue it fosters is in direct opposition to the negative self-talk characteristic of negative self-hypnosis. (Golden, Dowd & Freidberg, 1987, p. 51)

However, following Beck's work, subsequent "mindfulness and acceptance-based" CBT approaches have emphasised an alternative way of responding to negative automatic thoughts, derived in part from mindfulness meditation techniques such as those traditionally employed in Buddhism (Hayes, Follette & Linehan, 2004). Rather than attempting to dispute these thoughts or replace them with more rational, helpful alternatives, such "third-wave" approaches believe it is often more adaptive for clients to gain detachment from their thoughts and accept their troublesome feelings. This often involves an extension of the technique of psychological "distancing" from Beck's early cognitive therapy (Beck A. T., 1976).

Hence, one of the main ways in which hypnotherapy could benefit from modern CBT would be by incorporating strategies employed to gain psychological "distance" from negative automatic thoughts or morbid thought processes such as worry and rumination. As Barber and his colleagues observed, for example, the experience of hypnosis requires something resembling the willing suspension of disbelief, something that is comparable to normal absorption in reading a novel or watching a movie. In the imaginative experience of fiction, we refrain from reminding ourselves, that "this is just a story", "these are just words", "these are just actors", etc., and instead allow ourselves to respond "as if" the fictional events were real, to the extent that we may involuntarily laugh or cry, etc. (Barber, Spanos & Chaves, 1974, pp. 12–13). Barber pointed out that adopting an "uninvolved" and "distant" perspective on movies or novels can prevent emotions and other automatic reactions being evoked. In the same way, hypnotic subjects who remain distant and uninvolved do not respond as well to suggestions as those who actively imagine the things being described. Speaking of the analogy between watching a movie and listening to hypnotic suggestions, Barber and his colleagues, provide the following description of the distant and uninvolved style of responding.

> Given these kinds of attitudes, motivations, and expectancies, he may say to himself that this is just a movie and he is just watching actors perform their roles; he may remain continually aware that he is in an audience and that he is observing a deliberately contrived performance. Since he observes the movie in this uninvolved and distant manner, he does not think and imagine with the communications and he does not laugh, feel sad, empathize, or, more generally, feel, emote, and experience in line with the communications from the screen. We believe that this person resembles the subject who is *unresponsive* to suggestions in a hypnotic situation. (Barber, Spanos & Chaves, 1974, pp. 12–13, italics added)

However, most intriguingly, this account of what factors can prevent hypnosis from working also resembles accounts of meditation and mindfulness-based CBT techniques deliberately used to gain distance from negative automatic thoughts. It's a small step to propose the following rough analogy:

1. Hypnosis consists in prolonged focused attention upon expectant dominant ideas, to the exclusion of other experiences, taking them literally, and allowing yourself to respond "as if" the events they portray are real, using the same everyday cognitive and behavioural skills that allow imaginal involvement in books and movies, etc.
2. Dehypnosis largely consists in doing the *opposite* in response to negative automatic thoughts or autosuggestions, allowing them to fade naturally from the mind without attachment to them, continuing to be aware (mindful) of the breadth of other ongoing experiences rather than narrowing attention, reminding yourself that thoughts are just words or images in the mind and not the things they represent, and doing nothing in response to them that might perpetuate or elaborate them, such as analysing their meaning or struggling against them, etc.

When individuals worry or ruminate, they lose track of time and become less aware of their current surroundings in a way that resembles individuals in hypnosis. They elaborate on the content of their negative thoughts in great detail, for hours, chewing them over verbally in their minds, and in doing so they might be said to be writing their own "negative" hypnotic script and becoming imaginatively involved with it like someone reading a novel or movie script and becoming "lost in the story".

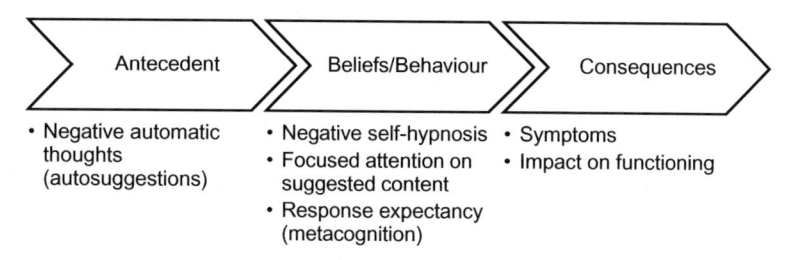

Antecedent	Beliefs/Behaviour	Consequences
• Negative automatic thoughts (autosuggestions)	• Negative self-hypnosis • Focused attention on suggested content • Response expectancy (metacognition)	• Symptoms • Impact on functioning

It might also be observed that meditation techniques are traditionally divided into *two* roughly distinct categories: "concentrative meditation" and "contemplative meditation". Braid originally saw hypnotism as resembling the concentrative meditation techniques that are common in Hindu yoga. By contrast, CBT has assimilated elements of Buddhist meditation techniques, which are more contemplative in style. We might say that hypnotism resembles concentrative meditation and dehypnosis resembles contemplative (or "mindfulness") meditation in many regards. Hence, chains of negative thoughts may be interrupted by doing the *opposite* of what cognitive-behavioural research has shown us that good hypnotic subjects do, that is, worry and rumination can be alleviated by a strategy that resembles meditation or mindfulness, a concept that is already widespread in the CBT field (Hayes, Follette & Linehan, 2004).

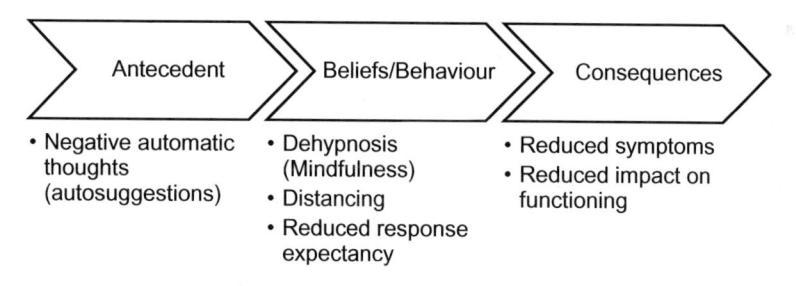

Antecedent	Beliefs/Behaviour	Consequences
• Negative automatic thoughts (autosuggestions)	• Dehypnosis (Mindfulness) • Distancing • Reduced response expectancy	• Reduced symptoms • Reduced impact on functioning

However, hypnotists in general have said little to date about the possibility of reversing negative self-hypnosis in this way, through a kind of dehypnosis. Hypnotherapists encourage subjects to become absorbed in "positive" or therapeutic ideas and images, imagining they are real, and allowing themselves to respond accordingly. By contrast, dehypnosis would consist in training clients to psychologically distance themselves from negative autosuggestions and suspend imaginative involvement with them, viewing them as transient events in the mind, words and pictures, and nothing more. Dehypnosis aims to "break the spell" of language, preventing negative automatic thoughts from developing into negative self-hypnosis, if you like, by reducing imaginal absorption and the receptive cognitive (or metacognitive) beliefs that allow thoughts to capture the imagination and evoke emotional suffering and other troublesome responses.

Nevertheless, at least one attempt has been made to integrate metacognitive theories, mindfulness, and cognitive-behavioural theories of hypnosis. Recently, the hypnosis researcher Steven Jay Lynn collaborated with the Buddhist teacher Lama Surya Das, among others, in an attempt to explore the possibility of combining elements of Buddhist mindfulness meditation practice, cognitive therapy, and hypnosis, drawing on recent research in cognitive psychology (Lynn, Das, Hallquist & Williams, 2006). Lynn et al. appeal to a cognitive model combining elements of Wells' influential metacognitive theory (Wells, 2009) and Lynn and Kirsch's own "response set" theory to explain the mechanism underlying mindfulness meditation and its relationship with hypnosis. They go on to summarise the relevance of hypnosis to mindfulness training as follows:

1. Suggestions can be used to motivate clients to persevere with meditation practice on a regular basis.
2. Suggestions can be used to generate a patient mind-set, so that when the attention naturally wanders this is seen as normal and accepted.
3. Suggestions can be given about acceptance of things that cannot be changed.
4. Hypnosis can be used to help people avoid identification with thoughts and feelings.
5. Hypnosis can help clients to become more actively accepting of certain unpleasant feelings.
6. Clients can be hypnotised to perceive negative thoughts as transient and unimportant.

They specifically recommend the use of the following hypnotherapy techniques in conjunction with mindfulness meditation:

1. Mental ("covert behavioural") rehearsal of previously avoided situations, as in exposure therapy.
2. Cue-controlled relaxation to help facilitate exposure to feared situations, as in applied relaxation.
3. The use of hypnotic desensitisation to facilitate relaxation during mental ("imaginal") exposure.
4. The use of hypnotic regression or reliving as a form of imaginal exposure to traumatic memories (as in PTSD treatment).
5. The use of suggestion to help clients tolerate the discomfort and repetition of exposure therapy.

They add that the most basic use of hypnosis in combination with mindfulness-based CBT would be in the use of suggestion to directly develop an ongoing state of mindfulness. Hence, paradoxically, they raise the possibility of using suggestions to induce mindfulness and undermine the suggestive power of automatic thoughts, such as the following: "Imagine that you are transparent, and disturbing thoughts and emotions cannot penetrate you or have any power to control your actions." Suggestions can be used to weaken (negative) suggestions, hypnosis to nullify (negative) self-hypnosis. In later chapters of the current volume, the use of mindfulness or "dehypnosis" strategies in cognitive-behavioural hypnotherapy will therefore be explored in rather more detail.

Overview of cognitive-behavioural hypnotherapy (CBH)

The approach recommended in this book focuses on the treatment of generic symptoms of stress and anxiety and draws upon four main traditions within cognitive-behavioural therapy, which are integrated in different ways with hypnotherapy.

1. Stress inoculation training (SIT), which provides a generic coping skills training framework for hypnotherapy as well as the implementation of certain mindfulness and acceptance-based strategies or "dehypnosis".
2. Exposure and response prevention (ERP) therapy, which provides a way of treating more severe anxiety.
3. Problem-solving therapy (PST), which provides a more flexible and strategic way of coping with a wide variety of problems.
4. Cognitive therapy, which provides a way of addressing faulty threat appraisals and other cognitive distortions, as well as psychological "distancing" techniques and strategies from mindfulness (contemplative) meditation traditions that can be reconceptualised as dehypnosis strategies.

Although diagnosis-specific conceptualisations and treatments are not included here, in favour of a more *transdiagnostic* perspective, the generic models of stress and anxiety employed naturally integrate with these, especially the approaches described in Beck's recent manual for cognitive therapy of anxiety disorders (Clark & Beck, 2010). Specific protocols for cognitive-behavioural hypnotherapy have also been published by other authors (Lynn & Kirsch, 2006; Alladin, 2008).

The first part of the book deals with the history and theory of hypnotism, first of all clarifying James Braid's original theory of hypnotism and then exploring modern cognitive-behavioural theories in more detail, highlighting the continuity between these two perspectives despite more than a century intervening. Not only is hypnosis very different from what many people assume, according to modern psychologists, but even its founder did not claim, for example, that hypnotism was a state of unconsciousness or sleep, etc. The second part of the book explores issues relating to assessment, conceptualisation, socialisation and skills training, as these subjects are not dealt with very well in most books on hypnotherapy. The third and final part describes the treatment approaches mentioned above in more detail, focusing closely on the various ways in which traditional hypnotherapeutic theory and practice can be profitably integrated with modern cognitive-behavioural therapy, within a broadly cognitive-behavioural reconceptualisation of hypnosis. Insofar as this cognitive-behavioural approach resembles central aspects of Braid's original theory of hypnotism, it might be reasonably described as a "return to Braid" or as a kind of "Neobraidism". Hence, it is to the history of hypnotism and the original theory and practice of Braid that we now turn.

CHAPTER TWO

James Braid and the original hypnotherapy

To understand modern hypnotherapy it's essential to have a basic grasp of the history of hypnotism. Unfortunately, that's an area which is surrounded by confusion. Hence, we must first consider how hypnotism originated, in opposition to Mesmerism, and how its essential nature was subsequently obscured by the tendency to confuse it with Mesmerism and the frequent use of certain misleading pieces of terminology. When key misconceptions are cleared away, the nature of the relationship between traditional hypnotism and modern cognitive-behavioural therapy (CBT) inevitably becomes more apparent.

James Braid (1795–1860) coined the English term "hypnotism", around 1841–1842, and is widely-considered to be the founder of both hypnotism and hypnotherapy. For example, Lynn and Kirsch, two of the leading cognitive-behavioural researchers in the field, open their recent textbook on evidence-based clinical hypnosis, by remarking: "Our use of the term hypnosis has its origin in the work of the nineteenth-century British physician James Braid" (Lynn & Kirsch, 2006, p. 6). A little-known fact is that Braid introduced "hypnotism" as an abbreviation for the longer-term "neuro-hypnotism", meaning sleep of the nervous system. This was the original expression coined by him to describe his discovery. Throughout his writings, Braid progressively developed a more specific psycho-physiological conceptualisation of hypnotism, eventually labelled the "monoideo-dynamic" model. This term literally denotes the seemingly automatic or reflex-like ("dynamic") power of focused attention on a single ("mono") train of thought or dominant cognition ("idea") to influence a wide range of behavioural and physiological responses (Braid, 1855, p. 81). He elsewhere refers to the monoideo-dynamic theory simply in terms of the "power of the mind over the body", for which he also coined the term "psycho-physiology". Braid's original theory and practice of hypnotism are sometimes referred to as "Braidism". As noted earlier, for convenience, we can perhaps refer to their reprisal in relation to modern psychological therapy as "Neobraidism" or as a "return to Braid."

The first complete edition of Braid's writings has recently been published, entitled *The Discovery of Hypnosis* (Braid, 2009). Shortly before his death in 1860, Braid summarised his final opinions on hypnotism in an article entitled "On Hypnotism." This has been dubbed Braid's "lost manuscript" because, although it contains many quotations from his earlier writings, after being translated into both French and German, the original English edition apparently disappeared, was all-but-forgotten, and has never been published. A backward translation was therefore made from the French and German editions, subsequently published with a brief report on its provenance in the most widely-referenced journal on hypnosis, *The International Journal of Clinical & Experimental Hypnosis* (Braid, 2009; Robertson, 2009). This article provides a concise summary of Braid's mature theory of hypnotism and is a far better account of his views than his original and best-known work, *Neurypnology* (1843). (A note on terminology: Braid used the word "hypnotism" to refer to the procedure, the discipline, and the condition of the subject, but never "hypnosis", so when discussing his writings his usage will generally be adopted.)

Braid was a Scottish surgeon who specialised in treating musculo-skeletal problems and eye conditions, particularly rectifying squints. He was influenced by one of the dominant movements in philosophical psychology of his day, known as the Scottish school of "Common Sense" realism, which emphasised naturalistic explanations in psychology and rejected speculative metaphysical theories. In the mid-nineteenth century, when medical science was still very much in its infancy, Braid was a staunch opponent of pseudoscience and known as a vigorous debunker of quack ("nostrum") remedies. He was a fierce opponent of Mesmerism, and coined the term "hypnotism" to distinguish his own opposing "common sense", psycho-physiological theory and practice. Braid concluded that hypnotism was primarily the result of selective focused attention upon an "expectant dominant idea", excluding intrusive thoughts or sensations, and that this could be induced and influenced by the interaction of multiple factors such as imagination, expectation, imitation, habitual associations, physical cues, and verbal suggestion, etc. He employed a variety of hypnotic strategies and practical techniques, several of which have been virtually forgotten today. However, his "eye-fixation" technique is still the best-known and most influential method of inducing hypnosis.

Braid believed, in opposition to the Mesmerists, that all hypnosis was essentially self-hypnosis and he therefore came to the view that his discovery bore greater similarity to ancient yogic meditation than it did to the "animal magnetism" of his predecessors. Unfortunately, after Braid's death, hypnotism gradually became more and more confused with Mesmerism, and subsequently mingled with quasi-Freudian theories about the "unconscious mind", which progressively obscured his original discoveries. Some key points are worth emphasising at the outset:

1. Braid never referred to the "unconscious mind", in fact he conceived of hypnotism as a form of conscious concentration and imagination.
2. He never referred to "hypnotic trance" and did not believe that hypnotism involved a trance-like state but rather emphasised its continuity with normal psychology, the term "trance" being reserved for a coma-like state rarely encountered in hypnotic subjects.
3. He did refer to "suggestion" but conceived of hypnotism as primarily a matter of autosuggestion or, as he put it, focused attention on "dominant ideas", that is, he would probably have agreed that "all hypnosis is essentially self-hypnosis".

4. He concluded that his theory of hypnotism had more in common with yogic meditation techniques than with Mesmerism.
5. Braid regretted his introduction of the term "hypnotism", albeit as an abbreviation for "neuro-hypnotism", because it misleadingly implies a state resembling sleep, and he emphasised that hypnotism was only accompanied by sleep-like amnesia in about ten per cent of his patients.
6. Braid strongly objected to the idea that people could be hypnotised against their will because, as he emphasised, subjects normally had to consent to the process and were conscious of what was being suggested to them, which they would typically reject if it seemed objectionable.
7. Braid's positive definition of hypnotism was that it consisted of "mental abstraction" or focused attention on an expectant dominant idea (or image), that is, selective attention to the idea or mental image of a response accompanied by the expectation of it occurring.

With the primitive means at his disposal, Braid adopted a vigorously empirical and scientific approach to developing his theory and practice, even more so than many twentieth century authors on hypnotism. Ironically, with the growing contemporary emphasis upon brief psychological therapies and evidence-based practice, Braid's fundamental orientation is back *en vogue* and a reappraisal of his work is long overdue. Braid's original hypnotism can, and should, therefore benefit from a *rapprochement* with modern evidence-based psychotherapy, especially the various forms of cognitive-behavioural therapy.

> I beg farther to remark, if my theory and pretensions, as to the nature, cause, and extent of the phenomena of nervous sleep, have none of the fascinations of the transcendental to captivate the lovers of the marvellous, the credulous and enthusiastic, which the pretensions and alleged occult agency of the Mesmerists have, still I hope my views will not be the less acceptable to honest and sober-minded men, because they are all level to our comprehension, and reconcilable with well-known physiological and psychological principles. (Braid, 1853, p. 109)

To summarise the main reasons for proposing a (partial) "return to Braid" in hypnotherapy:

1. Most of the problematic misconceptions in relation to hypnosis can be traced to a long-standing tendency to confuse Mesmerism with hypnotism.
2. Braid was a passionate skeptic and empiricist, who envisaged hypnotism as a "common sense" approach to psychological therapy.
3. Braid's original approach to hypnotism is appealingly simple and broadly consistent with modern cognitive-behavioural theory and practice.
4. Braid assumed that hypnosis explained psychopathology, to some extent, and attributed "hysteria" and other disturbances, in part, to spontaneous morbid ideas (i.e., autosuggestions), a very similar concept to Beck's negative "automatic thoughts".

As we shall see, in distinguishing hypnotism from Mesmerism, Braid reconceptualised it, based on the "ideo-motor" theory of his friend and ally William Carpenter, as a form of reciprocal interaction between "ideas" (cognitions) and motor responses ("behaviour"), which he subsumed under the general heading of "psycho-physiology." It's worth observing at the outset that the Victorian term "ideo-motor", central to hypnotherapy, happens to bear a similarity, by coincidence, to the modern term "cognitive-behavioural". Both can be taken to allude to the importance of cognitions or ideas in mediating behavioural (motor) responses or, in both cases, sometimes to the reciprocal interaction between cognition and behaviour.

Franz Mesmer and Victorian nostrum remedies

Many people, including many therapists and even hypnotists, falsely assume that hypnotism originated primarily in the work of the Austrian occultist and physician Franz Anton Mesmer (1734–1815). Mesmer was influenced by earlier practitioners who employed magnets for therapeutic purposes, placing them upon, or passing them across, the bodies of their patients. Mesmer himself found that he achieved similar results without the use of magnets, simply by passing his hands across the patient's body. Whereas most people would perhaps take this observation as evidence of the placebo effect or suggestion, Mesmer somewhat bizarrely concluded that his hands were magnetic; or rather that he must be channelling some mysterious form of biological "magnetism" through his own body and into that of his patients. The distinctive hand movements made by the Mesmerists became known as the "Mesmeric passes", because they typically involved repeatedly passing the hands across the surface of the body, at a slight distance, and in a somewhat theatrical manner.

Mesmer's doctrine was not entirely his own invention but derived from the writings of Paracelsus, Robert Fludd, and others (Bernheim, 1890, p. 14). However, he probably coined and certainly popularised the use of the term "animal magnetism" to distinguish this supposedly organic or biological version from ordinary "mineral magnetism". Nevertheless, many subsequent Mesmerists simply equated animal and mineral magnetism and assumed that ordinary magnets could control the flow of blood or function of the human nervous system. Braid carried out frequent informal experiments demonstrating that the reaction of some subjects to having a magnet, for example, held against their body was purely the result of expectation and suggestion; identical reactions occurred to fake (wooden) magnets and other placebos. In other words, Braid, Carpenter, and others, set about vigorously debunking Mesmerism and proving that its effects were due to the "power of the mind over the body" rather than any mysterious "magnetic" force. Hans Eysenck, one of the founders of behaviour therapy, who conducted early empirical research on hypnosis himself, therefore rightly observed:

> The terms "Mesmerise" and "hypnotise" have become quite synonymous, and most people think of Mesmer as the father of hypnosis, or at least as its discoverer and first conscious exponent. Oddly enough, the truth appears to be that while hypnotic phenomena had been known for many thousands of years, Mesmer did not, in fact, hypnotise his subjects at all. [...] It is something of a mystery why popular belief should have firmly credited him with a discovery which in fact was made by others. (Eysenck H., 1957, pp. 30–31)

Mesmer's patients would often experience violent emotional convulsions, fits or seizures termed "Mesmeric crises", which were supposed to bring about therapeutic results. (The Mesmeric "crises" were probably the forerunner of Freud and Breuer's concept of therapeutic "abreaction" in regression hypnotherapy and psychoanalysis.) In some cases these reactions may simply have been panic attacks or histrionic behaviour. Consequently, one of Mesmer's most illustrious followers, the French Marquis de Puysegur (1751–1825), made an important modification of technique in order to reduce the distress experienced by his patients. He began attempting to induce a more tranquil and relaxed condition termed "artificial somnambulism" because he believed (probably incorrectly) that it resembled the state of sleep-walkers. This innovation, the emphasis upon inducing a "somnambulistic" state resembling sedation or sleep, was part of the reason for the subsequent introduction of the problematic term "hypnotism", derived from the Greek word for "sleep", as we shall see.

Mesmerism spread widely throughout the following century and attracted numerous followers, many of whom introduced their own variation of the original theory and practice. In the Victorian era critics like Braid dubbed Mesmer's theories "occult", by which they actually meant approximately what we mean by "pseudoscientific" rather than specifically something magical or supernatural. However, from the outset Mesmer had indeed attributed supernatural qualities to animal magnetism, believing that it was somehow linked to astrology and the influence of the planets, and that it could be projected great distances, through walls or even across continents, stored in bottled water, or even bounced off mirrors. His followers, including the Marquis de Puysegur, continued to associate Mesmerism with claims of telepathy, clairvoyance, levitation, and other paranormal feats called the "higher phenomena". Consequently, Mesmerism was widely ridiculed as a "nostrum", that is, what we now call a "quack remedy." Sketches showing Mesmerists with the ears and tails of asses were not uncommon in popular publications, openly skeptical not only about the theory and practice of Mesmer's followers but regarding their personal character and integrity. The practice of Mesmerism closely resembles, and is probably a major precursor of and influence upon, several modern complementary therapies involving "subtle energy", etc. Moreover, the practice of animal magnetism generally appeared quite unreliable, it took at least half an hour, sometimes many hours, to induce most subjects, and only a minority of them were typically considered "sensitive" enough to fully respond.

Skeptics, of whom there were many, repeatedly attempted to debunk Mesmerism by demonstrating that the same reactions could consistently be induced by deception, that is, by falsely leading subjects to believe that they had been Mesmerised. For example, as its proponents claimed that animal magnetism travelled easily through walls, a subject might be (falsely) told that a Mesmerist in the next room was making passes, when he was not. Equally, when they were misled into believing they had *not* been Mesmerised, nothing ensued. For example, a Mesmerist might be asked to "magnetise" some water which could be given to a subject under the pretence that it was simply ordinary (un-magnetised) water. To a modern reader, it should be quite apparent that these experiments, although crude by contemporary scientific standards, constitute some of the earliest examples of "placebo controlled" studies in medicine. Collectively, the evidence of many such scientific experiments undermined the paranormal claims of the Mesmerists. However, they often did so by showing that real physical and mental reactions could be produced by creating the expectation that they would occur, or prevented by removing the same expectation. The most famous series of such experiments was carried out in 1784 by a committee of experts formed by the French Academy of Sciences, including Benjamin Franklin the American ambassador to France, who ultimately concluded that the results of Mesmerism were not due to "animal magnetism" but merely to the patients' "belief" and "imagination".

The vast majority of Mesmer's followers, therefore, believed that the Mesmerist (the "operator"), rather than the subject, was the one "in control" and causing the reactions. It was assumed that the Mesmerist's strength of will, or natural magnetism, determined the amount of influence he could exert over his patients rather than their attitudes or expectations. It should be noted that Mesmer's followers did not generally consider "self-mesmerism" or "self-magnetism" to be possible, because of the nature of their theory. They essentially considered the subject to be almost entirely passive while being "operated upon" by the Mesmerist. They believed that Mesmerism could operate by "silent willing", that is, without any communication at all between operator and subject—who could be in different rooms or even continents apart. As we shall see, the concept of "hypnotism" was introduced in direct opposition to these ideas, to correct the errors of the Mesmerists. However, the widespread confusion of hypnotism with Mesmerism has become a source of common misconceptions, which have actually been found to hinder the effectiveness of modern hypnotherapy insofar as they are liable to confuse and alienate clients—not to mention other professionals.

James Braid, the father of hypnotherapy

As noted above, the discovery of "hypnotism", as opposed to Mesmerism, is widely attributed to the James Braid. Braid began as a skeptic, dismissing all of the alleged effects of Mesmerism as due to misconception or even deceit. In November 1841, after attending several public demonstrations in a Manchester theatre by the Swiss Mesmerist named Charles Lafontaine, Braid and his friends mounted the stage in protest, crying "Humbug!", but were galled to discover that Lafontaine's subject, Mary, seemed to be exhibiting *genuine* physiological changes and a profound insensitivity to pain. The young girl's pulse had become unusually "small and rapid" while her eyes seemed involuntarily rolled back in their sockets and her eyelids had become temporarily cataleptic, making it difficult for her to open them. Braid tested Mary by forcing a pin between one of her nails and the end of her finger, during which tortuous experiment she appeared to remain asleep and impassive. Braid and his companions must have been left standing aghast on the stage before an audience in turmoil. This dramatic incident marks the birth of hypnotism, because it propelled Braid into a programme of vigorous clinical and experimental research that would occupy the remaining two decades of his life.

Braid, formerly a brash skeptic, now moderated his viewpoint and made the motto of his first book a quote from the influential Scottish philosopher of mind, Professor Dugald Stewart: "Unlimited scepticism is equally the child of imbecility as implicit credulity." Stewart was a key figure in the academic tradition termed Scottish "Common Sense" or "Realist" philosophy, which Braid aligned himself with. He claimed that the phenomena of Mesmerism should be salvaged by physicians adopting a more rational and scientific approach, while avoiding the worst excesses of its metaphysical speculations. Instead, he specifically encouraged them to develop a "doctrine of the bond between mind and body". (Braid coined the term "psycho-physiology" to designate his own research in the area of mind-body interactions.) Moreover, Stewart specifically encouraged physicians to investigate "the effect of *fixing and concentrating the attention*, in giving to ideal [i.e., imaginary] objects the power of realities over the belief", adding:

[Lord Francis Bacon had urged physicians] to ascertain how far it is possible *to fortify and exalt the imagination*, and by what means this may most effectually be done. The class of facts here alluded to, are manifestly of the same description with those to which the attention of philosophers has been lately called by *the pretensions of Mesmer* […]. (Stewart, 1827, italics added)

In other words, Stewart called for Mesmerism to be reconceptualised in terms of the subject's attention being fixated on certain ideas, with which her imagination becomes engaged. He saw heightened attention and imagination as providing a natural explanation of how suggestive ideas, words, and mental images, could evoke reactions similar to those experienced if the things imagined were real. In accord with Stewart's "Common Sense" agenda, therefore, Braid set about a programme of empirical research, repeatedly testing variations of the Mesmeric technique under different conditions with many different patients and often before various groups of scientists, academics, doctors, and surgeons. He was particularly drawn to the observation that subjects were apparently "Mesmerised" when Lafontaine gripped their thumbs and instructed them to fixate their gaze for a prolonged period on his eyes. Grasping for a more common sense explanation, Braid initially identified this fixation of the gaze as a key ingredient, which he soon realised involved a temporary fixation of the subject's attention.

Braid's initial experiments thoroughly confirmed his suspicion that a similar state of artificial "sleep" could be induced, without animal magnetism, simply by instructing subjects to remain completely motionless, breathe gently (as a way of reducing anxiety), and fix their gaze rigidly on a single "unexciting" object in a position causing strain to the muscles surrounding the eyes, until they were forced to close by the resulting fatigue, which seems normally to have taken around two minutes by Braid's initial method. This observation formed the basis of the classic "eye-fixation" hypnotic induction technique. Braid modified it in many ways, and many modern variations exist. The original version seems to have focused mainly on producing a powerful sense of muscular fatigue in the eyes, as they often began to water before closing and Braid describes the initial discomfort of this method as being too much for a handful of his clients. Braid, an eye surgeon, described this technique as requiring a "double internal and upward squint", to generate maximum strain upon the muscles of the eyes. He subsequently found it unnecessary to produce this intense strain in all clients, and made his technique gentler and more versatile by making more use of verbal suggestions.

Braid immediately began experimenting on other doctors and scientists, and giving public demonstrations of hypnotism with groups of subjects, etc. He soon proved that by a simple physical method, without any reference to "animal magnetism", or any attempt to employ it, he could not only induce the same physical and mental reactions found in Mesmerism, and bring about similar therapeutic improvements in patients, but do so more quickly and reliably, as even many Mesmerists admitted. Indeed, the Mesmerists were so disconcerted by these public demonstrations that they resorted to the somewhat desperate claim that Braid must be such a naturally powerful Mesmerist himself that he was projecting the force of animal magnetism into his subjects unconsciously, without *intending* to do so! However, Braid soon found that anyone could induce hypnotism, with little or no training, which further contradicted the basic assumptions of the Mesmerists. Moreover, despite carrying out repeated experiments, Braid concluded that it was impossible to produce the "higher phenomena", the supernatural powers, claimed by the Mesmerists. By character, Braid was the polar opposite of the flamboyant Mesmer; he was down-to-earth and vigorously empirical in his attitude. He proceeded as a skeptic and insisted on repeatedly testing his own assumptions, which led to many modifications of his theory and practice over the years. As such, Braid was arguably a (very early) forerunner of modern evidence-based practice in the psychological therapies.

Altogether, Braid published one full-length book and over fifty smaller booklets, essays, letters, and articles in the medical journals of his day. His writings were most frequently embraced by *The Medical Times* and published in other respected medical journals, including *The Lancet* and the *Association Medical Journal*, forerunner of the modern *British Medical Journal* (BMJ). However, Braid's great opponent and rival, John Elliotson, editor of *The Zoist*, the main journal of Mesmerism, repeatedly maligned him while refusing to publish anything Braid wrote. His first major work, *Neurypnology* (1843), was written less than two years after his discovery of hypnotism and sets out his initial observations in full, focusing upon the physiological phenomena of hypnotism, although his later writings culminate in a greater emphasis upon psychological factors such as suggestion. Braid coined the term "hypnotism" as an abbreviation for "neurohypnotism" (nervous sleep) which he defined in the opening pages of *Neurypnology* as a "peculiar condition of the nervous system, induced by a fixed and abstracted attention of the mental and visual eye, on one object, not of an exciting nature" (Braid, 2009, p. 290). "Neurypnology", the title of his first book, is an abbreviation of "neuro-hypnology" and was intended to mean, in plain English, the theory (or as he puts it "rationale") of neuro-hypnotism.

Hypnotism was originally defined, therefore, as a specific condition of nervous "sleep" (which perhaps meant neurological inhibition) induced by prolonged selective attention upon a single monotonous point of focus. As we shall see, Braid recognised from the outset that what he chose to call "nervous sleep" was not the same as normal sleep, and was usually accompanied by consciousness. He also clearly did not equate hypnotism with relaxation as he frequently, apparently in at least half of his clients, induced a state of rigid muscular catalepsy throughout the body during which he repeatedly claimed to observe a substantial increase in their heart rate, typically a doubling. Hence, although it is not particularly clear in his original book, Braid appears to have conceived of hypnotism primarily as a state of particularly intense selective attention ("mental abstraction") which could be associated either with profound physical relaxation ("nervous sleep") or tension ("catalepsy"), depending on the subject's focus of attention during the procedure. It is also not clear in Braid's early writings what his subjects focused their attention upon once their eyes closed. However, he later explains that after staring at an "unexciting object" such as the tip of his lancet case or the top of a wine bottle, for a few minutes, the patients' eyes would close and they would be directed to transfer the focus of their attention on to the sensation of drowsiness ("nervous sleep") or tension ("catalepsy"), which thereby became intensified, for a longer period of time, as required (Braid, 1852, p. 150).

The battle with Mesmerism

Hence, although many people, even today, assume that Mesmerism and hypnotism are the same thing and use the words interchangeably, Braid coined the term "hypnotism" precisely to emphasise the difference between his own theory and practice and that of the Mesmerists, that is, to refer to "the discovery I have made of certain peculiar phenomena derived and elicited by my mode of operating" (Braid, 1843, p. 290). In 1845, he wrote in *The Lancet*, "I adopted the term 'hypnotism' to prevent my being confounded with those who entertain these extreme notions, as well as to get rid of the erroneous theory about a magnetic fluid, or esoteric influence of any description being the cause of the sleep" (Braid, 2009, p. 10).

> For a considerable time I was of opinion that the phenomena induced by my mode of operating and that of the Mesmerisers, were identical; and, so far as I have yet personally seen, I still consider the condition of the nervous system induced by both modes to be at least analogous. It appeared to me that the fixation of the mind and eyes was attained occasionally during the monotonous movements of the Mesmerisers, and thus they succeeded sometimes, and as it were, by chance; whereas, by my insisting on the eyes being fixed in the most favourable position, and the mind thus riveted to one idea, as the primary and imperative conditions, my success was consequently general and the effects intense, while theirs was feeble and uncertain. However, from what the Mesmerisers state as to effects which they can produce in certain cases, there seem to be differences sufficient to warrant the conclusion that they ought to be considered as distinct agencies. (Braid, 1843, p. 294)

Braid goes on to argue that hypnotism is distinguished from Mesmerism because it places far greater emphasis upon an empirical approach and eschews the paranormal claims central to Mesmerism, for example, alleged phenomena such as telepathy and clairvoyance, and the notion of a supernatural force called "animal magnetism".

Responding to Dugald Stewart's appeal for a scientific alternative to Mesmerism, Braid summed up the Common Sense agenda in the conclusion to one of his booklets criticising Mesmerism and other Victorian subtle-energy therapies over their pseudo-scientific nature.

> My theory, moreover, has this additional recommendation, that it is level to our comprehension, and adequate to account for all which is demonstrably true, without offering any violence to reason and common sense, or being at variance with generally admitted physiological and psychological principles. (Braid, 1851, p. 199)

Indeed, Braid consistently appealed to scientific method and, in particular to a version of the principle known as "Occam's Razor", insisting that explanations of Mesmeric phenomena should first be tried "in accordance with generally admitted physiological and psychological principles" (Braid, 1852, p. 140). In other words, Braid argued that "common sense" psychological processes such as expectation, imagination, focused attention, and habit, provided a more parsimonious explanation for the effects under investigation than the introduction of a "new agency" in the form of animal magnetism.

Hence, he was forced to conclude, "It will be observed, for reasons adduced, I have now entirely separated Hypnotism from Animal Magnetism" (Braid, 1843, p. 288). This inevitably led to an ongoing conflict between Braid and several leading Mesmerists. It is true that Braid once toyed with the notion that "Hypnotism might therefore not inaptly be designated, Rational Mesmerism, in contra-distinction to the Transcendental Mesmerism of the Mesmerists" (Braid, 1850, p. 201) but he thought better of it and abandoned this idea. Moreover, Henry Brookes, a popular authority on animal magnetism was also quoted by Braid as writing:

> I am very glad you have at length found reason to change your original opinion as to the identity of your phenomena with those of Mesmerism. From the very first I freely admitted the value and importance of your discovery, but I could not admit that identity, and I blamed you for insisting upon it so hastily, and using such hard words against the animal magnetists, because they could not agree with you. I thought, and still think, you did wrong in that, and that you certainly did yourself injustice, for in fact you are the original discoverer of a *new agency*, and not of a mere modification of an old one. (Brookes, quoted in Braid, 1843, p. 289)

Even leading Mesmerists, therefore, including Brookes and the eminent surgeon Herbert Mayo, argued that Braid was the "discoverer of a new agency", of hypnotism, which they emphatically distinguished from Mesmerism. Widespread modern misconceptions about hypnosis, such as the notion that it involves controlling the mind of the subject by inducing a mysterious "trance" state, and is mainly due to the mysterious "power" of the hypnotist, are largely due to the popular confusion of hypnotism with Mesmerism. To make matters worse, this misunderstanding has long been deliberately fostered by stage hypnotists for theatrical purposes, that is, to generate a sense of mystique and dramatic effect (Barber, Spanos & Chaves, 1974). Moreover, it is the image of hypnotism that novels and films like to portray. When Count Dracula "hypnotises" a young virgin by staring deep into her eyes, in the old horror films, we are actually witnessing something loosely inspired by the practices of Mesmerism rather than by the hypnotism of Braid.

Braid and yogic meditation

One of the central points of difference between hypnotism and Mesmerism was that Braid had immediately observed that the "power" of inducing hypnotism was primarily attributable to the subject rather than the hypnotist; this is what Braid means when he repeatedly refers to hypnotism as "subjective" and "personal". (Braid definitely cannot mean "subjective" in the modern sense of being relative to the subject's conscious perspective, or merely imaginary, because he also stressed, vigorously and repeatedly, that hypnotism was a physiologically real phenomenon.) He quickly discovered that he could teach clients how to hypnotise themselves, and he made good use of "self-hypnotism", as he called it, in coping with his own attacks of rheumatic pain. There is no such thing as "self-mesmerism" or "self-magnetism", however, because the theory of animal magnetism fundamentally conflicts with the notion that its effects could be self-induced. Braid was therefore the first person to discuss the concept of self-hypnosis, as we understand it today. However, more than that, he considered the possibility of "self-hypnotism" to be central to our understanding of how all hypnotism works, even when apparently "induced" by a second individual acting as hypnotist. This subject-centred perspective, the emphasis on self-hypnosis, is also characteristic of modern cognitive-behavioural approaches to hypnotism (Lynn & Kirsch, 2006, p. 61). Braid's conclusion that all hypnotism is largely self-hypnotism must be emphasised, therefore, because it marks a very fundamental piece of common ground between the original approach and modern cognitive-behavioural theories of hypnosis.

Shortly before beginning his own practice of self-hypnotism, Braid became acquainted with several books describing Oriental meditation techniques practised by Hindu yogis and Muslim Sufis and he soon began publishing his reflections on the analogy between hypnotism and meditation. He immediately recognised that his own technique of hypnotism, "mental abstraction", bore much closer resemblance to the techniques of meditation than it did to the magnetic passes, etc., of Mesmerism. Meditation is normally self-induced, *like* hypnotism but *unlike* Mesmerism. Braid's interest in meditation really developed when he was introduced to the *Dabistān-i Mazāhib*, the "School of Religions", an ancient Persian text describing a variety of Oriental religious practices.

> Last May [1843], a gentleman residing in Edinburgh, personally unknown to me, who had long resided in India, favoured me with a letter expressing his approbation of the views which I had published on the nature and causes of hypnotic and mesmeric phenomena. In corroboration of my views, he referred to what he had previously witnessed in oriental regions, and recommended me to look into the "Dabistan," a book lately published, for additional proof to the same effect. On much recommendation I immediately sent for a copy of the "Dabistan", *in which I found many statements corroborative of the fact, that the eastern saints are all self-hypnotisers, adopting means essentially the same as those which I had recommended for similar purposes*. (Braid, 1844–1845)

Braid used this as further evidence against the Mesmerists, that is, proof that similar psychological and physiological states were widely regarded in other cultures as resulting from the behaviour of the individual subject, independently of any external force such as animal magnetism.

Hence, in his later writings, Braid stated that hypnotism was "entirely new" and his own "discovery" to the best of his knowledge, until he stumbled across the technique of meditation, which he conceded could be seen as its distant precursor (Braid, 1852, p. 137). Indeed, Braid eagerly admitted that "there is nothing new under the sun" and that the "vague, and confused, and dreamy idea" of hypnotism might have been around since ancient times. However, "It is only when an individual has been enabled, in some measure, to explain the nature and cause of certain phenomena, or at least to devise means for gaining such certainty and precision to processes and their sequences and relations, as shall give a definite form and practical bearing to the ideas, that they really come to merit the appellation of a *discovery*" (Braid, 1852, p. 138). On that basis, Braid defended his right to be recognised as the modern "author of hypnotism" and its discoverer, although he saw in yogic meditation and other practices the ancient Oriental precursor of self-hypnotism. Whereas the yogis Braid read of focused their attention on the tips of their noses, his own patients focused on some object or the tip of his finger. However, Braid's hypnotic patients were often instructed to focus their attention on the centre of their forehead instead, which he subsequently discovered to be identical to a common yogic meditation technique. Hence, both methods frequently involved intense, prolonged, focused attention upon a single object or idea, to the temporary exclusion of other thoughts or sensations. Hence, whereas modern psychotherapists have emphasised the similarities between their techniques and Buddhist, *contemplative* meditation, Braid, 150 years earlier, keenly drew attention to the parallels between hypnotism and yogic, *concentrative* meditation techniques.

William B. Carpenter and the ideo-motor reflex

About six years after his discovery of hypnotism, Braid was visited by Professor William Benjamin Carpenter (1813–1885) of the University of London and Royal Institution, who travelled up to Manchester to witness Braid's demonstrations of hypnotism first-hand (Braid, 2009, p. 235). Carpenter was a highly regarded academic and scientist, an authority in the nascent field of "mental physiology", a kind of distant Victorian forerunner of modern neuro-psychology. He shared Braid's skepticism about the supernatural claims of the Mesmerists and his desire to identify the true psychological and physiological basis of the phenomena in question. Carpenter introduced the concept of the "ideo-motor reflex" response, a primitive neuro-psychological model of suggestion and psychological automatism, which, as we shall see, Braid thoroughly assimilated as the basis of his revised conceptualisation of hypnotism.

From this point onward, Braid and Carpenter essentially became allies in the ongoing battle against the pseudoscientific doctrines and paranormal claims of the Mesmerists. Carpenter reported positively on Braid's technique of "hypnotic therapeutics" and his experiments; Braid embraced Carpenter's concepts and terminology regarding the psychology of suggestion. It is ironic given the traditional gulf between research and clinical practice, especially pronounced in modern hypnotherapy, that Braid's clinical work as a surgeon and general practitioner using hypnotism was so closely intertwined with the experimental studies he shared with Carpenter, the academic and scientist. Hypnotism was born out of this historical dialogue between scientific research and clinical practice and Braid was, in a sense, a Victorian psychological scientist-practitioner, although his methods were necessarily of a very primitive kind compared to modern psychotherapists and clinical psychologists. The Mesmerists certainly viewed the potent combination of Carpenter's reputation as a scientist and Braid's successful clinical demonstrations as posing a serious threat to the credibility of their own approach. John Elliotson, in particular, through his editorship of *The Zoist*, appears to have strongly opposed Braid and Carpenter as the enemies of Mesmerism, a controversy which Braid discusses at length in *The Critics Criticised* (1855). Elliotson continually attacked, and insulted, Braid in writing in an attempt to undermine hypnotism and strangle it at birth. It is remarkable that Elliotson is so often cited as a pioneer of hypnotism when in fact he was undoubtedly one of its staunchest and most aggressive opponents. The constant animosity of Elliotson prompted Braid to refer to the problem of *odium mesmericum,* a play of words on *odium theologicum* and *odium medicum*, by which he meant the irrational hatred of Mesmerists for their critics and those working on psychological techniques such as hypnotism.

Who discovered hypnotism?

At this point, it may be worth acknowledging that some disagreement does exist over Braid's claim to be the "author" or founder of hypnotism. Some scholars have noted that prior to

Braid's time, the Mesmerists Abbé de Faria and his follower Alexandre Bertrand also seemed to reject the concept of magnetism and to appeal instead to suggestion as the true explanation of Mesmeric phenomena. However, it was pointed out by Braid's early defenders that Faria and Bertrand's views "exercised no practical influence on Mesmeric theory" prior to the development of neuro-hypnotism (Bramwell, 1896, p. 38). Moreover, Faria in particular seems to have mixed his psychological observations with somewhat obscure mystical ideas in a manner totally alien to Braid's more empirical approach. This criticism regarding the issue of priority was actually mentioned to Braid and he responded by asserting that Faria had attributed the effects of Mesmerism solely to the imagination, whereas Braid emphasised the reciprocal inter-action between both mental and physical responses. He likewise concluded that Faria's technique, primarily involving verbal commands to "sleep", was fundamentally different from his own eye-fixation method, which was based upon the interaction between behavioural and cognitive factors (Braid, 1843, p. 288).

Braid's theory of hypnotism

Mental abstraction and monoideism

Hence, although Braid's earlier writings sometimes appear to emphasise physical processes and the concept of hypnotism as an unusual physiological state of nervous sleep, his later writings speak of it as a "mental theory", emphasising psychological processes (suggestion, imagination, expectation, etc.) and the concept of hypnotism as a form of mental focus (or selective attention, "abstraction") with important analogues in everyday experiences such as daydreaming or absent-mindedness. Indeed, within a decade of publishing *Neurypnology* (1843) he wrote that hypnotism "is essentially a state of mental concentration" (Braid, 1853, p. 92). The main reason for this shift in emphasis seems perhaps to have been Braid's observation that it was impossible to hypnotise certain mentally impaired clients because of their difficulty focusing attention. This conclusion was further reinforced by the fact that one of his best subjects found that she could not be hypnotised one day because the symptoms of a fever were affecting her concentration on that occasion (Braid, 1860, p. 67). Hence, Braid was gradually forced to conclude that mental focus, a psychological factor, was more important than eye-fatigue in inducing hypnotism. Some of his critics certainly perceived this as a *volte face* (Braid, 1851, p. 187).

However, it should be emphasised that the notions of neuro-hypnotism and mono-ideism are not quite as different as they may at first appear. Braid had always insisted that hypnotism was both induced and (normally) characterised by mental abstraction, single-pointed attention, and he was eager to emphasise that attention and inattention are two sides of the same coin. The more we become engrossed in a single impression, the more we tend to exclude other thoughts or impressions from our awareness, a phenomenon perfectly captured by the term "mental abstraction", meaning something like "selective awareness" in modern terms. Indeed, one of the key differences between hypnotherapy and modern psychotherapy, including cognitive-behavioural therapy (CBT), is that hypnotherapy places far greater emphasis upon managing the allocation of the client's attention during, for example, mental imagery or self-talk (autosuggestion) procedures. In his final "lost manuscript", therefore, Braid wrote:

> All that produces a strong excitation, all that modifies the preliminary state of the thoughts and the feelings, surely also modifies the mental and physical state of the individual, especially if it occurs with confidence, expectation, and concentration of mind. (Braid, 1860)

Braid was aware that certain problems might be better dealt with by focusing attention upon positive ideas, for example, self-confidence and assertiveness. Whereas others were better understood in terms of attention is being withdrawn, for example, distraction from acute pain and discomfort during surgery. However, removing awareness is often best achieved by focusing it on something else instead, for example, picturing a pleasant holiday scene in order to distract oneself from being in the dentist's chair. Braid took this for granted in his hypnotic eye-fixation induction which used focused attention upon any unexciting object, such as the top of a china ornament or the neck of a wine bottle, in order to temporarily "abstract" the client's attention from everything else and thereby induce a sense of inward mental focus and fading consciousness of the external environment. Braid compared hypnotism, in this regard, to the everyday phenomenon of absent-mindedness, in which someone may become so engrossed in a train of thought as to be oblivious to his environment for a while. The conceptualisation of "worry" and "rumination" as processes of thinking that capture attention, in a morbid way, has become a focus of recent research in cognitive-behavioural therapy (Wells, 2009). Worry and rumination resemble the states of reverie and absent-mindedness that Braid used to illustrate what he meant by hypnotism. Indeed, reconceptualising worry and rumination as processes resembling (spontaneous and unintentional) "negative self-hypnosis" (NSH) may provide an important way to link Braid's hypnotism to modern CBT, as noted earlier.

The expression "hypnotic trance"

Although the animal magnetists referred to the notion that some of their subjects entered a Mesmeric "trance", Braid never actually mentioned "hypnotic trance." In fact, virtually the only time he does make use of the word "trance" is in his book *Observations on Trance or Human Hybernation* (1850). This book speculates upon the alleged phenomenon of "human hibernation" in which people appear to have almost died but may subsequently return to their normal state. Braid refers to many anecdotal examples, most of which are rather dubious, including stories brought by from India about fakirs who claim to be able to be buried alive for many days by slowing down or suspending their vital functions.

Braid took these claims seriously and compared them to the medical condition known as "catalepsy" and the biological phenomenon of animal hibernation. At this time, the words "trance" and "catalepsy" were used synonymously in medicine to describe various loosely defined medical conditions resembling what we might now be classed as a coma or possibly catatonic psychosis. Braid prefaces his book, in fact, by quoting the medical writer Robert Macnish's definition of "trance". The full passage from Macnish's *The Philosophy of Sleep* (1830) defines the meaning of "trance" as follows:

> The most singular species, however, of suspended animation, is that denominated catalepsy, or trance. No affection, to which the animal frame is subject, is more remarkable than this. During its continuance, the whole body is cold, rigid, and inflexible; the countenance without colour; the eyes fixed and motionless: while breathing and the pulsation of the heart are, to all appearance, at an end. The mental powers, also, are generally suspended, and participate in the universal torpor which pervades the frame. In this extraordinary condition, the person may remain for several days, having all, or nearly all, the characteristics of death impressed upon him. [...] There is such an apparent extinction of every faculty essential to life, that it is inconceivable how existence should go on during the continuance of the fit. (Macnish, 1830, pp. 261–262)

Indeed, the English word "trance" appears to derive, via old French, from the Latin verb *transir*, meaning to depart, pass over to the other side, or die. Macnish thought this death-like condition could be induced by physical disease, but also by "a fit of terror" or by hysteria. It should be evident today, as it was to Braid, that this condition in no way resembles that of the typical hypnotic subject. Hence, proceeding upon the basis of Macnish's account, Braid uses the terms "catalepsy", "trance", and "hibernation" as equivalents. He believed that it was feasible that fakirs might be able to induce a similar state through regulation of their breathing and intense meditation techniques. In one passage, Braid did compare this death-like state to unusually profound hypnotic relaxation, writing of "the deep state of self-hypnotism, which I have likened to trance or hybernation in man". However, he clearly did not believe that a state resembling hibernation is at all common during hypnotism, that is, that it is the exception rather than the rule.

In other words, Braid did not refer to hypnotic "trance", except to suggest in passing that the deepest level of hypnotic sleep involved a profound relaxation and insensibility which could, tentatively, be compared to phenomena like hibernation, alleged burial alive, intense yogic meditation, and the death-like medical condition known as "catalepsy or trance." In his later writings, Braid refers to this state as "hypnotic coma", and implies that it occurs in a very small percentage of subjects:

> [...] let the term *hypnotic coma* denote that still deeper stage of the sleep in which the patient seems to be quite unconscious at the time of all external impressions, and devoid of voluntary power, and in whom no idea of what had been said or done by others during the said state of hypnotic coma can be remembered by the patient on awaking, or at any stage of subsequent hypnotic operations. (Braid, 1855)

Hence, by "trance" Braid meant a state of relaxation resembling an artificial coma and he clearly felt this was a rare and unusual effect, by no means the normal state of typical hypnotic subjects. He also perhaps wanted to distance himself from the use made by Mesmerists of the term "trance", which they tended to equate with clairvoyance and other supernatural powers. However, later writers on the subject typically confuse hypnotism with Mesmerism and so the term "trance" gradually crept into the language as a way of describing the hypnotic subject. The term "hypnotic trance" is therefore still popular with many hypnotherapists, especially the followers of Milton Erickson. However, many hypnosis researchers, especially those in the cognitive-behavioural tradition, consider it a serious hindrance both in scientific discourse and in explaining hypnosis to clients. For example, Clarke and Jackson, in an early textbook on cognitive-behavioural hypnotherapy, wrote, "One of the main barriers to the full acceptance of hypnosis has been the use of 'trance' as an explanation for the state from which hypnosis phenomena spring" (Clarke & Jackson, 1983, p. 31). Likewise, Lynn & Kirsch, two of the leading contemporary researchers, write:

> The idea that hypnosis involves a trance state may be the most pernicious of all popular ideas about hypnosis. Decades of research have failed to confirm the hypothesis that responses to suggestion are due to an altered state of consciousness, and as a result this hypothesis has been abandoned by most researchers in the field. (Lynn & Kirsch, 2006, p. 44)

As they also observe, among those researchers and clinicians who do continue to use the terminology of "hypnotic trance" the concept has been dramatically watered-down, to the point where it refers to something akin to mental absorption and is compared to everyday experiences such as being engrossed in a movie or a daydream. This would probably equate to what Braid meant by mental abstraction or focused attention but, like the cognitive-behavioural researchers today, he considered "trance" the wrong word to describe what normally happens during hypnotism.

Indeed, under normal circumstances, ordinary people virtually never refer to being engrossed in a story, watching a movie or reading a novel, as *literally* being in a "trance"—it's too strong a word for such a mundane experience. When hypnotherapists use the word "trance" in this very loose sense, it tends to confuse their clients, who normally expect it to mean something else. Moreover, when clients believe that they must enter a hypnotic trance it often creates problems for hypnotherapy. Many clients are frightened by this notion, and become defensive, whereas others develop unrealistic expectations of dramatic results which can lead to disappointment. Most of all, though, it tends to foster confusion regarding the client's role, as she sits listening to the hypnotist and wonders, "What am I supposed to be feeling?" In general, the concept can encourage her to adopt a "wait and see" attitude of extreme passivity which has been shown to reduce the effectiveness of hypnotic suggestions (Lynn & Kirsch, 2006, p. 45). Instead of explaining hypnotism as requiring "trance", it may therefore be preferable to say to some clients, for example, "It's a bit like doing meditation in some ways; you're just using your imagination to actively experience the things I describe but allowing yourself to do so with more confidence and focused attention than normal." Moreover, although hypnotism might resemble certain forms of "mental imagery", "attention training", or "meditation" techniques, etc., found in modern CBT, practitioners in that field never use the word "trance", which they would probably find inappropriate and misleading. Indeed, the use of that particular piece of terminology is almost certainly a major and totally unnecessary barrier to constructive dialogue between hypnotism and other psychological therapies.

Hypnotism distinguished from sleep

Braid also constantly struggled against the misconception that hypnotism entailed a state of unconsciousness or sleep, resembling general anaesthesia. He coined the term "hypnotism", as we have seen, as an abbreviation for "neuro-hypnotism", meaning sleep of the nervous system. Whatever Braid actually meant by this terminology it's clear that he did *not* mean sleep as ordinarily experienced. Nevertheless, the confusion of hypnosis with sleep, amnesia, and unconsciousness has become a perennial problem for hypnotherapists as popular representations of hypnotism in stage hypnosis shows and Hollywood films, etc., tend to portray the subject as being unconscious of her behaviour. Modern cognitive-behavioural therapists using hypnosis have testified to the stubbornness of this particular misconception:

> One, if not *the* major misconception associated with hypnosis, is that it is a form of sleep or involves a loss of consciousness. Patients presenting for hypnotic treatment will frequently express the view that they expect not to be able to hear anything or, alternatively, expect to be unaware of what is going on. This particular misconception appears hard to ablate by prehypnosis discussion. Even after detailed discussion on the issue, we have observed that patients express the "but I could hear everything around me" view after termination of a successful hypnosis episode. (Clarke & Jackson, 1983, p. 2)

In a sense, as Braid observed, hypnotism is actually the *opposite* of normal sleep because it entails prolonged conscious attention whereas sleep normally entails a diffuse awareness and "loss of power of fixing the attention" (Braid, 1852, p. 149).

Although roughly one in ten of Braid's patients did report experiencing amnesia he came to the surprising conclusion that they were nevertheless conscious of everything which had happened. Braid, and subsequently Bernhiem, were both forced to accept this interpretation of events because they found that amnestic subjects can subsequently remember what happened, in most cases, when it is suggested to them that they can do so. This phenomenon seems to prove that hypnotism is sometimes characterised by amnesia but *not* unconsciousness, although the two are very easily confused. Indeed, those clients who do experience spontaneous amnesia will often insist that they were asleep and unconscious throughout the process and this is a common cause of error among novice hypnotists. In addition to the fact that this amnesia seems reversible, which would be impossible if they had genuinely been unconscious, amnestic subjects also tend to answer questions, move in response to suggestions, etc., in a way which seems to prove that they can hear the hypnotist whether or not they remember doing so afterwards. Most noticeably, they virtually always hear, respond to, and *remember*, the final suggestions to emerge from hypnosis, which is difficult to explain if it's assumed they were truly unconscious throughout the procedure.

Braid was fond of quoting from *The Human Body* (1851), a book by Dr. J. J. G. Wilkinson, one of his own clients, and an enthusiastic convert to hypnotism, who expressed himself in infinitely more ornate language than his mentor. Braid quotes a "beautiful" and "elegant" description of hypnotism by Wilkinson, which he undoubtedly felt was, in some ways, superior to his own. It also constitutes one of those rare and valuable documents, a detailed self-report from the client of a famous therapist. Wilkinson described his understanding of the difference between sleep and hypnotism as follows, based on his personal experience of Braid's method:

> The atom of sleep is diffusion; the mind and body are dissolved in unconsciousness; they go off into nothing, through the fine powder of infinite variety, and die of no attention; common

sleep is impersonal. The unit of hypnotism is intense attention, abstraction—the personal ego pushed to nonentity. […] Patients can produce the hypnotic state upon themselves, without a second party; although a second will often strengthen the result by his acts or presence, just as one who stood by and told you that you were to succeed in a certain work would nerve your arm with fresh confidence.

Wilkinson likewise distinguished hypnotism from the supposedly telepathic process of Mesmerism. He continued:

The preliminary state (of hypnotism) is that of abstraction, and this abstraction is the logical premise of what follows. Abstraction tends to become more and more abstract, narrower and narrower; it tends to unity, and afterwards to nullity. There, then, the patient is, at the summit of attention, with no object left—a mere statue of attention—a listening, expectant life—a perfectly undistracted faculty, dreaming of a lessening and lessening mathematical point, the end of his mind sharpened away to nothing. What happens? Any sensation that appeals is met by this brilliant attention, and receives its diamond glare, being perceived with a force of leisure of which our distracted life affords only the rudiments. External influences are sensated, sympathized with, to an extraordinary degree, harmonious music sways the body into graces the most affecting; discords jar it as though they would tear it limb from limb; cold and heat are perceived with equal exultation, so also smells and touches. In short, the whole man appears to be given to each perception, the body trembles like down with the wafts of the atmosphere, the world plays upon it as upon a spiritual instrument finely attuned. (Wilkinson quoted in Braid, 1852, pp. 149–150)

Braid comments that Wilkinson himself merely entered the initial stage ("first conscious stage") of hypnotism. Although this is the most common type of hypnosis, experienced by the vast majority of Braid's clients, there were also conditions where the opposite happens to the attention and the subject does appear to be more asleep, or unconscious of his environment (Braid, 1852, p. 150). Although not amnestic, Wilkinson was clearly a gifted hypnotic subject, and given his striking way with language it is tempting to wonder whether he may have been an exceptionally "fantasy-prone" or highly creative and imaginative type. Highly responsive hypnotic subjects sometimes possess vivid imaginations, as reported by modern researchers in the field.

Difficulty with the word "hypnotism"

The word hypnotism means "sleep". However, as the majority of his clients were conscious during most of the procedure, Braid wondered whether it might be better to refer to them as typically experiencing a "sub-hypnotic state" or "partial hypnotism". Hence, the bulk of normal hypnotic subjects were distinguished from those who entered "full hypnotism", that is, the seemingly dissociated state accompanied by spontaneous reversible amnesia which hypnotists have tended to call "artificial somnambulism", borrowing the term from Mesmerism. However, Braid was keen to emphasise that this "partial" (conscious) hypnotism was normal (occurring in ninety per cent of cases) and perfectly sufficient for hypnotic therapy.

Nevertheless, this fumbling terminology was bound to cause confusion. Even in *Neurypnology*, his first major publication, Braid states that many subjects who experience the first, and most common, stage of hypnotism, consisting of nervous excitation and consciousness, "imagine they are not affected", despite increase in their pulse and changes in their external appearance and facial expression, and so he found it necessary to emphasise that "many instances of remarkable and permanent cures have occurred" in hypnotism of this kind, where the subject essentially remains conscious (Braid, 1843, p. 296).

In his later work, Braid elaborates on this point because it has clearly continued to cause confusion and resistance among his clients. Many modern hypnotherapists still struggle against the misconception that the client should be somehow "unconscious" or "asleep" during hypnotism.

> It is of great importance that it should be clearly understood by patients, that it is by no means generally requisite that they should lapse into the state of *unconsciousness* in order to ensure the salutary effects of the nervous sleep. Many imagine that unless they become torpid and insensible, no beneficial effect can ensue. This is a complete misapprehension, for the happy results of innumerable cases treated with the greatest success by hypnotism, clearly prove, that cases which had resisted all ordinary treatment by the exhibition of medicines and external applications, have readily yielded to the impression made on the nervous system by this peculiar influence, even when they were perfectly conscious of all that was done, and could remember, after awaking, every circumstance that had happened during the nervous sleep. This was strikingly verified in my own case, when I cured myself of a violent rheumatic attack by throwing myself into the nervous sleep for eight or nine minutes, from which I was aroused perfectly free from pain, although I had been perfectly *conscious all the while*. (Braid, 1853, p. 101)

Braid makes an important point here, which often helps to persuade clients. Self-hypnosis obviously requires *consciousness* and it would clearly be absurd to assume that it entails some kind of unconsciousness or sleep-like state. Braid's simple point about self-hypnosis actually leads to one of the best safeguards against this perennial misconception. The simple strategy of teaching the client how to do self-hypnosis and autosuggestion first, before commencing with hypnotherapy proper, that is, hetero-hypnosis, makes it even more difficult for her to confuse hypnosis with a state of unconsciousness resembling sleep. As we shall see, cognitive-behavioural approaches to hypnotherapy often adopt a skills training approach, which involves teaching clients how to use autosuggestion and self-hypnosis from the outset, in a highly collaborative manner. Socialisation of clients to the role of the hypnotic subject is generally much easier when self-hypnosis is taught first and used to provide the model for all subsequent hypnotism.

Braid actually went on to emphasise later in his career that subjects could even be hypnotised with their eyes remaining open in some cases (Braid, 1860, p. 70). This further drives home the point that hypnotic subjects were never *supposed* to be asleep or unconscious. As a result of the obvious confusion which terms like "hypnotism" and "nervous sleep" caused among his clients, however, Braid eventually came to modify his terminology.

> I am well aware that, in correct phraseology, the term *hypnotism* ought to be restricted to the phenomena manifested in patients who actually pass into a state of sleep, and who remember nothing on awakening of what transpired during their sleep. All short of this is mere reverie, or dreaming, however provoked, and it, therefore, seems highly desirable to fix upon a terminology capable of accurately characterising these latter modifications which result from hypnotic processes. This is the more requisite from the fact that, of those who may be relieved and cured by hypnotic processes of diseases which obstinately resist ordinary medical treatment, perhaps not more than one in ten ever passes into the state of oblivious sleep, during the processes which they are subjected to. The term *hypnotism*, therefore, is apt to confuse them, and lead them to suspect that, at all events, *they* cannot be benefited by processes which fail to produce the most obvious indication which the name imports. (Braid, 1855, pp. 80–81)

Indeed, as Braid implies in the passage above, most hypnotic subjects would describe their experience as resembling "reverie", "dreaming", "abstraction", or "concentration", rather than as "sleep" or even "trance". He therefore suggested the "partial hypnotic" states, which accounted for the vast majority of his patients, should be renamed "monoideism" rather than "hypnotism", to emphasise the role of conscious *concentration*, on a single imaginative theme, rather than the misconception that the procedure entails amnesia, unconsciousness, or sleep. Likewise, following their extensive programme of research on hypnosis, Barber and his colleagues reported that not one of their subjects had ever forgotten the events that occurred during hypnosis when it was suggested to them that they would remember and also that as long as suggestions for amnesia were not given, almost all subjects recalled the experience on emerging from hypnosis (Barber, Spanos & Chaves, 1974, p. 10).

Braid and hypnotic induction

Braid gave several brief descriptions of his eye-fixation method. His best-known account, from *Neurypnology* (1843), should be quoted in full because of its importance to our understanding of the topic:

> I now proceed to detail the mode which I practise for inducing the phenomena. Take any bright object (I generally use my lancet case) between the thumb and fore and middle fingers of the left hand; hold it from about eight to fifteen inches from the eyes, at such position above the forehead as may be necessary to produce the greatest possible strain upon the eyes and eyelids, and enable the patient to maintain a steady fixed stare at the object.
>
> The patient must be made to understand that he is to keep the eyes steadily fixed on the object, and the mind riveted on the idea of that one object. It will be observed, that owing to the consensual adjustment of the eyes, the pupils will be at first contracted: they will shortly begin to dilate, and after they have done so to a considerable extent, and have assumed a wavy motion, if the fore and middle fingers of the right hand, extended and a little separated, are carried from the object towards the eyes, most probably the eyelids will close involuntarily, with a vibratory motion. If this is not the case, or the patient allows the *eyeballs to move*, desire him to begin anew, giving him to understand that he is to allow the eyelids to close when the

fingers are again carried towards the eyes, but that the eyeballs *must be kept fixed, in the same position, and the mind riveted to the one idea of the object held above the eyes.* It will generally be found, that the eyelids close with a *vibratory* motion, or become spasmodically closed. After ten or fifteen seconds have elapsed, by gently elevating the arms and legs, it will be found that the patient has a disposition to retain them in the situation in which they have been placed, if *he is intensely affected.*

If this is not the case, in a soft tone of voice desire him to retain the limbs in the extended position, and thus the pulse will speedily become greatly accelerated, and the limbs, in process of time, will become quite rigid and involuntarily fixed. (Braid, 1843, p. 296)

He adds:

At first I required the patients to look at an object until the eyelids closed of themselves, involuntarily. I found, however, that in many cases this was followed by pain in the globes of the eyes, and slight inflammation of the conjunctival membrane. In order to avoid this, I now close the eyelids, when the impression on the pupil already referred to has taken place, because I find that the *beneficial* phenomena follow this method, provided the eyeballs are kept fixed, and thus, too, the unpleasant feelings in the globes of the eyes will be prevented. (Braid, 1843, p. 297)

And further:

That it is a law in the animal economy, that by a continued fixation of the mental and visual eye, on any object which is not of itself of an exciting nature, with absolute repose of body, and general quietude, they become wearied; and, provided the patients rather favour than resist the feeling of stupor of which they will soon experience the tendency to creep upon them, during such experiments, a state of somnolency is induced, accompanied with that condition of the brain and nervous system generally, which renders the patient liable to be affected, according to the mode of manipulating, so as to exhibit the hypnotic phenomena. As the experiment succeeds with the blind, I consider it not so much the optic, as the sentient, motor, and sympathetic nerves, and the mind through which the impression is made. (Braid, 1843, p. 297)

To this account he appended two important footnotes, the first states:

At an early period of my investigations, I caused the patients to look at a cork bound on the forehead. This was a very efficient plan with those who had the power of converging the eyes so as to keep them both steadily directed on the object. I very soon found, however, that there were many who could not keep both eyes steadily fixed on so near an object, and that the result was, that such patients did not become hypnotised. To obviate this, I caused them to look at a more distant point, which, although scarcely so rapid and intense in its effects, succeeds more generally than the other, and is therefore what I now adopt and recommend. (Braid, 1843, p. 296)

Braid distinguished between two main "stages" of hypnotism: the initial stage which consists of nervous arousal and increased alertness; and the later stage, characterised by catalepsy ("rigidity"), limited consciousness, sleepiness ("torpor"), and amnesia—similar in some respects to the "artificial somnambulism" of the Mesmerists. Braid emphasised the paradox that hypnotism seemed, at different times, to result in completely opposing psycho-physiological states. In his later work, it appears, as we shall see, that these are understood more as alternative forms of hypnotism rather than as stages or levels in a single process. His second footnote adds:

> I wish to direct especial attention to this circumstance, as from overlooking the fact of the first stage of this artificial hypnotism being one of excitement, with the possession of consciousness and docility, many imagine they are not affected, whilst the acceleration of pulse, peculiar expression of countenance, and other characteristic symptoms, prove the existence of the condition beyond the possibility of a doubt, to all who understand the subject. I consider it very imprudent to carry it to the ulterior stage, or that of torpor, at a first trial. Moreover, there is great difference in the susceptibility to the neuro-hypnotic impression, some arriving at the state of rigidity and insensibility in a few minutes, whilst others may readily pass into the primary stage, but can scarcely be brought into the ulterior, or rigid and torpid state. It is also most important to note, that many instances of remarkable and permanent cures have occurred, where it has never been carried beyond the state of consciousness. (Braid, 1843, p. 296)

From the outset, Braid seems to have emphasised that, once hypnotised, subjects could, with increasing ease and rapidity, be re-hypnotised without much need of a physical induction method, simply by evoking the memory of previously being hypnotised by means of the expectation that it is about to happen again.

> It is important to remark, that the oftener patients are hypnotised, from association of ideas and habit, the more susceptible they become; and in this way they are liable to be affected *entirely through the imagination*. Thus, if they consider or imagine there is something doing, although they do not see it, from which they are to be affected, they *will become affected*; but, on the contrary, the most expert hypnotist in the world may exert all his endeavours in vain, if the party does not expect it, and mentally and bodily comply, and thus yield to it. (Braid, 1843, p. 298)

Hence, Braid felt that with many subjects it was only necessary to use the eye-fixation induction once and that on subsequent occasions they could be hypnotised more and more easily by habit and association, that is, because they naturally recalled what it felt like when they were previously hypnotised. If you like, the initial physical process of eye-fixation is a behavioural strategy which creates a physical reaction, easily recalled and re-experienced on subsequent occasions by use of memory alone, without the need for repeating the physical strategy. Braid refers to this as "the law of habit and association" and in today's terms it would probably be compared to concepts such as classical conditioning. In most cases, it seems Braid did continue to repeat the induction at the start of each session but that he found it to work more and more quickly and effectively with repetition, the physical effect being reinforced by the memory of the last session.

Expectation

In his later writings, Braid explains that when the subject's eyes are closed, the intense focused attention cultivated during the eye-fixation is usually transferred on to the idea of muscular catalepsy, or some such bodily response. He also makes it quite clear that the essence of hypnotism consists in the induction of a focused state of attention.

> My usual mode of inducing the sleep is to hold any small bright object about ten or twelve inches above the middle of the forehead, so as to require a slight exertion of the attention to enable the patient to maintain a steady, fixed gaze on the object; the subject being either comfortably seated or standing, stillness being enjoined, and the patient requested to engage his attention, as much as possible, on the simple act of looking at the object, and yield to the tendency to sleep which will steal over him during this apparently simple process. I generally use my lancet case, held between the thumb and first two fingers of the left hand; but any other small bright object will answer the purpose. In the course of about three or four minutes, if the eyelids do not close of themselves, the first two fingers of the right hand, extended and a little separated, may be quickly, or with a tremulous motion, carried towards the eyes, so as to cause the patient involuntarily to close the eyelids, which, if he is highly susceptible, will either remain rigidly closed [a phenomenon now termed "eyelid catalepsy"], or assume a vibratory motion—the eyes being turned up, with, in the latter case, a little of the white of the eyes visible through the partially closed lids. If the patient is not highly susceptible, he will open his eyes, in which case request him to gaze at the object, etc., as at first; and, if they do not remain closed after a second trial, desire him to allow them to remain shut after you have closed them, and then endeavour to fix his attention on muscular effort, by elevating the arms if standing, or both arms and legs if seated, which must be done quietly, as if you wished to suggest the idea of muscular action without breaking the abstraction, or concentrative state of mind, the induction of which is the real origin and essence of all which follows. (Braid, 1852, p. 150)

It's important that Braid here clarifies that the hypnotist should "endeavour to fix his [the subject's] attention on muscular effort" and that maintaining selective attention ("abstraction") and concentration upon some such expectant dominant idea is essential to the hypnotic method because this was *not* made very explicit in his best-known work. It makes it clear that hypnotism was always conceived of primarily as a form of focused attention, which could be directed toward different responses, including tension (catalepsy), rather than a particular physiological state, such as relaxation. In his last manuscript, Braid briefly outlines his induction technique as follows:

> The fastest and surest method consists in causing the patient to fixate [her mind and gaze] upon any object of an unexciting nature; the object must be held above the face in such a manner as to be perceived distinctly by both eyes, and at the same time the individual must concentrate all of his attention upon the act to be accomplished. (Braid, 1860, p. 138)

The role of psychological ("subjective") factors is now clearer and eye-fixation involves focused attention upon the expectation of the suggested response occurring, that is, eyelid fatigue and closure.

> This process proved the subjective nature of the influence brought into play. What confirmed my conclusion was that the variety of objects which they were made to fix their gaze upon did not seem, in any way, to modify the symptoms determined. With certain very impressionable subjects, the results obviously depended on an expectation of some event; also any physical arrangement was enough to bring about the sleep; it took place when their attention was placed in expectation by the positive assertion that they would fall sleep; on the other hand, a moment later, one could subject them to the same condition without bringing on sleep, if, by suggestion or in any way whatsoever, one persuaded them that the physical conditions were currently ineffective. (Braid, 1860, pp. 138–139)

Hence, although Braid thought that eye-fixation had an inherent physical effect, this was powerfully modified by expectation, to the extent that it would either work or not, in some cases, depending upon the client's attitude and beliefs about the process. In other words, it is a behavioural strategy, the effects of which are powerfully cognitively-mediated by expectation and suggestion. In emphasising the crucial mediating role of expectation, here and elsewhere throughout his writings, Braid draws closer to Kirsch's cognitive-behavioural theory of hypnosis, based upon the concept of "response expectancy" (Kirsch & Council, 1989), which we shall discuss in more detail later.

In short, therefore, Braid conceptualised hypnotism as a state of focused attention upon a dominant idea or image (cognition), accompanied by the expectation that it would evoke the suggested response. From a modern perspective, one of the most notable things about this theory of hypnotism, the original theory, is the fact that it very clearly places central importance upon specific types of "metacognitive" thoughts and processes. "Metacognitions" are cognitions *about* cognitions, or thoughts about thoughts, etc. According to Braid, the essence of hypnotism consists in heightened attention to certain cognitions (dominant ideas and images) and the thought or belief that they are powerful enough to evoke the responses they suggest. Put crudely, hypnotism consists of focused attention and belief in the power of suggestion. This may become a kind of self-fulfilling prophecy, as the more strongly a subject believes that certain ideas are powerful suggestions, the more they function as powerful suggestions. The dominant ideas in question, it should be emphasised, are similar to what we would now call "autosuggestions". In Braid's model, ordinary suggestion ("hetero-suggestion"), delivered by a hypnotist, works by evoking dominant ideas, which arguably is like saying that all (hypnotic) suggestion entails a form of autosuggestion. The suggestions of the hypnotist are merely verbal cues or prompts, which may or may not activate autosuggestions within the mind of the subject and a receptive (hypnotic) attitude.

Observational learning and role-taking

Most modern hypnotherapists work one-to-one, in private. However, Braid, like the Mesmerists, usually worked in public, before a small group or a large audience. He often hypnotised several people in the same session, in the same room. Hence, he quickly became very aware that when one subject has been demonstrated to respond very well to hypnotism, others in the room tend to expect that they will respond similarly well, or to imitate the types of responses they've observed. This phenomenon of social imitation (or "vicarious learning") is now better known to stage hypnotists than to hypnotherapists because the former continue to hypnotise groups, in public. In fact, early hypnotists realised that it was pragmatic, under these circumstances, to exhibit their best subjects first, thereby providing suitable role-models for subsequent subjects to imitate. In an experimental setting, as Charcot's example famously showed, this would be folly because the results produced are contaminated by the subject's ability to observe others first. However, providing good role-models in a clinical setting is one way of potentially amplifying the positive results of treatment. Nowadays, of course, it is possible to show clients video clips of "model hypnotic subjects", making observational learning much easier to control. This is precisely what cognitive-behavioural approaches to hypnotic skills training, such as the Carleton skills training program (CSTP), have done (Gorassini & Spanos, 1999).

> [Whatever method is used] there can be no doubt of the fact that they will be rendered much more efficient by previously affording the patients an opportunity of watching others when submitted to the processes. The influence of sympathy and imitation are thus brought into play, and increase the susceptibility in a marked degree. Of this fact I have had many striking proofs. Where patients exhibit considerable resistance, therefore, it is always desirable to bring the power of sympathy and imitation to bear upon them, as well as the influence of direct auricular suggestion and expectation, excited by the confident tone and deportment in the operator so as to inspire them, as far as possible, with the conviction that the influence cannot be resisted. (Braid, 1852, pp. 150–151)

This observation, which has been made by many hypnotists since, appears to lend considerable support to socio-cognitive theories of hypnosis, such as Sarbin's, which reconceptualise hypnosis as a matter of the subject immersing herself in a socially-constructed role. Braid appealed to a basic "common sense" principle underlying his approach to suggestion, "the law of sympathy and imitation", to explain the ease with which subjects were hypnotised after observing others modelling the desired response. It's also clear that Braid conceived of "expectation" and self-confidence as key factors in determining hypnotic responsiveness. The value of observing others (models), learning how hypnotic subjects typically respond (role definition), being confident (self-efficacy) in their ability, and having a high level of expectation (response expectancy), are all typical factors emphasised in cognitive-behavioural theories of hypnosis.

Self-hypnotism and meditation

As we've seen, Braid was apparently the first person to employ self-hypnosis, although he referred to it as "self-*hypnotism*". Braid pounced upon the phenomenon of self-hypnosis as proof that hypnotism was the result of ordinary physical and mental processes and not dependent upon the mysterious occult power supposedly emanating from the "silent willing" (telepathy) of the Mesmerists.

> The experiments recorded [in Chapter Six of *Neurypnology*] of my having caused patients to hypnotise, manipulate, and rouse themselves, (by simply desiring them to rub their own eyes,)

and which produced results precisely the same as when done by anyone else, seem to me the most decisive proof possible that the whole results from the mind and body of the patients acting and re-acting on each other, and that it has no dependence on any special influence emanating from another. My first experiments on this point [i.e., self-hypnosis] were instituted in the presence of some friends on the 1st May, 1843, and following days. I believe they were the first experiments of the kind which had ever been tried, and they have succeeded in every case in which I have so operated. (Braid, 1843, p. 285)

Just over a year later, Braid resorted to self-hypnotism himself, as a means of coping with a severe bout of rheumatic pain.

It is commonly said that seeing is believing, but feeling is the very truth. I shall, therefore, give the result of my experience of hypnotism in my own person. In the middle of September, 1844, I suffered from a most severe attack of rheumatism, implicating the left side of the neck and chest, and the left arm. At first the pain was moderately severe, and I took some medicine to remove it; but, instead of this, it became more and more violent, and had tormented me for three days, and was so excruciating, that it entirely deprived me of sleep for *three nights successively*, and on the last of the three nights I could not remain in any one posture for five minutes, from the severity of the pain. On the forenoon of the next day, whilst visiting my patients, every jolt of the carriage I could only compare to several sharp instruments being thrust through my shoulder, neck, and chest. A full inspiration was attended with stabbing pain, such as is experienced in pleurisy. When I returned home for dinner I could neither turn my head, lift my arm, nor draw a breath, without suffering extreme pain. In this condition I resolved to try the effects of hypnotism. I requested two friends, who were present, and who both understood the system, to watch the effects, and arouse me when I had passed sufficiently into the condition; and, with their assurance that they would give strict attention to their charge, I sat down and hypnotised myself, extending the extremities. At the expiration of *nine minutes* they aroused me, and, to my agreeable surprise, *I was quite free from pain, being able to move in any way with perfect ease*. I say *agreeably* surprised, on this account; I had seen like results with many patients; but it is one thing to *hear of pain*, and another to *feel it*. My suffering was so exquisite that I could not imagine anyone else ever suffered so intensely as myself on that occasion; and, therefore, I merely expected a mitigation, so that I was truly agreeably surprised to *find myself quite free from pain*. I continued quite easy all the afternoon, slept comfortably all night, and the following morning felt a little *stiffness*, but *no pain*. A week thereafter I had a slight return, which I removed by *hypnotising* myself *once more*; and I have remained quite free from rheumatism ever since, now nearly six years. Was there the slightest room to doubt the value and efficacy of hypnotism in this case? (Braid, 1850, p. 217)

As noted earlier, Braid gradually came to see the phenomenon of self-hypnotism as evidence that his method of hypnotism might actually have had more in common with yogic meditation than with Mesmerism.

Inasmuch as patients can throw themselves into the nervous sleep, and manifest all the usual phenomena of Mesmerism, through their own unaided efforts, as I have so repeatedly proved by causing them to maintain a steady fixed gaze at any point, concentrating their whole mental energies on the idea of the object looked at; or that the same may arise by the patient looking at the point of his own finger, or as the Magi of Persia and Yogi of India have practised for the last 2,400 years, for religious purposes, throwing themselves into their ecstatic trances by each maintaining a steady fixed gaze at the tip of his own nose; it is obvious that there is no need for an exoteric influence to produce the phenomena of Mesmerism. […] The great object in all these processes is to induce a habit of abstraction or concentration of attention, in which the subject is entirely absorbed with one idea, or train of ideas, whilst he is unconscious of, or indifferently conscious to, every other object, purpose, or action. (Braid, 1846, p. 247)

Once this state of focused attention had been induced it could either be carried on toward a condition resembling sleep or else attention could be transferred onto a single dominant idea for therapeutic purposes.

Braid originally studied the effect of fixing the attention upon the gaze of another person, a practice common in Mesmerism. He then demonstrated that staring upon an inanimate object had the same effect, to which end he employed the top of a bottle, a cork strapped to the subject's forehead, a chandelier, the tip of the subject's own finger, his lancet case, and various ornaments and arbitrary objects. Braid mentions that the yogis of India are frequently described as fixing their gaze upon a part of their body such as the tip of their own nose, the centre of their forehead, or their navel. However, Braid recognised that physical fixation of the gaze was not essential, and that the words of a simple rhyme (like an Indian mantra) or the mental image of a bright star could serve a similar purpose as the object of mental fixation for inducing hypnotism. More or less anything, in fact, can be used as the object of concentration if the aim is to pacify the mind by contemplation of something monotonous, or even to induce a state of sleep.

All that is required for this is simply to place himself in a comfortable posture in bed, and then to close the eyelids, and turn up the eyeballs gently, as if looking at a distant object, such as an imaginary star, situated somewhat above and behind the forehead, giving the whole concentrated attention of the mind to the idea of maintaining a steady view of the star, and breathing softly, as if in profound attention, the mind at the same time yielding to the idea that sleep will ensue, and to the tendency to somnolence which will creep upon him whilst engaged in this act of fixed attention. Or it may be done with still more success, in certain individuals, by their placing some small, bright object in a similar aspect with a distant light falling thereon, the party looking at the object with open eyes, fixed attention, and suppressed [i.e., relaxed] respiration. Other modes of producing a state of mental concentration directed to some unexciting and empty thing, and thus shutting out the influence of other sensible impressions, may also prove successful for inducing calm sleep, by monotonising the mind—just as we see effected in the case of children, who are sent to sleep by rocking, patting, or gentle rubbing, or monotonous, unexciting lullabies—but none are so speedy and certain in their effects, with patients generally, as the modes which I have briefly explained. Mr. Walker's method of procuring "sleep at will", by desiring the patient to maintain a fixed act of attention, by imagining himself watching his breath issuing slowly from his nostrils, after having placed his body in a comfortable position in bed—and which was first published to the world by Dr. Binns, a few years ago—is essentially the same as my own method, which I had promulgated some time prior to the publication of the *first* edition of Dr. Binns's work on sleep. (Braid, 1852, p. 162)

As we have seen, Braid's theory of hypnotism held that by focusing the attention upon a repetitive idea or unexciting object a state resembling profound sleep could be induced, or that the opposite state, of muscular catalepsy could be induced by focusing attention upon the idea of rigid tension. These were the main responses he evoked for therapeutic purposes. However, as his experiments and his reflections on meditation show, he believed that any number of psychological or physiological changes could be induced by shifting the attention onto specific "dominant ideas" or mental images, which we would now call "autosuggestion." Nevertheless, Braid was emphatic that hypnotism was essentially an extension of ordinary psychological and physiological functioning. In particular, the effect of focused attention upon a dominant idea is merely a means of amplifying the familiar effects of suggestion and mental association which we observe in everyday life. He frequently referred to such common examples as the nursing mother producing milk on seeing or hearing her child crying, salivation caused by the thought of certain foods, shedding tears, blushing, anxious pallor and palpitations, fainting from disgust or losing appetite, etc., in response to mere ideas or information.

> If you wish to excite the feeling of nausea or vomiting, give the patient a mouthful of cold water, or draw the hand over the stomach, predicting aloud that he must necessarily vomit, as he had taken an emetic, or that the mere touch will be sufficient to produce the like effect; and if the patient is one of those subjects who has passed into the double-conscious ["full" hypnotic] state, or who is liable to manifest the power of suggestion during the waking condition, the desired effect was quite certain to follow. With all other patients a similar effect, but in a minor degree, may be realised, provided they can fix their thoughts steadfastly, and for a length of time, on the idea suggested. The same will be the result in respect to the action of the bowels, the tendency to void urine, exciting the secretion of milk in the nurse by directing the attention of the subject to the mammae, or talking within her hearing about her child; and the same of other functions, according to the mental direction and ideas suggested to the mind of the patient by words spoken aloud in his hearing, or otherwise. There is evidently an immediate increased determination of blood, and of increased sensibility, to whatever organ or function, or part, the mind of the patient is directed under such circumstances, especially if he is fully persuaded in his own mind, and expects such exciting results. Let anyone only reflect for a moment on the physiological phenomena of blushing. In this case the capillary circulation of the cheeks, or of the whole face and neck in some subjects, immediately assumes such a remarkable change as to paint the cheeks, face, and neck of a scarlet hue, even in those who have a pale complexion generally, from red globules crowding through vessels which, in their ordinary condition, admit chiefly the colourless part of the blood, or red globules in single file only. All this remarkable physical change is entirely due to mental emotion, and yet it is effected with a rapidity which could scarcely be equalled by the application to the parts so affected of the most violent mechanical or chemical stimuli. Again, pallor from mental emotion is the reverse of blushing, and is equally prompt in its response. Where, then, is the difficulty in comprehending why a dominant expectant idea in the mind of a patient should be

adequate to produce effects equally potent on other parts of the body, and on special organs, when strongly concentrated on such organs or parts? (Braid, 1853, pp. 93–94)

Braid had argued that the real physical and mental effects of "bread pills" and other placebo therapies, including homeopathy (which he criticised as a nostrum), were also due to expectation and dominant ideas.

He quotes from the English missionary William Ward's four-volume *A View of the History, Literature and Religion of the Hindoos* (1811), and inserts his commentary upon the effects of meditation recounted by the ancient teachers of yoga. Braid claims that these observations confirm "the fact of the Yogi being all self-hypnotisers, by inducing a state of intense abstraction, from a steady fixed gaze at an object, with a suppressed state of the respiration." For example, one of the applications of yogic meditation consists of evoking positive emotions to counteract opposing negative ones, a strategy frequently employed in modern psychotherapy.

Braid argues that when a yogi enters into this state of self-hypnosis, or meditation, his expectations and associations to the state, combined with a lively imagination and focused attention, will frequently result in a variety of dramatic subjective experiences, including hallucinations easily confused with supernatural phenomena. Modern practitioners of yoga, or other forms of meditation, may find in Braid's hypnotism a theory and practice more aligned with Western psychology and physiology. Despite the fact that hypnotism was, from its origin, compared with yogic meditation, this analogy has been subsequently neglected and has fallen into disuse. Modern hypnotherapy has evolved in a different direction, and is probably less similar to traditional eastern meditation techniques than Braid's original method was. However, modern CBT has embraced a variety of concepts and techniques influenced by Buddhist contemplative meditation. Braid's definition of hypnotism as a state of concentration upon a single idea (which he terms "mental abstraction" or "monoideism") lends itself to the comparison with concentrative meditation techniques. For example, reviewing the diverse range of meditation practices, Ornstein concluded:

> The common element in these diverse practices seems to be the active restriction of awareness to a single, unchanging process and the withdrawal of attention from ordinary thought. It does not seem to matter which actual physical practice is followed; whether one symbol or another is employed; whether the visual system is used or body movements repeated; whether the awareness is focused on a limb or on a sound or on a word or on a prayer. [...] The instructions for meditation are always consistent with this surmise: one is instructed always to rid awareness of any thought save the object of meditation, to shut oneself off from the main flow of ongoing external activity and to pay attention only to the object or process of meditation. Almost any process or object seems usable and has probably been used. (Ornstein, 1977, pp. 171–172)

From traditional meditation practices, hypnotists might learn the value of teaching clients to persevere with concentration upon a single object or idea, especially an idea of therapeutic value, although the state of general tranquillity induced by means of fixed attention upon an unexciting object, such as meditation upon the tip of the nose or a point on the ceiling, may also be beneficial in many cases. From hypnotism, on the other hand, meditation practitioners might learn more about the role of prior expectation, social imitation, mental imagery, and autosuggestion in determining the outcome of many meditation techniques.

Braid's theory of suggestion

Some scholars have incorrectly assumed that Braid mainly worked in a kind of physiological manner, by mobilising muscle groups, etc., and that he had virtually no concept of hypnotic suggestion. The emphasis upon verbal suggestion is normally attributed to Hippolyte Bernheim and his Nancy School, and the influence of their concept of hypnotherapy from the 1880s onward (Bernheim, 1890). However, throughout his career, Braid did acknowledge the role of verbal suggestion in hypnotism. Although he says relatively little about it in his earlier works, the emphasis upon this factor steadily increased, and in places he even indicates a sophisticated awareness of different *categories* of suggestion. Toward the end of his career, in summing up his work, Braid described hypnotism mainly as a vehicle for suggestion.

> The typical Mesmeric processes are very numerous, but, according to what I have seen on this subject and according to my ordinary manner of hypnotising, the true cause of the phenomena is simply this: the different methods used favour the production of this state of abstraction or fixation of attention, in which the mind is absorbed by a single idea. Then [in a deeper stage] the patient falls into indifference, he is closed, so to speak, to all foreign influences or impressions other than those called to his attention. In this state, his imagination becomes so vivid that any agreeable idea, developed spontaneously or suggested by a person to whom he accords, in a particular manner, his attention and confidence, takes on for him all the power of present events, of reality. The more frequently these phenomena are evoked, the easier and more convenient it becomes to evoke them; such is the law of association and habit. Indeed, the mind is in a state close to dreaming; the difference is that the patients not only think, but are still capable of putting their thoughts and desires into action. (Braid, 1860, p. 139)

Braid only gives a few verbatim examples of words spoken by him while hypnotising. In treating constipation, he passed his fingertips along the patient's abdomen to physically suggest the sensation of peristalsis and said "This will soon make the bowels act." (Braid, 1853, p. 105). In treating a patient whose menstruation had become irregular, he said, "Now, keep your mind firmly fixed upon what you know ought to happen", thereby instructing her to focus on the "expectant dominant idea" of menstruation (Braid, 1853, p. 106). However, it seems likely that more elaborate verbal suggestions must have been used by Braid at times.

Notably, moreover, Braid does not hesitate to draw a direct analogy between the art of hypnotic suggestion and the art of classical rhetoric (Braid, 1852, p. 154). From the outset it seems that he took it for granted that the verbal skills and techniques which make a man a great orator, lawyer, or actor are very similar to those which make him an effective hypnotist.

> Nor, after all, is this power of [hypnotic] suggestion, or persuasion, or concealed fascination, so remarkable or unaccountable as at first sight it appears to be. The secret of success with

all sophistical [i.e., rhetorical] writers and orators is of a similar nature. They make repeated appeals to the feelings, as well as to the reason, until the minds of their readers or hearers get bewildered and withdrawn from the true bearings of the main points of the case and the assumed, and apparent sincerity and energy, of the writer, and still more so of the orator, who, to his other aids of words and arguments, adds that of his physical manifestations, to captivate and carry his entranced hearers along with him, through the power of sympathy and imitation, and fixed attention, at last irresistibly moulds them to his will. (Braid, 1853, p. 105)

Likewise, following on from his "dramaturgical" model of hypnosis, as role-enactment, the social psychologist and hypnosis researcher, Ted Sarbin naturally assimilated concepts from the art of rhetoric.

Since Mesmer's time, hypnotists have employed linguistic devices, gestures, "passes", costumes, white coats, bedside manners, and even stage props in the service of the rhetoric of role enactment. A moment's reflection on the typical induction procedure makes clear that it is loaded with verbal and phonic rhetoric. The content may be directed to reassurance and rapport building, but the rhetorical style is different from ordinary conversation. (Sarbin, 1989, p. 408)

Moreover, contrary to the notion that he said little about it, Braid actually went further than most subsequent hypnotists in developing a system of classifying different modes of suggestion. In one of his later texts, he lists the following categories (Braid, 1852, p. 155).

1. Auditory suggestion ("the patients hear the ideas suggested when uttered in a language known to them").
2. Written suggestion ("when they see them written (which is sufficient to affect many)").
3. Sympathy and imitation ("when they can see, by ordinary vision, the movements made in their presence which it is intended they should be forced to imitate, through the power of sympathy and imitation").
4. Habit and association ("when they feel sensible impressions [i.e., physical sensations], associated with certain ideas or previous feelings").
5. MuscularSuggestion (when they feel impressions which "call subjacent muscles into action").
6. Spontaneous associations (when they feel impressions which "direct attention to the special organs of sense, which excites ideas corresponding with the functions of these different organs, or arouses former ideas arbitrarily or accidentally associated with such and such sensible impressions").

These forms of suggestion may distantly prefigure certain strategies and techniques in modern cognitive-behavioural therapy. For instance, aside from the use of spoken and written verbal suggestions, Braid's emphasis upon "sympathy and imitation" as a source of inter-personal influence pre-empts the concept of vicarious or observational learning through role-modelling emphasised in the work of social learning theorists such as Bandura. Braid's concept of "habit and association" is similar to Pavlovian conditioning theory and subsequent theories of habit formation in behavioural psychology leading to the use of conditioned "cues" in modern behaviour therapy. Likewise, Braid's technique of muscular suggestion clearly predates the James-Lange theory of emotion and William James' method of behaviourally acting "as if" cured. Braid's reference to spontaneous associations occurring when attention is directed to certain parts of the body might be interpreted as a precursor to certain forms of modern "indirect" suggestion.

The ideo-motor reflex (IMR)

As noted above, Carpenter proposed the influential "ideo-motor reflex" theory of suggestion, which became central to Victorian hypnotism. According to this view, under certain circumstances, ideas are capable of producing "unconscious muscular movements" by means of a kind of reflex response, that is, independently of direct conscious effort and in a seemingly involuntary or automatic manner. It's important to realise that the term "ideo-motor" refers to ideas, by which Victorian philosophers of mind meant mental images, memories, fantasies, thoughts, concepts, and more or less any kind of mental representation. The term "motor", of course, refers to muscular responses of the kind normally under voluntary control. The terms "idea" and "motor response", as used in Victorian philosophy and psychology, were essentially synonymous with the modern use of "cognition" and (overt) "behaviour." As noted above, the hyphenated term "ideo-motor" therefore bears a peculiar similarity to the modern expression "cognitive-behavioural." Although not identical concepts, there is a shared acknowledgment that cognitions (ideas) play a central role in shaping or mediating behavioural (motor) responses. Carpenter defines it thus:

> The continued concentration of Attention upon a certain idea gives it a *dominant* power, not only over the mind, but over the body; and the muscles become the involuntary instruments whereby it is carried into operation. [...] But it is the characteristic of the state of mind from which these Ideo-motor actions proceed, that the Volitional power is for the time in abeyance; the whole mental power being absorbed (as it were) in the high state of tension to which the Ideational consciousness has been wrought up. (Carpenter quoted in Braid, 2009, p. 118)

We might construe the underlying mechanism differently today, and socio-cognitive theories tend to place more emphasis on goal-directed striving. However, Carpenter, and Braid following him, interpreted the ideo-motor reflex theory in terms of an everyday ("common sense") observation which "like many other mental phenomena, has not attracted the notice it merits, simply because it *is* so familiar" (Carpenter quoted in Braid, 2009, p. 118). Hence, he illustrates it by reference to everyday examples, such as the fact that we do not think about the individual movements our mouth makes as we speak or the steps we take as we walk down a street, but merely allow ourselves to respond automatically to the intention to act. Our involuntary facial expressions are another familiar example of the power of an idea over the musculature of the body, to the extent, for example, that we may grimace visibly without even realising that we do so, when contemplating the memory of a painful experience.

It should be stressed that although Carpenter describes the movements caused by the "idea" as reflex-like, "unconscious" and involuntary, that does not exclude the possibility of a subject consciously and voluntarily choosing to entertain such an idea in the first place—as demonstrated by self-hypnosis and autosuggestion. If someone describes a disgusting scene to me, it might involuntarily make me cringe. However, I can also voluntarily imagine biting into a lemon and thereby evoke a seemingly "automatic" salivation response in my own mouth. Given that Carpenter provides examples such as the automotive movements of walking, made while absent-mindedly thinking of something else, it hardly seems that he intended the ideo-motor reflex to entail anything more unconscious or involuntary than many of our familiar everyday experiences.

Showing a surprising lack of awareness regarding their own history, hypnotherapists today often use the term "ideo-motor response" (IMR) to refer instead to a specific technique of physical suggestion in which a finger is made to twitch and rise. Although there are clearly limits to its explanatory power, the ideo-motor reflex is basically the original neuro-psychological theory of hypnotic suggestion. The study of hypnotism as understood by Braid, and also by Bernheim the founder of the Nancy School, was essentially an "ideo-motor" (or rather "ideo-dynamic") science. Carpenter actually provided a simple diagram in which he illustrated the basic ideo-motor reflex conceptualisation of suggestion (see below).

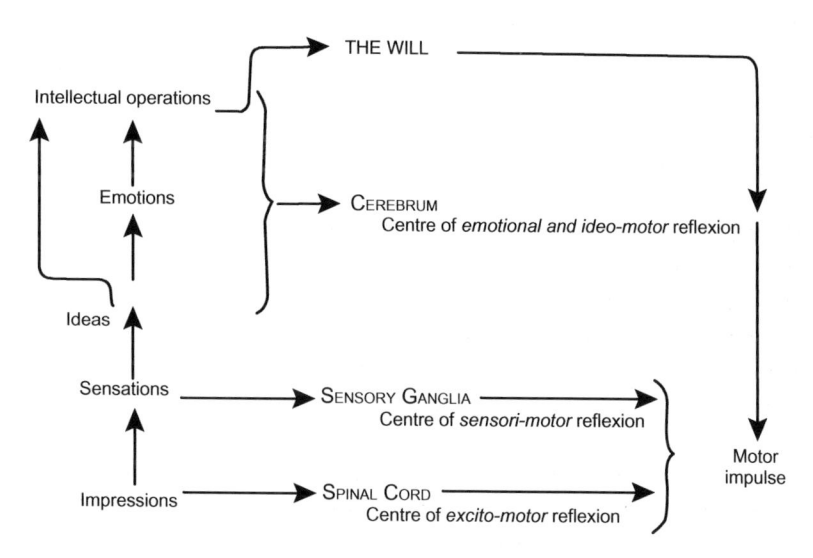

Figure 1. Carpenter's conceptualisation of the ideo-motor reflex.

The ideo-dynamic reflex

Carpenter's theory was modified by one of his associates, Dr. Daniel Noble, who pointed out that responses like lactation, lachrymation, and salivation could be evoked in a similar manner. These are *secretary* responses, rather than motor responses, so Noble coined the term "ideo-dynamic" reflex as a catch-all to include all physiological and behavioural reactions to ideas, "ideo-dynamic" meaning "the power of ideas" over the body. In addition, Braid pointed out that such ideas frequently *inhibit* muscular movement, rather than evoke it, as in the case of hysterical paralysis, so he adopted Dr. Noble's version of the terminology.

From their first meeting, around 1847, Braid rapidly assimilated Carpenter's theory and terminology into hypnotism, coining the term "monoideo-dynamic" to describe the underlying nature of hypnotism (Braid, 1855, p. 81). As noted above, Braid had concluded that the term "hypnotism" was somewhat misleading, inasmuch as it implies sleep, when in fact ninety per cent of his subjects remained conscious. Although he continued to use the term hypnotism in general, he felt it would be more accurate to describe most subjects as being in a state of focused attention on a single dominant idea, to the exclusion of any intruding or antagonistic thoughts or impressions. As such, "monoideism" is basically a technical term for what he had previously called "mental abstraction". The "mono" prefix which Braid introduced was meant to indicate that his method of hypnotism was now understood as a combination of Carpenter's ideo-dynamic theory of suggestion with the technique of concentration upon a single idea (or train of thought). The central mediating factor in hypnotism now became a cognitive or subjective one, focused attention (monoideism), rather than nervous sleep (neuro-hypnotism).

Many hypnotherapists today appear to be unaware that Braid's original theory of hypnotism was based on the ideo-motor conceptualisation developed by Carpenter. By contrast, André Weitzenhoffer, one of the best-known researchers in the field of hypnosis, and an opponent of the cognitive-behavioural tradition in hypnosis research, wrote of the ideo-dynamic formulation as follows:

> Few formulations regarding what the suggestion process is, exist that can be called a theory. The most widely accepted and influential so-called theory, still really a hypothesis, is known as the ideodynamic action theory, often being improperly referred to as the "ideomotor theory" and as a theory of hypnosis. Strictly speaking, it pertains directly only to suggested behaviour. It has nothing directly to do with hypnosis but, of course, indirectly it does. Of all the hypotheses that have been proposed regarding the production of hypnotic effects (understood as suggested effects), it is the one that comes closest to being a theory and more workers in the field have ascribed to it than any other hypothesis. (Weitzenhoffer A. M., 2000, p. 123)

Weitzenhoffer used the term "involuntary" to refer to responses that are not generally under the subject's control, such as digestive secretions, and "nonvoluntary" or "avolitional" for those responses that are normally voluntary but which appear to occur automatically, such as "arm levitation" in response to hypnotic suggestion.

> The term *automatism* [...] is essentially a synonym for these forms of behaviour. That is, suggestions are said to evoke automatisms. This *avolitional aspect is a key feature of suggestion* that shows up in all definitions and descriptions, one to which I have referred in the past as the "classical suggestion-effect", or more simply as the "suggestion-effect." The most widely accepted hypothesis regarding the physiological (really psychophysiological) mechanism underlying the suggestion-effect is a general cortical reflex action that has been called "ideodynamic action" [...]. The avolitional character of the response to suggestions is that

which distinguishes them as communications from other communications, such as requests, instructions, demands, commands, assignments, etc., that all elicit or call for willed behaviour. (Weitzenhoffer A. M., 2000, pp. 81–82)

Although sometimes it may be acceptable to speak loosely of the "ideo-dynamic" theory of hypnosis, the model really provides a specific hypothesis about the mechanism of action underlying suggestion in general. It is incomplete as an account of hypnosis but has historically provided the central hypothesis underlying Braid's "monoideo-dynamic" account of hypnotism (Braid, 1855) and many subsequent approaches.

Muscular suggestion

Within a year of his discovery, Braid travelled from his home in Manchester to deliver public demonstrations of hypnotism before the leading medical and scientific experts at the Hanover Square and London Tavern meeting rooms. Braid had tried many modifications of his eye-fixation induction technique, including asking subjects to turn their eyes to one side instead of looking upwards. However, in these public talks he exhibited a strange side-effect of this particular technique. According to Braid, it caused certain subjects, once hypnotised, to feel drawn to one side, turning their body around in the direction of their gaze (Braid, 2009, p. 384). It seems as though the physical sensation caused by turning the eyes to one side, when amplified by hypnotism, functioned as a kind of physical suggestion, evoking the desire to turn the body round. In this accidental discovery lies, perhaps, the seed of Braid's later theory of "muscular suggestion", a term he first introduced in 1844 and used several times in later works to describe this phenomenon (Braid, 2009, pp. 104, 216, 276).

> A familiar example of the influence of muscular expression or action reacting on the mind, may be realised by any sensitive person, even *during the waking condition*. Let him assume, and endeavour to maintain, any particular expression or attitude, and he will very soon experience that a corresponding condition of mind is thereby engendered. Now, such being the case during the waking condition, when the faculties of the mind are so much dissipated and diffused by impressions on the various senses, we can readily understand why the influence should be so much more energetic during Hypnotism, the peculiar features of which are high sensibility, with the whole energies of the mind concentrated on the particular emotion excited. (Braid, 2009, p. 264)

Braid compared this to the experience of actors shedding tears upon the stage, as a result of being completely immersed in their roles. Half a century later, Stanislavski's system of acting and later Strasberg's "method acting" approach would employ similar concepts in the training of actors. Stanislavski realised that the more the actor immersed himself in certain voluntary movements, facial expressions, mannerisms, and gestures, etc., the more easily he would be able to evoke the subjective feelings of the character portrayed, and *vice versa*. As Braid succinctly observed, muscular suggestion, combined with focus on certain ideas, can provide a means of controlling normally involuntary behaviour such as lachrymation, that is, shedding tears. Most people cannot cry at will, by simply making a decision to do so. However, by first adopting the facial expression, fitful sighs, and other mannerisms of someone in the throes of despair, they obviously stand a chance of evoking sad feelings and making tears begin to form.

Braid saw this method as a reversal or "inversion" of the normal causal sequence. We usually assume that feelings come first and cause facial expressions and other bodily reactions: I feel happy and consequently I automatically smile. However, Braid argued that constant association creates a two-way bond such that the behaviour can become the cause and the subjective feelings the effect: I smile and consequently I automatically feel happy. Psychologists will note that in his writings, which repeatedly formulate this "muscular suggestion" hypothesis, Braid clearly pre-empted the influential "James-Lange" theory of emotion by almost half a century. William James famously wrote:

> Whistling to keep up courage is no mere figure of speech. On the other hand, sit all day in a moping posture, sigh, and reply to everything with a dismal voice, and your melancholy lingers. There is no more valuable precept in moral education than this, as all who have experience know: if we wish to conquer undesirable emotional tendencies in ourselves, we must assiduously, and in the first instance cold-bloodedly, go through the outward motions of those contrary dispositions we prefer to cultivate. The reward of persistency will infallibly come, in the fading out of the sullenness or depression, and the advent of real cheerfulness and kindliness in their stead. Smooth the brow, brighten the eye, contract the dorsal rather than the ventral aspect of the frame, and speak in a major key, pass the genial compliment, and your heart must be frigid indeed if it does not gradually thaw! (James, 1884, p. 198)

It is quite possible that William James was actually influenced by Braid's ideas, perhaps via the medium of Bernheim's Nancy school, with which he was acquainted. In any case, Braid makes strikingly similar remarks about muscular suggestion in hypnotism.

> As we said, the position of the body significantly influences the emotions and sensations during the desired stage of hypnotism; also, whatever the passion which one wants to express by the attitude of the patient, when the muscles necessary to this expression are brought into play, the passion itself bursts forth suddenly and the whole organism responds accordingly. The upright body, the expanded chest, the contracted extensors, all that suggests the feeling of self-esteem, self-determination, resolve and unconquerable pride. As soon as one decreases the contraction of these muscles, that gives to the patient a depressed attitude, with sunken chest, the expression of the features changes in a very manifest way, the voice and the whole manner of being of the individual now express humility, abasement and pity. (Braid, 1860, p. 72)

As Braid writes in his earlier work:

> In this case there would be a sort of inversion of the ordinary sequence, what is naturally the consequence becoming the cause of cerebral and mental excitation. The following hypothesis will illustrate my meaning. It is easy to imagine, that putting a pen or pencil into the hand

> might excite in the mind the idea of writing or drawing or that stimulating the *gastrocnemius* [calf muscle], which raises us on our toes, might naturally enough suggest to the mind the idea of dancing, without any other suggestion to that effect than what arises from the attitude and activity of the muscles naturally and necessarily brought into play whilst exercising such functions. However, I would very much doubt the probability of stimulating the muscles of the leg exciting the idea of writing, or that placing a pen or pencil in the hand would excite the idea of dancing, without previous concert and arrangement to that effect. (Braid, 1843, p. 325)

However, the heightened focus of attention upon bodily sensations, and general state of expectation, in hypnotism could amplify this effect. Braid discusses, in particular, how by wrinkling the forehead of a subject with his fingers he could evoke internal feelings of sadness by changing the external facial expression. In developing this theory of "muscular suggestion", he repeatedly referred to Sir Charles Bell's concept of the "anatomy of expression", the minute study of facial expressions and how they relate to different states of mind.

> In this way, we influence the muscles of physiognomy [facial expression] and it is possible for us to arouse any passion or sentiment whatsoever; the contraction of the interconnected muscles, constituting "the anatomy of expression", evokes in the brain of the hypnotised person certain impressions just as these, in the waking state, determine the whole facial expression. It is thus merely a reversal of the usual order [of causation] between the emotions and their physical expressions. (Braid, 1860, p. 153)

Although arguably integral to hypnotism, Braid's concept of "muscular suggestion" has been all but forgotten. Similar ideas, largely derived from the James-Lange theory, have continued to have some limited influence upon behaviour therapists, for example, through Kelly's notion of fixed-role therapy or acting "as if" (Goldfried & Davison, 1976, pp. 136–157). Nevertheless, the concept of muscular suggestion is, as we shall see, possibly key to understanding traditional hypnotism.

The terminology can be made more consistent with modern psychotherapy simply by referring to "cognitive" and "behavioural" strategies used in hypnotism instead of "ideo-motor" and "muscular" suggestions. Two obvious examples of muscular suggestion in hypnotism should be noted, which Braid did not explicitly comment upon:

1. Acting "as if" concentrating. Remaining stationary and silent, while fixing the gaze upon a single point, for example, the behavioural strategy of staring at a point on the wall, during the classical eye-fixation induction, can be viewed as a form of muscular suggestion designed to evoke subjective feelings of intense mental concentration, hence Braid refers to "fixed and abstracted attention of the mental and visual eye" (Braid, 1843, p. 290).
2. Acting "as if" asleep or relaxed. Relaxing the skeletal muscles of the body, reclining, closing the eyes, breathing softly, and remaining silent and stationary for a prolonged period, during hypnotic relaxation, can be viewed as a muscular suggestion or behavioural strategy bound to induce further physiological relaxation and to evoke subjective feelings associated with sleep or relaxation.

Likewise, the concept of muscular suggestion can be applied to other behavioural strategies found in hypnotherapy such as slowly closing the eyelids (suggestive of sleep), taking a deep breath and exhaling a sigh (suggestive of relaxation), clenching the fist as a "cue" (suggestive of focus or determination), being instructed to open the eyes and stretch upon emerging from hypnosis (suggestive of awakening), etc. However, as we shall see, Braid concluded that hypnotism was better conceptualised in terms of the reciprocal interaction between muscular suggestion and verbal suggestion, or between the body and mind, which he termed "psycho-physiology". Over a century later, Barber and his colleagues arrived at a very similar conclusion, which they describe as the finding that verbal suggestions are more likely to succeed if they are somehow "coupled" with physical responses (Barber, Spanos & Chaves, 1974, pp. 28–29). For example, in the postural sway test a subject stands straight, feet together, eyes closed, and it is suggested verbally that they will sway backward. However, this behavioural strategy naturally leads the body to sway slightly, to maintain balance, creating the physical or muscular suggestion of being unbalanced. When the verbal (cognitive) and muscular (behavioural) strategies are coupled in this way, as Barber puts it, the effect is increased and subjects are more likely to actually fall backwards. Barber explains the eye-fixation induction in the same way, as a form of such "coupling" of cognitive and behavioural stimuli, which Braid would have called the reciprocal interaction between verbal and muscular suggestions.

Hypnotic triggers and cues

Although it is admittedly difficult to interpret his rather convoluted discussions on this point, Braid gradually arrived at the conclusion that certain trigger points could be created, by training and suggestion, which would allow the subject (or hypnotist) to evoke certain reactions, especially emotional responses such as laughter, singing, religious ecstasy, aggression, etc. Braid began by experimenting with trigger points on the scalp which phreno-mesmerists claimed were directly correlated with a wide variety of brain functions. However, he discovered that he could evoke the same responses, and more, by the use of suggestion and associate them with trigger points anywhere on the subject's body, not just their scalp.

> These manifestations may arise either from a previous knowledge of phrenology, or from a system of training *during the sleep*, so that they come out subsequently, as acts of memory, when corresponding points are touched, with which particular ideas had been associated through audible suggestion—which arbitrary associations may be equally, readily established by touching other parts of the body as by touching different parts of the head […] (Braid, 1855, p. 88)

Braid considered it a more "natural" method to manipulate the "anatomy of expression" so that the subject's facial expression, posture, and gestures, evoked the emotion by means of direct muscular suggestion. However, these responses could then be conditioned by the "law of habit and association" to be re-evoked by means of arbitrarily chosen trigger points, for example, pressing the base of the thumbnail, or the bridge of the nose.

The law of habit and association

Following the dominant philosophies of mind, such as the writings of the Scottish Common Sense school, Braid assumed one of the most basic laws of the mind to be the formation of habitual associations. This philosophical "law of habit and association" was an obvious precursor of Pavlov's research on conditioned responses, whose conditioning experiments with animals provided the original theoretical framework for early behaviour therapists such as Andrew Salter and Joseph Wolpe (Wolpe, 1958; Salter, 1949).

Braid repeatedly refers to a specific form of the "law of habit and association" which relates to "remembrance of past feelings" (Braid, 1852, p. 134). Indeed, hypnotism can often be self-induced by "the mere remembrance and expectation of the recurrence of past sensation" (Braid, 1852, p. 164). Braid repeatedly emphasised that once a subject had been hypnotised by eye-fixation they could subsequently be more easily hypnotised by the imagination alone, the impression of sleepiness and suggestibility having been "stamped" on the brain. The physical impression of eye-fatigue, once powerfully evoked, can easily be recalled and therefore re-experienced by means of habit and association.

Likewise, techniques of "sensory recall" in behavioural approaches to hypnotherapy have utilised the ability of subjects to re-evoke the memory of previously experienced sensations, which can be associated with specific cues (Kroger & Fezler, 1976, pp. 87–88). For example, by placing his hand repeatedly in very warm water, someone may learn to remember the feeling, perhaps by attaching a cue or trigger word to it, and thereby induce dilation of the peripheral blood capillaries in the hand, a technique sometimes used in the management of headaches.

The law of sympathy and imitation

The Scottish economist and political philosopher Adam Smith had outlined an influential theory of the laws of sympathy in the opening chapter of *The Theory of Moral Sentiments* (1759). However, an alternative account of sympathy and imitation, specifically in relation to Mesmerism, was developed by Dugald Stewart in *Elements of the Philosophy of the Human Mind* (1827). It is probably Stewart's philosophy of psychology that Braid has in mind on the many occasions when he refers to the laws of sympathy in accounting for the natural tendency to imitation found in hypnotic subjects and in the waking state.

Braid particularly related this concept to the imitation of the observable behaviour of others by hypnotic subjects, including their tendency to become more responsive to hypnosis after having first observed others being hypnotised in their presence. He also appeals to this concept as a way of explaining "mass hysteria" and the power of suggestion to implant negative fixed ideas (Braid, 1852, p. 160). In a curiously quaint example of this intensified imitation or modelling of behaviour during hypnosis, Braid described an informal demonstration carried out in 1847 which involved Jenny Lind, known as the "Swedish Nightingale", one of the most highly-regarded opera singers of the nineteenth century. Braid hypnotised a young woman, who happened to be a gifted hypnotic subject ("somnambule"), and in a demonstration before a group of observers, had her closely imitate the soprano's singing.

Two people present at this experiment did not want for some time to admit that they heard two voices, so perfect was the performance, from the point of view of the harmony and the pronunciation of Swiss, German and Italian songs. This patient accompanied Miss Jenny Lind, with as much success, in the improvisation of a long and difficult chromatic exercise that this great artist carried out to put to the test the capacities of the somnambule. (Braid, 1860, p. 76)

Braid's anecdote was supported by one of the observers who published his own account in *The Medical Times*. We're told that the girl in question, who worked in a warehouse and turned up in her overalls, could speak none of these foreign languages. Whether or not we accept this anecdote at face value, it serves to illustrate Braid's general contention that hypnotism was capable of enhancing behavioural modelling, at least with highly-responsive subjects. The original approach to hypnotism was, indeed, based upon recognition of the sometimes subtle and profound power of social imitation. For example, as we shall see below, Braid emphasised that changes in the demeanour and voice tonality of the hypnotist typically had a powerful influence upon the subject, which can also be seen as a form of modelling.

Verbal suggestion and voice tonality

Braid, of course, recognised that suggestions could be made verbally to subjects, either audibly or in writing. However, he also emphasised that the effect of verbal suggestions could be "modified by the tone of voice in which they are uttered" and quotes Wilkinson, again, as providing a particularly vivid anecdotal account of the experiments which led Braid to this conclusion.

> "What animal is it?" The patient will tell you it is a lamb, or a rabbit, or any other animal or thing. Does he see it? "Yes." "What animal is it now?"—putting depth and gloom into the tone now, and thereby suggesting a difference. "Oh!" with a shudder, "it is a wolf." "What colour is it?"—still glooming the phrase. "Black." "What colour is it now?"—giving the now a cheerful air. "Oh! A beautiful blue," spoken with the utmost delight. And so you lead the subject through any dreams you please, by variation of questions and of inflections of voice, and he sees and feels all as real. [...]
>
> Moreover, the patient's mind, directed to his own body, does physical marvels: he can do, in a manner, what he thinks he can. Place a handkerchief on a table, and beg him to try to lift it—observing, however, that you know it to be impossible—and he will groan and sweat over the cambric as though it were the anchor of a man-of-war. On the other hand, tell him that a fifty-six-pound weight is a light cork, to be held out at arm's length on his little finger, and he will hold it out with ease. (Wilkinson quoted in Braid, 1852, p. 151)

These comments and similar remarks made throughout Braid's writings make it clear that the notion that the hypnotist should speak in a "hypnotic monotone" is a myth, probably perpetuated by representations of hypnotism in fiction. Braid is clear that hypnotic suggestion is a rhetorical art and that the tone of the hypnotist's voice is as important as the words he uses, just as in ordinary communication. It is surprising to note how many modern hypnotists fall prey to this and other popular misconceptions about hypnotism, almost as though they are basing their understanding of the subject upon examples found in movies, novels, and popular culture generally, rather than on more credible sources, such as the historical, clinical, and research literature published in the field of hypnotism.

Elsewhere, Braid observed that generally speaking some verbal skill is required in hypnotism and whereas a "doubting tone of voice" or "hesitating manner" may undermine expectations, an "earnest and energetic, and confident and authoritative manner" is often more effective for both verbal suggestion and physical gestures (Braid, 1852, pp. 153–154). Barber's research subsequently provided empirical support for the view that suggestions delivered in a confident tone of voice were more effective than those delivered in a detached or "lackadaisical" manner (Barber, Spanos & Chaves, 1974). This observation concerning ineffectual ways of delivering suggestions may actually lend themselves to a positive understanding of *dehypnosis*. Likewise, when negative autosuggestions are repeated more slowly and in a doubting or detached tone of voice this may function in a manner resembling the "distancing" (or "defusion") techniques emphasised in cognitive therapy and more recent mindfulness and acceptance-based approaches (Beck A. T., 1976; Hayes, Strosahl & Wilson, 2012).

Reciprocal psycho-physiology

In his earlier writings, Braid often criticised the "imagination theory" but he was really objecting against the reduction of hypnotism to imagination alone, to the neglect of other factors such as genuine focused attention and the tangible physiological effects of the technique. The accusation that Mesmerism and hypnotism were all "just imagination" was common among certain skeptics of the period (Braid, 1852, p. 144). Braid responded by arguing that they were mistaken in trivialising the power of the imagination.

> Those who suppose that the power of the imagination and sustained mental attention directed to any part of the body is a mere *mental* condition, without being accompanied by any change in the physical organism, labour under a grave mistake. Sustained mental attention directed to any part changes both the sensation and circulation of the part so regarded, and in a more marked degree according to the imagination and belief of the patient. From this cause the most grave and fatal diseases may be engendered, and by withdrawing the attention, and fixing the train of thought on some new object or pursuit, relief and cures may be effected in cases which would utterly fail without such management of the mind. (Braid, 1851, p. 196)

Whereas others adopted a simpler psychological theory of hypnotism, which emphasised subjective factors such as belief and imagination, Braid consistently referred to "the reciprocal actions upon each other of mind and matter", that is, the circular interaction between the subject's mind and body (Braid, 1851, p. 190), which he eventually termed "psycho-physiology." This prefigures the modern emphasis upon cyclical interaction between cognitive (mind) and behavioural (bodily) factors, found in cognitive-behavioural therapy.

Braid's model of hypnotism, in terms of reciprocal "psycho-physiology", is based on a distinction between several paths of seemingly *automatic* influence. As we have seen, the general influence of the mind on the body is referred to as "ideo-dynamic", whereas the specific influence

(Behaviour) Muscular Response

(Cognition) Expectant Dominant Idea

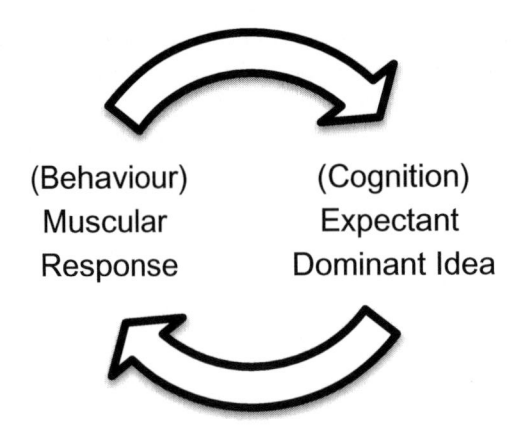

Figure 2. Braid's model of reciprocal cognitive-behavioural (ideo-motor) interaction.

of ideas on behaviour is labelled "ideo-motor", and the opposing influence, of behaviour on the mind, is called "muscular suggestion."

For example, in his debunking of spiritualists' table-turning, Braid argues that the expectant dominant idea of the table rotating caused an unconscious and automatic muscular movement to occur which progressively shifts the table, especially when a group of people had all laid hands upon the same surface and were (unwittingly) pushing in the same direction, thereby multiplying the physical force several times over. However, he adds that this initial ideo-motor response is further reinforced by the "suggestion conveyed to the mind by the muscular action which flowed from it" (Braid, 1855, p. 79). In other words, the initial expectation creates a muscular movement which in turn reinforces the expectation, creating additional

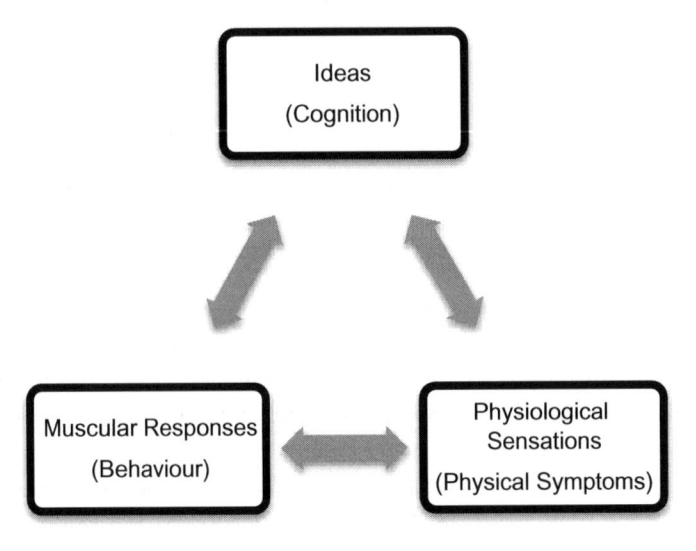

Ideas (Cognition)

Muscular Responses (Behaviour)

Physiological Sensations (Physical Symptoms)

muscular movement, etc., in a feedback loop. Braid therefore describes the table-turning illusion in terms of the "reciprocal actions and reactions" of mental and physical suggestions (Braid, 1855, p. 80).

A more familiar example to modern hypnotherapists would be Chevreul's pendulum experiment, which is often used in modern hypnotic skills training (Weitzenhoffer A. M., 2000, pp. 51–53). The pendulum swings in a certain direction because the mind of the subject is focused on the idea (or image) of it doing so, in an expectant way. However, this demonstration has been found to consistently work well because each actual swing of the pendulum creates a kinaesthetic sensation which further reinforces the expectation of it swinging, and so it tends to swing more and more as the result of the circular interplay between expectation (cognition) and performance (behaviour). This interaction between mental and physical factors may be particularly apparent in self-hypnosis training.

> The experiments recorded of my having caused patients to hypnotise, manipulate, and rouse themselves (by simply desiring them to rub their own eyes) and which produced results precisely the same as when done by anyone else, seem to me the most decisive proof possible that the whole results from the mind and body of the patients acting and re-acting on each other, and that it has no dependence on any special influence emanating from another. (Braid, 2009, p. 285)

Apparently influenced by his Christian faith, Braid expressed himself in thoroughly Cartesian language, assuming a "mind-body dualism", and implying that the mind was a metaphysically separate entity to the brain and the rest of the body. However, that metaphysical assumption need not impinge on the relevance of his ideas to scientific psychotherapy. Most of what Braid has to say about psycho-physiology and the ideo-dynamic response, that is, "the power of the mind over the body", can probably be reconceptualised in terms of certain high-level brain processes determining behavioural and emotional responses, rather than assuming that a separate reified entity called the "mind" somehow interacts with the body like a "ghost in the machine" (Ryle, 1949).

Braid and hypnotic therapy

Spontaneous autosuggestion and psychopathology

As we've seen, modern cognitive-behavioural hypnotherapists have reprised the notion of negative autosuggestion or self-hypnosis as a maintaining factor in certain psychological problems, aware of the obvious parallels between this, the position of the Victorian hypnotists, and Beck's notion of negative automatic thoughts (Beck A. T., 1976). Hence, the authors of one of the first explicitly cognitive-behavioural books on hypnotherapy wrote, "It is our view that many forms of psychopathology are at least partly the result of negative self-suggestions, or, negative self-hypnosis" (Golden, Dowd & Freidberg, 1987, p. 6).

Braid and Carpenter both immediately realised that many cases of both mental and physical illness could potentially be interpreted in terms of the influence of *involuntary* morbid ideas via the ideo-dynamic response. Cases of mass hysteria, hysterical paralysis, psychosomatic illness, psychosis, and emotional disturbance are all cited by them as resulting from fixation upon morbid ideas which subsequently exert an unhealthy effect upon the body. This obvious parallel between the causes and cures of, in particular, hysterical illnesses, naturally suggested a complementary theory of hypnotic psychopathology and therapy in which the morbid "dominant ideas" that cause (or maintain) the problem are directly addressed by suggesting opposing healthy ideas. Hence, emotional and psychosomatic conditions apparently caused by fixation on morbid dominant ideas were treated by Braid using opposing healthy ideas, in a manner somewhat prescient of modern cognitive therapy; "through the influence of suggestion, existing predominant ideas may be removed, and *any other ideas whatever produced in their stead*, which the operator chooses to indicate by word, look, or gesture" (Braid, 1852, pp. 144–145). Unlike cognitive therapy, though, Braid's hypnotism did not involve *disputing* negative thoughts or morbid dominant ideas.

Hence, Braid repeatedly emphasised the role of negative automatic thoughts ("involuntary dominant ideas") in various psychological problems especially so-called "conversion hysteria", employing hypnotherapy to "break down the pre-existing, involuntary fixed, dominant idea in the patient's mind, and its consequences" (Braid, 1853, p. 100).

> The most striking cases of all, however, for illustrating the value of the hypnotic mode of treatment, are cases of hysterical paralysis, in which, without organic lesion, the patient may have remained for a considerable length of time perfectly powerless of a part, or of a whole body, from a dominant idea which has paralysed or misdirected his volition. (Braid, 1853, p. 101)

Braid proceeded to describe how hypnotherapy opposes negative ideas with counter-acting suggestions.

> In such cases, by altering the state of the circulation, and breaking down the previous [negative] idea, and substituting a salutary idea of vigour and self-confidence in its place *(which can be done by audible suggestions addressed to the patient, in a confident tone of voice, as to what must and shall be realised by the process he has been subjected to)* on being aroused a few minutes afterwards, with such [positive] dominant idea in their minds, to the astonishment of themselves as well as of others, the patients are found to have acquired vigour and voluntary power over their hitherto paralysed limbs […]. (Braid, 1853)

Again, although Braid appears to have identified negative automatic thoughts and countered them with alternative, healthy and positive ones, he does not appear to have attempted to directly question or dispute the original unhealthy thoughts.

The founder of REBT, Albert Ellis, studied the writings of Coué as a young man (Ellis, 2004, p. 19) and negative cognition is repeatedly described in Ellis' early writings as a form of "negative autosuggestion." As noted earlier, musing over the therapeutic power of hypnotic suggestion, he wrote:

> The answer to this riddle, in the light of the theory of rational-emotive psychotherapy, is simply that suggestion and autosuggestion are effective in removing neurotic and psychotic

symptoms because *they are the very instruments which caused or helped produce these symptoms in the first place*. Virtually all complex and sustained adult human emotions are caused by ideas or attitudes; and these ideas or attitudes are, first, suggested by persons and things outside the individual (especially by his parents, teachers, books, etc.); and they are, second, continually *auto-suggested* by himself. (Ellis, 1962, p. 277)

Likewise, in one of his earliest books on cognitive therapy, Beck explicitly compares his cognitive theory of psychopathology to the Victorian hypnotists' theory of "hysterical" autosuggestion which he dubs "the illustration *par excellence* of the phenomenon of cognitive distortion in psychiatric disorders." Beck draws direct analogies between the mechanism underlying hypnotherapy and his own approach, concluding that the Victorian autosuggestion concept was more consistent with cognitive therapy than, for example, Freud's psychoanalytic theory (Beck A. T., 1976, pp. 207–208).

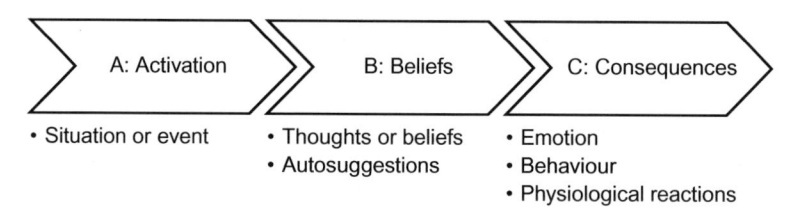

A: Activation — Situation or event
B: Beliefs — Thoughts or beliefs, Autosuggestions
C: Consequences — Emotion, Behaviour, Physiological reactions

Figure 3. ABC model (thoughts/autosuggestions).

Braid himself never fully developed his primitive ideational or cognitive model of psychopathology. However the basic concept of attributing symptoms to involuntary morbid ideas (negative automatic thoughts) is certainly to be found throughout his writings and his references to unhealthy ideas that have become "fixed" may even be compared to the notion of more enduring cognitive structures or processes in cognitive therapy. It is surprising that hypnotherapists were drawn away from explicitly conceptualising their clients' problems in terms of negative autosuggestion. This was partly due to the historical influence of psychoanalytic notions such as emotional or libidinal repression. However, reintroducing Braid's explicit emphasis on the concept of negative autosuggestion is particularly important to cognitive-behavioural hypnotherapy because it makes the treatment rationale more consistent with the conceptualisation of the client's problems, and also makes hypnotherapy more consistent with cognitive-behavioural models, such as Beck's, that emphasise the role of negative automatic thoughts, etc., in maintaining problems.

One of the advantages of the Victorian conceptualisation of hysteria as due to negative autosuggestion was that it allowed "experimental" hysterical symptoms to be induced and removed, using hypnotic suggestion. In modern psychology, many of these experiments would be considered unethical. However, if emotional or psycho-somatic problems are due to something resembling autosuggestion then there are perhaps still appropriate ways of exploring the underlying mechanism by both inducing and removing certain responses. For example, a very common hypnotic experiment involves suggesting to a subject that she cannot speak or move a limb, etc. Beck and his colleagues have noted the similarity between such hypnotic suggestions inhibiting movement and the kind of behavioural inhibition often reported by socially anxious clients, who find themselves "paralysed" by fear and unable to speak in certain social situations (Beck, Emery & Greenberg, 2005).

The two modes of hypnotic therapy

Braid used another quotation from Wilkinson to illustrate a basic distinction between two fundamental modes of hypnotherapy treatment. Wilkinson wrote, "As a curative agent, hypnotism contains two elements, each valuable in its kind":

1. Where it produces trance [sic.], it has the benefits of the Mesmeric sleep, or furnishes so strong a dose of rest, that many cases are cured by that alone.
2. The suggestion of ideas of health, tone, duty, hope, which produce dreams influential upon the organisation, enables the operator by this means to fulfil the indication of directly ministering to that mind diseased, which always accompanies and aggravates physical disorders. (Wilkinson, quoted in Braid, 1852, p. 148, formatting modified)

As explained elsewhere, "trance" was a word favoured by the Mesmerists, and never used by Braid to explain hypnotism. So the first element of hypnotherapy, sometimes known as "neutral hypnosis" today, is simply to induce the deepest possible state of relaxation. This was induced primarily by focusing attention on an "unexciting" or monotonous object, a method not unlike the "relaxation response" approach popularised in recent decades by Herbert Benson (Benson, 1975). The second element of Braid's hypnotic therapy involved focusing attention upon specific suggestions ("dominant, expectant ideas") of well-being. By producing "dreams", Wilkinson does not mean night-time dreams but rather a train of spontaneous images and ideas evoked by the suggestions given.

Braid himself makes comments which imply that some "deep" subjects become unconscious even of the hypnotist's suggestions or other stimuli and that the use of suggestion requires that the subject is only "partially engrossed" in hypnotism.

> As is the case in reverie or abstraction, so also is it in the hypnotic state—there are *different degrees* of mental concentration; so that from some of them, the patient may be aroused by the slightest impression—whilst in other stages, he can only be influenced by very powerful impressions on the organs of sense. Moreover, in the hypnotic condition, as in the state of reverie or abstraction, the subject may be so partially engrossed in his train of thought as to be susceptible of receiving suggestions from others—through words spoken or movements made in his presence—which shall involuntarily or unconsciously change his current of thought and action, without entirely dissipating his condition of mental abstraction. (Braid, 1852, p. 150)

As Braid appears to imply, here and elsewhere, for maximum hypnotic relaxation ("neutral hypnosis") to be maintained for a prolonged period, the subject may have to be left in silence as suggestions may have an inherently stimulating and distracting effect. In contrast to standard hypnotherapy, the subject's attention may have to remain focused upon a relatively monotonous and unexciting object or idea, rather than a stimulating series of evocative suggestions or images. For example, Braid refers the treatment of a patient with *delirium tremens*, suffering from hallucinations, who was induced into a "somnolent condition" and left to sleep in silence for twenty minutes, and then again until he awoke spontaneously, after which he was completely stable (Braid, 1853, p. 100).

Although it was common in Mesmerism, and clearly part of Braid's armamentarium, the notion of leaving subjects to rest in silence to maintain optimal relaxation largely disappeared from subsequent hypnotherapy. A notable exception may be found in the Soviet Union, where Pavlov's physiological theory of hypnotism as irradiated "cortical inhibition" was used as the basis for a similar hypnotic method employed on a large scale during the first half of the twentieth century for the treatment of a wide variety of medical and psychiatric conditions (Platonov, 1959).

> We have always used long-continued suggested sleep as an auxiliary therapeutic method. It is usually employed in more or less grave conditions as a concluding method after a course of psychotherapy and serves the purpose of restoring the function of the cortical cells and consolidating the therapeutic effect obtained.
>
> Even short suggested sleep not infrequently exerts a positive influence on the patient's nervous system. This is indicated by very numerous observations of many authors, as well as our own and those of our associates. In a number of cases even a state of light suggested sleep produces a certain therapeutic effect of itself, without any special suggestions. Thus, upon awakening from the very first suggested sleep some of our patients frequently report the disappearance of pain or unpleasant sensations. (Platonov, 1959, p. 234)

In a sense, Braid's method became divided into hypnotherapy East and West, at the start of the twentieth century, with different sides of the iron curtain pursuing opposing elements of his hypnotic therapy. More recently, the psychologist William E. Edmonston has made a bold attempt to vindicate the Pavlovian physiological theory of "neutral hypnosis", based on an extensive review of the relevant research, in his book *Hypnosis & Relaxation: A Modern Verification of an Old Equation* (1981). However, most modern researchers see relaxation as simply one response among others that can be suggested and not in any way *essential* to hypnosis.

Two modes of neutral hypnosis

Hence, Braid appears to have distinguished between the benefits of hypnotherapeutic suggestions, for confidence, health, etc., and the intrinsic benefits of the physiological state typically induced in hypnotism. Moreover, he actually appears to distinguish between two contrasting physiological states induced in hypnotism: relaxation ("somnolence") and tension ("catalepsy"). He induced either profound tension or relaxation selectively to meet the different needs of individual clients. "In certain cases, the muscles remained in a state of relaxation, breathing and circulation were peaceful; in others, there was catalepsy with laboured breathing and considerable acceleration of circulation" (Braid, 1860, p. 65).

It appears Braid would induce a deep "sleepy" state in some patients, for example, to reduce anxiety or physical tension. By contrast, he would use rigid catalepsy, with vigorous breathing and accelerated heart rate, to stimulate the body and perhaps to alleviate lethargy or depression. Braid induced catalepsy by raising the subjects' arms and legs, while they were seated, and asking them to focus completely on the sensation of rigidity in their limbs. It's not clear to what extent Braid supplemented this with additional instructions or suggestions but it sounds as though he often simply left the client to remain absorbed in either the sleepy or cataleptically tense condition for about five to ten minutes, sometimes much longer.

Hence, Braid emphasised, even in his later writings, that the use of suggestion during hypnotherapy to induce "expectant ideas" was not essential. Improvement was often better attributed to the physiological side-effects of the induction technique, or rather the physical condition induced.

> Whilst the expectant idea modifying or changing physical action is undoubtedly an important agent in most cases of hypnotic treatment, still it is not the *only* cause by which such cures are effected; as the altered condition of the circulation of the blood, and the quality of that fluid during the cataleptic or reverse condition of the body, as formerly explained, makes a powerful impression on the brain and spinal cord, and ganglionic system of nerves, as also on the heart's action, and must thus produce an alterative effect on the whole system, independently of any fixed idea or special train of thought in the patient's mind.
>
> In proof of the above statement, I could readily adduce cases in which no benefit had accrued to the patients when hypnotised with the *one* state of the circulation, and yet so soon as I threw them into the sleep, and acted on them in all respects as previously, *excepting as regarded the condition of the circulation during the sleep*, they were not only speedily benefited, but entirely cured. (Braid, 1853, p. 108)

In plain English, Braid is claiming that a patient might be induced into a relaxed-sleepy-lethargic state and left in silence for ten minutes, to no avail. However, by hypnotising them and inducing the opposite state, one of tension, rigidity, excitement, and catalepsy, and leaving them in silence to remain engrossed in it for ten minutes, they would sometimes obtain more benefit. It is tempting to draw attention to the *prima facie* similarity between Braid's selective use of tension or relaxation and Öst's modern applied tension and applied relaxation methods in the CBT field, which we shall return to in a later chapter (Öst, 1987; Öst, Sterner & Fellenius, 1989). However, Braid also argued that for relaxation to be induced optimally, attention should be focused on relaxing ideas but distracted from the body:

> If tranquilising is the object in view, let the patient remain in a recumbent and easy posture, with all the muscles relaxed to the utmost, and let the mind he sustained by encouraging expressions, and such as shall withdraw attention *from* the part most requiring to be tranquilised. If stimulation is required, then the limbs must be extended, and they will speedily pass into a rigid state, during which the circulation and respiration become much quickened, and by directing the patient's attention and expectation to any organ of sense, its function will naturally be quickened; and so of the function of any other organ or part of the body. Still, even in the state of excitement of the circulation and respiration, a suggested idea may

be made so completely to engross the patient's attention, as to subvert results which ought to have followed, and would have followed, but for this all-absorbing suggested idea.

The first point to be determined, therefore, in this hypnotic mode of treating suitable cases, is the same as is required in any other mode of treatment—viz., to endeavour, by careful examination, to ascertain what is the real nature and cause of the existing symptoms, and whether they require stimulating or depressing [i.e., tranquilising] measures to be adopted, locally or generally; and to what extent, in either direction, the excitement or depression ought to be carried. (Braid, 1852, p. 152)

As it happens, many hypnotists over the years have observed that depressed clients, who often suffer from lethargy and fatigue, not infrequently complain that deep relaxation hypnosis feels like "more of the same" and risks exacerbating their symptoms. Consequently, several modern hypnotherapists have recommended inducing active-alert states rather than sleepy-relaxed ones with such clients (Golden, Dowd & Freidberg, 1987). For similar reasons, sportsmen being hypnotised might complain that an induction designed to make them feel heavy, sleepy, and relaxed may seem to conflict with subsequent suggestions of motivation, enthusiasm, and excitement as they mentally rehearse running faster than ever before. For this reason, sports hypnotists have often dropped the sleep-relaxation suggestions and employed waking hypnosis or active-alert inductions instead.

Indeed, to be clear about this, although many people assume that "hypnosis = sleep" or "hypnosis = relaxation", this is demonstrably not true. Several studies have shown that when the traditional suggestions of "feeling sleepy and relaxed", etc., are replaced with suggestions of "feeling energetic and alert", the increase in subsequent suggestibility is pretty similar. Braid would have doubtless agreed as he repeatedly states that he doubled the heart rate of many (perhaps most) of his clients during hypnosis by inducing catalepsy, that is, an active-alert state. Despite his frequent use of the word "sleep", as we have seen, Braid repeatedly warns us that hypnotism should not be equated with sleep and that it takes many different forms, including variations where the subject's eyes remain open. Hence, hypnotic therapy was originally conceived of as benefitting patients either through suggestions of health and confidence, etc., or through the induction of a physiological state of either tension or relaxation, with or without additional suggestions. However, speaking strictly, it would probably be a mistake to refer to hypnotic relaxation as "neutral hypnosis", as Edmonston does, or to refer to hypnotic catalepsy in this way. Even Braid did not equate hypnotism with either of these two states but rather with monoideism, that is, focused attention upon a dominant idea (or cognition), accompanied by expectation, whether of tension, relaxation, or any other suggested response.

Summary of Braid's neuro-hypnotism

Braid neatly summarised his initial findings toward the end of his first book, *Neurypnology* (1843):

1. [Eye-fixation:] That the effect of a continued fixation of the mental and visual eye in the manner, and with the concomitant circumstances pointed out, is to throw the nervous system into a new condition, accompanied with a state of somnolence, and a tendency, according to

the mode of management, of exciting a variety of phenomena, very different from those we obtain either in ordinary sleep, or during the waking condition.
2. [Hypnotic stages:] That there is at first a state of high excitement of all the organs of special sense, sight excepted, and a great increase of muscular power; and that the senses afterwards become torpid in a much greater degree than what occurs in natural sleep.
3. [Nervous excitation and inhibition:] That in this condition we have the power of directing or concentrating nervous energy, raising or depressing it in a remarkable degree, at will, locally or generally.
4. [Heart rate:] That in this state, we have the power of exciting or depressing the force and frequency of the heart's action, and the state of the circulation, locally or generally, in a surprising degree.
5. [Muscular tone:] That whilst in this peculiar condition, we have the power of regulating and controlling muscular tone and energy in a remarkable manner and degree.
6. [General physiological effects:] That we also thus acquire a power of producing rapid and important changes in the state of the capillary circulation, and of the whole of the secretions and excretions of the body, as proved by the application of chemical tests.
7. [Therapeutic use:] That this power can be beneficially directed to the cure of a variety of diseases which were most intractable, or altogether incurable, by ordinary treatment.
8. [Pain control:] That this agency may be rendered available in moderating or entirely preventing, the pain incident to patients whilst undergoing surgical operations.
9. [Muscular suggestion:] That during hypnotism, by manipulating the cranium and face, we can excite certain mental and bodily manifestations, according to the parts touched. (Braid, 1843, p. 327)

Braid's notion of hypnotism as a "new condition" of the nervous system is moderated by his later writings which consistently emphasise the variety of psychological and physiological states found among hypnotic subjects and their continuity with ordinary states such as absent-mindedness, reverie, and concentration. Hence, I would suggest that Braid's early writings exhibit vocabulary more suggestive of a "special state" view of hypnotism, whereas in his later work there is increasing evidence of a shift in his thinking toward something more akin to modern cognitive-behavioural ("nonstate") theories of hypnosis.

In particular, Braid's writings are worth revisiting because they make it clear that hypnotism was originally conceived as a flexible cognitive state. If we substitute the word "cognition" for "idea", as I think we are entitled to, then it becomes easier to make a case for the relevance of "monoideism" to modern cognitive-behavioural therapy, insofar as it was conceptualised as an induced condition of selective attention focused upon a single dominant cognition, that is, the thought or image of a response, accompanied by heightened expectation of it occurring. Moreover, Braid makes it clear that he conceptualises hypnotism in terms of the subject's expectations and attention toward certain ideas (cognitions). That makes Braid's model of hypnotism essentially a "metacognitive" one, which focuses on beliefs and thinking processes we have in relation to cognitions, which correspond to the meaning of specific suggestions or autosuggestions. We shall return to the role of metacognitions later as this way of understanding hypnosis provides a powerful alternative to the outdated notion of "hypnotic trance" and a bridge to modern cognitive-behavioural theory and practice.

CHAPTER THREE

Cognitive-behavioural theories of hypnosis

Since its origin, hypnotism has been subject to a considerable amount of research, and revisions and improvements have been made to our understanding of it, particularly its therapeutic applications. Sometimes it has evolved as the result of fads, sometimes in the light of genuine scientific progress. In particular, we will examine the influence of psychological research derived from socio-cognitive and cognitive-behavioural theories of hypnosis. Doing so may serve to illustrate the extent to which Braid's original approach to hypnotism was on the right track and anticipated many modern concepts. In part, when we speak of "cognitive-behavioural" theories of hypnosis, this implies an emphasis on ordinary psychological processes rather than abnormal ones, such as an "altered state of consciousness" or "hypnotic trance". Braid's alignment with Scottish Common Sense realist philosophy of mind led him to approach the subject in a similarly down-to-earth manner.

Nevertheless, a long history of research and publications has led to the development of psychological theories of hypnosis which share certain concepts and postulates with those found in modern psychotherapy, especially cognitive-behavioural therapy (CBT). It is important to emphasise that what became known as the "cognitive-behavioural" theory of hypnosis must be distinguished from cognitive-behavioural therapy (CBT) techniques, although the latter are increasingly used in hypnotherapy. Indeed, although cognitive-behavioural theory and therapy are two different things, they naturally fit together and we shall attempt to explore the potential synthesis of traditional hypnotism, as practised by Braid, with cognitive-behavioural theories of hypnosis and CBT techniques. Although there is sometimes an inevitable ambiguity over what *is* and *is not* "hypnotism", it seems incontestable that the work of Braid at least has sufficient historical priority to be considered *bona fide* hypnotism. Indeed, we shall see that modern theories and practices were often foreshadowed, at least in part, by the original ideas of Braid and other Victorian hypnotists.

The state versus nonstate argument

The most important theoretical issue in the history of hypnosis research is known as the "state versus nonstate" debate. It revolves around the widespread assumption that hypnotic responses are primarily due to the induction of a "special" neurological or psychological state in the subject. In plain English, what is at issue is whether such a thing as "hypnotic trance" genuinely exists and adequately explains hypnotic responses. This is a controversial debate and still ongoing, although it has been observed that the two sides have tended to move progressively closer together and to appear less polarised than in the past. The nonstate point of view is particularly associated with cognitive-behavioural theories in hypnosis and this book will tend to broadly favour that viewpoint.

Braid moved from emphasis upon the notion of hypnosis as a peculiar physiological state toward a more multi-faceted position. As time went on, he placed less emphasis on the need for a formal induction technique, and greater emphasis on the continuity between hypnosis and ordinary psychological processes. In the late nineteenth century, the Salpétrière School headed by Charcot emphasised the notion of hypnotic trance as an abnormal neurological condition, divided into three consecutive stages, and linked to hysterical pathology. In fierce opposition to this viewpoint, Bernheim's Nancy school championed the "suggestion theory" which proposed that the "sleep" induced by hypnosis was just normal sleep or relaxation and that hypnosis was primarily a matter of ordinary suggestibility characterised by many "states" depending on the content of the suggestions Throughout the twentieth century, the debate became more subtle and led to a variety of different viewpoints linked to different psychological schools ranging from Pavlovian conditioning theory, and Freudian psychoanalysis, to social role-taking theory. It reached its peak, perhaps, in the 1960s and 1970s when research on hypnosis seemed to be sharply divided into two opposing perspectives. Nonstate viewpoints such as Sarbin's social psychological (role-taking) theory and the cognitive-behavioural perspective of Barber and his colleagues were contrasted mainly with Hilgard's "neodissociation" theory of hypnosis (Barber, Spanos & Chaves, 1974; Hilgard, 1977; Sarbin & Coe, 1972).

There were many other intermediate or alternative viewpoints at the time, and more have evolved since. It is often difficult to classify an author in terms of this dichotomy and the difference is frequently perceived as a matter of emphasis upon one set of factors or another, although use of the terms "trance" and "altered state" is naturally taken as a marker of the author's allegiance to a special state position. However, many clinicians who use the word "trance" seem to hold assumptions more consistent with the nonstate position. Nevertheless, the characteristic claims of the "special state" theory have been described as follows:

1. Hypnosis works because an altered state of consciousness called "hypnotic trance" has been induced.
2. The extent to which someone responds to suggestions, etc., depends on the "depth" of hypnotic trance induced.

3. It is often assumed by special state theorists that certain phenomena, such as anaesthesia, amnesia, or regression, are unique to hypnosis and require the induction of hypnotic trance.
4. It is also often assumed that subjective feelings of mental absorption, dissociation, relaxation, or disorientation correspond with the presence of hypnotic trance.

In contrast, nonstate or cognitive-behavioural theorists argue that the feeling of "hypnotic trance" is merely a consequence of certain suggestions or other procedures, a side-effect, which is not essential to hypnotic suggestibility or phenomena such as regression, etc. Moreover, feelings such as relaxation or detachment, which are commonly experienced during many other psychological techniques, are not considered to be markers of an abnormal, altered state of consciousness or "trance". Just because you feel "spaced out", it doesn't mean you're actually experiencing a "hypnotic trance", in other words (Lynn & Kirsch, 2006, p. 198).

Many people naturally assume that all hypnotists must believe that hypnotism works by inducing a hypnotic trance or "altered state of consciousness", as it is sometimes known. However, since the time of Braid, researchers have struggled to pinpoint any evidence for the existence of a special ("abnormal" or "unusual") hypnotic state. Some basic problems with this concept should be explained at the outset:

1. Hypnotists cannot directly observe the presence of a "hypnotic trance", so they normally try to *infer* its existence on the basis of observable behaviour and self-reports, such as the presence of amnesia, relaxation, etc., but these can all be explained without positing an altered state of consciousness.
2. Brain-imaging technology has signally failed to provide any clear-cut neurological evidence of anything which could be meaningfully called a "hypnotic trance" (Lynn & Kirsch, 2006, p. 199).
3. Research consistently shows that hypnotherapy is not dramatically more effective than non-hypnotic therapies such as CBT; it may have certain advantages but they are not as unique or remarkable as the notion of hypnotic trance tends to imply.
4. When hypnotised subjects are compared against control groups who have been given the same suggestion tests without a hypnotic induction, their scores are slightly (about fifiteen to twenty per cent) higher, but not dramatically so; hypnotic induction does not increase suggestibility by as much as trance-theorists would like.
5. When motivational scripts or instructions to become very active and alert (the opposite of relaxation) are substituted for a hypnotic induction, they produce a virtually identical increase in suggestibility to traditional hypnotic inductions, by modifying ordinary cognitive factors, that is, the attitude or mind-set of the subjects.
6. There are no "hypnotic phenomena" which cannot be replicated without the use of a hypnotic induction; hallucinations, amnesia, anaesthesia, regression, etc., have all been reproduced without using a hypnotic induction (Barber, Spanos & Chaves, 1974).
7. "Trance-like feelings" reported by hypnotic subjects are not unique to hypnosis; people report similar spaced-out feelings and unusual sensations during normal relaxation exercises and in many other settings; so "feeling hypnotised", in this sense, is not evidence

of being hypnotised. Such feelings are best seen as an arbitrary side-effect or consequence of hypnotic techniques, rather than markers of an underlying causal mechanism such as "hypnotic trance". They also correlate poorly with measurable responses to hypnotic suggestion tests.
8. Although, positively correlated to some degree, measures of hypnotic susceptibility are not a very strong predictor of treatment outcome; so being a highly-responsive hypnotic subject does not necessarily make you a good hypnotherapy client.
9. Many of the factors hypnotists routinely appeal to as characteristic of hypnotic trance, for example, focused attention or heightened expectation, are well within the bounds of ordinary psychology and cannot justifiable by regarded as "abnormal" or special in the way the expression "hypnotic trance" implies.
10. Neurological changes observed in hypnotic subjects don't seem to be very uniform, and vary between subjects and according to the tasks they're engaged in. There's too much variation in the neurological responses of hypnotic subjects to support the idea of a single altered state of consciousness, underlying all hypnotic responses.

Hence, as Lynn & Kirsch have put it, "most researchers have concluded that hypnotic responses are not due to a hypnotic state or trance" (Lynn & Kirsch, 2006, p. 4). As they also observe, William E. Edmonston's rigorous book-length review of the experimental literature suggests that the state of relaxation induced by traditional hypnotism is virtually indistinguishable from the "ordinary" relaxation induced by more conventional methods (Edmonston, 1981). Unlike cognitive-behavioural theorists, Edmonston drew the opposite conclusion: that hypnosis and relaxation were identical. However, *pace* Edmonston, this research arguably seems to show that traditional induction methods induce ordinary relaxation, not that hypnosis lacks any other distinguishing characteristics such as the cognitive set of the subject, etc. Historically, many hypnotherapists have equated "trance depth" with signs of relaxation, such as reduced respiratory rate and volume, relaxed facial expression, flaccid muscles, time distortion, etc. However, there is no evidence that these signs of relaxation correlate with heightened suggestibility (Kirsch, 1999, p. 220). Indeed, equating hypnosis with relaxation is deeply counter-intuitive insofar as "common sense" observations appear to suggest that people don't normally become dramatically more suggestible just because they're relaxed, whether physically or mentally. If relaxation typically heightened suggestibility then we'd expect many people to have noticed the fact over the course of human history, because relaxation is an everyday occurrence. Modern researchers do not measure hypnotic susceptibility in this way, by looking for signs of relaxation or "hypnotic trance", but rather by directly observing and evaluating hypnotic responses such as eyelid closure or arm levitation, etc. Moreover, as we will see below, hypnotism can also be induced by "active-alert" induction techniques, the opposite of the traditional "sleep-relaxation" approach.

A position some researchers have considered adopting is that "true hypnosis" is rare and that only highly-responsive ("virtuoso") subjects enter hypnotic trance. Even if this version of the special state theory was correct, and it is disputed, it would mean that the vast majority of ordinary hypnotherapy clients must be viewed primarily from a nonstate perspective.

Very few researchers would now maintain that the responses of normal hypnotherapy clients should be explained by placing greater emphasis upon an altered state of consciousness rather than ordinary social psychological and cognitive-behavioural factors such as expectation, attitudes, imagination, attention, compliance, motivation, cognitive-behavioural skills and strategies, etc.

Early history of the cognitive-behavioural position

The "behavioural" theories of hypnosis can be traced to Pavlov's physiological research in the late nineteenth century and his recommendations for the development of a hypnotic psychotherapy based on "cortical inhibition" and conditioned verbal reflexes. Pavlov's model of hypnotism subsequently became the basis for very large-scale implementation of Soviet hypno-psychotherapy programmes as documented by Platonov (1959). In the 1920s, one of the pioneers of behavioural psychology, Clark L. Hull commenced an influential programme of research on hypnosis, published as *Hypnosis & Suggestibility: An Experimental Approach* (1933). Hull concluded that he could find no essential features of the "hypnotic state" except an increase in suggestibility and no phenomena that could be produced in hypnosis that could not be produced by ordinary "waking suggestion", albeit to a lesser degree (Hull, 1933, p. 391). Hull's failure to demarcate "hypnotic trance" from normal suggestibility led early social psychologists to re-conceptualise hypnosis as an inter-personal construct comprising ordinary cognitive and behavioural factors.

However, Robert White's aptly-named 1941 article 'A preface to the theory of hypnotism' is usually cited as the origin of the social psychological and cognitive-behavioural tradition in hypnosis that undermined the popular concept of "hypnotic trance" (Lynn, Kirsch & Hallquist, 2008, pp. 113–114). White argued that research suggested hypnotic responses are primarily due to the conscious attitudes and voluntary efforts of the subject. In an oft-quoted passage, he defined hypnosis as follows:

> Hypnotic behaviour is meaningful, goal-directed striving, its most general goal being to behave like a hypnotised person as this is continuously defined by the operator and understood by the client. (White, 1941)

From White's perspective "hypnosis" becomes essentially a verb rather than a noun, a skill rather than a passive state, something the subject actively "does" rather than something that automatically "happens" to her as a result of "mechanical" induction rituals and suggestions.

White thereby set the agenda that hypnosis should "take its place as a chapter in social psychology". This was realised in the 1950s through a programme of research led by the social "role-taking" theorist Theodore Sarbin who explicitly rejected the concept of "hypnotic trance" in favour of what he subsequently called a "cognitive model of action", that is, of behaviour (Sarbin & Coe, 1972, p. 66). Sarbin proposed that behavioural responses were mediated by cognitive factors, primarily identification with social roles. Hence, Sarbin replaced the Victorian concept of "trance depth" with degrees of imaginative "role-involvement" and was the first researcher to combine cognitive factors from social psychology with behaviourism and formulate a fully-elaborated "nonstate" theory of hypnosis.

In 1974 one of the most widely-referenced texts in the history of hypnosis research was published by Theodore Barber, Nicholas Spanos, and John Chaves. Their detailed review of experimental research on hypnosis led them to follow Sarbin in rejecting the concept of "hypnotic trance".

> An alternative point of view, which is elaborated in the present text, might be labelled the *cognitive-behavioural viewpoint*. This approach proceeds to account for so-called "hypnotic" experiences and behaviours without postulating that the subjects are in a special state of "hypnotic trance". [...] From the cognitive-behavioural viewpoint, *subjects carry out so-called "hypnotic" behaviours when they have positive attitudes, motivations, and expectations toward the test situation which lead to a willingness to think and imagine with the themes that are suggested*. (1974, p. 5)

Barber's research team produced a wealth of empirical evidence supporting what they now christened the "cognitive-behavioural" theory of hypnosis. They also compared the processes involved in hypnotherapy and behaviour therapy, that is, Wolpe's "systematic desensitisation", and concluded that, once the concept of "hypnotic trance" was rejected, research on mediating factors suggested considerable overlap between the two approaches (1974, p. 141).

Sarbin and Barber were followed by other well-known researchers who developed different aspects of what is variously known as the "nonstate", "skeptical", "socio-cognitive" or "cognitive-behavioural" approach to hypnosis.

> Most members of these groups directly and indirectly credit Robert W. White for giving impetus to this school of thought. However, it was Theodore Sarbin, first, and later Theodore X. Barber (and from then on their students and collaborators) who were most responsible for the development of the cognitive-behavioural position. (Weitzenhoffer A. M., 1972, p. 112)

Modern cognitive-behavioural theories of hypnosis are typically divided into four broad categories, associated with different groups of researchers (Lynn & O'Hagan, 2009).

1. Identification with the socially-constructed role of the hypnotic subject, as first described by Theodore Sarbin.
2. Adopting a set of positive attitudes (cognitions) toward hypnosis, and active imaginative involvement in the process of suggestion, investigated by Theodore X. Barber and his colleagues.
3. The use of goal-directed "cognitive strategies", such as imagining certain things, to help respond to suggestions, described by Nicholas Spanos.
4. The role of expectancies, or "response sets", in generating hypnotic responses with the "automatic" quality found in aspects of daily life, emphasised by Irving Kirsch and Steven Jay Lynn.

When the "cognitive-behavioural viewpoint" and terminology are adopted innate similarities between hypnotherapy and CBT become increasingly apparent. We shall now proceed to examine some of these perspectives in more detail.

Sarbin and role-taking

In 1950, Theodore Sarbin published an article entitled "Contributions to Role-Taking Theory: Hypnotic Behaviour" which helped to thrust the state versus nonstate debate to the forefront of theoretical discussion of hypnotism (Sarbin, 1950). Sarbin argued that the concept of "role-taking" from social psychology could better explain the phenomenon of "hypnotic trance" than theories which attempted to identify hypnosis with a specific psychological or physiological state. Even Braid, albeit briefly, had made the explicit analogy between hypnotism and the experience of actors who shed real tears on stage, etc., by immersing themselves in their roles (Braid, 2009, p. 264).

Sarbin explicitly compares this model of hypnosis with the idea of an actor acting "as if" in order to fulfil a dramatic role. In Sarbin's original article he probably failed to emphasise sufficiently the fact that he was not suggesting hypnosis was a sham or that its effects were trivial. On the contrary, he clearly accepted that hypnosis can be a powerful tool for affecting the body and emotions. However, so can certain forms of acting, as can the socially-constructed rituals of pre-literate tribes. The difference between the ritual "trances" of the tribal shaman and the hypnotic subject on one hand, and the state of mind of an actor on the other, is down to the degree of subjective identification with the role being taken. However, there is no strict dividing line and some great actors may become more absorbed in their roles than some poor hypnotic subjects.

> From those studies of acting which have come to this writer's attention, it would seem that there is a great deal of overlap with hypnotic role-taking in this dimension, but there would be, on the average, less participation of the self in the role of actors as compared with hypnotic subjects. (Sarbin, 1950, p. 261)

Based on this "dramaturgical" or "social role-taking" model, Sarbin argued that the role-taking of the actor and of the hypnotic subject embodied similar characteristics (Sarbin, 1950, pp. 260–261). From this perspective, the ability to perform hypnotic responses depends upon three main variables:

1. Favourable motivation.
2. "Role-perception" (preconceptions of the role of hypnotic subject).
3. "Role-taking ability", the general ability to adopt a role through active imagination or acting "as if."

He notes that the same qualities apply, in a different way, to the performance of an actor and that introspective accounts and observer reports of theatrical acting reveal that the process involved shares several fundamental characteristics with hypnosis, which is better understood as *self*-hypnosis (Sarbin, 1950, p. 260). Sarbin also noted that whereas old theorists had argued that the personality of the deep hypnotic subject often seemed functionally "dissociated" or discontinuous from his normal personality, it was also common for certain gifted actors to be described as undergoing a transformation on stage in which they appeared temporarily possessed by a radically different persona. He cites research which shows that actors often report becoming oblivious to the audience and external events while engrossed in a role, losing themselves in the moment in a manner resembling the time-distortion, selective focus of attention, amnesia, etc., found in so-called "hypnotic trance".

In a study conducted in 1966, Sarbin compared the hypnotic responsiveness of a group of drama students to that found among a group of scientists, concluding that the results showed the actors to be significantly more responsive hypnotic subjects (Sarbin & Coe, 1972, p. 195). Indeed, Sarbin found a moderate positive correlation between the general role-taking ability of two sample groups and their hypnotic responsiveness. In other words, people who can "switch roles" easily, for example, who are good at "role-play" exercises in a classroom, tend to be good hypnotic subjects. However, there are different approaches to acting. It seems that actors versed in what Sarbin called "heated" methods, such as the Stanislavski system or Lee Strasberg's "method acting", were more likely to resemble hypnotic subjects than those who were more "technical" in their acting approach. Likewise, independently of Sarbin and his colleagues, Platonov reported that Soviet researchers carried out a large-scale study of suggestibility and found more highly-responsive subjects ("hypnotic virtuosos") among those they described as "artistic types", that is, musicians and actors.

> The observations conducted by Y. Katkov in a mass study of suggestibility of students of theatrical and musical schools really confirm that among this contingent there are relatively more people in whom the somnambulistic phase may be induced. (Platonov, 1959, pp. 46–47)

Platonov's own experiments, as we shall see below, also led him to conclude that only certain types of acting led to hypnotic-like responses, where the actor was internally absorbed in the experience, as in Stanislavski's system, rather than merely outwardly acting.

Indeed, Sarbin might have observed that Stanislavski's system of acting places considerable emphasis upon the actor being able to maintain a kind of dynamic relaxation while narrowing down his "circle of attention" to the imaginary roles and narrative unfolding on the stage. Stanislavski's own descriptions of his acting method are couched in psychotherapeutic terms which naturally reinforce the impression that his "psycho-technique" resembles self-hypnosis in Sarbin's sense of intense role-involvement.

> Observation of the nature of gifted people does disclose to us a way to control the emotion needed in a part. This way lies through the action of the imagination which to a far greater degree is subject to the effect of conscious will. We cannot directly act on our emotions, but we can prod our creative fantasy and [it] stirs up our emotion or affective memory, calling up from its secret depths, beyond the reach of consciousness, elements of already experienced emotions, and re-groups them to correspond with the images which arise in us. [...] That is why a creative fantasy is a fundamental, absolutely necessary gift for an actor. (Stanislavski, 1963, p. 75)

This perhaps sounds like a description of self-hypnosis. Likewise, Stanislavski distinguishes between merely "seeming" the character and actually "being" him or "living the role" (Stanislavski, 1963, p. 91). This is precisely what Sarbin meant by a high degree of role-involvement.

Of course, the stronger the overlap between hypnosis and non-hypnotic procedures, such as acting, the weaker the rationale becomes for practices unique to hypnosis, such as the formal induction method. Sarbin provides evidence from his own qualitative research which appears to show that the experiences that subjects have in hypnosis are significantly determined by their expectations about what is supposed to happen, that is, role-perception. Sarbin and others have provided evidence to show that when identical scripts are read to groups of subjects, with and without the formal hypnotic induction, similar responses tend to be observed. In other words, the use of a formal induction is now known to add little to the hypnotic responses exhibited. Indeed, although many hypnotherapists are convinced that the hypnotic induction is extremely important, they also tend to employ a wide variety of induction methods, with little in common. Surprisingly high levels of responsiveness to suggestions are found in groups who have not been explicitly "hypnotised" in this way, so it seems likely that hypnotherapists have erred by *under*-estimating the extent to which hypnotic suggestions can be effective in the absence of a formal induction procedure. Factors such as the "response expectancies" of the subject, her identification with the role of hypnotic subject, and voluntarily assumption of a receptive mind-set, may be more important than rituals such as eye-fixation, although these can still be useful, as we shall discuss later.

A superficial reading of Sarbin has led some people to assume he is trivialising the effects of hypnosis. However, even in his original article, Sarbin cited the early research of Edmund Jacobson and Johannes Schultz, the founders of Progressive Relaxation and Autogenic Training respectively, in support of his view that hypnotic role-taking can lead to enhanced control over normally involuntary bodily functions, that is, autonomic reactions such as heart rate and blood circulation which, among other things, constitute the basis of emotional reactions. Indeed, Sarbin carried out an experiment which appeared to show that when hungry hypnotic subjects enacted the role of someone eating imagined food, they were able to inhibit involuntary gastric contractions (Ullmann & Krasner, 1969, p. 89). Since that time, research on hypnosis has provided ample evidence of its ability to enhance control over emotions and physiological responses, in both experimental settings and in the treatment of emotional disorders and psycho-somatic conditions. Hence, Sarbin was careful to explicitly conclude his radical reconceptualisation of hypnosis in terms of "role-taking" theory by emphasising that despite his rejection of "hypnotic trance", nevertheless, "The effectiveness of hypnotism as a therapeutic procedure or as means of relieving suffering is not at issue" (Sarbin & Coe, 1972, pp. 246–247).

Imagination as muted role-taking

Moreover, although Sarbin reported research showing a correlation between abilities such as visualisation and role-taking ability he proposed the difficult concept that "imagination" is not a matter of "pictures in the mind", as people tend to naively assume, but rather a form of role-enactment in which behaviour is muted, or concealed from others. Hence, according to this interpretation, the common metaphor of imagination as consisting of "pictures in the mind" should be replaced with a perspective that sees imagining as attenuated and silent role-taking behaviour, a fully three-dimensional activity (Sarbin & Coe, 1972, p. 119). From Sarbin's point of view, all imagination is seen as a form of role-taking behaviour accompanied by intense conviction, that is, "believed-in imagining", as he came to describe it.

When Braid spoke of "expectant dominant ideas" in hypnotherapy, he typically seemed to be referring to the subject having an idea of acting, or responding, in some way. Braid does refer to the idea of an unexciting object regarding the method of induction, but regarding therapy he clearly assumed most of the ideas in question relate to bodily reactions or behaviour. In his final definition of hypnotism, his examples of ideas employed in monoideism are those of "being irresistibly drawn, repelled, paralysed, or catalepsed" (Braid, 1855, p. 81). In his book on *Hypnotic Therapeutics* he replaces a hysteric's morbid ideas with "a salutary idea of vigour and self-confidence" (Braid, 1853, p. 101). In one passage of *Neurypnology* he describes evoking ideas of "writing or drawing", "dancing", "friendship and shaking of hands", "nursing", "unyielding firmness", "veneration and benevolence", "eating and drinking", "the desire for something to smell at", "depressing emotions", etc., etc. (Braid, 1843, p. 325). In other words, Braid typically focused his subjects' attention upon expectant dominant ideas of role behaviour. In Sarbin's terms, Braid's subjects were engaged in role-enactment behaviour with a high degree of expectation and role-involvement. Sometimes this was "muted", and they remained seated and still, however, most of Braid's subjects physically (overtly) acted out the roles they were imagining. Their tendency to physically act out subjective states when encouraged to move around, doubtless, made Braid even more aware of the analogy between the kind of "imagination" involved in hypnotism and the kind employed by actors on the theatrical stage.

Indeed, speaking of hypnotism and related phenomena, Braid reports Carpenter's observation that the most suggestible subjects seemed to be particularly good at assuming roles, like an actor.

> Generally speaking those were most susceptible of this state whom were most prone to involuntary abstraction or reverie, and who had imagination sufficient to place themselves in the position of others. Those who might be induced to believe they were persons whom they really were not were generally those who had most imagination. By the power of imagination our best actors and actresses were enabled to identify themselves with the characters which they represented; and the assumption of character in the [hypnotic] states was only a similar condition. (Braid, 2009, p. 122)

(He actually says "electro-biological" rather than "hypnotic" but it amounts to the same thing in this context as the responses were considered equivalent.) Moreover, Braid's "law of sympathy and imitation" was used by him to explain how hypnotic subjects would tend to imitate role models. However, when modelling others, what we witness is primarily their overt speech and behaviour. Imitation therefore evokes another mechanism, muscular suggestion, which in turn helps us to evoke the "inner" experiences, especially the emotions, associated with taking on the role.

Acting and muscular suggestion

Braid's theory of muscular suggestion seems to be particularly relevant to the analogy with acting and role-taking. Indeed, as we have seen, Braid made the "reciprocal" inter-action between cognition and behaviour central to his theory of hypnotism as "psycho-physiology". Stanislavski, likewise, believed that physical action and imagination combine in the greatest actors to evoke a response from their whole being, their "entire nature", what Sarbin calls an "organismic" response, because the whole human *organism* is involved (Sarbin, 1950). Indeed Stanislavski states of the reciprocal interaction of the actor's internal imagination and his outward behaviour: "The union of these two actions results in organic action on the stage." What Sarbin calls deep organismic "role-involvement", Stanislavski refers to as the state of "I am …" in which the actor identifies completely naturally with his role (Stanislavski, 1963, p. 73).

Likewise, in a short article published immediately after *Neurypnology*, Braid explains in striking terms how muscular suggestion in hypnotism is simply the same process employed by actors but "with the whole energies of the mind" focused upon the dominant idea of the role to be enacted.

> A familiar example of the influence of muscular expression or action reacting on the mind, may be realised by any sensitive person, even during the waking condition. Let him assume, and endeavour to maintain, any particular expression or attitude, and he will very soon experience that a corresponding condition of mind is thereby engendered. Now, such being the case during the waking condition, when the faculties of the mind are so much dissipated and diffused by impressions on the various senses, we can readily understand why the influence should be so much more energetic during Hypnotism, the peculiar features of which are high sensibility, with the whole energies of the mind concentrated on the particular emotion excited.

He continues:

> It is no doubt, in a great measure, owing to the same cause, that our greatest actors and actresses have become so profoundly penetrated by touching scenes as to shed floods of tears during their impersonations of character—the just conception of the character first producing appropriate physical action, and this again reacting on the mind in the extraordinary manner which was manifested in [Sarah] Siddons and [Eliza] O'Neil [two distinguished Victorian actresses]. (Braid, 2009, p. 264)

These actresses "shed floods of tears", a normally involuntary secretory response, which their great talent for role-involvement and mental concentration had allowed them to render under voluntary control upon the stage, albeit indirectly says Braid, as a result of the genuine emotions evoked through reciprocal inter-action of their dominant idea ("conception") and physical action.

Moreover, experimental support for Braid's theory of muscular suggestion comes from an unexpected source. The Pavlovian hypnosis researcher, Platonov, carried out X-rays of Soviet actors to determine the effect of role-taking on physiological changes occurring in the stomach area. Two actors were asked to exhibit reactions of joy and then of terror. Platonov observed of the first actor, "These subjective experiences were vividly reflected in the whole picture of the gastric motoricity and at the same time in the total mimicry of the student." (1959, p. 213). The second actor's X-rays showed an absence of such internal physiological changes. However, upon interviewing him, it was established that he had been externally mimicking the requested emotions without attempting to reproduce the internal feelings associated with them. Platonov uses this as an example of the way in which physiological changes associated with emotion can be produced through autosuggestion. It appears to support Sarbin's contention that "heated" acting, rather than mere "technical" acting, resembles the kind of imaginative role-involvement found in hypnosis.

In connection with this, Platonov also reported a peculiar experiment, in which hypnotic subjects' bodies were moved to place them in emotionally expressive postures, as in Braid's "muscular suggestion" technique.

> The arms of the subject are put in a position corresponding to some particular emotional state expressed by this posture. The photographs [published by Platonov] show the external picture of various experiences of a person under the influence of change in the position of her arms effected by the hypnotist during suggested sleep. A corresponding mimic reaction connected with the particular position of the extremities immediately appears on the subject's face [clearly visible in the photographs]. The roentgenologic [x-ray] picture of motoricity of the stomach correspondingly changes at the same time.
>
> In this case kinaesthetic impulses formerly combined with various emotional states and connected with them by mimico-somatic reactions were now running to the cerebral cortex and served as the conditioned stimulus. This circumstance emphasises that the development of emotions is based on the conditioned reflex mechanism. (Platonov, 1959, p. 214)

In other words, when actors were placed in emotional postures during hypnosis this triggered genuine physiological and behavioural signs of the corresponding emotion. X-rays of the actors' stomachs showed that even their internal organs were affected, exhibiting involuntary changes associated with the emotional state.

Barber and cognitive-behavioural theory

Whereas Sarbin's work had mainly been conceptual, not discounting some important experimental findings, Barber and his colleagues followed this by engaging in a more systematic programme of research. Many carefully controlled studies were carried out which repeatedly examined different hypnotic phenomena, typically by comparing groups of subjects randomised across three conditions.

1. Those who had received traditional hypnotic inductions.
2. Those who had received special instructions instead designed to boost motivation.

3. Those who received neither induction nor motivational instructions but were simply told to imagine.

Barber's research team found that on standardised suggestibility scales, using various conventional tests, the group receiving traditional hypnosis scored slightly higher than the control group, who responded surprisingly well to "waking suggestions" without receiving any induction or preparation. However, the task-motivational subjects also scored equally high. Hence, hypnotic inductions "worked" but no better than a "cognitive-behavioural" pre-talk designed to boost motivation and imaginal absorption, etc. Moreover, Barber and his colleagues found the same held true for many hypnotic phenomena which, to varying degrees, could be reproduced without hypnotism among groups who had been motivated to try harder, including, age regression, amnesia, positive and negative hallucinations, anaesthesia, time distortion, physical endurance, etc. (Barber, Spanos & Chaves, 1974).

> Barber's extensive and systematic work was without a doubt the single most important factor in driving home the basic *ordinariness* of hypnotic responding, and therefore, its amenability to explanations that were framed in the terms used to account for other "ordinary" social behaviour. (Spanos & Chaves, 1989, p. 15)

Barber and his colleagues identified a range of antecedent factors related to hypnosis, situational cues such as:

1. The definition or presentation of the situation as "hypnosis".
2. The use of a hypnotic induction.
3. The wording of suggestions.
4. The tone of voice in which suggestions are delivered, mainly whether they were spoken confidently or in a detached "lackadaisical" manner.

These antecedents were linked to various consequences, mainly hypnotic responses, but Barber also noted the hypnotic "appearance" of subjects and self-reports of feeling hypnotised as consequences of the procedure, etc.

However, rather than assuming, in a stimulus-response manner, that hypnotic procedures (antecedents) automatically brought about hypnotic responses (consequents), Barber observed that these were mediated by the cognitions and behaviour of the hypnotic subject.

> From the cognitive-behavioural viewpoint, subjects carry out so-called "hypnotic" behaviors when they have positive attitudes, motivations, and expectations toward the test situation which lead to a willingness to think and imagine with the themes that are suggested. (Barber, Spanos & Chaves, 1974, p. 5)

Hence, Barber emphasised that hypnosis resembled certain everyday experiences of imaginative activity such as reading a novel or becoming engrossed in a movie, where favourable attitudes toward to the activity determine the level of absorption and the extent to which responses, such as emotions, are evoked in a way that feels like an "automatic" reaction. The concept of "hypnotic trance", as Barber put it, is just as misleading or obfuscating as an explanation of hypnotism as it would be if used to describe the experience of reading a book or watching a movie. Indeed, Braid had repeatedly tried to link his original account of hypnotism to a wide range of naturalistic observations, such as the emotional reaction of the audience to a great actor or orator, but subsequent authors tended to emphasise the abnormality of "hypnotic trance" and thereby alienate hypnotism from our familiar experience of suggestions or cues to imagine certain things evocatively.

Barber's principal conclusion was therefore that the effects of hypnotic suggestion are mediated not by the "depth of hypnotic trance" but rather by the "positive cognitive set" of subjects, especially their expectations, attitudes, and motivation. The family therapist, Daniel Aroaz, later coined the acronym "TEAM", adding "trust", another factor identified by Barber, to stand for:

Trust
Expectation
Attitudes
Motivation.

This acronym has been adopted by other authors describing cognitive-behavioural approaches to hypnotherapy because it also neatly captures the fundamentally collaborative ("team") nature of the relationship (Golden, Dowd & Freidberg, 1987). Many people, including many hypnotists, falsely assume that hypnosis is a non-collaborative procedure, again probably due to the widespread confusion between hypnotism and Mesmerism. Braid, as we have seen, emphasised the view that all hypnosis is essentially self-hypnosis and voluntarily engaged in by the subject for the achievement of her own goals, sometimes with the support and guidance of an external hypnotist.

Moreover, Barber's cognitive-behavioural theory held that in addition to the beliefs, or cognitive set, adopted by the subject, her behaviour during the hypnotic procedure affected her response. Subjects can be roughly classified in terms of their behaviour during hypnosis as follows:

1. *Negative* responses, such as thinking "this is pointless, it will never work, I don't want to do this".
2. *Passive* responses, called the "wait and see" attitude, misattributing responses solely to the actions of the hypnotist, etc., and therefore doing nothing to make them happen.
3. *Active-positive* responses, which involve "thinking along with suggestions" and actively imagining the things described and suggested by the hypnotist.

It might come as no surprise that subjects who respond negatively during hypnosis tend not to exhibit hypnotic responses, although there are some people who falsely claim, for example, that they can hypnotise subjects against their will. However, an even greater source of misconception comes from those who claim, for example, that the role of the subject is to do nothing, blank her mind, and allow the hypnotist to "talk directly to her unconscious", etc.

This leads to a passive, "wait and see", attitude which has also been found to *reduce* hypnotic responsiveness. Notably, that means the instructions given to clients by many hypnotherapists appear to be counter-productive and may actually undermine and *prevent* hypnotic responsiveness. It should be added that active-positive responders can be divided into two sub-groups:

1. Naturally good subjects. Those who spontaneously, and perhaps barely noticing, think and actively imagine in accord with suggestions.
2. Trained subjects. Those who have to be coached in adopting a similar response style and actively imagining suggested responses or goal-directed images that produce them.

Subjects who have to learn to actively imagine are likely to be more conscious of doing so and to feel their responses are less spontaneous or automatic. However, they appear to be able to acquire the ability to respond well to hypnosis in the majority of cases, with a small amount of practice and instruction. Barber's approach might be described therefore as consisting of two main elements:

1. *Beliefs*. The general positive "cognitive set" or hypnotic mind-set, consisting of expectation, favourable attitudes, and motivations, etc.
2. *Behaviour*. The specific covert behaviour or imaginative activity of the hypnotic subject, actively thinking along with suggestions and imagining the things described by the hypnotist.

In other words, Barber's cognitive-behavioural theory of hypnosis can be roughly simplified and illustrated as follows (Barber, Spanos & Chaves, 1974, p. 20):

As mentioned earlier, Barber further defined the favourable cognitive-set for hypnosis as follows (Barber, Spanos & Chaves, 1974, pp. 19, 49):

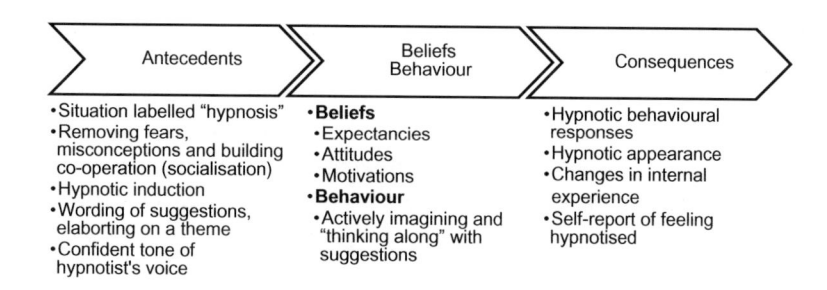

Antecedents	Beliefs Behaviour	Consequences
• Situation labelled "hypnosis" • Removing fears, misconceptions and building co-operation (socialisation) • Hypnotic induction • Wording of suggestions, elaborting on a theme • Confident tone of hypnotist's voice	• **Beliefs** • Expectancies • Attitudes • Motivations • **Behaviour** • Actively imagining and "thinking along" with suggestions	• Hypnotic behavioural responses • Hypnotic appearance • Changes in internal experience • Self-report of feeling hypnotised

1. *Expectancies*. The belief that one will be hypnotised and experience the suggested responses.
2. *Attitudes*. The belief that being hypnotised and responding to specific suggestions is worthwhile and valuable.
3. *Motivations*. Wanting to be hypnotised and experience suggested responses, here and now, in the current hypnotic situation.

Elsewhere in this volume this model has been assimilated with the concept of problem-solving orientation to describe the hypnotic mind-set, for the purposes of cognitive-behavioural hypnotherapy. Hence, Barber's observations can be reconceptualised as follows:

1. *Recognition.* Perceiving the situation as having been defined as "hypnotic" (one of Barber's antecedent variables) and suggestions as cues to respond accordingly.
2. *Attribution.* Attributing one's responses to active imagination and "thinking along with suggestions", as Barber puts it, along with the rest of the cognitive set, expectations, attitudes, and motivations, etc., as opposed to adopting a "wait and see" attitude by attributing responses to the actions of the hypnotist and the "unconscious mind", etc.
3. *Appraisal.* Evaluating the situation as worthwhile, valuable, and safe, which Barber labels "favourable attitudes", and contrasts with common misconceptions, removal of which constitutes another of his antecedents.
4. *Control.* Confidence in one's ability to actively imagine and "think along with suggestions" and the expectation, as Barber puts it, that suggested responses will occur.
5. *Commitment.* Motivation, as Barber puts it, to be hypnotised in response to the current situation, cues, and suggestions, etc.

The main differences here are that perception of the situation as having been defined as hypnotic and perceiving suggestions as cues to respond by active imagination (recognition) is emphasised as an important cognitive mediating factor, along with appraisal of the situation as safe, confidence in one's ability to fulfil the role of hypnotic subject, and attribution of hypnotic responses to causes that are not based on misconception and do not lead to a passive "wait and see" response style.

Active-alert hypnosis

If hypnosis is best conceptualised not as an altered state ("trance") but in cognitive-behavioural terms, as an extension of ordinary role-taking behaviour, or the assumption of a favourable "cognitive set", then what are we to make of the emphasis on "sleep" and "relaxation" in traditional hypnotic inductions? Whereas many, although not all, hypnotists favouring the "trance" conceptualisation have portrayed hypnosis as a special kind of "sleep" or "relaxation", adopting a role or assuming a positive mind-set does not appear to require relaxation of any kind. Braid himself did not believe that hypnotism necessarily involved sleep or relaxation. Most of his clients were physically tense or "cataleptic", their heart rates accelerated. Other influential figures in the history of hypnotism, such as Émile Coué, also abandoned the link between hypnosis and relaxation. Coué replaced the term "hypnotic suggestion" with "conscious autosuggestion", precisely to emphasise the fact, implicit in Braid's writings, that all hypnosis is essentially self-hypnosis and that hypnotism is a conscious procedure rather than something requiring sleep or unconsciousness, as the word "hypnosis" (meaning sleep) unfortunately implies. Albeit approaching the subject from a very different perspective, Milton Erickson also abandoned the view that hypnosis involves a state of relaxation or any resemblance to sleep. Nevertheless, if this is a misconception, it is still a very popular and deeply entrenched one, not only among the public but among many psychologists and even hypnotists.

In fact, several independent research studies have converged on the finding that so-called "active-alert" induction techniques are just as effective as traditional "sleep-relaxation" inductions. The most important example of this type of research was a study conducted by Ernest Hilgard in 1976 which adapted the Stanford Hypnotic Susceptibility Scale to produce two comparable versions, one employing the traditional sleep-relaxation suggestions and another employing suggestions of increasing energy and alertness (Banyai & Hilgard, 1976). Active-alert participants were asked to cycle on an exercise bike until their hearts were beating fast and they were sweating; whereas sleep-relaxation subjects were instructed to close their eyes, the active-alert group's eyes were to remain open and fixated on a point straight ahead. Both groups were tested using a modified version of the suggestion tests employed in the Stanford Scale, which had to be adapted for use on the exercise bikes. Scores were compared against a control ("waking suggestion") group which received the same suggestion tests but without any induction technique whatsoever. As is normally found, the group receiving the standard hypnotic induction, with suggestions of relaxation, scored slightly higher than the control group. However, so did the active-alert group. The researchers took this as evidence that whatever hypnosis is, it is *not* relaxation. Hilgard's own theory was that both groups must have experienced a state of psychological dissociation, which could be induced either through relaxation or through intense concentration. However, cognitive-behavioural theorists, who reject the "neo-dissociation" concept, view the finding as supporting their own view: that hypnosis simply cannot be equated with any "special" state and that responses are due primarily to the subject's favourable cognitive set.

Imaginal absorption and allocation of attention

A number of authors have suggested that heightened mental focus plays a central role in hypnosis. Terms such as imaginal absorption, role-involvement, or selective attention are used by different authors to express what Braid originally called "mental abstraction" or simply "concentration". Focus of this kind has two sides: selective attention to certain ideas (suggestions) and inattention to everything else, such as distractions or conflicting thoughts. As Braid himself seemed to realise, in some instances, such as coping with acute pain during surgery, the inattention to certain experiences may be more important than what is attended to. However, in most modern hypnotherapy, the emphasis falls upon focusing attention on certain ideas in order to evoke the responses they suggest.

In *Neurypnology* Braid suggested that despite their similarities, in some respects, hypnotism was the opposite of "reverie" or daydreaming, in which the mind and attention wander freely from one idea to the next. By contrast, the hypnotic method was described as follows: "I endeavour to rid the mind at once of all ideas but one, and to fix *that* one in the mind *even after passing into the hypnotic state*" (Braid, 1843, p. 361). Like Braid, some modern researchers have concluded that focused attention seems to be a central component of hypnosis. Clarke and Jackson reviewed the research on hypnotic responding from a cognitive-behavioural perspective, summing up their position as follows:

> The conclusion we reach is that hypnosis is one word for a configuration of cognitive changes, the most important of which is a focused attention. (Clarke & Jackson, 1983, p. xv)

They proposed a multi-factorial cognitive-behavioural theory of hypnosis which emphasised the importance of reducing anxiety and extraneous physical behaviour, focusing attention steadily upon relevant ideas and suggestions, shifting toward concrete representational thinking and away from critical reflection, and an increasing sense of the involuntary nature of responses (Clarke & Jackson, 1983, p. 31).

There is some obvious overlap and interaction between these factors. Insofar as physical inertia helps, it may be that it reduces nervous arousal, anxiety, and distraction. Likewise, it is well-known that anxiety can interfere with concentration. This is especially true of the kind of "performance anxiety" experienced by socially anxious individuals when engaged in an important and demanding task, such as fulfilling the role of a hypnotic subject. Relaxation does not seem to be essential to hypnosis, but it does seem to be often beneficial. Likewise, relaxation does not seem to be essential to concentration but it often seems to help, unless carried too far. It may be therefore that the primary elements in hypnosis are focused attention upon particular types of evocative (concrete) ideas, accompanied by a response set composed primarily of positive expectations. Relaxation and suggestions delivered by the hypnotist might help but are probably of secondary value, and in some cases might even be counterproductive.

In due course, we'll explore a way of reconceptualising hypnosis that aims to bring together these factors by drawing on established cognitive-behavioural concepts, derived from research on problem-solving and metacognition. However, although factors such as focused attention and the absence of misconceptions, etc., appear to be important, there's some reason to believe that they may have little effect if favourable expectations do not exist. For example, if someone is deeply focused on a suggestion to relax but has been led to expect that doing so will have the opposite effect, of making them more tense, then it is likely to do so. In this regard, *expectation rules hypnotism*. Moreover, the central role of expectation has been consistently emphasised throughout the history of hypnotism, from Braid's original writings onward, and has become particularly important in modern cognitive-behavioural research on the subject. Hence, it is to this subject and its relationship with non-hypnotic phenomena, such as the placebo effect, that we must now turn before proposing a revised cognitive-behavioural conceptualisation of hypnosis.

The placebo effect and response expectancy (Kirsch)

Sarbin's socio-cognitive theory of hypnosis emphasised the importance of role-related expectations, a point which others have seen as providing a bridge between role theory and phenomena such as the placebo effect. Expectations may relate to the way a socially-constructed role is enacted but also the predicted consequences of certain role-related behaviours.

The concept of expectancy is closely associated with that of role enactment. The concepts complement each other in that "expectancy" may be defined in terms of a verbal description of a role enactment likely to be reinforced in a given situation. […] Expectancy influences behaviour in situations such as hypnosis, psychotherapy, placebo and experimental research. (Ullmann & Krasner, 1969, p. 72)

The word "placebo" is Latin for "I will please." The term seems to have been used in medicine since the eighteenth century; though it was not until the mid-1950s that the "placebo effect" itself became an object of research and that expression became widely used. Inert substances have long been given to patients to pacify them, but little was known for certain about any actual therapeutic effect that doing so might have. Common placebo substances are sugar pills or saline (salt water) injections, which have no significant physical effect themselves but can be easily disguised as medicinal drugs. A common misconception is that because a treatment is called a "placebo" it can have no real benefit, or merely a temporary or superficial benefit. However, this does not seem to be the case and placebo control groups are employed in modern randomised controlled trials (RCTs) as standard because the improvement experienced as a result of placebo treatment is often genuine, and indistinguishable from the benefits of *bona fide* treatment. As Kirsch rightly points out, the placebo effect is the only psychological variable well-established and powerful enough to be routinely controlled for in modern medical research (Kirsch, 1999, p. 213). Researchers have routinely to control for placebo effects precisely because placebos are routinely effective for many individuals.

An important corollary of Kirsch's position is that research on the placebo effect, which in a sense means every single placebo-controlled study, should provide crucial information about the effectiveness of hypnotherapy. As it happens, some conditions respond better than others to placebos and there is a very noteworthy overlap between those which are most placebo-reactive and the conditions treated by psychotherapy, especially hypnotherapy. Depression, anxiety, psycho-somatic illness, and insomnia have been shown to respond well to placebos. Broken legs and cancerous tumours do not. However, initial research on the placebo effect focused on the comparison with anaesthetics (Beecher, 1955). Hence, "Of all the claims made for the placebo response, those that emphasise its power to relieve pain are the most well-established" (Evans, 2004, p. 27). Treatment of depression, anxiety, insomnia, pain, and psycho-somatic illnesses are areas where hypnotherapy has shown promise, perhaps because these conditions respond well to expectations of improvement, as is found in the placebo effect. However, it should be emphasised at the outset that neither hypnotism nor the placebo effect appear to be wholly reducible to the effects of expectation. For example, people who have been hypnotised repeatedly, or who have received real medication, may be subsequently more likely to exhibit expected (suggested) responses, and other factors such as attention and motivation appear to contribute to such effects. The placebo effect of replacing an initial active medication with an inert substance may be due, in part, to a process resembling Pavlovian classical conditioning, whereby the unconditioned physical response to medication has become associated to the stimulus of taking a certain type of pill.

It's long been noted that until the middle of the twentieth century a great many medical prescriptions were "pharmacologically inert", that is, placebos (Frank, 1961, p. 66). Likewise, a great many surgical procedures, which have long since been abandoned as useless, were nevertheless employed effectively in certain cases. Indeed, the majority of early hypnotists were physicians or pharmacists who had extensive experience of administering placebos on a daily basis, or certainly saw their colleagues prescribing many inert remedies. For example, the pharmacist Émile Coué developed his theory of "conscious autosuggestion" partly as a result of observing how his patients responded positively to hearsay about the latest remedies, regardless of their actual therapeutic value. Hypnotists have generally referred to the placebo, in fact, as a form of "waking suggestion", closely analogous to hypnotic suggestion. Indeed, if Braid had been familiar with the term, he would certainly have used it in relation to hypnotism, as he clearly compares it to the effect of "bread pills" and other pharmaceutically inert substances, which he often criticised as quack remedies or "nostrums".

Several authors have previously suggested that an approach to psychotherapy could be developed from psychological research on the placebo effect (Fish, 1973; Frank, 1961). Fish concluded that hypnotherapy provided an ideal setting for the application of placebo-based principles (Fish, 1973, p. 74). However, as Frank was keen to emphasise, the placebo effect may account for some aspects of psychotherapy better than others. In particular, Frank claimed to provide evidence that improvement in "social effectiveness" was less influenced by the placebo effect than emotional disturbance and certain stress-related health conditions (Frank, 1961, p. 72). Although he recognised that changes in affect and behaviour interact, as do other dimensions of clients' symptoms, Frank suggested that behaviour change might be more responsive to specific therapeutic strategies, such as assertiveness training, whereas emotional disturbance appears to respond well to non-specific, common factors in psychotherapy. An example would perhaps be that assertiveness training might be expected to improve socially-inhibited behaviour better than dream analysis (or tea-leaf reading), but that both, when delivered empathically, etc., might have beneficial (placebo) effects upon emotional states, for example, pacifying subjective feelings of anxiety, in some clients, particularly where favourable expectations are present.

However, little is known as yet about some factors which may influence the placebo effect. There is reason to believe that the authority or prestige of the prescribing doctor may contribute and that treatments perceived as more dramatic or powerful may have greater placebo effects, for example, injections are generally seen as more powerful than pills. One curious study in 1970 demonstrated that when anxiolytic drugs were administered to sufferers from anxiety disorders, different coloured pills brought about different responses. Green pills were most effective in reducing anxiety, and yellow pills least effective, even though they were chemically identical. Indeed green pills were twice as effective as either yellow or red pills in reducing symptoms of phobia. Even more intriguing was the fact that in treating depression as opposed to anxiety, yellow tablets were most effective. Red tablets were least effective in treating both anxiety and depression (Evans, 2004, pp. 36–37).

Non-blind placebo trial

In the 1960s, two researchers called Park and Covi published an unusual article entitled simply 'Nonblind placebo trial: An exploration of neurotic patients' responses to placebo when its inert content is disclosed' (Park & Covi, 1965). They selected fifteen neurotic participants, with a variety of mental and physical ailments, from the outpatient deptartment of a psychiatric clinic. Each patient was seen individually for two sessions only, once for a one-hour assessment and again for a fifteen to thirty minute prescription session. They were each given a bottle of placebo pills, without any active ingredients, to be taken three times per day. Patients were each read the following script at the second appointment:

> "Mr. Doe, at the intake conference we discussed your problems and it was decided to consider further the possibility and the need of treatment for you before we make a final recommendation next week. Meanwhile, we have a week between now and our next appointment, and we would like to do something to give you some relief from your symptoms. Many different kinds of tranquilisers and similar pills have been used for conditions such as yours, and many of them have helped. Many people with your kind of condition have also been helped by what are sometimes called 'sugar pills,' and we feel that a so-called sugar pill may help you, too. Do you know what a sugar pill is? A sugar pill is a pill with no medicine in it at all. I think this pill will help you as it has helped so many others. Are you willing to try this pill?" (Park & Covi, 1965)

Only one patient expressed reluctance to take part in the experiment. Of the remaining fourteen patients, thirteen showed signs of significant improvement across a battery of self-report and psychiatrist administered measures. An average forty-one per cent decrease in symptoms was reported, across different measures. The researchers note that this was greater than the improvement found in previous studies of *real* drugs, using the same measures. Four patients reported, indeed, that the placebo medication did them more good than anything they'd previously been prescribed. By contrast, the one patient who dropped out was subsequently assessed and found to have *increased* on the same measures of symptom severity.

Some patients were convinced they were receiving placebos, others convinced themselves that the script was a ruse and assumed the "sugar pill" must contain some active ingredient. Most notably, however, one patient actually compared knowingly taking the placebo pills to a kind of hypnotherapy.

> The patient indicated that she was quite suggestible, and she thought the treatment had been effective through a form of 'hypnosis' because she had been told so many times she would improve. (Park & Covi, 1965)

Perhaps she was right; at least her interpretation of the proceedings would accord with the notion of hypnosis as a "non-deceptive" placebo approach, and perhaps even with Braid's perspective on the relationship between hypnotic suggestion and placebos. Indeed, like Braid, the researchers conclude that the use of non-deceptive placebos could have psychotherapeutic implications, by using suggestion to heighten expectation in combination with other non-specific factors which the researchers describe as "support and reassurance" and giving the patient autonomy or responsibility for her own improvement (Park & Covi, 1965). These factors are also integral to cognitive-behavioural hypnotherapy.

It is therefore clear to see how this can be compared to the role of suggestion and related factors in hypnotherapy. It is crucial to understand that one of the main differences between hypnotic suggestion and the placebo effect, as traditionally employed, is that hypnotism is non-deceptive. Although there is broad agreement that the "power of the placebo" is a real, and often impressive, phenomenon, placebos cannot be routinely used in medicine because that would involve deceiving the patient, which is unethical. It's also ultimately futile because in the modern world such deception would be exposed over time. However, in hypnotism, at least in the cognitive-behavioural approach, the client is explicitly told that the effects are due to her own suggestion and imagination. Her informed consent and active collaboration are explicitly obtained at the outset and maintained throughout the course of treatment. Arguably, hypnotherapy is the only established way to harness the power of the placebo, by using suggestion explicitly, collaboratively, and without deception. The emphasis on deception in Ericksonian approaches has, to some extent, damaged this argument in favour of hypnotism. However, the growing emphasis on collaborative and transparent cognitive-behavioural approaches to hypnotherapy is bound to lend further support to the argument that hypnotism may be used in ways that capitalise on the wealth of evidence supporting the clinical value of the placebo effect.

Response expectancy

Irving Kirsch, one of the leading contemporary researchers in the field of hypnosis, has developed the "response expectancy" and "response set" interpretations of hypnosis. Kirsch's original "response expectancy" theory was developed in the 1980s and 1990s on the basis of Rotter's social learning theory (Lynn, Kirsch & Hallquist, 2008, pp. 121–123).

> According to this theory, expectancies for changes in subjective experience can affect experience directly and generate nonvolitional responses. More specifically, response expectancies are anticipations of automatic subjective and behavioural responses to particular situational cues, and they elicit automatic responses in the form of self-fulfilling prophecies. (Lynn, Kirsch & Hallquist, 2008, pp. 121–122)

These expectancies are dynamic, in that they readily change in response to events. They are, of course, cognitions and they most resemble the type of beliefs that Beck refers to as "predictions", closely related to the concept of apprehensive appraisals in anxiety. Kirsch therefore sees hypnotic inductions not as methods of "inducing trance" but rather as "expectancy modification procedures" or ways of inducing increased motivation and response expectancy (Lynn, Kirsch & Hallquist, 2008, p. 122). Indeed, following Kirsch we may define hypnosis, as a nondeceptive mega-placebo which means that:

1. Hypnosis is an enhanced version of the ordinary placebo effect and waking suggestion.
2. Unlike blinded placebo trials, hypnosis is non-deceptive (non-blind) because the client is told that she is receiving treatment by suggestion.

These two points are essential because expressions like "it's *just* a placebo" are too often used in dismissing or trivialising a therapy, and the deceptive nature of most placebos makes it unethical to use them in ordinary clinical practice. Moreover, as noted above, the routine use of deceptive placebos undermines the very trust which they depend upon for their effectiveness—it's ultimately self-defeating to deceive clients. In other words, hypnotic responses are seen as continuous with nonhypnotic response, except that they are strengthened by increased motivation and expectation. The ability to "think along with" or actively imagine responding, further increases expectation whereas trust and rapport between hypnotist and client may enhance motivation (Lynn & Kirsch, 2006, p. 24).

As Kirsch has noted, virtually all psychotherapy researchers have to recognise that expectation plays a central role in determining outcomes (Lynn & Kirsch, 2006, p. 24). Indeed, he cites the French Academy of Sciences' investigation of Mesmer as one of the first instances of hypnotic-like responses being explicitly attributed to expectation, although at the time this was taken by skeptics to constitute a refutation of the whole practice of Mesmerism (Kirsch & Council, 1989, p. 360). Similarly, today the problem persists that some readers may respond to the notion of attributing therapeutic improvement to expectation in a superficial way, by discounting its importance without due consideration.

It's perhaps important to clarify that if you firmly believed that hypnotism worked by means of a special state called "hypnotic trance" you might consider expectation to be a confounding *non*-hypnotic variable; whereas if you view hypnotism as a social construct (nonstate) you might consider expectation to be part of its essential nature. The "special state" view would conceptualise hypnotherapy as a means of inducing an altered state of consciousness; whereas the cognitive-behavioural view emphasises hypnotherapy as a means of increasing and shaping therapeutic expectations.

> Unlike special state theorists, cognitive-behavioural and social psychological theorists view expectancy as an essential part of the process by which hypnotic behaviour is generated. (Kirsch & Council, 1989, p. 361)

Put crudely, if hypnotism works by the same cognitive expectations as the placebo effect then it seems increasingly inappropriate to refer to "hypnotic trance" because, presumably, nobody would want to claim that the typical participants in a placebo controlled trial are all somehow in a hypnotic trance. Moreover, numerous studies have shown that the way subjects respond during hypnotism or other experiments is mediated by their cognitive expectations. For example, subjects who expect that hypnotism causes spontaneous amnesia are more likely to experience amnesia than those who do not. Even the ease or difficulty of responding to suggestions and the extent to which clients feel in control have been found to be affected by simple cognitive expectations, that is, influenced by what subjects are told before being hypnotised (Kirsch & Council, 1989, pp. 365–367).

Some studies have found a relatively small effect due to initial expectations, prior to hypnosis, but Kirsch rightly points out that this is because expectation changes during the process and an initially high expectation may suddenly reduce if the induction or therapy techniques no longer seem credible to clients, or their expectations clash with their initial experiences. For instance, a client who has a high expectation that hypnosis will be powerful but also expects (unrealistically) to be totally unconscious following the induction is likely to find that her misconceptions lead to disappointment which undermines her expectation relating to the final outcome of being hypnotised. Of course, this is a common experience reported by many hypnotherapy clients—due the therapists' failure to properly explain what to expect during the session. Hence, Kirsch's theory is adapted to predict that expectations cause automatic ("non-volitional") responses to hypnotic suggestion depending both upon how strong and how realistic (how "difficult") the expectation is; a strong expectation is useless if the subject expects some response to happen which is unrealistic or very difficult to achieve (Kirsch & Council, 1989, p. 371).

Moreover, as we have seen, hypnotists since the time of Braid have conceptualised both "cause and cure" in terms of suggestion. Hence, as well as offering a rationale for treatment the concept of response expectancy may also contribute to cognitive theories of psychopathology. Kirsch and Lynn cite studies which have implicated cognitive expectation in anxiety disorders, depression, sexual dysfunction, and drug use (Kirsch & Lynn, 1999, p. 59). As we shall see, Beck's cognitive model of anxiety and the cognitive models of stress from which it is derived conceptualise anxiety and stress as being maintained primarily by "appraisals" of the probability and severity of future harm, that is, dysfunctional *expectations*, which may escalate into "catastrophic predictions" about the anticipated future (Beck A. T., 1976; Clark & Beck, 2010; Lazarus R. S., 1966; Lazarus R. S., 1999).

Imagery and expectation

Kirsch's theory is largely consistent with other nonstate theories such as those of Sarbin and Barber, both of whom cite expectation as a central mediating factor in determining hypnotic responses. However, Kirsch places greater emphasis upon this factor than other researchers and has developed a more sophisticated theory of "expectation-related cognition" based on his research in this area. In particular, he believes that the effect of mental imagery is mediated by cognitive expectations. The ideo-motor reflex theory led many traditional hypnotists to assume that mental images causally evoke unconscious muscular movements in a fairly mechanical way. Barber had placed importance on both expectation and imagination in his nonstate model but he seemed to suggest that expectation is important largely insofar as it increases the subject's willingness to "think along with" and imagine the things being suggested by the hypnotist.

However, following Spanos' programme of research in this area, Kirsch points out that, for example, subjects can visualise their arm rising while still adopting a "wait and see" attitude, with no expectation that anything will happen, and in this instance it is unlikely to evoke an arm-levitation response. Equally, subjects can imagine one response (such as arm-lowering) while a contradictory expectation seems able to create another (such as arm-rising). However, that does not mean that mental imagery is pointless, only that cognitive expectation mediates its final effect.

> Although involvement in goal-directed imagery generally enhances hypnotic response, we believe that the causal link between imagery and expectancy is contrary to that proposed by Barber. From a response expectancy perspective, goal-directed imagery enhances responsiveness by virtue of its effects on expectancy. (Kirsch & Council, 1989, p. 375)

Imagery and expectation appear to interact and when working in unison they may increase the overall probability of a response occurring. However, Kirsch argues that expectation is the number one factor at stake. With this in mind, it is interesting to note that in Braid's later writings he increasingly refers not only to "dominant ideas", by which he includes both thoughts and images, but he uses the more specific term "expectant dominant idea". In doing so, he appears to be emphasising the role of expectation in the ideo-motor response. For Braid, always sensitive as an experimentalist to multiple factors, the "idea" of the ideo-motor response is not merely passive cognition or imagination of the response but a "lively faith", "confidence", or "expectant idea" that it will occur. Hence, mental focus and imagination combine with expectation as the principle psychological factors in Braid's original conceptualisation of hypnotism.

Involuntariness

Many people assume that the hypnotic subject is "under the control" of the hypnotist, that she cannot resist anything he suggests, and that her responses are unconscious and therefore automatic, like a robot, puppet, or zombie, as it's sometimes put. These preconceptions about hypnotism come largely from works of fiction, such as comic books and Hollywood movies, but also to some extent from the appearances fostered by stage hypnosis shows. The question of "involuntariness" has caused considerable difficulty in the field of hypnosis research because it is such a slippery concept. Apart from the conceptual difficulty involved in formulating a theory of hypnotic behaviour based on "involuntariness", there is also a practical difficulty in that it is not an easy concept to explain to subjects for the purposes of questioning them about their subjective experiences. When people are asked "Did you raise your arm voluntarily or did it rise by itself?" following an arm-levitation suggestion they will often reply "I'm not sure." Individuals often report that it is difficult for them to tell whether responses they make are voluntary or not, even after several attempts to scrutinise their subjective experience. This ambiguity may well be an important feature of hypnosis itself. However, on close inspection, it is also very difficult for people to discern the extent to which their everyday behaviour is voluntary. If a fly lands on my arm and I swat it away, did I do it intentionally or was it just a reflex? Could I have stopped myself or was it too automatic?

As Kirsch and Lynn observe, the children's game called "Simon Says" provides an excellent example of this problem (Kirsch & Lynn, 1999, p. 62). The premise is that the players have adopted an attitude (cognitive set) that they will follow any instructions prefixed by "Simon says ..." very quickly, but try to avoid falling into the trap of following any instructions which are not prefixed by those words. Of course, the whole point of this game is that once the response set is adopted it is surprisingly difficult for players to restrain themselves in time from automatically following the orders they're meant to be ignoring. If the instruction "Touch your toes" is called out (without "Simon says ...") the children will often start moving to touch their toes before they can stop themselves; is this voluntary or involuntary? The short answer is that we probably need to distinguish, as researchers like Lynn and Kirsch have, between different aspects of the question. In essence, most hypnotic subjects are, of course, voluntarily making the decision to be hypnotised in the first place, like those choosing to play the game "Simon Says". They may also voluntarily comply with some of the hypnotist's instructions, such as to imagine certain images or take a deep breath. Some responses such as their finger twitching in response to suggestion may seem automatic. However, they will often be able to resist or interrupt such suggestions, especially if they have been told beforehand that they will be able to defy them. So there are elements of automaticity in hypnotic responding, combined with elements of voluntary compliance, and many areas of ambiguity in-between.

As we've seen, in the early decades of the nonstate perspective, it was often (falsely) assumed that nonstate theorists were simply dismissing all hypnotism as mere social compliance. Although there is undoubtedly an element of conscious compliance in hypnosis, and also perhaps compliance of which the subjects themselves are somewhat unaware, as Braid suggests, most nonstate theorists accept that many hypnotic responses are, in some sense, automatic (Lynn & Kirsch, 2006, p. 26). Clearly some of the responses produced by hypnotic suggestion, such as changes in blood circulation, heart rate, and improvement in conditions like asthma, are not with the sphere of normal voluntary control. Studies have shown, for instance, that when they believe they are not being observed by the experimenters, hypnotic subjects tend to continue with their responses for a longer period of time than participants who have simply been asked to fake hypnosis. Moreover, one might expect experimental subjects who are merely complying with suggestion tests to pass all of them, whereas the vast majority tend to fail one or more items on standard suggestion scales, and most score in the middle region, passing some tests but failing others.

Hypnotic responses are genuine and have an ambiguously "automatic" quality to them, like automatically tying your shoelaces or humming a tune you overhear on the radio, and many similar occurrences we can point to in ordinary daily life. For example, as Carpenter once noted, we can all walk and daydream at the same time, "automatically" putting one foot in front of the other, without paying attention, deliberating, or making a conscious effort to move our feet. Hypnotic responses resemble this kind of everyday automaticity; they often have an "effortless" quality but can virtually always be interrupted, although it may sometimes take effort to do so. Hence, as Braid argued, it's unlikely that most individuals can be easily hypnotised to commit a crime, harm themselves, or do something else they find objectionable. Those who wish to sensationalise hypnotism, such as stage hypnotists, very frequently claim the opposite, but most researchers agree that hypnotic subjects normally retain control over their behaviour. Indeed, it may be that procedures that deliberately remove the "automatic" quality of hypnotic responses, such as repeating suggestions in a detached manner, or paying close attention to the procedure rather than the content of the ideas suggested, can be developed into dehypnosis strategies. Indeed, this may be part of the function of "distancing" or "defusion" strategies in cognitive therapy and modern mindfulness and acceptance-based CBT (Beck A. T., 1976; Hayes, Strosahl & Wilson, 2012).

Response sets

Although expectation appears to be a central factor in hypnotic responding, there may be more to say about how this functions. In the late 1990s, Kirsch and his colleague Steven Jay Lynn collaborated on the development of the social cognitive theory of preparatory "response sets", an integration of ideas from both their earlier work.

> Actions are prepared for automatic activation by response sets. Response sets are comprised of coherent mental associations or representations, and refer to expectancies and intentions

that prepare cognitive and behavioural schemas (i.e., knowledge structures), roles or scripts for efficient and seemingly automatic activation. Expectancies and intentions are temporary states of readiness to respond in particular ways to particular stimuli (e.g., hypnotic suggestions), under particular conditions. They differ only in the attribution the participant makes about the volitional character of the anticipated act. That is, we intend to perform voluntary behaviours (e.g., stopping at a stop sign); we expect to emit automatic behaviours such as crying at a wedding or, more relevant to our present discussion, responding to a hypnotic suggestion. (Lynn, Kirsch & Hallquist, 2008, p. 126)

This whole conceptualisation is based on the assumption that automaticity is a normal part of daily behaviour, such as when we "automatically" tie our shoelaces or whistle a tune, and that automatic responses in hypnosis are merely an unusual manifestation of this familiar everyday automaticity in behaviour. However, Kirsch modifies the earlier concept of response expectancy now to recognise that "although hypnotic responses may be triggered automatically, suggestion alone is not sufficient to trigger them" (Lynn, Kirsch & Hallquist, 2008, p. 127). Rather, behavioural responses to suggestions are triggered by subjective sensations that activate the expectation of them occurring. For example, arm levitation appears to be activated by sensations of lightness, which interact with suggestions and expectations to produce the automatic behaviour.

The response expectancy for arm levitation, for example, is that the arm will rise by itself. Yet a sufficiently convincing experience of lightness must be present to trigger upward movements. Subjective experiences thus have an important role in this theory of hypnosis. (Lynn & Kirsch, 2006, p. 25)

Often, it seems, a suitable bodily sensation must occur to trigger the expected behavioural response. Indeed, the expectation of a confirming sensation, such as the feeling of lightness, may be more important than the expectation of the behavioural response itself, such as the arm rising (Kirsch & Lynn, 1999, p. 63). Barber had earlier described the strategy of "coupling" suggestions with actual physical responses as part of the art of hypnosis (Barber, Spanos & Chaves, 1974; Braid, 1860).

Arguably, the interaction which these modern researchers identify between the sensations activating the response set and the increasing expectancy itself can be compared to Braid's original concept of a "reciprocal" interaction between the mind and body in the original theory of hypnotism. The sensation of lightness, in their example, activates the expectation that the arm will involuntarily rise, which in turn leads to increased movement and lightness in the arm, which again reinforces the expectation, etc., in a feedback loop. However, Braid's "psycho-physiological" theory of hypnotism provided a strikingly similar account of phenomena such as table-turning, 150 years earlier. Table-turning was a common practice of spiritualists, in which a group sat around a small card table, each person laying their fingers on the surface of the table, around its edge. By summoning spirits of the deceased, it was claimed, the table would turn or tilt, seemingly of its own accord. However, Braid and other skeptics, most famously the scientist Michael Faraday, set about debunking these claims through simple experiments showing that those seated around the table were unwittingly exerting force to collectively move or topple it.

Braid begins his account by reminding the reader of the ideo-motor reflex theory which states that "when the attention of man or animal is deeply engrossed or absorbed by a given idea, associated with movement, a current of nervous force is sent into the muscles which produce a corresponding motion", independently of volition. He continues:

> It is this very principle of involuntary muscular action from a dominant idea which has got possession of the mind, and the suggestions conveyed to the mind by the muscular action which flows from it, which led so many to be deceived during their experiments in "table-turning", and induced them to believe that the table was drawing them, whilst all the while they were unconsciously drawing or pushing it, by their own muscular force. (Braid, 1855, p. 79)

Later in this essay, Braid introduced the term "psycho-physiology" to describe "the reciprocal actions and reactions of mind and matter upon each other" in this way.

> I feel satisfied that the mental and physical phenomena which flow from said processes result entirely from the mental impressions, or dominant ideas, excited thereby in the minds of the subjects, changing or modifying the previously existing physical action, and the peculiar physical action thus superinduced re-acting on their minds […]. (Braid, 1855, p. 79)

He then states that this principle applies whether the initial expectation occurs spontaneously or is suggested by another either verbally or through physical manipulation causing certain sensory impressions. From the outset, therefore, Braid recognised the role of suggested ideas but also the importance of those ideas being confirmed and reinforced by subsequent physical sensations and visual observation of the table beginning to move slightly.

However, in *Hypnotic Therapeutics'* (1853) appendix on table-turning, Braid goes further and, with remarkable sophistication, proposes a theory which combines ideo-motor action, expectancy, and self-deception regarding voluntary behaviour.

> I believe the more strictly accurate mode of expressing the matter will be this […] that the ideo-motor principle *might* be adequate to effect the result *without* volition, or even in *opposition* to volition, provided the dominant idea was sufficiently vivid; but in these cases of table-moving, when honestly conducted, the ideational motor impulse is supplemented by *volition*, so *slightly* exerted as to be *unconscious* to the *persons so exercising it*; their attention and will being, as they suppose, entirely concentrated on the table, instead of on impinging the nervous force into the muscles, the action of which is required for producing the motion. The illusion, therefore, becomes complete, the force being partly ideational and partly voluntary, but partaking so slightly of the latter quality as not to be cognizant to the subjects engaged in the said experiments. (Braid, 1853, p. 112)

In relation to hypnotism, likewise, Braid repeatedly argued that following the initial physical experience of the eye-fixation induction, it became increasingly easy for subjects to be hypnotised by means of primarily psychological factors such as expectation and imagination alone.

> There is great difference in the susceptibility to the hypnotic impression, some becoming rapidly and intensely affected, others slowly and feebly so. Moreover, those who are naturally

highly susceptible, at length become so much so as to be liable to be affected entirely through the power of imagination, belief, and habit, i.e., the expectant idea will produce it in such subjects when no process whatever, either near or distant, is going forward; whereas if they are made to believe the contrary, through the requisite attention and expectation being otherwise engaged they may not become affected by processes which would naturally throw them into the sleep. (Braid, 1852, p. 150)

Hence, Braid did not argue that eye-fixation was necessary, only that by creating a powerful physical sensation, by means of this behavioural strategy, it became easier for the client to expect and imagine that she would be able to experience the same response again. As clients sometimes say, "Now I've been hypnotised once, I know what to expect next time."

Braid would acknowledge that expectation plays a role in the first session, especially if the subject had witnessed other people being hypnotised which would shape her expectation through the law of sympathy and imitation (vicarious learning). However, before the client "knows what to expect", other factors may become more significant, for example, the physical properties of the induction process itself. There is no doubt that intense eye-fixation, for example, can create powerful fatigue in the eyes which leads to very tangible sensations, and some observable physiological responses such as increased lachrymation or dilation and constriction of the pupils, etc. A handful of Braid's clients complained that it felt too painful and uncomfortable to follow his instructions because his original eye-fixation induction method involved considerable physical strain on the eyes. Although Braid describes this as inducing a peculiar physiological condition, it's actually a small step to re-interpret him as meaning that the unusual bodily sensations heighten expectation and may increase mental abstraction. When we feel relaxed and disorientated we tend to become less concerned with external events and more engrossed in, for example, the voice of the hypnotist, sensations in our body, and stream of consciousness going on inside. Indeed, Kirsch does acknowledge that "hypnotic inductions that produce minor sensory alterations and suggestions for active involvement in goal-directed imaginings", and other strategies used in hypnotism, can potentially enhance response expectancy (Kirsch & Council, 1989, p. 378).

To a variable extent, then, the way that a client responds to any given therapy intervention will be determined by the way she expects to respond, a "self-fulfilling prophecy", and the most effective strategies will often be those which clients come to find most credible and to believe have the power to help them. This is true of hypnosis and also of most cognitive and behaviour therapy techniques (Clarke & Jackson, 1983, p. 14). Of course, it is very unlikely that *everything* is reducible to the effect of "expectation", as this clearly falls flat when confronted with the many instances in which clients express genuine surprise at their "counter-expectational" responses. However, expectation is undoubtedly a powerful force in therapy, and one of the main ingredients which go into the treatment mix.

The nonstate Braid

Surprisingly, Kirsch and his colleague James R. Council pinpoint the German psychiatrist Albert Moll as the main precursor of the "response expectancy" theory among early hypnotists (Kirsch & Council, 1989, pp. 360–361). However, most of the views they attribute to Moll are definitely pre-empted in Braid's writings and so Kirsch may have overlooked the extent to which Braid made the concept of expectation central to hypnotherapy from the outset.

> As did other nineteenth-century theorists, Moll believed that a special altered state of consciousness was necessary for the occurrence of some hypnotic phenomena. However, unlike other state theorists, Moll afforded equal status to expectancy as an explanatory construct and believed that some genuine hypnotic effects did not require a trance state. His general emphasis was on the continuity, rather than the discontinuity, between hypnotic and nonhypnotic phenomena. Where possible, his inclination was to explain behaviour occurring in hypnotic contexts and similar behaviour occurring in nonhypnotic contexts as due to a single set of psychological mechanisms. Thus, Moll's theory can be considered a transitional approach between state and nonstate conceptions of hypnosis. (Kirsch & Council, 1989, p. 361)

Moll had read some of Braid's writings although he was primarily influenced by the French Nancy School of Bernheim (Moll, 1889). In any case, he's definitely something of a Johnny-come-lately as Braid, a much more significant figure in the history of hypnotism, had published numerous discussions of the role of "expectant ideas" in waking suggestion, hypnotism, etc., half a century before him.

Braid actually mentions "expectation", "expectant ideas", and "expectant attention" about eighty times altogether in his collected writings (Braid, 2009). Moreover, regarding psychopathology, Braid believed that hysterical crises, epileptic seizures, and other symptoms were often the result of the patient's morbid expectations functioning as self-fulfilling prophecies: "And in this way, also, some patients having predicted that certain effects will be manifested in their persons, at a certain time specified, the predominant idea will often realise the prophecy" (Braid, 1852, p. 152). Although Braid did not perhaps claim expectation was *essential* to hypnotic responses, he clearly implied that it was of absolutely central importance in most cases. In particular, in his later writings, Braid tends to refer to focused attention upon "dominant expectant ideas". As we've seen, although apparently unfamiliar with the expression "placebo effect" in the modern sense, he clearly alludes to "nostrum" (quack) remedies, which amounts to the same thing. Braid spent the latter decades of his life systematically debunking claims regarding Mesmerism, spiritualism, and various nostrum remedies, both in his writings and through numerous simple experiments. He did this precisely because of his interest in the power of the mind, through expectation and dominant ideas, to influence the body and behaviour, which became the basis of his theory of hypnotism. In modern parlance, the "placebo effect" was always seen as the main analogy for hypnotism.

> With such evidences as these cases afford of the power of a dominant expectant idea in changing or modifying physical action, either in the second-conscious [or "full"] hypnotic state, or in some subjects in the waking condition, there seems to be no reasonable ground to doubt the fact [...] I must not, however, omit to call attention to the cures effected by spells, charms, and amulets, sacred relics, and by various nostrums, as all these furnish powerful corroboration of the main position I am here contending for. (Braid, 1853, p. 108)

Indeed, this fundamental analogy with various manifestations of the placebo effect is very important to Braid's original theory of hypnotism, partly because responses to placebos don't seem like mere compliance or an unwitting desire to act *as if* cured. The physiological responses, and indeed symptom remissions, produced by placebos often seem to be well outside the sphere of normal voluntary control. The fact, for example, that skin conditions appear to improve as a result of placebos or hypnotic suggestion seems to show that something beyond normal volition is involved; the subject cannot normally "will" a wart to shrink, and Kirsch attributes these and other tangible physiological effects to response expectancy. We can, of course, expect things to happen that are outside of our normal sphere of willpower, but which may nevertheless come true as the result of expectation acting as a self-fulfilling prophecy. Kirsch therefore argues that rather than mere compliance or hypnotic trance, the most obvious mediating factor in hypnotism is cognition, that is, "expectancy-related cognition" (Kirsch & Council, 1989, p. 362).

Braid emphasised that his experiments debunking Mesmerism and similar approaches clearly demonstrated that when subjects, especially highly-suggestible ones, were asked to patiently focus their attention on various parts of their body with the "expectation of something being about to happen", they tended to experience whatever they expected to experience.

> But it is an undoubted fact that with many individuals, and especially of the highly nervous, and imaginative, and abstractive classes, a strong direction of inward consciousness to any part of the body, especially if attended with the expectation or belief of something being about to happen, is quite sufficient to change the physical action of the part, and to produce such impressions from this cause alone [...] Thus every variety of feeling may be excited from an internal or mental cause—such as heat or cold, pricking, creeping, tingling, spasmodic twitching of muscles, catalepsy, a feeling of attraction or repulsion, sights of every form or hue, odours, tastes, and sounds, in endless variety, and so on, according as accident or intention may have suggested. Moreover, the oftener such impressions have been excited, the more readily may they be reproduced, under similar circumstances, through the laws of association and habit. (Braid, 1846, p. 238)

Braid clearly states that focused attention on part of the body alone was often capable of producing various physiological responses and curious sensations. However, "fixity of attention, together with an expectant idea as to the peculiar result to be anticipated" considerably increased the probability of a response and also determined what response would occur (Braid, 1853, p. 94). In other words, paying attention to the body can lead us to notice spontaneous feelings of "heat or cold", "tingling", or can create actual "twitching" or tension ("catalepsy") or small movements, etc., and sometimes more dramatic or unusual sensations. However, when prolonged attention to the body is accompanied by an expectation that something specific will happen, for example, a finger twitching, that particular response is, of course, more likely to happen. Braid's experiments convinced him this could happen spontaneously and certainly without any "hypnotic induction". He therefore concluded that deliberate suggestions to experience similar responses were frequently effective without anything that might be described as a special "hypnotic state" or trance.

It should be noted that although Braid is often portrayed as a "special state" theorists, he lived long before this debate developed. In his earlier writings he did tend to refer to hypnotism as a "peculiar" or "abnormal" physiological state. However, as his career progressed, he placed more and more emphasis upon the interaction of multiple psychological and physiological factors in hypnotism and recognised a wider variety of responses in his subjects. He also increasingly emphasised the normality rather than abnormality of hypnotism, for example, saying of his techniques that "they create no new faculties; but they give us greater control over the natural functions than we possess during the ordinary waking condition", particularly the focusing of attention upon certain dominant ideas (Braid, 1853, p. 97). The words "imagination", "suggestion", "expectation", "association", "imitation", etc., feature more and more frequently in Braid's account of hypnotism as the years go on, and following his research on "waking" suggestion, he increasingly reports working with patients without the use of any hypnotic induction whatsoever.

> [I discovered] that the condition [of Mesmerism] arose from influences existing within the patient's own body, *viz.*, the influence of concentrated attention, or dominant ideas, in modifying physical action, and these dynamic changes re-acting on the mind of the subject, I adopted the term *hypnotism,* or nervous sleep, in preference to Mesmerism, or animal magnetism. This term has met with most favourable consideration from many able writers on the subject; still it is liable to this grave objection—that it has been used to comprise not a *single* state, but rather a series of stages or conditions, varying in every conceivable degree, from the slightest reverie, with high exaltation of the functions called into action, on the one hand, to intense nervous coma, with entire abolition of consciousness and voluntary power, on the other; whilst, from the latter condition, by very simple, but appropriate means, the subject is capable of being speedily partially restored, or entirely roused, to the waking condition. (Braid, 1855, p. 80)

As we've seen, Braid did not use the expression "trance" to explain hypnotism but simply referred to "mental abstraction", which he compared to absent-mindedness, reverie, and other ordinary psychological states. At the very least, his position was much closer to the nonstate view in spirit, despite his occasional reference to hypnotism as a "peculiar state", etc., which is probably little more than a figure of speech as he repeatedly emphasises that this "state", or rather multiplicity of states, is best explained by established psychological and physiological processes such as "mental concentration". Moreover, Braid happily conceded that most hypnotic phenomena can, especially with certain "sensitive" clients, be reproduced in the "waking" state, without the use of any induction technique whatsoever. Some of the reasons for considering Braid to be a precursor of modern cognitive-behavioural (nonstate) theorists rather than a special state ("trance") theorist, might be summed up as follows:

1. Hypnotism is an unusual application of normal psychological processes, familiar to Victorian "Common Sense" academic psychology, such as the laws of imitation, association, etc.
2. Hypnotism is closely-related to the placebo effect as observed in the effect of expectation in Victorian nostrum remedies, etc.
3. Hypnotism employs a variety of different "states", ranging from sleepiness to rigid catalepsy.

4. Hypnotism is construed as being closely analogous to Oriental meditation techniques, rather than involving a unique state of consciousness.
5. Hypnotic responses can be replicated without any hypnotic induction, in a normal state of conscious attention, especially with highly-responsive subjects.
6. The term "trance" is not employed to explain how hypnotism functions.
7. Instead, hypnotism is conceptualised in terms of ordinary cognitive factors such as expectation, imagination, and focused attention.

A modern conceptualisation of hypnosis is offered below, which draws primarily upon Braid's original theory of hypnotism but attempts to integrate it with the terminology of modern cognitive-behavioural theories of hypnosis. As mentioned earlier, we might perhaps describe this way of conceptualising hypnosis as a kind of "Neobraidism" or a cognitive-behavioural "return to Braid", as it arguably differs more in terminology than in essence from Braid's original theory of hypnotism.

Conclusion: a metacognitive model of hypnosis

From a cognitive-behavioural perspective it makes more sense to speak of hypnosis as functioning in terms of a typical cognitive set rather than altered state of consciousness, a "hypnotic mind-set" or "hypnotic attitude" rather than "hypnotic trance". Cognitive-behavioural researchers have previously conceptualised the hypnotic subject as a "creative problem-solving agent" (Lynn & Sivec, 1992). We might further define the cognitive set required for hypnosis as follows, drawing loosely upon the factors identified in research on problem-solving orientation.

1. *Recognition* of the cues for adopting a hypnotic mind-set (the induction) and experiencing hypnotic responses (the suggestions) from the outset, that is, noticing hypnotic suggestions, understanding their meaning, adopting selective attention toward them and inattention to extraneous distractions, etc.,– adopting a basic initial orientation toward suggestions and focusing on the task of hypnotic responding.
2. *Appraisal* both of suggestions as harmless and of suggested responses as desirable, that is, of hypnosis as essentially an "opportunity" rather than a "threat".
3. *Attribution* of hypnotic responses to the interaction between the receptive (hypnotic) mind-set and the ideas suggested, rather than misattributing their causation, for example, to the direct volition of the subject or an external hypnotist's words and actions—attributing responses to focused attention on dominant expectant ideas, in Braid's terms.
4. *Control* of responses is accurately appraised, as moderately high albeit indirect, that is,, the subject is self-confident about her intention to respond by being a "good hypnotic subject" and fulfilling that role ("self-efficacy") and has sufficient expectation of hypnotic responses occurring as suggested ("response expectancy").
5. *Commitment* to being hypnotised, both in terms of the time and effort realistically required, sometimes described as "favourable motivation", neither rushing nor avoiding being hypnotised.

In other words, a good hypnotic subject, rather than being "in a deep trance", is someone who adopts the right attitude or mind-set. She focusses on suggestions and forgets about distractions, assumes hypnosis is a positive opportunity and harmless, conceptualises the process accurately, without misconceptions, has confidence in her ability to play the role of hypnotic subject, and a high expectation of responding as suggested, and is motivated and committed to the process. By contrast, poor hypnotic subjects exhibit unfavourable attitudes, which can be classified according to the same schema:

1. *Recognition.* Failure to perceive the induction and suggestions as cues for adopting the right mind-set and exhibiting hypnotic responses; failure to understand their meaning, pay attention appropriately, or remain oriented to them to the exclusion of distractions. Difficulty concentrating or getting into a receptive "mind-set" can be due to many factors, for example, an unsuitable environment.
2. *Appraisal.* Viewing hypnosis or the suggested responses as threatening or undesirable. Anxiety about being hypnotised is a common source of inhibition in responding to suggestions.
3. *Attribution.* Misattributing the causation of hypnotic responses, for example, primarily to the "power of the hypnotist" (Mesmerism), the will of the subject (compliance), etc. Misconceptions about the nature of hypnosis and the cause of hypnotic responses are extremely widespread and often deeply entrenched. They often lead to an overly-passive ("wait and see") attitude rather than actively imagining the things being suggested, which is integral to the role of the hypnotic subject.
4. *Control.* Lack of self-confidence in one's ability to fulfil one's intention and adopt role of hypnotic subject, by assuming a receptive mind-set and failure to sufficiently expect the suggested outcome, are basic problems in hypnotism.
5. *Commitment.* Lack of commitment or motivation to be hypnotised and experience the specific responses suggested is widely regarded as fundamental obstacle to hypnotism. However, having unrealistic assumptions about the time and effort required to achieve certain outcomes, can also lead to difficulty. Impatience and rushing hypnosis are common problems, as are procrastination and avoidance.

This "hypnotic mind-set", or favourable cognitive set, interacts with specific cues or suggestions to activate specific hypnotic responses, which have a reciprocally reinforcing effect on the whole cognitive-set and also upon specific response expectancies.

The term "metacognition" refers to cognition about cognition, or thoughts about thoughts, and other psychological events. The hypnotic mind-set is definitely, to a large extent, metacognitive. It clearly involves the assumption of an attitude of receptivity toward suggested ideas (cognitions), which are appraised as important and capable of evoking hypnotic responses, under certain conditions. Belief in what Braid crudely termed the "power of the mind over the body" is a metacognitive belief, a belief about the nature and function of certain thoughts. Hypnotic responses are not "caused" by hypnotic suggestions. These merely act as the (optional) triggers that potentially cue the desired responses. The ideas they are associated with evoke hypnotic responses when accompanied by a suitably receptive mind-set, as described above. This broadly equates to Braid's original definition of hypnotism in terms of focused attention on a dominant expectant idea of some hypnotic response. Hypnotism can occur in the absence of external suggestions, through self-hypnosis, when self-instructions or images are used as cues for hypnotic responses. These will also be ineffective unless accompanied by attention, expectation, and the other factors described above as forming the typical hypnotic mind-set.

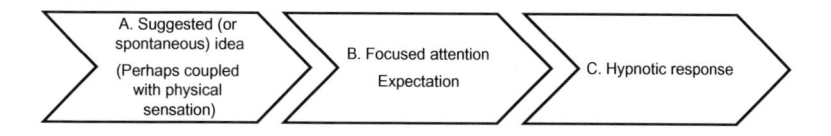

```
A. Suggested (or spontaneous) idea (Perhaps coupled with physical sensation) >> B. Focused attention Expectation >> C. Hypnotic response
```

As previously discussed, in relation both to Braid's theory of "reciprocal interaction" and Kirsch and Lynn's "response set" theory, hypnotic responding can best be understood as the subsequent cyclical interaction between cognitive and behavioural strategies or responses. Responsive hypnotic subjects tend to be actively engaged, either spontaneously or deliberately, in "thinking along with" suggestions by directly imagining the suggested responses happening or imagining things that indirectly evoke the responses. For example, when it is suggested that their arm feels rigid, they may imagine that it is turning into concrete or fixed to an iron bar. Often they are following the explicit or implicit instructions of the hypnotist, to imagine certain things, called "goal-directed fantasies", but particularly good subjects will spontaneously generate such imagery or modify the suggestions of the hypnotist to ensure they experience the suggested response. For this reason, the hypnotic subject has been previously conceptualised as a "creative problem-solving agent" by cognitive-behavioural theorists (Lynn & Sivec, 1992). Dehypnosis can be conceptualised in more or less the *opposite* manner, as involving procedures which expand attention beyond certain autosuggestions, or shift it on to the procedure rather than the content of suggested ideas, and interventions that lower the expectation of a hypnotic response occurring automatically. In dehypnosis, suggested ideas are seen as impotent and unimportant, viewed from a mindful but detached perspective, and responses are no longer evoked automatically. Given this understanding of hypnotism, in subsequent chapters, we'll examine how to approach assessment, conceptualisation, socialisation and skills training in a cognitive-behavioural approach to hypnotherapy, before proceeding to discuss basic treatment strategies and techniques.

Hypnotic orientation questionnaire

Please rate (0–100%) how strongly you agree with each of the following statements immediately following your hypnosis session, with reference to your experience at that time.

1. Recognition (orientation to suggestions as cues to respond)
"I viewed the induction and suggestions as signals to adopt a favourable attitude and respond by actively focusing my attention on the meaning of the words."

Rating (%):

2. Attribution (causal conceptualisation)
"I assumed that hypnotic responses were due mainly to my mind-set and active imagination rather than being caused directly by the actions of the hypnotist."

Rating (%):

3. Appraisal (appraising situation as opportunity rather than threat)
"I assumed that hypnosis and the suggestions given were completely safe"

Rating (%):

"I saw the procedure as being generally relevant and meaningful in terms of my personal goals."

Rating (%):

4. Control (self-efficacy & response expectancy)
"I was confident in my ability to fulfil the role of hypnotic subject and actively imagine the things being suggested."

Rating (%):

"I really expected that the suggested responses were going to happen."

Rating (%):

5. Commitment (motivation & time/effort appraisal)
"I really wanted to participate in this procedure and to experience all the things being suggested."

Rating (%):

"I was patient and committed to persevering with my role as hypnotic subject until the responses occurred."

Rating (%):

PART II

ASSESSMENT, CONCEPTUALISATION, AND HYPNOTIC SKILLS

CHAPTER FOUR

Assessment in cognitive-behavioural hypnotherapy

This chapter, and the one following, provide a basic, generic overview of assessment and case formulation in cognitive-behavioural hypnotherapy. The inclusion of hypnosis only entails slight modifications to common CBT approaches, which are well-documented elsewhere (Grant, Townend, Mills & Cockx, 2008; Persons, 2008). However, some counsellors and therapists who use hypnosis will be less familiar with structured approaches to assessment and cognitive-behavioural case conceptualisation. As this area is not well described in many books on hypnotherapy, and because there are some minor adjustments worth including, I have chosen to include a chapter discussing assessment and conceptualisation sufficiently to provide a very basic introduction. However, I would suggest that readers consult the texts referenced for more detailed information and guidance.

Many practitioners using hypnotherapy assess clients primarily in the initial session, which typically lasts around fifty minutes. Other practitioners employ longer sessions, or more of them, to complete the initial assessment and conceptualisation process (Westbrook, Kennerley & Kirk, 2007, p. 54). For example, Chapman provides an example of clinical hypnosis in CBT where two sessions are dedicated to preparation for treatment (Chapman, 2006, p. 76). This is bound to vary depending on the therapist and their circumstances, for example, whether the client has already been thoroughly assessed commencing treatment. Although hypnotherapists will probably tend toward simpler and more concise approaches to both assessment and conceptualisation, and briefer treatment plans, things should not be abbreviated at the expense of "essentials" such as the assessment of risk factors and contra-indications, etc.

The therapeutic relationship

Bordin's well-known analysis of the components of the "working alliance" in psychotherapy, divides it into three key areas, which apply to virtually all modalities of treatment, including both CBT and hypnosis (Bordin, 1979).

1. Bond of trust between therapist and client.
2. Agreement on therapy goals.
3. Agreement on therapy tasks.

These latter two aspects are sometimes overlooked in discussions of the therapeutic relationship. However, they are particularly important and intimately linked to the bond of trust between therapist and client. It doesn't matter if therapist and client like and trust each other; if they completely disagree about what they're trying to achieve together and how best to go about doing it then there will be no working alliance between them. The goals and tasks, or treatment plan, are linked to other key components of the assessment and formulation process, as follows:

1. "What is the main problem?" (Problem definition).
2. "Why is it a problem?" (Problem formulation).
3. "What is the main goal?" (Goal definition).
4. "How are we going to achieve the goal?" (Treatment plan).
5. "Why do we expect that plan to work?" (Treatment rationale).

Cognitive and behavioural therapies have always emphasised the important role played in treatment by similar factors in the therapeutic relationship. Although it has sometimes been assumed that they neglect this area, this is essentially a misconception. Indeed, Beck provided a specific "cognitive formulation" of the therapeutic relationship, in terms of collaborative agreement on the following components (Alford & Beck, 1997, p. 79).

1. Mutual expectations for the therapy.
2. The agenda for each individual session.
3. A shared conceptualisation of the client's problems and goals.
4. The nature of the client's diagnosis or presenting problem.

This clearly resembles Bordin's earlier definition of the working alliance in terms of trust, and mutual agreement on the tasks, and goals of therapy.

Hypnotherapists, likewise, have always emphasised the central importance of the relationship in treatment. The Mesmerists referred to the profound connection between operator and subject as "rapport", by which they actually meant to imply a bond so intense that the subject would temporarily be oblivious to distractions. The dramatic nature of this relationship was questioned by early hypnotists and researchers, such as Clark L. Hull, but the emphasis on the role of the relationship has endured to this day (Hull, 1933). Barber concluded from his programme of research into hypnosis that trust in the hypnotist and positive attitudes and expectations about the procedure were important mediating factors in determining the outcome of experiments on hypnosis (Barber, 1969).

Positive attitude. During the course of his life, the subject has acquired the view that being "hypnotized" or responding to suggestions is exciting, useful, worthwhile, or valuable.

Positive motivation. Right now, in the immediate test situation, the subject wants to be or tries to be "hypnotized" or to have the experiences that are suggested.

Positive expectancy. The subject believes that he himself can be "hypnotized" or can have the experiences that are suggested (Barber, Spanos & Chaves, 1974, p. 49).

As noted earlier, these and other client factors identified in Barber's research were summarised in the acronym "TEAM" (trust, expectations, attitude, motivation) coined by Daniel Araoz in his writings on hypnosis (Araoz, 1982).

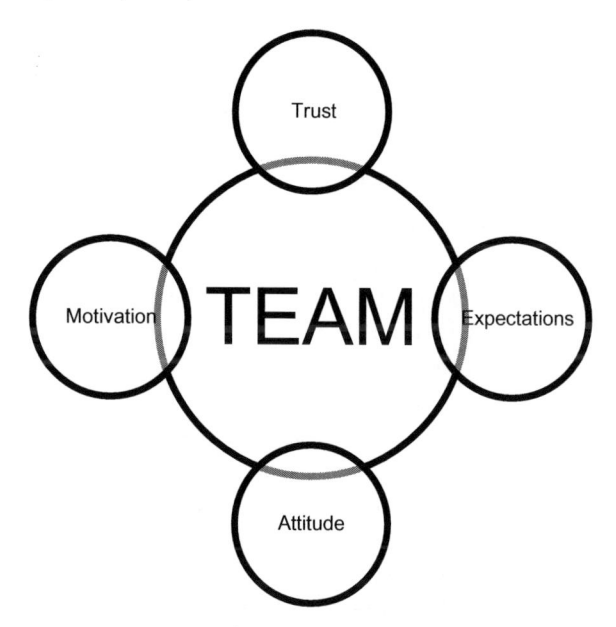

According to Araoz, clients must trust themselves to respond to hypnosis and trust the therapist they're working with. They must have realistic expectations about the therapy, rather than viewing it as a panacea or quick fix and realise that being hypnotised is a learnable mental skill, which they can expect to get better at with practice. They should have an attitude of curiosity about the procedure and about their responses and a collaborative mind-set, uninhibited by misconceptions or unfounded fears about hypnosis. Finally, they should be motivated to achieve their goals by completing the tasks required in hypnotism (Araoz & Negley-Parker, 1988, p. xvi). The cognitive-behavioural approach to hypnotherapy is therefore fundamentally, and necessarily in most cases, a collaborative "team effort."

By comparison, the collaborative nature of most traditional CBT leads to an emphasis on Socratic (questioning) rather than didactic (lecturing) styles of interaction. Socrates famously feigned ignorance saying "I know only that I know nothing", as a deliberate rhetorical strategy or ruse ("Socratic irony") to engage others in a searching enquiry. The typical cognitive-behavioural therapist is rather like the television detective Columbo whose trademark strategy, akin to a modern Socrates, was to feign befuddlement and ask carefully-chosen questions to get to the bottom of things. Instead of lecturing "didactically", or spoon-feeding her answers, the therapist should, therefore, generally prefer to help the client tell her story and arrive at her own conclusions by the judicious use of questioning, including frequently asking for clarification and checking his understanding.

Therapists often seem to absorb certain dogmas about the best approach to adopt when working with clients that deserve to be questioned. One is the notion that it's inappropriate to interrupt a client. However, clients will often expect to be gently interrupted when they're wandering off the subject, and potentially wasting their own session time. They may even resent the therapist for failing to manage the session time better, by allowing them to ramble needlessly. Hence, Lazarus writes:

> One of my trainers once told me that interrupting a client was counterproductive. "Whatever the client is talking about is important and significant to that person." Nonsense! Clients often ramble or babble on tediously about irrelevant matters. They may discuss trivial events as a smokescreen, hiding and blotting out the real issues. There are gentle and effective ways of cutting into the flow. (Lazarus A. A., 1981, p. 59)

This is more of an issue when hypnotherapy is being employed, as allowing the client to spend too much time talking unnecessarily will make it very difficult to dedicate sufficient time to the most typical hypnotic techniques during a standard fifty-minute session. The role of the therapist using hypnotism tends to be a little more directive and didactic, in some respects, than in traditional CBT. Where clients are either overly-reticent or verbose, Lazarus recommends the "single-word technique." "If you were allowed only a single word to describe your problems, what would that word be?" The client can then be asked to expand the word into a single sentence. Finally, the therapist may simply ask the client to elaborate and tell him more about the single sentence offered (Lazarus A. A., 1981, pp. 49–50).

In any case, the development of a healthy working alliance is just as important in cognitive-behavioural approaches to hypnotherapy as in standard CBT. The relationship obviously begins to develop from the first meeting onward, which also happens to be the phase during which initial assessment and conceptualisation occurs. However, the relationship must then be maintained throughout the course of therapy by dealing appropriately with any problems, or "ruptures", which may arise. That's typically best done by adopting a transparent and collaborative stance, although different tactics will be required depending upon the personality of the client and the circumstances. Regular feedback from clients on the relationship and how, in general, they feel the sessions are going, is an important safeguard against some problems in the relationship and can be used to identify difficulties early on and address them before they cause more serious harm to the working alliance.

Assessment

Therapeutic assessment is an essential precursor of all hypnotherapy. In research contexts, semi-structured clinical interviews are often employed as these have been found to have good reliability in determining diagnosis. ADIS-IV is particularly well-suited to assessment of anxiety disorders (Brown, Nardo & Barolow, 1994) and this has been recommended as a standard diagnostic assessment preceding cognitive therapy for anxiety (Clark & Beck, 2010, p. 131). The brief *Interview Guide for Evaluating DSM-IV Psychiatric Disorders* contains specific questions for diagnosis and an outline of the Mental Status Examination (MSE) (Zimmerman, 1994). However, the nature and extent of the assessment process will obviously vary depending on the needs of the client, nature of the problem, context of treatment, and other factors. For example, Lynn et al. emphasise that both psychological (therapeutic) assessment and assessment of hypnotic susceptibility should precede clinical hypnosis:

> At a minimum, the psychological assessment should include information pertinent to the client's mental and physical status, life history, and current psychological problems and dynamics. Important areas of inquiry include the client's treatment motivation, needs, character structure, life situation, history of dissociative and posttraumatic reactions, resources, perceived strengths and weaknesses, and beliefs and misconceptions about hypnosis. (Lynn, Kirsch, Neufeld & Rhue, 1996, p. 14)

As Sanders and Wills observe, the assessment format cannot be rigidly prescribed because CBT practitioners working in different contexts and coming from different backgrounds will adopt different approaches:

> Rather it is a series of coat hooks on which to hang information as it is assimilated, and people will use it according to their core training. Counsellors, for example, may be more likely to use it in a less didactic and more "conversational" [...] style with their clients; psychologists or medical therapists may be more structured, thoroughly covering the questions in a systematic manner; and nurse therapists may integrate such an assessment with a clinical interview or mental state examination. (Sanders & Wills, 2005, p. 80)

Hypnotherapists, especially working with subclinical problems or ordinary "stress", etc., may likewise adopt an abbreviated assessment procedure. In this chapter, we will assume a relatively simple and general-purpose model of assessment derived from other psychological therapies, particularly CBT.

Goals and agenda-setting

The generic goals of the assessment and conceptualisation phase of treatment (Beck J. S., 1995, p. 26; Meichenbaum, 1985, p. 27) can be summarised roughly as follows:

1. Develop a collaborative relationship (working alliance) with the client
2. Develop a definition of the client's main problem(s)
3. Gather assessment information through interviewing, imagery-based recall, self-monitoring, questionnaires, etc.
4. Identify risk issues and contra-indications and respond appropriately

5. Identify the client's preconceptions about hypnotherapy and current interpretation of her problem
6. Socialise the client to the treatment model being employed and her role in hypnotherapy
7. Develop an initial "working hypothesis" or conceptualisation of the problem
8. Educate the client about her symptoms and about hypnosis, if offered, and alternative treatment options
9. Agree short and long-term goals for treatment
10. Evaluate treatment options and agree a treatment plan, including homework, and obtain the client's informed consent to proceed
11. Anticipate possible setbacks and obstacles to treatment and plan how to cope with them
12. Identify strengths and opportunities and instil a sense of hope in relation to outcome.

These goals can be achieved in a number of ways and naturally shape the structure and agenda of the initial sessions. As so many things need to be achieved in the assessment and conceptualisation phase, it helps if therapist and client share a clear vision of the agenda for each session.

Agenda-setting is normal practice at the beginning of most CBT sessions, from the assessment onwards. It's particularly important, however, for the initial assessment session in hypnotherapy. Clients seeking hypnotherapy usually come with problematic misconceptions about the nature of the treatment and this leads to confused expectations prior to the initial session. Setting a clear agenda helps to dispel some of those misconceptions from the outset, for example, the idea that the client will simply be hypnotised and told she feels better, etc. Agenda-setting provides an opportunity to let the client know in advance "what she's in for" during the first and subsequent sessions. Again, because clients often come with confused ideas and unanswered questions, outlining the agenda typically triggers further questions about the nature of hypnosis and these can either be answered briefly or put on the session agenda for more detailed discussion in due course, as appropriate.

Collaborating on the agenda involves checking that the client understands and agrees with the items contributed by the therapist and seeking her input by asking, for example, "What are the main things you want to discuss today?" Often the main "targets" for the session identified by the client will fit in well with the therapist's own agenda. For example, at the start of the initial assessment clients often say, "I just want to know how therapy works really", which the therapist should normally already be planning to cover anyway. The client's feedback on homework will often generate some of the main topics for subsequent session agendas. Of course, sometimes the therapist and client may have different views about what needs to be the focus of a session, and this should be brought into the open and discussed together. Agreement on the session agenda can be seen as a specific example of the kind of general agreement upon tasks and goals that Bordin thought essential to the working alliance (Bordin, 1979).

The order in which assessment information is gathered, and questions are asked, should vary according to the circumstances rather than being assumed to follow a rigid sequence (Westbrook, Kennerley & Kirk, 2007, p. 53). In general, however, especially for hypnotherapy which is usually a brief approach, it may be preferable initially to prioritise focussing upon a specific, typical example of the client's main current problem and the principal maintaining factors, etc., rather than placing too much emphasis on the client's history and speculation over early predisposing factors.

Structure and agenda for initial session

In some cases a client will already have received a formal diagnostic assessment prior to commencing treatment, although this may not always be the case, for example, where the therapist or counsellor is working with less severe problems. Where a client has already been formally assessed in this way, a typical outline for the initial session in cognitive therapy, modified to include reference to hypnotherapy, might be as follows (Beck J. S., 1995, pp. 26–27).

1. Collaboratively set the agenda, and provide a rationale to the client for doing so
2. Check the client's mood and briefly review any outcome measures completed
3. Briefly review the main presenting problem and whether anything has changed in the period since any previous contact or evaluation occurred
4. Develop a problem list and treatment goals
5. Evaluate the client's expectations for therapy and socialise her to the cognitive model and cognitive-behavioural hypnotherapy
6. Educate the client about her symptoms and about hypnosis, correcting misconceptions.
7. Set initial homework, for example, reading handout, self-monitoring, using self-hypnosis CD, etc.
8. Provide a summary of the session (or ask the client to summarise what the main points they remember are and fill in any gaps)
9. Obtain feedback from the client ("How do you feel our session went today?").

Once the therapist has outlined, in a few sentences, the time frame and basic structure of the agenda, the client should be asked, for example, "Is there anything else you want to put on the agenda for today's session?" As noted above, often the client's items can be linked to things the therapist already planned to cover as part of the standard agenda, for example, a client might say "I wanted to know how many sessions it will take", which can be covered in discussing the treatment plan and client's expectations. There may be circumstances where a more thorough initial assessment may be required, perhaps requiring more time, for example, a longer session or more sessions. A more detailed outline of some example questions that might be asked during a generic semi-structured initial assessment, might be as follows (Clark & Beck, 2010, p. 138; Kirk, 1989; Meichenbaum, 1985, p. 33).

Problem definition

Client's definition of the problem

1. Summarise what you already know about the problem from other sources and check this is correct with the client and whether anything has changed
2. "Can you describe the problem in your own words?" (Problem definition)
3. (If there are multiple problems, draw up a "problem list" and prioritise the main one).

Severity, frequency, duration, triggers, and impact of symptoms

1. "How serious do you feel the problem is? Rate severity of symptoms 0–100 per cent." (Severity)
2. "How often does the problem occur?" (Frequency)
3. "How long do the symptoms last?" (Duration)
4. "What is the range of situations in which the problem occurs?" (Extent)
5. "What specific external or internal events seem to trigger the problem?" (Triggers)
6. "Which of these situations or events are most distressing? Can you rank their severity?" (Hierarchy)
7. "How does this problem interfere with other areas of your life? Health? Work? Finances? Relationships? Leisure time? Daily routine?" (Impact).

History and scope of the problem

1. "When did this first begin to be a problem?" (Onset)
2. "Are you aware of anything that may have led to the problem beginning?" "What was happening in your life at that time when it first started?" (Precipitants)
3. "What's the problem's history since it began? Has it ever gone away, got better, or worse?" (Course)
4. (If appropriate enquire about previous episodes of the same problem).
5. "Do you remember any earlier childhood events that might have contributed in any way to the problem?" (Predisposing factors)
6. "Has anyone in your immediate family ever experienced this or any other psychological problem?" (Family history)
7. "Have you ever had any other psychological problems or received any other psychiatric treatment?" (Psychiatric history)
8. "Have you ever had any form of psychological therapy or counselling before? How well did it work?" (Previous therapy).

Client's definition of her goals

1. "What are your goals for therapy? How will you know when you've achieved them?" (Goal definition or list)
2. "How else would your life be improved if you solved this problem?" (Impact of goals)
3. "What, if anything, might prevent you from achieving that goal?" (Obstacles).

Conceptualisation of problem

Modulating factors ("Modifiers")

1. "What makes the problem worse?" (Aggravating factors)
2. "What makes the problem better?" (Relieving factors).

Client assumptions about causes and cure

1. "What do you think originally caused your problem?" (Client interpretation of onset)
2. "What do you think causes your problem to continue?" (Client interpretation of maintaining causes)
3. "Do you avoid any situations or activities because of the problem?" (Avoidance)
4. "What else have you tried to do in the past to cope with or solve the problem?" (Coping strategies)
5. "Do you do anything to try to protect yourself or seek safety when the problem occurs, or beforehand?" (Safety-seeking)
6. "How well are those ways of coping working out for you overall, in the long-run?"
7. "What do you think the solution to your problem is?"

Analysis of specific situation (using direct questioning or imagery-based recall)

1. "Can you give me a recent, typical example of the problem occurring and describe exactly where you were and what was happening?" (Antecedent situation)
2. "Were there other people involved? What were they doing?" (Interpersonal factors)
3. "How did you feel emotionally?" (Affect)
4. "What sensations, if any, were you aware of in your body?" (Sensations)
5. "What did you feel like doing? What did you actually do?" (Behaviour)
6. "Did you do anything to try to protect yourself or seek safety?" (Safety-seeking)
7. "What were your initial thoughts?", "What did you think next?" (Cognition)
8. "Did any images come into your mind during that situation?" (Imagery)
9. "What did you fear might happen?" (Feared outcome)
10. "Did you do anything to avoid or control your thoughts or feelings?" (Experiential avoidance)
11. "What do you feel that situation might say about you as a person?" (Personal meaning)
12. "How typical was that situation of the problem in general?"

Additional information

Further assessment

1. Brief mental state examination (MSE) and risk assessment
2. Assess medication and substance use
3. "What personal strengths or resources do you have that might help you cope with the problem?" (Strengths & assets)
4. "Pick three words that you would use to describe yourself." (Self-concept)
5. "Is there anything else you think I need to know about the problem in order to be able to help you?"
6. Summarise problem and check understanding with client. (Summary of problem).

Education & socialisation

1. "What do you know about this approach to therapy?" (Expectations)
2. Socialise client to basic cognitive-behavioural hypnotherapy approach (Socialisation)
3. Educate the client about her symptoms, etc. (Psycho-education)
4. Develop conceptualisation and share working hypothesis (Initial conceptualisation)
5. Discuss the treatment options and rationale in terms of the conceptualisation (Treatment rationale)
6. Collaborate with the client regarding treatment strategies (Treatment plan)
7. Set initial homework, for example, reading, thought record, self-hypnosis CD, etc. (Homework/Self-monitoring).

Summary & Feedback

1. "Is there anything else you want to ask me or tell me about before we finish?", "Is there anything else you think I might need to know to be able to help you?"
2. "What are the main points you're taking away from our session today?" (Client summary)
3. Summarise session, filling in gaps in client's account (Present final therapist summary)
4. "How do you feel the session went overall?" (Elicit Feedback).

This is a rough guide only but hopefully it will provide some context for the subsequent discussion of treatment. First, however, we should explore some aspects of the assessment in more detail.

Mood check and outcome measures

At the start of the initial assessment and subsequent sessions, the client should be asked to provide a brief update on how she's been feeling since the last contact with the therapist, for example, "How have you been since we last spoke?" In addition to briefly reviewing any outcome measures completed, etc., the client's mood can be checked in many ways, for example, by asking her to rate from 0–100 per cent how anxious she has been on average (Beck J. S., 1995, p. 29). If it's not apparent, clients should generally be asked why they think any reported changes in their problems have occurred, for example, "Why do you think your anxiety was lower this week than last week?"

Some form of baseline measure of the client's symptoms should normally be obtained during the assessment phase so that subsequent progress can be observed. A comprehensive collection of validated outcome measures for anxiety disorders and symptoms can be found in the *Practitioner's Guide to Empirically Based Measures of Anxiety* (Antony, Orsillo & Roemer, 2001). A similar volume is available for depressive disorders and symptoms (Nezu, Ronan, Meadows & McClure, 2000). Because they are copyrighted, individual copies of some of these forms, including the Beck Anxiety Inventory (BAI) and Beck Depression Inventory-II (BDI-II), must be purchased for use with clients. However, others are sometimes made available at no cost for clinical use. The Clinical Outcomes in Routine Evaluation Outcome Measure (CORE-OM) is a multipurpose outcome measure that assesses a range of typical symptoms seen across different diagnoses and can be used with most clients (Barkham, et al., 2001). CORE-OM is available for use free-of-charge and can be downloaded from the internet (www.coreims.co.uk).

Some forms may be administered before or during assessment (pre-treatment), sometimes also again mid-treatment, post-treatment, and possibly at a follow-up session weeks or months later, to evaluate progress at different points in time. Some outcome measures are suitable for completion on a weekly basis, prior to each treatment session, to provide a session-by-session record of client progress. Where possible, the therapist should briefly review outcome measures as soon as they are returned and provide some basic feedback to reinforce the client for the effort involved in completing them, although a more thorough inspection of the written responses will sometimes have to wait until after the session has finished. It has been suggested that the "time-series" research design, which monitors the outcome measures of a single case, or a small number of cases, at regular intervals, such as every day, may be particularly well-suited for hypnotherapists to employ in their clinical practice as a means of studying the effectiveness of their approach (Borckardt & Nash, 2008).

Life history

Clients will often, rightly or wrongly, attribute their problem to events occurring around the time of onset. However, they are sometimes less able to identify predisposing factors, preceding onset, perhaps occurring in childhood, that may have "set the stage" for the problem and made them vulnerable to it developing. Information should be sought in relation to the life history of clients, such as negative life events that may have contributed to vulnerability. Their history in relation to childhood development, family relationships, school, sexual experiences, and employment should be investigated as appropriate to the case. Their history in relation to medical problems, psychiatric problems, medication use, and substance abuse, should also normally be investigated. Arnold Lazarus has developed a comprehensive Multimodal Life History Inventory, which some hypnosis practitioners have used to gather relevant data from the client, potentially saving considerable session time (Chapman, 2006, p. 77; Lazarus A. A., 1981, pp. 227–240). Kuyken et al. have also, more recently, published a detailed "aid to history taking" form for clients to complete as a way of saving time during assessment sessions (Kuyken, Padesky & Dudley, 2009, pp. 327–339). A brief set of questions are included at the end of this chapter.

Diagnosis and medication

Sometimes hypnotherapy is used as an adjunct to other evidence-based psychological therapies for clients with diagnosable psychiatric disorders. However, it is also frequently used to treat milder (subclinical) problems such as mild-moderate (subphobic) fears, ordinary stress reactions, social anxiety or shyness, low self-esteem, or lack of assertiveness, etc. Where the client has received a diagnosis or her symptoms potentially meet diagnostic criteria, this should provide an initial guide to treatment and be given paramount importance in assessing the client's needs.

Where a client is receiving medication this needs to be established during the assessment. Of course, no recommendations about changing medication use should be made by the practitioner using hypnosis unless he is qualified to do so. The therapist should be aware, however, of the medication the client is receiving, whether they are using it appropriately, and any reactions, side-effects, or interactions with psychological treatment strategies that may be relevant.

Mental State Examination (MSE)

The mental state examination (MSE) is a standard brief assessment procedure used in psychiatry and CBT (Zimmerman, 1994). It's seldom discussed in the hypnotherapy literature, perhaps because aspects may be less relevant to some of the issues treated with hypnosis, such as nonclinical issues like study skills or sports performance improvement and subclinical stress-related problems, etc. Grant et al. summarise the following elements of mental state examination in CBT (Grant, Townend, Mills & Cockx, 2008, pp. 15–16).

1. *Appearance.* Anything notable about the physical appearance or behaviour of the client, that is, whether they appear unkempt, underweight, agitated, anxious, depressed, etc.
2. *Speech.* Any abnormalities in style of speech, such as slow and halting, pressured, rapid, barely audible, high-pitched, etc.
3. *Mood.* The client's recent mood as reported by her and observed by the assessor, for example, are they anxious, depressed, angry, etc.
4. *Appetite.* Any abnormalities or changes in appetite, increases or decreases in appetite or in weight, etc.
5. *Sleep.* How many hours sleep does the client get on average? Any recent changes, difficulty getting to sleep, awakening during the night, waking too early, or with the quality of sleep, etc.
6. *Sex drive.* Is sex drive normal? Have there been any recent changes?
7. *Anhedonia.* Does the client take pleasure in a range of activities? Have there been recent changes? Does the client still enjoy the things she used to?
8. *Irritability.* Does the client report feeling irritable or agitated?
9. *Self-worth & self-image.* Does the client have low self-esteem? How does she see herself; how does she think others see her?
10. *Hopelessness.* How does the client view her future, optimistically or pessimistically?
11. *Risk/self-harm/suicide.* Are there any indications of risk to self or others? Particularly suicide risk, which should be assessed in detail, for example, history, plans, intent, means, protective factors, etc.
12. *Psychosis.* Any evidence of psychotic symptoms, for example, hallucinations, delusions, disordered thinking or behaviour, etc.
13. *Concentration.* Does the client have any difficulty concentrating? Any recent changes?
14. *Orientation.* The three main orientation factors: Is the client aware of the time/date, the location, and the name of the therapist present?
15. *Memory.* Does the client have any problems with memory? Any recent changes?

Other considerations may include the client's attitude toward the therapist, her level of conscious alertness, psychomotor activity (nervous tics, retardation, agitation, etc.), soundness of judgement (ability to make safe and reasonable life decisions), insight into the problematic nature of her symptoms, etc. Expression of affect is labelled "full range" (if normal), and abnormalities including affect that is "restricted" or "constricted" (narrow range of emotions expressed), "blunted" (emotions present but their expression is muted), "flat" (lack of emotion), "labile" (rapid swinging between emotions) or "inappropriate" (for the topic or setting). Thought process is classed as normal or "goal-directed", where the patient remains on relevant topics, whereas abnormal processes include "circumstantial thought" (excessive detail), "tangential thought" (going off the subject), "loose associations" (jumping around topics illogically), "perseveration" (repeating the same thing), etc. Leahy and Holland also provide a summary of the main MSE elements in their CBT guide to treating anxiety and depression (Leahy & Holland, 2000, pp. 5–6).

Risk and contra-indications

Suicidal ideation should normally be checked with all clients as a standard part of assessment, along with other potential risk factors. The way that risk is handled will depend on the circumstances but adequate assessment and management must, for obvious reasons, normally be prioritised above most other agenda items. Dobson and Dobson recommend the following initial question for suicide risk assessment in CBT: "On bad days, do you sometimes think that life is not worth living?" This is followed by other questions about risk, depending on the individual client's presentation, such as:

> What keeps you going on bad days?
> Are there people that you think of when you are having thoughts of harming yourself?
> "Do you ever hurt yourself separately from thoughts of suicide?" (Use examples).
> (Dobson & Dobson, 2009, p. 24)

Where suicidal ideation is present, for instance, it's common to seek further information on the content, frequency, and strength of current suicidal thoughts. Questions should also be asked about the history of previous suicide attempts, methods employed, seriousness of attempts, harm caused, family history of suicide, current availability of means (guns, pills), protective factors such as relationships with children or other family members, the client's expectations for the future and hopes for treatment, etc.

Considerable disagreement has always existed over specific contra-indications to the use of hypnotism. Lynn et al. list the following types of client as examples of those potentially unsuitable for clinical hypnosis (Lynn, Kirsch, Neufeld & Rhue, 1996, p. 15).

1. Clients vulnerable to psychotic breakdown
2. Clients who have paranoid resistance toward being influenced or controlled by others
3. Unstable dissociative or post-traumatic clients
4. Clients with a borderline personality structure.

Clients with obsessive-compulsive disorder (OCD) may also be unsuitable for hypnotherapy insofar as they have been found to score lower than normal, or clients with other disorders, on scales measuring hypnotic susceptibility (Spinhoven, Van Dyck, Hoogduin & Schaap, 1991).

Suitability for cognitive-behavioural hypnotherapy

Safran and Segal have developed the Suitability for Short-Term Cognitive Therapy (SSCT) rating scale, which contains items that may serve well as a guide to assessing suitability for cognitive-behavioural hypnotherapy (Safran, Segal, Vallis, Shaw & Samstag, 1993). It includes the following items:

1. Accessibility of automatic thoughts
2. Awareness and differentiation of emotions
3. Acceptance of personal responsibility for change
4. Compatibility with cognitive rationale
5. Alliance potential (in-session evidence), that is, ability to work with the therapist
6. Alliance potential (out-of-session evidence), that is, ability to form positive relationships in general
7. Chronicity versus acuteness, that is, longer duration problems may be less suitable
8. Security operations, that is, extensive avoidance and safety-seeking may be less suitable
9. Focality, that is, ability to remain focused on the main problem
10. General optimism/pessimism about therapy.

Many different researchers have attempted to quantify the role of client characteristics in determining the outcome of treatment more generally. Clarkin and Levy provide a wide-ranging review of the research in this area, which attempts to bring together the findings of other authors (Clarkin & Levy, 2004). Evidence in this area is mixed because client factors probably interact with each other and with treatment and therapist factors to determine outcome. Client variables are often divided into diagnostic factors, socio-demographic factors, and personality factors. As Clarkin and Levy note, several client diagnostic characteristics have attracted attention as possible predictors of treatment outcome (Clarkin & Levy, 2004, pp. 198–202).

1. *Severity of symptoms*. In general, with some exceptions, there seems to be good evidence that more severe symptoms indicate poorer treatment outcome.
2. *Functional impairment*. People with similar symptoms may experience very different degrees of impairment to social or cognitive functioning, in relationships, work, study, etc. In general, functional impairment also indicates poorer outcome in treatment.
3. *Co-morbidity*. The presence of other psychiatric diagnoses, including personality disorders, is sometimes described as increasing "complexity" and also tends to suggest poorer outcome. Although there's little research in this area, the presence of chronic pain or general medical conditions, may also predict poorer outcome in psychotherapy.

So-called "socio-demographic" variables such as gender, race, and age do not seem to be typically correlated with differences in treatment outcome and there is little evidence to show that matching therapist and client on these variables makes much difference. However, clients who have lower socioeconomic status may tend to have poorer outcomes (Clarkin & Levy, 2004, p. 203).

Personality factors have particularly attracted the interest of psychoanalytic researchers and discussion of certain key terms permeates some of the literature. Some of the main concepts in this area are as follows (Clarkin & Levy, 2004, pp. 205–207).

1. *Client expectancies*. There is good evidence in general to show a correlation between positive expectations for treatment and positive outcomes. Moreover, Kirsch's research in this area has developed the concept further with particular relevance to the mechanism of hypnotic suggestion.
2. *Readiness to change*. Prochaska and DiClemente's (1983) trans-diagnostic model of change processes has been influential across different models of psychotherapy and there is good evidence to support the conclusion that clients who have passed the stage of contemplation and arrived at a stage of "readiness for change" are more likely to benefit from psychotherapy, although this research has focused mainly on habit disorders, which might be compared to the role of commitment and motivation in the hypnotic mind-set.
3. *Ego strength*. The concept of ego-strength is defined as the presence of positive personality traits (strengths of character) which allow individuals to develop adaptive ways of coping with anxiety and their ability to retain a secure sense of their own identity despite conflict and suffering. Hartland's well-known "ego-strengthening" hypnosis script is an attempt to directly develop these qualities through suggestion. With some exceptions, ego strength has generally been found to predict better treatment outcomes.
4. *Psychological mindedness*. The quality of being "psychologically minded" refers to clients' ability to understand their own problems and those of other people from a psychological point of view, and equates to something like "insight". There is more mixed evidence in relation to this concept but it still holds some promise as a predictor of treatment outcome.

In addition to these general characteristics, other client variables such as hypnotic susceptibility may be predictive of outcome for certain forms of hypnotherapy, although research in this area has somewhat produced mixed findings.

Hypnotic susceptibility (hypnotisability)

As noted earlier, pooled evidence from six randomised controlled trials (RCTs) has found, on average, a modest ($r = 0.44$) positive correlation between hypnotic susceptibility and treatment outcome (Flammer & Bongartz, 2003). Researchers have found specific correlations between hypnotic susceptibility and treatment outcome for conditions including the following (Lynn, Kirsch, Neufeld & Rhue, 1996, p. 16).

1. Asthma
2. Obesity
3. Nicotine dependence

4. Somatoform disorders
5. Post-traumatic stress disorders
6. Phobias.

Moreover, certain psychological disorders, including phobias, eating disorders, and dissociative disorders, have been found to be associated with higher than normal levels of hypnotic susceptibility (Lynn, Kirsch, Neufeld & Rhue, 1996, p. 17).

Hypnotic susceptibility can be assessed formally using standardised scales. The most frequently cited scale in the research literature is the Stanford Hypnotic Susceptibility Scale (SHSS), of which there are several versions, the most relevant being Form C (Weitzenhoffer & Hilgard, 1962). However, the kind of scales used in research are not popular in clinical practice, probably because they typically take around an hour to administer. A briefer but more controversial tool called the Hypnotic Induction Profile (HIP) is suitable for clinical practice (Spiegel & Spiegel, 1978). Hypnotic susceptibility can also be informally assessed, however, by using any number of traditional hypnotic suggestion tests, such as Chevreul's pendulum experiment, eye-closure, eyelid catalepsy, rigid arm catalepsy, etc. (These are discussed in detail in the chapter on hypnotic skills training in the current volume.)

Summary and feedback

The assessment and all subsequent sessions should end with the therapist offering a summary of what's been covered. It's also useful to ask at the end of the assessment, "Do you think there's anything else I need to know to be able to help you?" The end-of-session summary in each session should be followed by some kind of check for client feedback, ideally using an open question such as, "How did you find today's session?", "What was most useful?", or "Did you have difficulty with anything we covered?"

Time permitting, it can be valuable to have clients summarise what they have learned from the session and the instructions they are taking away, etc. For example, "What are the main things you're taking away from the session today?" Meichenbaum refers to this as a "comprehension check" and in relation to his own coping skills training approach, stress inoculation training (SIT), suggests approaching it sometimes as a more rigorous role-reversal exercise where the client assumes the position of the therapist to demonstrate how she would teach what she's taken from the session to a hypothetical client (Meichenbaum, 1985, p. 41). This is a particularly useful way of checking the client's comprehension of homework tasks, including self-monitoring, and the rationale for them, that is, "Can you role-play the part of another therapist explaining to an imaginary client exactly *how* she's going to do this homework and *why* it's relevant to the problem we've been discussing?"

Typical agenda for subsequent sessions

The typical structure of subsequent cognitive-behavioural hypnotherapy sessions is broadly the same as for traditional CBT, except that clients tend to expect greater emphasis on hypnosis and to experience hypnotherapy in most sessions. Generally speaking, the latter half of the session will normally be dedicated to the use of hypnotic rehearsal of coping imagery, imaginal exposure, or similar techniques.

Example session agenda

1. Brief update and review of the intervening period, check on the client's anxiety episodes (frequency and intensity) and outcome measures
2. Bridge from previous session and collaborate on setting the rest of the agenda, usually just one or two main items
3. Review feedback on homework, what has been learned
4. First main session item, for example, additional skills training in self-hypnosis following on from homework or traditional cognitive therapy work, etc.
5. Second main session item, for example, use of hypnotherapy for rehearsal of mental imagery, etc.
6. Agreeing next homework assignment, for example, using a self-hypnosis recording
7. Client provides a summary of main points covered in session and feedback on how session went and what was helpful/unhelpful.

In other words, the initial update and mood check, review of homework, setting next homework, and final summary and feedback are "standing items" that are included as standard in most session agendas. The client and therapist might acknowledge these and discuss them if necessary but the main question is how the rest of the time, in the middle of the session, will be spent, that is, what the main target issues and interventions are for the session. Often this will be carried over from the previous session or determined by the overall treatment plan but this should be discussed collaboratively with the client and other issues for discussion may be raised by them.

Client life-history form

Personal details

When providing information, try to be as concise as possible at this stage and focus on the key things your therapist needs to know. You can always add more detail later.

Name	
Age	Date of birth
Country of birth	Sex
Marital status	Occupation
Email	Contact telephone(s)
Postal address	

Problem(s) and goal(s)

Briefly summarise the three main problems for which you're seeking help:
1.

2.

3.

What are the three main goals you want to achieve by the end of your therapy?
1.

2.

3.

How do you expect your therapist might help you achieve those goals?

Problem domains

Please provide brief details of any other problems you're currently experiencing in the areas below.

Work/study
Relationship with spouse/partner
Relationship with rest of family
Relationships with friends
Financial/legal problems
Social life/leisure activity
Sex life
Physical health/fitness
Mental health

Mental health profile & history

Please answer all of the questions below concisely, giving details where possible.
1. Has anyone in your family ever experienced psychiatric problems?

2. Has anyone in your family ever made a suicide attempt?

3. Have you ever experienced any psychiatric problems?

4. Are you currently receiving any psychiatric medication? Name? When started? Dose?

5. Have you ever made any suicide attempts? How? When?

6. In the past four weeks, have you had any suicidal thoughts? How strong was your intention to act on them?

7. Have you ever harmed yourself in any other way? How? When?

8. How would you describe your mood/emotions in general over the past four weeks?

9. Do you have any problems with sleep? How many hours do you typically sleep?

10. How would you describe your appetite and diet?

Physical health/substance use

1. Do you have any other health problems currently?

2. Have you had any notable or relevant health problems in the past?

3. Are you currently taking any other prescription or over-the-counter medication?

4. Any other notable information about your current physical or mental health?

5. Do you smoke? How many times per day?

6. Do you drink alcohol? How many units per week?

7. Do you use any illegal recreational drugs? What? How much? When?

8. What is your GPs name and practice address?

Relationships and personal history

Family/relationships

Please summarise details of your father, mother, any siblings, and any other significant people in your life, e.g., children, spouse/partner, ex-partners, etc. Mark with an asterisk (*) people who currently live with you.

First Name	Relationship (How related?)	Sex/Age (Deceased?)	Location (Country, town)	Comments (How do you get on?)
	Father	M,		
	Mother	F,		

Work and education

1. What are your main academic and vocational qualifications?

2. Briefly describe your experience of school as a child?

3. Briefly describe your experience of any subsequent education or study?

4. Briefly summarise what your current job entails, including your job title and employer:

5. Briefly summarise your previous work history, including any problems:

Life events

1. Did you ever experience any kind of physical, sexual, or emotional abuse as a child? (Give details.)

2. Have you experienced any kind of abuse as an adult? (Give details.)

3. Briefly summarise any other traumatic or particularly disturbing events that happened in your past:

4. How would you describe your childhood in general? Did you experience any other notable problems?

CHAPTER FIVE

Case formulation in cognitive-behavioural hypnotherapy

Case conceptualisation or "clinical formulation", as it is sometimes known, is central to modern psychotherapy although fewer references are made to it in the literature of hypnosis. Conceptualisation is the centrepiece of modern psychotherapy, especially CBT, and has been described as the "bridge from assessment to treatment" (Dobson & Dobson, 2009, p. 32). The effects of psychotherapeutic intervention differ fundamentally from those of taking medication, for example, insofar as it depends to a greater extent upon the rationale given for the treatment and the language used to formulate the conceptualisation (Alford & Beck, 1997, p. 96). Some attempts have previously been made to combine cognitive-behavioural case formulation with the use of clinical hypnosis and Chapman has argued that this provides the best way to integrate hypnosis fully within a CBT approach (Chapman, 2006).

As either an alternative or adjunct to formal diagnosis, case formulation attempts to provide a theoretically-derived explanation of the client's presenting problems and possibly other underlying factors. It forms a progressively refined "map" or "picture" of the client's problems by offering a "working hypothesis", usually developed collaboratively, regarding the cause and nature of her symptoms. The working hypothesis, which forms the heart of the conceptualisation, is normally derived from theory-based models of different types of problem. The conceptualisation is tested out by adopting a fundamentally experimental attitude toward implementation of the treatment plan, which is modified in the light of therapeutic progress and other emerging information. In other words, testing of the working hypothesis takes place in an atmosphere of "collaborative empiricism", broadly emulating basic scientific method.

> A case formulation is a theory of a particular case. A cognitive-behavioural case formulation is an idiographic (individualised) theory that is based on a nomothetic (general) cognitive-behavioural theory. (Persons & Davidson, 2001, p. 86)

The most influential nomothetic models in the field of cognitive-behavioural therapy are Beck's cognitive model of depression and the various models of anxiety derived from it (Beck, Rush, Shaw & Emery, 1979; Beck, Emery & Greenberg, 2005; Clark & Beck, 2010). The collaborative development of a conceptualisation helps the client to answer the question "Why is this happening?" Part of its main function is therefore to help develop and guide the treatment plan and provide the client with an explicit rationale for homework, etc. Indeed, by learning how to contribute to her own conceptualisation, the client becomes progressively more able to assume the role of therapist toward her own problems. Moreover, in many cases the improved understanding it brings may be of considerable therapeutic value in itself. It may also help the client to predict certain problems and to prevent relapse in the future, following the termination of treatment.

The practice of conceptualisation is not very explicit in Beck's original writings on cognitive therapy (Beck A. T., 1976; Beck, Rush, Shaw & Emery, 1979) but much more explicit models are now extremely common in CBT. Conceptualisations can be developed and shared with clients either in a few paragraphs (or more) of writing, perhaps on a structured form, or with the aid of a diagram, or some combination thereof. Generally speaking, most CBT practitioners now prefer to employ simple diagrams as these are easier to make use of collaboratively with clients during sessions, for example, by drawing them on a board or filling in blanks together on a diagram printed on paper, etc. Conceptualisation diagrams appear to have become increasingly complex over the past couple of decades and they can often appear like "Spaghetti Junction" or computer circuit boards, at first glance. However, the more complex diagrams can usually be simplified by breaking them down into parts, which can be shared with the client more easily in the early stages of treatment (Clark & Beck, 2010). The formulation for any given case should, as the saying goes, be as simple as possible but no simpler. Novice therapists might be better to start by focusing on conceptualisation approaches such as the basic "ABC" diagram below, etc. It should be emphasised that the process of formulation is intimately linked with clinical supervision because good formulations are much easier to share and discuss with supervisors, and the supervisor's role will naturally involve collaborating with the therapist in reflection upon, and developing conceptualisations presented when discussing, individual clients.

Many therapists, including most of those using hypnosis, may employ broadly "cognitive" or "behavioural" techniques without linking them to an explicit conceptualisation. It may therefore be argued that the emphasis on an explicit cognitive-behavioural conceptualisation is what differentiates cognitive-behavioural therapies from other therapeutic models. Cognitive-behavioural hypnotherapy should, therefore, also proceed from a similar conceptualisation approach. There are many different approaches to conceptualisation, derived from different theoretical models of different problems and diagnoses, particularly in the cognitive-behavioural literature. The two most influential approaches to case formulation in CBT are derived from Jacqueline Persons and Judith Beck, although Aaron Beck's recent manual for anxiety also contains detailed case conceptualisation forms and diagrams (Beck J. S., 1995; Clark & Beck, 2010; Persons, 2008).

Case-level formulation

The application of Persons' case conceptualisation approach to cognitive-behavioural hypnotherapy has been discussed at length by Chapman (Chapman, 2006). Persons distinguishes between three levels of formulation: the case (or person), the problem (or syndrome), and specific situations (Persons & Davidson, 2001, p. 87). Case conceptualisation, at the broadest level, often develops gradually, as a picture of the whole person develops out of conceptualisations of specific situations and individual problems. According to Persons, the whole case conceptualisation should be divided into five main domains, which can be summarised in a standard written format:

1. Problem list
2. Diagnosis (where appropriate)
3. Working hypothesis
4. Strengths and assets
5. Treatment plan. (Persons & Davidson, 2001, p. 89)

The initial assessment phase attempts to ascertain much of this information, although the case conceptualisation will continue to be revised and developed throughout treatment. As Persons acknowledges, psychiatric diagnosis and treatment plan are not, strictly-speaking, part of the cognitive-behavioural formulation itself. Diagnosis is normally included on the same documentation because disorder and formulation tend to be very closely related, and the information is therefore particularly relevant. The treatment plan is normally included because it follows very closely from the rest of the formulation, particularly the central working hypothesis, which provides its rationale. In Persons' approach, the treatment plan consists of the treatment goals (which follow largely from the problems prioritised on the list), the modality of treatment (such as cognitive-behavioural hypnotherapy), the frequency and duration of sessions, the key psychological interventions planned, any adjunct therapies (such as medication), and any anticipated obstacles that could prevent the client from following the plan and attaining the goals (Persons & Davidson, 2001, p. 99).

In the field of clinical hypnosis, in relation to his "cognitive hypnotherapy" approach, Alladin has described a similar eight-step case formulation process (Alladin, 2008, p. 25). A modified version based upon this approach to cognitive-behavioural hypnotherapy might consist of the following steps.

1. *Triggers*. Identify specific trigger situations encountered in the past and those which the client anticipates in the future, especially short-term trigger events (within the next two weeks) which the client can instigate herself.
2. *Presenting problem*. Identify the client's presenting problem as specifically as possible, across multiple dimensions, for example, by using a descriptive conceptualisation such as the five aspects model.

3. *History.* Explore the history of the problem, the client's perception of its origin, etc., and look for recurring cognitive and behavioural themes.
4. *Formal diagnosis.* Identify possible diagnoses, for example, using DSM-IV-TR.
5. *Working hypothesis.* Formulate a working clinical hypothesis to explain possible causation or onset and the inter-action between current maintaining factors across different modalities, especially cognitive and behavioural factors.
6. *Assess strengths & risks.* Identify client's strengths, assets and resources, and any obstacles, threats or risks which they may encounter over time. This may resemble a SWOT analysis, looking at current Strengths and Weaknesses and future Opportunities and Threats.
7. *Treatment goals.* Therapist and client should mutually agree time-limited goals for therapy, stated in concrete terms, that is, SMART goals: Specific, Measurable, Achievable, Relevant, and Time-limited.
8. *Treatment plan.* Formulate a staged treatment plan to achieve the treatment goals, based on the working hypothesis.

The centrepiece of the whole case conceptualisation approach is the "working hypothesis", which derives from the problem list and upon which the treatment plan is based. The working hypothesis can be written up in the form of several paragraphs, which attempt to summarise and explain the relationship between the main problems, and their affective, behavioural, and cognitive elements, that is, drawing upon the same information included in typical conceptualisation diagrams (see below). CBT authors have increasingly emphasised the value of briefly assessing the client's strengths and assets, as these may influence the working hypothesis and treatment plan (Kuyken, Padesky & Dudley, 2009). Moreover, acknowledging the client's positive characteristics can help counterbalance over-emphasis of the "negative" side of things, due to extended discussion of her problems. In fact, with some clients, it can be useful to carry out something like a brief SWOT analysis by enquiring about personal Strengths, Weaknesses, Opportunities, and Threats, that might be relevant to the treatment.

Problem list

The first step in case formulation is normally to obtain a clear statement of the main presenting problem, or a comprehensive list of problems, from the client. Insofar as possible, this should be phrased in behavioural terms, and made specific and concrete. Persons has also emphasised the value of making the problem list as thorough and inclusive as possible (Persons, 2008). At the level of the initial problem list, descriptions normally have to be kept short, and so problems are usually summarised in one or two brief sentences. Where appropriate problem descriptions may also include brief specific reference to key thoughts, behaviours, or emotions.

Problems listed may include, for example, symptoms of anxiety or depression, etc., as well as problems with finances, work, relationships, physical health, accommodation, social life, leisure activities, etc. (Although with brief hypnotherapy, assessment often needs to be quite focused and concise because of time constraints.) The client may be simply asked, "Can you help me draw up a list on the board here of all the problems that you currently have that might be relevant to your therapy?" Making it clear that you're developing a list, by drawing it on paper or a board helps the client to keep things brief enough at this stage, as further discussion can be deferred until later. Sometimes it can be helpful to ask clients to review their problem list for homework and reflect on whether they want to modify or add any items. The other assessment questions will also help both therapist and client to collaborate on a sufficiently comprehensive list.

Example problem list

1. General worry about work-related problems.
2. Problems getting to sleep most nights and tiredness the next day.
3. Anxiety in anticipation of meetings.
4. Low self-esteem and tendency to self-criticise.
5. Lack of assertiveness skills in response to problems at work.
6. Arguments with husband/wife/partner, and tension in the relationship.

Developing the initial problem list is often followed by a brief process of "problem reduction" or simplification, that is, looking for common denominators, etc. (Beck A. T., 1976, pp. 225–229). Clients often arrive at therapy complaining of the fact that they feel overwhelmed by so many problems and this sense of being bombarded with problems heightens their distress and undermines their hope for the future. Yet when asked to list their main problems, they typically produce a relatively brief list of key points, often around half-a-dozen main headings. "There are several problems here but *not* 'hundreds' of them", the therapist might observe. Moreover, when multiple problems are listed the expert knowledge and experience of the therapist often come into play insofar as he may be able to reduce them to aspects of one or two underlying issues. In the example above, the therapist might observe that several of these problems are potentially related as symptoms of Generalised Anxiety Disorder (GAD) or chronic worry. Developing the conceptualisation will further assist the therapist and client in reducing problems by identifying their relationship and placing emphasis on the key maintaining factors.

Once a list has been drawn up, problems should be prioritised. This requires further collaboration between therapist and client. There may be different reasons for choosing to prioritise a specific problem:

1. *Significance or seriousness.* The client or therapist may feel that a particular problem is especially serious or significant, for example, suicidal ideation or substance abuse.
2. *Urgency.* An anticipated event may be looming, for example, a job interview, and time limitations may suggest that it should become the focus of assessment and treatment.
3. *Client preference.* The client may simply have a strong preference to focus upon or discuss a particular problem.
4. *Expediency or simplicity.* The therapist may feel that a particular aspect of the problem would be simpler or easier to address first, and select an "easy target" to focus the treatment upon initially, which may help to "graduate" tasks and build the client's confidence.

Once a problem is identified as a priority, similar criteria may be applied to prioritise specific situations or incidents that relate to the problem chosen (see below). Key problems can be developed into goal statements, as discussed below. Judith Beck, by comparison, emphasises the development of a "goal list" early in therapy (Beck J. S., 1995, p. 32).

Goal definitions

Clients often initially express their goals for treatment as "To feel better" or "To not be anxious", etc. However, these are not helpful statements because they are too vague. They can, however, be translated into a more detailed description of the desired outcome and broken-down, where necessary, into several, more specific, component goals. Mutual agreement on goals is an essential component of the working alliance in therapy (Bordin, 1979). However, it is important to bear in mind that the therapist or client may feel a need to modify the goals during later stages of treatment, and they may have to be periodically reviewed.

Treatment goals are usually defined in ways that are as specific and measurable as possible, while remaining meaningful and relevant to the client. They can be defined using the SMART acronym, of which there are several variations, such as the following:

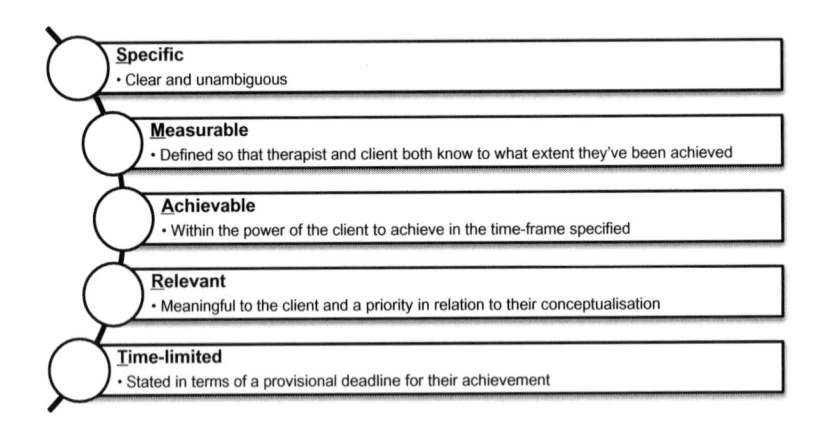

Specific
- Clear and unambiguous

Measurable
- Defined so that therapist and client both know to what extent they've been achieved

Achievable
- Within the power of the client to achieve in the time-frame specified

Relevant
- Meaningful to the client and a priority in relation to their conceptualisation

Time-limited
- Stated in terms of a provisional deadline for their achievement

However, the SMART approach is not suited to all treatment goals and some flexibility is therefore required in relation to setting goals primarily involving affective or cognitive change rather than behaviour (Dobson & Dobson, 2009, p. 61).

End-of-treatment goals should be agreed, which will describe what needs to happen for the therapist and client to be satisfied that treatment can be concluded, for example, eliminating panic attacks and being able to engage in all previously avoided activities, etc. These overall goals normally need to be broken down into subordinate goals (Leahy & Holland, 2000, pp. 6–7). For example:

1. Completion of tasks or acquisition of skills such as facing feared situations, increasing rewarding activities, or developing assertiveness or problem-solving skills.
2. Reduction in specific symptoms such as reducing anxiety by fifty per cent on subjective ratings during certain feared situations or eliminating compulsive apologising.

3. Improved functioning, for example, better performance in college assignments, improved daily routine, or gaining employment.
4. Cognitive changes such as reduced frequency or duration of certain thoughts or reduced ratings of the strength of negative beliefs in general or in problem situations.

In order to know that goals are being achieved, they must somehow be measurable and evidence of changes in behaviour, where possible, tends to be emphasised over subjective ratings of changes in affect or cognition, although these may often be combined. For example, someone who has social phobia might aim to initiate at least one conversation each day with colleagues, while experiencing anxiety below thirty per cent on a subjective rating scale. The ultimate goal of treatment is sometimes, particularly in clinical trials, quantified as a reduction below clinical cut-off levels on a standardised outcome measure such as the Beck Depression Inventory (BDI), although some therapists prefer to emphasise overt behavioural goals.

Goal elaboration

The development of specific treatment goals overlaps with a therapeutic intervention employed in hypnotherapy. The client may be asked to develop a "script" or story in which she describes her future self in as much detail as possible, coping with or having overcome her main presenting problem and having achieved her desired outcome at the end of treatment. This script can be written freely as a story or developed in a semi-structured manner, for example, by asking the client to provide as much detail as possible on a form including headings such as:

1. What is the main situation or event that you want to respond differently to?
2. What do you want to feel emotionally in that situation? (Affect)
3. What bodily sensations would you hope to experience? (Sensation)
4. What would you say and do differently? (Behaviour)
5. What would you be thinking or saying to yourself? (Cognition: Thoughts/Self-Talk)
6. How would you view yourself as a person? (Cognition: Self-Concept)
7. What impact would these improvements have on your life in general?
8. What impact, if any, would they have on your relationships?
9. What impact, if any, would they have on your work?
10. What impact, if any, would they have on your health?

The client will normally need some collaboration from the therapist to develop a draft copy of her "script" into something more satisfactory and comprehensive. The therapist can easily ask questions to press the client for more detailed information, where necessary. There are three main benefits to doing so:

1. The client and therapist will develop a clearer statement of the treatment goals.
2. The client will often experience some therapeutic benefit from the process of repeatedly reviewing and elaborating the script over time.

3. The script can easily be adapted for use as a hypnotherapy suggestion script, which may be employed during treatment sessions or recorded as a self-hypnosis routine that the client can listen to for homework.

Providing the client with a form containing the questions above to reflect on and complete, in order to elaborate upon her treatment goals, can be a useful initial homework assignment.

Formulation models

Formulation models are generally either "cross-sectional" (or "situational"), giving a snapshot of one or more particular situations analysed into certain components, or "longitudinal" (or "developmental"), describing the chronological development of a problem over time. A rough distinction can also be made between:

1. *Descriptive* conceptualisations, which simply analyse a situation into its elements, such as the three or four systems models below.
2. *Explanatory* or "maintenance" conceptualisations, which attempt to explore the function of certain elements, usually cognitions or behaviour, in maintaining a problem.
3. *Chronological* conceptualisations, which divide a problem into discrete temporal stages, usually either in terms of longitudinal or developmental factors or more short-term phases of a problem, such as before, during, or after social situations, etc.

It's often advisable to begin with a basic cross-sectional formulation as this rests on the more explicit aspects of the client's problem, which lead naturally into a basic functional or explanatory conceptualisation, such as the ABC models below. Longitudinal conceptualisation, by contrast, tends to involve speculation, making inferences, about the past and the client's non-conscious cognitive structures, her underlying beliefs and assumptions and related constructs such as "schemata."

Situational analysis

It is central to most cognitive-behavioural hypnotherapy to identify specific situations in which the client's symptoms are triggered. There are several reasons for this:

1. Focusing upon specific, concrete examples helps therapist and client to communicate more clearly and avoids abstraction, confusion, and misunderstanding.
2. Discussion of concrete examples often helps the client to heighten her own awareness of triggers and symptoms.
3. Many mental imagery techniques, particularly in hypnosis, will require the use of a specific scene related to the problem which the client must be able to picture in her mind's eye; this should be identified and evaluated in advance.

As Beck notes, discussion of the range of trigger situations tends to follow on naturally from compiling a problem list (Clark & Beck, 2010, p. 137). It can also be useful to have the client spend a few minutes developing a list of previous and anticipated trigger situations, people, or events. The therapist can then help them to pick one to focus upon in treatment, employing similar criteria to those mentioned above in relation to prioritising the problem list.

Sometimes a past event in which the client manifested symptoms may be most revealing and in some cases this may even become the focus of treatment, especially in PTSD where past events may reverberate in the present as intrusive memories. However, in the majority of cases it is more pragmatic to focus upon an anticipated event, in the near future, as the assessment then becomes a preparation for the use of mental rehearsal and other techniques designed to help the client cope better with forthcoming events. Moreover, the anticipated trigger situation selected as "target" or focus of treatment should normally be an event within one or two weeks, for the simple reason that the client should be able to observe her improvement between sessions and report back to the therapist. Further, the selection of a target situation which the client can instigate helps to guarantee that it will be experienced between sessions. For example, the client may say her anxiety is triggered by people being aggressive toward her. Whether or not this will happen between sessions may appear to be in the hands of fate, leaving it up to chance whether the client can practice coping skills or monitor improvement, etc. However, she may be able to instigate a conversation with someone who dislikes her and whom she generally avoids talking to, as a test of her progress.

Once a specific situation has been identified, the client should be encouraged to describe it in vivid, detailed, and concrete language. The features of a specific situation, put simply, can best be investigated by the some variation of the classic "W" questions.

1. *What* exactly happened?
2. *Where* did it happen?
3. *When* did it happen?
4. *Who* was involved?
5. *How* did you respond (in terms of thoughts, actions and feelings)?

Therapists generally prefer to ask "how?" rather than "why?" questions; the latter are more "hit-and-miss" and often encourage the client to engage in speculation rather than sticking to the facts. On the other hand, sometimes it can be useful to obtain the client's assumptions about "why" she experiences problems in certain situations and to compare this against the cognitive-behavioural conceptualisation as an aid to further socialisation to the model being employed. Finally, the therapist may wish to probe further into the situation with exploratory questions aimed at narrowing down the focus on to specific factors in the situation which act as triggers. For example, the therapist might ask, "What is the worst part of that situation for you?", "What is it in that situation that *really triggers* your anxiety?", "What would make that situation even worse?", "What would make the situation better or easier to cope with?" These provide ways of isolating specific critical factors which may become the focus of treatment.

The specific triggers or antecedents in a situation may be either internal or external and can also be considered to fall into one of three main categories: environmental, interoceptive, and cognitive triggers (Clark & Beck, 2010, p. 137).

1. *Environmental* triggers include features of the external situation, which seem to trigger the problem response, for example, in many specific or social phobias.
2. *Interoceptive* triggers are bodily sensations, such as chest pain, etc., and particularly associated with panic attacks and health anxiety.
3. *Cognitive* triggers are thoughts, impulses, or images, etc., which appear to trigger the response, particularly in OCD or PTSD.

Although the measurement or rating of problems and hierarchy construction isn't strictly-speaking part of the process of conceptualisation, we will briefly address these areas below because they follow naturally from the descriptive analysis of specific example situations in the treatment of anxiety.

Measurement

One of the earliest and most common measures employed in behaviour therapy and hypnotherapy is the Subjective Units of Disturbance (SUD) scale (people often say "distress" or "discomfort", which amounts to the same thing). This was a simple percentile scale which clients are asked to use to rate their anxiety in response to various real, anticipated, or imaginary situations. It can be "calibrated" by asking clients to think of the most upsetting thing that could happen to them in life, the genuine worst-case scenario, and agreeing to rate that as 100 per cent on the SUD scale. Other images or situations can then be rated by comparison to that benchmark. Many hypnotherapists use a 0–10 scale for simplicity.

It may also be useful to use measures of "self-efficacy" (Bandura) or sense of mastery, etc., especially when treatment focuses on the acquisition of coping skills or behaviour change. The client can be asked to rate "How confident are you that you can cope successfully with that situation?" as a percentage or 0–10. A similar question, especially useful when teaching self-hypnosis and other coping skills, would be, "How confident are you that you can use that technique effectively now?" Clients can also be asked to rate their level of belief in certain positive or negative self-statements, autosuggestions, or beliefs. For example, "When you repeat that statement to yourself right now, how true does it seem as a percentage?" In Beck's approach to anxiety, though, ratings are based on appraisals of probability and severity of threat, that is, how likely and how catastrophic a future event is estimated to be (Clark & Beck, 2010). As we shall see, Beck also refers to a "dual belief system", distinguishing between appraisals of threat made when anxious, or during a threatening situation, and those made when non-anxious, or at a distance in space and time from perceived threat.

These different, affective, behavioural, and cognitive measures can be used selectively with different clients, with different therapy techniques, or with the same client at different times.

Affect SUD scales used to measure levels of anxiety, or other feelings such as anger, depression, etc. Positive affect scales can also be used to measure levels of pleasure, happiness, etc.

Behaviour Self-efficacy scales can be used to measure how confident the client is that she can do some task or use some skill effectively, or break some bad behavioural habit.

Cognition   Simple ratings of belief can be used to evaluate how true a statement seems to the client, during an anxious episode versus when at a distance from it. More specific appraisals of the probability and severity of harm are emphasised in Beck's cognitive therapy for anxiety.

The ratings given by clients in relation to relevant cognitions and behaviours will vary depending on the extent to which their "anxiety mode" is activated (see below). Ratings should therefore be sought "when your anxiety is at its peak" versus "when you are at a distance from the situation or event."

Graded hierarchy construction

A central component of early behaviour therapy, especially systematic desensitisation, was the construction of detailed "hierarchies" of ten or twenty scenes graded in ascending levels of anxiety. This was often a laborious process, taking place over several sessions. The therapist usually begins simply by asking the client to "brainstorm" situations which present the same problem. Normally, however, the therapist will use his ingenuity to help the client identify scenes, or modify them, to construct a satisfactory hierarchy of images. There are several ways of doing this:

1. *Time distance*. The client creates imaginary scenes ranked according to time distance from a dreaded event, for example, an hour before a job interview, ten minutes before the interview, ten seconds away, etc.
2. *Spatial distance*. The client creates scenes based on spatial distance from the thing feared, for example, a dog is pictured on the other side of the park, walking on the other side of the street, walking right up to him, etc.
3. *Content*. The content of the image is modified to reduce or increase anxiety, for example, rehearsing a presentation before the mirror, reciting it to a friend, delivering it to a small group of friends, to a huge audience at a conference.

It is well-established that greater chronological and spatial distance from a feared object or event tends to reduce anxiety. (In many cases, of course, such as approaching an airport, spatial and chronological distances reduce hand-in-hand.) The content of imagery can be modified in innumerable realistic or unrealistic ways to "tweak" the level of anxiety, for example, changing it to a black and white picture instead of colour, including the presence of the therapist for emotional support, employing a distressing word rather than an actual image, etc. Most hierarchies probably involve a combination of spatial, temporal, and content-related differences between items.

Over time, therapists in general have abbreviated the process of hierarchy construction considerably, compared to Wolpe's original systematic desensitisation method (Wolpe, 1958). It is useful, in most cases, to construct a simple hierarchy of about six to ten items, ranked according to their difficulty. Clients can be asked, however, how close to the top of the hierarchy they want to begin. In severe cases of anxiety, of course, clients may wish to focus on less challenging items first. However, with simple mild-to-moderate phobic anxiety clients will often be able to begin by picturing the most anxiety-provoking scene, or one close to the top of their hierarchy. When assigning tasks for clients between sessions, for example, real-world exposure, it is usually necessary to construct more careful hierarchies and without the therapist present, clients may wish to begin lower down the ranking and work their way up. For example, a socially anxious client might construct a list of situations where she wishes to assert herself and rank them according to difficulty. Although some clients benefit from being "pushed to challenge themselves", within reasonable bounds, others will make better progress by starting with small steps, at the bottom of their list, and working toward tackling the more challenging items over time.

Another feature of hierarchy construction is that lists of scenes were traditionally divided into different "themes". To pick a simple example, a client who fears both moths and spiders might construct two hierarchies: one for moths and another for spiders. Some clinicians and researchers have argued that this is also unnecessary, as anxiety reduction tends to generalise to loosely related situations, especially when the client is led to expect this, and the anxiety-reduction is attributed to general-purpose coping skills which he is employing. Hence, in some cases, a hierarchy could be constructed composed of different insects, or even containing totally unrelated scenes such as social anxiety situations. It's also possible to create a hierarchy by gradually eliminating unnecessary coping skills or safety-behaviours, for example, low difficulty tasks might be completed while using relaxation techniques as a temporary "crutch" to be abandoned on subsequent tasks.

Three/four systems (ABC model)

Three-systems (ABC) conceptualisation

One of the most important conceptualisation models for this approach to cognitive-behavioural hypnotherapy, distinguishes between the three "response systems" of affect, behaviour, and cognition. In the 1920s, the psychotherapist and hypnotist Charles Baudouin employed a three-dimensional model. He even labels the categories "ABC", although in a different sequence from the one used elsewhere in this volume, and so I have taken the liberty of switching the letters to make them consistent with the format used here. Baudouin writes, "A simple classification is the following:"

> A. Instances belonging to the *affective* domain (joy or sorrow, emotions, sentiments, tendencies, passions);
>
> B. Instances belonging to the active or *motor* domain (actions, volitions, desires, gestures, movements at the periphery or in the interior of the body, functional or organic modifications);
>
> C. Instances belonging to the *representative* domain (sensations, mental images, dreams, visions, memories, opinions, and all intellectual phenomena). (Baudouin, 1920, p. 41, my italics)

He specifically argues that different types of hypnotic suggestion or autosuggestion can engender affects (A), motor behaviour (B), and representations (C, cognitions). This can be expressed in another simple "ABC" acronym:

1. *Affect*. The client's mood and emotions, under which we can subsume, for convenience, conative factors such as desires and aversions as well as physical sensations.
2. *Behaviour*. External (overt) behaviour, including audible speech; the things we say and do.
3. *Cognition*. Thoughts, whether verbalised or unspoken, especially those of a verbal nature; may be closely associated with mental imagery.

Other cognitive-behavioural hypnotherapists have embraced the familiar three-dimensional orientation.

> In our view, therapeutic results are more enduring if symptom amelioration includes the modification of thoughts, feelings and behaviour patterns that maintain the symptoms. (Golden, Dowd & Freidberg, 1987, p. 7)

This simple affective, behavioural, and cognitive (ABC) distinction not only helps us keep in mind the inter-dependence of maintaining factors, but helps us to analyse the relationship between different modes of therapeutic treatment.

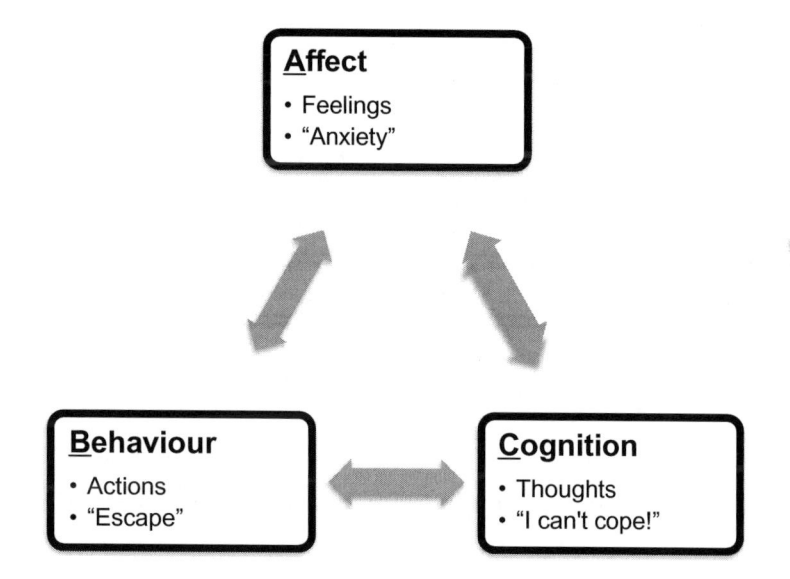

Affect
- Feelings
- "Anxiety"

Behaviour
- Actions
- "Escape"

Cognition
- Thoughts
- "I can't cope!"

Likewise, the original daily thought records employed by Beck and his colleagues as homework assignments employ columns to record the situation (date/time) and the client's corresponding affect (emotions), behaviour, and cognitions (automatic thoughts). As Persons points out, this form can be regarded as the basis of a kind of "mini-formulation" at the level of the specific situation (Persons & Davidson, 2001, p. 88).

Sometimes physical sensations or symptoms may be incorporated into this diagram, for example, by noting them in the centre (Stern & Drummond, 1991, p. 14). However, many therapists prefer to further distinguish between "feelings" in the sense of emotions and bodily sensations. For example, Donald Tosi and his colleagues combined REBT and hypnotherapy to develop a hybrid cognitive-behavioural hypnotherapy approach called "rational stage directed hypnotherapy" (RSDH), later renamed "cognitive experiential therapy" (CET). Their approach distinguishes between emotional, physiological, and behavioural consequences of irrational beliefs (cognitions), extending Ellis' original "ABC" model into a five-factor "ABCDE" model (Tosi & Baisden, 1984, p. 156).

A. Activating event or situation
B. Cognitive function
C. Affective responses
D. Physiological responses
E. Behavioural responses.

This kind of descriptive conceptualisation approach is also called a "five aspects" or "hot-cross bun" model because it refers to four aspects of the client's response, the fifth aspect being the environmental triggers (Greenberger & Padesky, 1995, p. 4). Specifying physiological symptoms or bodily sensations as a distinct category can be especially useful with problems centred on reactions to specific bodily sensations such as panic attacks or health anxiety.

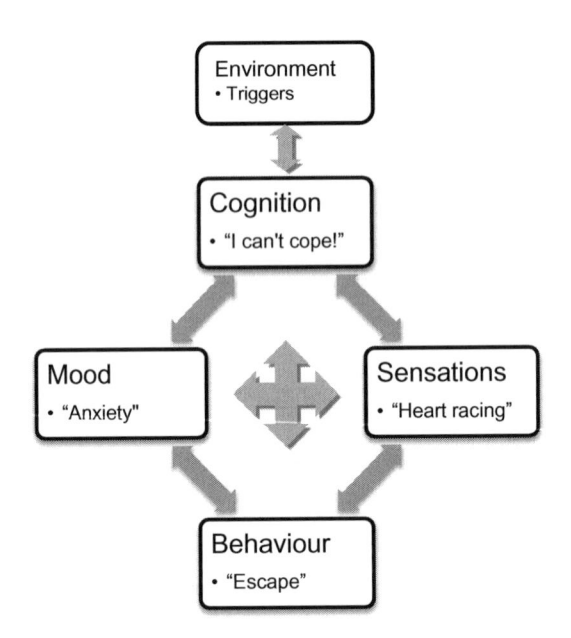

```
           Environment
           • Triggers
               ↕
           Cognition
           • "I can't cope!"
         ↙    ↕    ↘
   Mood              Sensations
 • "Anxiety"        • "Heart racing"
         ↘    ↕    ↙
           Behaviour
           • "Escape"
```

Although this is undoubtedly a very common, generic, and popular way of diagramming clients' problems, it does have some obvious flaws, which have been highlighted in the literature (Westbrook, Kennerley & Kirk, 2007, pp. 61–62). The main problem, arguably, is that the therapist may be tempted to simply draw lines between the boxes without clarifying exactly what the relationships might be between these elements. Moreover, different "cognitions", "behaviours", etc., are sometimes lumped together in a way that potentially obscures crucial differences between their subtypes and interactions between them. For example, Beck's model of anxiety has always distinguished between thoughts which appraise the seriousness of a threat (primary appraisal) and those which appraise one's ability to cope with it (secondary appraisal) (Beck A. T., 1976, pp. 63–64). These thoughts may typically occur at different stages and interact importantly with each other. There are many distinctions to be made between different types of behaviour, for example, automatic versus deliberate, helpful versus unhelpful, overt versus covert, etc. The functional relationship between the relevant elements of the conceptualisation therefore needs to be investigated collaboratively with the client in more detail over time.

Functional analysis (ABC model)

Several different "ABC" models are used in psychotherapy, especially within the CBT tradition. Functional analysis (or "behavioural analysis") in CBT is derived from the operant conditioning approach to behavioural psychology. It tends to focus, in a relatively simple manner, on the immediate chronological sequence of events surrounding a problem behaviour. The function of the behaviour is analysed in terms of the antecedent stimuli which trigger it and the consequences that increase its future probability of recurring, that is, reinforcing it. We naturally think of this in terms of simple reward and punishment, for example, a dog being given a treat for raising its paw or being beaten for chewing the slippers. However, the process of "negative reinforcement" is particularly important to CBT conceptualisation, whereby a behaviour is "rewarded" not by some positive occurrence but rather by the negation or non-occurrence of something aversive. The most obvious example of negative reinforcement would be anxiety or tension being relieved by escape behaviour, that is, leaving a feared situation. The more often this happens, the stronger the desire to flee the situation will become in the future, through constant negative reinforcement. Similarly, the behaviour of smoking a cigarette may temporarily relieve the discomfort caused by nicotine cravings, strengthening the habit over time, again through continual negative reinforcement. A simple "Antecedents-Behaviour-Consequences" (ABC) diagram, representing the most basic form of functional analysis, might look as follows:

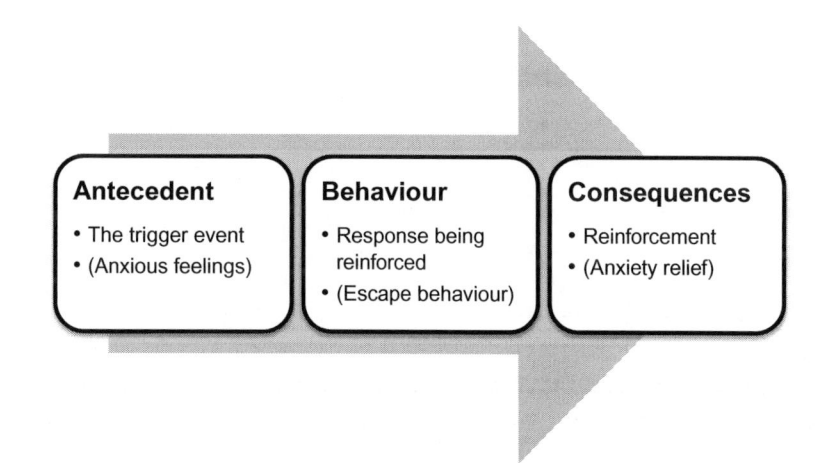

Antecedent
- The trigger event
- (Anxious feelings)

Behaviour
- Response being reinforced
- (Escape behaviour)

Consequences
- Reinforcement
- (Anxiety relief)

It's also useful to distinguish between the short and long-term consequences of behaviour. The issue of long-term consequences should be raised early in treatment simply by asking: "How's that working out for you in the long-term?" Long-term negative consequences of a maladaptive behaviour can typically be divided into worsening of symptoms, such as anxiety, and impact on functioning across different domains of life, such as work, relationships, leisure, etc.

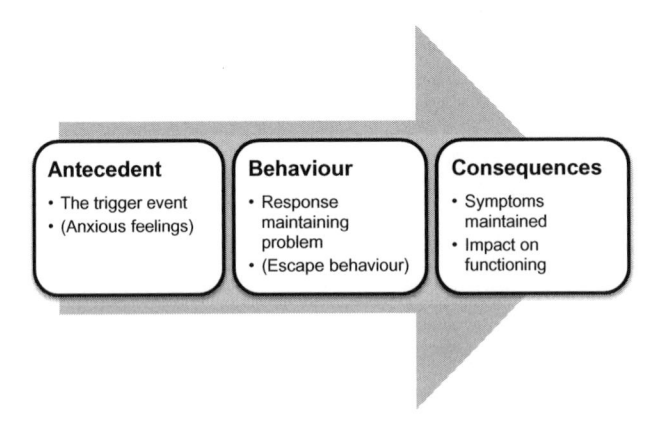

Antecedent
- The trigger event
- (Anxious feelings)

Behaviour
- Response maintaining problem
- (Escape behaviour)

Consequences
- Symptoms maintained
- Impact on functioning

This type of conceptualisation is extremely useful early in therapy, as a means of evaluating the client's existing coping strategies and safety-seeking behaviours, etc.

Activation-beliefs-consequences (ABC)

Albert Ellis, the founder of rational-emotive behaviour therapy (REBT), developed a very popular cognitive conceptualisation approach referred to as the "ABC model", which stands for "activation" (or "activating event"), "beliefs", and "consequences" (Ellis, 1962). This approach was adopted in early cognitive therapy and widely used in other forms of CBT (Beck, Rush, Shaw & Emery, 1979).

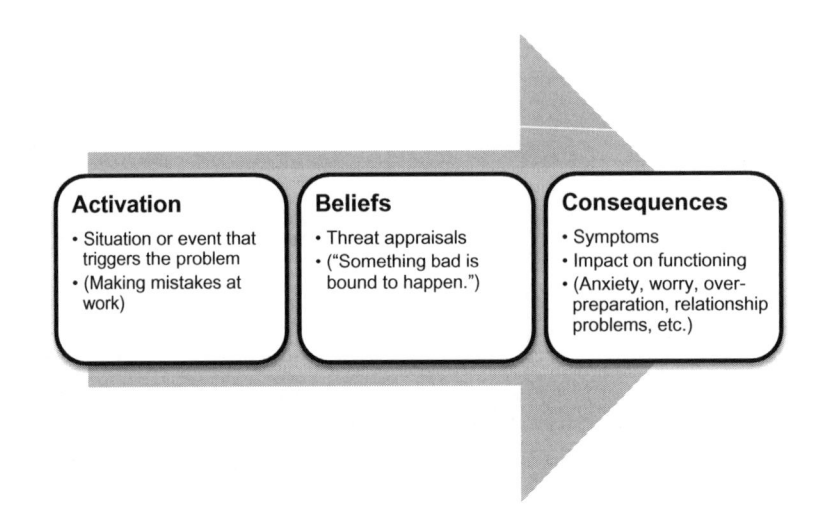

Activation
- Situation or event that triggers the problem
- (Making mistakes at work)

Beliefs
- Threat appraisals
- ("Something bad is bound to happen.")

Consequences
- Symptoms
- Impact on functioning
- (Anxiety, worry, over-preparation, relationship problems, etc.)

The same model can easily be adapted to cognitive-behavioural hypnotherapy by discussing the concepts of "negative autosuggestion" or "negative self-hypnosis" as equivalent to mediating beliefs in CBT.

Basic longitudinal conceptualisation

It is essential in any psychotherapy to make a fundamental distinction between remote ("distal") and recent or ongoing ("proximal") causal factors, that is, the reasons why something happened in the first place, and the reasons why it still continues. The cardinal question of modern psychotherapy is not "Why did I become like this?" but "How am I maintaining this?" or perhaps "Why haven't I simply grown out of it over time?" However, information on the history of a problem and its development is often of great value to the conceptualisation.

Perhaps the most basic form of "longitudinal" conceptualisation, describing the chronological development of a problem, distinguishes between predisposing, precipitating, and perpetuating factors (Stern & Drummond, 1991, p. 15). In other words, vulnerability, onset, and maintenance are distinguished in the history of the client's problem. This also allows the problem to be understood more in biographical terms, within the broader context of the client's life history.

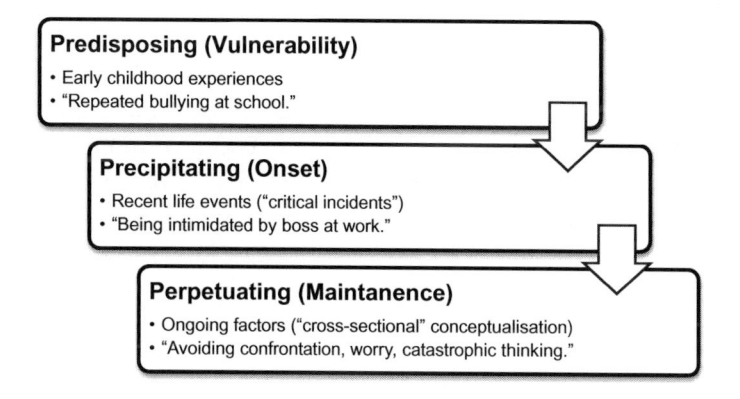

Predisposing (Vulnerability)
- Early childhood experiences
- "Repeated bullying at school."

Precipitating (Onset)
- Recent life events ("critical incidents")
- "Being intimidated by boss at work."

Perpetuating (Maintanence)
- Ongoing factors ("cross-sectional" conceptualisation)
- "Avoiding confrontation, worry, catastrophic thinking."

Major predisposing ("vulnerability") factors include family history and early childhood experiences. For example, a family history of depression or loss of a parent in childhood may increase the risk of an individual subsequently developing depression. Family history may contribute to a problem because of genetic heredity or because of the interpersonal influence of the family upon the child's development. It would be a mistake to assume, as some hypnotherapists employing regression still appear to, that individual traumatic experiences in childhood are the only or even the most common predisposing factors for psychological problems in adulthood. Modelling or vicarious learning (e.g., of a parent's dysfunctional behaviour) may contribute to the development of some problems. Other problems, including many phobias, may be related to the absence of certain learning experiences, for example, lack of exposure to certain feared situations in childhood.

Major precipitating factors ("precipitants") are more easily identified by most clients by asking them, for example, "What was happening in your life when the problem started?" or "What do you think the main thing might have been that triggered the problem?" A distinction should be made between events that occurred when the first major episode initially began and precipitants of subsequent episodes or that contributed to an ongoing problem by exacerbating it.

Major perpetuating ("maintaining") factors are identified in most cross-sectional conceptualisations. These should normally include an analysis of the interaction between cognitions, affect, sensations, and behaviour, of different types, in relation to specific situations or events (as discussed above). The detailed cross-sectional descriptions produced by several situation analyses should typically be used to identify common cognitive themes and behavioural patterns, which can be explicitly linked to the longitudinal conceptualisation by reference to the hierarchical relationship between underlying beliefs and situation-specific thoughts and appraisals, etc. (Beck J. S., 1995).

The cognitive hierarchy and levels of conceptualisation

Clients typically present with specific problems which can usually, albeit with some effort, be linked to specific problem (trigger) situations in their life. For instance, a woman presents with a lack of confidence and the therapist establishes, through sensitive and persistent questioning, that this takes the form of anxiety triggered in social settings where she is expected to speak aloud; a specific example given by her might be speaking to customers on the telephone at work. These concrete "samples" or examples of her problem provide the bedrock for constructing a bottom-up assessment of her more general traits. Focusing initially upon specific situations and responses can help to ground the therapy and avoids the confusion often caused by ambiguity in the consulting room. However, with many clients, it is important to also assess their wider functioning and more general personality traits.

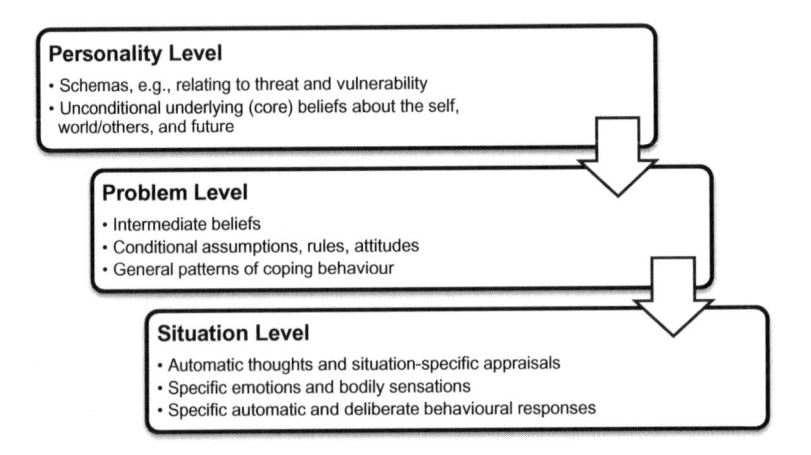

Personality Level
- Schemas, e.g., relating to threat and vulnerability
- Unconditional underlying (core) beliefs about the self, world/others, and future

Problem Level
- Intermediate beliefs
- Conditional assumptions, rules, attitudes
- General patterns of coping behaviour

Situation Level
- Automatic thoughts and situation-specific appraisals
- Specific emotions and bodily sensations
- Specific automatic and deliberate behavioural responses

When reviewing both the client's childhood experiences, and major negative life events, it's useful to ask, "What conclusions do you think you might have drawn about yourself, at the time, based on that experience?" (Sanders & Wills, 2005, p. 47). Similar questions can be used to address the three elements of Beck's cognitive triad by asking the clients what their experiences may have led them to believe about themselves, the world/other people, or their future. It's therefore also possible for the therapist to briefly conceptualise the relationship between hypothetical cognitive structures, using a simple diagram, as follows, that distinguishes between the level of character or personality (core beliefs), the overall problem (rules, assumptions, coping patterns), and the specific situations affected (Persons & Davidson, 2001, p. 87). This is similar to the widely employed hierarchical cognitive conceptualisation approach adopted by Judith Beck, which distinguishes between core beliefs stemming from childhood, intermediate beliefs and patterns of coping across situations, and situation-specific thoughts, actions and feelings (Beck J. S., 1995).

Hypotheses about core beliefs and intermediate rules and assumptions can be derived from direct questioning, sources of evidence such as self-report questionnaires, and especially by looking for common themes across several descriptive conceptualisations of specific situations (Beck J. S., 1995).

Richard Lazarus' "transactional" model of stress

In *Psychological Stress and the Coping Process* (1966) Richard Lazarus laid the foundations of the "transactional" (person-environment) model of "cognitive appraisal" in stress, which Beck and his colleagues subsequently developed into the main cognitive model of anxiety (Beck, Emery & Greenberg, 2005, pp. 37–41; Beck A. T., 1976, pp. 63–64). This was followed by the publication of another influential book, *Stress Appraisal and Coping*, co-authored with Susan Folkman (Lazarus & Folkman, 1984). The technical term "appraisal" is emphasised by Lazarus, and subsequently in Beck's cognitive model of anxiety, because it is intended to denote "an evaluation of the personal significance of what's happening", in terms of one's "well-being", and to do so better than alternative expressions such as "belief", "automatic thought", or "perception" (Lazarus R. S., 1999, pp. 74–75). Appraisals are usually very rapid, situation-specific, and may occur outside conscious awareness, much like Beck's concept of "automatic thoughts."

This person-environment transaction or "seesaw" model of stress interprets the level of anxiety experienced as a function of the extent to which the appraisal of perceived threat (or damage to one's goals) in a specific situation outweighs the individual's appraisal of his ability to cope and to deflect or minimise harm, that is, his self-confidence in the face of a perceived threat (Beck A. T., 1976, pp. 63–64). Hence, Beck and his colleagues sum up the anxious client's thinking as: "Something bad is going to happen that I won't be able to handle" (Beck, Emery & Greenberg, 2005, p. 201). Put crudely, someone extremely low in confidence, seeing herself as weak and helpless, may feel anxious and overwhelmed even by a minor threat. Equally, even someone high in confidence, seeing herself as strong and capable, will feel anxious when faced with a threat they perceive as imminent and extremely dangerous, for example, potentially life-threatening. The degree to which the "seesaw" transaction between coping and threat tips *toward* threat and *away* from coping is sometimes referred to as the level of perceived "risk" (Beck A. T., 1976, p. 248) or the "risk-resources equation" (Pretzer & Beck, 2007, p. 468).

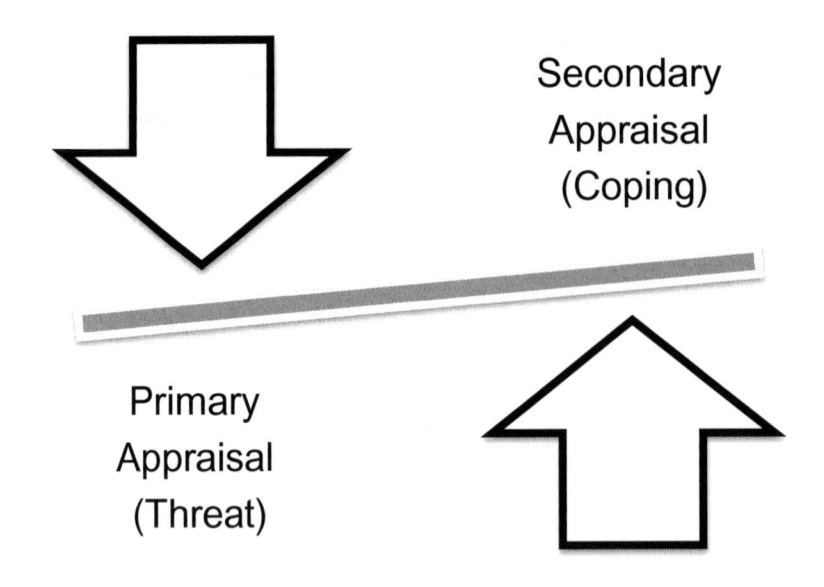

[Diagram: a balance scale tipped with "Primary Appraisal (Threat)" (down arrow) on the lower left and "Secondary Appraisal (Coping)" (up arrow) on the upper right.]

Lazarus construed appraisal of threat and coping as based upon assumptions about one's goals (and their hierarchy), general beliefs about oneself and the world, and one's personal resources (Lazarus R. S., 1999, p. 70). In particular, he emphasised that personal goals are fundamental to stress and anxiety, as demands are stressful to the extent that they conflict with or impinge upon one's perceived interests. In other words, by "threat" we normally mean a threat to one's goals or "vital interests", as Beck puts it (Beck, Emery & Greenberg, 2005). "The important principle here is that, if there is no goal commitment, there is nothing of adaptational importance at stake in an encounter to arouse a stress reaction" (Lazarus R. S., 1999, p. 76). General goals, and specific intentions in the situation, determine the perceived relevance of threat. Assessment of personal goals and concerns is emphasised more in the conceptualisation of generalised anxiety disorder (GAD), where anxiety tends to range across a variety of different threats to a number of personal goals (Clark & Beck, 2010, pp. 419–420).

Lazarus' "transactional" model of stress distinguishes between the following logical steps; although these components may closely interact and do not necessarily occur in this order:

1. Primary cognitive appraisal (of threat)
2. Secondary cognitive appraisal (of coping)
3. Problem-focused coping
4. Emotion-focused coping
5. Reappraisal of threat and coping.

"Primary appraisal" of threat in Lazarus' model, which is logically rather than chronologically "primary", involves a near-instantaneous evaluation of the extent to which a situation is relevant to and threatens one's personal goals and situation-specific intentions (Lazarus R. S., 1999, p. 75). According to this model, primary appraisal involves evaluating the relevance of a threat to our well-being, in terms of personal goal commitments, and initial predictions of the outcome (Lazarus R. S., 1999, p. 76). In considering the concept of stress more broadly, Lazarus distinguished between three types of primary appraisals: "harm/loss", "threat", and "challenge." These terms denote actual "harm" or "loss", which has already occurred, the uncertain possibility of future "threat", and more normal "challenges", which may be seen as a positive experience or opportunity (Lazarus R. S., 1999, p. 76). Cognitive therapy of anxiety is mainly concerned with the concept of exaggerated "threat" appraisal, which may be replaced by the appraisal of the situation as a more mundane "challenge". This shift in the quality of the appraisal, from seeing environmental demands as challenges rather than threats, is explicitly emphasised in the problem-solving therapy (PST) concept of developing a positive "problem orientation", that is, encouraging the client to view problems more confidently and optimistically as mere challenges-to-be-overcome rather than severe threats-to-be-avoided (D'Zurilla & Nezu, 2007). Indeed, some recent cognitive therapy interventions focus on encouraging clients to think of threat and challenge (or "opportunity") as opposite ends of a continuum rather than different categories, and to appraise their problem situations as being located part-way along the continuum, that is, as simultaneously both threatening and challenging rather than exclusively one or the other (Robichaud & Dugas, 2006, pp. 296–297).

"Secondary appraisal", which logically follows, involves an evaluation of one's relevant "coping options" and abilities. "Secondary appraising refers to a cognitive-evaluative process that is focus on what can be done about a stressful person-environment relationship, especially when there has been a primary appraisal of harm, threat or challenge" (Lazarus R. S., 1999, p. 76). Cognitive appraisal of coping, judging the options, tends to precede *actual* coping. However, the distinction sometimes becomes blurred as "an active search for information and meaning on which to predicate action" can constitute a form of coping response itself (Lazarus R. S., 1999, p. 76). The potential for just thinking about coping in more constructive way (secondary appraisal) to form a kind of coping response in itself may be compared to the role of systematic problem-solving procedures in PST, or the development of "coping plans" in cognitive therapy, which may sometimes reduce stress or anxiety prior to the chosen behaviour being implemented (Clark & Beck, 2010; D'Zurilla & Nezu, 2007). Indeed, what primary appraisal initially evaluated as a "threat", secondary appraisal can turn into a mere "challenge".

> The more confident we are of our capacity to overcome obstacles and dangers, the more likely we are to be challenged rather than threatened and vice versa, a sense of inadequacy promotes threat. Because confidence in ourselves varies greatly among different people, individuals differ in whether they are more prone to experience threat or challenge. We can think of this tendency as a personality trait and a concept like self-efficacy [from Bandura] applies. (Lazarus R. S., 1999, p. 77)

Beck's model of anxiety describes this trait-like predisposition to secondary appraisal of poor coping (low "self-efficacy") in terms of a general cognitive schema of personal vulnerability, which becomes activated in certain situations. However, the appraisals derived from this schema can be modified. Lazarus describes the kind of questions implicitly evaluated in secondary appraisal as follows:

"Do I need to act?"
"When should I act?"
"What can be done?"
"Is it feasible?"
"Which option is best?"
"Am I capable of doing it?"
"What are the costs and benefits?"
"Do the costs exceed the damage, and might it be better not to act?"
"What might be the consequences of each alternative type of response, say, acting or not acting?"
(Lazarus R. S., 1999, p. 78)

This way of describing spontaneous secondary appraisal clearly resembles the prescriptive steps of problem-solving therapy (D'Zurilla & Nezu, 2007). In other words, secondary appraisal can also be carried out consciously and systematically as a way of deliberately coping with stress and one may even be trained in deliberate reappraisal of coping.

Actual "coping attempts" normally follow cognitive appraisal of demand (threat) and coping. Coping efforts are then reappraised in terms of their influence upon the situation, that is, whether things have improved or got worse as a result of what one did in response. Lazarus and his colleague Susan Folkman had originally defined coping as "constantly changing cognitive and behavioural efforts to manage specific external and/or internal demands that are appraised as taxing or exceeding the resources of the person", which Lazarus summed up simply as meaning, "coping is the effort to manage psychological stress" (Lazarus R. S., 1999, pp. 110–111). However, the relational model also made an important distinction between two modes of coping (Folkman & Moskowitz, 2004, p. 751; Lazarus R. S., 1999, p. 77;114;).

1. "Problem-focused" (or "instrumental") coping, which targets the *actual* transaction, either by changing something about oneself or the demands of the environment, for example, problem-solving or planning steps, etc.
2. "Emotion-focused" (or "palliative") coping, which targets the emotional distress caused by the transaction, for example, through avoidance, distraction, use of drugs or alcohol, or reassurance-seeking, etc.

It is difficult to make a clear-cut distinction between coping skills on the basis of whether they are emotion or problem-focused because most can be either or both at once, for example, physical exercise can be used as a distraction or way of elevating mood but it can also solve practical problems such as unfitness or wanting to lose weight, etc. However, the distinction has been used extensively in the stress literature. Nevertheless, more recently researchers in the stress field have proposed a distinction between these and other broad categories of coping (Folkman & Moskowitz, 2004, p. 752).

3. "Meaning-focused" coping (or "positive reappraisal"), which involves active cognitive restructuring of the perceived meaning of the situation by trying to see the positive side of things, considering alternative views, modifying causal attributions, drawing on personal values, beliefs, and goals to reinterpret events, employing humour, acceptance, etc.
4. "Seeking social-support", which may consist either of instrumental (practical) support or emotional support, etc.

In a broad overview of the literature on stress and coping, Folkman recently concluded:

> We have found that coping is strongly associated with the regulation of emotion, especially distress, throughout the stress process. We have found that certain kinds of escapist coping strategies are consistently associated with poor mental health outcomes, while other kinds of coping—such as the seeking of social support or instrumental, problem-focused forms of coping—are sometimes associated with negative outcomes, sometimes with positive ones, and sometimes with neither, usually depending on characteristics of the appraised stressful encounter. […] And we have learned that coping skills can be taught through cognitive-behavioral therapies. (Folkman & Moskowitz, 2004, pp. 747–748)

One natural tendency is for emotion-focused coping to predominate when situations are appraised as being unchangeable (Lazarus R. S., 1999, p. 121). The idea that matching coping style to appraisal of controllability should lead to better coping outcomes is sometimes termed the "goodness of fit" hypothesis.

> Theoretically, appraisals of control call for greater proportions of active, instrumental problem-focused forms of coping, and appraisals of lack of control call for more active or passive emotion-focused coping. (Folkman & Moskowitz, 2004, p. 755)

Lazarus cites the Serenity Prayer used in Alcoholics Anonymous as a neat example of the considerations in secondary appraisal of coping (Lazarus R. S., 1999, p. 80).

God grant me the courage to change what can be changed, the serenity to accept what cannot be changed, and the wisdom to know the difference.

However, there is currently mixed support for the "goodness of fit" hypothesis in the stress and coping research literature (Folkman & Moskowitz, 2004, pp. 755–756). There is some tentative support for the more general hypothesis that increased "coping flexibility", or the use of a wide repertoire of coping strategies across different situations rather than a narrow or rigid style of coping, may be associated with greater well-being (Folkman & Moskowitz, 2004, p. 756). Moreover, there has been some emphasis on the problematic nature of certain emotion-focused coping strategies.

> In the majority of studies of coping and adjustment, emotion-focused coping has been associated with higher levels of distress. (Folkman & Moskowitz, 2004, p. 761)

However, "emotion-focused" coping may be an overly broad category and recent literature on stress and coping makes a more refined distinction between emotional "avoidance" and "emotional approach" types of coping. Hence, Beck emphasises the careful evaluation of the client's reliance on emotion-focused coping, as opposed to problem-focused, as part of cognitive therapy assessment for anxiety disorders (Clark & Beck, 2010, pp. 148–149). He recommends doing this by asking clients to complete detailed checklists reporting the frequency and perceived effectiveness of different types of coping strategies.

Lazarus also distinguished between "cognitive coping", which involves positive reappraisal of the person-environment relationship, and behavioural attempts at coping (Lazarus R. S., 1999, p. 77). However, having distinguished these various components, Lazarus subsequently emphasised the fact that they actually tend to occur as different aspects of a single transaction (Lazarus R. S., 1999). In most situations, coping naturally consists of both problem-focused and emotion-focused strategies, and tends to involve both cognitive reappraisal and behavioural coping responses, in various combinations (Lazarus R. S., 1999, p. 78). The *Ways of Coping Questionnaire* has been used to conduct research on different coping styles, which have been analysed into the following broad factors (Lazarus R. S., 1999, p. 115).

1. Confrontive coping, that is, putting up a fight for what you want, trying to persuade other people to change, expressing anger, etc.
2. Distancing, that is, making light of a situation, refusing to dwell on it, trying to forget about it, etc.
3. Self-controlling, that is, trying to keep feelings to yourself, not telling others, trying not to act impulsively.
4. Seeking social support, that is, talking to others for information, to get help, or for advice, etc.
5. Accepting responsibility, that is, self-criticism, attributing the problem to your own actions, promising to handle things differently in future, etc.
6. Escape-avoidance, that is, wishing the situation would go away, wishing for a miracle, avoiding other people, etc.
7. Planful problem solving, that is, making more effort to fix things, making and following an action plan, making practical changes, etc.
8. Positive reappraisal, that is, adapting (growing) positively as a person, learning from the experience, developing faith, etc.

Lazarus claimed that one of the main generalisations that can be drawn from the research literature is that in any given situation, on average, people would use almost all of the strategies listed above to cope with stress (Lazarus R. S., 1999, p. 119). Planful problem solving and positive reappraisal have generally been found the most reliable forms of coping with stress, which loosely support problem-solving therapy and cognitive therapy, respectively (Lazarus R. S., 1999, p. 122). However, other strategies are sometimes better. Indeed, Lazarus concluded from the extant research on stress and coping that "no universally effective or ineffective coping strategy exists". Different coping strategies are good or bad for different people, and different problems, under different conditions, and at different times, including at different chronological stages in the development of a problem.

> It is not valid to assume that the way an individual copes with one threat will be the same as that chosen for a different threat. The evidence, in fact, tells us otherwise. A *key principle*

is that the choice of coping strategy will usually vary with the adaptational significance and requirements of each threat and its status as a disease, which will change over time. (Lazarus R. S., 1999, p. 111)

This observation is fundamental to flexible multi-component coping skills approaches such as stress-inoculation training (SIT) and problem-solving therapy (PST), which will be discussed in later chapters in relation to cognitive-behavioural hypnotherapy (D'Zurilla & Nezu, 2007; Meichenbaum, 1985). Both of these forms of cognitive-behavioural therapy eschew "cookbook" approaches to managing stress or anxiety, based on formulaic techniques, and focus instead on helping clients to systematically identify, apply, and evaluate different coping skills for different problems, within a more versatile methodological framework.

Finally, reappraisal of threat refers to the subsequent modification of initial emotional responses by "cognitive coping" or reinterpreting the personal meaning of the situation.

Reappraising is an effective way to cope with a stressful situation, perhaps one of the most effective. However, it is sometimes difficult to distinguish from an ego defense [or cognitive avoidance], such as denial. When the personal meaning of what is happening fits the evidence, it is not an ego defense, but one of the most durable and powerful ways of controlling destructive emotions. (Lazarus R. S., 1999, p. 116)

In other words, it is sometimes difficult to distinguish between genuine cognitive restructuring, of the kind espoused in cognitive therapy, and maladaptive attempts at thought-control or cognitive avoidance such as "trying to think positively" or thought suppression, etc. This concept of reappraisal therefore denotes the main stage at which cognitive therapy normally intervenes.

Lazarus' relational model of stress and coping is usually employed during the conceptualisation stages of several cognitive-behavioural approaches, including stress-inoculation training (SIT) and problem-solving therapy (PST). However, it also forms the basis of the more elaborate, generic model of anxiety, and its diagnosis-specific variations, currently proposed by Beck and his colleagues for use in cognitive therapy (Clark & Beck, 2010). One limitation of Lazarus' original model is that it has little to say about *positive* emotions, which may be significant as subsequent research has emphasised the presence of both positive and negative emotions in coping with even extreme stress (Folkman & Moskowitz, 2004, pp. 747, 764–765).

Beck's original cognitive model of anxiety

From the outset, Beck has referred to the cognitive model as "turning anxiety on its head", reversing the tendency of clients to overlook the role of the "head", or cognition, and focus instead on their anxious feelings or symptoms (Beck, Emery & Greenberg, 2005, p. 6). In cognitive therapy the term "fear" is used to refer to the immediate (automatic) cognitive appraisal of threat, whereas "anxiety" refers to the ongoing emotional response to the appraisal (Beck, Emery & Greenberg, 2005, p. 9). This is consistent with common usage insofar as people speak of "fearing" events in the future, without necessarily feeling "anxious" until they are near at hand. Fear, the automatic appraisal of threat as impending, has always been at the heart of Beck's cognitive model of anxiety (Clark & Beck, 2012, p. 15). Cognitive therapy therefore focuses on identifying the client's "core fear", the faulty appraisal of threat that underlies irrational or excessive anxiety (Clark & Beck, 2012, p. 27).

Following on from Lazarus' influential "transactional" model of cognitive appraisal in the stress response, in his first book on cognitive therapy, Beck summarises the cognitive model of anxiety as follows:

> We label anticipation of damage fear, and the unpleasant emotional reaction anxiety. If a person feels confident in his ability to cope with or repel the threat, anxiety is minimized. It is increased when he considers the potential damage to his domain as imminent, highly probable, and highly destructive. Anxiety may be further increased by uncertainty with regard to when the harm may occur. (Beck A. T., 1976, p. 63)

Different forms of anxiety may, to some extent, be distinguished in terms of problems which primarily relate to danger versus coping. For example, GAD clients may perceive themselves as helpless and inadequate, and overwhelmed by daily hassles, which are not particularly "serious" or life-threatening, suggesting that appraisal of coping is the dominant problem. By contrast, clients with panic attacks may believe they are going to die immediately of a heart attack, when they feel certain trigger sensations, which is mainly an issue of faulty threat appraisal. Of course, most clients tend both to exaggerate threat and to trivialise their coping ability, although the emphasis obviously differs.

The cognitive model of anxiety interprets it as a "vicious cycle" or "spiral" in which fear, or an initial appraisal of threat, leads to behavioural and physiological symptoms of anxiety, and possibly problems in the environment, particularly negative responses from other people, which are appraised as further signs of both threat ("I'm going to have a heart attack!") or vulnerability ("I can't cope!"). This, of course, increases fear and anxiety, which escalates symptoms, and so on, represented in the simplified diagram below (Beck, Emery & Greenberg, 2005, pp. 46–48).

Anxiety mode and "dual belief system"

The concept of a "dual belief system" is integral to the cognitive model of anxiety, particularly in relation to phobia (Beck A. T., 1976, pp. 161–165). Phobics exhibit a marked discrepancy between appraisals of threat and vulnerability when the anxious mode is activated, and threat is near, and the same appraisals when in a non-anxious mode, when threat is distant. In his first book on cognitive therapy, Beck made a simple but important observation which is easily replicated by any therapist conducting behavioural experiments that involve exposure to feared situations: the probability and severity appraisals of anxious clients become progressively greater as they approach the threat situation.

> I have tested this observation many times by asking phobic patients to estimate the probabilities of harm. At a distance from the phobic situation, for example, a patient may state that the possibility of harm is almost zero. As he approaches the situation, the odds change. He goes

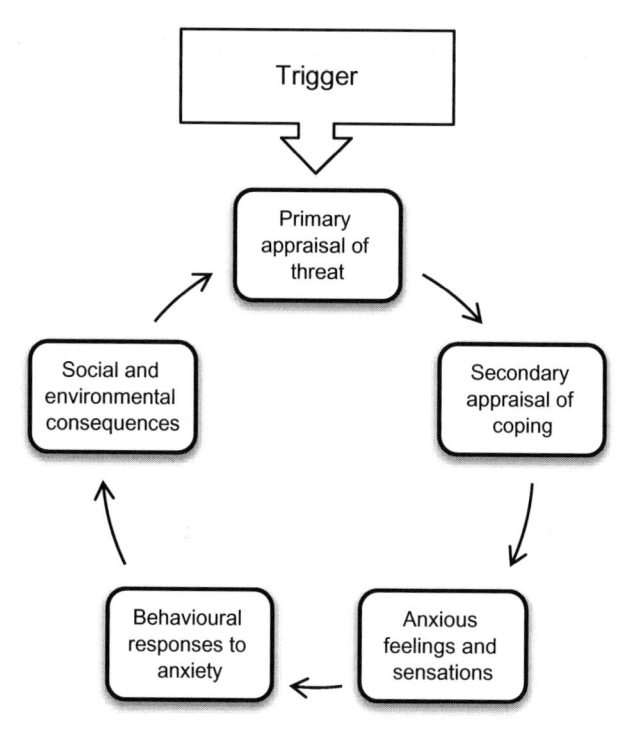

Figure 4. Simplified vicious-cycle model of anxiety.

to 10 percent, to 50 percent, and finally in the situation, he may believe 100 percent that harm will occur. (Beck A. T., 1976, p. 164)

For example, someone who fears flying may rate the probability of his plane crashing as less than one per cent when relaxed, in the therapist's consulting room, but this rating would typically increase, maybe even to 100 per cent, during a flight, at the peak level of his anxiety—logically, however, the probability should remain the same regardless of his proximity to the perceived threat. Beck recommends that the case conceptualisation for anxiety, as standard, includes information on the client's appraisals of threat and coping when anxious versus when non-anxious. Beck defines the concept of a "mode" as follows:

> Under ordinary circumstances, the cognitive set [i.e., schema] varies in response to changes in the nature of the stimulus situation. If the content persists over diverse situations, the set is reflecting the bias of a superordinate organizing principle labelled the "mode." The mode is a subsystem of the cognitive organization and is designed to consummate certain adaptational principles relevant to survival, maintenance, breeding, self-enhancement, and so on. Thus, we have a depressive mode, a narcissistic mode, a hostility mode, a fear (or danger) [i.e., threat] mode, an erotic mode, and so on. (Beck, Emery & Greenberg, 2005, p. 59)

These can be compared to the concept of a "normal" or "confident" mode. The anxious mode, with which we are primarily concerned here, is also referred to as the "primal threat mode", to emphasise its evolutionary heritage. The concept is therefore related to the primitive "fight-or-flight" response. It's fundamental to the cognitive model of anxiety that appraisals of threat and vulnerability in the anxiety mode, when threat is perceived as near, will tend to be more distorted than appraisals made in the non-anxious mode, sometimes referred to as the "dual belief system" of anxiety.

The final stage of Beck's conceptualisation process involves asking the client to rate the level of threat and her ability to cope as judged when she is feeling anxious versus when she is feeling "normal", that is, relatively safe and relaxed, etc. This usually illustrates quite clearly how judgement is distorted during activation of the anxiety mode, as clients will tend to rate the threat level as lower and their ability to cope as higher when they have some distance from the situation or event, and are able to reflect upon it more calmly. The therapist should emphasise this difference in order to help socialise clients to the cognitive model and to normalise the fact that the thoughts that they experience at the peak of their anxiety may seem much less convincing (or even absurd) when talking normally in the consulting room, which can otherwise seem like a contradiction and confuse them.

> The phobic person seems to hold simultaneously two sets of contradictory beliefs about the probability of the occurrence of harm when in the situation he fears. When removed from the feared situation, he beliefs the situation is relatively harmless: the fear he experiences is proportional to the amount of objective risk in the situation. As he approaches the phobic situation, he becomes increasingly anxious and perceives the situation to be increasingly dangerous. [...] His belief switches from the concept "it is harmless" to "it is dangerous." The notion that phobic individuals can have contradictory beliefs about a feared situation—"dual belief systems"—has been ignored in much of the technical literature on phobias. (Beck, Emery & Greenberg, 2005, pp. 127–128)

It's frequently observed that phobic clients in particular tend to appraise feared situations quite realistically and even deny experiencing any negative automatic thoughts or images, yet when confronted with exposure, when their anxiety is aroused, the same clients "change their tune" and report powerful and convincing thoughts and images of some feared catastrophe. As Beck puts it, appraisals of the probability of actual harm may be very low (less than thirty per cent) when the threat is still at a distance but when they are in the feared situation, this may rapidly escalate and even approach a feeling of 100 per cent certainty that "something bad is going to happen."

Schemas of threat and vulnerability

The anxiety mode is driven by "schemas" (or "schemata", i.e., templates) or underlying cognitive meaning-making structures, which typically lie beyond normal conscious awareness, the content of which can be expressed in the form of beliefs or predictions (Antony & Swinson, 2000, p. 241). The principal schemas which are activated in the anxiety mode are those related to threat and personal vulnerability or helplessness. When an individual enters a situation she does so "prepared in advance" by the activation of cognitive "schemas", which orient her to potential sources of threat or vulnerability. In some cases, this may lead to a biased appraisal of the probability and severity of threat, etc., and problems with maladaptive anxiety (Beck, Emery & Greenberg, 2005, p. 54). The schemas are implicit cognitive structures, used to assign meaning to the situation. The most important schemas in relation to anxiety, according to Beck's conceptualisation, are those relating to two closely-related factors:

1. *Threat*, that is, signs of potential danger or harm to the individual's vital interests.
2. *Vulnerability*, that is, signs of personal weakness, helplessness, or inability to cope in relation to the perceived dangers.

Beck defines anxious "vulnerability" as follows:

> In this context, vulnerability may be defined as a person's perception of himself as a subject to internal or external dangers over which his control is lacking or is insufficient to afford him a sense of safety. (Beck, Emery & Greenberg, 2005, p. 67)

In his self-help guide, Beck recommends that clients who struggle to identify thoughts about helplessness simply ask themselves whether they feel like they're "losing control" when anxious (Clark & Beck, 2012, p. 35). If so, exploring specifically how they feel they've lost control or what they've lost control over will often shed light on their appraisal and schemas of vulnerability.

"Self-confidence" can be defined as a contrasting (positive) type of appraisal, consisting of positive appraisals of one's assets, resources, sense of control, and coping ability in relation to overcoming a threat (Clark & Beck, 2010, pp. 48–49). Likewise, the appraisal of a situation as a "threat" can be contrasted with the appraisal of "safety" or of demands as "challenges" or opportunities for growth. In relation to Beck's "cognitive triad" model, anxiety threat schemas mainly relate to the world and other people, whereas vulnerability relates primarily to one's implicit *self*-concept; both threat and vulnerability appraisals relate to themes of uncertainty about future problems. As Beck writes, "In anxiety, the self is seen as inadequate (because of deficient resources), the context [i.e., world] is thought to be dangerous, and the future appears uncertain" (Alford & Beck, 1997, p. 16). Beck does not explicitly say so here but future-related (apprehensive) automatic thoughts in anxiety tend to centre upon themes of catastrophic worst-case outcomes ("What if?" thinking) as well as the uncertainty of threat.

In the original cognitive therapy manual for anxiety, Beck et al. emphasised the role of "major concerns" (core beliefs) in the anxious client's treatment and distinguished between three broad clinical themes "derived from his sense of vulnerability", that is, acceptance, competence and control (Beck, Emery & Greenberg, 2005, p. 289, 293). The interpretation of vulnerability appraisals in terms of these subordinate themes can often help to make sense of the client's fears. These major concerns are associated with beliefs or assumptions, which may be unspoken, but nevertheless guide feelings and behaviour. For example, clients may assume "If people criticise me it means they reject me" (acceptance), "I must succeed at work" (competence), or "If I can't cope with my feelings something awful might happen to me" (control). Although cognitive therapy emphasises the restructuring of specific automatic thoughts to begin with, as common themes emerge the focus shifts on to modification of underlying assumptions and "schemas" or major anxious concerns.

Beck's revised cognitive model of anxiety

Beck has revised his cognitive model of anxiety and presents a modified version in his recent treatment manual *Cognitive Therapy of Anxiety Disorders* (Clark & Beck, 2010) based on Clark and Beck's "three-stage, schema-based, information processing model of anxiety" (Beck & Clark, 1997). The three-stage model of anxiety provides a trans-diagnostic conceptualisation, applicable generically to different anxiety disorders. It distinguishes between:

1. The initial "orienting mode" in which signs of danger are registered, biased by selective attention toward and interpretation of threat.
2. The primal threat mode, characterised by the dominance of highly "automatic" cognitive-physiological-behavioural responses.
3. The subsequent activation of a more reflective mode, making greater use of slightly slower and more strategic (deliberate, or "controlled") cognitive and behavioural coping responses.

In other words, "The processing, driven by the activation of cognitive schemas, moves from being automatic and unconscious to conscious and strategic" (Beck, Emery & Greenberg, 2005, p. xv). Beck provides an excellent analogy for the initial orientation to threat, that of the "coast watchers" in England during the Second World War, whose job was to watch the skies for sightings of German bombers approaching across the channel. These people had to become highly-attuned to the threat they were looking out for in order to spot the earliest possible signs of an attack and raise the alarm. The anxious individual is already prepared to spot signs of danger in certain situations, but this preparation for threat can lead to biases of attention and interpretation and "false positive" alarms.

In addition to the concept of preparation and initial orientation, a broad distinction is made between two overlapping styles of subsequent cognitive (information) processing:

1. *Automatic* processing is more effortless, involuntary, and unintentional, non-conscious or partially conscious, relatively fast, difficult to control, rigid, and stereotypical, etc.
2. *Strategic* processing is more effortful, voluntary, and intentional, more fully conscious, slower, more amenable to control, more able to adapt to novelty and complexity, etc.

The three-stage reaction to anxiety is triggered by the initial orienting mode, or "early warning detection system", which operates outside of conscious awareness and automatically registers potential signs of danger, assigning attentional priority to them, at a relatively instantaneous rate of processing, driven mainly by the cues without much high-level cognitive involvement (Beck & Clark, 1997, p. 51). In anxiety, the main problem is that the orienting mode has become excessively attuned to detect signs of personally-relevant threat, thereby predisposing the individual to over-react by activating the automatic primal threat mode, when they are not in genuine danger. The primal threat mode is an evolutionary survival mechanism that consists of the activation of a cluster of schemas relating to immediate preparation for danger and the search for safety, and the somewhat more conscious "primary appraisal" of threat through automatic apprehensive thoughts and images. Basic underlying distortions in cognitive processing occur at this stage due to further selective bias toward the awareness and interpretation of potential threats and an increasing "intolerance of uncertainty." This is associated with a tendency to over-estimate the probability and severity of danger, that is, catastrophic thinking (Beck & Clark, 1997, p. 53). Finally, the "secondary elaboration" stage, or reflective mode, is activated, bringing into play greater processing of the "self-in-relation-to-the-world", evaluation of coping, and activation of the "metacognitive" mode of thinking about thinking (Beck & Clark, 1997, p. 53). At this stage, anxiety may be affected in one of three main directions:

1. Anxiety escalates even further because of worry as the primal threat mode continues to dominate cognitive processing and to distort reappraisal of threat upward and coping downward.
2. Anxiety reduces temporarily and because the primal threat mode creates a drive toward maladaptive defensive behaviour such as escape, avoidance, or safety-seeking.
3. Anxiety reduces more adaptively because the constructive mode is activated and threat and coping are reappraised in a more balanced and realistic manner, which cognitive therapy tries to encourage. (Beck & Clark, 1997, p. 53)

As this model suggests, cognitive therapy aims both to reduce worry and other unhelpful elaborative thinking processes and to prevent cognitive and behavioural avoidance and other maladaptive defensive responses. Instead it promotes the realistic and constructive elaborative reappraisal of threat severity and probability, and one's coping ability and signs of safety or rescue. The central rationale is that this should lead to the deactivation of the primal threat mode and reduction of automatic anxiety thoughts, physiological symptoms, and defensive reactions, etc. Hence, cognitive therapy can be seen, to some extent, as building upon

Initial Registration Phase (Orienting Mode)
• Non-conscious orientation and attentional bias to threat stimuli
• Rapid recognition of external and internal threat cues

Automatic Fear Response (Primal Threat Mode)
• Automatic apprehensive thoughts
• Automatic physiological (autonomic) responses
• Automatic defensive behaviours (safety-seeking)

Strategic Coping Response (Reflective Mode)
• Deliberate coping behaviour (safety-seeking)
• Worry and re-appraisal of threat and coping ability
• Deliberate thought-control strategies

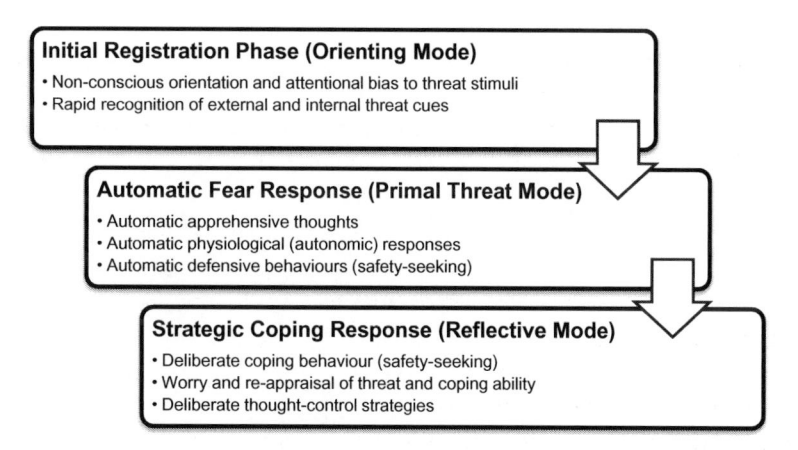

Figure 5. Clark and Beck (1997) Three-stage model of anxiety.

natural and spontaneous ways of overcoming excessive anxiety, through rational and realistic reappraisal of threat, which already occurs in most cases of ordinary psychological functioning (Beck & Clark, 1997, p. 55).

This leads to a comprehensive case conceptualisation approach combining information derived from the initial clinical interview with standardised measures, self-monitoring forms, observation of the client during the session, and other sources of information. However, Beck assumes it will generally take two to three sessions on average to complete a full case conceptualisation, and that it will be updated somewhat throughout treatment (Clark & Beck, 2010, pp. 157–158). In hypnotherapy, assessment and formulation may have to be a somewhat abbreviated version of this because treatment often takes place over fewer sessions than standard CBT. Fortunately, Beck provides a simplified model, which is shared with clients, and might serve as an initial approach from which a more detailed conceptualisation can be progressively developed in subsequent sessions (Clark & Beck, 2010, p. 193). Hence, a simplified version for use with clients in cognitive-behavioural hypnotherapy might be represented as follows:

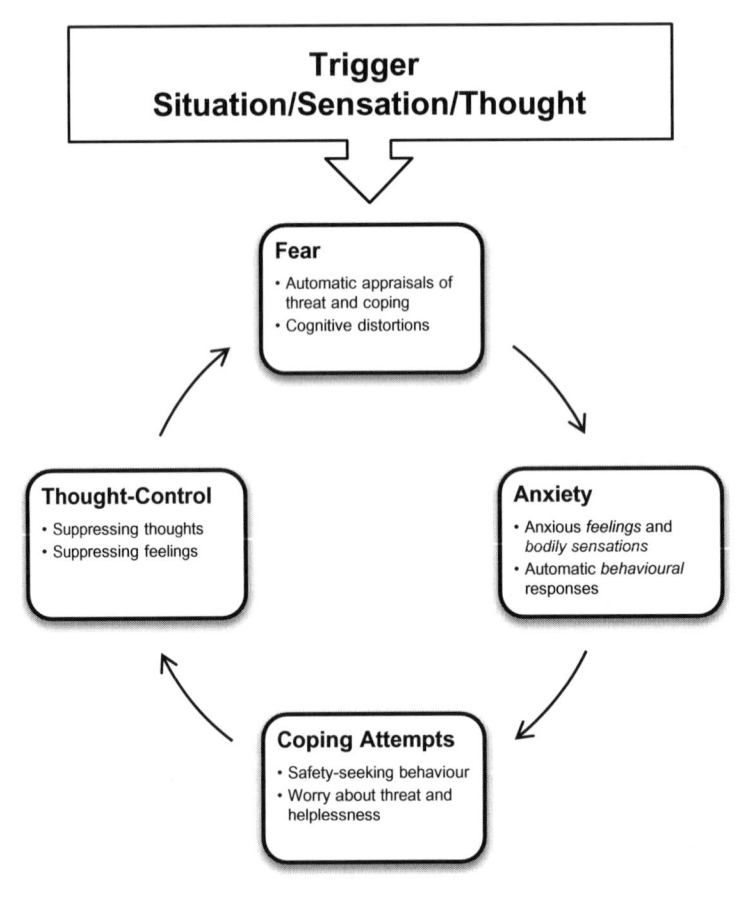

Figure 6. Simplified cognitive model of anxiety (revised).

More detailed analysis for cognitive case conceptualisation can be derived from the model and questions described below.

Immediate fear response

According to Beck, conceptualisation of the immediate fear response must answer three main questions:

1. What is the range of situations and events that trigger the fear response?
2. What is the core schema (appraisal) of threat to the self?
3. What is the immediate defensive or inhibitory behavioural response to the perceived threat? (Clark & Beck, 2010, p. 136)

The situations identified may be characterised in terms of the role of either environmental, interoceptive, or cognitive triggers for the fear response. These triggers activate the threat schema, which typically leads to specific automatic anxious thoughts or "first apprehensive thoughts", defined by Beck as, "brief, sudden, and completely automatic thoughts or images that something bad or unpleasant is about to happen, or at least could happen, to persons or their valued resources" (Clark & Beck, 2010, p. 141). They often take the form of "What if?" questions about some anticipated catastrophe, that is, something "bad" that might happen.

Automatic thoughts and images

These immediate threat-related thoughts and images are difficult to assess because they just "pop" or "flash" into the mind. Clients are often unaware of their existence afterwards, when no longer anxious, and focus instead on reporting their subsequent responses

Situations
- External (environmental) triggers.
- Internal (cognitive or interoceptive) triggers.

Automatic Apprehensive Thoughts
- Thoughts and images related to primary appraisal of threat.
- Probe with questions: "What's the worst that could happen?"

Physiological Sensations
- Symptoms of autonomic hyperarousal, etc.
- Catastrophic interpretations of bodily sensations.

Automatic Inhibitory/Defensive Behaviours
- Cognitive and behavioural avoidance, compulsions, safety-seeking, etc.
- Flight (escape), freeze, faint responses, etc.

Primary Cognitive Processing Errors
- Main types of thinking errors.
- Specific examples of errors.

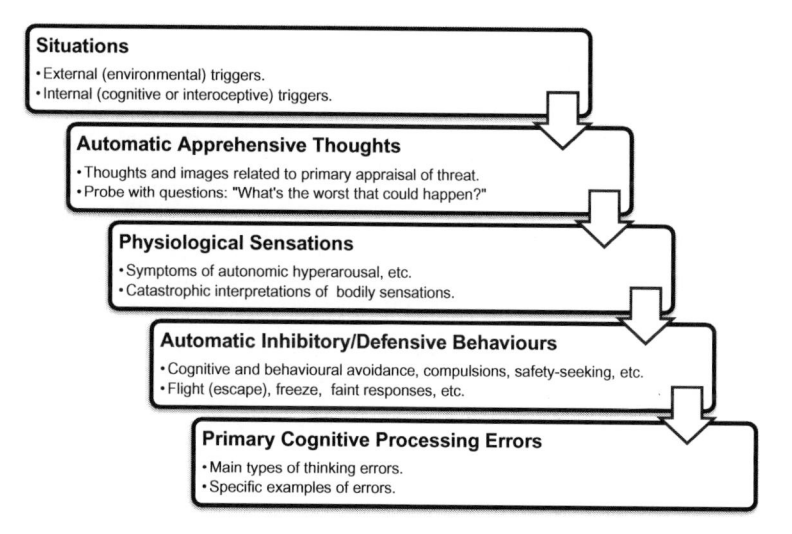

Figure 7. Clark and Beck (2010) Conceptualisation of immediate fear response.

(Clark & Beck, 2010, p. 141). Hence, clients will report "just feeling nervous", without being able to identify the thoughts accompanying their feelings. This is why careful self-monitoring is particularly important to Beck's cognitive therapy, in gathering the "raw data" of fleeting automatic thoughts, which otherwise evade notice. Moreover, when not currently anxious, the client may dismiss possible automatic thoughts as "stupid" or "ridiculous" because they no longer seem based on plausible fears, perhaps even making them somewhat embarrassing to recount. Clients may say, for example, "I don't really believe that" or "I couldn't have really been thinking that, surely?", "It seems absurd now", etc. Beck emphasises that clients need to be socialised to accept the fleeting and easily-missed nature of immediate apprehensive thoughts in anxiety. Questions can be used during assessment to help collaboratively identify the critical thoughts in the immediate fear response. For example:

"What would be the worst that could happen in this situation?"
"What's so bad about the situation?"
"What could be harmful?"
"What's not right or feels disconcerting about the situation?"
"What could change about the situation that might ease your anxiety?"

Again, clients may need to be encouraged to suspend evaluation of what's probable or realistic in order to better identify their own automatic thoughts, which are often quite irrational and unrealistic. Although with different types of anxiety it is sometimes necessary to probe for specific types of thought, the client should be encouraged to express them in her own words (Clark & Beck, 2010, p. 142). As noted earlier, Lynn and Kirsch have likewise pointed out that catastrophic expectations and expectations of anxiety responses are central features of anxiety disorders and panic attack. They therefore describe anxiety disorders as "self-confirming expectancy disorders", in which a fear of fear creates the problem through response sets similar to those underlying hypnosis, that is, through a form of negative autosuggestion or self-hypnosis (Lynn & Kirsch, 2006, p. 138). Autosuggestions or expectations of experiencing anxious responses (anxious response-expectancy) can perhaps be considered as equivalent to what Beck means by exaggerated appraisal of their probability and severity (Clark & Beck, 2010).

In addition to identifying specific cognitive "events" (images, thoughts, or appraisals), the therapist should help the client to identify specific "thinking errors", or cognitive processes (distortions), which her individual thoughts typically exhibit. Anxiety tends to be associated with a selective awareness and interpretation of the problem situation, biased toward the perception of certain threats, and this naturally leads to various cognitive distortions, such as "tunnel vision" for threat, exaggerating the probability of danger, overlooking evidence of safety or coping ability, etc.

Automatic physiological responses

It is also essential to enquire about the client's physiological symptoms and bodily sensations during specific incidents, that is, symptoms of autonomic hyperarousal during periods of anxiety. For example, dry mouth, weak legs, trembling, nausea, breathing difficulty, increased heart rate, increased blood pressure, feelings of faintness, sweating, dizziness, etc. The therapist might also investigate, for example, how these vary in different situations, how long they last, if they are interpreted as signs of danger, how much distress they cause, what is done to relieve them, etc. In particular, catastrophic interpretations of bodily symptoms are central to the conceptualisation of panic attacks and health anxiety. Difficulty with "thinking" or concentration, one of the most frequent complaints in anxiety, can be seen as a correlate of the automatic allocation of attention to perceived sources of danger, due to anxious arousal, and the general narrowing of the scope of attention, making normal voluntary control of thinking processes extremely difficult. Catastrophic misinterpretations of physical sensations are central to panic disorder and also to health anxiety, and even some cases of social anxiety disorder.

Automatic behavioural responses (defensive/protective behaviours)

When someone is presented with imminent danger, they may automatically ("instinctively") stiffen, freeze, inhibit speech or cry out, or grab nearby objects or another person for help, without "thinking" or consciously meaning to do so. The client's "immediate inhibitory responses" as Beck calls them, consist primarily of "escape, avoidance, freezing or fainting" and other "subtle defensive reactions" or automatic safety behaviours (Clark & Beck, 2010, p. 146). Like automatic thoughts, these defensive behaviours can be so rapid or inconspicuous that they are easily overlooked by the client herself, who made need help properly identifying them. Typical examples include, behavioural avoidance (avoiding certain situations or activities) and cognitive avoidance (suppressing certain thoughts), but also escape or flight from the situation, avoiding eye-contact, reassurance seeking, freezing, fainting, or automatic safety behaviours such as gripping objects or other people for safety. The ultimate automatic defensive behaviour is arguably the "emotional fainting" response, which is characteristic of a total sense of helplessness in the face of overwhelming and imminent threat, constituting a kind of deep-rooted evolutionary "fail safe" mechanism (Beck, Emery & Greenberg, 2005, p. 51). In an absolute emergency, the primitive circuits of the brain will simply "kill the power" and hope that solves the problem. The emotional fainting response is often feared, especially during panic attacks, but seldom actually occurs except in blood-injection-injury type phobias, where the brain is perhaps fooled into responding as though a grievous wound had been inflicted. (We may have evolved this response because of its survival value: an animal which is attacking, because surprised or defending its territory, may have no motive to continue the attack and inflict further injury when its victim plays dead.)

Beck illustrates the concept of defensive behavioural inhibition by reference to the age-old observation that although a man may walk steadily along a plank of wood when laid on the ground, he falters and wobbles when the same plank is laid across a deep river or between two high buildings (Beck, Emery & Greenberg, 2005, p. 75). The same example has frequently been used by hypnotists to illustrate the "power of suggestion", that is, the fear of a precipitous fall, to inhibit or "paralyse" voluntary movement. Beck et al. use exactly the same analogy to explain the power of the audience in social phobia, which he says can be "likened to that of a hypnotist", adding:

> The socially anxious person can be hypnotized into believing that he cannot open his mouth, that he cannot think clearly, that he cannot stand erect. He is, in a sense, hypnotized into

believing that his brain and organs of articulation are paralyzed. (Beck, Emery & Greenberg, 2005, p. 307)

As we've seen, in the Victorian era, "hysterical paralyses" were attributed by Braid to morbid dominant ideas or autosuggestions. It is natural therefore to conceptualise anxious inhibitory responses as the result of negative autosuggestion or self-hypnosis when using a cognitive-behavioural approach to hypnotherapy.

In his conceptual model of stress, which is closely-related to the generic model of anxiety, Beck also emphasises the role of "behavioural inclinations" or action tendencies (Pretzer & Beck, 2007, p. 466). In response to stress, or presumably anxiety, the individual's schemas activate a powerful inclination to physically act in primitive ways, that is, to fight or flee. Although these inclinations or impulses may create a muscle-set in preparation for physical behaviour this is normally "muted" or inhibited, and does not lead to actual overt fighting or fleeing behaviour. Hence, clients may report that they "felt like punching" someone or "felt like running away", without doing either of these things. Nevertheless, direct observation, or close questioning, may reveal that they tense muscles in particular ways or, for example, visibly clench their fists, hunch their shoulders, or shrink back, often in an automatic and non-conscious manner. Again, this can be compared to the classic Victorian examples of the ideo-motor reflex response, and conceptualised as a process of negative autosuggestion. Raising awareness of these subtle manifestations of behavioural inclination can help the client notice incipient signs of stress or anxiety and adopt a coping orientation toward them, treating them as cues to respond differently and "nip anxiety in the bud". Beck emphasises the behavioural inclination is not necessarily a consequence of emotion because, for example, someone may act automatically in a crisis without "having time to feel anxious", that is, without self-reported affect (Pretzer & Beck, 2007, p. 469).

Strategic processing and secondary appraisal

Following the immediate, automatic fear response, the client gradually begins to enter a second phase of reflection or "elaborative reappraisal" of the situation, which is more accessible to conscious awareness and deliberate control.

> Anxiety is always the result of a two-stage process involving the initial activation of threat followed by a slower, more reflective processing of the threat in light of one's coping resources. (Clark & Beck, 2010, p. 147)

These more deliberate, elaborative thinking processes are responsible for the persistent nature of some anxiety. According to Beck, the key questions are, at this stage, how might the client's reflection upon the situation actually *increase* her anxiety and how effective is it as an attempt to reduce anxiety or switch off her "anxiety mode."

Because elaborative thinking is more amenable to conscious control, this is the level at which cognitive therapy initially targets change, by altering "what happens next" following an anxious appraisal of threat. However, this subsequently impacts upon the more automatic initial thoughts and images experienced in anxiety (Clark & Beck, 2010, p. 148). Beck divides elaborative processing into five key areas:

1. Evaluation of coping abilities, leading either to a sense of confidence or helplessness.
2. Deliberate safety-seeking behaviour, which tries to create a sense of being "protected" or "secure" against perceived threats.
3. Activation of the opposing "constructive mode", that is, adaptive coping, problem-solving and cognitive strategies, such as realistic reappraisal of threat and coping, etc., which reduce fear naturally.
4. Cognitive coping and worry, that is, what the client worries about, how frequently, and for how long.
5. Threat and vulnerability reappraisal in the "normal mode" after anxiety has subsequently abated, in a safe environment, is likely to be less biased, as is appraisal of coping.

Strategic behavioural coping (avoidance & safety-seeking)

Central to the cognitive model is the research finding that certain forms of "emotion-focused" coping, that is, attempts to suppress anxiety, may be counter-productive in the longer-term, whereas "problem-focused" coping strategies, which seek to rectify the actual source of the anxiety, are often more associated with improved well-being and positive feelings (Clark & Beck, 2010, p. 148). The therapist needs to identify the client's deliberate coping strategies and to help her re-evaluate how effective they are short-term versus long-term as a means of reducing anxiety. This may also take the form of evaluating the "pros and cons" of certain strategies. Some strategies employed in response to anxiety involve attempts to seek safety, which may allow the client to feel temporarily free from harm and even to reduce her anxiety. It's important to distinguish between the initial "automatic" and subsequent "strategic" attempts at safety-seeking, which are more conscious, voluntary, and deliberate. Conceptualisation should

Behavioural & Emotional Coping Strategies
- Evaluate behavioural and emotional coping strategies
- Evaluate safety-seeking behaviour

↓

Worry Symptoms
- Triggers and duration of worry
- Main worry content/themes

↓

(Meta-) Cognitive Coping Strategies
- Evaluate thought-control strategies
- Frequency and perceived effectiveness of thought-control

↓

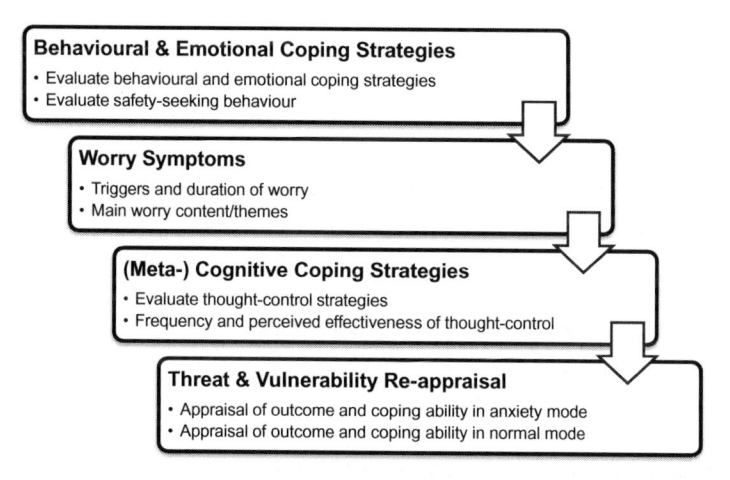

Threat & Vulnerability Re-appraisal
- Appraisal of outcome and coping ability in anxiety mode
- Appraisal of outcome and coping ability in normal mode

Figure 8. Clark and Beck (2010) Conceptualisation of secondary reappraisal in anxiety.

ideally aim to determine to what extent such behaviours in response to anxiety, such as taking anti-anxiety medication or complementary therapies, make clients "feel safer", how they predict they would feel if they had to stop doing them, and how much control or choice they have over the behaviour.

Since the 1990s, the concept of "safety-seeking behaviours" has assumed a central role in the conceptualisation of most problems, especially anxiety disorders (Salkovskis, 1991). Beck defines safety-seeking as follows:

> [Safety-seeking is] any cognitive or behavioral response intended to prevent or minimize a feared outcome. It is also an attempt to reestablish a feeling of comfort or calm and a sense of being safe. (Clark & Beck, 2012, p. 46)

This concept, in a sense, is an extension of the notion of avoidance behaviour in anxiety. Indeed, overt "avoidance" of encountering anxiety-provoking situations and experiences and attempts to "escape" from them once encountered are the most common forms of safety-seeking. However, avoidance can take more subtle forms as well and anxious people usually do many things to try to "protect" themselves from the danger they sense. For example, someone who is agoraphobic will probably completely avoid entering certain situations, such as walking through a crowded shop, where she might fear some catastrophe or having a panic attack. However, she may enter certain situations on condition that she is able to seek safety in other ways. For instance, she might seek safety by clinging on tightly to someone, often a spouse, to try to prevent the feared catastrophe of fainting. She may also plan "escape routes" from the situation, for example, remaining close to the exit, as another way of reassuring herself that she can find a route to perceived safety. Someone with social phobia might over-prepare for presentations to try to minimise the perceived risk of making a mistake and he may avoid eye-contact with other people when speaking if this makes him feel temporarily safer. Moreover, these behaviours may become habitual themselves and continue in the absence of anxiety. However, all of these safety-seeking behaviours are predicated on the assumption that there is a real danger against which the client needs to protect herself.

One of the main problems with safety behaviours is that they prevent assumptions about the feared situation from being disconfirmed by experience. CBT practitioners often tell their clients an old joke to illustrate this point, and socialise them to this aspect of the conceptualisation model.

> Once there was a man who walked around town with a little mouse in his pocket. Someone asked him, "Why do you carry the mouse around with you?" He replied, "Because I need it to scare away the elephants of course!" The other person pointed out that there were no elephants in town to which he received the answer: "Exactly! See how well it works?"

This is a kind of superstitious thinking; the impression that the mouse is keeping elephants at bay is clearly an illusion. I pick this example, incidentally, because we can imagine the man trying to give a rationale to justify his safety behaviour: "I've heard people say elephants are scared of mice!" Clients often give weak or fallacious reasons for their unhelpful strategies.

However, there's no real connection between the behaviour and the non-occurrence of the feared outcome, it's just a coincidence. Likewise, there may be no real connection between clinging on to someone and not fainting or between over-preparing and not being humiliated by an audience (other factors might be more important). Clients can be asked how the man in the joke could be convinced that he doesn't need the mouse to protect him from elephants. They will usually recognise that the only real solution would be for him to go into town without his mouse (safety behaviour) and see what happens. Likewise, the only way the client can really prove to herself that her safety behaviours are unnecessary, and her fears are groundless, would be to abandon them completely and see what happens in the feared situation. Moreover, it's more difficult for anxious clients to process evidence of safety than potential signs of threat, and so the use of "false" safety-seeking behaviours is a quick and easy way to create a sense of security while avoiding the harder work of discovering and assimilating genuine evidence of safety in the environment (Clark & Beck, 2012, p. 47).

It's particularly important to identify safety behaviours properly because they frequently sabotage the therapy, and they are often overlooked by therapists during the assessment phase. What prevents clients from proving to themselves that they're actually safe already and have nothing to fear? Careful questioning and self-monitoring is often required. At assessment, the client might be asked, for example:

- What situations do you avoid, delay, or try to get out of? (Make a list.)
- When you're in an anxious situation do you try to get away or end them quickly? How?
- What do you do to try to protect yourself or feel safer in anxious situations?
- What have you started doing since the problem began that you didn't do before?
- What would you do differently in these situations if you had no anxiety at all?
- What would you do differently if you knew for certain you were completely safe already?

On the other hand, conceptualisation should also take account of adaptive coping, that is, the clients' strengths and resources and the extent to which they are already able to do some of the things CBT might recommend. In particular, how often do clients already face their fears ("spontaneous exposure") rather than avoiding them? How much control do they exert over maladaptive responses? How capable are they of problem-solving or re-appraising more realistically the seriousness and probability of the feared outcome or their own ability to cope with it?

Worry and thought-control

Worry is central to generalised anxiety disorder (GAD) but is also common in other forms of anxiety. It appears to contribute significantly to the persistent activation of the anxiety mode. The frequency and duration of worry should therefore be determined, along with the nature of the worry content, which may tend to broadly correspond to the triggers for anxiety, or to encompass other themes. In cognitive therapy, worry is defined as follows:

> [Worry is] a persistent chain of repetitive, uncontrollable thinking that focuses on uncertain future negative outcomes. It involves repeated mental rehearsal of possible solutions that fail to resolve the sense of uncertainty about an impending threat. (Clark & Beck, 2012, p. 48)

Worry tends to consist of catastrophic "What if?" questions as well as "How will I cope?", that is, more conscious, prolonged, and elaborative thinking about appraisals of threat and vulnerability. Worry itself has been seen as a form of "cognitive avoidance", as it often takes the form of attempts to plan for and avoid future catastrophes (that seldom really happen). Moreover, research has shown that worry tends to be verbal in nature and that it may actually suppress physiological arousal by acting as a means of avoiding more concrete and specific thoughts about underlying fears (Borkovec & Sharpless, 2004). In other words, by asking a series of verbal questions about threat and coping, jumping around from one perspective to another, the individual may avoid prolonged exposure to visual images of threat. However, focusing for a prolonged period on mental imagery ("worrying visually") typically causes anxiety to peak but then allows it to habituate naturally, reducing in a more lasting way, and permitting rational reappraisal of the feared outcome ("decatastrophising"). For this reason, worry is often treated by using a form of imaginal exposure to worst-case scenarios.

Likewise, deliberate attempts at thought suppression or inhibition ("blocking") of emotional expression may be factors contributing to the maintenance of anxiety. This may take the form of distraction, relaxation, positive thinking, or simply trying to suppress thoughts and feelings. An internal struggle against automatic thoughts is particularly common in obsessive-compulsive disorders but plays a part, to some extent, in most forms of anxiety. Thought-control tends to backfire by forcing more attention, ironically, to be allocated to the very thought being suppressed, sometimes creating a "rebound effect" whereby it occurs more frequently in the future, perhaps especially when anxiety recurs. Thought control can be viewed as a form of "experiential avoidance", the avoidance of unpleasant internal experiences, a concept even more central in recent mindfulness and acceptance-based approaches to CBT (Hayes, Strosahl & Wilson, 2012). Clients who seek hypnotherapy are often looking for more ways to control their thinking and the therapist must be careful not to simply contribute to maladaptive attempts at thought control and emotional suppression.

Reappraisal of threat and coping

One of the most obvious factors in the appraisal of coping is that the client may believe (rightly or wrongly) that she lacks certain skills or resources necessary to cope with the perceived threat (Beck, Emery & Greenberg, 2005, p. 69). For example, a client with social phobia may have a social skills deficit and actually not know what to say or do in response to "difficult" conversations, in which case assertiveness training may increase confidence (self-efficacy) and reduce anxiety. However, some clients may be perfectly capable of being assertive but simply lack the confidence to do so without inhibition, under-estimating their coping ability. Hence, perceived deficits in coping skills may be realistically or unrealistically appraised by the client, something the conceptualisation needs to take into account.

Moreover, activation of the anxiety mode may lead to biased recall, whereby clients under-estimate the extent to which they have coped with similar problems in the past, and focus disproportionately on past failures (Beck, Emery & Greenberg, 2005, p. 68). For instance, when anxious, the blood phobic client may remember the one occasion she fainted when visiting a doctor, and having an injection, and forget or trivialise numerous other occasions where she has been able to manage her anxiety and tolerate similar procedures. Likewise, biased attention to and interpretation of potential signs of failure, incompetence, weakness, etc., in the current situation contribute to further escalation of anxiety. In other words, a fundamental shift occurs in attention from one's strengths and skills onto one's weaknesses and mistakes, etc., and a switch occurs from approach behaviour and problem-solving to self-protection and escape from the situation (Beck, Emery & Greenberg, 2005, pp. 69, 71).

Collaborative conceptualisation

Where possible, a simplified version of the conceptualisation, often using a basic diagram such as an ABC model or vicious cycle, should be shared with the client early in treatment. The client can be helped to participate more fully in the process of therapy by contributing to the conceptualisation from which the treatment rationale is derived. This process may overlap with early socialisation experiments designed to introduce the client to basic hypnotic skills and demonstrate some of the key concepts underlying treatment, such as the nature of focused attention and autosuggestion. Once the client has a basic working knowledge of some of the basic assumptions employed in treatment she will be better able to contribute to the ongoing refinement of the conceptualisation and treatment plan. In the next chapter, therefore, we shall look at the process of anticipatory socialisation in cognitive-behavioural hypnotherapy, especially teaching initial self-hypnosis skills, which will lead us into discussion of the extant research on hypnotic skills training in general.

Cognitive conceptualisation of anxiety (worksheet)

Modified for cognitive-behavioural hypnotherapy, based on Clark & Beck's revised cognitive therapy for anxiety, from their treatment manual (Clark & Beck, 2012) and self-help guide (Clark & Beck, 2012).

1. Orientation to anxiety triggers
(Main external or internal triggers: situations, thoughts, sensations, etc.)

2. Automatic fear responses (negative self-hypnosis)
Automatic thoughts (autosuggestions) about threat (content of core fear)

Appraisal of probability (%) and severity (%) of threat when anxious

Key cognitive errors

3. Deliberate coping responses
Thoughts about helplessness and vulnerability (appraisal of coping)

Safety-seeking, avoidance, and unhelpful coping strategies

Worry content and duration

Thought-control (experiential avoidance)

Rational reappraisal (realistic autosuggestion)
Appraisals of probability (%) and severity (%) of core fear when non-anxious

Alternative, when non-anxious, account of threat probability and severity

Alternative, when non-anxious, account of coping ability and genuine signs of safety

CHAPTER SIX

Socialisation and hypnotic skills training

If we reconceptualise hypnosis in terms of a particular, favourable cognitive set, or "hypnotic mind-set", rather than the concept of "hypnotic trance", an altered state of consciousness, certain practical consequences follow. Cognitive factors such as expectation and focused attention on appropriate ideas and strategies can be developed through education and skills training. The traditional "hypnotic induction" takes on a new meaning and is seen more as a opportunity for adoption of the relevant set of attitudes rather than a mechanical way of inducing an "altered state" or "trance". Understanding the role of the hypnotic induction better also allows us to be more flexible about the technique used and focus instead upon the underlying processes, which can be utilised in a variety of different ways.

Following the initial assessment, the next step is usually to progressively educate the client about the method of cognitive-behavioural hypnotherapy and to socialise her to the role of "hypnotic subject", as reconceptualised within this approach. This typically involves some discussion, correction of misconceptions, fostering a suitably favourable attitude, and the use of various initial "suggestion experiments" to begin helping the client develop a practical understanding of hypnosis from her own experience. This naturally leads into the process of training in *self*-hypnosis, which provides an introductory homework assignment that tends to be an important initial part of the overall treatment plan in hypnotherapy.

In this approach, there is also considerable overlap between training in self-hypnosis skills and being induced into hypnosis by an external hypnotist ("hetero-hypnosis"). Typically, when working collaboratively, there is no need to use hypnotic inductions in the traditional, formal sense, because once the client has been trained to enter self-hypnosis she can simply be explicitly asked to do so at the start of therapy sessions. It's widely recognised by hypnotherapists that asking a client to induce self-hypnosis, and perhaps providing some verbal instructions and encouragement, can be indistinguishable from certain common approaches to "hetero-hypnotic" induction, that is, inductions performed by the hypnotist. For example, once a client has been taught how to induce self-hypnosis through eye-fixation, using a variation of the Braid method, she can be asked simply to look at the ceiling and hypnotise herself by suggesting that her eyes feel heavy and want to close. However, this can be very similar to the standard process whereby the hypnotist induces eye-closure through external suggestions, especially where these are phrased "permissively", for example, "Just imagine your eyes feel tired and allow them to grow heavy and close, in your own time." Indeed, permissive suggestions of this kind can easily be viewed as instructions for the client to engage in self-hypnosis rather than hetero-suggestions *per se*, as they more explicitly attribute agency to the subject rather than an external hypnotist.

However, all traditional direct hypnotic suggestions are best understood as implicit invitations to imagine what is being suggested. The suggestion "Just allow yourself to imagine your eyelids growing heavy and let them close" is no different to "Your eyelids are growing heavy and closing", if the client is socialised to her role in a way that makes it clear these words are merely an invitation to imagine what is being described rather than a direct command to her "unconscious mind", etc. Arguably, much confusion has been caused by the fact that hypnotists do not always explicitly state the fact that direct suggestions are invitations to use the imagination, as if in brackets they were saying: "(Just allow yourself to imagine you're experiencing what I'm about to describe): Your eyelids are growing heavy and closing." This is often taken for granted, though, and does not need to be laboriously repeated prior to every suggestion. Nevertheless it is probably a common error among many hypnotists that they fail to explain this part of their role to every client and therefore to socialise them adequately in anticipation of hypnosis. From the outset, Braid very explicitly defined hypnotism as focused attention upon an expectant dominant idea. However, he did not prefix every suggestion with the words, "Please focus your attention on the idea that I'm about to suggest and expect your body to respond automatically." He perhaps explained the subject's role to them, in this regard, before commencing the hypnotic induction, but this is not made explicit in his writings.

Socialisation to cognitive-behavioural hypnotherapy

The hypnosis researcher Martin Orne introduced the notion of "anticipatory socialisation" from social psychology to the field of psychotherapy in his original article on the subject (Orne & Wender, 1968). Beck cited this as providing evidence that "preliminary coaching of the patient about the type of therapy selected" tends to enhance treatment effectiveness (Beck A. T., 1976, p. 220). Hence, the process of anticipatory socialisation has become integral to standard cognitive therapy. However, socialisation is, in a sense, even more important in cognitive-behavioural hypnotherapy where the client's attitudes, expectations, and freedom from misconception and anxiety, are central to the whole method. This process usually begins during the initial assessment and proceeds through the subsequent construction of a shared conceptualisation, reinforced by homework exercises and reading handouts, etc., and often continuing to some extent throughout the whole course of treatment.

Socialisation in CBT typically begins by helping the client to understand how her thoughts appear to influence her emotions, and perhaps also the relevance of behaviour such as avoidance or safety-seeking in maintaining problems. More simply, the "cognitive model" can be presented as the view that "people's emotions and behaviours are influenced by their perception of events" (Beck J. S., 1995, p. 14). Especially in REBT and early cognitive therapy, this was explained by reference to the famous quotation from the Stoic philosopher Epictetus:

> The truths of Stoicism were perhaps best set forth by Epictetus, who in the first century A.D. wrote in the *Enchiridion*: "Men are disturbed not by things, but by the views which they take of them." (Ellis, 1962, p. 54)

This saying of Epictetus has become a "hallmark" of REBT and is "even given to clients during the early sessions, as a succinct way of capturing the starting point" (Still & Dryden, 1999, p. 146). Following Ellis, Aaron Beck and his colleagues claimed that the "philosophical origins" of cognitive therapy also lay in the ancient Stoic tradition, and used the same quotation to illustrate their cognitive model of depression.

> Epictetus wrote in *The Enchiridion*: "Men are disturbed not by things but by the views which they take of them." […] Control of most intense feelings may be achieved by changing one's ideas. (Beck, Rush, Shaw & Emery, 1979, p. 8)

However, nowadays, many other anecdotes and examples, which are perhaps more familiar to the client, can be used to convey the same basic point as part of the initial socialisation procedure. For example, the client may be introduced to the metaphor of wearing "rose- tinted" or "grubby-coloured" glasses, and how this might change her perception of the world. This is usually followed by further analysis of a specific situation and her responses, for example, beginning to introduce other elements such as her physical behaviour and bodily sensations, and examining how these interact with thoughts and emotions experienced at the time in question, as illustrated in the basic conceptualisation diagram below.

A common strategy in CBT is to ask the client about her thoughts about the session while in the waiting room outside, which has been referred to as providing a "base camp" from which further cognitive conceptualisation can proceed (Sanders & Wills, 2005, pp. 82–83). These often consist of negative predictions or "What if?" thoughts evoking mild anxiety. These thoughts and feelings can be contributed by the client to a simple initial ABC diagram to help her reconceptualise her feelings and behaviour in terms of the cognitive mediation model. As Ellis puts it, clients typically enter therapy conceptualising their own problem in terms of stimulus-response (A causes C) language and the initial process of socialisation involves helping them to reconceptualise it in terms of their thoughts and beliefs (A plus B causes C).

In cognitive-behavioural hypnotherapy, the central role of mediating beliefs, or rather the specific thoughts associated with them, can be compared to "negative self-hypnosis". Hence, the client can be helped to reconceptualise her problem in terms of hypnosis by exploring whether her feelings and actions might be mediated by focused attention upon dominant expectant ideas, as Braid put it, of a morbid or unhelpful nature. As we saw earlier, Beck and Ellis both initially compared negative cognitions to the old Victorian hypnotists' idea of morbid autosuggestion, or what is often now called "negative self-hypnosis".

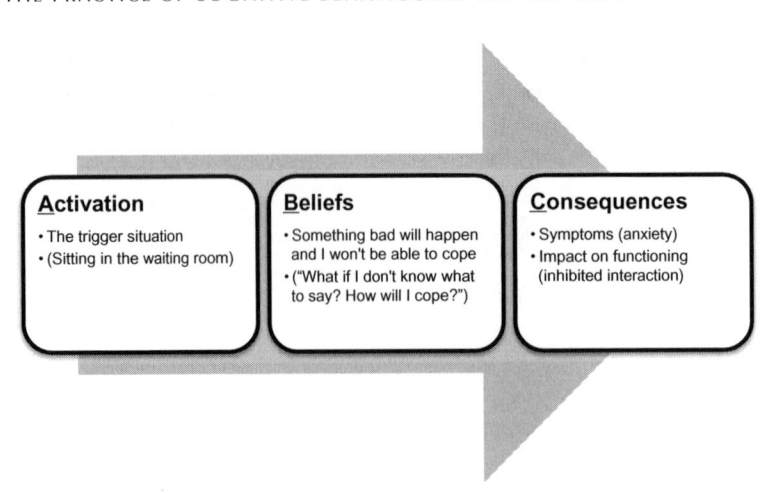

Activation
- The trigger situation
- (Sitting in the waiting room)

Beliefs
- Something bad will happen and I won't be able to cope
- ("What if I don't know what to say? How will I cope?")

Consequences
- Symptoms (anxiety)
- Impact on functioning (inhibited interaction)

This can be elaborated in simple steps and stages, for example, by adding her behaviour, and discussing how these three ingredients of the situation might interact with each other. For example, the client may have tried to make herself feel better by reading a magazine to distract herself. This may or may not work. Perhaps it worked for a moment but increased her sense of being unprepared, fuelling the recurrence of more automatic thoughts about not knowing what to say. This can be developed progressively into a more detailed conceptualisation diagram, which will help the client to understand how her problem is to be reconceptualised and, subsequently, how the treatment rationale follows from this information. During initial socialisation, the client can also be asked what would happen to her feelings if she were thinking differently or what someone who initially feels anxious but copes well with it might be saying to herself.

Helping the client to understand the role of negative automatic thoughts, or autosuggestions, is particularly important to cognitive-behavioural hypnotherapy because by normalising the process of autosuggestion and linking it to a familiar example from the client's own life, it helps to undermine common misconceptions about the nature of suggestion in hypnotherapy and remove some of the unhelpful mystique associated with hypnotism. The therapist might say: "Perhaps you could see this as a kind of hypnotism or autosuggestion that you're already doing automatically, without realising it, only involving *unhelpful* thoughts rather than helpful ones of the kind we might explore later in therapy." This can develop into a wider discussion of the role of thoughts and actions in maintaining symptoms such as anxiety or depression, and particularly in hypnotherapy, it may be useful to supplement this by using mental imagery exercises of the kind described below.

Socialisation to hypnotherapy: mood induction

Clients can be socialised to the cognitive hypnotherapy model very easily by using more "experiential" techniques. For example, simply asking them to close their eyes and imagine themselves in a problem situation while focusing on the content of their most distressing thoughts for a few moments. (It's perhaps notable that this experiment doesn't tend to work well unless the client is clearly instructed to focus attention continually on the thought-content or ideas.) Either a recently experienced example or an anticipated situation will suffice. The client should be asked what effect it has on her feelings to focus on the negative thoughts and possibly to rate the intensity of her emotional response as a percentage. This usually demonstrates very easily the power that certain thoughts have to contribute to the problem by causing anxiety or similar negative emotions or even bodily sensations. This usually takes less than a minute and the therapist should immediately proceed to ask the client to do the opposite and observe her response. In other words, to hold the external situation constant in her mind, while focusing attention instead on a more realistic and constructive appraisal of it, in the form of a short phrase or sentence repeated while imagining things. Again the client should be asked to describe her feelings, which will normally have reduced in intensity or changed in a positive direction, and possibly to re-rate the intensity of the original negative emotion in percentage terms.

> "Could you just close your eyes for a moment and imagine that you're in the situation you describe earlier, as if it's happening right now: in the waiting room outside. Really imagine seeing what you saw and hearing what you heard, doing what you did and feeling what you felt. When you've got that just nod your head … [Wait.] Now just repeat that negative thought to yourself: 'What if I say the wrong thing? Making a mistake would be awful.' Continue to imagine being in that situation and focus on thinking that thought. Pay close attention to how you experience it, what emotions you feel and any sensations in your body … So what do you notice? How does it make you feel? How upsetting is that feeling from zero to 100 per cent? What would be the longer-term consequences if you continued to think that way in similar situations in the future?"
>
> "Okay, now just set that thought aside, but remain in the same situation, while thinking an alternative thought, something more helpful perhaps. Focus your attention on the alternative we discussed earlier: 'I'll probably be fine and even if I make a mistake it doesn't really matter.' Does that seem realistic enough? What happens? How do you feel if you give all of your attention to that alternative perspective on things? So how upsetting does the situation seem now, rated zero to 100 per cent? So how much difference do your thoughts make to your feelings and actions in this situation? What would be the long-term consequences of viewing things differently in the future? So what do you think might be useful for us to do in these therapy sessions to help you change?"

This is a very simple, economical, and powerful way of demonstrating the effect of thoughts, or autosuggestions, upon feelings, and the wider impact on the problem in general. However, it should not be used to imply that cognitive-behavioural hypnotherapy is merely about "positive thinking". The emphasis should be upon realistic rather than wishful thinking. One remedy for this is to ask the client to identify:

1. The worst-case scenario or most negative way of thinking about events.
2. The best-case scenario or most positive way of thinking about events.
3. The most rational and realistic way of thinking about events, which may somewhere fall in-between these two extremes.

Moreover, it should be borne in mind that the relationship between positive and negative thoughts is not straightforward. Someone who is capable of powerful *positive* thoughts and feelings may be equally capable of powerful *negative* or destructive ones. Indeed, most people vacillate between these poles to some extent. In other words, rehearsing positive thoughts does not, by itself, necessarily weaken negative ones. The client should therefore be helped to understand that developing psychological distance from negative thoughts and beliefs and directly challenging them will be integral to most cognitive hypnotherapy, although there is also a role for rehearsing new alternative ways of thinking that are more realistic and constructive, but not for naive positive thinking of the "Pollyanna" variety.

To the final question above, the client is likely to answer that if she could somehow change her thinking then her feelings would improve and that this would be of long-term benefit to her ability to function in different areas of life. The therapist, at this stage, need only reassure the client that CBH consists of a variety of simple techniques that are designed precisely to help her modify her thoughts and beliefs in a lasting way. The specific details of the treatment plan can then be progressively developed, following on from a more detailed conceptualisation of the client's problem. However, the next step, which bridges socialisation to treatment in CBH, typically involves teaching the client self-hypnosis and training her in hypnotic skills and attitudes. In fact, the process of training in self-hypnosis follows very easily indeed from the mood induction technique above. The therapist might ask: "What would happen if you were even more focused upon those ideas, for even longer, and were even more confident in expecting them to influence your feelings and actions?" The client will usually recognise that prolonged or repeated focus of attention on autosuggested ideas, accompanied by high expectation or confidence, will have a more powerful suggestive effect. That allows the therapist to lead neatly into suggesting different strategies and techniques for focusing attention more systematically and confidently upon autosuggestions, that is, structured training in self-hypnotic skills. Clients can be socialised to the role of mindfulness-based techniques in dehypnosis by means of experiments such as repeating a negative autosuggestion slowly, with pauses between words, while developing a sense of psychological distance, as if taking a step back several paces, metaphorically, from the words and focusing attention on the process of articulating them, how they sound, rather than upon their meaning. Clients may also benefit from techniques that involve alternating hypnotic focused attention and expectation with mindfulness and detachment from verbal thoughts or suggestions.

Normalising self-hypnosis

In addition to the use of simple (ABC) conceptualisation diagrams and imagery experiments, simple analogies with everyday phenomena can be used to help socialise the client to self-hypnosis. If hypnotism does not work because of an abnormal altered state of consciousness ("trance") then it would be surprising if the skills employed in hypnosis, or self-hypnosis, lacked any clear analogy with everyday psychological processes. It may be helpful to stress to clients that "Hypnosis is much easier than you realise, you've probably done similar things many times without calling it 'hypnosis'". One of the most mundane analogies, which is both perpetually overlooked and extremely important, is the relationship between self-hypnosis and ordinary relaxation. Some people are better at relaxing than others. Some people discover their own strategies and become more skilled at using them, perhaps without ever discussing them or reflecting on the process. Relaxation, everyone would probably agree, can be induced somewhat more deeply than normal by focusing attention on ideas, such as mental imagery, especially if this is done confidently and expectantly, perhaps for a prolonged period. Few people have immediate and direct voluntary control over their body to the extent that they would by sheer willpower alone, that is, by just making the decision to do so, be able to deeply relax most of the muscles, lower their heart rate, and perhaps fall asleep. However, most people can probably learn to take more control over their body in this regard by practicing simple imagery and autosuggestion.

Typical strategies, found in therapy books, are often little more than "common sense" to many people who feel they "could have figured them out for themselves." For example, by taking time to progressively imagine each part of the body relaxing in turn, moving attention gradually from the idea of the foot relaxing, for example, to the ankle, then the calf, the thigh, etc., the whole body can be relaxed more deeply than normal. Some people find these things easier than others but most people can get better with practice. Yet the underlying skills involved are very similar, if not identical, to the skills involved in learning most hypnotic responses. Most people wouldn't really consider ordinary relaxation to be anything as dramatic as hypnosis, but actually this seems to be a clear example of the ideo-motor reflex, the use of the imagination to evoke bodily responses. Keeping these "naturalistic" analogies in mind can help clients to appreciate that they probably already know much more about doing hypnosis than they realised at first. As we've seen, Braid explicitly compared hypnotism to many everyday examples of suggestion, such as blushing or pallor in response to a story, actors shedding tears onstage by being immersed deeply in their roles, or mothers lactating at the mere thought of their baby crying.

To take a second and more striking analogy, sexual arousal has been suggested as an analogy for self-hypnosis in more or less the same way (Diamond, 1989, p. 383). Perhaps all masturbation, at least insofar as it involves the use of fantasy for arousal, in the absence of a sexual partner, is a kind of self-hypnosis. Many people fantasise *during* sex, or learn in therapy to use their mind to overcome sexual problems such as frigidity or impotence. However, masturbation probably provides an even clearer example of imagination, focused attention, abstraction, expectation, "coupling" subjective ideas with physical sensations, etc. These are used to evoke subjective feelings of sexual arousal, and genuine physiological reactions perhaps even leading to orgasm. Indeed, to take a crude example, most men cannot simply say "erection on!" or "erection off!" to themselves, click their fingers, and produce or remove instantaneous tumescence because it is not an entirely voluntary response. However, it can be brought under voluntary control by using indirect means, suitable "cognitive strategies" such as arousing fantasies or memories. It may therefore require attention to be focused reasonably well for an appropriate length of time on suitably erotic ideas and images. Intrusive thoughts or sensations would perhaps need to be excluded or ignored. There is also perhaps a reciprocal interaction between physical sensations and imagined ideas, which may reinforce each other, as in Braid's psycho-physiological account of hypnotism. Finally, some degree of confidence or expectation, like Bandura's self-efficacy, or Kirsch's response expectancy, presumably plays a role, if only because someone racked with doubt about his ability to do so would probably find it difficult to engage in the process of sexual fantasy.

This sexual metaphor is actually a very good analogy for the use of self-hypnosis to overcome anxiety, where the involuntary physiological response is not sexual orgasm, but lowering of heart rate, and stabilising of other physiological responses such as trembling, sweating, increased blood pressure, etc. In Beck's terminology, the activation of the sexual mode can be compared to the de-activation of the anxiety mode. So much mystique has accrued around hypnotism because of the association with the occult and stage hypnosis that it's incredibly difficult for many people who "can't see the wood for the trees" to realise that it employs basic psychological skills which they already possess and use every day in some shape or form. We can make much better use of these skills, though, and learn new strategies, or benefit from coaching and practice, in a way that potentially allows us to do more impressive and unusual things such as dissociating from pain during surgery or helping our body to heal certain physical illnesses. However, one of the most fundamental and important uses of hypnotherapy lies in its ability to help us overcome everyday fear and increase self-confidence.

Cognitive-behavioural theory & skills training

Writing in the foreword to Roger Strauss' book on self-hypnosis, T. X. Barber described four major insights that developed out of the "hypnosis renaissance" of the 1970s (Straus, 1982, pp. ix–xi).

1. Self-hypnosis was realised to be a much broader and more important concept that had previously been assumed because hypnosis in general was increasingly understood to depend upon active goal-directed imagination of the kind employed during self-hypnosis.
2. Self-hypnosis was shown to be, to a large extent, a learnable skill, which can be taught using familiar behavioural training methods such as psycho-education, coaching, modelling, shaping, and reinforcement, etc.
3. Self-hypnosis gradually lost its "aura of mystery" as researchers explored the cognitive and behavioural strategies involved, and their similarity to other processes.
4. The value of self-hypnosis was understood to reach beyond psychotherapy and into other domains of life such as education and everyday self-management of emotion and behaviour for positive psychological functioning.

As we've seen, Braid defined hypnotism mainly in terms of the subject's mental focus upon expectant dominant ideas, the role of the hypnotist being mainly to help guide her attention. Consequently, for Braid, all hypnosis was fundamentally self-hypnosis. He quotes his friend Dr. Wilkinson's succinct account:

> Patients can produce the hypnotic state upon themselves, without a second party; although a second will often strengthen the result by his acts or presence, just as one who stood by and told you that you were to succeed in a certain work would nerve your arm with fresh confidence. (Wilkinson quoted in Braid, 1852, p. 149)

This way of describing early hypnotism makes it clear that the hypnotist was cast somewhat in the role of a guide or coach, rather than someone "controlling" the mind of the subject. Many subsequent authors have emphasised the role of the hypnotist in a manner harking back to the supposed "external" influence of the Mesmerist. However, modern cognitive-behavioural models of hypnosis stand out as being in agreement with Braid. "Ultimately, patients are responsible for generating suggestion-relevant imagery, experiences, and behaviours" (Lynn & Kirsch, 2006, p. 61). Braid therefore used the term "dominant idea" (autosuggestion) far more than "suggestion". In the original hypnotherapy, the role of the hypnotist was largely to function as an instructor or guide and the power of suggestion laid primarily within the subjects themselves. Hence, Braid consistently refers to pre-existing or spontaneously occurring ideas in the subject's mind as one of the main sources of her responses. The suggestions of the hypnotist, in Braid's model, generally operate through the mediation of the subject's own expectant ideas and images. Hence, in this approach, training in self-hypnosis ("auto-hypnosis") is fundamental to all clinical hypnosis, even when subsequently induced by an external hypnotist ("hetero-hypnosis").

It's a universal and basic observation, beyond dispute, that some people respond more dramatically to traditional hypnotism than others. Many researchers previously assumed that hypnosis was related to a "stable trait", a fact apparently supported by the small amount of change found in hypnotic susceptibility scores when subjects were tested and retested up to twenty-five years later using standard measurement scales for hypnotic susceptibility. However, others, mainly influenced by cognitive-behavioural theories of hypnosis, challenged this idea and following the work of Sarbin and Barber, a variety of cognitive-behavioural "skills training" methodologies for hypnotic subjects, influenced by the social learning theory of Albert Bandura, evolved in the 1970s (Diamond, 1989). Hypnotherapists sometimes glibly, and wrongly, state that the "state versus nonstate" argument is just an "academic debate" and doesn't have any practical significance. In fact the adoption of a nonstate or cognitive-behavioural conceptualisation of hypnosis has very important practical benefits. The most obvious of these is that it is intimately linked to the development of hypnotic skills training procedures that have demonstrated their ability to enhance the responsiveness of hypnotic subjects, something of undeniable importance to the clinical practice of hypnotherapy. For most applications of hypnotherapy, high levels of suggestibility are unnecessary. However, poorly responsive subjects will probably benefit from basic research-based hypnotic skills training procedures such as being encouraged to actively imagine suggested ideas, adopting less perfectionistic standards for achieving mental imagery or physical responses, increased emphasis on rapport between therapist and client, and learning a repertoire of "cognitive skills" such as various mental imagery techniques designed to evoke suggested responses (Lynn, Kirsch & Hallquist, 2008, p. 131).

According to Diamond, one of the pioneers of this approach, "cognitive skills methodology relies on advances in modern cognitive behavioural psychology and hypnotherapy" in order to achieve the goal of training clients to evoke and make use of their mental abilities in ways that are outside their normal sphere of control (Diamond, 1989, p. 382). Early attempts to train hypnotic subjects were followed by an extensive programme of research led by Nicholas Spanos at Carleton University in Canada, in the 1980s, which produced the Carleton skill training programme (CSTP), the most empirically-supported methodology for enhancing hypnotic responses. In a nutshell, according to Spanos, in the CSTP approach the client is instructed in specific tactics, such as mental imagery, designed to produce specific responses, and is given the opportunity to observe models demonstrating the behavioural and cognitive responses desired (Gorassini & Spanos, 1999, p. 151).

The CSTP has been supported by numerous studies as an effective means of increasing hypnotic responsiveness among initially low-responding subjects. Participants are first given standard hypnotic susceptibility scale tests and those which score low are then trained to respond to a range of suggestions, including simple motor tests like arm-lowering but also cognitive suggestions such as visual and auditory hallucinations and amnesia, before being retested in full. CSTP basically asks clients to role-play their responses to suggestions while interpreting them as automatic, in order to generate a kind of willing self-deception which seems to generalise to future experiences of being hypnotised (Gorassini & Spanos, 1999).

Authors involved in this skills training methodology consider hypnotic responses to be primarily mediated by a learnable repertoire of cognitive skills or strategies (Diamond, 1989; Gorassini & Spanos, 1999).

> The cognitive skills model is distinguished by its emphasis on the lack of a formalised hypnotic induction ritual, the more permissive, cooperative, and nonauthoritarian orientation, and the individualised, idiographic, and actively participatory approach to induction, suggestion, and training in cooperation with the [subject]. (Diamond, 1989, p. 394)

In a sense, some awareness of hypnotic skills training has been implicit in hypnotism from the outset. As we have seen, Braid explicitly recognised that when hypnotic subjects observed others they were liable to respond in a similar manner through the "law of sympathy and imitation". He also noted the practice effect in hypnotism, observing that clients who had been hypnotised repeatedly tended to become better at responding. Moreover, as discussed earlier, Braid conceptualised hypnotism in naturalistic terms, as focused attention on a dominant expectant idea, something more easily learnable than an abnormal altered state of consciousness might appear to be. Most importantly, though, Braid repeatedly stressed that all hypnotism was "personal" and "subjective", by which he meant that all hypnosis is ultimately self-hypnosis and due to the cognitive and behavioural strategies employed by the subject rather than the skill or power of an external hypnotist.

Cognitive-behavioural strategies

In a sense, the ideal hypnotic response to suggestion can be compared to the ability to become deeply absorbed in the content of a story, so much that it evokes physical and emotional reactions. This narrative or dramaturgical analogy can be useful in skills training. For example, CSTP places considerable emphasis upon training clients in the use of specific "cognitive" (or "subjective") strategies, which are taught in this way. In the brief version of CSTP the instructions to clients are summed up in two sentences.

> Make the responses that are suggested, but pay no attention to the fact that you are making them. Instead, devote your full, undivided, and continuous attention to the stories [i.e., the suggestions]. (Gorassini & Spanos, 1999, p. 171)

For example, during training in arm-levitation, subjects are instructed to respond to the suggestions as follows.

> In response to this suggestion, you must do everything that is required of someone making believe such a thing. You must lift your arm up, and you must imagine that the arm is really a hollow balloon that is being pumped up full of helium, rising by itself, and anything else you wish to imagine that is consistent with such a make-believe situation. Of course, your arm will not really go up by itself, you must raise it. However, you can make it feel like it's going up by itself by focusing on the make-believe situation, that your arm is hollow and being filled with helium. (Gorassini & Spanos, 1999, p. 152)

Spanos' socio-cognitive approach to hypnotism was originally based on the assumption that most hypnotic responses were in fact voluntary behaviours but that subjects deceived themselves into believing that they were automatic. This is fundamentally different from the claim that hypnotic subjects are simply faking or consciously complying with suggestions because the end result of successful self-deception is that the subject genuinely feels as though, for example, his eyes have closed or his arm has lifted because of the power of suggestion. As we have seen, other cognitive-behavioural researchers have argued that hypnotic responses are genuinely automatic, in the same way as the placebo effect and other phenomena (Kirsch & Lynn, 1999). Nevertheless, there is considerable overlap and consistency between these viewpoints. A modified version of the original process was therefore developed called the Connecticut CSTP, based on response expectancy theory (Gorassini & Spanos, 1999, p. 147). This differed from the original self-deception procedure in that it refrained from telling clients to intentionally produce responses, or role-enact, while persuading themselves that they were happening automatically, and instead emphasised the subject's expectations of genuinely responding automatically. In the original version, therefore, the arm is meant to rise due to volition but the subject fools themselves into believing it is automatic. The "response expectancy" (Connecticut) version of this removes the comments about voluntary compliance ("You must lift your arm"). In this version, then, the response is attributed to expectancy, which the mental imagery (cognitive strategy), is meant to reinforce.

Hypnosis may employ both cognitive and behavioural strategies, by "coupling" ideas with physical responses in order to enhance their effectiveness. However, the behavioural strategies in the original CSTP simply involve doing (enacting) the physical response voluntarily. Very much like Braid, the CSTP emphasises to the client the reciprocal interaction of mental (cognitive) and physical (behavioural) stimuli in hypnosis. Braid's "muscular suggestion" can be combined with the ideo-motor response to constitute converging cognitive and behavioural strategies (or stimuli) for suggested "arm-levitation" as follows:

1. *Cognitive.* The subject focuses attention upon the expectant dominant idea of the arm rising, for example, employing the kind of goal-directed imagery described by Spanos, something quite similar to what is normally understood by self-hypnosis or autosuggestion.
2. *Behavioural.* The subject presses her hand flat against a hard surface and then focuses her attention on the initial sensations of lightness naturally created when it's slowly released and

allowed to rise. Alternatively, as in the original CSTP, the subject might simply voluntarily lift her arm slowly, while imagining that it is happening of its own accord.

One advantage of voluntarily lifting the arm is that it creates a physical sensation which helps to reinforce the mental image and expectation that it will continue to rise, that is, to "kick start" the process. However, other behavioural strategies, such as the one above or straining the eyes to produce tiredness, can be employed instead of mere voluntary movements. In some cases, the subject may be asked to begin by voluntarily making a suggested movement, such as arm-levitation, and then gradually imagine that it's happening more and more automatically, until she genuinely feel as if the movement is happening of its own accord, something we might describe as "fading voluntary compliance" with suggestions.

Cognitive set (hypnotic mind-set)

As previously discussed, Barber replaced the concept of hypnotic trance with that of a positive cognitive set, which we have defined in terms of factors derived from cognitive-behavioural research on problem-solving. These attitudes should be evaluated and a positive mind-set explained and fostered with clients at the outset and throughout training.

1. *Recognition.* "Think of the induction as your cue or signal to adopt a positive and receptive mind-set; you should then focus your attention completely on the suggestions and view them as cues to actively imagine the responses being described."
2. *Appraisal.* "It's important that you view hypnosis as a positive opportunity rather than anything threatening and also that you see the process, and the suggestion experiments we're doing, as a way of ultimately helping you to achieve your personal goals."
3. *Attribution.* "Although people are often confused about how hypnosis works, psychologists believe it's mainly due to your own conscious attitudes and expectations rather than anything an external hypnotist does."
4. *Control.* "The more confident you feel about following the instructions and fulfilling your role as hypnotic subject, and the more you expect the ideas you focus upon to cause the suggested responses, the easier you'll find hypnosis."
5. *Commitment.* "It's important to be motivated and to really want to by hypnotised and invest the time and effort required, being keen to respond but patient with yourself."

The attitude of the client is perhaps the most important factor in determining how she will respond to the practical exercises described below so explicit attention to it should not be neglected.

The naive, popular conception of hypnotism, shared by a great many hypnotherapists, is that techniques such as eye-fixation somehow induce or cause a "hypnotic trance". In fact, the relationship between the "induction" procedure and the hypnotic mind-set or orientation may, in a sense, be the inverse of this, the mind-set preceding the induction technique rather than following it. Most hypnotic induction techniques involve a physical suggestion such as eyelid closure. It may be more accurate to say that in anticipation of responding to this, or similar techniques, good subjects will rapidly, perhaps automatically, adopt the right mind-set or attitude, focusing their attention appropriately and adopting a confident and expectant attitude, because they realise this will be required for them to experience the suggested response in a few moments' time.

The hypnotic mind-set, in other words, is voluntarily adopted in anticipation of the need to respond to hypnotic suggestions. Suggestions such as those of eyelid closure or magnetic palms serve as good induction procedures because they are brief and allow the client to immediately observe the desired response, confirming that she has adopted a favourable mind-set. For some people this may happen automatically and effortlessly, others may require training or just repeated opportunities to practice. As Braid noted, though, it becomes so habitual with practice that most subjects no longer require the induction technique at all and can simply be asked to put themselves into hypnosis by recalling the appropriate mental attitude, once learned. The induction therefore provides helpful confirmation that the subject has put herself in hypnosis; it does not, in some mechanical way, put the subject into hypnosis or induce a "trance", though.

Trial-and-error learning

An important aspect of most skills training approaches is that hypnotism is broken down into component skills that can be practiced independently and repeated opportunities are given for trial-and-error learning, through reinforcement by means of the therapist praising successive approximations to the desired style of responding. This is helped by focusing on "easy" suggested responses before "harder" ones and upon responses such as simple physical movements or relaxation, which are easily observed, providing immediate feedback. The opportunity to practice in steps and stages fits neatly with the whole collaborative atmosphere of CBH and makes it easier for the client to assume greater responsibility for her responses, and therefore to make more use of self-hypnosis in the future to prevent relapse, without the aid of an external hypnotist. Typical steps might involve training in eye-fixation and closure, relaxation, arm heaviness, arm levitation, rigid arm catalepsy, etc., as we shall see below. In general, suggestions of physical movement that are coupled with behavioural strategies have the highest response rate (e.g., eyelid closure, arm lowering, etc.), followed by "challenge" or "inhibitory" suggestions (e.g., "you cannot bend your arm") and those suggesting movements that conflict with bodily sensations (e.g., arm levitation). However, "cognitive" suggestions, for hallucinatory experiences and post-hypnotic suggestions tend to have poorer response rates on average.

Role-modelling

Braid, as we have seen, repeatedly emphasised the importance of the "law of sympathy and imitation" in training hypnotic subjects. Unlike modern hypnotherapists, he often hypnotised patients in the presence of others, who tended to respond more easily after witnessing a successful demonstration. Similarly, in CSTP, subjects first observe video clips of model hypnotic subjects demonstrating each suggestion test and commenting on their subjective experiences.

The role-model actually provides a "running commentary", talking aloud while responding to suggestions, for example, during arm-levitation, she says:

> It's going up by itself. It feels hollow. I can see the pump. I can feel the arm being pumped up. It's really light. It's moving up by itself. It's getting even lighter. It's going up by itself. It just keeps getting lighter and is going up by itself. It's just getting lighter and lighter. (Gorassini & Spanos, 1999, p. 153)

This is followed by a brief discussion between the role-model and her therapist where the model comments in more detail on her experience. For example, a brief excerpt reads:

> You really have to let yourself get into it. That really made the difference, like you said it would. Like, I didn't just sit back and say, "Hey, I'm just imagining all this." Commenting on it would have just ruined the feeling. I just did it. I just let myself get totally engrossed in imaging my arm as hollow and being pumped up, and when I did, it all felt like it was really happening. […] There's a real knack to it. I found myself getting better and better at it as I practised. (Gorassini & Spanos, 1999, p. 154)

Hence, observational learning of the kind emphasised by Bandura plays an absolutely central role in increasing the subject's sense of self-efficacy, that is, her belief that she can do it, as well as her role-perception, her understanding of what the subject is meant to be doing and experiencing during the tests, that is, what highly responsive subjects commonly imagine and tell themselves while responding and what it feels like to them (Gorassini & Spanos, 1999, p. 153).

Theoretically, role-modelling should be more effective if it uses real subjects who resemble the client being trained, rather than using the therapist, for example, as a role-model. However, often, in clinical practice, it's the therapist who serves as a role-model by demonstrating suggestion tests briefly to the client and describing what it feels like and how to produce the responses. Seeing role-models struggle a bit but overcome potential obstacles should also increase clients' self-efficacy more than modelling mastery, that is, people who seem to find it *too* easy to respond to suggestion tests. The models should seem as credible as possible and again, theoretically, viewing more than one model should produce better results. When subjects learn hypnosis in a group there is greater opportunity for modelling other people although care has to be taken to prevent the opposite effect whereby one or two overly cynical subjects can influence the rest of a group contagiously in a negative direction by fostering self-doubt.

Cognitive-behavioural skills training in hypnotherapy

Almost any traditional suggestion test can be turned into an experiment for hypnotic skills training. For example, Golden et al. (1987, pp. 14–18, 133–134) provide a detailed cognitive-behavioural protocol for hypnotic skills training in the clinical setting, based partly on Salter's seminal article on the subject (Salter, 1941). Their approach includes the following suggestion experiments:

1. *Hand heaviness.* The eyes are closed and arms held out straight ahead while the subject imagines holding a heavy weight in the dominant hand.
2. *Hand levitation.* The arms are held out and the subject imagines something which makes one of the hands feel light causing it to rise.
3. *Chevreul's pendulum.* The subject holds a pendulum and imagines it moving in different directions.
4. *Rigid arm-catalepsy.* The subject holds out one of her arms and tenses it rigid while imagining it cannot bend.

There is considerable scope for variation in the choice of techniques used in hypnotic skills training. These are some of the easier ones. It is surprising that more of them do not mention the possibility of using Braid's eye-fixation induction as a skills training exercise because doing so has many advantages, not least that it easily lends itself to use as a self-hypnosis induction technique. An alternative combination of exercises might therefore be as follows, including initial socialisation procedures:

1. *Cognitive set.* Discussion of the role of the hypnotic subject, the "hypnotic mind-set", and analogies with everyday experiences of suggestion.
2. *Bucket and balloon.* The subject stands upright with both arms stretched out in front, closing her eyes, clenching her fists, and turning the right hand palm upwards. She is then to imagine that her right hand is holding the handle of a heavy bucket, making it feel tired and sink down, while their left arm is resting on a large inflatable ball that is gradually expanding, making it feel light and rise. After a few moments she can open her eyes and observe the difference in position of their arms, it being normal for the "heavy" arm to have moved more than the "light" one, which neatly illustrates the reciprocal interaction between behavioural and cognitive strategies, as holding the arms out makes them tire naturally and it's easier to imagine a heavy arm growing heavier than to imagine it growing light and floating.
3. *Eye-fixation.* The client repeatedly (three to four times) looking upward to strain the eyes slightly and employing different strategies to make them feel tired and close, such as imagining they're extremely tired and have been looking for a long time, imagining a bright light is shining into the eyes, imagining heavy weights attached to the eyelids, repeating verbal suggestions in the mind such as "My eyelids are growing heavy, sleepy, and tired ... they're closing, closing, closing ..."
4. *Three deep breaths.* The client takes three deep breaths, holding each for as long as is comfortable. On the exhalation she is to instruct herself to "relax" or "let go", as a form of autosuggestion, and see how deeply she can relax by using her imagination in this way. She should repeat this a few times, experimenting with different cognitive strategies such as the image of taking a step down a flight of stairs into deeper levels of relaxation with each out-breath.
5. *Magnetic palms.* The client holds her hands close together, palms about an inch apart. She is then to imagine they are powerfully drawn together, using cognitive strategies such as repeating the words "My hands are moving together, drawn closer and closer and closer ...",

imagining a magnetic force pulling her palms or fingertips together, picturing a rubber band around her hands pulling them together, imagining someone else pressing her hands together, etc.
6. *Mood induction.* Experimentation with negative and positive cognitions during mental imagery, by focusing on autosuggestions as a means of evoking corresponding changes in emotion.

Once the client has the basic "knack" of autosuggestion and understands the correct mental attitude she can be instructed in a simple self-hypnosis procedure such as using eye-closure, followed by three deep breaths to relax, and then repeating a helpful coping statement or auto-suggestion while mentally rehearsing a problem situation.

Chevreul's pendulum experiment

This is traditionally one of the most popular ideo-motor experiments. It's one of the easiest suggestion tests and most people experience it on their first attempt, especially young children. You can easily make a pendulum from a piece of thread and a wedding ring. However, many New Age suppliers sell cheap bronze dowsing pendulums, which are much better suited to the job. Before using a pendulum, though, it's important to properly explain to the client that it is not being used for "dowsing" but simply as a traditional way of teaching people how to use auto-suggestion to make it swing. Braid developed his theory of hypnotism precisely by debunking supernatural methods such as pendulum dowsing, which he argued were due to simple suggestion and the ideo-motor reflex response.

The effect generally seems to be improved if the arm holding the pendulum is as free as possible and comfortable, with the elbow resting on some surface. Looking at the pendulum itself rather than the hand, and rather than closing the eyes, usually makes it easier. The pendulum should be on a string or chain roughly eight inches long and the pendulum should be heavy enough to swing easily. It should be suspended over a flat surface, perhaps a sheet of paper with a circle or a cross drawn upon it, the tip of the pendulum no more than a couple of centimetres from the surface. As it often takes a minute or so for the pendulum swing to develop, this gives the client time to become tense or assume it's not working. Ask the client to deliberately set the pendulum swinging in a straight line first by using the other hand to set it in motion. Now suggest that it will change direction or begin to circle instead and the response will be quicker because the pendulum is already in motion. It can also considerably aid the response if the hypnotist gestures alongside the pendulum with his hand, indicating the rough movement it is to make. This appears to work well as a kind of non-verbal suggestion. Alternatively, move your finger alongside the pendulum, keeping perfect time, and suggest to the client that it's being drawn along by your finger like a magnet; which can also work surprisingly well.

Lynn and Kirsch describe a clever variation of the pendulum experiment which they seem to think works even better with some poorly responsive clients. A line is to be drawn on a piece of paper and the pendulum suspended above it. The subject then counts backward from 1,000 in steps of seven while trying to prevent the pendulum from swaying along the line. They believe this tricky counting often brings about a cognitive overload which prevents the client from unwittingly inhibiting the natural response (Lynn & Kirsch, 2006, p. 50). Asking clients to deliberately swing their pendulum in a straight line over a circle and try to prevent it from straying into an ellipse motion can also work well. Lynn and Kirsch also suggest that the client should be instructed to imagine the pendulum swinging in one direction while the therapist gives opposing suggestions to prove to the client that she is in control and teach her that hypnosis works mainly by her active imagination rather than the hypnotist's suggestions (Lynn & Kirsch, 2006, p. 47).

Sucking a lemon (Pavlov's dogs)

A favourite demonstration of many stage hypnotists was to take a lemon, cut it in half, and pretend to suck the juice while suggesting to the audience that they could taste it in their own mouths and were beginning to salivate. This is obviously a sensory and secretory response rather than a motor response and it is because of this kind of phenomenon that Braid and others replaced Carpenter's term "ideo-motor response" with "ideo-dynamic response", which refers more generally to the power of the mind, or ideas, over the body.

One reason why this test tends to work well is that it takes advantage of an unconditioned reflex response. In fact, this is precisely the reflex which Pavlov conditioned his dogs to associate with the sound of a bell. Pavlov sometimes sprayed small amounts of a harmless acidic fluid on the dogs' tongues to produce the response he sought. Any acidic taste tends to evoke salivation, such as the taste of citric fruits or vinegar. The smell and sight of various substances, or of other people eating them, functions like a conditioned stimulus for salivation, and Pavlov himself stated that hypnotic suggestion was an exemplary demonstration of this kind of conditioned reflex response manifested in humans. Salivation is more pronounced when people are hungry; it therefore seems the response to this suggestion can sometimes be strengthened by first suggesting that the subjects are very hungry.

The eye-fixation induction

Braid's original induction, as described earlier, needs little modification as a contemporary technique. It should be presented in a more collaborative style, so that the client's role, actively imagining the sensations and physical eyelid closure, is made more explicit. Different strategies may be suggested to the client as means of inducing eyelid heaviness, for example:

1. Recall what it felt like the last time you were very tired and your eyes felt like closing.
2. Imagine you've been staring at the ceiling for a long time and your eyelids are very tired indeed.
3. Tell yourself, "My eyelids are growing heavy, they're closing, closing, closing ...", and focus on the meaning of those words.
4. Imagine a bright light shining into your eyes, or a gentle breeze blowing against them, that makes them feel like blinking and closing.
5. Relax all the muscles around your eyes, in your forehead, face, and scalp, and allow that relaxation to spread into the eyes.

6. Imagine that your eyelids are like two heavy velvet curtains, or that it feels as though weights are pulling them down.
7. Imagine that with each exhalation of breath, your eyelids are relaxing just a little bit more deeply.
8. Count from five down to zero, and imagine that as you do so, your eyelids are growing more heavy and beginning to close.
9. Start to close your eyes voluntarily, just a little, and imagine that it's becoming more automatic and they continue to close down further all by themselves.
10. Imagine that you're very sleepy and nodding off as if your eyelids feel like closing.

The hypnotist can easily demonstrate eye fixation and closure to the client, modelling the response for her to imitate. The client can also be asked to repeat the exercise three to four times. Hull demonstrated a clear practice effect in his early behavioural experiments with eyelid closure, the response time roughly halving on each repetition (Hull, 1933). If the client begins with her eyes closed for a minute or so, before opening her eyes slowly to commence the eye fixation experiment, she will also tend to respond more quickly, her eyes already being somewhat relaxed from the time spent with them shut. A suitable patter for use in a skills training approach, would be as follows:

> Just close your eyes for a moment and relax ... Relax your eyes ... Relax your face ... Relax your whole body ... Allow yourself to let go more deeply on each and every out-breath ... [Pause] In a moment, I'm going to ask you to look up at the ceiling and to use your imagination to make your eyelids feel heavy and close ... You can do this easily just by really imagining the things I'm describing, and focusing your attention on the idea that the suggested response is happening ... Now, turn your eyes upward and slowly raise your eyelids ... Look up at the ceiling overhead ... Just elevate your gaze enough to strain a little, not too much ... Now just find a point on the ceiling and keep your gaze fixed right there ... As you do so, notice what your eyes feel like and how that sensation gradually changes ... Imagine your eyelids are beginning to grow tired and heavy, more tired and heavy with each and every exhalation of breath ... Use your imagination to make your eyelids feel like closing ... As I now count from five down to zero, with each and every number, allow the muscles of your face and head to relax more deeply, and let that relaxation spread over the eyes and into the eyes, until they begin to close ... Starting now ... five ... four ... three ... two ... one ... zero ... closing all the way down ... Now just let go completely and go deeper into hypnosis ... Relax the eyes ... Relax the face ... Relax the whole body ... Keep letting go more deeply with each and every exhalation of breath ...

Staring at the ceiling constitutes a behavioural strategy that inevitably makes the eyes feel tired. Most people could do this for a long time before having to close their eyes. When suggestions of relaxation and eyelid closure are coupled with the behavioural strategy, though, the eyes tend to close within about twenty seconds or so. The use of suggestion and imagination greatly amplifies the physical sensation of heaviness created by straining the eyes and accelerates the rate of eyelid closure. With practice, of course, it becomes unnecessary to strain the eyes at all and even Braid noted that some clients (perhaps less than ten per cent) find it too uncomfortable and prefer not to use this method. The "strain" should normally be very slight, though, and in no way severe or painful. The client may, alternatively, just stare at a fixed point straight ahead and employ the same sort of suggestions.

Self-hypnosis and relaxation ("neutral hypnosis")

The self-induction of progressively deeper levels of hypnotic relaxation (sometimes called "neutral hypnosis") should also be included under the heading of hypnotic skills training experiments. This is a natural progression from the other exercises, for example, building upon the feelings of heaviness, eye closure, etc., and spreading similar sensations throughout the rest of the body. It helps to provide clients with a sense that their skills training is working towards something which is both of therapeutic value and more recognisable as a mode of traditional self-hypnosis. Clients often achieve considerable satisfaction from the sense that they have been working toward this goal.

It has often been overlooked that the depth of physical relaxation induced in self-hypnosis is itself a powerful "convincer", and provides the client with tangible evidence that she is a "good hypnotic subject." The unusually deep sensations of relaxation and observable changes in breathing, heart rate, muscle tone, etc., provide just as much confirmation that the client is responding properly to his own autosuggestions as do the traditional arm heaviness, levitation, catalepsy tests, etc. The therapist may also observe and draw the client's attention to more subtle psychophysiological effects such as dilation of the pupils, dilation of the peripheral blood capillaries, speech inhibition, time distortion, etc.

Some people are inclined to refer to this process of inducing relaxation as "self-hypnosis" itself but doing so is quite misleading. It is better construed as an effect or test of suggestion, a hypnotic response. The client should be encouraged to identify "hypnosis" with focused attention and expectation, etc., the mediating factors which occur during all of the preceding exercises. In a sense, all deliberate autosuggestion is self-hypnosis, insofar as it involves putting oneself into the role of hypnotic subject and adopting the appropriate attitudes and state of attention. Hypnosis is no longer equated with relaxation or sleep. It can clearly be induced in active and alert states, an observation central to modern research and the practice of cognitive-behavioural hypnotherapy.

The Mesmerists would often induce a state of "artificial somnambulism" in their subjects and leave them to rest in quiet for several hours. When Braid first introduced hypnotism he seems to have made limited use of verbal suggestion preferring instead to induce catalepsy by physical manipulation or simply to focus upon deepening the superficially sleep-like state he calls "nervous sleep." In the Soviet Union, for several decades, hypnotic therapy consisted largely of the induction of profound relaxation. Verbal suggestions from the hypnotist were seen as potential distractions so subjects were often left in silence in a darkened room for around an hour to relax in peace.

As we have seen, this notion of hypnotism devoid of specific therapeutic suggestions is sometimes termed "neutral hypnosis." Platonov used this approach with many hundreds of Soviet clients, and monitored the effects using various physiological measures during his work in Pavlovian laboratories (Platonov, 1959, p. 234). This went beyond typical hypnotic relaxation. Apart from the fact that all stimuli were withdrawn, including the presence of the hypnotist, the initial suggestions were somehow phrased to emphasise the notion of a recuperative state deeper than normal sleep (Platonov, 1959, p. 78).

In the vast majority of cases, Platonov's clinic apparently employed short sessions of direct hypnotic suggestion, followed by around an hour of deep hypnotic rest in silence, for about five or six sessions.

> Experience has shown that 1 hour of this state, in most cases, provided maximum rest for the entire organism. This prolonged state of suggested deep rest is extraordinarily beneficial not only to the cortical dynamics and the entire higher nervous activity as a whole, but also to the functional state of all tissues and organs and the entire vegetative and endocrine system. (Platonov, 1959, p. 79)

Whereas the reduction in heart rate found in novice meditators has been reported to be in the region of only three beats per minute, Platonov reported an average reduction of eight to ten beats per minute in his own use of neutral hypnosis, based on Pavlovian principles. This is also broadly consistent with another Soviet physiological study he cites:

> Thus, by studying the pulse and respiration in 24 subjects during suggested sleep (67 studies) A. Tsinkin came to the conclusion (1930) that in the state of deep suggested sleep the pulse slowed down by 6 to 12 beats per minute, while during weak or medium suggested sleep it slowed down by 3 to 7 beats per minute. (Platonov, 1959, p. 54)

Platonov and his colleagues applied this method to the prevention of hypertension, treatment of ulcers, and other physical conditions, but also in the treatment of neuroses. Although this approach is seldom used in modern hypnotherapy it is easy to envisage the potential benefits, especially for stress-related illnesses and anxiety disorders. Few modern clients will want to pay their therapist to leave them in a dark room in silence for an hour while he reads the newspaper outside! This method would perhaps be more suitable for use between sessions, perhaps facilitated by the use of a self-hypnosis recording.

Hetero-hypnotic induction

By presenting self-hypnosis as a prelude to hypnotherapy proper (hetero-hypnosis) the client circumvents many common misconceptions and the therapist "can settle into the congenial role of a coach, facilitator, or advisor, rather than an authoritarian figure" (Lynn & Kirsch, 2006, p. 61). There are few essential differences between self-hypnosis and hetero-hypnosis, although the presence of an external guide, providing instructions and suggestions, obviously does have some practical consequences. Erika Fromm and her colleagues concluded from detailed research that attention was generally less focused in self-hypnosis than in hetero-hypnosis and that imagery tended to be more vivid, spontaneous, and to play a more significant role in self-hypnosis (Fromm, Brown, Hurt, Oberlander, Boxer & Pfeifer, 1981). They also found, as most therapists would probably expect, certain hypnotic phenomena such as regression and hallucination to be more successful in hetero-hypnosis.

When subjects are hypnotised using a standard induction method, such as eye-fixation and suggestions of relaxation, and given a series of suggestion tests, such as those used in the Stanford Scales, a very small minority (less than five per cent) score zero, a small minority score top marks by passing all twelve tests, and the vast majority of us come somewhere around the middle, creating a roughly bell-shaped distribution of responsiveness. At first glance, that makes it look as though conventional hypnotism is moderately effective on average at increasing suggestibility. However, only if we make the basic error of assuming that the baseline response rate to suggestion tests is zero, that is, "compared to nothing." In fact, it's quite easy just to remove the induction and deepening part at the start of the Stanford Scales and deliver the rest of the suggestion tests as "waking suggestion" control measures. When this is done, the big surprise is that it makes such little difference to the outcome, people still tend to pass about half the suggestion tests, and some people still score very high. In other words, the use of a classical induction increases the number of suggestion tests responded to by about fifteen to twenty per cent. As Lynn and Kirsch put it, someone who scores six out of twelve in the waking condition might go up to about seven out of twelve when tested again with a hypnotic induction (Lynn & Kirsch, 2006, p. 41). This is a fairly consistent experimental finding. These subjects generally do report "feeling slightly spaced out", etc., just like normal hypnotherapy clients, so it's not simply that they don't feel hypnotised.

Moreover, when we try doing other things to increase their response rate, such as trying to increase their motivation to concentrate or giving them suggestions that induce the opposite of sleep-relaxation, a highly active-alert state, a virtually identical increase in the average score is generated. Hence, there seems to be little difference in this regard between alternative induction techniques (although traditional eye-fixation is probably the method about which most is known.) In other words, hypnotic inductions do work, but probably not dramatically. They work enough to justify using them but most of the benefits of hypnotherapy probably come from other factors such as the way the subsequent suggestions are delivered. To put it crudely, from a nonstate perspective, hypnotism is more the art of *suggestion* than the art of *inducing trance*. Likewise, when hypnotherapy was the only brief psychological therapy, it was easy to assume that the treatment results it achieved were due mainly to the "trance", because it was being compared against nothing. However, now that there are many non-hypnotic brief psychotherapies, such as CBT, anyone can see that although different therapies jostle for position as the treatment of choice, hypnotherapy and CBT probably have broadly similar effects, on the average, and neither is massively more effective than the other, or than many other styles of therapy. Hypnotherapy cannot credibly pretend to be dramatically more effective than CBT in treating anxiety or insomnia, for example.

Noticeably, however, hypnotherapy is more or less the only psychological therapy which makes any reference to "inducing a trance". In hypnotherapy a client might close her eyes, relax, picture their goals, and think positively. In certain forms of CBT, the client might be asked to close her eyes, relax, rehearse coping imagery, and repeat coping statements internally. There may be negligible difference between the two processes except the name "hypnosis" versus "CBT" and the use of an induction technique in the former. Most hypnosis researchers would argue that there are benefits to calling the process "hypnotic" and continuing to employ induction techniques, but it is not necessary to do so, and the added benefit of doing so is not normally dramatic. There are of course some clients who simply dislike hypnosis or for some other reason will respond negatively to it, and are better suited to non-hypnotic therapy. Likewise, there are some clients who benefit little from CBT, or anything else, but respond beautifully following a hypnotic induction. The hypnotic induction, though, is probably overrated and just one small part of the skilled hypnotherapist's armamentarium. Even Braid, perhaps, would have agreed with this observation, as he did not feel it necessary or advisable to employ eye-fixation with many clients and worked with them in the "vigilant" or "waking" condition instead.

Many novice hypnotherapists encounter unresponsive clients and say, "I don't think I'm getting them deep enough into hypnosis." In reality, this is probably a red herring and the real problem is not the "depth of trance" but the lack of mutual understanding between client and therapist. Virtually anything the therapist is trying to do "in hypnosis" should work, albeit to a lesser extent, without hypnosis. If it's not working at all then there's more likely to be a problem with the working alliance or the type of therapy techniques being used. In brief, hypnotherapists should be flexible, and adapt their approach to the needs of the client without becoming overly-fixated on the notion of "getting them deeper" into a trance. Where an alternative to the traditional eye-fixation technique is required, the hypnotist can use a wide variety of alternatives, such as the magnetic palms suggestion, suggestions of relaxation, or simply asking the client to close her eyes and put herself in hypnosis, signalling when she's ready to continue by nodding her head. However, for the most part, when hypnotism appears "not to work" it's due to the cognitive set of the subject, lack of confidence, motivation, expectation, trust in the hypnotist, or understanding of the hypnotic subject's role, etc. Discussing these things with the client and coaching her in hypnotic skills in order to help her learn the correct mind-set is generally a better approach than simply switching from one induction or deepening technique to another, in the hope that eventually something will work, without attempting to change the client's attitudes.

Hypnotic "deepening" techniques

The widely-held assumption, shared by many members of the public and even many hypnotherapists, that deepening relaxation and sleepy feelings in hypnosis increases the depth of a "trance" state which leads to greater suggestibility seems to be little more than a common misconception. Responses can be induced and deepened in hypnosis, and some changes may facilitate suggestion, to varying degrees, in different individuals, in different ways, and to different extents.

This misconception is probably fostered by the confusion between neutral and applied hypnotherapy. There may be reason to believe that unusually deep states of sleepy relaxation can be induced very effectively in hypnosis, as in the former Soviet Union, but doing so does not necessarily increase responsiveness to other hypnotic suggestions and may even be counter-productive in some respects. If someone is so relaxed they can hardly move a muscle, they are unlikely to respond as well to suggestions of energy, motivation, and enthusiasm, as someone who is in an active, alert, and focused psychophysiological state already. Hence, "alert hypnosis" is now often preferred by modern hypnotists when motivating depressed clients or enhancing sportsmen's performance (Golden, Dowd & Freidberg, 1987).

The ambiguity and confusion over the essential nature of hypnosis infects the popular concept of "going deeper into trance." What exactly is being "deepened" in hypnosis if not hypnotic trance? Most clients report depth of hypnosis based on their level of relaxation or alertness, when active-alert suggestions are given (Golden, Dowd & Freidberg, 1987, p. 27). However, relaxation in itself does not appear to correlate with heightened suggestibility. Nevertheless, if clients perceive deep relaxation as evidence that they are responding well to suggestions, this may increase their confidence and level of expectation in a way that increases subsequent suggestibility—not because hypnosis is a state of relaxation but because their expectations of relaxing were satisfied.

Most "deepeners" used by hypnotists therefore fall into one or more of the following categories, depending on what they seem primarily to be trying to "deepen" or increase.

1. *Role-involvement*. Techniques which suggest, directly or indirectly, that the client is going deeper into hypnosis and therefore imply that the client should increasingly adopt the role of a more responsive person, for example, direct suggestions such as "You are now going much deeper into hypnosis and respond more easily to positive suggestions."
2. *Relaxation*. Techniques which deepen physical or mental relaxation, for example, fractional muscle relaxation.
3. *Mental focus*. Techniques which deepen mental absorption by focusing attention, for example, encouraging the client to become engrossed in complex mental imagery or suggesting "You are becoming more and more absorbed in the sound of my voice."
4. *Dissociation*. Techniques which deepen subjective feelings of benign dissociation, for example, suggesting that the client is floating out of her body, etc.
5. *Expectancy*. Techniques which deepen faith in the process and increase response expectancy, for example, convincing demonstrations such as the arm-levitation technique.
6. *Confusion*. Followers of Erickson believe that "confusional inductions" causing disorientation in the client's mind can enhance responsiveness, though this is not a central aim of traditional hypnotism—of course, clients themselves do not normally report that they equate "depth of hypnosis" with their level of confusion!

As can be surmised, many hypnotists feel the distinction between "induction" and "deepening" techniques is somewhat arbitrary, as most deepeners can be used at the beginning of a session to induce hypnosis, and most induction techniques can be adapted for use during hypnosis as deepeners. Moreover, most deepening techniques seem to be roughly equivalent in terms of their effectiveness (Lynn & Kirsch, 2006, p. 62). The techniques most commonly used in research on hypnosis are Braid's classic eye-fixation induction, the counting deepener, and direct suggestions of fractionated relaxation, etc., so arguably we know more about these methods than any others.

However, over the years the author has informally collected data from groups of subjects attending workshops who were asked to rate their "depth of hypnosis" following various scripted techniques. The main finding, which stands in need of genuine empirical validation, is that traditional-style deepeners are consistently rated higher in terms of participants' subjective ratings of effectiveness. In particular, eye-fixation, the counting deepener, fractionated muscle relaxation, and to a lesser extent taking three deep breaths and "speech inhibition", outperformed other induction/deepening techniques in this respect. Suggestion tests such as arm catalepsy and Vogt's method of fractionation by repeated re-induction consistently performed badly as deepeners and most complex imagery was pretty "hit and miss". In short, simple, traditional methods which are easily recognisable to clients as "hypnosis" and which do not challenge them to respond or require opening their eyes, seemed to be the most reliable, according to the ratings gathered. "Placebo deepeners", that is, various deepening techniques which were plucked out of thin air or designed to be unlikely to work tended to work moderately well, about as well as many of the published techniques aside from the better ones mentioned above. One of the "placebo" deepeners tested, for example, asked subjects simply to visualise walking around an empty room, another asked them to roll their eyes back for a few minutes—neither of these were expected to have any inherent value. In one case, the author read a short story about a monkey, picked at random from a children's book, to a group of students who were told they were listening to a Neo-Ericksonian hypnosis script with specially-chosen metaphors and hidden suggestions for their unconscious minds. The group found their subjective responses during this (sham) exercise to be similar to the experience of listening to a "real" Neo-Ericksonian hypnosis script, taken from a book on hypnotherapy. It appears that often hypnotists may invent a technique which appeals to their own pet theory or personal preference, use it with a few clients, find that most of them "go a bit deeper"—maybe a minority don't like it, maybe a few respond superbly—and from this they conclude they've discovered a new deepening script and publish it for others to use! However, it's quite possible that they would have encountered the same results by asking their clients to rub their tummy and pat their head as a deepener—or perhaps something less obviously silly. These informal observations are also consistent with Barber's overall view, derived from his research programme, that although relaxation probably contributes little directly to hypnotic responsiveness, hypnosis is not relaxation; nevertheless relaxation-based inductions and deepeners do particularly seem to appeal to subjects, perhaps because they meet their expectations of hypnosis, and may therefore increase their subsequent responses (Barber, Spanos & Chaves, 1974).

As a general rule of thumb, it's a good idea to ask clients for feedback and discuss with them what they find helpful during hypnosis. It's not clear whether Braid and other early Victorian hypnotists had an explicit idea of "hypnotic deepeners" as they often seem simply to have performed an induction and treated clients for five to ten minutes before emerging them. Some modern clients, especially good subjects who have been hypnotised several times, don't appear to see the point of "deepening techniques" and may prefer simply to have a short induction and get "straight to work" on the therapy suggestions. It's possible that the main function of deepeners in the initial stages of therapy is to satisfy client expectations and provide them with some evidence of the classic suggestion effect, that is, impressive "spaced out" feelings due to unusually deep relaxation. If the client thinks "That felt strange; I'm not normally able to do that on my own!" it probably increases her self-efficacy and confidence in the therapy.

Emerging from hypnosis

Braid used to abruptly clap his hands beside the client's ear or blow in her eyes to "awake" her—not a strategy any modern hypnotist would be likely to imitate! The emerging technique should be conducted slowly enough for the client to regain her orientation, etc., unless you plan to re-hypnotise her again shortly. The most important element of the "emerging" technique is probably the *suggestion* that the client is emerging from hypnosis. You might ask what it is exactly that the client is "emerging" from if we've discarded the concept of a hypnotic trance. The answer is actually quite simple. Although we don't need to posit a special state to explain hypnotism, clients do experience various bodily sensations and other changes as a result of the suggestions given. They're usually, even in nonstate approaches, guided into relaxation—partly because this is so useful in managing anxiety problems. Hence, if that were the case, clients would be emerging from relaxation and regaining a sense of alertness. They may also be very engrossed in mental imagery or a sense of fantasy, for example, during regression, dream work, or mental rehearsal. In these cases, clients may need to gradually "emerge" from fantasy and regain their sense of orientation.

Braid called the procedure of emerging subjects from hypnotism "dehypnosis" and we can compare it in some ways to the deliberate process of dehypnosis applied to spontaneous negative self-hypnosis or negative autosuggestions. Narrowly focused attention is replaced by a shift or expansion of attention on to the external environment, as the client emerges from hypnosis. In a similar manner, mindfulness or dehypnosis strategies may encourage clients to acknowledge but expand their awareness beyond negative automatic thoughts, to encompass a wider variety of contrasting stimuli, by spreading their attention through their whole body and into the room around them. As we have seen, focusing attention narrowly on the meaning of a suggestion tends to be more evocative. By contrast, when an idea exists in consciousness alongside many other ideas and experiences, as just one small corner of a broad attentional sweep, it appears to have less "suggestive" power. This can be illustrated by asking clients to try to suggest relaxation to themselves in a state of focused attention and then alternate this with the same suggestion employed while scanning the room and trying to take in as many different aspects of the environment as possible. The latter condition tends to be less effective and clients may say they were "too distracted" to give sufficient attention to the suggestion. In this way, an analogy can be made between the typical process of emerging from hypnosis by opening the eyes and re-orienting attention to the present moment and the current environment, in a broader way, and the process of dehypnosis applied to negative autosuggestions by holding them in awareness while expanding attention beyond them, and widening its scope. A useful metaphor for this is to imagine that the thought is written on a window pane, so that the client can acknowledge its presence while looking beyond it, and taking in the view of the world outside in a more flexible and expansive state of attention, grounded in the reality of the present moment.

The question "Can I get stuck in hypnosis?" is common among anxious clients, unfamiliar with the subject. Every hypnotist knows this is impossible. As with so many misconceptions about hypnotism, a complex research-based answer to this question, though possible, is better replaced with a "common sense" response. If people could "get stuck" in hypnosis, we'd all know about it already. There would be videos and photographs of hundreds of dust-covered hypnotic subjects stacked up in psychiatric hospitals, awaiting some magical cure for being "stuck in trance". It should be obvious that this problem doesn't exist.

The notion of "hypnotic trance" as an abnormal altered state of consciousness lends itself to the fear of being somehow "stuck" in hypnosis. By contrast, if hypnosis consists of voluntarily adopting a receptive attitude and orientation, then it's difficult to see how one could get "stuck" in it any more than it's possible to get stuck in the attitude of empathising with someone or listening to a story. One consequence of clarifying this, and abandoning the mythic notion of "trance", is that the process of "hypnotic termination" or emerging from hypnosis becomes considerably less significant and mysterious.

It's been frequently observed by many hypnotists that subjects tend, after standard emerging techniques, to continue to be quite suggestible. This makes more sense, perhaps, if we assume that what was "induced" was a sense of confidence, expectation, and mental focus. Counting to five and opening your eyes doesn't necessarily remove that orientation to suggestions. Neither is it particularly problematic, though. It's true that where subjects feel disoriented or deeply relaxed, it's important to help them regain their normal reality orientation before leaving the clinic, especially, for example, if they're riding a motorcycle home. However, in general, the most important part of emerging from hypnosis is simply the instruction to "emerge from hypnosis", and perhaps giving the client time to do so, by counting from one to five.

Hypnotic suggestion

It is important to stress that hypnotic suggestion does not normally involve deception or delusion. On the contrary, cognitive-behavioural researchers have chosen to refer to traditional hypnotic styles of suggestion as "imaginative suggestion" because they are really best construed as invitations for the subject to imagine the experiences being described (Lynn, Kirsch & Hallquist, 2008, p. 112). Indeed, hypnotic suggestions often consists of describing "as if" experiences. For example, a client may be invited to imagine that her arms feel "as if" they have turned to lead to evoke feelings of heaviness and relaxation, which is a fundamentally different thing from actually believing that her arms have literally turned to lead.

The common misconception of hypnotism, that it is a form of mind-control or brainwashing, is linked to this idea that suggestions typically create delusions rather than acting as prompts for willing imagination. The fact that the subject typically agrees to imagine the things being described can, once again, be captured in the saying: "All hypnosis is self-hypnosis." As Lynn and Kirsch emphasise, although suggestions are traditionally phrased in such a way as to directly portray the suggested experiences as real ("Your arm is as rigid as a steel bar"), it would be more accurate to say that the hypnotic situation normally defines the role of the subject as being to imagine these experiences "as if" they were real, treating them as metaphors rather than taking them as literal descriptions (Lynn, Kirsch & Hallquist, 2008, p. 113).

The basic "rules" of traditional suggestion are widely-understood in the literature of hypnosis. These are no more than common sense principles designed to assist the subject in evoking appropriate responses, through the wording of suggestions in ways that are conducive to imagination. They can be summarised as follows:

1. *Meaningful and evocative.* Suggestions must be meaningful and evocative for the individual being hypnotised. There's obviously no point hypnotising someone in Latin, for example, if it's a language they don't understand. However, words such as "confident" or "assertive" are understood intellectually by many clients without necessarily evoking any emotional or imaginative response. Note that this may clash with the claims of those who believe suggestions are directed to the "unconscious mind" rather than the conscious mind, particularly the followers of Milton Erickson, who have a very different concept of hypnotic suggestion.
2. *Present tense.* Suggestions phrased in the present tense tend to be more evocative. Note that as virtually all therapy clients seek to make changes that will generalise to future situations outside of the consulting room this creates a basic problem for phrasing suggestions. "How can I suggest that I will feel more confident next Friday, but phrase it in the present tense?" The answer is simply that clients will typically have to imagine themselves in the future situation "as if" it is happening now, thereby allowing changes to be rehearsed and phrased in the present tense.
3. *Positively phrased.* Suggestions should be phrased (grammatically) in the positive to avoid the problem of evoking ideas and feelings in reaction to thoughts being verbally negated. For example, it's better to say "allow yourself to feel more calm and relaxed" rather than "allow yourself to feel less tense and anxious", etc.
4. *Personally relevant.* Suggestions should be relevant to the client's goals and values, and she should be motivated to respond to them, which means that they should suggest reactions the client is open to, and willing to experience.
5. *Repeated in different words.* Suggestions are normally repeated but as repeating a word or phrase tends to quickly lead to it losing its evocative power, it is the underlying theme that is repeated while the words are usually varied and elaborated into a script, that is, a single idea like growing in confidence in social situations is suggested in many different ways, that complement and reinforce each other.

There are a number of other principles to be aware of when employing verbal suggestion. One of the most important is the simple observation, consistently supported by research on hypnosis, that some types of suggestions are statistically much more likely to be successful than others. This should perhaps be obvious to anyone who has any experience of hypnosis but its implications are seldom discussed in the literature of hypnotherapy. A good hypnotist will develop a script, or series of suggestions, which are creatively designed to make the most use of the responses most easily evoked. "Easier" types of suggestion will tend to be used first, before introducing types that are typically "harder" to respond to.

Research on hypnosis generally distinguishes between three main categories of suggested response, which can be ranked as follows:

1. *"Physical"* or behavioural suggestions (simple ideo-motor responses), such as arm-lowering or eyelid closure, etc., which tend to have much higher response rates than other types of suggestion.

2. *"Challenge"* suggestions, or suggestions of behavioural inhibition, which involve suggesting that some behaviour will be impossible and challenging the client to try to defy the suggestion, such as suggesting arm-rigidity and challenging the client to try to bend her arm, or suggesting "eyelid-catalepsy" and challenging the client to try to open her eyes. These are moderately effective but considerably less so than simple ideo-motor suggestions, made without challenging the client to defy them. They are typical of stage hypnosis, and some experiments, but less common in hypnotherapy where some clients dislike the connotation of being "controlled" by another person.
3. *"Cognitive"* suggestions, which generally refer to suggested hallucinations or delusions, such as truly believing that a fly is buzzing around the room, etc. These are also common in stage hypnosis and some experiments but not in hypnotherapy and have the lowest success rate on average.

To this it might be added that "post-hypnotic suggestions", suggestions of a delayed response intended to occur after having emerged from hypnosis, also have a low statistical success rate on average. Although techniques such as challenge, post-hypnotic, and hallucinatory suggestions are well-known, popularly associated with hypnotism, and often referred to in relation to experimental hypnosis and stage hypnosis, they are seldom important to hypnotherapy, which is fortunate because they are not particularly reliable interventions. The main alternative to the traditional post-hypnotic (future-tense) suggestion is mental ("imaginal") rehearsal in which the client imagines being in a future situation, as if now, while *present*-tense suggestions are given and responded to, in the consulting room. Traditionally-worded post-hypnotic suggestions may be of some value as an adjunct to this technique but they should seldom be used by themselves.

Finally, it is well-known that the effectiveness of suggestions can be understood in terms of how consistent they are with the subject's expectations and how believable they seem at the time. This is closely related to the concurrent experience of the subject and the use of specific behavioural strategies to evoke real bodily sensations. This phenomenon, labelled "coupling" by Barber, is perfectly illustrated by the "bucket and balloon" suggestion experiment. The subject is asked to close her eyes, stretch out both arms in front of her, close her hands, and turn her right-hand palm upward. She is asked to imagine that she is holding the handle of a heavy bucket in her right hand and that her left hand is resting on a giant balloon, which is being inflated, causing it to feel light and rise. Responses to this experiment vary but typically the right (heavy) arm will lower somewhat and the left (light) arm will rise, although less so. This clearly illustrates the basic principle that suggestions are most effective when they are consistent with bodily sensations and other expectations. The arms are placed in a position in which gravity is bound to make them *both* grow heavy and tired, albeit slightly, which we can describe as a behavioural strategy or Braid's "muscular suggestion". Suggestions of heaviness in the right arm, therefore, need merely amplify the naturally-occurring sensations of heaviness in that position. Suggestions of lightness in the left arm are considerably less effective, although they do still generally work, because they have to compete with the natural feelings of heaviness also being experienced in that arm.

In other words, suggestions should normally be worded so that they are "coupled with" and build upon physical responses the subject is likely to have anyway or at least so that they avoid directly conflicting with her experience. This takes some creativity. For example, by asking the client to take a deep breath and hold it, then suggesting she will feel a more profound sense of relief and relaxation each time she exhales, the hypnotist builds upon the natural physical sensations of "respiratory relief", which is more likely to succeed than merely suggesting that tension is disappearing. Braid conceptualised this aspect of hypnotism from the outset in his "reciprocal interaction" theory of suggestion, discussed earlier, according to which muscular suggestions (behavioural strategies) reciprocally interact with dominant ideas (cognitive strategies) to create a powerful feedback loop. Kirsch and Lynn describe something similar in their modern cognitive-behavioural "response set" theory of hypnotism, as we have also seen. The hypnotist should bear this principle in mind and attempt, where possible, to construct suggestions that are complemented by behavioural strategies and therefore more likely to be effective. The most obvious example of this occurs in the standard eye-fixation induction where the behavioural strategy of looking up at the ceiling to strain the eyes causes a natural sensation of tiredness in the eyelids, which verbal suggestions (cognitive strategies) then amplify, creating a circular interaction between physical response and mental expectation, through coupling.

We have now explored the initial stages of treatment, including assessment, conceptualisation, and socialisation, and the wider issues of hypnotic skills training, including the use of inductions and suggestions in hypnosis. We have seen how central the collaborative philosophy is to cognitive-behavioural hypnotherapy, and the value of socialisation and training in basic hypnotic skills, including self-hypnosis. The final section of this book will proceed to explore the subsequent application of these basic skills as part of the treatment plan by looking at key emotional, behavioural, and cognitive aspects of therapy. We shall begin, however, by exploring a basic skills training approach to cognitive-behavioural hypnotherapy itself, which adapts established frameworks for coaching clients in the selection and use of basic coping skills, such as applied relaxation or more recent mindfulness and acceptance-based strategies. Skills training, and the "learning" orientation, are a theme running through this approach, starting with initial socialisation experiments but also pervading the whole treatment plan, as we shall now see.

PART III

COGNITIVE-BEHAVIOURAL HYPNOTHERAPY

CHAPTER SEVEN

Applied self-hypnosis and coping skills

Following on from socialisation of the client to cognitive-behavioural hypnotherapy, and initial hypnotic skills training, the therapist can easily progress to teaching self-hypnosis as a coping skill, tailored to suit the client's needs and preferences. What we shall call "Applied Self-Hypnosis" (ASH) or the "coping skills" approach to self-hypnosis is probably the simplest cognitive-behavioural framework for hypnotherapy. Indeed, earlier texts on cognitive-behavioural hypnotherapy have explicitly presented self-hypnosis as a versatile coping skill that can be applied by clients across a wide range of situations (Golden, Dowd & Freidberg, 1987, p. xi). The approach adopted here attempts to build upon the established research on hypnotic skills training and coping skills methodologies in CBT (Gorassini & Spanos, 1999; Meichenbaum, 2007). Self-hypnosis is widely taught in hypnotherapy as a generic coping skill and it is logical to do so early in treatment as a way of further socialising the client to her role. A simple but comprehensive cognitive-behavioural framework for doing so is presented below, modelled upon established treatments for mild to moderate stress and various subclinical issues. However, this initial approach can easily be expanded to treat more serious clinical problems, which the following chapters attempt to do by adding more rigorous exposure therapy, problem-solving, and cognitive restructuring strategies for anxiety.

Stress-inoculation training (SIT)

In the late 1960s and early 1970s Donald Meichenbaum attempted to reconcile the early cognitive therapy approaches of Aaron Beck and Albert Ellis, among others, with the principles and techniques of conventional behaviour therapy. Meichenbaum drew upon the earlier work of Soviet researchers such as Vygotsky and Luria in developing a social learning model of cognitive and behavioural change. This led to the introduction of an early cognitive-behavioural therapy called "cognitive-behaviour modification", which incorporated an emphasis on cognition in the form of internal speech (Meichenbaum, 1977). This approach shared many common elements with other cognitive-behavioural therapies, especially Beck's "cognitive therapy", although it was originally more indebted to behavioural psychology and experimental research on self-talk. Compared to Beck's approach, Meichenbaum placed somewhat less emphasis on evaluation of irrational beliefs and schemas and more emphasis on problem-solving and training in a range of cognitive and behavioural coping strategies (Meichenbaum, 1977, pp. 197–198). Meichenbaum's approach also placed slightly more emphasis on the *function* of cognition, whether it helped adaptive coping, rather than on its objective truth or falsehood. It involves teaching clients to coach themselves through stressful situations by using their own helpful self-instructions and coping statements alongside specific coping skills.

A particular application of cognitive-behaviour modification, called "stress-inoculation training" (SIT) was subsequently developed by Meichenbaum and his colleagues in the 1970s as a versatile therapeutic framework, emphasising training in multiple cognitive and behavioural coping skills for stress-related problems (Meichenbaum, 1985; Meichenbaum, 1977). SIT evolved in response to early behaviour therapy approaches to the treatment of anxiety, particularly Wolpe's systematic desensitisation, but differed in conceptualising treatment largely in terms of training in several coping skills, which were chosen from a "menu" of options, for both treatment of current psychological stress and prevention of future problems. Meichenbaum described SIT as a flexible and individually tailored form of cognitive-behavioural therapy that provided a generic framework and set of guidelines for learning coping strategies rather than a specific one-size-fits-all treatment formula (Meichenbaum, 2007). Hence, SIT itself isn't strictly-speaking a specific "therapy technique" but rather a versatile approach to training clients in a wide variety of individually-tailored coping strategies. Nevertheless, it also provides an ideal framework for delivering training in individual types of coping skill, such as applied relaxation, or self-hypnosis. This method was specifically designed to improve appraisals of coping (self-efficacy) by enhancing the client's coping-skills repertoire or, as Meichenbaum puts it, to transform learned helplessness into learned resourcefulness (Meichenbaum, 1977, p. 159). In other words, it offers a systematic approach to training clients in self-hypnosis strategies and building their skill and confidence in applying them to challenging real-world situations.

SIT is based upon the central metaphor of "inoculation", which forms the basis of the treatment rationale presented to clients during the socialisation phase (Meichenbaum, 2007). This important analogy was actually derived from the earlier work of the hypnosis researcher Martin Orne (Orne, 1965). The client is deliberately exposed to stressors in graduated doses, to build up her psychological resilience, figuratively "immunising" or "inoculating" herself toward more severe stress in the future. In this way, clients are trained to cope *prospectively*, in anticipation of future stressors. Meichenbaum defined the general principle as being that a client's resilience to stress can be enhanced by means of exposure to stimuli, either in imagination or in reality, that are strong enough to activate coping abilities without being powerful enough to actually overwhelm her (Meichenbaum, 1977, p. 182). SIT typically entails repeated exposure to traumatic memories or anticipated threats, while building up coping abilities. Hence, in addition to a form of graduated exposure, SIT involves training in the application of additional coping strategies. The primary treatment goals in SIT are to help the client build a broad, flexible repertoire of coping strategies and improve her skill and confidence in using them in a variety of stressful situations.

In older approaches, coping skills such as cue-controlled relaxation are often presented as ways to rapidly control or eliminate anxiety. However, in modern CBT, in order to avoid the problem of experiential avoidance, the emphasis is more on the use of coping skills to endure, or accept, anxiety and other unpleasant feelings without trying to escape the situation or engage in "false" safety-seeking behaviours. For example, while remaining in a challenging situation, clients may be taught how to "relax into" their anxious feelings, letting go of any struggle against them, until they abate naturally through habituation, rather than trying to "relax them away". Indeed, sometimes SIT has been explicitly combined with more prolonged exposure techniques, based on a habituation model. For example, Isaac Marks incorporated the use of SIT in combination with exposure therapy for phobias (Marks I. M., 2005, pp. 150–155, 181–188).

> The essence of dealing with fear is learning to ride it until the storm passes. In stress immunisation [SIT] how to do this is taught as a deliberate skill. It's like learning how to drive a car. To cope with stress we don't just mutter good things to ourselves. We become aware of the worrying things we say or do that cramp our style and upset us. Then we develop positive rules and strategies to adopt when in trouble. Finally we learn to use these repeatedly in all sorts of different problem situations. We practise these again and again until we automatically bring them into play whenever we feel frightened. (Marks I. M., 2005, p. 154)

However, partly as a means of improving generalisation of treatment outcomes, the emphasis in SIT typically falls more upon the development of adaptive coping responses to stressful situations, rather than merely habituation. Hence, "Stress immunisation [SIT] involves preparing for difficulties, learning what these will be, what can be done to overcome or reduce them, and rehearsing possible solutions" (Marks I. M., 2005, p. 166). One rationale for this is that whereas simple habituation may reduce anxiety in response to a specific anxiety-provoking stimulus, repeated application of coping strategies, across a variety of similar situations, may lead to growing skill and confidence, greater generalisation of improvement, and better relapse-prevention.

SIT differs from more cognitivist approaches such as Beck's cognitive therapy or Ellis' REBT, although they all emphasise the role of client's spontaneous "self-statements" or automatic thoughts. It involves greater time spent on directly rehearsing changes in self-talk during performance, often in parallel to the use of behavioural coping strategies, which self-instructions are coupled with, and designed to complement. The emphasis is more upon rehearsing adaptive ways of thinking and acting in graduated steps and stages whereas, for example, Beck's cognitive therapy places greater emphasis on questioning the evidence for thoughts. In other words, although there is considerable overlap between cognitive therapy and SIT, Meichenbaum's approach is more concerned with whether self-statements and behavioural strategies are *helpful* in *coping* with stress rather than whether they are *realistic appraisals* of the situation. Hence, it is sometimes said that SIT is more of a constructive approach, which centres on developing new and better ways of coping with stress, whereas cognitive therapy focuses on modifying existing cognitive structures and removing factors responsible for maintaining emotional disturbance (Rachman & Wilson, 1980, pp. 208–209). As Meichenbaum put it, whereas the cognitive therapies of Beck and Ellis focus on tackling the presence of maladaptive self-talk (automatic thoughts), and associated beliefs, coping skills approaches focus more on tackling the absence of specific coping skills and attempting to rectify this by training the client in helpful new strategies, systematically building her skill and confidence when applying these in the real world (Meichenbaum, 1977, p. 194). However, the difference is essentially one of emphasis as SIT has much in common with other CBT approaches.

As noted, SIT is a flexible multi-component treatment approach and normally adapted for different problems by incorporation of different conceptualisations and coping skills, etc. For example, Meichenbaum describes a specific application of SIT for clients with multiple phobias, consisting of psycho-education and discussion about anxiety reactions, followed by modelling and then behavioural rehearsal of coping skills and associated self-instructions, which were then applied to various stressful situations, with positive reinforcement for the client's efforts (Meichenbaum, 1977, p. 157). More specifically, these clients were taught to conceptualise their phobias in terms of a cognitive model of emotion commonly used in SIT that distinguishes between four chronological phases: preparation, exposure, coping with feeling overwhelmed, and reflection afterwards. Specific coping strategies involved collecting factual information about the object of the phobias (including rats and snakes), learning tension-release relaxation techniques, controlled breathing, self-monitoring of anxious thoughts, coping statements designed to counter them, worry prevention, and self-instructions for motivation and focus, etc. (Meichenbaum, 1977, pp. 154–155).

Similarly, hypnotherapy and autosuggestion techniques can easily be assimilated within the broad SIT framework as can modern mindfulness and acceptance-based approaches. For example, applied self-hypnosis based on a similar coping skills approach might consist of the following stages and coping strategies, depending on the needs of the client:

1. **Assessment, conceptualisation, and socialisation**
    a. Assessment of the client, her problem, and existing coping style.
    b. Psycho-education about the treatment and client symptoms and socialisation to hypnosis and the treatment approach.
    c. Conceptualisation of the client's problem in terms of negative self-hypnosis (NSH) and unhelpful autosuggestions, occurring at four stages (before, during, at critical points, and after), explained in terms of a simple "vicious cycle" diagram.
    d. Imagery-based recall techniques to gather information and heighten awareness of early-warning signs, with initial training in "distancing" (dehypnosis) strategies.
    e. Self-monitoring of negative automatic thoughts (autosuggestions) and raising awareness of early-warning signs of symptoms occurring.
2. **Skills acquisition and rehearsal**
    a. Evaluation of existing coping skills in terms of their helpfulness in the longer-term, and modification or elimination of unhelpful strategies.
    b. Evaluation of possible alternatives such as hypnotic, dehypnotic, and nonhypnotic coping strategies, for example, hypnotic relaxation, autosuggestions for coping, dehypnosis or "distancing" strategies, etc.

    c. Modelling and coaching in chosen coping skills, perhaps including training in basic hypnotic skills or mindfulness (dehypnosis) strategies

    d. Rehearsal of skills for homework, for example, by listening daily to a recording and recording progress and observations

3. **Application and generalisation**
    a. Application of coping skills in imagination, for example, coping imagery used in hypnosis in anticipation of real situations
    b. Application of coping skills during real-world (*in vivo*) graduated exposure, across a range of challenging situations
    c. Rapid-frequent application of abbreviated coping skills, such as brief cue-controlled relaxation, autosuggestion, or brief mindfulness exercises, regularly throughout the day, across a range of situations, for increased generalisation
    d. Anticipation of future high-risk situations and early-warning signs of relapse, and problem-solving potential setbacks (relapse prevention)
    e. Development of a final summary of the conceptualisation and revised coping plan for future reference (therapy blueprint).

Although this framework may look complex at first, it's actually very simple, flexible, and intuitive when applied in practice. In a sense, any existing attempt to train clients in self-hypnosis as a coping skill will probably already be doing many of these things. However, it would probably also benefit from expanding to include any missing or neglected elements, which are identified in the framework above as being of general value and importance.

Research on stress-inoculation training

SIT was designed for both clinical and nonclinical problems and recognises that stressors may range from situations that are acute and time-limited to those which are chronic and continual, and vary across a number of dimensions (Meichenbaum, 2007). Hence, the range of stressful situations targeted can include time-limited and chronic (ongoing or recurrent) stressful situations, as well as stress caused by current, anticipated, or past events, ranging from minor aggravations to severe traumas. Research studies have, in particular, applied SIT to the treatment of various forms of stress, pain, and anxiety. It has been employed with a wide variety of professional groups, including probation officers, nurses, teachers, military personnel, psychiatric staff members, disaster and safety workers, and with individuals coping with transitions such as unemployment, joining the military, re-entering college, etc. (Meichenbaum, 2007). Rachman and Wilson provided an early review of thirty-four controlled outcome studies on self-instruction and SIT, published between 1971 and 1979, covering a wide range of problems and client groups, including some psychiatric conditions, such as schizophrenia and agoraphobia, and many non-clinical problems such as non-assertiveness, fear of snakes, public speaking nerves, test anxiety, etc. (Rachman & Wilson, 1980, pp. 209–220). They concluded that the overall pattern of results was very encouraging, adding:

> SIT was compared with various control conditions and alternative forms of treatment including systematic desensitization, behaviour rehearsal, EMG biofeedback, and operant conditioning

procedures. The findings suggest that SIT was significantly superior to control conditions in most studies and equalled or out-performed comparison treatments in others. (Rachman & Wilson, 1980, p. 217)

A more recent meta-analysis of SIT's effects on anxiety and performance in a variety of settings, examined thirty-seven different studies, including 1,837 participants. The authors concluded:

> Results indicated that stress inoculation training was an effective means for reducing performance anxiety, reducing state anxiety, and enhancing performance under stress. Furthermore, the examination of moderators such as the experience of the trainer, the type of setting in which training was implemented, and the type of trainee population revealed no significant limitations on the application of stress inoculation training to applied training environments. (Saunders, Driskell, Johnston & Salas, 1996)

This review reported the number of practice sessions across different research studies to fall in the range one to ten for different applications. However, Meichenbaum states that in clinical practice the typical number of SIT sessions is typically eight to fifteen, followed by booster and follow-up sessions over a three to twelve month period (Meichenbaum, 2007). Duration of treatment is therefore broadly similar to hypnotherapy, or perhaps slightly longer on average, although less severe problems generally require fewer therapy sessions.

Meichenbaum has published a brief, systematic treatment manual for practitioners entitled *Stress Inoculation Training* (1985), outlining the method. This was intended to provide a very flexible cognitive-behavioural methodology for the delivery of coping skills in contrast to the many popular "stress management" approaches which adopt a more prescriptive or "cookbook" approach. SIT approaches things from a different perspective, by providing a generic model for the selection and systematic application of diverse coping skills. Moreover, Meichenbaum's generic SIT treatment manual was intended to stimulate further research into more specific applications. For example, an earlier manual describes SIT applied to the treatment of various types of pain in considerable detail (Turk, Meichenbaum & Genest, 1983). However, as noted, the general-purpose SIT approach also provides a convenient framework for developing a flexible "coping skills" approach to training in *self-hypnosis*, from a cognitive-behavioural perspective. The rest of this chapter will therefore explore the integration of cognitive-behavioural skills training approaches to hypnosis with the generic coping skills framework provided by SIT, in relation to therapeutic strategies for stress and anxiety symptoms.

Applied self-hypnosis (ASH)

Applied hypnotic coping-skills approaches for stress management, and the treatment of related problems such as anxiety disorders, can perhaps best be modelled on SIT. Rather than simply providing additional coping strategies, though, there are ways in which these approaches might be more closely integrated. For instance, the use of relaxation, mental (coping) imagery, and coping statements or self-instructions for stress inoculation, which often resemble autosuggestions of the kind used in self-hypnosis, may be interwoven with a wide variety of coping strategies and provide ways to facilitate rehearsal and skills acquisition. However, in doing so, we must be careful to avoid the prescriptive "single component" approach to stress reduction Meichenbaum warned against (Meichenbaum, 1985, p. 21). Hypnotism should be seen as merely one among many possible approaches, capable of being integrated within a stress-inoculation framework. In other words, stress-inoculation training is perhaps better seen as providing a generic conceptual framework for hypnotherapy, rather than the other way around. SIT also makes use of a broad spectrum of cognitive-behavioural interventions including cognitive restructuring, problem-solving, role-play, mental rehearsal, self-monitoring, self-instruction, self-reinforcement, and environmental changes, etc. However, hypnotherapy is itself an extremely technically eclectic approach, and really more of a framework for delivering specific interventions than a specific technique. What hypnotism brings to the table, as it were, is not only a repertoire of coping strategies but a broader framework for facilitating training by means of inducing a responsive mind-set to suggestions and mental imagery, in particular.

Meichenbaum stressed the complexity of the relationship between stress and coping, and the difficulty of predicting whether a particular coping strategy will be helpful or unhelpful for a given client or circumstance (Meichenbaum, 1985, p. 14). Instead, the SIT approach is based on the guidance that the therapist should propose coping strategies cautiously, presenting the evidence in a balanced way, and helping the client to evaluate the pros and cons of different approaches in a collaborative manner, leading to the construction of a flexible, tailored treatment plan based on a careful functional analysis of the client's problems (Meichenbaum, 1985, p. 15). The client should also be helped to evaluate her past history of relevant coping and current coping strategies.

Because of the observation from basic research in the stress field that different stressors appear to require different coping strategies, which may vary at different times, it is typically recommended that a "flexible coping repertoire" should be cultivated (Lazarus R. S., 1999). Hence, multiple strategies are assessed using a relatively simple three-stage behaviour-analysis and problem-solving model (Meichenbaum, 1985, p. 15). For example, typical questions that help therapist and client to collaboratively evaluate relevant treatment options, in terms of specific coping strategies, might include:

1. *Problem-identification.* What is the specific problem, how does it function, and what specific goals can the client realistically hope to achieve?
2. *Response enumeration.* What ways of coping have been tried in the past? What existing coping strategies are being used? What "menu" of relevant coping strategies can be gleaned from the literature on similar problems? What's worked in the past for other people with similar problems? What else can the client think of that might be worth trying?
3. *Response evaluation.* How are the client's existing strategies working out in the long-run? Which alternative strategies would be easiest to learn and apply? Which strategies would be most likely to help achieve the client's goals? What would be the short-term and long-term consequences of particular strategies? What are the pros and cons of each option? Can some

strategies be combined for cumulative effect? Which two to three coping responses would seem like the best option to begin learning and testing out in practice?

As Meichenbaum points out, left to their own devices, people who struggle with stress often persist in employing ways of coping that are ineffective or even exacerbate the problem so careful evaluation of the workability of different strategies is important. The therapist may help the client to begin evaluation of her existing coping strategies through simple questions such as: "How's that way of coping been working out for you in the long-run?" The later chapter on problem-solving training (PST) will provide a much more comprehensive account of problem-solving methodology that may be relevant in some cases. However, for the selection of stress-related coping strategies, a simple process of evaluation and decision-making is often sufficient.

In relation to applied self-hypnosis, therapists may choose to offer clients a range of hypnotic, dehypnotic and nonhypnotic strategies to consider, based upon a cognitive-behavioural conceptualisation of their problem. Chosen strategies are then rehearsed, perhaps using hypnotic inductions to enhance mental rehearsal or self-hypnosis recordings for daily practice, etc. Strategies are then tested out during graduated exposure to progressively more stressful tasks. Generalisation of improvement in coping skills is actively encouraged, in collaboration with the client, by rehearsing a range of different tasks and situations, especially ones closely-related to the treatment goal. As treatment proceeds, coping skills such as self-hypnosis may need to be abbreviated, for example, by replacing them with the use of cues or hypnotic triggers, for example, the client may learn rapid cue-controlled relaxation techniques or two to three minute mindfulness strategies. As with problem-solving training, emphasis is placed on contingency planning (backup plans) and preparing for potential setbacks in the future.

Applied self-hypnosis process goals

The process goals of applied self-hypnosis are therefore similar to those of SIT (Meichenbaum, 1985, p. 22). They can be summarised as follows:

1. Clients are taught to conceptualise stress or anxiety, typically according to Lazarus' basic transactional model of stress, from which Beck's cognitive model of anxiety is also derived.
2. The concept of negative self-hypnosis (NSH) is used to reconceptualise problems in terms of spontaneous negative (unhelpful) autosuggestions and associated beliefs.
3. Clients are taught to self-monitor and record their thoughts (autosuggestion), actions, and feelings, in order to gain psychological distance from them and improve awareness.
4. Clients are taught, following self-monitoring, to regard the "early warning" signs of stressful or maladaptive responses as cues for the utilisation of coping skills.
5. Existing coping strategies are functionally evaluated, in terms of their overall workability, and new alternatives are suggested based on the model and the client's creative problem-solving.
6. Clients are trained in a simplified form of the "problem-solving" approach, involving problem definition, generation of alternatives, decision making, and implementation and evaluation of proposed coping strategies.

7. Problem-focused (instrumental) and/or emotion-focused (palliative) coping strategies are considered, including a range of hypnotic, dehypnotic, and nonhypnotic techniques, for example, hypnotic relaxation or coping imagery, distancing, cognitive restructuring, etc.
8. The coping skills identified for training are modelled and rehearsed, perhaps using hypnosis as an adjunct to training, for example, to mentally rehearse coping strategies.
9. Application of coping skills through graduated exposure using imaginal, role-play, and/or real-world (*in vivo*) tasks is employed to progressively build the client's repertoire of coping skills and self-confidence ("self-efficacy"), again perhaps using hypnosis for mental rehearsal of coping skills.
10. Generalisation is explicitly encouraged, often through abbreviation of coping skills and frequent daily practice, and clients are helped to anticipate future setbacks (relapse prevention) and prepared to cope with unexpected stressors in the future (contingency planning), building psychological resilience to stressful situations.

Meichenbaum's SIT guidelines also stressed the importance of developing a healthy working alliance and the need for adopting a flexible approach, tailoring things to the client's individual needs and preferences (Meichenbaum, 1985, p. 20). Clients are praised for their efforts, as well as their successes, and encouraged to praise and reinforce themselves congruently as well. These are, of course, also extremely important factors when using teaching self-hypnotic coping skills. Ideally, the whole atmosphere of training should be collaborative and experimental, a team effort, where therapist and client work side-by-side and in an open-minded manner, formulating hypotheses about the most adaptive ways of coping and testing them out systematically in practice.

Hence, the overall SIT framework has been seen as a means of increasing "self-efficacy" and improving self-appraisal of coping ability, central to cognitive conceptualisations of stress and anxiety. In particular, providing clients with a repertoire of coping skills, which they have played a role in choosing on the basis of a shared conceptualisation, is one way of enhancing their perceived control over stressful or threatening situations (Rokke & Rehm, 2001, p. 178). However, the basic coping skills approach is probably best-suited to cases where coping ability is appraised as inadequate but the challenges faced are viewed fairly realistically, such as mild to moderate, or subclinical, stress-related problems. The role of cognition should typically be evaluated, particularly to identify the presence of exaggerated threat appraisals, which are typically more prominent in more sever anxiety disorders. Where clients are experiencing faulty threat appraisals, in addition to learning coping strategies, greater emphasis on cognitive therapy of the kind developed by Beck, and described in a later chapter of the current volume, may be necessary.

Situations which are perceived as unpredictable and uncontrollable tend to be more stressful and anxiety-provoking. However, by learning a repertoire of adaptive coping skills, including both "palliative" and "instrumental" strategies, and self-instructions to guide them, clients may acquire an increased sense of control over their circumstances. Although they are often contrasted with older "self-control" or "coping skills" approaches, mindfulness and acceptance-based strategies emphasised in modern "third-wave" approaches to CBT can be assimilated within this framework (Hayes, Follette & Linehan, 2004). Strategies like cognitive distancing, mindfulness meditation, and active acceptance of unpleasant feelings can be presented as one set of options alongside others, allowing the client to compare strategies and choose between them, perhaps after testing them out. Hence, with these broad aims in mind and following the SIT framework, applied self-hypnosis is roughly divided into three logically-distinct phases of training: assessment, skills-acquisition, and application.

Assessment, conceptualisation and socialisation phase

The assessment, conceptualisation, and socialisation phase of applied self-hypnosis resembles the various approaches discussed in earlier chapters of the current volume. However, it may be worth recapping and expanding here on certain aspects of particular relevance to applied self-hypnosis and the general coping skills orientation. For example, for coping skills to be developed, it is particularly important that complex problems should be broken down into sub-goals and the client should be encouraged to differentiate between *changeable* and *unchangeable* aspects of the situation, that is, those aspects under her control and those not (Meichenbaum, 2007). One way of doing this is to have the client complete a simple two-column "control appraisal" form, in relation to her specific problems and goals, with one column headed "under direct control" and the other headed "not under direct control". This quintessentially "Stoic" method will be discussed in more detail in the later chapter on cognitive therapy. However, it is particularly useful here because ultimately the client's own actions are the only things directly under her control, focus upon which helps to socialise her to the importance of evaluating her current coping behaviour and testing out alternative ways of behaving.

As we've seen, the coping skills approach also requires careful assessment of the client's current ways of coping and evaluation of their workability. In many cases, clients can be conceptualised as "stuck" in coping styles that may have been helpful in the past but have somehow become maladaptive or excessive, such as worrying, safety-seeking, distraction, or avoidance. Moreover, applied self-hypnosis also carefully examines the client's cognitions, in the form of internal self-talk that accompanies coping behaviour. Hence, two fundamental questions are posed in the assessment stage, modified from SIT (Meichenbaum, 1977, p. 249).

1. What is the client *actually* doing and saying (suggesting to herself), which appears to interfere with helpful (adaptive) outcomes?
2. What is the client *failing* to do and say (suggest to herself), which could potentially lead to more helpful (adaptive) outcomes?

SIT was one of the first cognitive or behavioural therapies to really emphasise the importance of developing a shared conceptualisation of the client's problem at the outset of treatment (Meichenbaum, 1977, pp. 151–153). At different stages of the problem, a cross-sectional (situational) conceptualisation may be developed, which basically differentiates between the client's thoughts, actions, and feelings, in response to the stressful situation. More specifically, description of the situation should include reference to person-environment factors such the internal or external triggers for the stress response, and predisposing factors like schemas of threat and vulnerability, lack of social support (or other interpersonal problems), and actual coping abilities available. The main automatic thoughts and images of interest are those which involve distorted, schema-related appraisals of threat and coping, as these can be viewed as mediating the activation of the "primal threat mode", as Beck puts it, which we might also label the "stress mode". Stress mode activation consists of emotions, bodily sensations, and automatic behavioural inhibition or mobilisation.

Beck's cognitive therapy approach to stress management particularly emphasises the importance of "behavioural inclinations" or action tendencies that may not be fully discharged and can lead to chronic problems, for example, being "prepared for action" and activating muscles ready to fight or flee without relevant overt behavioural responses occurring (Pretzer & Beck, 2007, p. 478, 479). Finally, more deliberate, strategic attempts at coping, either cognitively or behaviourally, can be identified, which typically fall into the broad categories of problem-focused (instrumental) or emotion-focused (palliative) strategies, from which some authors distinguish social-support seeking and other interpersonal strategies, or meaning-making and cognitive reappraisal of the situation. Because the client's overt attempts at coping tend to have an impact on the situation, whether helpful or unhelpful, this process can be conceptualised as a cycle, circle, or spiral, in which the impact of coping on the situation is repeatedly reappraised and either maintains or de-activates the stress mode.

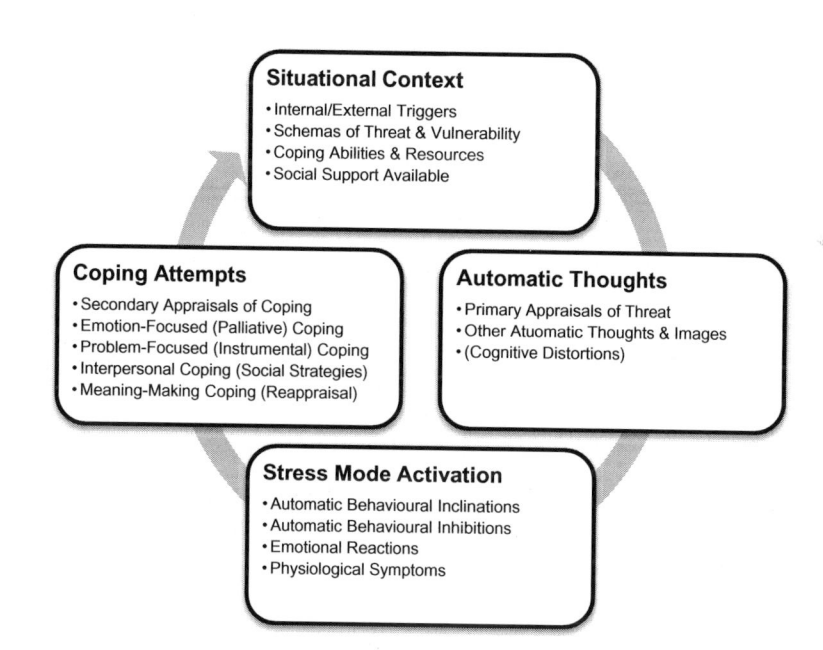

Situational Context
- Internal/External Triggers
- Schemas of Threat & Vulnerability
- Coping Abilities & Resources
- Social Support Available

Automatic Thoughts
- Primary Appraisals of Threat
- Other Atuomatic Thoughts & Images
- (Cognitive Distortions)

Stress Mode Activation
- Automatic Behavioural Inclinations
- Automatic Behavioural Inhibitions
- Emotional Reactions
- Physiological Symptoms

Coping Attempts
- Secondary Appraisals of Coping
- Emotion-Focused (Palliative) Coping
- Problem-Focused (Instrumental) Coping
- Interpersonal Coping (Social Strategies)
- Meaning-Making Coping (Reappraisal)

This stress conceptualisation is similar to the "clock face" or "vicious cycle" approach advocated by Meichenbaum, except that, consistent with Beck's generic models of anxiety and stress, it views escalation of emotion as following appraisal of threat, rather than the other way around (Clark & Beck, 2010, pp. 32, 176–177, 193; Meichenbaum, 2007, p. 503; Pretzer & Beck, 2007, p. 480). Moreover, it is worth noting that Beck identifies the following potential causes of stress (Pretzer & Beck, 2007, p. 480).

1. The actual demands of the situation may exceed the individual's coping ability.
2. The individual may over-estimate the demands of the situation or under-estimate her coping, and thereby distort the risk-resources ratio.
3. The individual may catastrophe or exaggerate the consequences of failure to cope.
4. The individual may attempt to cope with the situation in ways that are maladaptive and backfire.
5. Certain fears or beliefs may inhibit the individual from using relevant coping skills.
6. There may be a lack of adequate social support.
7. Certain fears or beliefs may inhibit use of existing social support.

The assessment and conceptualisation are designed not merely to provide information but to heighten the client's self-awareness of her ongoing response patterns and to stimulate them to modify her thoughts and actions (Meichenbaum, 1977, pp. 251–252). This initial stage of treatment also involves the development of a working alliance conducive to guiding the client through the process of repeated exposure to stressors required for "stress inoculation" to occur.

Applied self-hypnosis particularly emphasises the use of "imagery recall" methods to gather detailed information in assessment. The client is often asked to close her eyes and relive recent, typical examples of stressful situations, recounting the sequence of relevant thoughts, actions, and feelings, and any common cognitive themes (Meichenbaum, 1977, p. 249). The use of imagery-based recall can also be very helpful in raising awareness of "early warning signs", low-intensity signs of incipient problems, which normally go unnoticed. For example, after describing a recent stressful situation, the client can be asked to "rewind" slightly and describe in detail what was happening just prior to the problem being noticed, and as it began to take hold. Spotting early-warning signs and treating them as "cues to cope", allows the client to introduce alternative coping styles earlier in the cycle of distress, when it is likely to be most effective.

As in other forms of CBT, self-monitoring outside of sessions is also emphasised as a means of gathering information on typical stressors and responses, that is, thoughts, behaviours, and feelings, etc. However, research in the stress and coping field has shown that retrospective reports of coping are unreliable. Correlations between daily reports of stressful events and coping and weekly retrospective reports are relatively poor (r=0.47–0.58) (Folkman & Moskowitz, 2004, pp. 749–750). Hence, to avoid the problem of retrospective reports distorting information, clients are usually encouraged to keep daily records of problems, or coping strategies, made as close as possible to the actual events. Records should ideally be tailored for the individual client's needs. The example below encourages clients to record different stressful situations, any early-warning signs spotted such as muscular tension, the main feelings (rating their intensity), the most upsetting thoughts, and the main behaviour they engaged in, including any existing coping attempts, rating how helpful or "workable" it would be if continued these ways of thinking and acting in the long-term.

Self-monitoring record				
Date/Time/Situation	Earliest signs	Feelings (Intensity %)	Thoughts (Helpful %)	Behaviour (Helpful %)

In addition to carrying out a detailed cognitive-behavioural analysis of the problem situations, the emphasis in this stage is on developing a strong working alliance, socialising the client to her role in the training, setting treatment goals, and educating her about the nature of stress and the application of the "transactional" conceptualisation to her problems. Reconceptualisation basically involves providing the client with a framework for interpreting her problem, presented in broadly "layman's" terms, which the client fleshes out the content of collaboratively with the therapist. Perhaps controversially, Meichenbaum believed that the scientific basis of a particular conceptual model was relatively unimportant compared to its face validity to the client (Meichenbaum, 1977, p. 151). Indeed, there is little evidence to support the notion that sharing different conceptualisations contributes to treatment outcome (Kuyken, Padesky & Dudley, 2009). Whether or not some approaches are significantly better than others, one of the main advantages of any form of conceptualisation appears to be that it teaches clients to divide their problem up into different aspects (for example, thoughts, actions, feelings) and chronological stages (for example, before, during, after). This allows the client to begin considering the relationships between these multiple basic factors rather than viewing her problem, in all-or-nothing terms, as a kind of homogenous "lump" of stress or anxiety (Meichenbaum, 1977, p. 153). As the proverb says, "Divide and conquer."

Although the conceptualisation model in SIT has been varied to suit different problems and client groups (Meichenbaum, 1985, p. 48) it generally conceptualises stress based upon the influential "transactional" (or "seesaw") model of Richard Lazarus, described earlier (Lazarus R. S., 1999; Meichenbaum, 2007). This happens to be the same underlying model from which Beck's cognitive therapy of anxiety and a number of other cognitive-behavioural treatment approaches, including problem-solving therapy (PST), are derived (Clark & Beck, 2010; D'Zurilla & Nezu, 2007). The transactional model conceptualises stress reactions as being cognitively mediated by the relationship between appraisals of personal coping ability and appraisals of situational demands, as we have noted earlier in the chapter on conceptualisation. Clients should generally be made aware, for example, that although stressful "life events" do appear to have negative effects, the interaction ("transaction") between stressful events and coping responses appears to be a better predictor of whether or not stress will cause long-term problems or not. Lazarus summed this up by noting that the correlation with illness generally found in research on negative life events, "improves prediction over chance by less than 10% and is, therefore, too low to have practical value" (Lazarus R. S., 1999, p. 51). The role of cognitive appraisal, coping skills and problem-solving in determining the response to stress is therefore usually emphasised in the conceptualisation phase. As noted above, for milder problems the emphasis may fall upon appraisals of coping ability in relation to realistic appraisals of demands or threat. However, with more severe anxiety, greater attention is usually paid to threat appraisals as these may be highly distorted. Nevertheless, most clients who suffer from stress or anxiety, to a greater or lesser extent, will tend to distort their appraisals both of threat and of coping, and the two are often closely intertwined and not entirely distinct.

Moreover, in addition to developing a shared conceptualisation of the problem, more didactic psycho-education about the nature of stress *symptoms* is provided at this stage. Stress is normalised and the client is encouraged to see her reactions as relatively understandable and natural. Focus is shifted on to the "here and now" and current coping with stress rather than dwelling on the past. Throughout applied self-hypnosis, the client should be helped to develop a sense of resilience and "learned resourcefulness" and to see problems as difficult challenges-to-be-coped-with rather than overwhelming threats-to-be-avoided. Likewise, setbacks are anticipated and seen as normal and temporary, that is, as learning opportunities rather than catastrophic reasons for relapse. Hence, the hypnotic coping skills approach fosters a general problem-solving orientation, as in Meichenbaum's approach. The aim is not to eliminate stress but rather to encourage clients to adopt the role of active problem-solver in relation to their goal of finding a more helpful and adaptive way of coping with stress (Meichenbaum, 1985, p. 30).

Indeed, the role of the hypnotist and trainer himself is that of a "creative problem solver" rather than someone rigidly following a stepwise treatment protocol. However, the basic distinction between emotion-focused (palliative) and problem-focused (instrumental) coping from the stress literature should be borne in mind (Lazarus R. S., 1999). Problem-focused coping attempts to address the perceived source of the stress, fixing the problem about which the client is upset, whereas emotion-focused coping tries to manage the emotional reaction to events by targeting distressing thoughts and feelings. The most beneficial strategy will vary depending largely on whether the situation is seen as changeable and under the client's control or not. Where problem situations cannot be resolved, individuals will tend to focus on managing their emotions (emotion-focused coping) instead of trying to manage the situation (problem-focused coping). However, the majority of problems tend to require a combination of both coping styles. It should also be emphasised that mindfulness and acceptance-based approaches can be evaluated alongside other coping strategies and may be used in combination with many traditional behavioural strategies such as relaxation skills or assertiveness strategies, etc. Following initial "control appraisal", as described above, the client is likely to conclude that some aspects of the problem are outside her direct control and probably need to be accepted, at least for the time being. By contrast, those aspects under direct control, her own actions and primarily her coping behaviour, should be "owned", evaluated, and improved, in order to render them more workable for the longer-term. However, a rough distinction can be made between emotion-focused coping styles that involve attempts at self-control, the avoidance or elimination of unpleasant thoughts and feelings, and those involving mindfulness and acceptance of internal experiences. The former style of coping is often less workable in the longer-term, especially with severe anxiety, where "experiential avoidance" may frequently backfire. In general, mindfulness and acceptance-based strategies (including distancing and dehypnosis) may be preferable styles of emotion-focused coping.

Clients are also encouraged to reconceptualise their stress responses by differentiating between several components and chronological phases of the stress and coping cycle. Clients, as in other CBT approaches, are helped to distinguish between environmental triggers and their thoughts, actions, and feelings in response to them. As noted earlier, Meichenbaum particularly emphasises the chronological conceptualisation of coping responses in terms of four phases as a generic part of conceptualisation in SIT, namely: preparation, confrontation, coping with critical moments, and reflection or reinforcement afterwards (Meichenbaum, 1985, p. 48).

This model can be applied to a wide variety of stressful situations. For example, in relation to hypnosis for childbirth, the stages might be distinguished as follows:

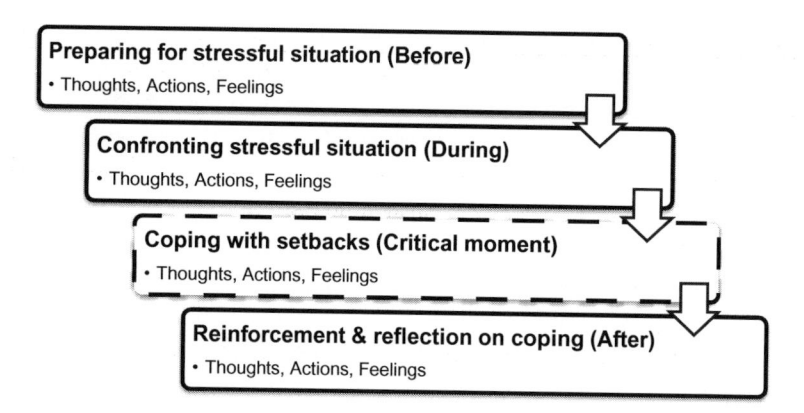

```
┌─────────────────────────────────────────────┐
│ Preparing for stressful situation (Before)  │
│ • Thoughts, Actions, Feelings               │
└─────────────────────────────────────────────┘
        │
        ▼
    ┌─────────────────────────────────────────────┐
    │ Confronting stressful situation (During)    │
    │ • Thoughts, Actions, Feelings               │
    └─────────────────────────────────────────────┘
            │
            ▼
        ┌─────────────────────────────────────────────┐
        │ Coping with setbacks (Critical moment)      │
        │ • Thoughts, Actions, Feelings               │
        └─────────────────────────────────────────────┘
                │
                ▼
            ┌─────────────────────────────────────────────┐
            │ Reinforcement & reflection on coping (After)│
            │ • Thoughts, Actions, Feelings               │
            └─────────────────────────────────────────────┘
```

1. Preparation for labour, that is, the period of pregnancy, which involves coping with a variety of problems as well as preparation for childbirth itself.
2. Confronting the experience of labour, that is, exposure to the onset of labour itself and the potential stressors involved with giving birth.
3. Coping with critical moments, that is, dealing with contractions and possibly certain medical interventions or high-anxiety moments, including panic sensations.
4. Reflection after childbirth, that is, looking back on how coping strategies worked out after the baby is born, savouring positive experiences, learning from events, and reinforcing constructive ways of coping.

As noted earlier, the client is encouraged to carefully assess the subtle signs of incipient anxiety or distress ("low-intensity" or "prodromal" cues) that can arise during any of these four stages of exposure to potential stressors, that is, to spot the early warning signs of potential emotional problems. She can then prepare to combat stressful responses by "nipping them in the bud", or "short-circuiting" them, that is, employing adaptive coping skills and strategies at the earliest opportunity in the chain of responses (Meichenbaum, 1977, p. 153). In relation to childbirth, this might entail identifying what constitutes a likely early warning signal of potential problems, such as negative automatic thoughts, and responding with an appropriate coping response. For instance, the parturient woman might spot signs of worry such as frowning or thinking "I can't do this" and respond immediately by using relaxation and rehearsal of helpful autosuggestions or coping statements, such as: "I *can* do this; lots of other people do it; it's what nature designed my body to do!"

Other challenging situations may be more recurrent, for example, social anxiety may be conceptualised in terms of before, during and after stages as follows:

1. Preparation for social encounters, involving worry and anticipatory anxiety about social situations, and perhaps over-preparation and other unnecessary or maladaptive coping attempts.
2. Confronting social situations, involving excessive self-focused attention and behavioural inhibition in response to stressful social experiences.

3. Critical moments during encounters, involving social gaffes, the overwhelming urge to escape from the situation or even situationally cued panic attacks, etc.
4. Reflection afterwards, involving morbid rumination of the worst aspects of the situation and negatively biased recall and interpretation of events (often called "the post-mortem").

Hence, Meichenbaum conceptualises the "story" of the client's stress and coping cycles by distinguishing between the *before*, *during*, and *after* of exposure to a stressful task or situation, with the optional insertion of an additional phase that only occurs when setbacks or particularly "critical moments" arise and feelings of distress risk becoming overwhelming (Meichenbaum, 1977, p. 153). The concept of planning to cope with potential setbacks or critical moments can be compared to the notion of "contingency planning" in problem-solving, that is, "What is the backup plan if things seem to be going wrong?"

> The essential ingredient of SIT is the tracking of self-statements (what clients say to themselves) at each of the four phase. Once statements that exacerbate anxiety (e.g., "This is too much for me!") are identified, new coping self-statements can be substituted (e.g., "I know I can handle it"). (Salovey & Singer, 1991, p. 373)

During each of these chronological stages, clients faces different demands, which call for different coping responses. Their stress and coping at each stage can also be conceptualised most simply in terms of thoughts, actions, and feelings. More specifically, Lazarus' transactional model can be used to conceptualise stress in terms of the difference between their cognitive appraisals of threat (or harm/loss) versus coping, their actual coping attempts, and physiological symptoms of emotional disturbance (Lazarus R. S., 1999).

As noted above, this may easily be developed into a slightly more sophisticated "vicious cycle" model of stress and coping, which describes the "micro-level" of responses within particular chronological phases in terms of a more rapid sequence of events, typically: initial orientation to triggers, automatic appraisals of threat, automatic emotional and behavioural reactions, and then more deliberate ("strategic") coping attempts (including maladaptive efforts such as "false" safety-seeking) and additional thoughts appraising the difficulty of coping, etc. Having reconceptualised the client's problem in terms of distinct stages and affective, behavioural, and cognitive components, it becomes easier to identify and proceed to develop the specific coping skills that appear most relevant. In a coping skills approach to hypnotherapy, a variety of both hypnotic and non-hypnotic skills are learned through practice and then applied to real-life problems and stressful situations.

Skills acquisition and rehearsal phase

During the coping-skills acquisition stage of applied self-hypnosis, clients may learn new cognitive and behavioural coping skills or further develop their existing repertoire of strategies. As noted earlier, coping strategies can be divided, for convenience, into hypnotic, dehypnotic (mindfulness), and nonhypnotic categories. The self-monitoring procedures employed in the preceding conceptualisation and assessment phase, used to pinpoint problematic thoughts, actions, and feelings, naturally leads on to the identification of counteracting thoughts (self-statements) and actions (coping skills), which can be used to de-automatise and short-circuit the problematic chain of responses (Meichenbaum, 1977, pp. 154, 223). Moreover, spotting low-intensity cues, or "early warning signs", allows them to be used as "cues to cope", and initiate new coping strategies and self-instructions in the place of old, unhelpful ones (Meichenbaum, 1977, p. 223).

Particularly where the client possesses existing skills but these are inhibited by internal (cognitive) or external (social) factors, applied self-hypnosis can focus on using interventions such as cognitive restructuring to help clients remove such inhibitions and make full use of their existing coping skills, for example, by correcting faulty appraisals of threat or vulnerability. Different skills may be required to either cope with different aspects of the emotional stress response (thoughts, actions, feelings) or to solve practical or interpersonal problems, at different stages in the development of the situation (before, during, at critical moments, and after). So the conceptualisation provides an important guide to the development of coping strategies at multiple levels.

The client may be asked what suggestions she has for ways of coping with stress and what coping strategies she has tried in the past either successfully or unsuccessfully, which follows on naturally from the earlier assessment phase (Meichenbaum, 1985, p. 53). As we have seen, a particularly helpful question for the therapist to ask, sometimes repeatedly, is "How's that way of coping working out for you in the long-run?" This question not only elicits useful information, and helps clients to evaluate the function of their behaviour, but it also potentially heightens their attention to the consequences of their actions in a way that helps shape subsequent behaviour in adaptive directions. Following on from the conceptualisation, a number of alternative techniques are offered to clients from a "menu" of options; this is done selectively so as to avoid overwhelming them with choices, and they are encouraged to test out and evaluate different ways of coping with stress (Meichenbaum, 1985, p. 54). These include both problem-focused ("instrumental") and emotion-focused (or "palliative") coping strategies, and potentially also mindfulness and acceptance-based strategies. Applied self-hypnosis, like SIT, may encourage clients to consider the "goodness of fit" between coping strategies and situations, in terms of using problem-focused coping to deal with changeable aspects of a situation and emotion-focused coping for unchangeable problems (Meichenbaum, 2007). The main cognitive-behavioural approaches that SIT draws upon are:

1. Relaxation skills training based on Jacobson's Progressive Muscle Relaxation and a variety of other methods (Bernstein, Borkovec & Hazlett-Stevens, 2000; Jacobson, 1938).
2. Cognitive restructuring based mainly on Beck's approach (Beck, Rush, Shaw & Emery, 1979).
3. Problem-solving training based on Goldfried & D'Zurilla's approach (Goldfried & D'Zurilla, 1971).
4. Self-instruction training based on Meichenbaum's earlier approach to "guided self-dialogue", particularly coping statements and self-reinforcement (Meichenbaum, 1977).

And these are also influences that applied self-hypnosis training can assimilate. To take a more specific example, Marks' combination of prolonged self-exposure therapy and "stress immunisation" (stress inoculation), which is based on Meichenbaum's approach, suggests that clients write down self-instructions, for using coping skills such as those listed below, on small cue-cards to be taken out and read aloud as soon as the initial signs of anxiety are spotted (Marks I. M., 2005, pp. 181–182).

1. Diaphragmatic breathing
2. Brief tension-release muscle relaxation
3. Picturing the worst-case scenario deliberately (decatastrophising)
4. Accepting the anxious feelings
5. Encouraging oneself to endure exposure, inhibiting escape
6. Picturing a pleasant scene
7. Distancing oneself from fearful thoughts
8. Rational responses to automatic anxious thoughts
9. Questioning the evidence for automatic anxious thoughts
10. Reminding oneself that the feelings are temporary.

For instance, Marks provides the following self-instructions for questioning automatic thoughts, to be read aloud from a cue-card, "I'll challenge my thoughts that I'm going mad or losing control and prove that I won't." For muscle relaxation the instructions state, "I must tense all my muscles as much as I possibly can, then relax them, then tense them again, then relax them again, until slowly I feel easier in myself" (Marks I. M., 2005, pp. 181–182). This list of coping strategies includes *acceptance* of anxious feelings and *distancing* from fearful thoughts, strategies favoured in more recent mindfulness and acceptance-based CBT but which have long been present to some extent in earlier cognitive and behavioural approaches.

Beck likewise argues repeatedly in favour of prolonged exposure so that anxiety may decline naturally over time, through habituation. However, he also states that coping strategies may be of value during exposure insofar as they are used to prevent premature escape and "false" safety-seeking behaviour and instead allow the client to remain in the situation for longer rather than being used to suppress anxiety (Clark & Beck, 2012, p. 138). He warns that if anxiety appears to reduce too quickly or easily when using a coping strategy it may potentially be a sign that it's functioning as a form of maladaptive avoidance or safety-seeking. Nevertheless, Beck lists the following potentially helpful coping skills for use during self-exposure to feared events:

1. Challenging anxious thoughts using Socratic questions and substituting a more rational and realistic alternative way of thinking about events.
2. Focusing attention on completely accepting individual physical symptoms and sensations, rather than struggling against them.
3. Deliberately look around the environment, making an effort to fully process evidence of safety that one might otherwise have overlooked (deliberate safety-cue processing).
4. Controlling breathing by maintaining a normal respiratory rate, around eight to twelve breaths per minute, avoiding holding one's breath or hyperventilating by breathing too rapidly.

5. Relaxing mentally or physically, although Beck specifically cautions against using this to avoid anxious feelings completely, rather than to endure them until they naturally abate.
6. Picturing oneself gradually coping with and then mastering the situation, either before entering the situation or at the beginning of the task.
7. Engaging in physical activity and giving all of one's attention to it, channelling one's nervous energy into focused action, again being cautious that this is not used to avoid anxiety.

Beck also refers to the use of the AWARE acronym, mentioned earlier, as a guide to coping during self-exposure to anxious situations (Clark & Beck, 2012, p. 142). This can be seen as resembling a set of mindfulness and acceptance-based coping skills, instructing the client to:

Accept anxiety rather than struggling against it
Watch anxious thoughts and feelings from a detached perspective
Act as if non-anxious by approaching feared situations and remaining in them without escape or safety-seeking behaviour
Repeat these tactics systematically, until anxiety declines to an acceptable level
Expect to make progress, adopting a realistic and optimistic attitude.

Hence, a simple menu of potential coping skills, for use during exposure to phobia, that could be presented within an applied self-hypnosis approach might include:

1. Using brief autosuggestions for physical relaxation of different parts of the body.
2. Using hypnotic triggers (cue-controlled relaxation) to relax the whole body rapidly.
3. Direct verbal autosuggestions to focus attention on the present moment and external environment and broaden it flexibly in a non-anxious manner.
4. Direct verbal autosuggestions that feelings are being accepted as harmless and transient, and that one can ride them out and motivational autosuggestions to remain in the situation.
5. Dehypnosis or distancing strategies to prevent negative automatic thoughts from turning into negative self-hypnosis.

Like traditional hypnotherapy, SIT has tended to favour the incorporation of relaxation techniques, which Meichenbaum refers to as the "aspirin" of stress management (1985, p. ix). He notes that although SIT adopts a flexible orientation and the strategies taught vary, most trainers have tended to start with relaxation skills training because it is easily learned by most clients and is often very appealing and intuitive to them as a way of coping (Meichenbaum, 1985, p. 55).

Relaxation techniques are not essential to hypnotherapy, and their use in CBT has recently waned in popularity because in some situations they are deemed unnecessary or possibly even counter-productive. Nevertheless, many clients prefer to use relaxation and may obtain benefit from this approach, which SIT emphasises should be carefully evaluated for its suitability and tested out in practice in each individual case. Because the emphasis in the SIT approach is generally upon training clients to develop more skill and confidence in relation to their own coping repertoire, relaxation is introduced as an active coping skill that requires practice and is applied in response to self-monitoring of tension in a range of situations, rather than a passive activity, such as listening to calming music in a quiet environment, etc. In particular, Meichenbaum recommended that Wolpe's more passive stimulus-response approach, systematic desensitisation, should be modified by presenting relaxation as an active coping skill, controlled by deliberate self-instruction and coping imagery:

> The coping-imagery procedure requires that while visualizing a scene from the hierarchy, the client is to see himself coping with anxiety by slow deep breaths, relaxation, and self-instructions. In other words, in the coping-imagery procedure the client visualizes both the experience of anxiety and also ways to handle and reduce this anxiety. (Meichenbaum, 1977, p. 121)

The therapist might, for example, instruct the client to use the words "let go" as a very short self-instruction, combined with a simple breathing technique, as follows:

> See yourself in that situation as if it's really happening right now. Allow yourself to experience some anxiety. Now imagine that you're using the coping strategies you learned earlier to cope with your anxiety. Take a deep breath and fill your lungs. Now exhale slowly as you say the words "let go" to yourself. Really try to relax away the tension as you exhale and just accept any remaining feelings of anxiety. You're getting better with practice. Notice how good it feels to know you can control your responses. Now just fade the image and relax ... in a moment, we'll repeat that again.

The main point here is that the client is taught to perceive the use of imagery and self-instruction as ways of guiding her in developing personal coping skills rather than passively assuming that the therapist is doing something to reduce the anxiety for her. In the context of hypnotherapy, active coping skills training would equate to teaching autosuggestion rather than employing standard (hetero) hypnotic suggestion.

Coping imagery, in which the client experiences some anxiety but treats it as a cue to employ coping strategies, has been found more effective than "mastery imagery", in which the client imagines already having overcome the problem (Meichenbaum, 1977, p. 122). It's a common strategy in behaviour therapy to train clients to identify early or low-intensity antecedents of anxiety and think of them as cues or signals to immediately employ a coping response. "Symptoms" such as anxious thoughts, actions, or feelings, can be treated as cues for the deliberate instigation of coping responses, which can be referred to as adopting a general-purpose "coping orientation" or "coping mind-set" in response to environmental demands or symptoms of stress (Meichenbaum, 1977, p. 123). In traditional behaviour therapy, acquisition of coping skills is understood in terms of behavioural learning theory, which typically emphasises the following techniques:

1. *Instruction.* "Psycho-education" involving written and verbal information is usually provided at the beginning of training, especially concerning the rationale for specific coping strategies in relation to the conceptualisation developed.

2. *Modelling.* Demonstration by the therapist or others, or verbal examples, video clips, etc., demonstrating acquisition of the skills.
3. *Coaching* (prompting). Verbal prompting and guiding of behaviour as it is being rehearsed
4. *Shaping.* Reinforcement of "successive approximations", whereby the skill to be acquired is broken down into smaller steps with each being learned in turn.
5. *Behaviour rehearsal.* Repeated practice using the complete skill in the session, in imagination, during role-play, or between sessions as homework, etc.
6. *Feedback.* Providing evaluation of the outcome of training, perhaps using established questionnaires to rate progress, biofeedback, etc.
7. *Reinforcement.* Deliberate praise and reward from the therapist and from the client herself for the efforts made and focus on amplifying the natural reinforcing quality of the actual results obtained and sense of achievement from the skill learned.

These same learning principles are applied to hypnotic skills training, as described in an earlier chapter. Hence, we might say that a cognitive-behavioural or collaborative skills training approach to hypnotherapy consists in training the client in two sets of skills:

1. General self-hypnosis skills, and fulfilling the role of the "good hypnotic subject".
2. Stress and anxiety coping skills, and fulfilling the role of the adaptive and confident individual.

Below are some examples of general categories of coping strategies, most of which may be combined with hypnosis, roughly categorised as follows:

Problem-focused coping

- Problem-solving (methodologically)
- Behavioural rehearsal of different solutions
- Assertiveness skills
- Other social and communication skills
- Sleep hygiene
- Time management and activity scheduling
- Physical exercise and dietary changes
- Obtaining social-support in addressing a practical problem
- Seeking further information about solving a problem.

Emotion-focused coping (self-control)

- Physical relaxation (progressive muscle relaxation)
- Mental relaxation (using self-hypnosis, suggestion, imagery or meditation)
- Cognitive reappraisal of threat/safety
- Cognitive reappraisal of vulnerability/coping
- Behavioural experiments, testing underlying schemas and assumptions

- Prolonged exposure to the feared event, either in imagination or in reality
- Response prevention (blocking or dropping safety-seeking behaviours)
- Repeated emotional review (Raimy).

Dehypnosis (mindfulness and acceptance-based strategies)

- Distancing unhelpful or anxious thoughts from reality, viewing thoughts as hypotheses, etc.
- Distancing oneself from one's thoughts and feelings, taking a "step back" from them, etc.
- Acceptance of unpleasant feelings, such as anxiety
- Expanding attention in the "here and now", throughout the body or external environment.

Common unhelpful coping and safety-seeking

- Avoidance of specific feared situations, events, or activities (behavioural avoidance)
- Withdrawal from activity or social encounters in general
- Escape from feared situations before anxiety has naturally declined
- Subtle avoidance, such as averting gaze or distracting attention
- Safety-seeking behaviour, that is, irrational or unnecessary attempts to protect against perceived threat
- Reassurance-seeking that's repetitive or compulsive
- Checking repeatedly for signs of safety
- Over-thinking, in the form of prolonged worry or rumination
- Threat-monitoring, or excessive attention to possible sources of danger
- Thought-control or excessive attempts to distract from thoughts or suppress them, etc.
- Emotional suppression or trying to block or avoid strong feelings
- Misuse of drugs and alcohol to suppress feelings
- Venting through aggressive or antisocial speech or actions, escalating arguments, etc.

Training in hypnosis can be used to generally facilitate more adaptive coping strategies by allowing the client to rehearse using them in imagination, in a focused and vivid manner, along with the use of coaching and direct verbal suggestions. A close analogy of this can be found in the use of relaxation as a coping skill, rehearsed in imagination in the technique known as "self-control desensitisation", which forms part of the applied relaxation approach (Öst, 1987). However, Beck's description of using techniques such as time-projection imagery for decatastrophising and cognitive restructuring, and many other techniques, can easily be rehearsed in hypnosis and taught to clients as self-hypnosis techniques. Alternatively self-hypnosis recordings can be made to help clients rehearse coping skills in a hypnotic mind-set, using vivid mental imagery and focused attention, etc.

Self-instruction training

In addition to teaching specific coping skills of the kind list above, Meichenbaum was particularly concerned with training clients in the use of "self-instructions", which he defined as a form of conscious "internal dialogue" or "self-statements" that typically take place when the normal automaticity of behaviour is interrupted by a problem in the performance of some task (Meichenbaum, 1977). He was originally influenced by the research of Soviet developmental psychologists, such as Vygotsky and Luria, who viewed thought as evolving during childhood through a natural process of internalising social speech. This internal dialogue constitutes a stream of cognitive events, which can consist of imagery, expectations, attributions, appraisals of oneself or the situation, or possibly task-irrelevant or interfering thoughts (Meichenbaum, 1985, p. 6).

Vygotsky's main contribution to developmental psychology was his attempt to explain how crucial aspects of childhood development were socially learned ("culturally mediated") and incorporated by the child through a process of "internalisation" based upon his interaction with parents, peers, and other significant social figures. Vygotsky thought children's play was central to their ability to develop the use of their imagination and thinking, instead of merely reacting to their immediate environment. Play thereby helped children to achieve greater self-control ("self-regulation") over their impulses and emotions. Obviously, any attempt to explain how speech is used to regulate one's own emotion and behaviour should be relevant to the study of autosuggestion and hypnosis. The use of these developmental theories by Meichenbaum in his cognitive behaviour modification approach therefore highlights an important area of overlap between hypnotherapy and early CBT.

Vygotsky observed that after evolving through the early phase of "crib talk" or baby babble, children begin to think aloud by first using "social speech" to communicate with their parents and other adults. Around ages two to five, the child increasingly begins to talk to *himself* as if talking to another. This self-talk initially resembles social speech, that is, the child talks to himself using words and phrases that he might use when talking to another person. Vygotsky refers to this as the child gradually adopting "social attitude" toward himself. However, this self-talk gradually becomes compressed, modified, and adapted to suit the purpose of emotional and behavioural self-control. After increasing in frequency during the preschool years it subsequently declines and becomes progressively quieter around the age when starting school, progressing through murmurs or whispers, until it finally occurs only in the imagination as internal ("covert") speech. Stages in the natural childhood internalisation of social speech can therefore be summarised as follows:

1. *External social speech*. The child talks aloud to other people, for example, adults and other children.
2. *External self-talk (social)*. The child talks aloud to himself in a manner resembling social speech.
3. *External self-talk (modified)*. The child talks aloud to himself in a modified manner.
4. *Internal self-talk*. The child talks to himself in his imagination, without speaking aloud.
5. *Compressed internal self-talk*. The child thinks by using private, modified and abbreviated self-talk.
6. *Silent thought*. The child thinks without necessarily using either external or internal speech.

Vygotsky believed that speech formed an important vehicle for thinking and that this progression from social speech to completely private speech helped to explain the formation of human thought processes and their relationship with the development of the imagination. This does not mean that thought and speech are the same thing but rather that speech contributes greatly to the formation and development of thinking. Social speech is the basis from which private self-talk develops but these two forms of speech, private and public, develop in different directions because they come to fulfil quite different functions. Private speech is central to self-control and adapted to the purpose of helping direct and control our thoughts, feelings, and actions. It tends to be much more concise than external speech, and may consist of rapid, repetitive or disorganised words and phrases rather than grammatically correct sentences. It is notable that adults suffering from certain mental health problems, or under extreme stress, tend to revert to exhibiting *audible* self-talk, muttering under their breath, thinking aloud, talking out loud to themselves, etc.

Meichenbaum combined elements of Vygotsky's theory of the internalisation of social speech with the practice of behaviour therapy. In doing so, he explicitly made use of the hypnosis researcher Theodore Sarbin's theory of imagination as "muted" role-enactment. Sarbin had argued that the popular concept of "imagination" is thoroughly embedded in the Cartesian dualist philosophy of mind, which is essentially the default philosophy ("folk psychology") taken for granted in modern culture and language. However, Cartesianism has historically attracted considerable criticism from academic philosophers, on the basis that it is logically incoherent, on close inspection. Sarbin therefore proposed a non-Cartesian (non-dualist) theory of the imagination which views imagination as muted role-enactment characterised by varying degrees of role-involvement, that is, "believed-in imagining".

> In order to gain some leverage on a theory that would extend our understanding of imagining as the important element in hypnosis (interpreted here as believed-in imagining), a bold hypothesis is suggested to replace the hypothesis of pictures in the mind. The hypothesis, sketched in broad strokes is this: The concept of imagination was constructed by our linguistic ancestors as the consequence of a [conceptual] category mistake, an illicit transformation of a metaphor to a literal entity. [...] The commonly held view of imaginings as pictures in the mind is an unwarranted belief—a belief developed out of the Cartesian view of the dualistic nature of man. (1972, p. 113)

Hence, Sarbin argues that the notion of "imagination" as "pictures in the mind" was originally a figure of speech but gradually lost the "as if" quality of metaphor and became concretised (reified) into a literal description.

By contrast, borrowing a concept from the Kantian philosopher Hans Vaihinger, Sarbin argues that what we call "imagination" would be more accurately described as "hypothetical instantiation" or "acting as-if". Human beings are capable of varying degrees of hypothetical instantiation ("as if" behaviour), positing an instance of some absent object, which exists only hypothetically. Sarbin therefore proposed a three-stage model of child development, similar to Vygotsky's perspective, to account for the child's acquisition of the "as-if" skill or believed-in imagining:

1. *Imitation.* The child learns by social imitation, copying the actions of another person who is present.
2. *Role-taking.* The child subsequently learns to imitate the speech and actions of other people by playing "let's pretend" in their absence. This is the beginning of hypothetical behaviour, where the client uses imaginary objects, for example, playing "mother" and setting a table with imaginary cups and plates.
3. *Imagination.* The childhood achievement of muting speech, learning to talk to themselves covertly, begins simply by learning to whisper or mutter under the breath. Gradually the child learns to silence the sound of his speech, and subsequently to conceal all visible muscular movements associated with speech.

According to Sarbin, the activity of imagining things, as in hypnosis and mental imagery techniques in CBT, actually consists in such "muted, attenuated role-taking" (Sarbin & Coe, 1972, p. 118). He also reported empirical research showing a correlation between abilities to use mental imagery and role-taking ability. Hence, "The older metaphor of imagining, pictures in the mind, is replaced by muted or attenuated three-dimensional action, silent role-taking, and is conceptually continuous with overt role-enactment" (Sarbin & Coe, 1972, p. 119).

For Sarbin, therefore, hypnosis is a form of adult (muted) role-enactment in which clients behave "as if" they are experiencing things which are suggested by the hypnotist or auto-suggested by themselves. In doing so, however, they may change their body's physiology in ways that are not normally possible, for example, lowering their heart rate or changing hormone production, etc. They may also learn to identify with certain roles rehearsed as part of the process of hypnotherapy, such as to "act as if confident" or "as if non-anxious". This may generalise to their sense of identity and behaviour outside of the consulting room, and may even become more or less permanent, which is essentially the aim of treatment. A risk, from this perspective, would be that clients who think of hypnosis as being about "visualisation" in a Cartesian way would make the mistake of rehearsing seeing certain images while continuing to say unhelpful things and feel unhelpful feelings, etc. For instance, clients might practice seeing themselves boarding an aeroplane but continue to tense their muscles and tell themselves, "Oh my God, it's going to crash!" This role-rehearsal would probably fail because the role-taking was not "organismic", involving the whole person at once, but rather incomplete, conflicted, involving harmful thoughts and feelings.

Moreover, based on the Soviet developmental theories and drawing on Sarbin's theory of believed-in imagining, Meichenbaum carried out a series of experiments which explored the role of self-talk in self-regulation and cognitive-behavioural therapy with children, adolescents and adults. Meichenbaum simply wondered whether the developmental progression of thought and language described above could provide the rationale for a therapeutic approach and set about an impressive programme of research, which basically led to the conclusion that it could indeed (Meichenbaum, 1977, p. 23). For example, he found that talking aloud helped pre-school children to perform certain tasks, but hindered older children who tended to have internalised and compressed their self-talk already. He also found that although self-talk became internalised with age, it also becomes more task-related. Children who performed well in behavioural tasks tended to show a higher ratio of task-relevant self-talk, whereas those who struggled showed more unhelpful self-talk unrelated to the task at hand (1977, pp. 20–21).

Research which shows that older children and adults exhibited less self-talk when performing successfully and that asking them to talk aloud hinders performance might seem to suggest that this strategy is unhelpful. However, as Vygotsky had argued, to understand a psychological process we need to view it within its historical context, and see the bigger picture. Meichenbaum found that although self-talk hindered adults at first it could be faded out gradually, in a manner resembling the preschool child's stages of development, and that doing so was ultimately helpful to adults as well as older children. Meichenbaum therefore emphasised that deliberate self-talk constitutes a preparatory stage for the internalisation of skills and attitudes which become spontaneous over time (1977, p. 67). Again, it's notable that self-talk tends to reappear when older children, or even adults, are under stress or engaged in particularly difficult tasks. These observations led Meichenbaum to recommend that verbal self-instructions should be abbreviate and "faded" over time until they were more or less eliminated as unnecessary. The same principle may apply to the use of autosuggestions in hypnotherapy, which perhaps are more useful as a temporary bridge to coping, and should be progressively faded out of use, so that the client may learn to cope without the need for a running commentary, which tends to bring a certain degree of self-consciousness to bear on the majority of tasks.

Meichenbaum's original research focused upon training hyperactive and impulsive children to control their behaviour. In a typical training sequence used with children, instructions are internalised in the following stages (Meichenbaum, 1977, p. 32):

1. *Self-instruction modelling.* An adult performs the task while talking aloud, modelling helpful self-instructions.
2. *Overt instruction.* The child performs the same task, while being actively prompted and coached by the adult's verbal instructions.
3. *Overt self-instruction.* The child performs the task without adult guidance, relying on her own self-instructions, said aloud.
4. *Faded overt self-instructions.* The child whispers her self-instructions, while repeating the task again, "fading" the verbal prompts.
5. *Covert self-instruction.* Finally, the child performs the task in silence, while repeating her self-instructions privately, in her imagination.
6. *Repetition.* This process was repeated over several sessions using graded tasks according to the behavioural principles of "shaping", or successive approximation.

The types of self-instruction given were initially divided into broad categories, such as:

1. *Problem definition.* "Okay, what do I have to do? You want me to copy the picture. I have to draw slowly."
2. *Focusing attention and guiding responses.* "Carefully, draw the line down. Now down some more and to the left."
3. *Self-reinforcement.* "Good. I'm doing well."

4. *Self-evaluation and error-correction.* "I made a mistake, that's okay; I can just go on slowly." (Meichenbaum, 1977, p. 32)

Hence, Meichenbaum described the use of self-instruction as being designed to nurture active problem-solving attitudes and specific behavioural coping strategies (Meichenbaum, 1985, p. 70). The emphasis is on identifying specific self-instructions, or forms of self-talk, that are workable and helpful in terms of achieving adaptive goals. In contrast to this approach, as Beck pointed out, cognitive therapy focuses more on the modification of underlying beliefs and correcting faulty appraisals of situations, primarily in terms of their rationality and consistency with the evidence (Alford & Beck, 1997, pp. 60–61).

The research showed that impulsive children clearly benefitted from self-instruction training. Role-modelling was more effective when accompanied by deliberate imitation and self-talk. A similar programme of training was subsequently found effective in helping adult schizophrenics to be more "relevant and coherent" when speaking to others. Several studies subsequently showed that healthy adults could benefit from self-instruction, for example, college students were trained to enhance their creative thinking. For instance, Meichenbaum's self-instruction approach was shown to be more effective in this regard than Eugene Gendlin's "focusing" method, a humanistic psychotherapy approach popular at the time. Hence, Meichenbaum specifically suggested self-instruction training could be used in conjunction with D'Zurilla and Goldfried's problem-solving therapy (Meichenbaum, 1977, pp. 64–65).

However, although it may be helpful to conceptualise problems in terms of antecedent thoughts, people often act without explicit internal dialogue of any kind and self-talk tends to become conscious only when a problem is encountered or choices must be evaluated and decisions made (Meichenbaum, 1985, pp. 6–7). Nevertheless, introducing self-talk can be an important mediator of change, partly because it helps to increase self-awareness and "deautomatise" habitual thoughts, actions and feelings (Meichenbaum, 1977, pp. 210–211). Hence, "forced cognitive mediation" is an important stage in therapy, that is, the client is asked to speak aloud, in order to heighten awareness of her unhelpful "automatic" thoughts and deautomatise them. Once again, this aspect of early behaviour therapy can be compared to some of the strategies employed in more recent mindfulness and acceptance-based approaches to CBT, for example, slowly repeating automatic thoughts aloud or prefacing them with "I notice that I am having the thought that ...", etc. (Hayes, Strosahl & Wilson, 2012). Meichenbaum reasoned that if self-control developed naturally in childhood through the internalisation of social speech then children with behavioural problems could perhaps artificially replicate this process by modelling the speech of others and gradually internalising it in the form of self-instructions (Meichenbaum, 1977, pp. 22–23). Although children initially talk to themselves aloud, especially when trying to cope with difficult tasks or control their own emotions and behaviour, this fades into whispered self-talk, before becoming completely internal or imagined (muted) dialogue.

Hence, he was keen to emphasise that although skills and self-control can be learned in this way, talking aloud can interfere with skills once learned. "Once the verbalization, to use Vygotsky's term, goes 'underground' it is best to leave it there" (Meichenbaum, 1977, p. 20). In other words, in adult therapy, self-instructions are intended to be transitional aids to learning coping skills and modifying underlying cognitive structures; like stabilisers on a bicycle, their use is intended to be temporary because once competence has been achieved they potentially get in the way of more spontaneous, skilled responses. Again, this is consistent with the observation that raising awareness of negative automatic thoughts, or autosuggestions, and verbalising them in a detached way (distancing) can help to prevent their influence, which we might consider a strategy of *dehypnosis*.

By contrast, though, helpful cognitions were internalised by repeating them in a focused and congruent manner, while gradually compressing them and fading the explicit verbalisations. Words by themselves were not effective unless accompanied by the appropriate feelings and intentions. If repeated "parrot fashion" the benefits were minor compared to more "organismic" and committed forms of self-instruction in which the accompanying intentions and feelings were also activated (Meichenbaum, 1977, p. 64). In other words, self-instructions are most effective when the whole person is engaged congruently and a favourable attitude or mind-set is adopted, just like in hypnotherapy. However, Meichenbaum vigorously opposed the reduction of self-instruction training to "positive thinking" of the kind found in much popular hypnotherapy and self-help literature (Meichenbaum, 1985, pp. 71–73). Likewise, in cognitive-behavioural hypnotherapy, suggestions and self-statements emphasise realistic and adaptive thinking rather than positive thinking. For example, Clark and Jackson, in their early book on cognitive-behavioural hypnotherapy, argued that the inclusion of Meichenbaum's self-instruction techniques was particularly useful in the treatment of social phobia. Hypnotherapy was used by them, in combination with cognitive therapy, to expose clients in fantasy to hypothetical "worst-case" scenes of social evaluation and anxiety, while rehearsing coping, a kind of "decatastrophising" imagery technique, which we shall return to in a later chapter (Clarke & Jackson, 1983, p. 257).

In Meichenbaum's training approach, the relevant attitudes and emotions were role-modelled by the therapist along with the appropriate use of self-talk. He also employed "Socratic dialogue", like Beck, as a way of helping clients to evaluate their self-talk and develop more constructive things to say to themselves. This might involve posing questions that encourage rational reflection and evaluation on the part of the client. Moreover, self-statements are not assumed to work in a "magical" way but rather to provide support for active coping efforts, using specific behavioural strategies of the kind described earlier.

> Self-instructions can play two primary roles in governing desired behaviours. In the acquisition of new skills, self-instructions can serve as useful cues for the recall of appropriate behaviour sequences or for redirecting and correcting behaviour errors. In the correction of maladaptive behaviour, self-instructions can interrupt automatic behavioral or cognitive chains and can prompt the use of more adaptive responses. Self-instructional skills will probably not be effective in the absence of requisite behavioral skills, but may be very useful in the learning of new skills and in enhancing the performance of adaptive responses. (Rokke & Rehm, 2001, p. 179)

Indeed, having initially employed this approach in combination with basic operant conditioning strategies, Meichenbaum attempted to combine self-instruction training with other traditional behaviour therapy techniques such as desensitisation, modelling, and aversion therapy.

His overall conclusion, based on several studies, was that previous behaviour therapists had under-estimated the role of private speech and cognitions in mediating the outcome of their methods. Meichenbaum observed that a number of studies appear to show that self-talk, a form of covert (private) behaviour, can be modified by using principles common in older forms of behaviour therapy where they were used to modify overt (public) behaviour, including modelling, imagery, classical conditioning, and operant reinforcement (Meichenbaum, 1977, p. 108). Hence, although Meichenbaum did emphasise the role of cognition in behaviour therapy, unlike Beck and Ellis, he felt that clients' cognitions could be modified by relatively simple training methods based on traditional conditioning methods applied to speech (Meichenbaum, 1977, p. 110). It's important to emphasise that the subject learns to use the instructions congruently, focusing on their meaning, rather than repeating the words absent-mindedly or insincerely (Meichenbaum, 1977, pp. 88–89). However, with encouragement from the trainer, the client gradually begins to achieve her goals, which helps to reinforce and maintain the new self-talk and associated attitudes.

This is probably closer to the perspective generally adopted in using traditional hypnotism, where suggestions are used to modify thinking without necessarily employing extensive weighing-up of evidence, of the kind employed in Beck's cognitive therapy. In applied self-hypnosis, therefore, clients can be trained in the modification of self-talk construed as a form of negative autosuggestion and self-hypnosis, replacing unhelpful verbal statements with more helpful self-talk, a manner loosely modelled on the early cognitive-behavioural approach of Meichenbaum. This is also not unlike the approach adopted in established hypnotic skills training protocols except that in applied self-hypnosis the coping behaviour and cognitive strategies, such as verbal autosuggestion or mental imagery, being modified directly relate to therapeutic outcomes. What Meichenbaum's research appears to show is that behavioural coping skills, of many different kinds, can be enhanced through training in verbal self-instructions, in terms of treatment outcomes, generalisation of coping skills, and long-term maintenance of improvement (Meichenbaum, 1977, p. 108). Sometimes this resembles the client internalising the verbal coaching of the trainer and, in a sense, becoming her own internal coach or guide, as she employs specific behavioural skills such as relaxation, assertiveness, or exposure to feared events, etc. However, this would also lend further indirect support to the important contention that training in cognitive-behavioural hypnotherapy, which also involves congruent rehearsal of self-statements (autosuggestions), may enhance standard CBT approaches. If congruent self-instructions can *enhance* most behaviour therapy techniques, as Meichenbaum interpreted his research as showing, then presumably coupling hypnotic autosuggestions with strategies from behaviour therapy could do so as well, functioning in a similar manner.

Moreover, in Meichenbaum's approach metaphorical or coping imagery is sometimes pictured while using verbal self-instructions and this can enhance their benefits (Meichenbaum, 1977, pp. 93–95). For instance, children were taught to imagine themselves approaching challenging tasks slowly "like a turtle" whereas adults are typically asked to picture themselves employing coping strategies. This approach to training children in self-instructions became the basis of later research on treating adult psychiatric patients, such as schizophrenics, with similar methods. It was ultimately applied, usually as part of the broader SIT approach, with clinical anxiety, such as phobias, and non-clinical stress-related problems such as exam nerves, public speaking anxiety, etc. When used as part of stress inoculation, with adult populations, the process of self-instruction training is usually simplified and abbreviated somewhat, though. The emphasis on congruent coping statements alongside relevant coping imagery bears an even closer resemblance to training in self-hypnosis and other hypnotherapy techniques.

> The rehearsal of these strategies, under imaginal or in vivo conditions with input, modelling, and feedback from the therapist, should also be planned. Many cognitive-behavioural therapies can be expanded and perhaps enhanced by the inclusion of self-instructional strategies. Strategies such as relaxation training, systematic desensitization, and assertion training can all include a self-instructional component. (Rokke & Rehm, 2001, pp. 180–181)

Part of the appeal of self-instruction training, therefore, is that it is potentially a simple method of augmenting almost any other cognitive-behavioural therapy approach, for example, self-instructions can easily be coupled with exposure therapy or problem-solving, and doing so may enhance treatment effects and improve generalisation in many cases (Meichenbaum, 1977, p. 108). For example, Meichenbaum recommended that systematic desensitisation could be enhanced by training the client simply to use the words "relax" and "calm" as self-instructions to guide the client in deliberately "relaxing away" remaining feelings of tension (Meichenbaum, 1977, p. 120). Although similar "cue" words are used in Öst's applied relaxation method, they are conceptualised as conditioned stimuli rather than as self-instructions in Meichenbaum's sense (Öst, 1987).

In mindfulness and acceptance-based approaches, self-instructions are often used as an aid to meditation-like techniques. For instance, prefacing distressing thoughts with the phrase "Right now I notice myself having the thought that …" can create a sense of psychological distance from them. Likewise, repeating the phrase, "Right now, I am aware of …" and naming and describing aspects of the environment can focus attention on to the here and now. During worry-postponement strategies, the client may say, "I'm not going to think about this any longer, just accept the thought and come back to it later at my specified time." These are all statements or instructions given to oneself to help guide attention and adhere to a strategy. Once again, the use of self-instruction resembles the client internalising the role of a coach or trainer, giving herself explicit guidance on how to respond adaptively to a difficult situation. She progressively becomes her own "internal coach" or therapist with regard to applying mindfulness and acceptance, or other cognitive-behavioural strategies.

Developing coping statements

In relation to applied self-hypnosis training, of course, it's natural to talk about *helpful* and *unhelpful* autosuggestions. However, self-instructions in Meichenbaum's approach do serve a wider range of functions than typical autosuggestions or suggestions in hypnosis. The function of self-statements may actually extend to guiding actions, focusing of attention, self-praise, raising and answering appropriate questions, etc. Self-statements or instructions of this kind have been studied and employed in many different experimental and applied settings but are used in SIT primarily as a means of coping with the stress response and feelings of anxiety, etc.

> The discussion of the client's stressful experience provides the basis for the development of coping self-statements. If the client's thoughts can make stress worse, then it is not a big step for the client to suggest that different thoughts (self-statements) can be employed at each phase to reduce, avoid, or constructively use stress. In a collaborative manner, the trainer and the client consider possible coping self-statements. (Meichenbaum, 1985, p. 70)

Beck et al. describes a similar "TIC/TOC technique" in the cognitive therapy of anxiety, which involves teaching clients to identify "task-interfering cognitions" and replace them with "task-oriented cognitions" (Beck, Emery & Greenberg, 2005, p. 278). Likewise, a simple two-column form can often be used for applied self-hypnosis with one column headed "unhelpful autosuggestions" (or old thoughts) and another headed "helpful autosuggestions" or (new thoughts). After identifying some of the main negative automatic thoughts or autosuggestions that interfere with adaptive coping, the client is asked to generate alternative coping statements, which directly replace them, and support the use of adaptive coping strategies and behaviour in the face of challenging situations. The table below has some simple examples:

Unhelpful autosuggestions (old)	Helpful autosuggestions (new)
"I can't cope!"	"I can cope as long as I take my time."
"I don't know what to do!"	"I've learned how to relax rapidly use a cue word."
"What if it doesn't work?"	"If I need to use it, I've got a backup plan in reserve."
"This is awful!"	"It's not the end of the world."
"I hate feeling anxious."	"Anxiety is harmless, just accept it and let go."
"I need to get out of here now!"	"Be patient and wait for it to abate naturally."
"I'm going to be overwhelmed with anxiety."	"Take a deep breath, pause, and use my cue-word to let go of as much tension as I can."

In particular, negative automatic thoughts or autosuggestions can be treated as "early-warning signs" and cues to respond quickly with alternative, counter-acting self-instructions.

Hence, following Meichenbaum's application of the Soviet developmental research on internalisation of social speech, self-instruction training as part of stress-inoculation can be viewed in terms of three main stages (Rachman & Wilson, 1980, p. 208).

1. *Self-monitoring*. The client is trained to self-monitor unhelpful (maladaptive) thoughts in the form of self-talk.

2. *Therapist modelling.* The therapist models adaptive coping behaviour while talking aloud, verbalising relevant self-instructions for preparation, confrontation, coping with setbacks, and self-reinforcement.
3. *Self-instruction.* The client then performs the target behaviour while talking aloud and verbalising relevant self-instructions in place of the previous anxious self-talk. Self-statements are gradually made covert (internal) and faded completely, in graduated steps, while the therapist provides prompting, feedback, and reinforcement.

Self-instructions, according to Meichenbaum's approach, are usually based on typical examples recommended for specific problems or client groups, which the individual adapts and tailors to suit her needs. Meichenbaum concluded that statements regarding themes of control and competence were particularly effective for most clients, both themes acknowledged in the cognitive therapy of anxiety, along with themes of social acceptance (Beck, Emery & Greenberg, 2005; Meichenbaum, 1985, p. 70). As we've seen, one of the main adjunctive techniques recommended by Marks during traditional exposure therapy is the use of coping statements, based on the SIT approach developed by Meichenbaum (Marks I. M., 2005, pp. 150–155; Meichenbaum, 1985). Another example can be taken from Beck's original cognitive therapy manual for anxiety, in which the following advice is given on self-instruction training:

> A patient can also help to overcome his fears of entering anxiety situations through verbal self-instruction. In this procedure, one actively repeats to oneself phrases that represent important concepts developed in therapy: "Stay with the situation"; "Stay focused on what you're doing"; "The anxiety level will go down"; "What is my purpose"; "Don't evaluate yourself"; "Anxiety is uncomfortable but not dangerous"; or, "What others think of me is none of my business." Many patients find catchphrases helpful when they approach a feared situation. Some examples are, "The lion will disappear when I face him"; "Face what you fear"; "I need to take risks"; "this will pass"; or, "I have to accept the anxiety." The patient repeats these catchphrases in a self-confident and self-assured manner. (Beck, Emery & Greenberg, 2005, pp. 269–270)

Again, it's notable that Beck et al. refer here to the use of self-instructions for active *acceptance* of anxious feelings in an early approach to cognitive therapy, although mindfulness and acceptance-based responses are just one of several coping styles here.

As noted earlier, coping statements are often written on small cue-cards that the client can carry around to act as a reminder, perhaps being read over prior to certain situations as a kind of "mini coping-plan". For example, Marks advises clients to write down coping tactics on a cue card to be read aloud to themselves as soon as they notice signs of anxiety developing. These include self-instructions for abdominal breathing, tension-release relaxation, enduring prolonged exposure, cognitive disputation, etc. (Marks I. M., 2005, p. 181). Meichenbaum and others also refer to the use of cue-cards or even contracts based on simple acronyms that provide a more structured framework for constructing sets of self-instructions and coping strategies (Meichenbaum, 1985, p. 71). This approach follows from the client's conceptualisation and lends itself equally well to hypnotherapy, where the terms of the contract or revised coping plan might be expressed as follows, with examples in brackets below:

Brief coping plan (revised)

1. **Trigger situations**
When I am in a typical "high-risk" situations such as the following:
(Job interviews and meetings at work.)

2. **Cues to cope**
Or when I notice "early-warning signs" such as these:
(Clenching my jaw, thinking "I can't cope!", self-consciousness, or feeling my heart pounding.)

3. **Coping strategies**
I will pause what I'm doing and instead treat these as my "cues to cope", and immediately respond by using the following rational coping strategies:
(Take three deep breaths and say my autosuggestion "let go" as I recall what it feels like to relax deeply and then expand my attention more on to the external situation and other people.)

4. **Self-instructions & suggestions**
I will coach myself through things by using the following verbal "self-instructions" and suggestions:
("I can do this as long as I take things slowly and use the strategies I've learned. Take a few breaths and relax, remain in the situation and accept your feelings so they can begin to reduce naturally, give all of your attention to the external situation for a while.")

As noted earlier, different coping statements and strategies may be appropriate at different chronological stages, particularly before, during, or after a stressful event. Below is a summary of generic guidance on developing self-instructions for applied self-hypnosis, adapted from Meichenbaum's original manual for SIT and based on the four chronological stages discussed above in relation to conceptualisation (1985, pp. 72–73).

1. **Preparing for stressor**
Focus on specific preparations for task or rational problem-solving and planning. Distance from negative anticipatory thinking, accept feelings of anticipatory anxiety, and confine worry to specified worry-time. Eliminate or reduce avoidance and preventative safety-seeking behaviour. Employ mental rehearsal or self-hypnosis recordings and practice coping skills in preparation for event. Set up backup plans ("Plan B") to prepare for possibility of becoming extremely stressed and feeling overwhelmed or if initial coping strategies fail.

2. **Confronting and handling stressor**
Prolong exposure to real-world situation, while dropping unnecessary safety-seeking behaviour. Expand attention flexibly throughout external "here and now" situation, remaining focused on task. Actively accept feelings and view them as harmless and transient. Let go of any struggle against them. Distance from unhelpful thoughts and repeat coping statements, such as "I can handle this, as long as I take my time and use my strategies", etc. Employ learned coping strategies where appropriate, along with self-instructions and autosuggestions.

3. **Coping with feelings of being overwhelmed**
(This stage does not always occur.) Remain in situation and keep attention on present moment and external situation. Stop escape or safety-seeking behaviour, if necessary, using "blocking" strategies. Pause, slow down, and continue to distance from thoughts and accept feelings, allowing them to come and go naturally—"ride it out." Patiently repeat use of coping strategies, or switch to "backup plan" and employ a different strategy.

4. **Evaluation of coping efforts, and self-reward**
Look back over experience and evaluate what has been learned, what worked well and what did not. Take a balanced perspective and recognize small gains, don't belittle gradual progress. Praise self for trying, for effort rather than just for success. Keep trying, don't expect perfection. Reflect on what you could do differently next time. Write down notes for recall later and then set aside. Eliminate or reduce any unhelpful rumination.

A range of statements are typically developed for each stage of coping based on the assessment and conceptualisation of the client's problem and typical examples can be drawn from previous clients with similar problems or the clinical and research literature on the subject. The therapist may present the client with a list of examples and collaborate with her on reviewing them, choosing any that seem appropriate, or developing others tailored to the client's needs (Meichenbaum, 1985, p. 74). Self-statements that affirm coping ability, such as "I can handle this, I've learned several good strategies I can use …" tend to work particularly well. Braid likewise used, as a slogan for early hypnotism, a well-known Latin quotation from the poet Virgil meaning: "They can because they believe they can." It is typically helpful to couple these statements of self-efficacy with a focus on specific tactics rather than general strategies, although some combination may work well. Also, self-statements that remind the client to focus on the present during difficult tasks rather than allowing herself to have "What if?" thoughts about catastrophic outcomes often help.

For example, Meichenbaum divided the self-statements used throughout different stages of coping with clients who suffered from multiple phobias, into the following categories based on their purpose (Meichenbaum, 1977, pp. 155–156):

1. Reappraise the reality of the situation, that is, the probability and severity of threat
2. Replace negative thoughts and images with rational and realistic ones
3. Accept physical symptoms of anxiety as normal, harmless and temporary
4. Re-interpret symptoms as cues or opportunities for coping, that is, as a challenge rather than signs of danger (threat)
5. Motivate yourself to confront and tolerate the phobic situation
6. Cope with intense fear, without escaping the situation
7. Reflect on coping performance and praise and reward efforts.

In general, it's useful to consider self-statements such as the following:

1. Motivate the client to persevere patiently, reminding her of her goals and reasons for making an effort, linking her actions to personal values ("This is important to me because I want to set a good example to my kids!")

2. Pose specific questions that it's useful to try to answer to deal with the problem ("Now what do I need to do next?")
3. Focus attention on the present moment, the task-at-hand, and external environment ("Notice where you are and what you're doing right now.")
4. Distance from unhelpful thoughts ("Right now I'm aware that I'm having the thought that something bad is going to happen; just notice that thought and take a step back from it.")
5. Optionally, reappraise the situation in more realistic and confident terms, as a challenge rather than a threat ("Where's the evidence something bad is likely to happen? Remember all the reasons I listed that show I'm exaggerating the risk; remember all the reasons I have to be confident I can cope.")
6. Actively accept unpleasant feelings ("Let go of any struggle and just allow your feelings to come and go naturally; they're just feelings, I don't need to do what they're telling me.")
7. Treat symptoms as cues to cope ("I notice that I'm becoming tense, that's my signal to pause and use the strategies I've learned …")
8. Remind her to employ certain coping strategies and guide her through them ("Now just use that strategy I've been rehearsing.")
9. Interpret setbacks, or feelings of anger, fear, sadness, or frustration, as signals to pause, slow down, and repeat coping strategies ("Take your time, try again.")
10. Offer reassurance that situations, feelings, or mistakes are not catastrophic and encouragement to remain in the situation until it's over ("It's not the end of the world, just stay with things for a while longer and let the feelings run their course.")
11. Affirm her ability to cope ("I can do it!"), possibly depending on the use of some strategy ("I can do this if I take my time …")
12. Praise or otherwise reward her for individual steps accomplished ("Well done, that's a big step forward!").

This list incorporates some elements of more recent mindfulness and acceptance-based CBT, which can be combined with many traditional forms of behaviour therapy. However, approaches such as applied relaxation have proven successful using a very limited set of coping strategies. In a simplified approach, the client may just be taught how to use self-hypnosis to prepare for stressful events by rehearsing them in a relaxed and confident state of mind and then to employ cue-words to relax rapidly during exposure to the real situation and use brief autosuggestions such as: "I can handle this, just relax and take things slowly …"

Self-instruction and autosuggestion

One of the most obvious points to address in terms of combining hypnotherapy with SIT is the question of how self-instruction in SIT relates to autosuggestion in hypnotherapy, as noted briefly above. Indeed, Meichenbaum was forced to address a similar issue in considering the accusation (or misconception) that self-instruction was just another form of "positive thinking." He specifically refers to Coué's New Nancy School and the writings of Baudouin, as well as other forms of "positive thinking", which he is keen to distinguish from self-instruction (Baudouin, 1920; Coué, 1923; Meichenbaum, 1977, pp. 159–162). However, he also recognised that the New Nancy school of "conscious autosuggestion", closely linked to the hypnotherapy of that period, employed procedures that "came quite close to modern-day behaviour therapy interventions" (Meichenbaum, 1977, p. 160).

His research had shown that banal repetition of verbal formulas was ineffective compared to the self-instruction approach. Encouraging the use of a "litany" of verbal formulas such as "Every day in every way I'm getting better and better" tends to lead to rote-repetition without the necessary feelings attached. Meichenbaum found this "emotionless patter" to be ineffective as a means of self-regulation and emphasised that in addition to "saying the right things to yourself", clients needed to "try out" self-statements in progressively more challenging real-world situations, testing them out in the face of adversity (Meichenbaum, 1977, pp. 161–162). He therefore identified several specific problems with the "affirmation" or "positive thinking" approaches to autosuggestion:

1. Autosuggestions are often too general or vague and not individualised enough to be effective in evoking specific responses.
2. Autosuggestions that are rehearsed without graded exposure to specific anxiety situations do not appear to be as effective.
3. Autosuggestions may be repeated in a "rote" manner (like a "psychological litany") without relevant emotions or intentions being rehearsed.

To be effective, self-talk needed to be specific to the client and their situation, supported by relevant emotions and intentions, and actively rehearsed in the presence of anxiety-provoking imagery or situations.

Nevertheless, all of these issues are very easily addressed. A recurring problem with hypnosis is the popular misconception of it as a method of "talking to the unconscious mind", which usually implies passivity on the part of the subject. This fallacy has to be resolved at the outset of any form of cognitive-behavioural hypnotherapy, and the client socialised to the fact that her active conscious attitude is a critical factor in determining how she responds to suggestions. In other words, suggestions and autosuggestions in hypnotherapy are much closer to instructions and self-instructions than it might appear at first. Clients are expected to mean what they say and either deliberately enact strategies requested of them or evoke responses through active expectation and imagination, which is arguably what Braid originally meant in describing hypnotism as focused attention on dominant, expectant ideas and images. As we've seen, Barber's research on hypnosis found that suggestions given in a "lackadaisical" or disinterested manner were ineffective compared to those repeated confidently and congruently, which closely parallels Meichenbaum's findings on self-instruction training.

The relevance of Meichenbaum's approach to cognitive-behavioural hypnotherapy is perhaps most obvious when he discusses the application of SIT to coping with pain because he explicitly draws upon the research, concepts and treatment strategies reported in the hypnosis literature, including the writings of Sarbin, Barber, and Spanos, the three most influential cognitive-behavioural hypnosis researchers of the period (Meichenbaum, 1977, pp. 172, 177–178). Individual coping strategies for managing pain, typically involving "goal-directed fantasies" incompatible with experiencing pain, were employed as coping skills in SIT and supported by self-instructions in a manner directly based upon the use of autosuggestion and mental imagery in *hypnosis* for pain control. For example, clients chose their own strategies, based on typical examples, including relaxing deeply and imagining being somewhere else while employing self-instructions such as "Just breathe deeply and use one of the strategies", "Relax; you're in control" (Meichenbaum, 1977, p. 177).

One of the main differences between self-instructions and hypnotic suggestions is that the former are not necessarily phrased in the positive grammatically. For example, a hypnotist might suggest: "Let yourself relax" rather than "Don't panic!" However, Beck et al. also explicitly recommend the use of "positive self-instruction" as a way of helping clients to relieve anxious symptoms early in treatment, and that these should be phrased, for example, as "Carry the milk carefully" rather than "Don't spill the milk" (Beck, Emery & Greenberg, 2005, p. 245). When hypnotists recommend the use of positive suggestions, they therefore mean suggestions phrased in the positive grammatically rather than suggestions of a wishful or Pollyanna nature. As noted previously, following Beck, a simple remedy for the tendency to wishful (unrealistic) positive thinking among clients is simply to ask them to describe:

1. *The worst case.* The most negative way of thinking about the level of threat and one's coping ability in a stressful situation.
2. *The best case.* The most positive way of thinking or most-desired outcome
3. *The most-likely case.* The most rational and realistic way of interpreting events or their outcome.

The most-likely case can be used as the basis for developing a balanced and realistic appraisal of the situation, along with an optimistic but realistic affirmation of one's coping ability. Applied self-hypnosis, as a cognitive-behavioural approach, tends to favour the more rational and realistic form of self-talk, although these should generally be phrased evocatively and in the positive grammatically for hypnotic suggestions to be effective. Rather than simply suggesting "Things will probably be okay", it may be more helpful to help the client articulate genuine signs of safety in the environment in more detail than normal and to affirm their ability to cope realistically with events.

It is also true that while most of Meichenbaum's self-statements take the form of instructions for *voluntary* responses whereas hypnosis frequently employs suggestions and autosuggestions designed to evoke more automatic or *nonvolitional* responses. Nevertheless, instructions for voluntary responses and suggestions for automatic ones are normally intertwined in hypnotherapy, for example, "Take a deep breath and exhale slowly" (instruction) and "All the tension is melting away" (suggestion). It is therefore sometimes difficult to distinguish *instructions*, in this sense, from *suggestions*. More specifically, hypnosis typically consists of an initial instruction about engaging in a cognitive or behavioural strategy to be voluntarily complied with. For example, instructions for voluntarily imagining "goal-directed fantasies", such as "imagine a helium balloon attached to your arm", are followed by suggestions intended to evoke automatic responses, such as "your arm is now growing lighter and rising in the air." However, Meichenbaum does acknowledge that "self-statements" can influence involuntary physiological responses such as autonomic arousal and specifically refers to the experimental use of hypnosis in this respect (Meichenbaum, 1977, pp. 207–208). In relation to applied self-hypnosis training, we can roughly distinguish between self-instructions for voluntary behaviour, voluntary behaviour itself, and autosuggestions aimed at evoking automatic responses, the "classic suggestion effect." Indeed, we might do so in a way that broadly correlates with our basic distinction between affect, behaviour, and cognition, as follows:

1. *Affect.* Autosuggestions for nonvolitional responses, such as direct suggestions of self-confidence, relaxation, habituations, etc.
2. *Behaviour.* Coping strategies engaged in voluntarily, such as goal-directed fantasies (relaxation or coping imagery) and overt behavioural strategies such as tensing and relaxing muscles or engaging in assertive behaviour, etc.
3. *Cognition.* Self-instructions for engaging in voluntary coping strategies, that internalise the interpersonal coaching instructions of the therapist, for example, "Just take your time and allow yourself to accept the feelings …".

This is only a very rough distinction. It is often difficult to tell apart instructions that guide voluntary behaviour and suggestions that evoke more automatic responses. For instance, "I can handle this if I take things slowly", might be both an instruction to act in a certain way and a suggestion that evokes helpful feelings, etc. Likewise, many voluntary coping strategies have a suggestive effect. Employing an assertiveness strategy may be adaptive but it also entails acting "as if" confident and can be construed as a form of "muscular suggestion" of the kind described by Braid, as explained in earlier chapters. *Acting* confidently, or even imagining acting confidently, can make you *feel* confident, in other words.

However, the more elaborated lists of coping statements become, the more self-instructions are added, and the more they begin to resemble what Beck and other cognitive-behavioural therapists calls a comprehensive "coping plan" or script (Clark & Beck, 2010). In modern cognitive therapy, "coping plans" and scripts are used to summarise problem-solving strategies for specific situations in detail, often as part of "decatastrophising" interventions, as we shall see in due course. Recently, Meichenbaum has adapted SIT to incorporate elements of a constructive narrative perspective (CNP), which assumes that humans fundamentally experience their lives in terms of a narrative, script, or "story" they construct about things (Meichenbaum, 2007). This includes the "story" clients develop about stressful life events and their attempts to cope with them. Clients are helped to become more aware of their existing narratives or self-stories and how these impact on their stress and coping. They are then helped to construct a more adaptive narrative, re-appraising and finding meaning in stressful events, and planning more adaptive problem-solving and emotion-focused or acceptance-based coping styles. In addition, therefore, to developing skill and confidence in using specific coping strategies, SIT also involves helping the client to construct a new "life story" that moves them on from the role of "victim" to a sense of themselves as someone who is a "survivor" or even "thriving" despite adversity.

Narrative perspectives have also played an important part in the history of the cognitive-behavioural theory of hypnosis. In particular, as we've seen, Sarbin's early research introduced an influential reconceptualisation of hypnosis in terms of the dramaturgical model of "role-taking" theory (Sarbin, 1950; Sarbin & Coe, 1972). According to this view, hypnosis itself involves the enactment of a socially-constructed role, requiring abilities on the part of the client analogous to those of an actor immersing himself in a performance. However, the whole process of hypnotherapy can also be conceptualised in terms of the construction and imaginative rehearsal of a role embedded within a narrative structure, consisting of the "hypnotic script" or imagery employed. In other words, going beyond the use of individual coping statements or autosuggestions, applied self-hypnosis may focus on building a more detailed coping plan or script with the client that may take the form of a hypnotic script, allowing her to rehearse assuming the role of someone who copes better with stress and perceives events in a more constructive way. Returning to our example of childbirth, this might be applied by helping the client to develop a story or script describing the sort of mother she would like to be or how she would like to cope with the process of labour, etc. Scripts and stories can easily be developed collaboratively into self-hypnosis recordings for use as homework, with some help from the therapist.

Application (exposure) and generalisation phase

In the final phase of applied self-hypnosis training, coping skills, such as hypnotic relaxation, dehypnosis (distancing), helpful autosuggestions, etc., are applied in a progressive manner to a range of stressful tasks, in a manner somewhat resembling graduated exposure therapy. Application is conducted through a combination of imaginal, role-play, and *in vivo* exposure techniques, in different contexts, targeting a variety of stressors. Hence, SIT involves graduated exposure but derived more from a cognitive-behavioural coping-skills training model, rather than simply emphasising habituation to feared events. It is designed to help develop skill and confidence in relation to one's coping ability in a way that generalises across a wide range of potential situations and therefore leads a broader sense of emotional resilience than typically results from prolonged exposure to individual threats (Meichenbaum, 1985, p. 17).

For example, someone with a dog phobia may overcome that fear through prolonged exposure alone. However, doing so won't necessarily make them much better at coping with other stressful situations in life, in the future, like exam situations or public speaking, etc. By contrast, the use of specific coping strategies during exposure can lead to the client acquiring a skill that can be applied in many different situations, for the rest of her life, which is likely to increase self-confidence. Meichenbaum (Meichenbaum, 1977, p. 149) actually quotes the hypnosis researcher Martin Orne's earlier article 'Psychological factors maximizing resistance to stress with special reference to hypnosis' as his inspiration for the graduated "stress-inoculation" approach:

> One way of enabling an individual to become more resistant to stress is to allow him to have appropriate prior experience with the stimulus involved. The biological notion of immunization provides such a model. If an individual is given, the opportunity to deal with a stimulus that is mildly stressful, he is able to do so successfully (mastering it in a psychological sense), he will tend to be able to tolerate similar stimulus of somewhat greater intensity in the future. [...] It would seem that one can markedly affect an individual's performance in the tolerance of stress by manipulating his beliefs about his performance in the situation [...] and his feelings that he can control his behaviour. (Orne, 1965, pp. 315–316)

Confrontation (or exposure) to stressful situations or events is therefore graduated, starting with training in using the coping skills in relation to mildly stressful situations. Once basic coping strategies have been acquired they can be applied in four main ways, as appropriate:

1. Imaginal rehearsal, picturing a feared situation while using the strategy.
2. Role-play rehearsal, for example, assertiveness or communication skills, etc.
3. Real-world (*in vivo*) rehearsal, during exposure to feared situations.
4. Rapid-frequent rehearsal of coping skills during a variety of different situations and activities.

Clients can also be instructed to test out their skills in response to spontaneously occurring "daily hassles", taking every opportunity to develop their ability to cope with stress. Exposure typically involves a combination of imaginal, role-play, and *in vivo* (real-life) tasks, ranked in an ascending hierarchy of difficulty. Forms should be tailored for recording homework assignments involving rehearsal and application of coping skills. For example, the simple self-monitoring form below can be used following the one described earlier, to record feelings, such as anxiety, and rate their intensity before and after the use of coping strategies learned, along with any helpful coping statements or self-suggestions used. The client can record what she learned, particularly information that might disconfirm or modify her schemas of threat and vulnerability following the experiment.

Coping skills record					
Date/Time/ Situation	Feelings (Before %)	Coping strategies	Suggestions	Feelings (After %)	Observations (What did you learn?)

Self-instructions are typically used by the client to remind them of their coping skills, motivate and guide them through their use, and reinforce themselves by praising their own efforts.

Coping imagery

The use of mental imagery is also employed in stress-inoculation training as a means of preparation for subsequent *in vivo* exposure. The combination of mental imagery, relaxation, and self-statements obviously bears a strong similarity to ordinary hypnotherapy. Indeed, Meichenbaum derived his mental imagery approach to stress-inoculation training from Wolpe's systematic desensitisation, which was itself originally a hypnotic technique (Meichenbaum, 1985, p. 76; Wolpe, 1958).

> As in desensitization, the client is asked to imagine coping with progressively more threatening scenes while relaxed. However, instead of following Wolpe's practice of terminating the scene when the client experiences stress, in SIT the client is asked to imagine coping with the

stressful situation. The scenes highlight low-intensity intrapersonal and interpersonal cues that signal the onset of a stressful situation or a stressful reaction. The goal is to have clients learn to notice, even anticipate, signs of distress, so that they can become cues that produce coping responses. To maximize the similarity between imagery rehearsal and real-life experiences, coping imagery is employed. Coping imagery involves clients imagining themselves becoming stressed, having stress-engendering thoughts and feelings, and then coping with these difficulties using the coping skills they have acquired. (Meichenbaum, 1985, p. 77)

The use of coping, as opposed to mastery imagery, is emphasised, by which it is meant that the client rehearses feeling stress and struggles at first, before using her coping skills to recover from a temporary setback. This has been found superior to mastery imagery, in which clients are simply asked to imagine themselves having already acquired competence and mastered the situation completely. Meichenbaum gives the following brief illustration:

You can feel the tenseness building in your arms, your breathing becomes heavier (trainer uses the client's stress symptoms). As you begin to barrel up the stairs, you are able to pause just for a moment, take a slow deep breath, and, as you exhale slowly, you are able to gain your composure as you climb the stairs. See yourself coping with your stress … Relax … Good. (Meichenbaum, 1985, pp. 77–78)

The client is encouraged not only to picture her coping behaviour, and use of relaxation and other strategies agreed in advance, but to employ coping statements or self-instructions in the image rehearsed. Coping imagery also allows the client repeated opportunities to practice patient acceptance of unpleasant feelings of anxiety and psychological distancing from distressing thoughts.

Generalisation of improvement

Meichenbaum emphasised that what the client says to himself about the outcome of confronting his stressors, at this stage, is critically important because his reflections on the experience will determine maintenance and generalisation of the new coping behaviour being applied to the situation (Meichenbaum, 1977, pp. 224–227). This raises the question as to whether the outcome constitutes evidence that might change underlying cognitive structures (schemas) as in Beck's concept of behavioural experiments or "empirical hypothesis testing". Altering covert speech during exposure to stressful situations is integral to the stress-inoculation approach but this leads to an examination of the outcome that follows experimenting with certain changes in behaviour, which in turn allows underlying schemas to be modified (Meichenbaum, 1977, p. 226). In other words, repeated exposure to threatening situations while experimenting with the use of coping strategies can easily be construed as a behavioural experiment, as in Beck's cognitive therapy. From a coping skills perspective, particularly useful debriefing questions to ask following experimentation with new behaviour and ways of coping might include:

1. "What did you actually do to cope?"
2. "What actually happened?"

3. "What worked well and what didn't?"
4. "What might you do differently next time to cope better?"
5. "So how would that way of coping probably work out for you in the long-run?"
6. "What else did you learn about coping with this situation?"
7. "What does this say about your coping ability in general?"
8. "From 0–100 per cent, how would you now rate your confidence in your coping ability?"

Changing attitudes in this way can lead to improvement across a wider range of situations. Generalisation is also encouraged by having clients rehearse a variety of different coping skills in response to different types of stressor, in different environments, and through the use of cognitive interventions such as self-instruction and cognitive restructuring. For example, by learning to relax very rapidly, using a cue-word, clients can be asked to relax for at least one minute in each waking hour of the day, to develop their skill and confidence and a more generalised sense of relaxation across multiple tasks and situations.

Maintenance of improvement

Application and exposure are also supplemented by relapse-prevention strategies, and proactive anticipation of potential setbacks in the future. Sessions may be "faded", progressively reducing their frequency, and booster sessions and follow-up assessments conducted as well as attention to maintenance of improvement and follow-through. Moreover, as treatment progresses the therapist's role should be "faded", as the client gradually internalises it and takes over greater responsibility for her therapy, becoming her own internal coach or therapist with the aim of "making the therapist obsolete" insofar as possible. This is marked by the client gradually becoming more active in setting agendas and influencing the course of subsequent therapy sessions. Maintenance can also be aided by arranging "booster sessions" as required and providing clients with a "blueprint" of the conceptualisations and treatment, based on reflective evaluation of what worked and what didn't. The use of recordings in hypnotherapy can also be helpful as clients have a permanent source of help ready-to-hand if they need a reminder or booster in the form of self-hypnosis.

Relapse prevention typically involves identifying high-risk situations or early "warning signs" of possible relapse and helping the client to plan ways of coping and rehearse them, perhaps generating a written "relapse prevention plan" (Pretzer & Beck, 2007, p. 493). A typical cognitive therapy relapse prevention form might be used, containing questions such as the following, which can follow on from the client's existing "revised coping plan" as described above (Pretzer & Beck, 2007, p. 494).

1. What situations have been hard to cope with in the past?
2. What situations are hard to cope with currently?
3. What situations are likely to be hard to cope with in the future? (High-risk situations)
4. How do you propose coping with them?
5. What thoughts, actions, or feelings, etc., might be initial indications that you're having problems? (Early warning signs)

6. How do you plan to respond if you spot those signs?
7. If that doesn't work what could you try next? (Backup plan).

This kind of written plan can be combined with the client's conceptualisation diagram and other notes to provide a record of their understanding of the problem and plan for maintaining improvement in the long-term. The main thing is that the client is encouraged to plan for relapse and to reflect on their options in a rational problem-solving manner.

Applied hypnotic relaxation

This section and the next will provide a more detailed account of two of the most important coping skills that may be incorporated within the cognitive-behavioural hypnotherapy framework for applied self-hypnosis:

1. Applied hypnotic relaxation
2. Applied "dehypnosis" or mindfulness.

Relaxation is not essential to SIT; it is just one coping strategy among others. However, it is probably the most commonly employed strategy, especially in relation to managing anxiety. By the 1970s, several different relaxation "coping skills" approaches to the treatment of stress and anxiety had evolved in response to Wolpe's original systematic desensitisation technique (Wolpe, 1958). Meichenbaum provided a review of the main approaches, highlighting their common factors, which helped to define the preferred method used in SIT (Meichenbaum, 1977, pp. 143–150). These later approaches generally differed from traditional progressive muscle relaxation (Jacobson, 1938) and systematic desensitisation (Wolpe, 1958) insofar as they were more multifaceted and emphasised the client's *active* role in learning and applying coping skills (Meichenbaum, 1977, p. 147). Likewise, adopting a flexible approach to self-hypnosis and autosuggestion can actually open up a wide variety of possible relaxation techniques for use with different clients, involving autosuggestions and mental imagery strategies of many kinds.

Criticisms of relaxation techniques

Although behaviour therapy largely originated in the use of systematic desensitisation, a relaxation-based technique (Wolpe, 1958), in recent decades there has been a widespread move away from using relaxation as a standard intervention in the treatment of anxiety disorders. First of all, "exposure therapists", like Isaac Marks, reported finding that exposure to feared situations was equally beneficial with or without prior relaxation training. Initial relaxation training in systematic desensitisation, which used to take place over the first four to six sessions, was seen as unnecessarily laborious:

> This approach [systematic desensitisation] is easy to learn, but takes so long to help sufferers overcome their fear that more efficient forms of exposure are now usually recommended.

> Relaxation turns out to be unnecessary—though sufferers like doing it, relaxation does not speed recovery and the time is better spent just doing exposure if possible. (Marks I. M., 2005, p. 145)

However, Marks *does* still recommend the use of both abdominal breathing and tension-release relaxation as brief coping strategies, insofar as they allow clients to prolong exposure and overcome the urge to escape (Marks I. M., 2005, p. 181). Self-instructions for these techniques are to be written on cue cards which are read aloud at the first sign of tension.

> Keep your fear level manageable, by very slow deep breathing with your hand on your tummy, or tensing and relaxing your muscles, or doing mental arithmetic, solving crossword puzzles, counting the beads on a rosary, or whatever else you find useful. (Marks I. M., 2005, pp. 187–188)

Nevertheless, some behaviour therapists have rejected the use of relaxation immediately prior to exposure, as in systematic desensitisation, because it is believed that habituation can only occur properly if the anxiety response is able to reduce by a sufficient degree, usually thought to be about half its initial level. If the client is already so relaxed that little anxiety is evoked to begin with then there's not much scope remaining for a reduction to occur and this is thought to be necessary for permanent extinction of the anxiety to take place (Rosqvist, 2005, p. 54). Indeed, certain authors have gone so far recently as to suggest that "relaxation during exposure is contraindicated, generally" (Rosqvist, 2005, p. 55).

However, there is still mixed evidence, confusion, and controversy in this area. Beck's position in his recent treatment manual for anxiety disorders is as follows:

> The role of relaxation training in treatment of anxiety disorders continues to generate considerable debate. The long-established tradition of teaching progressive muscle relaxation to relieve anxiety may still have some efficacy for the treatment of GAD and possibly panic disorder, especially when the more systematic and intense applied relaxation protocol is employed. However, relaxation training for OCD and social phobia is unwarranted, although it may still have some value in PTSD for those with heightened generalized anxiety. (Clark & Beck, 2010, p. 267)

As Beck implies, systematic forms of relaxation training often appear to be more beneficial than hasty attempts to relax as a safety-seeking behaviour or form of experiential avoidance. Moreover, as Bryant observes in his discussion of cognitive-behavioural hypnotherapy for anxiety:

> Although the potency of relaxation techniques in actually reducing clinical anxiety is arguable, many clinicians provide relaxation because it can give a sense of self-mastery and symptom reduction, and may encourage compliance with therapy. Hypnosis can facilitate the relaxation process by deepening the relaxation exercises that are embedded in the hypnotic induction, directing the individual to focus attention on the specific muscle groups or emotional

responses that are being relaxed, and providing imagery to enhance the relaxation experience. (Bryant R. A., 2008, p. 538)

Indeed, Beck still recommends the frequent use of relaxation techniques, such as progressive muscle relaxation and meditation, as part of cognitive therapy for stress management (Pretzer & Beck, 2007, p. 492) and also, with some reservations, in his recent self-help workbook for anxiety (Clark & Beck, 2012). In short, relaxation-based coping strategies may be best-suited for mild or subclinical problems rather than the more severe anxiety disorders and the therapist should be careful to evaluate their use to make sure the client is not becoming dependent upon relaxation as a form of safety-seeking or experiential avoidance. It's partly for this reason, that an alternative, mindfulness and acceptance-based, strategy is described below, following this section on applied hypnotic relaxation.

Overview of applied hypnotic relaxation

Currently, the most evidence-based relaxation approach is the "applied relaxation" protocol developed in Sweden by Lars-Goran Öst and his colleagues (Öst, 1987). It originated out of Jacobson's progressive muscle relaxation, Wolpe's systematic desensitisation, and the variety of "coping skills" approaches to anxiety management that evolved in the 1970s. Öst was also influenced by Meichenbaum's broader SIT approach, which applied relaxation resembles and can be combined with. Applied Relaxation normally involves systematic training in muscle relaxation skills and subsequent abbreviation of them into a rapid coping skill, which is applied to stressful situations. The original protocol spans about ten to twelve weekly sessions. The overall framework closely resembles that of SIT, except that progressive muscle relaxation is prescribed as the main coping strategy rather than the client being presented with a "menu" of options to evaluate and choose from.

Öst introduces clients to a simple triple-response conceptualisation model of anxiety (or stress), similar to the generic ABC (affect, behaviour, cognition) model described above, that distinguishes between physiological sensations, behaviour, and cognitive (subjective) responses. The emphasis during assessment and conceptualisation is on helping the client spot "early-warning signs", particularly common physiological sensations such as muscles tensing or heart rate increasing, and environmental antecedents such as typical events or situations that are associated with elevated stress. Although it has been abbreviated and delivered in different formats, the typical skills acquisition stages are as follows:

1. Full routine of tension and release muscle relaxation
2. Abbreviated tension-release relaxation
3. Relaxation by recall ("release only") and counting, which involves a procedure described as "indirect suggestion" and resembling self-hypnosis in some respects
4. Rapid cue-controlled relaxation
5. Differential relaxation, involving recalling the experience of relaxation during a variety of activities, selectively relaxing any unnecessary tensions from the body.

Tension-release training can be presented as a precursor to self-hypnosis training in order to provide the client with a physical experience to recall by means of subsequent autosuggestions. It also provides an opportunity to "couple" suggestions of relaxation, as described by Barber, with a behavioural strategy that naturally creates muscular relaxation before fading the physical techniques and increasingly using recall only. However, in many cases clients can learn to relax simply by using simple hypnotic inductions, deepeners, and autosuggestions of relaxation. The standard eye-fixation hypnotic induction involves tension of the muscles around the eyes and relaxation, followed by counting. The counting technique used in applied relaxation is virtually indistinguishable from the traditional hypnotic method. In the "release only" phase, the therapist verbally prompts the client to "Breathe with calm, regular breaths and feel how you relax more and more for every breath ... Just let go ... Relax your forehead ... eyebrows ... eyelids ... jaws ... tongue and throat ... lips ... your entire face ...", etc. (Öst, 1987). These clearly resemble hypnotic suggestions and some authors provide more elaborate suggestions to clients during applied relaxation that bear even closer similarity to hypnotic scripts (Bernstein, Borkovec & Hazlett-Stevens, 2000). The client then scans her body for any remaining tension and tries to relax completely, possibly reverting back to the behavioural tension-release strategy if necessary.

Hence, a simple format for training in Applied Hypnotic Relaxation might be similar to the above but with minor modifications:

1. *Optionally*, begin by training in abbreviated progressive muscle relaxation, using tension-release.
2. Self-hypnosis skills training, involving eye-fixation and counting deepener, followed by direct autosuggestions of relaxation in different parts of the body.
3. Rapid cue-controlled relaxation, using a cue-word as a hypnotic trigger to recall the feelings of deep relaxation experienced during earlier training.
4. Differential relaxation training, involving the use of the hypnotic trigger or cue during a variety of situations and activities.

In short, training in a formal self-hypnotic relaxation routine, first through coaching in the therapy session and subsequently by listening to a short recording daily at home, leads to the development of a brief coping skill, using a cue-word or hypnotic trigger, which can be used to apply relaxation rapidly during imaginal exposure or in real-world situations.

This is not a new idea, however. Many hypnotherapists will be familiar with similar approaches and self-hypnosis has even been used in this way as part of cognitive-behavioural treatment. For example, the English psychiatrist Philip Snaith developed an early protocol for a cognitive-behavioural form of self-hypnosis training, which was explicitly linked to SIT and other coping skills approaches but employed a hypnotic relaxation technique loosely based on Schultz's Autogenic Training. He called this method Anxiety Control Training (ACT) (Snaith, 1974; Snaith, 1981, pp. 208–227). It involved verbal feedback of relaxation responses to the client in hypnosis, coupling them with sensations already being experienced, etc. The client then practices a brief autosuggestion technique at home, for example, repeating "My arms are becoming heavy and limp" or "I am becoming calm and still", focusing on the bodily sensation suggested for about ten minutes twice daily and perhaps also visualising a calm and relaxing scene. After three to four sessions, the therapist introduces anxiety-provoking imagery and the mental rehearsal of a coping skill. After initial relaxation the client is asked to imagine herself in an anxiety-provoking situation and to take three to four deep breaths to control her anxiety, reinforced with suggestions that she is becoming more skilled and confident at doing so. Following this initial training in coping imagery, the client is advised to incorporate anxiety-provoking imagery into her self-hypnosis practice sessions at home. However, the procedure presented below is somewhat more systematic and draws more closely upon applied relaxation and stress-inoculation training, both of which have substantial empirical support as we've seen above.

Self-monitoring and awareness training

Applied hypnotic relaxation naturally begins with the use of self-monitoring and imagery-based recall techniques to raise awareness of early-warning signs of stress, and related problems. This also provides an opportunity to identify unhelpful thinking in general, including negative automatic thoughts or negative autosuggestions, and unhelpful coping strategies. From this basic information, alternative ways of coping can be identified along with more helpful ways of thinking, such as adaptive coping statements. The client can be asked to summarise her typical unhelpful self-talk (autosuggestions) when confronting the problem and to develop alternative helpful coping statements (helpful autosuggestions), using a simple two-column form like the one described earlier. This should also serve as an opportunity to both raise awareness of early warning signs of impending stress or anxiety and to practice basic mindfulness and acceptance skills (dehypnosis) prior to the application of hypnotic relaxation techniques. In short, the client can be encouraged to observe thoughts from a distance when writing them down, viewing them as transient events in the mind, and to accept feelings by letting go of any struggle against them or attempt to control or eliminate them, including through the use of experiential avoidance, safety-seeking behaviour, etc.

Example hypnotic relaxation skills-acquisition script

This is an abbreviated example of a hypnotic induction and suggestion script for training in applied hypnotic relaxation. A similar procedure may be administered by the therapist or provided on a recording for the client to listen to daily, for a few weeks, during the initial coping-skills acquisition stage. The following script is of the kind that might be used on a recording and should normally be tailored to suit the client's needs and preferences, for example, by collaboratively choosing a cue-word and suggestions that seem appropriate and helpful to her. The first segment of the script below provides an example of an appropriate induction, followed by suggestions of relaxation loosely modelled upon Schultz's Autogenic Training and similar approaches:

> Just close your eyes, take a moment to make yourself comfortable, and relax completely ... [Pause] Now slowly turn your eyes upwards and open your eyelids ... Fix your gaze on a

point on the ceiling overhead … In a moment, I'm going to begin counting from five down to zero … As I do so, just imagine your eyelids are growing so heavy they feel like closing, and allow them to grow heavy and close … Beginning now … Five … Four … Three … Two … One … Zero … Let your eyelids close all the way down as you begin going into hypnosis … Relax your eyes … Relax your face … Relax your whole body … Good. Now with each and every exhalation of breath, imagine you're letting go and relaxing more deeply, in your body and in your mind … [Pause]

In a moment, I'm going to begin repeating a series of simple suggestions that describe feelings of relaxation. You can use these suggestions to guide you as you become progressively more skilled and confident at deeply relaxing … Just allow yourself to patiently imagine the sensations being described as if you're actually feeling them while listening to the words … Begin now by focusing your attention first on both of your legs … Your legs are becoming heavy and warm … Your legs are becoming heavy and warm … Your legs are becoming heavy and warm … [Pause] Now both your arms … Your arms are becoming heavy and warm … Your arms are becoming heavy and warm … Your arms are becoming heavy and warm … [Pause] Now the trunk of your body, your chest, back, and abdomen … Your chest, back and abdomen are becoming relaxed … Your chest, back and abdomen are becoming relaxed … Your chest, back, and abdomen are becoming relaxed … [Pause] Now your neck, and shoulders … Your neck and shoulders are becoming limp and relaxed … Your neck and shoulders are becoming limp and relaxed … Your neck and shoulders are becoming limp and relaxed… [Pause] Now your facial muscles … Your facial expression is becoming calm and peaceful … Your facial expression is becoming calm and peaceful … Your facial expression is becoming calm and peaceful … [Pause] Now your breathing … Your breathing is becoming peaceful and relaxing … Your breathing is becoming peaceful and relaxing … Your breathing is becoming peaceful and relaxing … [Pause] Now your whole body as one … Your whole body is becoming completely relaxed … Your whole body is becoming completely relaxed … Your whole body is becoming completely relaxed … [Pause] Good. Now just keep relaxing more and more deeply with each and every exhalation of breath … [Pause]

In a moment, I'm going to begin counting from five down to zero again … This time, as I do so, just imagine that you're counting along with me in your mind … As we count, just allow yourself to let go and relax more and more deeply with each number, until by the time we've reached zero, you're relaxing as deeply as you can imagine right now … Beginning now … Five … Four … Three … Two … One … Zero … Good. Just continue to let go and relax more deeply with each and every exhalation of breath … [Pause]

Next, the following suggestions and instructions can be provided for the development of an abbreviated coping strategy:

Patiently, with practice, you're learning what it feels like to relax more thoroughly, throughout your body, and to let go of the muscles more deeply … You're becoming more skilled and confident at relaxing deeply … It's becoming easier and easier for you to remember this feeling of deep relaxation and experience it at other times and places, just by choosing to recall the sensation of letting go profoundly in the body and the mind …

Now you can learn how to recall those sensations of relaxation, the feeling of letting go, more quickly and easily by associating them with a signal you give yourself, which we call a hypnotic trigger or cue. You can use any words you like but for the sake of this exercise I'm going to assume you're using the cue-words "Let go ..." [This is for a recording, modify the cue-words to suit the client's preference.] To begin with, I want you just to focus on your breathing for a minute or so, particularly the out-breath ... Each time you exhale, repeat the words "Let go ..." in your mind ... Say the words in a relaxing way and focus on making a progressively stronger link, a mental association, between the words and the feelings of profound relaxation ... I'm going to give you a few minutes to continue making that link in silence, beginning now ... [Pause for about one to two minutes, or about twenty breaths.] Good. Now you can fade the words from your mind and just continue relaxing in silence.

Finally, I'm going to help you to rehearse using your cue-words, just as you might use them to recall profound relaxation in a real-life situation ... In a moment, I'm going to ask you to take three deep breaths, slowly, holding your breath for as long as is comfortable before each exhalation ... As you breathe in, I want you to think of the word "Tense" as you'll automatically tense your muscles when holding your breath, that's just natural ... Then, as you exhale, I'm going to ask you to think of your cue-words "Let go ..." and to release any tension and relax completely, all over again, by recalling the sensation of letting go ... Beginning now ... Take a deep breath in as you think the word "Tense" ... Hold your breath for as long as is comfortable ... Then exhale slowly, let go completely all over again, and think of the words "Let go ..." Breathe naturally, for a while longer, letting go and relaxing more deeply on each and every out-breath as you think of the words "Let go ..." [Pause for about 30 seconds.] Now take a second deep breath in as you think the word "Tense" ... Hold your breath for as long as is comfortable... Then exhale slowly, let go completely all over again, and think of the words "Let go ..." Breathe naturally, for a while longer, letting go and relaxing more deeply on each and every out-breath as you think of the words "Let go ..." [Pause for about thirty seconds.] Take a third deep breath in as you think the word "Tense" ... Hold your breath for as long as is comfortable ... Then exhale slowly, let go completely all over again, and think of the words "Let go ..." Breathe naturally, for a while longer, letting go and relaxing more deeply on each and every out-breath as you think of the words "Let go ..." [Pause for about thirty seconds.]

Good. Once you've finished it's a good idea to practice using those cue-words to relax as rapidly and deeply as possible. Over time, you should practice doing so in a variety of different situations and before, during, or after a variety of different activities. By doing so, not only will you become more skilled and confident at relaxation but you'll probably find yourself becoming more relaxed throughout the day, adopting a more relaxed way of life in general.

Finally, the following segment is used to emerge from hypnosis:

In a moment, I'm going to begin counting from one up to five, and as I do so, you can now allow yourself to emerge from hypnosis and relaxation, focusing on the room around you, where you are and what you're doing ... Beginning now ... One ... Starting to emerge from hypnosis and relaxation ... Two ... Feeling more alert and focused on the external situation ...

> Three ... Focusing your eyes and beginning to breathe a little more deeply ... Four ... Ready to open your eyes ... Five ... Take a deep breath and open your eyes as you emerge fully and completely from hypnosis ... Now just take a moment to regain your orientation to the room around you and when you're ready begin to practice using your relaxation skills in different situations, relaxing by taking three deep breaths and using your cue-words to rapidly recall the feeling of complete relaxation.

Clients rehearse this once with some modelling, coaching, instruction, and feedback in the therapy session before being given a recording to listen to daily. After two to three weeks of daily practice, they usually begin applying the brief (cue-controlled) relaxation coping strategy, first in their imagination, as below, and then in real-world stressful situations.

Example applied hypnotic relaxation script

The coping skills or self-control approach to desensitisation basically assumes that the client has gone through a skills acquisition stage in which she's learned how to relax rapidly by using cue-words, and developed some skill and confidence in doing so. The following self-hypnotic desensitisation script basically allows her to rehearse using her coping skills during imaginal exposure to a stressful situation. Mental rehearsal of coping skills can be used either in anticipation of a real-life situation or to reduce anxiety provoked by purely hypothetical worries. A range of fictional situations can even be employed simply to provide an opportunity to strengthen coping ability and inoculate against stress in general. A typical hypnotic procedure might begin with the induction technique, suggestions of relaxation, and counting technique, described above. This would be followed by repeated exposure to a stressful situation, evocation of anxious thoughts and feelings (or other troublesome responses such as anger), and repeated practice in using the cue-words or other coping skills to counteract anxiety. Delaying the use of the coping skill slightly also provides a valuable opportunity to practice exposure to and acceptance of unpleasant feelings, before reducing them. In some cases, it may be a better long-term strategy to imagine letting go of any struggle against unpleasant feelings and "relaxing *into*" them instead of trying to "relax them *away*", as practicing acceptance may be helpful where avoiding unpleasant thoughts and feelings, such as worry and anxiety has become a problem ("experiential avoidance").

The script below asks the client to signal when she's ready to continue, which is the ideal way to control the timing of the procedure. On a recording this would have to be replaced with a pause, typically of around ten to twenty seconds. The therapist should take a subjective rating of disturbance (SUD) from zero to ten, when the client is imagining the scene to be targeted, before beginning. This can then be checked again after every repetition of the scene. At first it may be best simply to focus on learning the basic relaxation skill but over time helpful coping statements and imagery can be incorporated by asking the client to see herself coping better with the situation and telling herself helpful statements and instructions, for example, "I can do this, just take your time, I'm relaxing and letting go of all the tension ...", etc. The therapist will usually have to remind the client of the specific details in addition to making general suggestions like the ones below. An induction and suggestions of relaxation are first employed, for example, as in the first segment of the preceding script. Next, suggestions are given for the rehearsal of the coping strategy in imagination, as follows:

> Now you've relaxed in hypnosis, I'm going to help you to develop greater skill and confidence in using your coping strategy. In a moment, I'm going to simply ask you to repeatedly imagine the stressful situation we agreed earlier. As you do so, I want you to really imagine that you're there, as if it's happening right now, and you're experiencing things through your own eyes rather than from a distance. Allow yourself to fully experience any stressful or unpleasant thoughts and feelings ... Just notice them and let them come and go freely, without trying to struggle against them in any way. After a few moments, you're then going to use your coping strategy to relax as deeply as possible. [Pause]
>
> Now just imagine yourself in that situation, as if it's happening right now ... Allow yourself to really experience and accept any unhelpful thoughts and unpleasant feelings that tend to occur ... Just nod your head when you're satisfied you've got those feelings and can accept them ... [Wait] Now remain in that scene but use your coping strategy to let go of any tension that you can voluntarily release ... Beginning now ... Take a deep breath in and hold your breath for as long as is comfortable ... Then exhale slowly, let go completely all over again, and think of the words "Let go ..." Breathe naturally, for a while longer, letting go and relaxing more deeply on each and every out-breath as you think of the words "Let go ..." Picture yourself relaxing in the scene and coping better and better with things ... Imagine telling yourself helpful coping statements like the ones we discussed earlier ... [Pause for about fifteen seconds.] Now take a second deep breath in and hold your breath for as long as is comfortable ... Then exhale slowly, let go completely all over again, and think of the words "Let go ..." Breathe naturally, for a while longer, letting go and relaxing more deeply on each and every out-breath as you think of the words "Let go ..." Picture yourself coping and imagine telling yourself helpful statements ... [Pause for about fifteen seconds.] Take a third deep breath in and hold your breath for as long as is comfortable ... Then exhale slowly, let go completely all over again, and think of the words "Let go ..." Breathe naturally, for a while longer, letting go and relaxing more deeply on each and every out-breath as you think of the words "Let go ..." Picture yourself coping and imagine telling yourself helpful statements ... [Pause for about fifteen seconds.] Good. Now from zero to ten how uncomfortable do you feel now while imagining yourself in that scene? [Wait for response.] Okay. [Repeat this paragraph three to four times or until anxiety is reduced by about half.]

The client can then be emerged from hypnosis as normal, with some additional suggestions for improving skill and confidence in using her coping strategies, as in the final segment of the preceding script.

It's a small step to then see how similar coping skills can be employed in real-life situations. Doing so should be at a pace that is appropriate for the client and normally graduated along a hierarchy of difficulty or anxiety experienced. Prolonged exposure to feared situations tends to reduce anxiety through habituation, although coping skills such as relaxation often help and appear to dramatically reduce the typical amount of time required. On the other hand, relaxation can sometimes be used as a form of experiential avoidance and may become too much of an "emotional crutch" in some cases, as noted above. The next chapter will therefore discuss the basic principles of exposure therapy in more detail, returning to the issue of coping skills at some points. In addition to its application to specific challenging situations, rapid-frequent use of relaxation coping skills throughout the day, across a wide variety of situations, perhaps for one to three minutes during each waking hour of the day, may help lead to a greater degree of generalisation and even a more relaxed attitude toward life in general.

Applied dehypnosis (mindfulness and acceptance)

Overview of applied mindfulness

A similar approach can be adopted toward training in basic mindfulness and acceptance strategies. As noted above, Beck's early writings on cognitive therapy contained reference to a strategy referred to as psychological "distancing", which involves learning to be mindful of thoughts and to experience them as psychological events rather than confusing them with external reality (Beck, 1976). This concept was taken up by the founders of acceptance and commitment therapy (ACT), which was originally called "comprehensive distancing" (Hayes, Strosahl & Wilson, 2012). They developed the idea further, making it one of the central processes in their own approach to therapy, renaming it "defusion." Distancing or defusion is therefore a central process in modern mindfulness and acceptance-based approaches to therapy but is not a novel concept in the CBT field.

In his first book on cognitive therapy, *Cognitive Therapy and the Emotional Disorders* (1976), Beck clearly defined the concept of "distancing" as follows:

> Some patients who have learned to identify their automatic thoughts recognize their unreliable and maladaptive nature spontaneously. With successive observations of their thoughts, they become increasingly able to view these thoughts objectively. The process of regarding thoughts objectively is labeled *distancing*. (Beck, 1976, pp. 242–243)

He elsewhere repeats this view, that merely helping clients to become more aware of their automatic negative thoughts "tends to be accompanied by greater objectivity (distancing)" insofar as the client increasingly spots that their thoughts are not in accord with reality and corrects them spontaneously (Beck, 1976, p. 258).

Later, in their technical account of cognitive theory, Beck and his colleagues explicitly equate the clinical technique of distancing with the theoretical concept of "metacognition", or thinking *about* thinking, stating that distancing constitutes an active, self-regulatory process that involves switching to a metacognitive level of processing information (Alford & Beck, 1997, p. 65). He explicitly defined it as follows:

> "Distancing" refers to the ability to view one's own thoughts (or beliefs) as constructions of "reality" rather than as reality itself. (Alford & Beck, 1997, p. 142)

Beck had originally explained that the term "distancing" came from the literature on projective tests such as the Rorschach test. Some individuals are "carried away" by strong emotional reactions to ambiguous pictures and view the ink-blots, etc., as though they were literally equivalent to the things they take them to represent. Others are more able to "take distance", perceiving the ink-blot merely as an ink-blot (Beck, 1976, p. 258). As Beck goes on to explain, when someone automatically equates his thoughts with reality his distancing is described as poor. By contrast, his distancing is good, when he can view his thoughts as hypotheses or inferences, rather than facts. He therefore described distancing as the ability to distinguish between "I believe" and "I know".

Moreover, in their 1985 manual for anxiety disorders, Beck and his colleagues refer to helping clients achieve psychological distance from anxious thoughts and feelings by referring to themselves in the third person throughout the day ("Bill is feeling anxious, he's worried others are judging him negatively ...") to develop an objective stance on their feelings (Beck, Emery & Greenberg, 2005, p. 194). Elsewhere, in this manual, Beck and his colleagues refer to distancing in terms of developing "self-observation" and the ability of the client to "watch myself watch myself", to be self-aware of his awareness.

In his later, theoretical text on cognitive therapy, Beck linked distancing to "perspective taking". Hence, one technique for facilitating psychological distance is to have the client take the perspective of other people, who may disagree with her beliefs, and thereby distance herself from them temporarily. This approach is used with schizophrenic delusions in cognitive therapy but also with other disorders and for subclinical problems (Alford & Beck, 1997, p. 143).

In short, the following strategies are described by Beck and his colleagues as basic "distancing" strategies in standard cognitive therapy:

1. Writing down negative automatic thoughts on a daily thought record.
2. Writing thoughts on a blackboard and literally viewing them from a distance.
3. Viewing thoughts as inferences or hypotheses instead of facts, distinguishing between "I believe" and "I know".
4. Referring to your thoughts and feelings in the third-person ("Bill is having anxious feelings, he's thinking that people are criticising him ...").
5. Using a counter to keep a tally of specific types of thoughts, seeing them as habitual and repetitive.
6. Self-observation, being aware of your own awareness, noticing how you observe your thoughts.
7. Shifting perspectives and imagining being in the shoes of other people, who might disagree with your beliefs and view things differently.

Distancing is one of several initial symptom-relief strategies used to reduce anxiety prior to the systematic disputation of cognitions (Beck, Emery & Greenberg, 2005, p. 232). It formed part of the multi-component "AWARE" strategy described in Beck's cognitive therapy for anxiety (Beck, Emery & Greenberg, 2005). The same strategy has also been incorporated into Beck's most recent publication, a self-help workbook for anxiety disorders, where it its use in conjunction with exposure-based therapy is emphasised (Clark & Beck, 2012). The "AWARE" strategy instructs clients to:

>**A**ccept your anxious feelings and allow them to decline naturally
>**W**atch your thoughts and feelings from a distance

<u>A</u>ct "as if" non-anxious, remaining in situations and dropping "false" safety-seeking behaviour
<u>R</u>epeat these strategies, perhaps through repeated imaginal review (Raimy's method)
<u>E</u>xpect to make progress, in a realistic and optimistic manner.

Distancing strategies therefore constitute an important basic skill in cognitive therapy and form an integral part of the broader concept of mindfulness. Emphasis upon distancing and mindfulness was combined in Beck's cognitive therapy with acceptance of emotions, through strategies such as Victor Raimy's "repeated review" method, an imagery technique which combines well with hypnotism. In addition, active acceptance of anxious feelings, seeing them as transient and harmless, letting go of any struggle against them and allowing them to run their course, is integral to most forms of exposure. This can be facilitated by simple strategies such as imagining "breathing through" the sensations, while allowing them to come and go freely. Likewise, mindfulness and acceptance can be used to counter the narrowing of attention on to threatening sensations and increased self-focus that is associated with anxiety, by expanding awareness beyond them, throughout the body, and outward to the external environment, in a manner similar to emerging from hypnosis, or what has traditionally been called "dehypnosis", since the time of Braid.

Self-monitoring and awareness training

Self-monitoring strategies can play an important role in the development of psychological "distance" or mindfulness. The practice of writing thoughts down in automatic thought records was described by Beck and his colleagues as a simple method for achieving distance and objectivity in relation to them (Beck, Rush, Shaw & Emery, 1979, p. 164). There's a knack to writing down thoughts concisely and looking at them on the paper, slowly and patiently, with mindfulness and a sense of psychological distance from them, before putting the form away and symbolically letting go of the thoughts for the time being. Likewise, by counting the number of times certain automatic thoughts occur, using a golf or knitting counter, the client starts to view them as stereotypical and repetitive in nature. Hence, the client may learn to distance herself and say, "There's another anxious thought; just count it and then let it go" (Beck, Emery & Greenberg, 2005, p. 196). According to Beck, the anxious client is to patiently accept the thoughts, observe them, and then let them go, rather than struggling against them. Similarly, by recording automatic thoughts or writing them up on a chalkboard and *literally* viewing them from a distance, the client can be helped to gain psychological distance or detachment from her distressing ideas (Beck, Emery & Greenberg, 2005, p. 191).

Moreover, spotting unpleasant feelings early makes it easier to actively accept them, abandoning any struggle against them, and to allow them to abate naturally before they have escalated into a full-blown episode of heightened distress. In general, keeping records and self-monitoring can be construed as a form of awareness training, designed to help clients notice their reactions to different situations and to provide them with the opportunity to change course and respond differently or simply "do nothing" in response to triggers that would normally be associated with automatic emotional reactions such as anxiety. Increasing awareness of the ingredients of anxiety and its stages makes it easier to dismantle the experience and accept its components individually, rather than viewing them as a unified "lump" of emotion, which is likely to be experienced as more overwhelming.

Example dehypnosis skills-acquisition script (repeated review)

Raimy's basic method of repeated cognitive review can be very easily integrated with hypnosis and naturally lends itself to training in the distancing and acceptance skills. These three strategies (distancing, acceptance, and repeated review) were originally central to the symptom-relief repertoire of skills in the initial phase of cognitive therapy for anxiety. When we apply mindfulness and acceptance during imaginal exposure we end up with a technique that procedurally resembles hypnosis (or rather "dehypnosis") and many other forms of skills rehearsal using mental imagery. Suggestions can be recorded that facilitate dehypnosis by using mindfulness and acceptance strategies, *reversing* the factors which have been established as central to the hypnotic mind-set, such as imaginal absorption, response expectancy, etc. (Lynn, Das, Hallquist & Williams, 2006). See the later chapter on cognitive therapy for more discussion of the "repeated review" approach.

The script below provides a concise example of how Raimy's "repeated review" technique can be used in hypnosis, along with suggestions for cognitive distancing and emotional acceptance. This procedure can be used in early sessions, following imagery-based recall of recent, typical events, to help the client obtain initial symptom relief and to acquire the basic cognitive therapy skills of distancing and acceptance of feelings, described by Beck and his colleagues as the first step in cognitive therapy of anxiety (Beck, Emery & Greenberg, 2005, p. 232). After establishing a particular situation that's linked to anxiety, or other distressing emotions, the therapist can take the client through a simple mindfulness "induction" routine such as the following:

> Pause for a few moments to become more mindful and self-aware. Notice how you're currently using your body and your mind, right now, in the present moment. Take a step back from your thoughts and allow yourself to acknowledge and accept any unpleasant feelings you might be having, such as tension, pain, or anxiety. Be aware of yourself as the detached observer of your thoughts and feelings. Throughout life you've experienced literally millions of different thoughts and feelings and observed many different things. Your current thoughts and feelings are transient, just what you happen to be experiencing right now, sooner or later your attention will move on to other things, and then sometimes it may return to these experiences again.
>
> For now, just be aware of what you're currently experiencing, from moment to moment, without evaluating it, analysing it, or interpreting it. You can have your eyes open or closed, be standing or sitting, it really doesn't matter. Just allow yourself to pause and become mindful of your experience for a few moments. If your mind wanders, that's fine, just acknowledge the fact and bring your awareness patiently back to the exercise you're doing.

This can be followed by instruction in the repeated review of emotional imagery:

> Now I'd like you to review that whole sequence of events very patiently, a few more times, from beginning to end ... Don't try to change anything; don't try to stop anything from

changing ... Sometimes things may change spontaneously just by being observed ... As you go through events, though, do slow things down a little and practice distancing from your thoughts and actively accepting your feelings ... Distance reality from your thoughts, by noticing what you're thinking, as you think it, and realising that your thoughts are just hypotheses, just thoughts rather than facts ... Distance yourself from your thoughts by taking a step back, metaphorically, in your mind, and viewing them in a more detached way, you are not your thoughts or feelings, you're the conscious observer of them ... Allow yourself to patiently accept your feelings as harmless and transient, opening up and fully experiencing them by letting go completely of any effort to control or suppress them ... Take your time and review that situation from start to finish, as if it's happening right now and you're really there, seeing things through your own eyes ... [Pause] As you go through the scene, just briefly describe what happens this time and how you feel ... [Wait] What else did you notice about the whole experience this time? [Wait] From 0–100% how distressing was it to imagine? [Wait]

Okay, now slowly go through the whole experience once again, from just before you noticed the earliest warning signs, through the peak, to the end, once it's over ... Again, patiently watching your thoughts from a distance while you accept your feelings and let go of any internal struggle with them ... [Pause] As you go through the scene, just briefly describe what happens this time and how you feel ... [Wait] What else did you notice about the whole experience this time? [Wait] From 0–100% how distressing was it to imagine? [Wait]

Okay, now slowly go through the whole experience just one more time, from just before you noticed the earliest warning signs, through the peak, to the end, once it's over ... Again, patiently watching your thoughts from a distance while you accept your feelings and let go of any internal struggle with them ... [Pause] As you go through the scene, just briefly describe what happens this time and how you feel ... [Wait] What else did you notice about the whole experience this time? [Wait] From 0–100% how distressing was it to imagine? [Wait]

You will probably find it helpful to repeat this exercise daily, reviewing your thoughts and feelings, by imagining the situation in detail, at least 3–4 times ... You can use this repeated review in your imagination as an opportunity to practice both distancing from your thoughts and actively accepting your feelings ... You should carefully observe and note down what effect that has upon your problem, both immediately and over time ... As your distress reduces, and you begin to feel more confident, you can also consider how you might solve problems and cope differently with similar situations in the future ...

The client can then be "emerged" by expanding attention through their body and into the external environment, resuming their orientation to the reality of the present moment.

Now gradually begin to expand your awareness beyond those experiences. Continue to be aware of your breathing and any part of your body that you've been attending to but, in addition, allow your awareness to begin spreading through the rest of your body, throughout the trunk of your body, your arms, your legs, your neck and head. Become aware of your whole body as one, and continue to accept any unpleasant sensations you're experiencing but also begin to notice what else you're experiencing, more and more, progressively widening the sphere of your attention. Not trying to avoid or control unpleasant experiences but rather expanding beyond them.

Now gradually spread your awareness out further beyond your body and into the room around you, where you are and what you're doing right now. Continue to notice how you're using your body and mind as you look slowly around you. As you finish the exercise and begin interacting with the external world and perhaps other people, take that sense of mindfulness and self-awareness with you into your environment and any tasks at hand. If you continue to notice any unpleasant sensations, that's fine, just accept them, let go of any struggle against them, and gently expand your attention beyond them to the world around you and the way you're interacting with life as you move into action.

This dehypnosis procedure can also be adapted for use on a self-hypnosis or "mindfulness meditation" recording, which the client may benefit from listening to daily for a week or two. In other words, it can function as a more formal skills training procedure, prior to introducing more rapid and portable mindfulness and acceptance-based coping skills such as the strategy described below.

Example applied dehypnosis script

"Mini-meditation" techniques such as the "three-minute breathing space" (3MBS) in mindfulness-based cognitive therapy (MBCT) can be employed to provide an opportunity for rapid-frequent practice of coping skills throughout the day and in a variety of settings. We can think of this as injecting a short burst of more profound mindfulness in-between ordinary daily activities. It's natural to think of the shift in focus of attention involved as narrowing briefly on to some anchoring point or "centring device" such as the breath and then widening to the present moment and the task at hand, as a way of concluding the exercise and continuing, mindfully, with daily activity. The following brief exercise incorporates elements from several mindfulness and acceptance-based therapies. It uses the same induction (first) and emerging (last) segments as the preceding script but sandwiched in the middle is a brief acceptance-based coping strategy:

Step one involves mindfulness of the here and now ... Pause for a few moments to become more mindful and self-aware. Notice how you're currently using your body and your mind, right now, in the present moment. Take a step back from your thoughts and allow yourself to acknowledge and accept any unpleasant feelings you might be having, such as tension, pain, or anxiety. Be aware of yourself as the detached observer of your thoughts and feelings. Throughout life you've experienced literally millions of different thoughts and feelings and observed many different things. Your current thoughts and feelings are transient, just what you happen to be experiencing right now, sooner or later your attention will move on to other things, and then sometimes it may return to these experiences again.

For now, just be aware of what you're currently experiencing, from moment to moment, without evaluating it, analysing it, or interpreting it. You can have your eyes open or closed, be standing or sitting, it really doesn't matter. Just allow yourself to pause and become mindful of your experience for a few moments. If your mind wanders, that's fine, just acknowledge the fact and bring your awareness patiently back to the exercise you're doing.

Step two involves grounding attention in the breathing ... Now gradually narrow your focus of attention on to the sensations of your breathing. Don't try to change your breathing, don't try to stop it from changing, just breathe naturally. Accept what your breathing feels like and make room for it to do whatever it wants, let go of any desire to change or control it. Notice the sensations of your breathing, the rise and fall of your belly, perhaps movements in your chest, or even your shoulders. Become aware of even the smallest sensations that accompany your breathing, feelings you may not have noticed before. Keep paying attention to your breathing to help ground your attention in the reality of the present moment.

If you're aware of any unpleasant feelings anywhere in your body, just allow yourself to accept them patiently and let them come and go as they please, or to remain the same. Let go completely of any struggle against them and instead study them from a more detached perspective. Combine awareness of the breath with awareness of the body by imagining your breath continually passing right through that part of your body where the unpleasant feelings are happening. Use your breath to centre your attention on that part of your body for a while. As you breathe in and out, continue to actively accept those sensations and allow yourself to fully experience them. Let go completely of any struggle against them. Make room for the feelings to run their course, or come and go freely by imagining a sense of space opening up around them. You are not your breath, you are not those sensations, you are not your emotions or even your thoughts; you're the detached observer of all of these things, viewing experiences from a distance as they come and go without struggle.

Step three involves expanding awareness throughout the body ... Now gradually begin to expand your awareness beyond those sensations. Continue to be aware of your breathing and any part of your body that you've been attending to but, in addition, allow your awareness to begin spreading through the rest of your body, throughout the trunk of your body, your arms, your legs, your neck and head. Become aware of your whole body as one, and continue to accept any unpleasant sensations you're experiencing but also begin to notice what else you're experiencing, more and more, progressively widening the sphere of your attention. Not trying to avoid or control unpleasant experiences but rather expanding beyond them.

Now gradually spread your awareness out further beyond your body and into the room around you, where you are and what you're doing right now. Continue to notice how you're using your body and mind as you look slowly around you. As you finish the exercise and begin interacting with the external world and perhaps other people, take that sense of mindfulness and self-awareness with you into your environment and any tasks at hand. If you continue to notice any unpleasant sensations, that's fine, just accept them, let go of any struggle against them, and gently expand your attention beyond them to the world around you and the way you're interacting with life as you move into action.

These and other basic coping skills can be employed to facilitate cognitive restructuring, behaviour change, and emotional habituation, etc. This approach may suffice for many clients, particularly with mild to moderate stress or anxiety. However, the following chapters provide a much more detailed account of standard cognitive and behavioural strategies combined with hypnosis. These more thorough interventions may be of value with clients who have more complex or severe problems. The division of the following chapters is based on a rough distinction between feelings, actions, and thoughts, not unlike the format adopted in Beck's original manual for anxiety (Beck, Emery & Greenberg, 2005). In brief, the chapter on *affect* explores the role of exposure-based interventions in more detail, the chapter on *behaviour* describes a detailed problem-solving methodology for use in hypnotherapy, and the one on *cognition* examines the role of Beck's cognitive therapy in conjunction with hypnosis, particularly through the use of mental imagery techniques.

CHAPTER EIGHT

Affect: hypnotic exposure therapy

Everyone knows what it means to be "exposed to danger". In behaviour therapy and CBT the term "exposure" is used to refer to the presentation of situations or events, which the client unrealistically and mistakenly perceives as significantly threatening or experiences as *unnecessarily* anxiety-provoking.

> In its simplest form, exposure treatment consists merely of advice to sufferers to expose themselves every day to a situation they find rather difficult and to record their daily actions in a diary which the therapist reviews at the next visit. As they gain confidence, they can set themselves fresh targets to achieve from one week to the next. (Marks I. M., 2005, p. 144)

As conceived within modern cognitive therapy for anxiety, exposure has been defined as follows:

> [Exposure is] systematic, repeated, and prolonged presentation of external objects, situations, or stimuli, or internally generated thoughts, images, or memories, that are avoided because they provoke anxiety. (Clark & Beck, 2012, p. 129)

Over the past decades, a great many techniques have evolved that make use of exposure principles. Most anxiety treatment in CBT involves systematically graduated, repeated, and prolonged exposure to feared situations or events, either external or internal, which initially provoke anxiety and a strong urge to avoid them or escape (Clark & Beck, 2010, p. 238). Indeed, exposure is widely considered to be an "essential" component of any effective treatment for anxiety, especially specific phobias (Antony & Swinson, 2000, p. 191). Although sixty per cent of adults report phobia-like fears, only 11.25 per cent of the adult population appear to meet DSM-

IV-TR diagnostic criteria for specific phobia (Leahy & Holland, 2000, p. 214). That suggests that over eighty per cent of such fears are sub-phobic in nature and may be more easily treatable.

Although the term "exposure therapy" is sometimes used to refer to specific behaviour therapy protocols, it is also sometimes used more generally to refer to any treatment strategy that involves confrontation with anxiety-provoking stimuli, including exposure-based "behavioural experiments" in cognitive therapy for anxiety (Clark & Beck, 2010). Hypnosis has been long used for imaginal exposure and as preparation for real-life (*in vivo*) exposure. Indeed, hypnosis and imaginal exposure therapy combine very easily and self-hypnosis recordings are ideal ways to deliver imaginal exposure homework. Autosuggestion can be used prior to and during *in vivo* exposure, as with coping statements and self-instruction. Imaginal exposure works best when it is prolonged and realistic. However, prolonged realistic imagination with focused attention is virtually a definition of hypnosis. Moreover, hypnosis appears to be an effective way to vivify mental imagery, increase focused attention, and prolong the duration of exposure, because of time distortion, etc.

Behavioural exposure therapy

The origin of exposure and desensitisation

The earliest clear example of systematic exposure-based therapy, based on behavioural psychology, is found in two articles published in 1924 by Mary Cover Jones, a colleague of J. B. Watson, one of the pioneers of behaviourism (Jones, 1924a; Jones, 1924b). She described the treatment of children, aged three months to seven years, suffering from a variety of phobias using a technique called "the method of direct conditioning." One of these articles is a detailed case study of the treatment of a rabbit phobia in a child named Peter, conducted under laboratory conditions. The other describes in detail her observation on different methods of therapy by conditioning applied in the treatment of a group of seventy children with phobic anxiety. She tried a variety of verbal and conditioning techniques in combination with repeated *in vivo* exposure, concluding as follows:

> In our study of the methods for removing fear responses, we found unqualified success with only two. By the method of direct conditioning, we associated the fear-object with a craving-object, and replaced the fear by a positive response. By the method of social imitation we allowed the subject to share, under controlled conditions, the social activity of a group of children especially chosen with a view to prestige effect. (Jones, 1924b)

In other words, she concluded the techniques most effective were those later known as "reciprocal inhibition", juxtaposing anxiety with a stronger response that inhibits it (in this case appetite), and "participant modelling", approaching the feared object and handling it with guidance from more confident peers. Her main technique in the treatment of Peter was to feed him, as a means of pacifying him, while repeatedly exposing him, *in vivo*, to a graded hierarchy of situations related to his fear of rabbits. However, it was several decades before others began to develop these initial findings into a fully-fledged system of behaviour therapy.

In Britain, according to Hans Eysenck, behavioural exposure therapy originally developed out of the psychoanalyst Alexander Herzberg's "active psychotherapy" approach in the 1940s.

> In this, patients with specific fears and anxieties were given graduated tasks, starting with relatively easy tasks producing little anxiety, and working up to more and more difficult ones. Thus a patient showing a fear of open spaces would be instructed to set foot outside his door and take two or three steps in either direction and then go back. If he found this too stressful, he might be accompanied by his wife or friend. Gradually the range would be extended to five or six steps, then to ten, then to twenty, then to going to the end of the street, then going round the square. Gradually the patient would work up towards complete freedom of fear under these circumstances. The therapist would of course always be ready with reassurance and advice, but these graduated tasks were a most important part of the treatment approach. (Eysenck H. J., 1977, p. 111)

The application of graduated task assignment to phobias, etc., is not clearly set out in Herzberg's book *Active Psychotherapy*, although it's probably implied by his more general remarks about treating "neuroses" (Herzberg, 1945). This was followed by the development of Joseph Wolpe's "systematic desensitisation", the most influential technique of early behaviour therapy (Wolpe, 1958). Systematic desensitisation involved the use of either hypnotic suggestions of relaxation or training in progressive muscle relaxation, followed by systematic exposure to imagery of feared events, while in a deeply relaxed state, in order to create a conditioned inhibition of anxious arousal by repeatedly juxtaposing anxiety triggers with relaxation.

However, in 1948, immediately prior to the advent of modern behaviour therapy, the psychotherapist Lewis Wolberg had published his two-volume *Medical Hypnosis*, one of the most influential clinical textbooks on hypnosis of that period, which pre-empts the use of early behaviour therapy techniques such as systematic desensitisation and imaginal exposure (Wolberg, 1948a; Wolberg, 1948b). Although he was an eclectic psychodynamic therapist, specialising in the use of hypnosis, Wolberg described the use of several hypnotherapy techniques based directly on behavioural psychology, which he refers to as "hypnotic desensitization", "reconditioning", and "exposure" to phobias.

> Fears that are conditioned through chance associations may, under hypnosis, occasionally be reconditioned by associating strong pleasure stimuli with the situation that inspires the phobia. [...]
>
> Another means of treating phobias is by desensitization. Under hypnosis the patient is given suggestions to expose himself gradually to the terrifying situation. The aim in desensitization is to get the patient to master his fears by actually facing them. It is essential for the individual to force himself again and again into the phobic situation, in order that he may finally learn to control it. [...] The hope is that the conquering of graduated doses of his fear will desensitize him to its influence. (Wolberg, 1948a, p. 235)

His chapter entitled "Hypnosis in Reconditioning" opens by explaining that this form of behavioural hypnotherapy was based upon the precedent set by Mary Cover Jones and other psychologists in applying conditioning principles to the treatment of anxiety-related problems.

Wolberg describes the case of a patient who successfully overcame her intense phobia for oranges through hypnotic imagery of pleasant experiences and direct suggestions, used to facilitate graduated exposure. Exposure occurred initially in the form of imagery in hypnosis, picturing herself in an orange grove, followed by physical (*in vivo*) exposure to drinking progressively stronger concentrations of orange juice (Wolberg, 1948b, pp. 213–214). Wolberg also described the use of exposure-based hypnotherapy for social phobia, based on a behavioural conceptualisation of the problem. In the case of one highly socially phobic and avoidant patient, relaxing imagery of a pleasant scene, during hypnosis, was followed by an imagined conversation with another person. To this scene, progressively more and more people were added, in a graduated manner, increasing the difficulty for the client in steps and stages, again during hypnosis, until he pictured himself speaking in a group of people without anxiety (Wolberg, 1948b, p. 215).

Wolpe had evidently read *Medical Hypnosis* as he cites it as the basis for his own use of the "arm-levitation" induction (Wolpe, 1990, p. 181). Although he later increasingly substituted progressive muscle relaxation, Wolpe initially used hypnosis to induce relaxation and described this technique as "hypnotic desensitisation", like Wolberg before him. Hence, the cardinal technique of early behaviour therapy for anxiety appears to have been prefigured by and perhaps derived from Wolberg's earlier behavioural hypnotherapy technique. *Medical Hypnosis* (1948a) was, in fact, published exactly ten years prior to Wolpe's first major book on behaviour therapy, *Psychotherapy by Reciprocal Inhibition* (1958), although Wolpe also published some initial journal articles on hypnotic and nonhypnotic desensitisation during the mid-1950s (Wolpe, 1954). However, Wolberg's *hypnotic* "reconditioning" and "desensitization" techniques were part of a more eclectic approach than Wolpe's systematic desensitisation. Wolberg sometimes incorporated pleasant imagery, direct suggestions, combination of imaginal and real-world (*in vivo*) exposure, and even directions to focus more attention externally on pleasant aspects of the conversation in social phobia, all of which feature in subsequent cognitive-behavioural therapy approaches.

The basic rationale for exposure

From the origin of behaviour therapy in the 1950s onward, there has been a proliferation of techniques used to treat anxiety that emphasise presentation, in reality or imagination, of the things feared. Researchers were naturally inclined to try to reduce the apparent effect of these different approaches to their common factors. Isaac Marks, in particular, is associated with the bold claim, now established as orthodoxy, that the most important ingredient in most anxiety treatment is simply repeated, prolonged, exposure to the feared stimuli. Hence, Marks went so far as to claim that, "all therapist-assisted strategies, such as desensitisation or flooding in fantasy, or prolonged exposure in vivo, are simply elaborate manoeuvres toward persuading patients to expose themselves to the ES [evoking stimulus]" (Marks I. M., 1981,

p. 66). It can now be said that "Exposure-based interventions are among the most studied and effective components of cognitive-behavioural therapy" (Dobson & Dobson, 2009, p. 103). Despite this, practitioner surveys have found that cognitive-behavioural therapists report surprisingly low rates of actually using exposure-based techniques (Dobson & Dobson, 2009, p. 106).

Nevertheless, there has long been a general consensus among clinicians and researchers that "exposure therapy is hard to beat" when it comes to the treatment of most forms of cued anxiety, especially specific phobias. Even Beck, the founder of cognitive therapy, highlights the importance of exposure, a behavioural intervention, as "the single most effective intervention for therapeutic change across the anxiety disorders" (Clark & Beck, 2010, p. 235). This has also long been recognised in the cognitive-behavioural literature on hypnotherapy:

> The case for exposure as the indispensable element in the treatment of phobic anxiety is difficult to resist. [...] We would go as far as to say that without exposure there can be no significant improvement in phobic disorders. (Clarke & Jackson, 1983, p. 196)

The mechanism by which exposure works is traditionally construed by behavioural therapists in terms of classical conditioning principles as a form of "habituation" or "extinction". Habituation has been described as "the backbone upon which all exposure treatment is built" (Rosqvist, 2005, p. 41). The process of habituation of anxiety might be seen as a kind of *vis medicatrix naturae*, or natural healing process, by which the human organism corrects or "unlearns" maladaptive anxiety. It should also be noted that, from the outset, behaviour therapists have emphasised that qualities of the therapeutic relationship, such as the warmth, empathy, and congruence of the therapist and the provision of a safe environment, probably contribute to the reduction of anxiety during some exposure procedures. This is generally a positive ingredient in treatment, so long as the client is not allowed to become overly-dependent upon the presence of the therapist.

However, as we've seen, although Beck and other cognitive therapists recognise the central importance of exposure, and accept many of the principles of the behavioural approach, especially in the treatment of specific phobias, they tend to combine this with an emphasis on cognitive factors, such as the client's automatic thoughts and underlying beliefs about threat and vulnerability in the feared situation (Clark & Beck, 2010). Hence, exposure in cognitive therapy tends to be conceptualised, in part, as a behavioural experiment designed to modify underlying threat schemas, although Beck and other cognitive therapists *also* recognise the phenomenon of habituation as a central mechanism in exposure-based therapy for anxiety (Clark & Beck, 2010). Indeed, beliefs *about* habituation may provide a close bridge between behaviour therapy and cognitive therapy, such as the client's acceptance of beliefs such as:

- "Anxiety will decline naturally if I allow the feelings to run their course."
- "Struggling against my anxiety just makes things worse."
- "If I try to escape from situations that make me anxious, I'll just prevent myself getting over it."

Socialisation to exposure-based therapy, even in Beck's *cognitive* therapy, consists in teaching the client about the natural phenomenon of habituation, correcting misconceptions, and improving motivation to remain in anxiety-provoking situations long enough, despite feelings of anxiety and urges to escape or engage in safety-seeking behaviours (Clark & Beck, 2010; Clark & Beck, 2012).

Socialisation to exposure-based therapy

As Marks puts it, "The essence of dealing with fear is learning to ride it until the storm passes" (Marks I. M., 2005, p. 154). This requires courage and motivation on the part of most clients because it goes against their natural instinct to flee or protect themselves in response to anxiety. Typically, in a CBT approach, the rationale for exposure should incorporate four key elements (Antony & Swinson, 2000, p. 194):

1. An account of how exposure actually works, that is, either by habituation or by disconfirming beliefs about threat and vulnerability.
2. An explanation of why previous attempts or "naturally-occurring" exposure may not have worked in the past.
3. Basic guidelines on how exposure therapy, including self-directed exposure homework, should be carried out.
4. Evaluation of the "costs and benefits" of exposure versus avoidance.

The behavioural approach dominates the conceptualisation of specific phobias, and so it is probably best to begin by considering the role of habituation in such cases, although cognitions may also be important, particularly in conditions more complex than specific phobias. The inherently "self-limiting" nature of anxiety, its natural tendency to habituate, can be easily illustrated to clients by focusing on an observable physiological phenomenon such as increased heart rate.

> When someone who is afraid of heights stands on the balcony of a high building, and becomes anxious, what do you think happens to their heart rate? That's right. Their heart rate will normally increase quite sharply, perhaps to *double* its normal resting level. Suppose they had to remain in the situation, though, and couldn't escape. What would happen to their heart rate over time, if we just kept waiting and waiting?

This simple question often causes clients to scratch their heads. Sometimes they want to say that anxiety continues, unabated, or that it increases, but they also tend to have the conflicting thought that it *must* eventually go down again, somehow.

> "What goes up must come down." Of course, their heart rate won't normally remain at double its resting level permanently; the increase will start to wear off even if they remain in the situation. It will tend to increase very sharply when they enter the situation then, after a while,

begin to gradually reduce. How long do you think that might take? Could anything *interfere* with it reducing?

This can lead on to a useful discussion. Reduction in heart rate to baseline level might occur in specific phobias within about fifteen to twenty minutes during exposure, whereas for more complex or severe problems like agoraphobia it may take over an hour (Marks I. M., 1981).

Imagine someone did manage to endure being on that balcony long enough for their anxiety to "wear off" and their heart rate to return, more or less, to its normal level. What do you think would happen if they visited the balcony not just once, but every day, and on each occasion, they tolerated their anxiety until their heart rate went back to normal, or at least reduced substantially, before leaving? What would happen to their anxiety level *eventually*, over time?

This line of questioning tends to lead on to the observation that the initial level of anxiety is likely to be less severe as exposure is repeated and may abate more quickly. Most clients can arrive at this conclusion themselves with the aid of simple Socratic questioning. Some authors explain the rationale for imaginal exposure to clients by drawing an analogy with watching a "scary" movie several times, which normally means that it becomes less frightening with each viewing. Imaginal exposure can easily be compared to viewing a movie of a "scary" incident in the mind's eye until it stops provoking anxiety (Antony & Swinson, 2000, p. 193). The need to reverse avoidance and approach one's fears can be explained to clients by referring to the old adage, or cliché, that if you fall off your horse the best thing to do is get right back on it again (Marks I. M., 2005, p. 140). People will often recognise that after a car accident, in a similar manner, drivers are generally advised not to postpone things too long but to get back behind the wheel again as soon as they are able.

Many clients, perhaps even the majority, will initially react to the concept of exposure therapy by discounting it with comments like, "Yes but I've been trying to do that for years and it doesn't seem to be working." In some cases, where actual behavioural avoidance is low, such as among people who are socially anxious but frequently endure social situations where they feel extremely uncomfortable, it will be more important to elaborate on the exposure therapy rationale. Otherwise the client will struggle to understand how "facing their fears" actually differs from what they already find themselves doing. There are several reasons why "spontaneous exposure" or the client's deliberate attempts, before treatment, to "face their fears" may not have been helpful (Clark & Beck, 2010, p. 240). These should be discussed sufficiently for the client to understand the difference and embrace the exposure therapy rationale, at least in the spirit of a collaborative experiment.

Unhelpful (naturally-occurring exposure)	Helpful (exposure therapy)
Unplanned and unsystematic	Planned and systematic
Unpredictable and uncontrollable	Predictable and controllable
Anxiety too *high* or too *low* to be therapeutic	Graded exposure starting from *moderate* level
Briefer exposure leading to sense of defeat	Prolonged exposure leading to sense of mastery

Occurs infrequently	Occurs regularly, i.e., daily
Ended by escape during high anxiety	Ended once anxiety has reduced substantially
Accompanied by avoidance and safety-seeking	Prevention of avoidance and safety-seeking
Accompanied by negative automatic thoughts	Automatic thoughts are properly questioned
Attempts to avoid or suppress thoughts and feelings	Acceptance of feelings and focus on feared situation

Likewise, Marks provides five "Golden Rules" of exposure therapy for his clients, which help to address this problem of socialisation to the treatment approach (Marks I. M., 2005, p. 183).

1. Remember that anxiety is very unpleasant but fundamentally harmless, that is, fears of physical (e.g., heart attack) or mental (e.g., nervous breakdown) catastrophes are unfounded.
2. Avoid trying to escape from feared situations and events because this simply maintains the problem.
3. Encourage yourself to face your fears as often as possible because practice makes perfect, that is, the more often you face your fears the more easily you will overcome them.
4. The longer you face them the better because anxiety is temporary and will reduce naturally if you remain for long enough in a feared situation, that is, "what goes up must come down."
5. The more quickly you confront your worst fears, the more quickly your anxiety will reduce.

If the client discounts the potential benefits of exposure the therapist should check whether she has followed these "golden rules" in the past and is distinguishing clearly between helpful and unhelpful forms of exposure as described above.

Likewise, as noted previously, Beck's current cognitive therapy for anxiety recommends use of the "AWARE" acronym, from the original 1985 cognitive therapy manual for anxiety disorders, as a self-help guide during exposure (Clark & Beck, 2012, p. 142).

> **A**ccept feelings of anxiety and let go of any struggle against them
> **W**atch your anxious thoughts and feelings from a distance, as a detached observer
> **A**ct courageously, as if non-anxious, despite your anxious feelings, approaching the feared situation and remaining in it without trying to escape or seek safety
> **R**epeat these steps, persevering until your anxiety reduces substantially
> **E**xpect to make progress, adopting a realistic and optimistic perspective, assuming that anxiety can be tolerated and overcome to some extent through repeated exposure.

This guidance is somewhat similar to the type of strategies emphasised in more recent mindfulness and acceptance-based approaches to CBT, which developed Beck's concept of "distancing" from negative automatic thoughts and combined this with other mindfulness practice, sometimes employed during exposure-based interventions (Hayes, Follette & Linehan, 2004).

Motivation for exposure

Part of socialisation to the exposure approach normally involves evaluation of the client's level of motivation and attempts to ensure they are sufficiently motivated to act against their fear.

It should be emphasised to clients that exposure therapy, especially regular self-exposure to challenging situations, requires considerable determination, perseverance and patience (Marks I. M., 2005, p. 142). Indeed, the initial meeting with the therapist can be seen as a form of exposure, which many potential clients would feel an urge to avoid, and clients therefore deserved to be praised for taking this first courageous step. They are already being much braver than the many people who "suffer in silence" without approaching anyone for help.

It is also important to reassure clients that the treatment is effective, and to provide accurate information on the likelihood of success, where possible. In their review of outcome studies on treatment for specific phobia, for example, Roth & Fonagy conclude that overall:

> The efficacy of systematic desensitization and exposure techniques has been widely researched, with strong evidence that the latter is more effective than the former, particularly when exposure is prolonged to the point at which anxiety is markedly reduced. Clinically significant improvement is achieved in 70–85% of cases. (Roth & Fonagy, 2005, p. 155)

However, systematic desensitisation and applied relaxation also appear to be effective evidence-based interventions, especially for specific phobias and, as Marks noted, some clients may prefer these more relaxation-based approaches, where appropriate. Cognitive interventions have not been extensively studied in the treatment of specific phobias, partly because the efficacy of exposure is so well established and incorporation of cognitive interventions does not appear to have much additive value, except in certain cases (Roth & Fonagy, 2005, p. 156). The situation differs when it comes to other forms of anxiety, such as GAD or social phobia, where there is more reason to believe that cognitive factors such as catastrophic worry and fear of negative evaluation predominate and that cognitive interventions may be of value or even essential to the treatment, often in addition to exposure therapy. The combination of cognitive interventions and exposure constitutes a good illustration of a truly "cognitive-behavioural" approach.

Types of exposure

Strictly speaking, any treatment is a form of exposure if it requires the client to face their fears, either in reality or in their imagination. However, there are many different ways of doing this, known by very different names. First of all, it is common to make a basic distinction between:

1. *Situational* exposure, also known as "real-world", "live", "overt", or "*in vivo*" exposure, in which the client faces the thing feared in reality, often outside of the consulting room.
2. *Imaginal* exposure, also known as "symbolic", "covert", or "*in vitro*" exposure, in which the client merely pictures the thing feared.

However, in subsequent decades, a third type of exposure can be added:

3. *Interoceptive* or "internal" exposure, in which the client exposes himself to physical sensations in his own body which trigger anxiety, usually in the treatment of panic attacks.

In some cases, instead of anticipated real-world situations, a form of imaginal exposure may be used to target internal cognitive cues such as memories and intrusive thoughts or fantasies, etc. With problems such as social anxiety or low self-esteem, role-playing scenarios with the therapist may also constitute a form of exposure, which could be considered a form of *overt* imagination in contrast to the *covert* imagination of passive "mental imagery" techniques. Moreover, video clips and photographs are also often used very effectively as forms of exposure.

Imaginal exposure is more effective than one might assume; there is a surprising tendency for anxiety reduction experienced during imaginary scene presentation to transfer to the real world. Nevertheless, there is a general consensus among researchers and clinicians that the more realistic exposure is the more beneficial and lasting its effects tend to be, that is, real-world situational exposure is the "gold standard", particularly for more severe or complex anxiety disorders such as agoraphobia and OCD (Antony & Swinson, 2000, p. 192). However, most hypnotherapists combine both approaches. Clients can often be *prepared* for situational exposure between sessions by the use of imaginal exposure in the consulting room. Although imaginal exposure is proven to be effective without hypnosis, in the context of behaviour therapy, one reason for introducing hypnosis is that it tends to encourage clients to experience mental imagery as more realistic and therefore a step closer to real-world exposure. Moreover, exposure-based interventions have been employed within hypnotherapy for at least half a century and almost certainly prior to the development of behaviour therapy, as we have seen.

To a large extent, different anxiety disorders can be distinguished in terms of the type of events or situations that trigger anxiety and therefore the type of exposure that therapy tends to emphasise (Dobson & Dobson, 2009, p. 105; Leahy & Holland, 2000, p. 283). For example:

- Specific phobia usually requires *in vivo* exposure to the sight of, or physical contact with, a feared object, event or situation, etc.
- Social phobia mainly involves fear of making a social gaffe or being the centre of attention.
- Generalised anxiety disorder (GAD) entails chronic worry about multiple imaginary catastrophes, which can be exposed to in imagination.
- Posttraumatic stress disorder (PTSD) often entails memories of a traumatic event which are the cues for anxiety and targets for exposure.
- Panic disorder often involves bodily sensations that are interpreted catastrophically ("I'm having a heart attack") and "interoceptive" exposure.
- Agoraphobia, in addition to panic attacks, often requires exposure to situations that the client typically avoids, being away from sources of help (safety signals) and abandonment of safety-seeking behaviours, etc.
- Obsessive-compulsive disorder (OCD) may involve exposure to distressing thoughts or images or to feared situations and the prevention of compulsive "neutralising" responses such as hand-washing, etc.

In some cases, particularly in OCD, it may be helpful to view anxiety as cued by *not* doing something, such as not compulsively washing one's hands after touching something thought to be contaminated with germs. Hence, it should be clear that different types of anxiety disorder also tend to require treatment to involve the prevention of certain maladaptive responses used automatically or deliberately to try to cope with anxiety, as otherwise exposure is incomplete and habituation or cognitive modification may be undermined. We will return to discussion of this subject in more detail under the heading of "response prevention" below.

Hierarchy construction

As discussed in a previous chapter, assessment for anxiety normally involves the construction of a "hierarchy" of feared situations or events, which forms a bridge between assessment and treatment as it is integral to the implementation of most exposure therapy. During assessment, the range of things which evoke anxiety should have been identified and this list is typically developed into one or more lists of items ranked according to the severity of distress experienced. In modern CBT, hierarchies typically consist of about ten to twenty items related by a single "theme". For example, a client with blood-injection-injury type phobia might develop a single hierarchy based around the specific theme of a forthcoming blood test and another hierarchy containing a more general list of related events that are feared, such as seeing television programmes about hospitals or hearing people talking about injuries, etc.

Hierarchy item	Disturbance (SUDs)
Watching blood being taken from arm	90%
Having needle inserted	80%
Preparing to have needle inserted, talking to nurse	80%
Sitting in waiting room before having blood taken	60%
Arriving at hospital for blood test	50%
Booking date for blood test	30%
Imagining having blood test	30%
Talking aloud about blood test	25%

Ranking items according to the anxiety that would be experienced *if* the client faced them perhaps fails to distinguish very well between those situations that are faced and those avoided. For that reason, some therapists ask clients to combine ratings of anxiety and avoidance in a single figure or to at least indicate those items on the hierarchy that are typically avoided (Clark & Beck, 2010, p. 268; Leahy & Holland, 2000). Moreover, as briefly noted in an earlier chapter, the ranked items on a hierarchy can be identified and structured in a number of ways:

1. By proximity in spatial distance or location, for example, seeing a feared animal at different distances, or being at different locations, such as leaving home, arriving at the airport, etc., in the process of boarding a flight.
2. By proximity in time, which is often related to spatial distance, for example, the day before an exam, the morning of the exam, waiting to enter the hall, about to commence writing, etc.
3. By the scale or severity of the threat, for example, speaking to friends, speaking to strangers, speaking to a formal audience, etc.

4. By the presence or absence of moderating factors, for example, for an agoraphobic to walk through the street with a companion versus alone, with or without therapist assistance, during the day or at night, etc. (Potentially including safety-behaviours or coping strategies that would be dropped further up the hierarchy.)
5. By types of exposure involved, for example, talking aloud about a feared situation, visualising it in the imagination, observing someone else in the situation, or entering the situation (*in vivo*) oneself.

There are a number of other considerations that may be relevant to the construction of hierarchies. Evolutionary perspectives on anxiety as a primitive survival response suggest that there may be some relationship between the proximity of danger and different phases of the response sequence: freeze, flee, fight, and faint (Rosqvist, 2005, p. 31). Animals tend to freeze when they are initially spotted by a predator, at a distance, in order to reduce the probability of being detected. By comparison, it's particularly noticeable that in social phobia, automatic behavioural inhibition, or "freezing" and "clamming up", tends to occur when people feel they have become the "centre of attention." When threat seems more imminent, animals abandon the "freeze" response and take "flight" to escape the situation, if possible, and this response predominates in most anxious situations among clients. When an animal cannot flee, it will initially retaliate to defend itself, exhibiting defensive aggression, or putting up a "fight". Some defensive coping behaviours during anxiety may be related to this mode of response, for example, "snapping" at people, etc. When the animal is completely overwhelmed, "fainting" may be the last option. This response is rare in anxiety disorders except in blood-injection-injury type phobia, which may be because the sight of blood and injury signal to an anxious animal that it is wounded and fighting a losing battle. In these circumstances, the body may automatically trigger the emotional fainting response because this sometimes stops animal attacks and prevents further injury, for example, if an animal is attacking because surprised or defending its territory, rather than for food, it may have no motive to continue attacking once its victim "plays dead."

There's some evidence to suggest that the more "predictable" a feared situation is and the more the client feels "in control" of the process, the more likely they are to benefit from exposure (Antony & Swinson, 2000, pp. 198–200). However, as real-life situations are often unpredictable and outside of the client's control, later exposure therapy sessions may be designed to incorporate slightly more use of spontaneous factors. For example, where the therapist uses role-play with a socially-anxious client as a form of exposure he may initially agree what will be said (low hierarchy) but work toward saying anxiety-provoking things the client is less prepared for, role-playing more spontaneous content, "without a script". However, the fact that exposure will involve unpredictable elements or factors outside the client's control should normally be discussed and agreed collaboratively in advance. For instance, "This time I'm going to make things a bit more challenging by playing the role of an angry customer again but without telling you in advance what I'm going to be complaining about, so it's a little more unpredictable, is that okay?" However, recent research on anxiety has also suggested that some clients are particularly intolerant of uncertainty, risk, and ambiguity, and that behavioural experiments should be specifically engineered to expose them to uncertainty systematically as part of treatment (Robichaud & Dugas, 2006).

Imaginal exposure is generally less anxiety-provoking and so it is often used as preparation for real exposure, that is, as a lower hierarchy item. Likewise, observing another person doing something is often a preliminary to the client performing the same task, and so "modelling" can often be used as a lower hierarchy item. Even the use of relaxation or safety-seeking behaviours can sometimes be treated as lower hierarchy exposure tasks, as crutches to be dropped later, if that helps the client to begin facing situations otherwise completely avoided. However, these lower items must be presented as preparation, or "stepping stones", and not allowed to become ways for clients to procrastinate and postpone facing their more important fears.

Intensity of exposure

Exposure can be brief or prolonged, lasting anything from five seconds to several hours, and brief exposures may be repeated many times in a single session. However, there is reason to believe that exposure should be continued until *after* anxiety abates, which would make duration a function of the intensity of the anxiety experienced, that is, the more anxious the client the longer exposure may take. Consequently, it is also common to distinguish between forms of exposure therapy based upon the intensity of the anxiety which the client is allowed to experience.

1. *Flooding*, in which clients are exposed to very high levels of anxiety for prolonged periods, until it abates.
2. *Graduated* (moderate) exposure, in which clients are exposed to moderate levels of anxiety, often using cognitive or behavioural strategies to actively reduce their anxiety.
3. *Desensitisation*, in which clients are repeatedly exposed to very low levels of anxiety until they are extinguished, before progressing in small steps to more challenging items along a graduated hierarchy.

Most therapists employ moderate graduated exposure, largely because many clients are averse to the notion of flooding, and because systematic desensitisation, in its original form, may be too slow-moving for them. Moreover, when clients are asked to engage in situational exposure between sessions it is often without the presence of a therapist and therefore flooding is not a realistic option, whereas systematic desensitisation may, again, be too gradual to be practical. A simple alternative is to ask the client to face the most anxiety-provoking situation which both they and the therapist mutually agree they are able to safely cope with, without feeling overwhelmed. Although clients appear to benefit from facing their greatest fears early in treatment, the percentage who drop out appears to be greater, and so exposure that is graduated may ultimately be more effective because clients are more likely to comply with what's being asked of them (Clark & Beck, 2010, p. 242). Ultimately, clients appear to benefit more from exposure, at some stage, which goes beyond the level of difficulty they are likely to face in real life. For example, a client with blood-injection-injury phobia who struggles to endure blood tests and injections might be exposed to these in imagination, role-play, and subsequently in reality, but they may also benefit from exposure to more extreme situations such as observing thoracic surgery taking place, etc., which goes beyond what they are likely to encounter in everyday life. Exposure to highly anxiety-provoking items will tend to modify appraisals of threat more profoundly, to be more convincing to clients, and to help protect against relapse in the future (Antony & Swinson, 2000, p. 209).

Moreover, although "exposure" is the explicit focus of certain important therapy techniques, it seems clear that a wide variety of different interventions necessarily entail some degree of direct or indirect exposure to anxiety-provoking experiences, often implicitly or incidental to other aims. For example, mental rehearsal of coping skills tends to entail picturing situations which currently arouse anxiety. Assertiveness training is another clear example of an approach that invariably requires some degree of exposure to the feared social situations, through imagination or role-play and then in reality. Even assessment has been seen as involving some degree of exposure, which is often required to rate anxiety before and after treatment. For example, even research participants with social anxiety who receive placebo therapy may be assessed by asking them to give a short presentation, before and after the pseudo-treatment. However, doing so often means that they will experience at least two opportunities to expose themselves to public speaking in a safe environment, and this "measurement effect" may account for improvements observed in the absence of active treatment.

There is considerable evidence that *pure* exposure, by itself, is very effective in anxiety treatment. Debate continues over the role of adjunctive interventions combined with exposure, as in stress inoculation training. However, psychotherapy research is complex enough, but once the effect of exposure itself is controlled for it becomes increasingly difficult to measure the remaining effects of adjunctive strategies and interventions. The difference, for example, between pure exposure and exposure combined with coping statements is likely to be both small and variable. Benefits may reside in the maintenance of improvement over months or years but, again, this becomes harder to measure because of the requirement for long-term follow-up with a sufficient numbers of participants. Finally, to further complicate matters, it is unlikely that all other relevant variables can be adequately controlled during attempts at pure exposure. For example, even if the therapist doesn't tell the client to do so they may engage in their own reappraisal of threat, coping statements, relaxation, distancing, coping imagery, etc., using what have been called "spontaneous additions" to the treatment protocol. The repeated emotional review technique introduced by Raimy and adopted in Beck's original cognitive therapy for anxiety as an initial symptom-reduction strategy, has the advantage of allowing therapist and client to observe and evaluate a range of spontaneous improvements that can happen during repeated exposure to mental imagery. Moreover, the mere presence of the therapist, and his personal qualities, may influence the client's behaviour and level of relaxation during exposure, as may the context in which exposure takes place, such as viewing a video clip in the perceived "safety" of an environment like the consulting room. However, as always, the gold standard for exposure is real-world (*in vivo*) confrontation of the main feared situations, without the use of unnecessary avoidant or safety-seeking strategies.

One of the most successful studies using *hypnotic* exposure was carried out by Marks on a group of psychiatric outpatients who experienced significant reductions in phobic anxiety when hypnotherapy was combined with relaxation and coping suggestions (Marks, Gelder & Edwards, 1968). Again, clients seem to find the use of relaxation, coping skills and coping statements, etc., credible and appealing. There are indications from a wide variety of studies that each of these components can potentially contribute to the treatment of anxiety, although it is far from clear how they interact or what their relative merits are in different cases. As noted, recent mindfulness and acceptance-based CBT approaches have placed greater emphasis on distancing from thoughts, actively accepting feelings, etc., during exposure-based techniques (Hayes, Follette & Linehan, 2004; Roemer & Orsillo, 2009). To some extent, the clinician will still have to depend upon his judgement and feedback from clients when choosing exactly how to tailor different anxiety management strategies to individual cases.

Frequency, duration and latency of exposure

The frequency and duration of exposure will vary to some extent depending upon the nature of the client's diagnosis, the specific nature of the things exposed to, and the style of exposure being employed, etc. However, more frequent and prolonged forms of exposure tend to generally be more effective. When exposure is sporadic or infrequent, as is often the case with spontaneous naturally-occurring exposure, it can effectively mean that clients are "starting again from square one" when re-entering the feared situation. Typically, clients should be expected to expose themselves to their fears *in vivo* every day or at least five days per week. When exposure is too brief or infrequent there is a risk that clients will respond negatively, especially if they are exposed to fears and stop prematurely, that is, "escape" from the anxiety before it has significantly abated, as this is likely to contribute to maintaining the problem. It's generally accepted that the evidence supports "massed" over "spaced" frequency of exposure, meaning that lots of exposure in a short period of time tends to be slightly preferable to spacing it out over a longer period (Antony & Swinson, 2000, p. 201). For this reason, exposure sessions are often "prolonged" compared to other forms of CBT, lasting one to three hours, depending on the type of exposure and severity of the problem. Recently, some researchers have found initial evidence that commencing with massed exposure and gradually spacing it out may be more effective. This is termed an "expanding spaced exposure schedule" and there are some signs that it may reduce anxiety as rapidly as traditional massed exposure but better prevent the *return* of anxiety at follow-up (Antony & Swinson, 2000, pp. 201–202). However, as we shall see, some exposure-based interventions are briefer, although perhaps due to the inclusion of other treatment factors such as relaxation coping-skills, belief modification, or mindfulness strategies, etc.

Another way to increase the frequency of exposure is through self-directed homework, which should be incorporated into most treatment plans. Antony and Swinson recommend that homework should ideally consist of "long" exposure sessions carried out three to six times per week, combined with briefer exposure sessions conducted periodically throughout the day, as frequently as possible (Antony & Swinson, 2000, p. 201). Of course, one convenient way of doing this is to combine several longer *in vivo* exposure sessions per week with more frequent imaginal exposure, perhaps using a fifteen to twenty-minute self-hypnosis recording, once or twice per day. With imaginal exposure, the frequency can potentially be more than once per day because the duration is typically shorter and imaginal exposure is usually more convenient and easier to arrange, etc. Sometimes different forms of exposure may be combined.

The duration of *in vivo* exposure for more severe anxiety disorders like agoraphobia is typically up to ninety minutes, or more, in traditional behaviour therapy, during which anxiety may be rated every fifteen minutes or so. In many cases, thirty to sixty minutes is sufficient and for relatively simple problems such as moderate specific phobias, anxiety may sometimes reduce adequately in less than twenty minutes. Marks, one of the main proponents of the behavioural approach, summed up his experience regarding the duration of exposure as follows:

> In a lucky minority of sufferers just a few minutes of exposure to the things that terrify them reduce the fear, usually in those who have had their problem only for a few weeks or months and are really determined to get the better of it. More commonly, the fear starts to diminish within half an hour after the start of the exposure, even in people with very long-standing phobias. Rarely, several hours may be needed for the fear to start abating. (Marks I. M., 2005, p. 139)

The basic rule of thumb adopted in most forms of CBT is that exposure should continue until anxiety has reduced by at least half, for example, from seventy per cent to thirty-five per cent or less (Clark & Beck, 2010, p. 242). Hence, less severe anxiety will often require shorter periods of exposure. When a client "escapes" from exposure before anxiety has actually habituated (which they will have a strong urge to do), this risks increasing their anxiety on future occasions, although they may still benefit if they can resume exposure again within a minute or so (Antony & Swinson, 2000, p. 200). However, especially where relaxation or cognitive methods are used, anxiety also appears to reduce with repeated (massed) brief imaginal exposure, of perhaps twenty to thirty seconds each, as in systematic desensitisation (Wolpe, 1990), stress inoculation training (Meichenbaum, 2007), applied relaxation (Bernstein, Borkovec & Hazlett-Stevens, 2000), eye-movement desensitisation and reprocessing therapy (EMDR) (Shapiro, 1997), or Raimy's method of repeated cognitive review (Beck, Emery & Greenberg, 2005; Raimy, 1975). Where brief imaginal exposure is used though, it is normally repeated at least three to four times, for several images over a period of about fifteen to thirty minutes, and sometimes, as in EMDR, for up to sixty minutes or more in total.

Hence, where exposure has to be brief, it can usually be prolonged by employing repeated ("massed") presentations of the feared stimulus, returning to the scene, in a short space of time, which is often the case in certain forms of imaginal or interoceptive exposure. For example, exposure to bodily sensations associated with panic attacks might occur by breathing through a straw for a couple of minutes, which would normally have to be repeated about five times in a row, that is, taking about 15–20 minutes, with pauses, and be repeated about three times per day. In the original cognitive therapy manual for anxiety, Beck et al. recommend that "repeated review", a form of imaginal exposure involving repeated visualisation of a feared situation, should be carried out between sessions for periods lasting about fifteen to thirty minutes, within which time anxiety was typically reported to reduce sufficiently (Beck, Emery & Greenberg, 2005, pp. 252–253). Likewise, systematic desensitisation, traditionally employs repeated "scene presentation" in fantasy (imaginal exposure) for periods of merely fifteen to twenty seconds, interspersed with twenty to thirty second relaxation pauses, about thirty times, for a total period of about fifteen to thirty minutes per session (Wolpe, 1990, pp. 173–175). However, whereas modern graduated exposure typically starts with items rated about seventy per cent on a SUD scale (Antony & Swinson, 2000, p. 201) traditional desensitisation never presented items rated more than twenty-five per cent. Low-anxiety scenes were presented while the client was in a relatively deep state of muscular and autonomic relaxation because desensitisation was based on a "reciprocal inhibition" model rather than "habituation". In this approach, three to four brief presentations in a relaxed state are typically sufficient to reduce the reported SUD level to around zero, after which the next scene on the hierarchy is presented (Wolpe, 1990, p. 175).

As noted above, graduated exposure to more anxiety-provoking scenes without preliminary relaxation is now more common because it has been found to be effective in a shorter period of time, although some clients may prefer the slower relaxation-based approach. Whereas systematic desensitisation, or reciprocal inhibition, assumes that long-term anxiety reduction is brought about mainly by the repeated pairing of mild anxiety with profound relaxation, graded exposure therapy based on a habituation model assumes that substantial reduction in anxiety from a higher initial level, by prolonging exposure, is the mechanism by which more permanent reduction is achieved. Over time, behaviour therapists using desensitisation began presenting scenes at higher levels of initial anxiety, abbreviating the preliminary relaxation training and placing more responsibility on the client for "relaxing away" their anxiety, which led to the development of more "coping skills" oriented approaches such as stress inoculation training and applied relaxation, among others (Meichenbaum, 1985; Öst, 1987). Some approaches to graduated exposure, including Marks', incorporate the use of relaxation as a coping skill for some clients, and when they do so this very closely resembles the "coping skills" approach to desensitisation, so there is actually considerable overlap between certain forms of exposure therapy and coping skills approaches like stress inoculation training (Marks I. M., 2005; Meichenbaum, 2007).

Hence, partly because the anxiety evoked is often less severe than in most *in vivo* exercises, periods of graded imaginal exposure tend also to be briefer, often lasting less than thirty minutes, although some authors recommend thirty to sixty minutes (Antony & Swinson, 2000, p. 193). However, ratings of anxiety, using a SUD scale, can be obtained at regular intervals throughout to monitor progress. It follows from this that imaginal exposure will often take up most of the time in sessions where it is being used. Likewise, *in vivo* exposure sessions may need to be longer than average, depending on the severity and complexity of the problem, often taking from one to three hours with problems like severe agoraphobia.

The term "latency" is used to describe the time delay between the signal or opportunity to begin exposure and the actual approach or presentation of the feared stimulus. In other words, it refers to hesitation or procrastination, avoidance of beginning the procedure, which is believed by behaviour therapists to exacerbate subsequent anxiety (Rosqvist, 2005, p. 48). Clients should not be "rushed" into beginning an exposure task but they should also be prevented from too much hesitation or procrastination once they've decided to begin a task. They should be encouraged to "start as they mean to go on", "get down to business", and initiate the actual exposure in as timely and unhesitant a manner as possible. Likewise, in anxiety disorders characterised by extensive anticipatory worry, such as GAD and social phobia, anxiety does not typically reduce despite prolonged thinking about feared events in the lead up to them. In fact it tends to persist and leads individuals to enter situations with an already heightened level of anxiety and negatively-biased appraisal of threat and coping.

Other factors in exposure

The wider the variety of stimuli the client is exposed to within a particular theme the more likely improvement is to generalise and the lower the risk of relapse or return of anxiety (Antony & Swinson, 2000, p. 202). For example, a client who has a phobia for dogs would probably achieve more robust reductions in anxiety if exposed to a variety of different dogs, behaving in different ways, etc. Likewise, relapse is less likely when exposure is conducted in a range of different contexts or environments, especially when exposure includes the context in which the client is most likely to actually encounter the feared event in everyday life, that is, in a naturally-occurring setting (Antony & Swinson, 2000, pp. 202–203). For example, a client with fear of public speaking may benefit from role-playing presentations, etc., but they are likely to obtain the most enduring benefit by exposing themselves to speaking in meetings at work, if that is where their anxiety typically arises. In general, exposure should aim to target as closely as possible the real situations and challenges the client is likely to face in their daily life, outside of the consulting room, and after treatment has ended.

Exposure and response prevention

"Response prevention" was originally introduced as an adjunct to exposure therapy for obsessive-compulsive disorder (OCD). The terminology is normally associated with the treatment of OCD where it has long been established as the treatment of choice.

> However, when viewed more broadly as the prevention of maladaptive coping responses that contribute to the persistence of anxiety, response prevention can be an important treatment component for any of the anxiety disorders. […] In essence any therapeutic intervention that seeks to suppress the expression of safety-seeking responses in the context of anxiety arousal is a form of response prevention. (Clark & Beck, 2010, p. 251)

Hence, Beck recommends that "exposure and response prevention" should actually be seen as a more *generic* approach extended to all forms of anxiety, particularly to the prevention of avoidance and "safety-seeking" behaviours that are central to the maintenance cycles described in most modern conceptualisations of anxiety. Moreover, Beck extends the concept of response prevention beyond overt behavioural responses to encompass the prevention of cognitive coping strategies such as thought-suppression as well. "Response prevention, then, is a robust intervention strategy designed to eliminate problematic behavioural, that is, emotional and cognitive responses that lead to premature termination of exposure to a fear stimulus" (Clark & Beck, 2010, p. 251). Hence, all exposure-based therapy must normally entail response prevention, in the broad sense, starting with the prevention of escape behaviour and extending to more subtle forms of avoidance, including thought-suppression and emotional-suppression (experiential avoidance) and maladaptive safety-seeking behaviour.

As Beck puts it, "The goal of any exposure intervention is to provoke anxiety or distress and allow it to decrease spontaneously without recourse to avoidance, neutralization, or other forms of safety seeking" (Clark & Beck, 2010, p. 247). A common problem during exposure therapy is that the client, either deliberately or automatically, "cheats" and reduces their anxiety through cognitive or behavioural avoidance of the threat or attempts to secure an artificial sense of safety. Safety-seeking strategies also prevent normal exposure from happening and thereby interfere with the natural human capacity for habituation and emotional processing. Therapy therefore seeks to help clients prevent their use.

> Most therapists seem to agree that whatever form the exposure takes, for improvement to occur the patient should not block, dissociate, or discount, what is happening during exposure treatment, but should actively engage with and process the working stimuli. (Marks I. M., 1981, p. 56)

Anything that reduces anxiety, albeit temporarily, is prone to be powerfully "negatively reinforced" by the relief it brings, creating an increasing urge to repeat the strategy again in the future, which may become compulsive and difficult to resist. Beck tends to refer collectively to these strategies as "defence" behaviours and other authors have acknowledged some overlap with psychodynamic accounts of "defence mechanisms" (Dobson & Dobson, 2009, p. 109). Put simply, in response prevention, "The overall strategy is to have the client do the opposite of what he is inclined to do" (Beck, Emery & Greenberg, 2005, p. 259). This might be described as acting "as if" non-anxious, exhibiting approach behaviour and dropping avoidant and safety-seeking behaviours. Doing so entails accepting feelings of anxiety and usually also distancing from negative automatic thoughts, as recommended in the cognitive therapy "AWARE" strategy discussed earlier. The therapist should therefore help the client to carefully evaluate the full range of behaviours that she engages in, externally or internally, in response to anxiety or threatening situations, in order to identify those potentially responsible for maintaining symptoms.

Behavioural avoidance, escape and safety-seeking

Behavioural *avoidance* might take the obvious form of the client simply procrastinating, delaying things, making excuses, "calling in sick", or otherwise avoiding engaging in exposure to begin with. *Escape* occurs when exposure is terminated prematurely by fleeing or giving up before anxiety has abated. Subtle forms of behavioural avoidance or escape are more problematic and may be quite difficult to detect, for example, averting the gaze, blocking the ears, walking more quickly past a threatening situation, etc. According to the cognitive model of anxiety, escape is undesirable for four main reasons (Clark & Beck, 2010, p. 194).

1. It prevents the client from discovering that nothing dangerous happens, that is, disconfirming their appraisals of threat and establishing evidence of safety.
2. The sense of relief experienced constitutes "negative reinforcement" and, at a primitive level, rewards avoidance and strengthens subsequent urges to avoid or escape similar situations, as well as other maladaptive behaviours.
3. Escapkje constitutes a failure to cope with the situation and evidence of helplessness and vulnerability, further strengthening these schemas and reducing self-esteem and self-confidence (or "self-efficacy").

4. The relief experienced may increase future sensitivity to signs of danger and thereby maintain or even increase anxiety, sometimes referred to as an "incubation effect" of escape from high levels of anxiety (Eysenck & Martin, 1987, pp. 18–19).

Some strategies, termed "safety-seeking" behaviours, are used by clients, either automatically or deliberately, to achieve a false sense of safety, that is, as precautions against danger or to protect against threat during exposure. These are unnecessary if the perceived threat is being exaggerated anyway and their use creates a problem in that the non-occurrence of the feared outcome is mistakenly attributed to the safety strategy employed. For example, some clients become very dependent upon holistic remedies, which they believe help them to cope with anxiety. They feel temporarily safer when using these methods but doing so may prevent them from benefitting fully from exposure therapy, by preventing their fears from being properly disconfirmed by the experience. Safety behaviours that function as unnecessary "crutches" should be identified systematically throughout therapy and are normally "banned", or at least substantially reduced, especially during exposure. Key safety-seeking behaviours were first identified in relation to certain disorders such as OCD, where their function may sometimes be more obvious. For example, constant reassurance-seeking is a common form of maladaptive safety-seeking:

> In treatment, therefore, relatives have to learn not to be reassuring, so that the questions are not kept going by repeated temporary reductions of anxiety through reassurance. (Marks I. M., 1981, p. 85)

Early cognitive therapy for anxiety emphasised behavioural escape and repeated checking and reassurance-seeking as the two most significant "protective" mechanisms (Beck, Emery & Greenberg, 2005, pp. 258–259). However, therapists must be on the lookout for anything that allows the client to discount the outcome of exposure-based behavioural experiments by saying: "Yes, nothing catastrophic happened, but *only* because I did xyz to keep myself safe."

Some forms of subtle covert avoidance are more difficult to detect and may involve more or less anything that takes the client's attention away from the threat cues in the situation being exposed to, thereby preventing genuine exposure from taking place and distorting the information processed on the basis of the experience (Beck, Emery & Greenberg, 2005, p. 274). For example, focusing one's attention on non-threatening parts of a situation in order to avoid the feared parts, thinking of something else, or distorting imagery during imaginal exposure, may become an obstacle to exposure therapy. Clients are therefore asked to keep their attention focused on the most feared aspects of the situation. The tendency for clients to become distracted has long been countered in behaviour therapy by, where appropriate, asking them to describe aloud the feared aspects of the situation or imagery they are being exposed to, which allows the therapist to monitor the extent to which they are attending to relevant threat cues, etc. (Clark & Beck, 2010, p. 243). The rationale for focusing on threat cues should be understood by the client and she may be intermittently reminded by the therapist to keep paying attention to them or, more indirectly, helped to focus by means of frequent questions about her experiences. However, in Beck's cognitive therapy approach to exposure, it is also important that the client is able to *broaden* the scope of their attention to notice genuine evidence of safety in the environment as selective attentional bias often inhibits normal processing of safety signals (Clark & Beck, 2010). Similarly, clients should be discouraged from attempts to suppress or control distressing thoughts and feelings ("experiential avoidance"), but rather to accept them and allow them to abate naturally rather than fighting with them or fleeing from them.

Cognitive and emotional avoidance (experiential avoidance)

In addition to avoiding *external* threats, many clients learn to avoid unpleasant *internal* experiences, particularly feelings of anxiety and fearful thoughts, etc. Animals are presumably unable to wrestle with their thoughts and feelings in this way and simply avoid situations and activities that have aversive consequences, such as those provoking anxiety. However, humans are able to observe their thoughts and feelings with greater self-consciousness, and this allows them to transpose the urge to avoid or eliminate from external events on to internal experiences associated with them. As noted earlier, this has been referred to as "experiential avoidance" (Hayes, Follette & Linehan, 2004). Experiential avoidance can take many forms and may entail avoidance, escape, or attempts to control bodily sensations, emotions, thoughts, urges, etc. Attempts at control and avoidance are even more problematic in the internal world than they are in relation to external events, because internal experiences are often inescapable and, ironically, may even become more salient, perseverative and recurrent through attempts to eliminate them.

In Beck's generic model of anxiety, discussed earlier, attempts at thought-control and the suppression of feelings constitute the final stage of the model, following maladaptive attempts at safety-seeking and escape. In particular, when an individual fails to solve an external problem or to escape from perceived threat they may assume their only remaining option is to endure the situation, "through gritted teeth" as it were, while suppressing their internal cognitive and emotional responses. However, attempts to control thoughts and feelings can backfire, especially in the longer-term, and may be the most important maintaining factor in more serious disorders. Clients will often report using certain strategies commonly recommended in different therapy and self-help approaches such as relaxation, positive thinking, distraction, and disputing thoughts. However, they do so in a way that's maladaptive, ineffective and driven by a desire to *escape* threatening internal experiences.

Raising awareness of experiential avoidance and its unhelpful consequences is essential in most cases of anxiety. The client must usually be helped to drop these strategies, although at first they may be very reluctant to do so. Hence, at the beginning of Beck's original approach to anxiety, symptom-focused strategies included *distancing* from fearful thoughts and *acceptance* of anxious feelings. These strategies allow clients to experience thoughts and feelings rather than struggling against them, which often brings an ironic reduction in distress and improvement in control over processes such as worry. Raimy's "repeated review" technique, to be discussed in more detail later, was also recommended by Beck et al. for use alongside distancing and acceptance, and can provide a vehicle for training in exposure to feared situations, through mental imagery, while developing the ability to distance from thoughts and actively accept anxious feelings, letting go of any unhelpful struggle against them. Another useful strategy that helps socialise clients to this aspect of therapy involves imagining an "effort to control" dial, marked zero to ten and initially set at five, which the client can turn up and down while observing the effect on their experience. For example, the therapist might ask: "What happens if you turn up the dial to ten and imagine a very strong desire to control your thoughts and avoid thinking about your problems?" Most clients will readily observe that a strong desire to control anxious thoughts and feelings tends to backfire by creating more tension and, ironically, drawing more attention to the experiences they're trying to avoid. It's important to note that acceptance of internal experiences often requires distancing from thoughts, so that the client is accepting the fact the thought is occurring rather than the content or meaning of the thought itself (Hayes, Strosahl & Wilson, 2012). Accepting the internal experience as "I am *having thoughts* about failure" while maintaining psychological distance is fundamentally very different from accepting the thought-content "I *am* going to fail!"

Modifying coping strategies

Beck asks clients to complete a detailed checklist of cognitive or behavioural coping strategies and to evaluate how effective they are as means of reducing anxiety in the short-term, and to what extent they may contribute to perpetuating it over the longer-term. This is similar to asking the client to carry out a "cost-benefit" analysis of the short and long-term consequences of the behaviour, which is the approach adopted by some other therapists. However, in many cases it suffices to ask the client "How's that working out for you?" Clients may observe that their coping strategies often help them "feel better", bringing temporary relief from anxiety, whereas the therapist might point out if the course of their problem hasn't shown an improvement over time. A useful distinction between "*feeling* better" and "*getting* better" can be made, to simplify the distinction between short and long-term consequences. Many things that people do when distressed help them to "feel better" temporarily but they seldom help them to "get better" in the long-term and may even make things worse. The most basic form of relief comes from behavioural avoidance or escape from anxious situations, which will make most people "feel better" briefly but is, of course, unlikely to help them "get better" in the long-run.

Essentially, the client should be helped to realise that the short-term benefit of temporarily reducing anxiety, through avoidance, etc., is outweighed by the long-term costs, the harm that is done in terms of fuelling the underlying problem and interfering with the client's ability to function and quality of life. The two main long-term problems are that reliance on avoidant strategies and safety-seeking means clients will prevent natural habituation and emotional processing from occurring and also prevent themselves from discovering that the probability and the severity of the feared outcome are much lower than they assume (Clark & Beck, 2010, p. 253). Of course, when these "crutches" are abandoned, anxiety will tend to initially be much higher and that is something the client must be prepared to anticipate and cope with. For some clients, safety-behaviours may be difficult to abandon and a compromise is to allow them to be retained at first and gradually eliminated as confidence increases (Antony & Swinson, 2000, p. 205).

Response "blocking" and habit-reversal

Some maladaptive coping responses are under voluntary control and can easily be abandoned by clients, as soon as they understand the rationale for doing so. Others are more automatic or compulsive and there may be an overwhelming urge to continue using them, even in the presence of the therapist. Clients can simply be asked to rate how much control they believe they have over these responses, from 0–100 per cent. Although initial ratings may not be accurate, as clients can either over-estimate or under-estimate the difficulty of abandoning their old habits, re-evaluating their level of control after attempts at response prevention will lead to a more realistic appraisal. In addition to enhancing motivation to block the response and training the client to be more aware of the earliest signs of the behaviour occurring, two simple cognitive and behavioural strategies are often employed (Clark & Beck, 2010, p. 254).

1. Cognitive coping statements or self-instructions can be employed by the client that affirm their sense of self-efficacy ("I can do this!") and the importance or personal value of blocking maladaptive coping ("I'm doing this because it's important to me to remain in these situations and be a good role-model to my kids!").
2. Competing behavioural responses can be used that are directly incompatible with the behaviour being blocked, for example, clenching the fists for one to three minutes until the urge to bite one's fingernails to cope with anxiety has abated.

These safety-behaviour "blocking" strategies closely resemble techniques such as those used as a central component of Habit-Reversal Therapy in traditional behaviour therapy (Azrin & Nunn, 1977). These methods can readily be coupled with autosuggestion and presented as a form of *self-hypnotic* coping skill, designed to prolong exposure by blocking automatic safety-seeking and escape behaviours rather than as a means of reducing anxiety directly.

However, Beck also recommends using "paradoxical intention" as the most preferred intervention, where the client is instructed to do the *opposite* of their safety-seeking behaviour and deliberately acts in a way that powerfully disconfirms the assumption upon which safety-seeking is predicated (Clark & Beck, 2010, p. 254). This might involve acting "as if" *non*-anxious, while accepting feelings of anxiety and distancing from fearful thoughts, as described in the "AWARE" strategy above. As Beck notes, the most common maladaptive behavioural responses are simple avoidance and escape from the feared situation, and the exposure therapy prescription to engage in repeated, prolonged exposure, or approach to the perceived threat, can be seen as a form of paradoxical therapy insofar as it requires the client to do the *opposite* of what they usually assume will make them feel safe, in order to prove to themselves that nothing catastrophic actually happens.

Thought-control, anxiety-management and exposure

Most hypnotherapy places considerable emphasis upon anxiety-management strategies such as "relaxation", "positive thinking", or "positive imagery", etc. However, Beck states simply: "In most instances it would be better to refrain from deliberate anxiety management" (Clark & Beck, 2010, p. 245). These strategies may be counter-productive in some cases, especially with more severe forms of anxiety. Most obviously, where anxiety management techniques prevent genuine exposure to threat cues from happening, for example, by asking clients to forcefully or unrealistically visualise the situation as being less threatening, this runs contrary to the principles and rationale of most exposure therapy and is likely to be counter-productive.

For instance, clients have sometimes heard self-help advice recommending that they try imagining the audience naked while giving a presentation if they suffer from "nerves", etc. This can be seen as a form of distraction from the real situation. It is also probably driven by a false assumption that anxiety is intolerable and will continue to escalate without reducing naturally given enough time, etc. Additional costs may include problems such as overloading cognitive resources and thereby impairing performance, particularly in social situations, etc. Common maladaptive coping strategies of this kind are often learned from therapists or self-help books and this may also make clients reluctant to abandon them.

Nevertheless, as in stress inoculation training, there is some role for anxiety management techniques with less severe problems, in general stress management, and sometimes in facilitating the early stages of exposure therapy. However, some caution is needed insofar as the use of these techniques may hinder long-term improvement in certain cases by interfering with the natural process of exposure and habituation. For example, research on the effect of "distraction" and "thought suppression" techniques during exposure has yielded mixed results with some studies showing that these strategies can interfere with the benefits of exposure. Hence, it's typically recommended that clients do not try to distract themselves or suppress their anxiety during exposure but rather give all their attention to the reality of the present moment, and the object of their fear, while accepting their feelings and acknowledging their thoughts in a detached (distanced) way, because struggling against anxiety often has the paradoxical effect of worsening it, just as trying to fall asleep often keeps insomniacs awake longer (Antony & Swinson, 2000, p. 204).

Indeed, even some proponents of hypnotherapy are hesitant to prescribe coping strategies such as self-hypnosis for certain clients to use during exposure. Bryant reports a case where a client was trained in self-hypnosis prior to *in vivo* exposure for fear of flying.

> We did not ask her to complete her self-hypnosis during the flights because we did not want her to learn that she felt safe because of the self-hypnosis (or reliance on the hypnotist's voice). It is possible that self-hypnosis can become a safety behavior that people rely on to reduce their distress. This reliance on some behavior (such as self-hypnosis) can impede the learning that flying itself is not immediately dangerous. (Bryant R. A., 2008, p. 545)

However, in other cases, anxiety-management coping strategies can be seen as initial crutches to help clients tolerate graduated exposure and progressively faded from use as they ascend the hierarchy of feared situations. Even if the client "feels safe" because of self-hypnosis or coping skills she will still potentially, in some respects, have the opportunity to learn from exposure that feared outcomes do not happen. Ideally, though, most therapy for anxiety should culminate in the client facing the feared situation without the need for safety-behaviours or coping strategies to avert perceived threats or control anxious thoughts and feelings.

Cognitive therapy and exposure

As noted above, although exposure therapy originally developed as a form of *behaviour* therapy, it constitutes a central component of almost all forms of cognitive therapy for anxiety. For example, Beck describes exposure as "one of the most powerful therapeutic tools available to the therapist for the reduction of fear and anxiety" (Clark & Beck, 2010, p. 238).

> Behavioural interventions play a critical role in cognitive therapy of anxiety disorders. In fact it is difficult to imagine an effective cognitive treatment for anxiety that does not include a significant behavioural component. (Clark & Beck, 2010, p. 266)

Hence, Beck refers to the "cognitive reconceptualisation of behavioural treatment" (Clark & Beck, 2010, p. 236). The role of exposure, in particular, is reinterpreted from the standpoint of the cognitive, or "information-processing", model of anxiety as essentially a way of "disconfirming fearful predictions" (Antony & Swinson, 2000, p. 195). From this point of view, direct experience of the feared situation provides an opportunity for "reality testing" and the correction of faulty appraisals of the probability or severity of threat, and possibly also reappraisal of one's coping ability. It is particularly important that unhelpful safety-seeking behaviours are prevented, as by creating a sense of safety these prevent the client from potentially disconfirming unfounded appraisals of danger. A distinction must therefore be made between coping responses that are potentially helpful and those that serve to maintain the problem.

Because cognitive therapy proceeds from a cognitive *conceptualisation* of anxiety, developed collaboratively with the client, it will also tend to involve presentation of an explicit treatment rationale based, to some extent, upon the cognitive model. This means socialising the client to the view that faulty threat and vulnerability schemas are central to the problem and that the goal of exposure is to process information in a way that modifies these underlying cognitive structures (Clark & Beck, 2010, p. 239). In other words, the client should be helped to understand that the purpose of exposure is to prove to herself, in the middle of an anxiety episode, that nothing catastrophic will happen and that she can cope with any problems that do arise, in order to help her adopt a more realistic and adaptive perspective on the actual situation and switch off the fight-or-flight response, etc.

Many key principles of exposure therapy are "carried over" from behavioural approaches into cognitive therapy for anxiety. However, Beck also argues that two new therapeutic implications follow from the cognitive model of exposure (Clark & Beck, 2010, p. 238).

1. Exposure should activate relevant cognitive schemas and appraisals of threat and vulnerability, to at least a moderate degree, in order for optimal therapeutic change to occur.
2. Exposure should present disconfirming information, that is, therapeutic improvement will be greater to the extent that the client focuses upon and fully processes information about the experience that corrects exaggerated appraisals of threat or vulnerability, etc.

In other words, relevant schemas of threat and vulnerability should be moderately activated and systematically disconfirmed by exposure, functioning as a behavioural experiment, which empirically tests the underlying hypotheses. This differs from purely behavioural models of exposure by placing greater emphasis on the relevant schemas being involved in the encounter with the feared situation and the outcome being adequately observed and reflected upon by the client. For example, selective attention, distraction, or misinterpretation of the experience could interfere with the therapeutic process.

Exposure as behavioural experiment

Especially in relation to anxiety, particularly phobic anxiety, cognitions in general are more powerfully modified by personal experience, that is, exposure, than by verbal persuasion or Socratic questioning, etc. (Antony & Swinson, 2000, p. 195). Cognitive approaches to the treatment of anxiety therefore tend to focus on the role of exposure as a form of "behavioural experiment." Hence, exposure based on the cognitive model will normally target specific thoughts or beliefs for change, and this will be agreed with the client in advance. The procedure is essentially conceptualised as a form of "empirical hypothesis testing" experiment, composed of the following stages:

1. Identify target cognition.
2. Prescribe behavioural (exposure) experiment.
3. Self-monitor experience and outcome.
4. Evaluate results.

Beck encourages clients to identify the key cognition to be tested simply by asking what the most feared or worst outcome of the exposure task might be (Clark & Beck, 2012, p. 144). Afterwards, the results are usually reported to the therapist during his review of the client's homework and considerable emphasis is placed upon evaluating the extent to which the experiment undermines the target cognition and supports an alternative one. Beck suggests that the alternative cognition developed could be written down on a "coping card" to be used by the client during subsequent exposure to similar situations (Clark & Beck, 2010, p. 237).

It's a good idea to help the client evaluate the costs and benefits of exposure versus avoidance early in therapy, as part of the process of socialisation to the treatment rationale. When this is done carefully, clients will often identify perceived "disadvantages" that are essentially feared (catastrophic) outcomes, for example, "I might have a heart attack", "I might lose control", "I might faint", "I might make a fool of myself", etc. This is an "added bonus" from the point of view of the cognitive therapist because these fearful cognitions can then be directly tackled using standard cognitive therapy interventions. It also highlights the fact that predictions of feared outcomes often need to be identified early in exposure treatment and addressed precisely because they constitute perceived "disadvantages" or motives for avoidance and noncompliance with the treatment plan. Equally, when noncompliance occurs and clients refuse to participate in therapist-directed exposure or, more often, avoid doing self-exposure homework, the therapist should take this as a signal that negative thoughts or beliefs need to be identified and addressed, for example, "If I try to do this homework, I'll just make myself worse", etc.

When developing the hierarchy, Beck asks clients to also identify the core anxious thought or feared outcome associated with each item, where possible, and to record this in an additional column, so that each entry on the hierarchy describes the situation or event feared, the level of anxiety/avoidance, and the core anxious thought (Clark & Beck, 2010, p. 468). This information is not likely to be easily available for all items when the hierarchy is first drawn up, though, and will probably need to be added as treatment continues. In many cases, the core fear may be identical or similar across most of the items on a single-themed hierarchy. However, for more varied fears, such as those found in social phobia and generalised anxiety, this procedure may be more useful. Also, gathering this information helps to provide a bridge between construction of a hierarchy and collaborative development of relevant behavioural experiments based on exposure.

Hence, Beck describes cognitive restructuring during exposure as a technique in which exaggerated threat appraisals are disputed by the client taking note of evidence, in the current situation, that danger is not as great as first thought and also that anxiety will decline naturally over time (Clark & Beck, 2010, p. 245). The belief that anxiety is uncontrollable is arguably manifested in common automatic thoughts described by anxious clients relating to themes of helplessness, for example, "I've tried but I can't tolerate my feelings long enough to stay in the situation!" There is an overlap here between cognitive and behavioural models of anxiety insofar as clients frequently do not initially believe what the behavioural model tells us about habituation, that is, that the best way to cope with anxiety may simply be to do nothing but accept it, endure the situation, and wait for the feelings to naturally subside. Arguably one of the most adaptive coping statements would therefore affirm key beliefs about natural habituation: "I can do this, all I need to do is accept that I feel anxious and hang in there long enough for the feeling to gradually wear off ..."

Interoceptive exposure and panic attacks

"Interoception" refers to the perception of stimuli originating within the human body. The term "interoceptive exposure" (IE) is used in CBT to refer to exposure to bodily sensations, most commonly those associated with panic attacks such as hot flushes, disorientation, chest tightness, difficulty breathing, etc. Generally speaking, where panic attacks are present, it often makes sense to address them before other aspects of an anxiety disorder because an uncontrolled panic attack can typically cause relapse in relation to other treatment gains.

Most traditional exposure therapy targets the *sight* of feared external situations, and sometimes involves other senses such as hearing, touch, or even smell. However, panic attacks are considered to present a special case because they can be conceptualised as involving catastrophic interpretation of internal bodily sensations rather than external events. Exposure therefore involves evoking the feared sensations themselves.

> Although this approach is mainly associated with panic disorder, some authors have proposed that it may also be applicable to problems such as social phobia and specific phobia, which often also involve anxiety about bodily sensations. (Antony & Swinson, 2000, p. 209)

Four main aspects of interoceptive exposure can be distinguished (Antony & Swinson, 2000, p. 210).

1. Socialising the client to the treatment rationale.
2. Inducing the bodily sensations or symptoms.
3. Assigning interoceptive exposure homework exercises.
4. Combining interoceptive exposure with situational exposure.

The rationale for interoceptive exposure is essentially similar to traditional exposure therapy and can be conceptualised either in behavioural (habituation) or cognitive (hypothesis testing) terms. However, with interoceptive exposure it is particularly important to assess any contra-indications to specific exercises; for example, clients with asthma should not be asked to hyperventilate, etc. Symptom-induction techniques need to be tried out in the consulting room first to establish which ones are most appropriate for the client. Whichever exercise is chosen it should create sensations that approximate to those experienced in the real setting and evoke moderate anxiety, in a relatively safe and controllable manner (Antony & Swinson, 2000, p. 211). Three of the more common interoceptive exposure exercises are as follows:

1. Spinning around on a swivel chair for about sixty seconds to produce feelings of dizziness and derealisation, etc.
2. Hyperventilation for about sixty seconds to induce breathless feelings and light-headedness, etc.
3. Breathing through a very narrow straw for a couple of minutes to produce feelings of difficulty breathing, heart racing, etc.

However, many alternatives are available. For example, Antony and Swinson provide a list of *seventeen* exercises (Antony & Swinson, 2000, pp. 212–213).

When suitable exercises have been identified and rehearsed under the therapist's supervision these are assigned as homework to be rehearsed on a frequent basis, as with traditional exposure therapy. As these are typically short exercises, lasting a minute or so, unlike entering a feared situation which can be easily prolonged for hours, each session of self-exposure will normally have to consist of a set of about five repetitions (or "trials"), with short breaks between, in order to suitably prolong exposure (Antony & Swinson, 2000, p. 215). As this means a whole set may only take about ten to fifteen minutes, sets should be repeated frequently, for example, three times per day. For example, a client might be asked to hyperventilate for about a minute, then take a break for a minute or so, about five times in a row, and to do this three times every day, meaning the hyperventilation exercise is actually conducted fifteen times per day in total. Homework forms are provided to help monitor these sessions and identify and dispute the automatic thoughts, or catastrophic interpretations, associated with the sensations evoked. Finally, after practising at home, self-exposure should be carried out in more naturalistic settings, in the presence of feared situations or objects, integrating interoceptive and situational exposure, for example, by hyperventilating on a crowded train carriage. Interoceptive exposure of this kind is often difficult to combine with *hypnosis* and may be better conducted as normal, in conventional CBT, even where hypnotherapy forms part of the overall treatment approach.

Hypnotic exposure therapy

In some forms of anxiety, the role of cognition of the self-talk variety has been questioned. For example, small infants and animals, *without* the use of language, can clearly develop phobic anxiety responses similar to those found in adult humans. In PTSD the increased startle reflex seems to be triggered in a very rapid and reflexive manner by loud noises or reminders of the trauma, without much time for verbal appraisal of the situation, in a manner also resembling heightened startle responses found in animals and infants. As Wolpe and other behaviourists pointed out, in many simple phobias, such as snake phobia, phobic anxiety can be triggered by mental imagery or photographs, etc., where the client clearly understands that the threat is *not* real. This presents a challenge for Beck's claim that anxiety is primarily due to cognitive appraisal of threat as highly *probable* and *severe* (Beck, 1976; Clark & Beck, 2010). Moreover, where dysfunctional beliefs or self-talk are reported in phobias, they often appear to be more the *result* rather than the *cause* of behavioural and emotional reactions (Clarke & Jackson, 1983, pp. 242–243).

In their early textbook on cognitive-behavioural hypnotherapy, Clarke & Jackson therefore emphasise the distinction between phobias which stem from a genetic predisposition, and appear to be naturally-occurring fears of a heightened sensitivity, and more "cognitive anxieties", such as social phobia or fear of negative evaluation by others, which have a more significant cognitive overlay. They recommend hypnosis combined with traditional exposure therapy for specific phobias where the cognitive element is less prominent.

> For these etiologies, behaviour therapy techniques which facilitate safe exposure must form the centrepiece of therapy. While information and reassurance are not unimportant, phobias must be understood as "stupid" reactions which are not particularly amenable to rational analysis. Hypnosis is a technique that can function in many ways as an important adjunct to imaginal exposure techniques. (Clarke & Jackson, 1983, p. 184)

As they note, *even* Albert Ellis, the founder of REBT and one of the pioneers of the cognitive-behavioural tradition, wrote, "Pure cognitive restructuring works relatively poorly for any kind of phobia" (Ellis, 1979, p. 162). Although traditional hypnotherapy does not place so much emphasis upon *in vivo* exposure, many established hypnotherapy techniques can be described as forms of imaginal exposure. These have an important role as a preparation for *in vivo* exposure between sessions and in contexts where *in vivo* exposure is not appropriate.

Hypnotic imaginal exposure

As noted earlier, most behaviour therapists recommend that *in vivo* exposure is employed in preference to imaginal exposure, especially for more severe or complex anxiety disorders such as agoraphobia or OCD (Antony & Swinson, 2000, p. 192). However, imaginal exposure may be preferable in a number of circumstances, for several reasons:

1. Where the target of exposure is itself a thought, memory, or image, exposure will naturally be conducted in imagination, for example, in reliving certain memories experienced in PTSD.
2. Where regular *in vivo* exposure is difficult or impossible to arrange, for example, in fear of flying, thunderstorms, childbirth, etc.
3. Where the feared events are so distant in the future or remote from specific circumstances that *in vivo* exposure is not possible, for example, worry about remote events in generalised anxiety disorder, etc.

4. Where preparation for a specific event is important, for example, in public speaking anxiety, etc.
5. Where it is difficult to arrange *in vivo* exposure during sessions, the therapist may prefer to use imaginal exposure.
6. Where the feared events would be dangerous or unethical to instigate or expose the client to in reality, for example, traumatic incidents, car crashes, etc.
7. As a lower hierarchy item, in preparation, if the client is too afraid or unwilling to begin *in vivo* exposure straight away.

These sessions also tend to be shorter than *in vivo* exposure and are therefore more convenient for the therapist to conduct within the confines of their consulting room, in a normal fifty minute session. Because imaginal exposure tends to be easier and briefer, it also has the advantage of allowing exposure to more *catastrophic* or threatening scenarios, approximating to the "flooding" approach (Clark & Beck, 2010, p. 250). Moreover, facing the "worst-case scenario", sometimes called the core or underlying fear, early in therapy has several advantages in terms of cognitive therapy. For example, it allows "decatastrophising" or re-evaluation of the probability and severity of the client's ultimate fears to begin.

Cognitive avoidance is a special problem during imaginal exposure because it can be harder to detect than during *in vivo* sessions (Clark & Beck, 2010, p. 249). Clients are normally urged to keep focusing on the relevant aspects of the feared image. An important benefit of hypnosis is that it may potentially help to prevent this by facilitating increased focus upon the exposure imagery while withdrawing it from distractions. Clients in hypnosis frequently report that they feel highly absorbed in whatever they are imagining and unaware of or indifferent to external distractions. Hypnosis also appears capable of enhancing the vividness, detail, and realism of mental imagery. A further benefit may be that hypnotic suggestion can be used to enhance expectations regarding the benefits of exposure and tolerance for anxiety during the procedure. Imaginal exposure techniques do generally lead to a reduction in anxiety during real-world exposure and have been found to have lasting benefits up to nine years after treatment has been completed (Marks I. M., 1981, p. 60).

Embedding emotive imagery

One of the first modifications made to Wolpe's systematic desensitisation by other behaviour therapists, especially in the treatment of children, seems to have been the introduction of additional imagery which was designed to evoke emotions counter to anxiety. For example, Lazarus described the case of one young boy, frightened of the dark, who was to imagine being in progressively more distressing scenes of darkness while accompanied by his favourite superhero (Lazarus A. A., 1971). Of course, the presence of another figure may encourage imitation, role-modelling of their behaviour, but it also appears capable of having a reassuring effect or to arouse emotions of pleasure or excitement, antagonistic to anxiety.

Clarke and Jackson describe the use of "embedding techniques" during exposure therapy, in which clients are asked to picture themselves in a pleasant relaxing scene and then "have a daydream" about the phobic situations, or watch it on a movie or television screen, that is, to embed the feared image within another, anxiety-inhibiting, scene. They call this embedding a "scene-within-a-scene" technique. It is common for therapists to ask clients to imagine themselves in a *cinema* while watching a movie clip of themselves in anxiety-provoking situations. There's perhaps a certain lack of creativity there. Cinemas aren't usually particularly relaxing environments. The client, by contrast, could just as easily imagine herself relaxing in a beautiful garden, on a summer's day, having her shoulders massaged, while watching a movie clip of herself in a stressful situation!

Hypnotic desensitisation

Hypnotherapists have long used forms of imaginal exposure which juxtapose relaxation and anxiety-provoking imagery based on the rationale, derived from behavioural learning theory, that where relaxation is sufficiently profound it can lead to a conditioned inhibition of anxiety (Wolberg, 1948a). As we have seen, Wolpe later developed "hypnotic desensitisation", as he initially referred to it, into the cardinal technique of early behaviour therapy, systematic desensitisation (Wolpe, 1958). It was therefore natural for subsequent cognitive-behavioural hypnotherapists to adopt a modern "hypnotic desensitisation" approach, which incorporates coping imagery and helpful coping statements (Golden, Dowd & Freidberg, 1987, pp. 49–51). Indeed, more modern forms of systematic desensitisation, derived from Goldfried's "coping skills" approach, are still used in recent CBT protocols and bear an even closer resemblance to established hypnotherapy techniques (Borkovec & Sharpless, 2004; Goldfried & Davison, 1976;Öst, 1987). A similar approach called "Applied Hypnotic Relaxation" has been described in the earlier chapter on applied self-hypnosis and coping skills, however, so we won't go into more detail here.

Exposure scripts

Cognitive-behavioural therapists have attempted to compensate for the problem of subtle avoidance by asking clients to write down a detailed description of the feared situation and their anxious response to it, referred to as a "disaster" or "fear imagery" script (Clark & Beck, 2010, p. 249; Rosqvist, 2005, p. 60). Fear imagery scripts are stories or "narratives" about the feared situation, which focus on information that is emotionally significant and evokes activation of the anxiety mode and relevant threat and vulnerability schemas. For instance, Rosqvist provides the following guidance on developing a "disaster script" in CBT (Rosqvist, 2005, p. 64):

1. The script should be phrased in the first person ("I feel …", etc.).
2. The script should be phrased in the present tense, even if it refers to a future or past situation.
3. It should involve as many of the client's senses as possible, in order to be more vivid, realistic, and emotionally evocative.

Likewise, imaginal exposure often involves asking clients questions during the procedure, designed to maintain their focus and make the imagery more evocative and realistic (Antony & Swinson, 2000, p. 193). For example:

1. What are you feeling?
2. What are you thinking?
3. What physical sensations are you experiencing?

4. What are you doing now?
5. What are you hearing, seeing, or smelling?

These guidelines and strategies are virtually *indistinguishable* from those employed in the formulation of imagery or suggestion in traditional hypnotherapy. Hence, the increasing use of "scripts" in cognitive therapy obviously encourages analogies to be drawn with the use of "scripts" in hypnotherapy, although there are sometimes interesting differences in technique. Most importantly, fear imagery scripts are designed collaboratively, by the therapist Socratically guiding the client in a process of personal discovery, whereas hypnosis scripts are often written by the therapist, and used in a relatively prescriptive manner.

In CBT, the therapist will normally develop a script with the client and then help her to rehearse using it in session before assigning it as a self-exposure homework exercise. The client will normally read the script out loud before closing her eyes and trying to continue imagining the scene, perhaps opening her eyes again periodically to re-read the script as necessary, maintaining imaginal exposure for up to thirty minutes or so. Of course, in some cases it may be preferable to have the client listen to a recording of the script, made either in her own voice or by the therapist. The therapist could also read the script to the client, which would clearly resemble the kind of procedure used in traditional hypnotherapy. Beck suggests that these scripts can be used for "audio habituation training", a technique derived from behavioural approaches to exposure.

> A recording of the fear scenario is made on a CD so that the fear scripts I presented repeatedly without interruption. The client is instructed to listen to the CD and to get into the scenario depicted as fully as possible. The CD is allowed to play repeatedly for 20–30 minute exposure sessions. (Clark & Beck, 2010, p. 250)

This method increasingly resembles the use of self-hypnosis recordings, which have long been given to clients for homework. One advantage of the hypnotherapy approach is that countless scripts have been developed and are widely used by hypnotherapists to help clients develop the appropriate mind-set of focused attention and disregard for distractions, etc., as a preliminary to the prescribed imagery. The use of recordings like this has considerable potential for enhancing the benefits of self-exposure homework assignments using mental imagery, as well as in the preparation of clients for *in vivo* exposure to related situations.

Treatment

Exposure in most cognitive-behavioural hypnotherapy should normally begin with a moderate item on the hierarchy, low enough to act as a "test run" to help the client build confidence but high enough to activate the anxiety mode to some extent. However, exposure should not be employed, of course, on items that are too low on the hierarchy to be worthwhile working on or too high for the client to bear. Ideally, the therapist should demonstrate (model) as much of the technique as possible before instructing the client to begin exposing herself. Graded exposure in hypnotherapy will typically begin with a moderately anxiety-provoking situation and proceed as quickly as possible up the hierarchy toward the client's most severe and relevant fears.

Once the client has started to accept the cognitive rationale, and a cognitive conceptualisation has been shared, exposure interventions can target thoughts and appraisals in the form of a behavioural experiment. During exposure, where possible, cognitive therapists probe for faulty appraisals of threat and vulnerability by enquiring repeatedly about automatic thoughts and images and helping the client to identify alternative interpretations of the situation (Clark & Beck, 2010, p. 240). Likewise, clients should typically be encouraged to closely monitor their thoughts and appraisals during both real and imaginal exposure homework between sessions. In particular, clients should repeatedly re-evaluate their predictions concerning the core feared outcome, in terms of its probability and severity, and their own ability to cope with any difficulties they encounter.

The treatment plan for exposure is often divided into the following stages (Leahy & Holland, 2000, pp. 284–285).

1. *Preparation*. The client must be prepared by sharing the initial working hypothesis, explaining the treatment rationale, and evaluating her motivation and commitment to graded self-directed exposure. It's not unusual for clients to drop out of treatment simply because of the urge to avoid facing their fears. At this stage, the client may also be prepared by initial training in any relevant coping skills such as response prevention techniques or coping statements, etc.
2. *Creation of hierarchy*. It may take one or more sessions to develop an accurate hierarchy of the feared situations and agree the order in which items are to be addressed. The hierarchy must be accurate because treatment is so dependent upon its use.
3. *Initial exposure*. The initial exposure session is distinguished because it normally takes place during a therapy session, either in the consulting room or outdoors. This session acts as information gathering, by direct observation, for the therapist and further preparation of the client for self-directed exposure.
4. *Self-directed exposure*. Subsequent exposure will normally be mainly self-directed, without the therapist present, and conducted on a daily basis between sessions. The client self-monitors the exposure tasks and their anxiety levels, etc., which are recorded on a homework form to be reviewed at the start of each subsequent therapy session. Exposure is repeated until anxiety has reduced to a negligible level, at which point the client moves up the hierarchy to the next item, facing a more difficult challenge, until all anxiety in all targeted situations has been addressed.

It's often impractical for therapists to accompany clients outside of the consulting room, especially on a repeated basis, to engage in *in vivo* exposure. Ideally, exposure should take place at least once per day. Fortunately, self-directed exposure appears to be about as effective as exposure directed by a therapist (Leahy & Holland, 2000, p. 283). Homework is therefore a particularly important component of most exposure therapy and hypnotherapy lends itself well to enhancing homework assignments. Clients should be asked to continue self-directed exposure (or "self-exposure") between sessions, normally on a daily basis. Homework should be recorded on an appropriate form. For example, traditional behavioural approaches to exposure involve recording information such as the following (Marks I. M., 1986, p. 56).

Exposure homework record					
Date/Time/Task	Duration (Min.)	Anxiety before (0–100%)	Anxiety during (0–100%)	Anxiety after (0–100%)	Comments (Coping tactics?)

It's not unusual for clients to avoid engaging in self-exposure homework tasks, or to miss planned therapist-directed exposure sessions, for example, by calling in sick. Typical reasons for noncompliance with homework include:

1. Lack of motivation, that is, perceived discomfort outweighs perceived benefits.
2. Scepticism about the perceived treatment rationale.
3. Confusion or ambiguity about the homework plan.
4. Catastrophic beliefs about the possible risks of exposure to a feared situation.
5. Lack of confidence (self-efficacy) with regard to the task.
6. The exposure task is inconvenient or impractical to arrange.

It's therefore important for the therapist and client, collaboratively, to try to anticipate potential obstacles to the treatment plan. First and foremost, the client should be properly socialised to the treatment and should understand the conceptualisation of her problem and how this relates to the treatment rationale and planned interventions. Where possible, moreover, the therapist should be present to direct exposure in the early stages, or on the first occasion, but clients will normally be able to engage in self-directed *in vivo* exposure between sessions without supervision, especially if they have the support of a friend or spouse, etc. It is also helpful to get clients to verbally summarise their homework plan and to have it written down in concise form, so that the instructions are unambiguous and clear. Exposure homework should be carefully planned so that, where possible, the client knows exactly what tasks to perform, where and when to perform them, and how to record them. Ideally, specific times each day should be agreed for self-directed exposure between sessions (Antony & Swinson, 2000, p. 198).

Motivation is particularly important for self-directed exposure. Clients may be helped to consider their motives, or to carry out a cost-benefit analysis of avoidance versus exposure. The presence of another person offering encouragement may help motivate the client. It's often important for clients to reinforce their efforts through praise, regardless of how successful they have actually been. Some clients will report that they comply with homework on "good days" but not on "bad days", when feeling ill or anxious. It's important that this does not reduce the frequency of exposure too much or that it becomes a form of avoidance, so it's generally advisable to encourage clients, within reason, to persevere with their homework even, and perhaps especially, on "bad days" (Antony & Swinson, 2000, p. 198).

Providing recordings, such as self-hypnosis CDs or MP3 s containing imaginal exposure or desensitisation procedures, constitutes an extremely useful adjunct to treatment in sessions. Recordings including imaginal exposure exercises, based upon a systematic desensitisation approach similar to cognitive-behavioural hypnotherapy, have been found to be as effective as desensitisation sessions conducted in the presence of a therapist (Marks I. M., 1981, p. 60; Wolpe, 1990, p. 215). However, hypnotherapy can also be of benefit in terms of motivating clients to engage in exposure and helping them to adopt an appropriate mind-set toward the task. For example, suggestions can be given about remaining in the situation for long enough, abandoning unnecessary safety-seeking behaviours, focusing attention on the reality of the present environment, accepting feelings, distancing from thoughts, and acting "as if" non-anxious in other regards, etc. Hypnosis itself is associated with heightened focus of attention in a way that may facilitate prolonged or repetitive imaginal exposure during sessions or when listening to recordings. Moreover, as we have seen, where coping skills are deemed appropriate, hypnosis can contribute in a number of ways, through the use of relaxation, autosuggestion, or coping imagery, etc., as long as the client does not misuse these as forms of safety-seeking or experiential avoidance. However, although anxiety is often the central concern of clients, it is not the only problem they typically face. The next chapter will provide a more flexible and comprehensive approach to problem-solving, integrated with hypnotherapy, in order to help clients address specific obstacles and thereby go on to become more skilled and confident problem-solvers in general.

CHAPTER NINE

Behaviour: Problem-Solving Hypnotherapy (PSH)

> The important thing is not so much to know how to solve a problem as to know how to look for a solution.
>
> (Skinner, 1971)

Problem-solving therapy (PST) originated in the 1970s as a form of cognitive-behavioural therapy (CBT) that focused on helping individuals to improve their general confidence and skill when it comes to solving their own problems (Goldfried & D'Zurilla, 1971). It is often referred to as "Social Problem-Solving", although the term "social" merely denotes problem-solving in the real (social) world, rather than specifically social or interpersonal problems. (However, PST does excel as an adjunct to assertiveness or social skills training.) It draws on psychological research on problem-solving abilities in experimental settings and combines elements of behavioural self-management and coping skills training, which fundamentally emphasise the client taking over the role of the therapist and co-ordinating her own therapeutic strategies. It is a relatively brief, simple, action-oriented, and pragmatic approach to therapy that has been used for a very wide variety of client groups and issues and seems to hold promise as quite a general-purpose therapeutic strategy. It is also particularly useful in managing crises, building resilience, and relapse prevention. PST provides a generic framework for the planned implementation of specific coping strategies and can therefore flexibly assimilate strategies from cognitive therapy, hypnotherapy, and many other approaches. Meichenbaum distinguished between "coping skills" approaches to CBT, such as his stress inoculation training, that emphasise training in adaptive responses to stressful situations, and problem-solving approaches that emphasise "standing back" from stressful situations and more systematically analysing the problem to evaluate possible solutions (Meichenbaum, 1977, p. 195). However, he noted that these two styles of CBT overlap insofar as problem-solving in anticipation of stressful situations is naturally followed, in many cases, by more systematic training in coping skills to be applied during confrontation of the stressor.

We've already explored how hypnotherapy can be combined with coping skills approaches such as SIT to help clients prepare for stressful situations. However, hypnotherapy also appears to combine very well with PST. The standard PST approach emphasises the adjunctive use of "visualisation" in several different forms, throughout each of its stages. Hypnosis is particularly helpful as a way of assisting clients to develop a positive "problem-solving attitude" ("orientation"), in exploring alternative solutions through shifting perspective using mental imagery, evaluating the consequences of proposed solutions through "age progression" ("time projection" imagery), and in preparing chosen solutions through imaginal rehearsal ("covert behavioural rehearsal"). PST also provides a way for hypnotherapists to work within a cognitive-behavioural model with simplicity, and in a way that allows the client to take a more active role in determining the course of treatment. We will explore the specific relationship between hypnosis and problem-solving in more detail below, after describing the standard PST procedures.

Most of the relevant research has focused on the finding that depression tends to be associated with problem-solving deficits and a substantial body of clinical outcome research now demonstrates that PST is effective in the treatment of clinical depression (Bell & D'Zurilla, 2009). More recently, growing research has supported the relevance of "negative problem orientation" (see below) to the maintenance of generalised anxiety disorder (GAD) and the efficacy of a CBT protocol emphasising problem-solving training for GAD (Robichaud & Dugas, 2006). Beck's revised cognitive conceptualisation of GAD also emphasises the role of "negative problem orientation" and *failed* problem-solving attempts in relation to pathological worry (Clark & Beck, 2010, p. 400;418). Worry often appears to involve the prolonged and fruitless search for a solution that will provide safety from the perceived threat of harm (Clark & Beck, 2010, p. 414). In the UK, an abbreviated version of PST has been developed called problem-solving therapy for primary care (PST-PC), which is delivered in one one-hour session and five thirty-minute sessions, spread over twelve weeks, that is., a total of three-and-a-half hours (Mynors-Wallis, Gath, Lloyd-Thomas & Tomlinson, 1995). Moreover, similar approaches to problem-solving, decision-making, and the collaborative resolution of conflict have been used in business settings (Bolton, 1979, pp. 238–257).

Various assessment tools have been used to evaluate problem-solving ability and related constructs, most notably the *Social Problem-Solving Inventory-Revised* (SPSI-R), a fifty-two-item (or twenty-five-item short form) self-report scale, with good psychometric properties. SPSI-R is used to evaluate the following five dimensions (D'Zurilla & Nezu, 2007, p. 26; Maydeu-Olivares & D'Zurilla).

1. Problem Orientation (PO)
    a. Positive Problem Orientation (PPO)—adaptive
    b. Negative Problem Orientation (NPO)—maladaptive
2. Problem-Solving Skills (PSS)
    a. Rational Problem Solving (RPS)—adaptive
    b. Impulsivity/Carelessness Style (ICS)—maladaptive
    c. Avoidance Style (AS)—maladaptive.

The main clinical textbook describing the generic approach is *Problem-Solving Therapy* by D'Zurilla and Nezu (2007). There is also an accompanying self-help book, *Solving Life's Problems* by Nezu, Nezu, and D'Zurilla (2007). The authors provide a generic problem-solving training manual from which they encourage readers to develop their own individual manuals for more specific applications, which is one of the major sources for this chapter on what I would propose calling "problem-solving hypnotherapy" (PSH) (D'Zurilla & Nezu, 2007, pp. 95–148). The conceptualisation of the hypnotic subject as a creative problem-solver and application of elements of the problem-solving methodology to hypnotic skills training has been discussed in an earlier chapter. Here we will describe in comprehensive detail the integrative problem-solving hypnotherapy approach. The overall appeal of the problem-solving approach and its relevance to hypnotherapy is well-captured in the following remarks:

> Problem-solving represents a logical, systematic, and reasonably easily learned approach which can be used to help patients in many psychiatric and non-psychiatric settings [and clients with ordinary stress and "everyday hassles"]. It has the advantage of being based on common-sense principles, and is therefore attractive to patients as well as to therapists. Problem-solving is sometimes the only treatment approach that needs to be used. However, it can be an adjunct to other psychological and physical treatments. (Hawton & Kirk, 1989, p. 425)

Although PST was developed as a stand-alone cognitive-behavioural therapy, it is also commonly integrated with other forms of CBT (Dobson & Dobson, 2009, pp. 82–83). Overall, there appears to be considerable potential for combining PST and hypnotherapy. Both are brief therapy techniques, potentially based on a similar cognitive-behavioural orientation. Indeed, long before problem-solving therapy or CBT developed, the hypnotherapist Lewis Wolberg outlined the use of problem-solving methods in hypnotic "rational persuasion" psychotherapy in the well-known clinical textbook *Medical Hypnosis* (1948b). He described a relatively primitive approach, which emphasised the importance of helping the client to remain committed to his personal goals, even in the face of aversive feelings.

> It is necessary to review all possible solutions for the problem at hand. Next, the best solution is chosen even though this may seem inadequate in coping with all aspects of the problem. A plan of action must then be decided on. It is then necessary to proceed with this plan of action immediately, and to abandon all worry until the plan is carried out as completely as possible. Above all the person must stick to his plan of action, even if he finds it distasteful.
> If the person himself cannot formulate a plan, the physician may help him to do so. The patient should be told that it is better to concern himself with a constructive plan than to get tangled up in the hopelessness of an apparently insoluble problem. Until he can work out something better, it is best to adjust himself to the present situation, striving always to externalise his energy in a constructive way. (Wolberg, 1948a, p. 182)

The therapist therefore works collaboratively with the client to help him review all possible solutions to his problem, to choose the best available one, and to form an action plan and see it through to completion. Elsewhere Wolberg describes something resembling a "SWOT analysis" in business (Strengths, Weaknesses, Opportunities, Threats) where the patient is encouraged to evaluate his own personal "assets and liabilities", or strengths and weaknesses. This is used to help him reformulate his personal goals in life in a more realistic way, taking full advantage of his genuine resources.

> The physician teaches the patient to regard his symptoms as the product of emotions and distorted goals in life. He outlines for the patient the disturbed attitudes and strivings which get him into difficulties with people. Next he helps the patient apply the knowledge about himself to immediate life situations. An evaluation is made of the patient's assets and these are compared with his liabilities. From this the patient often learns that he has concentrated upon his liabilities more than on his assets. He may come to the realisation that he has been so provoked by his failures that he has minimised any good qualities that he possesses. Indeed when his assets are brought to his attention, he may be surprised that he has accepted them without realising their proper value. He may gradually become cognisant of how exclusively he has focused his attention on his bad features, blotting from his mind his good points. Redirecting his attention on the latter gives him new goals toward which to strive. This may break up a vicious chain of frustration and despair. An investigation of the patient's objectives may disclose ambitions that he is unqualified to fulfil which have contributed to his sense of defeat. An attempt is made to modify these ambitions within the range of the patient's capacities, energies and environmental opportunities. (Wolberg, 1948a, p. 203)

Wolberg even provides a transcript of a group hypnotherapy session based on Paul Dubois' "rational persuasion" approach to psychotherapy, an early twentieth century precursor of modern cognitive therapy. The script contains many instructions for coping strategies and ego-strengthening suggestions, as well as hypnotic suggestions for developing a positive problem-solving orientation, based on the methods mentioned above:

> I will abolish worrying and thinking too much about myself. If anything comes up that needs solution, I will immediately review all possible courses of action and choose the one that seems to be best. Once I have made up my mind, I shall follow the plan I have evolved. (Wolberg, 1948b, pp. 183–184)

About two decades after Wolberg's account of problem-solving in hypnotherapy, a number of more explicit problem-solving approaches developed which fit within the broad cognitive-behavioural framework, drawing on a large body of experimental literature on problem-solving. "Social problem-solving therapy" (or "training"), as it is sometimes known, began to develop in the late 1960s and early 1970s mainly through the work of therapists and researchers such as D'Zurilla, Nezu, and Goldfried (D'Zurilla & Nezu, 2007; Goldfried & D'Zurilla, 1971). A second approach developed roughly in parallel to PST under the name Interpersonal Cognitive Problem Solving (ICPS), first documented in Spivack, Platt & Shure's *The Problem-Solving Approach to Adjustment* (Spivack, Platt & Shure, 1976). Meichenbaum's stress inoculation training (SIT) approach also places emphasis on problem-solving (Meichenbaum, 1985) as does Beck's cognitive therapy for depression (Beck, Rush, Shaw & Emery, 1979), and several current forms of CBT incorporate elements of the problem-solving approach along with cognitive restructuring and other components.

PST is often conceptualised as a generic approach to coping with stress, a very broad concept. However, this approach was also found relevant to many specific emotional problems of the kind treated in psychotherapy and a number of studies seem to identify a correlation between problem-solving skill deficits and psychopathology. Indeed, a central assumption underlying PST is the view that much "psychopathology" is better understood in terms of dysfunctional or maladaptive coping strategies, which lead to symptoms such as anxiety and depression and create additional problems in different domains of living (D'Zurilla & Nezu, 2001, p. 219). Hence, PST has been used to help clients with a range of diagnosable mental health problems, particularly depression and generalised anxiety, but also as a way of addressing stress among different groups and in relation to different circumstances, such as coping with various medical conditions, with pain, or with issues like overeating or substance abuse. Problems coping with a variety of situations in daily life can arguably be best addressed through a fairly generic training approach that helps the individual to become more skilled and confident at solving problems in general (Goldfried & D'Zurilla, 1971, p. 109). PST can be used both preventatively and remedially, that is, to stop problems occurring again in the future by dealing with the antecedent causes or to directly remove the symptoms after they have occurred. PST may also serve as a post-treatment strategy for relapse prevention and maintenance of improvements. However, it is also used for dealing with "daily hassles" and everyday stressful situations. Those with specific, identifiable problem-solving deficits are most likely to benefit; however, most clients can gain some benefit from this approach.

Whereas other CBT approaches sometimes place more focus upon acceptance of the external situation and changing internal responses, that is, thoughts and feelings, PST focuses more on mobilising behaviour to make practical changes to certain external situations. Moreover whereas traditional behaviour therapy and some current forms of CBT incorporate systematic training in specific prescribed coping strategies, such as progressive muscle relaxation or assertiveness, PST provides a more flexible framework within which clients are helped to creatively identify, evaluate, plan, and implement the use of whatever strategies appear to suit their individual needs. D'Zurilla and Nezu emphasise that it requires "conscious, rational, effortful and purposeful activity"; relative to many other therapy approaches, the client's role is to be more active and pragmatic. Indeed, the client is encouraged to become her own therapist, and to generalise the skills learned, applying them throughout her life.

Hence, PST places more emphasis upon planning than do other coping-skills approaches, such as stress inoculation, which emphasise rehearsal and training of specific strategies. However, Meichenbaum recommended problem-solving should be used as an adjunct to other coping skills within the framework of stress inoculation training (Meichenbaum, 1977, p. 195). The "problem situation" is defined as any (current or anticipated) life situation which requires some response from the client, but to which no effective or adaptive response is immediately obvious. Skinner defined a problem in behavioural terms as follows, "A person has a problem when some condition will be reinforcing but he lacks a response that will produce it" (Skinner, 1974, p. 123). Problem-solving in Skinnerian terms should therefore increase the frequency of reinforcement, which is considered particularly important in the "behavioural activation" approach to treating depression (Kanter, Busch & Rush, 2009; Lewinsohn, Munoz, Youngren &

Zeiss, 1986). However, Skinner also observed that in situations where the consequences are perceived as important and two or more potential solutions ("choices") are perceived as about equally probable, in terms of their effectiveness, problem-solving may also be (negatively) reinforced because it constitutes an "escape" from the "aversive" condition of indecision (Skinner, 1974, pp. 124–125). As we shall see, an important new form of CBT for generalised anxiety disorder (GAD) focuses on the central maintaining factor of anxiety being "intolerance of uncertainty", which is treated through a combination of imaginal exposure, prevention of maladaptive behavioural responses, and problem-solving (Robichaud & Dugas, 2006).

PST basically assumes that much "psychopathology" consists of failure to cope adequately with stressful events, and problem-solving can be seen as a general-purpose creative coping strategy that helps to build resilience against stress and consequent emotional disturbance (D'Zurilla & Nezu, 2007, p. 61). Research on middle-aged and elderly community residents has suggested that thirty-four per cent of the variance between daily problems and anxiety is accounted for by problem-solving ability, particularly negative problem-orientation, and that the interaction between daily problems and problem-solving ability accounts for fifty per cent of the variance in anxiety overall (D'Zurilla & Nezu, 2007, p. 70). Other studies have provided support for the view that negative problem-orientation may contribute to anxiety directly and also indirectly, by exacerbating worry (D'Zurilla & Nezu, 2007, pp. 80–81). After reviewing the extant research on worry and problem solving, Barlow concluded:

> Taken together, these findings suggest that individuals who worry excessively and/or meet criteria for GAD are likely to have little confidence in their ability to solve problems or in their control over outcomes, although they exhibit no clear self-reported deficits in their ability to problem solve. (Barlow, 2002, p. 492)

Worry tends to take the form of abstract verbal processing, which may replace the processing of more concrete imagery and specific information that's conducive to adaptive problem-solving (see below).

With regard to the empirical support for PST as a treatment, a substantial body of evidence favours its efficacy across a wide range of problems and client groups. A recent meta-analytic review of problem-solving therapy identified thirty-one controlled studies, involving a total of 2,895 participants (Malouff, Thorsteinsson & Schutte, 2007). The authors concluded that PST was significantly more effective than placebo or treatment as usual ("medium" effect size compared to both, $d = 0.54$) across a range of client groups and issues including major depression, dysthymia, conduct disorder, obesity, alcoholism, substance abuse, back pain, etc.

Problem-solving methodology

Terminology

Clients can be socialised to the model by explaining that problem-solving is like planning and then taking a journey, or navigating your way through a maze. The "problem" is where you start from ("what is"). The "goal" is your destination ("what should be"). The possible "solutions" are the paths you can potentially follow to get from start to destination or from problem to goal ("how to get there"). There may be several routes from problem to goal or, as the old saying goes, "There's more than one way to skin a cat." More specifically, in the PST approach a "problem" is basically defined in the broadest possible terms as any situation demanding a response, which is not currently available due to certain obstacles (D'Zurilla & Nezu, 2007, pp. 12–13). A *solution* may consist either of situation-specific cognitive or behavioural coping responses, or some combination thereof, which solve the problem and achieve the goal. Solutions are ways of coping with either a problem situation ("problem-focused coping") or with one's emotional reaction to it ("emotion-focused coping"), or some combination thereof (Nezu, Nezu & Perri, 1989, p. 29).

Conceptualisation: the relational/problem-solving model of stress

The social problem-solving model has been integrated with Richard Lazarus' influential "relational" (or "transactional" model) of stress, which, as we have seen, was also the basis of Beck's original cognitive model of anxiety (Beck A. T., 1976; D'Zurilla & Nezu, 2007, pp. 61–71; Lazarus R. S., 1999, pp. 58–59). We have discussed these models in detail in the earlier chapter on conceptualisation but will elaborate here on the relationship between problem-solving and the transactional model of stress.

Problem-solving approaches can be seen as methodologies for resolving stressful situations. From this perspective many different "mental health" problems are viewed as stemming from maladaptive or failed attempts to cope with stressful life events or everyday hassles. Remedial treatment of many problems may involve training in problem-solving but problem-solving may also be effective as a form of prevention by building resilience to stress and a flexible repertoire of coping skills and strategies. Lazarus' model of stress emphasises the interaction between four main factors:

1. Primary appraisal of demands (threat).
2. Secondary appraisal of coping.
3. Coping attempts (emotion-focused or problem-focused).
4. Reappraisal (of demands and coping).

According to the "relational/problem-solving" model of stress, the client "cognitively appraises" the stressful problem-situation in terms both of the degree to which it threatens to harm her well-being ("primary appraisal") and her ability, and range of options, to cope with it ("secondary appraisal") (D'Zurilla & Nezu, 2001, pp. 220–221). "Coping" consists both in clients' ability to self-regulate their emotional responses ("emotion-focused coping") and their ability to solve practical problems ("problem-focused coping"), although one or the other may predominate. Reappraisal involves reflection on the outcome of coping and attempts to re-evaluate the threat or find another coping strategy. In the language of PST, "problems" are typically the demands (or threats), "solutions" are the coping strategies, and the process of rational "problem-solving" is linked to Lazarus' concept of reappraisal.

Problem-solving can be seen as a flexible and generic coping strategy, which can improve appraisals of coping with stressful events across a range of different situations and thereby reduce the stress reaction to perceived environmental demands (D'Zurilla & Nezu, 2007, p. 9).

> The relational/problem-solving model retains the basic assumptions and essential features of Lazarus' relational model of stress. However, these features are cast within a general social problem-solving framework, and problem solving is given an expanded and more important role as a general coping strategy. Within this model, stress is viewed as a function of the reciprocal relations among three major variables: (1) stressful live events, (2) emotional stress responses, and (3) problem-solving coping. (D'Zurilla & Nezu, 2001, p. 220)

Notably, "planful problem-solving", adopting a systematic approach to solving practical problems, was found by Lazarus to be one of the most reliable coping styles in research reported in the stress literature. More importantly, Lazarus emphasised that in general the main lesson to be learned from research on coping and stress is that there's no one-size-fits-all, that is, different coping strategies prove effective or ineffective for different clients, facing different problems, under different circumstances, at different stages of a problem's progression. PST gets around this difficulty by training clients to dynamically identify and evaluate their own coping strategies rather than focusing on training them in specific strategies in a prescriptive manner. The emphasis is therefore on flexibility and generalisation of high-level ("metacognitive") coping skills. As the cliché goes, "Give a man a fish and you feed him for a day; teach a man to fish and you feed him for a lifetime." Give a man a coping strategy and you help him to overcome a handful of stressful situations; teach him to creatively problem-solve, and generate his own coping plans, and you make him more resilient to future stressors.

As Lazarus notes, the relational model of stress can be seen as resembling the Serenity Prayer's advice to "serenely accept" (emotionally-focused coping) things that we cannot change, while "courageously changing" (problem-focused coping) the things we *can*, and having, of course, the wisdom (cognitive appraisal) to know the difference (Pietsch, 1990). When a problem-situation is appraised as solvable, or under the subject's control, problem-focused coping naturally tends to predominate. By contrast, when the problem-situation seems uncontrollable or unsolvable emotion-focused coping tends to predominate. Goal-setting at the start of problem-focused therapy may therefore be comprised of either:

1. *Problem*-focused goals. Changing the situation itself, trying to resolve a practical problem.
2. *Emotion*-focused goals. Changing the way the client *feels* about the situation, coping with the emotional response.

It has to be emphasised that whereas Lazarus and other writers tend to equate the term "problem solving" with "problem-focused coping", the PST methodology does not and treats *emotion*-focused coping strategies, such as cognitive restructuring, distraction, relaxation, etc., as potential solutions in exactly the same way as in solving practical external problems (D'Zurilla & Nezu, 2007, p. 65;102). However, as Lazarus emphasised, in most cases emotion-focused and problem-focused coping strategies tend to be combined, although one or the other will normally predominate at any given time. PST can be used either to develop ways of coping at a practical or emotional level. Likewise, in previous chapters we've explored a variety of coping strategies. However, following recent research supporting mindfulness and acceptance-based approaches in CBT, it might be better to distinguish clearly between emotion-focused coping involving self-control or avoidance of unpleasant internal experiences, such as relaxing to suppress anxiety, and more acceptance-based strategies, such as distancing from negative automatic thoughts and accepting unpleasant feelings until they abate naturally (Hayes, Strosahl & Wilson, 2012). As previously noted, in some cases it appears that relaxation and similar emotion-focused coping skills work well as means of regulating anxiety, whereas in other cases it they can backfire and lead to more problems. The client and therapist therefore need to carefully evaluate the function of coping strategies in terms of their probable long-term consequences.

The use of PST easily complements Beck's conceptualisation of anxiety or Lazarus' model of stress, particularly insofar as improving skill and confidence in problem-solving can improve appraisals of ability to cope ("self-efficacy") in the face of stress or perceived danger. This approach works best when problem situations are fairly realistically appraised and practically solvable. In general, the stress management literature does indicate that problem-focused coping tends to be more effective in the long-term than emotion-focused coping, although there is considerable variation among individuals and the demands of specific situations (D'Zurilla & Nezu, 2007, p. 63). However, if the problem is conceptualised as involving exaggerated appraisals of threat, or maintaining factors such as safety-seeking behaviours, the problem-solving approach can easily be based upon a shared cognitive formulation of anxiety, for example, by generating alternative ways of modifying threat appraisals, different behavioural experiments, or ways of preventing safety-seeking behaviour, or strategies for developing mindful acceptance, etc. In standard PST, the client tends to conceptualise their own problem in more common sense language. On the other hand, cognitive therapy normally socialises clients to a conceptualisation that draws on specific research-based models of anxiety, that is, to a problem formulation including elements that may not be obvious at first to the client, such as the potentially counter-productive long-term consequences of escape, safety-seeking or thought-control strategies (Clark & Beck, 2010).

Overview of treatment structure

So what sorts of specific "problems" are addressed by PST? D'Zurilla and Nezu give the following example problem and goal definitions, where goals are phrased as "What can I do …" questions.

> [Depression] "My girlfriend has just informed me that she is ending our relationship because she no longer loves me. I am feeling extremely depressed and inadequate. What can I do to make myself feel better?
>
> [Tension-induced pain] "I am sitting at my desk trying to complete a difficult report that is due tomorrow, but I cannot concentrate because I have a terrible headache. I have already taken aspirin, but it has not worked. What can I do to relieve my headache pain?"

[Overeating] "I am sitting at home alone watching TV, and I have a strong urge to go out and buy some ice cream, but I know that I have already reached my calorie limit for the day. What can I do to keep myself from giving in to the urge to go out and get some ice cream?" (D'Zurilla & Nezu, 2001, p. 223)

The specific aims of cognitive-behavioural problem-solving have been defined as follows (Hawton & Kirk, 1989).

1. To help clients identify relevant problems, especially those related to symptoms being treated such as anxiety or depression.
2. To help clients appraise their existing resources for coping with problems and address deficits in coping skills.
3. To improve problem orientation and enhance the client's sense of control over their problems (self-efficacy).
4. To help clients action plan solutions to relevant problems and apply them by confronting their problems.
5. To provide clients with a general-purpose coping strategy for building resilience toward future problems (stressors) and prevention of relapse.

The PST approach developed by Goldfried & D'Zurilla, and subsequently by Arthur and Christine Nezu, the most widely-used method, focuses on training clients in two main areas, as mentioned above:

1. *Problem-orientation*, or the client's basic set of attitudes toward problems in general.
2. *Problem-solving style*, or the generic skills and strategies employed in solving problems, sometimes termed "problem-solving proper".

In addition, this original distinction was recently revised into a "five-dimensional" model on the basis of a number of research studies, including factor analyses conducted on large student samples (D'Zurilla & Nezu, 2007, pp. 21,24). This five-factor model, as used in the SPSI-R, distinguishes between two forms of problem orientation:

1. *Positive* problem orientation (adaptive).
2. *Negative* problem orientation (maladaptive).

It also distinguishes between three problem-solving styles:

1. *Rational*, which is functional and adaptive, and the style clients are trained to employ.
2. *Avoidant*, which is common with anxiety, and involves procrastination and avoidance of planning or confrontation with problems.
3. *Careless/impulsive*, which involves rushing into tackling problems in a messy way or handling them complacently.

A functional or "rational" problem-solving style consists of four generic component skills or strategies, which occur in the following sequence.

1. *Problem definition and formulation*, the ability to identify and formulate the problem adequately.
2. *Generating alternatives*, the ability to brainstorm solutions.
3. *Decision making*, the ability to evaluate the consequences (pros and cons) of different solutions and choose the best option.
4. *Solution implementation and verification*, applying an action plan, self-monitoring the outcome, evaluating what happened, reinforcing efforts, and adapting to feedback.

Where problems concern other people, that is, are of a social or inter-personal nature, special consideration of the motives and possible responses of others is essential, and in some cases problem-solving may be conducted collaboratively with the input of other affected parties. Clients in PST must learn these skills first, sometimes by considering hypothetical problems, and then be guided through their successful application to real-life problems. The steps can be roughly summarised in terms of the following questions, which can be provided on a cue card as a guide and reminder to clients.

> **Cue card for problem-solving**
>
> 1. *Problem*: What specifically is the problem? How is it a problem? What specifically is your goal?
> 2. *Brainstorming*: What possible solution strategies and specific tactics can you think of?
> 3. *Decision*: What are the pros and cons of your best options? What specifically will you do and when?
> 4. *Action*: Do it! What happened? How well did it work? What did you learn? Reward your efforts! What next?

Likewise, D'Zurilla & Nezu have introduced the "ADAPT" acronym to help clients remember that PST is about adapting behaviour to meet the demands of stressful situations and to act as a reminder to adopt a positive problem orientation and use the four rational problem-solving skills (D'Zurilla & Nezu, 2007, pp. 96–97; Nezu, Nezu & D'Zurilla, 2007, pp. 11–12).

*A*ttitude: Adopt a positive and optimistic problem-solving attitude (orientation) from the outset and throughout all the steps.

*D*efine: Develop a clear, objective, and accurate definition of your problem, goals, and any obstacles.

*A*lternatives: Brainstorm a variety of alternative solutions for overcoming your problem and achieving your goal.

*P*redict: Weigh up the pros and cons (consequences) of your options and choose the best solution.

*T*ry it out: Put your best solution into practice, evaluate the outcome, praise or reward your efforts, and try again until the problem is solved.

We will examine each of these elements below beginning with the underlying problem orientation or attitude. However, first it may be helpful to consider some factors that are considered common pitfalls or general facilitative strategies. Based upon the use of problem-solving methods in industry, Robert Bolton identified the following traps to be avoided (Bolton, 1979, pp. 252–254).

1. Not handling interfering emotions first.
2. Not defining the problem properly, especially the specific goals desired.
3. Evaluating or clarifying (elaborating) during brainstorming, which leads to digressions.
4. Not working out the nitty-gritty details, that is, the specific steps for implementing the chosen solution.
5. Not following-up to see that the action plan has been implemented, including verification and reinforcement of efforts.

Moreover, it should also be mentioned that PST introduces clients to a number of principles and strategies, designed to facilitate the whole process. D'Zurilla & Nezu refer to research suggesting that human attentional capacities are easily overwhelmed when trying to process complex information, a limitation that may interfere with problem solving. They propose the following three general strategies to compensate for this (D'Zurilla & Nezu, 2007, p. 108).

1. *Externalisation.* Information should be written down where possible, for example, using the forms typically provided in therapy or drawing diagrams, etc., because this is believed to relieve the cognitive burden of having to continually internally display information, freeing more cognitive resources for analysis and evaluation.
2. *Visualisation.* Processing mental imagery where possible appears to facilitate problem solving in a number of ways, and "visualisation" is easily turned into a hypnotic technique, which can help by making problem definitions more concrete and complete, by use of time projection to evaluate consequences, and covert behavioural rehearsal to prepare action plans, etc.
3. *Simplification.* Problem-solving can be helped by sticking to the principle of making things as simple as possible, but no simpler, as this will speed up the whole procedure and aid the cognitive processes involved—"Keep It Simple Stupid" or "Keep it Sweet and Simple" (KISS).

These three strategies are integral throughout PST and help to address common pitfalls. Several "visualisation" techniques are employed throughout different stages of PST. However, the developers of PST actually provide a complete "visualisation script" in their self-help manual, discussed below, which very closely resembles a hypnotherapy script, although not labelled as such (Nezu, Nezu & D'Zurilla, 2007, p. 107). The emphasis upon the principle of "visualisation" as an aid throughout problem-solving clearly integrates well with Cognitive-Behavioural Hypnotherapy. Hypnosis typically involves the use of focused attention on mental imagery, accompanied by an expectant or confident cognitive set, which in this context can be compared to positive problem orientation.

The value of writing things down ("externalisation") often needs to be "sold" to clients, as it may feel easier to them not to bother keeping records. However, especially in the early and middle stages of training, carefully documenting problem-solving and solution implementation, etc., appears to contribute substantially to the whole process. To improve adherence, therapists should make certain that clients understand what is to be recorded and the rationale for doing so, which can be aided by completing an example entry on certain homework forms during the therapy session. It is particularly important in PST, as in other forms of CBT, to consistently reinforce homework, through appropriate praise and encouragement, which should generally refer to the effort made rather than the outcome.

"Simplification" and adaptiveness are important because, as critics have pointed out, following the PST approach too rigidly or laboriously may be counter-productive (Haaga & Davison, 1991, pp. 279–280). It's usually beneficial to take things slowly at first so that clients can learn the component skills properly but "rough screening" of alternative solutions, abbreviated decision-making, simplification, and rapid problem-solving, are more appropriate to some situations, for example, which dynamic or unpredictable changes may call for quick responses. Another way of viewing this is that in some situations, problem-solving may have to rely on rapid, automatic information processing, which may nevertheless be improved by prior training or by the activation of positive problem orientation schemas:

> A more radical variation on PST would emphasize mainly the initial, orientation stage, elaborating the remaining stages only for especially refractory problems. For most problems, the problem solver's attitude may be more significant than the particular meta-cognitive methodology used. (Haaga & Davison, 1991, p. 280)

However, in most cases, training in the rational problem-solving skills does seem to add something to positive problem-orientation, and there may be a reciprocal relationship between improved orientation and improved enactment of the problem-solving skills.

Moreover, problem-solving *proper*, going through some of the component steps, often plays a role in "decatastrophising" techniques in cognitive therapy. Here the focus is on having the client problem-solve and develop a "coping plan" for dealing with the feared worst-case scenario or with more realistic, likely-case scenarios (Clark & Beck, 2010, pp. 207–209, 430). The therapist helps the client use problem-solving skills to work out a written action plan for coping with feared events, which is reviewed repeatedly between sessions, whenever the relevant catastrophic ("What if?") thoughts resurface. (See the chapter on cognitive therapy in this volume for a more detailed account.) A simplified problem-solving approach can also be applied to "response prevention", for example, by helping the client to consider different ways to inhibit safety-seeking and other maladaptive strategies, such as by using "blocking strategies" or perhaps replacing them with more adaptive, alternative responses (Clark & Beck, 2010, pp. 254–255). As the main intervention for most anxiety is exposure and "response prevention", Beck defines "adaptive" coping responses as those which aid the client in inhibiting maladaptive responses while prolonging genuine exposure and focused attention on threat cues long enough for natural emotional processing to take place and anxiety to reduce (Clark & Beck, 2010, p. 255).

Finally, problem-solving and creativity skills training have been studied in relation to verbal self-instruction techniques. Meichenbaum dedicated a section of his original textbook on cognitive-behaviour modification to detailed discussion of self-instruction training for "creative problem-solving" (Meichenbaum, 1977, pp. 58–68). After reviewing some of the early research in this area, he provided a detailed set of example self-instructions for creativity and problem-solving, based on a synthesis of different themes in the creativity literature, which includes many strategies and concepts found in modern problem-solving therapy (Meichenbaum, 1977, p. 63). For example, these include self-statements like the following, designed to help induce and maintain an "attitudinal set" for creativity:

> Size-up the problem. What do you have to do?
> Be creative.
> Break away from the obvious, the commonplace.
> Quantity helps breed quality.
> Defer judgement and evaluation until you've finished brainstorming alternatives.
> Don't limit yourself to the first answer you think of.
> There's no right or wrong answer; it doesn't matter what other people think.
> Let your ideas play; let one suggestion lead to another.
> Good, you're getting the idea.

Different self-instructions will be suited to different stages of problem-solving. However, the concept of a general attitudinal set for creativity can be compared to the notion of positive problem-orientation below. After systematic training in self-instructions for creative problem-solving, Meichenbaum observed that subjects developed a "generalized set" to approach everyday problems in a more creative manner, and they began spontaneously generalising their new strategies to the solution of novel problems and different situations. On the basis of this observation concerning the apparent ease with which self-instructions can be used to develop a generalised creative problem-solving attitude, Meichenbaum explicitly recommended that self-instruction training could be combined with Goldfried and D'Zurilla's original problem-solving therapy approach (Goldfried & D'Zurilla, 1971; Meichenbaum, 1977, p. 65). Hence, this sort of verbal statement can be discussed with clients, who may be encouraged to develop their own self-instructions to be memorised, or written on cue cards, and repeated, congruently and meaningfully, as self-guidance during problem-solving.

Problem orientation

"Problem orientation" refers to the overall attitude of the individual toward problems in general, and the individual's perception and appraisal of problems. A distinction is made between positive and negative problem orientation. It is essential that the client adopt a positive overall problem-focused orientation before beginning the process. Developing a positive problem-orientation or "problem-solving attitude" crudely involves being confident and optimistic about coping with problems. However, more specifically, D'Zurilla and Nezu have distinguished between five different components of problem-orientation (D'Zurilla & Nezu, 2007, p. 22).

1. *Problem recognition*, that is, spotting and responding to problems when they occur.
2. *Problem attribution*, that is, attributing problems to specific causes.
3. *Problem appraisal*, that is, estimating the severity of problems and their relevance for well-being (Lazarus' "primary appraisal" of demands).
4. *Perceived control*, that is, estimating your control over or ability to cope with problems ("secondary appraisal" of coping, or Bandura's "self-efficacy" and "outcome expectancy").
5. *Time/effort commitment*, that is, estimating the amount of work required to solve a specific problem and willingness to commit to it.

For example, in plain English, a *positive* problem orientation might be said to consist of the following characteristics (D'Zurilla & Nezu, 2001, p. 225):

1. Recognising a problem accurately when it occurs and treating this as a signal ("cue") to "stop and think", that is, to begin problem-solving proper.
2. Belief that problems are a normal and inevitable part of life and the ability to accurately attribute problems to specific causes, while avoiding extremes such as falsely attributing problems to global and stable personal defects.
3. Appraising new problems as "challenges" (opportunities for growth) rather than as overwhelming "threats" to be avoided.
4. Self-confidence in one's ability to cope effectively with such problems and belief (optimism) that there is a solution to be found.
5. Realising that complex problems may require substantial time and effort to resolve them, being willing to act in a timely manner and to inhibit impulsive behaviour when solving stressful problems.

Of these, problem-solving confidence or "self-efficacy" is perhaps the most important factor. These broad "orientation" factors are also conceptualised as "cognitive schemas" like those referred to in Beck's cognitive therapy (Clark & Beck, 2010; D'Zurilla & Nezu, 2001, p. 214). Problem recognition activates the other schemas, in a manner similar to the "orientation" or recognition phase in Beck's revised three-stage model of anxiety (Clark & Beck, 2010). Moreover, "problem appraisal" and "perceived control" broadly correspond with Beck's notions of schemas of "threat" and "vulnerability" (helplessness) in the cognitive model of anxiety (Clark & Beck, 2010). This is not surprising as the Beckian model of anxiety and the problem-solving model of stress both draw upon Richard Lazarus' concepts of primary and secondary appraisal (Lazarus R. S., 1999). Indeed, during standard cognitive therapy for anxiety, the client would normally address most of these beliefs and appraisals, in some sense. As in Beck's cognitive therapy, the client may sometimes be asked to view the subsequent steps of problem-solving proper as a form of behavioural experiment ("empirical hypothesis testing"), that is, to adopt a "try it and see" attitude toward solution implementation and test out specific predictions about the outcome of their chosen behaviour. As we've seen earlier, the concept of problem orientation can be used to reconceptualise the positive cognitive set for hypnosis identified by Barber and other cognitive-behavioural researchers, providing a detailed problem-solving model of hypnosis.

Moreover, the concept of "negative problem orientation", a set of dysfunctional attitudes toward coping with problems, is central to an influential cognitive therapy model of generalised anxiety disorder (GAD) developed by Michel Dugas and his colleagues in Quebec (Koerner & Dugas, 2006, pp. 207–208; Robichaud & Dugas, 2006, pp. 296–298). Clients with GAD have been found to have higher levels of negative problem orientation than those with other anxiety disorders, or than is found in the normal population. Although they may possess problem-solving skills, GAD clients often seem overwhelmed by even small problems or daily hassles. Indeed, researchers have found that decreased self-confidence in one's problem-solving ability tends to lead to a subsequent *increase* in catastrophic thinking and worry, which suggests a possible causal role for negative problem orientation in the development of pathological worry (Davey, 2006, pp. 168–169). There is also some correlation between "intolerance of uncertainty" and worry, which may interact with negative problem orientation to interfere with the process of problem-solving proper and maintain or exacerbate subsequent worry and anxiety (Koerner & Dugas, 2006, p. 208). These clients are often characterised by intense frustration at their failed attempts to solve problems or cope better with them, leading to an overwhelming sense of "personal inadequacy" or "incompetence" (helplessness) and further inhibition of constructive problem-solving behaviour, especially solution implementation (Davey, 2006, pp. 167–168).

> The therapist explains that it is human nature to avoid threatening situations and approach opportunities. As such, so long as patients view problems as purely threatening and doubt their own abilities, they will necessarily refrain from solving their problems even if they are good problem solvers. (Robichaud & Dugas, 2006, p. 296)

Indeed, in anxious individuals who are intolerant of uncertainty, negative problem orientation may lead to potential solutions being prematurely rejected, because they are not "perfect" or certain solutions, effectively turning attempts at problem-solving into pathological unproductive worry. This inhibition of constructive problem-solving is conceptualised by Beck, following Rachman, as a repeatedly failed "search for safety", which contributes to maintaining the sense of pervasive vulnerability in GAD (Clark & Beck, 2010, pp. 414–415; Rachman S., 2004). Hence, Beck's revised cognitive therapy for GAD also specifically emphasises cognitive restructuring of the negative problem orientation, and training in problem-solving skills, but only where worry relates to a more realistic feared outcome (Clark & Beck, 2010).

Another cognitive conceptualisation of GAD is that these clients are basically trying to use worry to solve their problems but failing to do so because the anxiety of mentally facing their fears causes them to think in vague, abstract, *verbal* terms rather than employing concrete *imagery* or elaborating on the specific details of their worries (Koerner & Dugas, 2006, p. 212; Butler, Fennell & Hackman, 2008, p. 185). As the "visualisation" principle of PST implies, concrete mental imagery appears to provide more specific information, which facilitates the process of problem solving. Worry can be construed as a form of cognitive avoidance, which keeps things vague enough to moderate anxiety, but does so at the expense of inhibiting natural emotional processing and constructive problem-solving. Although GAD may present an extreme example of negative problem orientation, some of the observations made in the special cognitive therapy protocol developed for this condition may be applicable more generally (Robichaud & Dugas, 2006).

> The therapist makes a distinction between viewing "threat" and "opportunity" as opposite ends of a continuum rather than as discrete categories. The patient is charged with attempting to find a challenging aspect, or opportunity, in the problem so as to move the situation away from 100% threatening on the continuum, and toward a balance between threat and opportunity. [...] In this manner, although the threatening aspects of the situation are not ignored, the patient can see a benefit to solving the problem. (Robichaud & Dugas, 2006, pp. 296–297).

For these clients, cultivating the overall problem-solving attitude or orientation may be more important than the specific problem-solving skills used. However, there may be a reciprocal interaction between one's attitudes toward problem-solving and practical attempts to develop and utilise the specific skills above. By maintaining the right orientation and repeatedly applying these skills to specific problems, the overarching goal of problem-solving therapy is achieved, which is not just the solution of individual problems but long-standing and generalised improvement in one's underlying problem-solving confidence and ability, across diverse situations.

In other words, the goal of problem-solving therapy isn't just to solve individual problems but to make the client a better problem-solver in general. Hypnotic techniques such as self-hypnosis, the use of "ego-strengthening" type scripts, and mental rehearsal, are ideal ways of helping the client to cultivate and maintain a positive problem orientation (see below). It is also sometimes helpful to have clients evaluate their own problem orientation as a homework exercise between sessions and worksheets have been developed for doing so (Nezu, Nezu & Perri, 1989, p. 146). As it's difficult for most people to properly evaluate their own cognitive distortions at first, the therapist will probably have to carefully review this kind of self-report form with clients and discuss the reasons for each rating and their comments.

Problem orientation evaluation

Describe the problem? (Where, when?)

Briefly describe how you actually responded? (Thoughts, actions, feelings?)

Rate problem orientation

Rate your agreement with each statement below (0–100%) and describe underneath why you chose that number:
1. "I recognised the problem early-on and used my feelings (or other early-warning signs) as cues to begin constructive problem-solving." (%)
2. "I saw the problem as a normal part of life and accurately attributed it to its specific causes." (%)

3. "I saw the problem as a challenge to be coped with rather than as a threat to be avoided." (%)
4. "I was confident in my ability to solve the problem and optimistic that a solution did exist." (%)
5. "I was realistic about the time required to solve the problem and willing to invest enough effort." (%)

Spotting specific problems is part of problem orientation (problem recognition) and the PST protocol emphasises the importance of teaching clients to interrupt their automatic, habitual response chains by using the "Stop and Think!" strategy. The client is taught to respond to cues that indicate a problem is occurring, especially feelings of distress or frustration, by visualising a *"STOP"* sign and using self-instructions to "stop and think" before responding further, possibly supported by the use of a cue card with the words "Stop and Think." This simple cue or self-instruction is meant to remind the client to do two things, aimed at interrupting and modifying existing maladaptive response patterns (Nezu, Nezu & Perri, 1989, p. 154).

1. *Stop*: Inhibit impulsive responses or maladaptive (cognitive or behavioural) coping strategies early on, which could be seen as a form of "response prevention".
2. *Think*: Remind yourself of self-instructions for positive problem-orientation ("I can do this, if I take it slowly", etc.) and to engage in the four stages of rational problem-solving.

This coping skill is mentally rehearsed during sessions by having the client repeatedly picture herself in example situations where a problem occurs and responding by picturing the stop-sign image and using the self-statement to "stop and think"; of course this imaginal rehearsal of the coping skill can be conducted using hypnosis (D'Zurilla & Nezu, 2007, pp. 122–123). It should be emphasised that the purpose of this technique isn't to *suppress* upsetting thoughts but for the client to cue herself to pause and engage her constructive problem-solving skills.

As noted above, the process of worry has been conceptualised by some researchers as *failed* problem-solving. Some therapists prefer to speak of all worry as maladaptive, compared to rational problem-solving, whereas others think it better to verbally distinguish "helpful" and "unhelpful" ways to worry. In his book, *The Worry Cure*, Robert Leahy therefore encourages clients to differentiate productive from unproductive styles of worry (Leahy, 2005, p. 93). As worry tends to focus on perceived *problems*, there is some justification for comparing the concept of "unproductive worry" to negative problem orientation:

Unproductive worry

1. Dwells on unanswerable questions (or unsolvable problems).
2. Involves long chains of events leading to distant catastrophes.
3. Rejects potential solutions because they are not "perfect", that is, intolerant of uncertainty or risk.
4. Prolongs thinking in an attempt to reduce anxiety, that is, an endless search for safety.
5. Fails to distinguish between what can be controlled and what cannot.

According to Leahy, *productive* worry, by contrast, exhibits the opposing characteristics by focusing on problems that are plausible and realistic and the generation of immediate practical solutions. Productive worry is tolerant of uncertainty and does not dwell on hypothetical catastrophes in the distant future ("What if?" scenarios). I would add that productive worry and positive problem orientation probably focus on probabilities rather than possibilities, that is, on the most likely-case scenario rather than worst-case scenarios. To help manage unproductive worry, some CBT authors also recommend teaching anxious clients to use a simple "decision tree" or flowchart model (Butler, Fennell & Hackman, 2008, p. 186).

Worry decision tree

1. What are you worrying about? (Problem definition)
2. Can you actually do anything about it?
   a. No. Stop worrying and do something else to distract yourself. (End.)
   b. Yes. Work out what you could realistically do and make an action plan. (Problem-solving)
      i. Can you do anything practical right now? (Solution implementation)
         1. No. Plan when you are going to do it. Now stop worrying and do something else to distract yourself. (End.)
         2. Yes. Do it now. Now stop worrying and do something else to distract yourself. (End.)

Problem recognition and attribution require identifying whether the problem demands emotion-focused or problem-focused coping, that is, whether the problem is a practical and solvable one or whether it is a distant or unsolvable problem that demands emotional coping strategies rather than attempts to change the situation itself. Generally, the client should identify their problem thoughts, actions, and feelings as signals that an antecedent practical problem exists rather than assuming that their responses constitute the problem to be solved (Nezu, Nezu & Perri, 1989, p. 63). For example, if someone feels depressed about problems communicating in their relationship, labelling their feelings of depression as the problem to be solved (emotion-focused coping) should normally be a last resort. It will generally be preferable, and more adaptive, to make attempts to solve the practical (external) problems with communication or the relationship first (problem-focused coping) (D'Zurilla & Nezu, 2001, p. 223). The worry decision-tree model above assumes "distraction" as an emotion-focused coping strategy but in PST the client will normally be encouraged to evaluate alternative emotion-focused coping strategies and the specific tactics required to implement them, for example, "What specific techniques could you use to distract yourself?", "What other strategies might you want to consider instead of distraction?" For most clients, mindfulness and acceptance-based strategies may be superior initial responses to worry rather than attempts at distraction or thought-suppression, although the workability of different strategies should be carefully evaluated in collaboration with the client where possible (Hayes, Strosahl & Wilson, 2012).

One way of facilitating problem recognition is to think of "problems" as whatever we worry about. Similarly, clients can be asked to complete a form or checklist, rating their satisfaction with different domains of life, and explaining briefly the reasons for their ratings. This can help to "start the ball rolling", by generating more problems for the list, and provides an overview of the main problems in different areas of the client's life. Rating satisfaction seems to make it much easier for people to articulate their problems by asking themselves the question, "Why isn't it 100 per cent?" The developers of PST refer to a similar approach as "casting a problem horoscope" (Nezu, Nezu & Perri, 1989, pp. 147–148). This starts by looking at examples of problems across a range different areas of life, following which the therapist may help the client draw up a more conventional "problem list", focusing on the most relevant issues identified from the initial broad sweep (Hawton & Kirk, 1989, pp. 409–410).

Problem-domain analysis form

Rate your satisfaction in each of the following life domains. If it's below 100%, outline your main problems.

Problem domains

Work/Study (%)

Family (%)

Friends/Socialising (%)

Spouse/Partner (%)

Financial/Legal circumstances (%)

Interests/Hobbies (%)

Mental/Physical health (%)

Personal development (%)

Other areas of your life (%)

Developing a positive problem orientation, particularly problem recognition, leads on naturally to the following stage: problem definition and formulation.

Problem definition and formulation

Whereas problem orientation involves general beliefs about problems and coping, problem definitions are more concrete and situation-specific. (This loosely parallels the distinction between general schemas and specific appraisals of threat and vulnerability in Beck's cognitive model of anxiety.) Problem definition and formulation essentially involve developing a clear statement of the main problem, coming up with a specific statement of a relevant goal, and identifying what obstacles make it a problem to achieve the goal. It is the foundation upon which the subsequent components of problem-solving are built and the component of rational problem-solving style with the strongest empirical support (D'Zurilla & Nezu, 2007, p. 31). Definitions should therefore be as complete, objective, and accurate as possible. The PST literature tends to quote the philosopher John Dewey in this regard, who said, "A problem well-defined is half solved."

Problem definition therefore means stating one's problems and goals accurately, concisely, and objectively, without reference to too many assumptions or using too much emotive language. Problem definitions should aim to capture the heart or essence of a problem as clearly as possible and goals should be "SMART", that is, Specific, Measurable, Achievable, Relevant, and Time-limited. Vague definitions of problems or unrealistic goals are common reasons for failed problem-solving. Obstacles should be identified, as part of the problem formulation, as these explain "why the problem is a problem", that is, what currently prevents the client from solving the problem and achieving their goal. Defining a problem effectively can be broken down into five different steps (Nezu, Nezu & Perri, 1989, p. 71).

1. Seeking out the relevant facts.
2. Describing those facts clearly and concisely.
3. Separating out any unfounded assumptions or irrelevant information from the known facts.
4. Identifying what makes the problem a problem, for example, anticipating obstacles that might prevent the problem from being solved and the goal achieved.
5. Setting specific, measurable, achievable, relevant, and time-limited goals (SMART goals).

Sometimes it can be easier to state the goal first and then the problem. It's important that the client does not make the common error of confusing the problem her goal or a solution, for example, "My problem is that I want to earn more money." This is probably an assumed solution to an implicit and undefined problem, that is, "Why is what you earn at the moment causing a problem? What would you gain by earning more money?" The client may find that having gone through these steps, and specified the goal and potential obstacles, her original definition of the problem has to be revised, which tends to be a sign that some healthy reflection and reappraisal is occurring.

Clients are helped to define the problem situation by "sticking to the facts" and using concrete and unambiguous language, suspending the use of rhetoric or emotive language where possible and obtaining any information that's lacking. They are encouraged to answer the "W" questions, for example, as described in the form below (D'Zurilla & Nezu, 2007, p. 124). Where necessary, this can be set as a preliminary homework exercise, with the client encouraged to "seek out all the relevant facts" about the situation and their responses to it.

Problem definition: Asking the "W" questions

1. What does or doesn't happen that's particularly troubling you?
2. Where does the problem happen? Where are you when it happens?

> 3. Who is present when the problem occurs? Who is responsible for the problem? Who is affected by it?
>
> 4. When does the problem happen? When did it first begin? When does it need to be resolved by?
>
> 5. How do you respond to the problem? What are your typical thoughts, actions, and feelings at the time?
>
> 6. Why does the problem happen? (What causes it?) Why is it still a problem? Why do you respond the way you do?
>
> Summarise your definition of the problem:
>
> Rate your satisfaction with your definition of the problem (0–100%):
>
> If necessary, revise your definition of the problem below:

Problems can also be defined as the difference between "What is?" and "What should be?" Some reference to goals is therefore helpful in formulating problems completely. Goals in problem-solving therapy are often articulated as questions beginning "How can I …?" or "What can I do to …?" (D'Zurilla & Nezu, 2007, p. 129). Goals should ideally be defined according to the "SMART" acronym, where possible, as setting unrealistically demanding or complicated goals, which are not easily attainable, is a common tendency among anxious and depressed clients, who are prone to "set themselves up for failure." In some cases this may lead to a cycle of repeated efforts followed by failure to attain unrealistic standards, which may lead to a generalised sense of helplessness, lack of control, or incompetence (Nezu, Nezu & Perri, 1989, p. 81).

Sometimes it may be important to look for deeper underlying problems or goals. Problem-solving should not focus on problems that are too superficial. Once an initial goal is identified, the underlying need can be identified by repeatedly asking, "What do you want to achieve that for?" in a manner resembling the "downward arrow" technique used in cognitive therapy (Burns, 1980; D'Zurilla & Nezu, 2007, pp. 128–129) This age-old technique for identifying underlying needs or goals can be found even in the writings of Aristotle. Several factors have been identified by Nezu et al. as common obstacles to problem-solving, which the client can sometimes be asked about directly, as follows (D'Zurilla & Nezu, 2007, p. 128).

> **Some problem formulation questions**
>
> What's the problem ("what is")?
>
> What's your goal ("what should be")?

> What causes the problem?
>
> What obstacles prevent you from achieving your goal? Why haven't you achieved it already?
>
> To what extent are the following factors contributing to the problem (0–100%).
> Try to describe underneath specifically how these might be obstacles to achieving your goal.
> 1. Novelty or unfamiliarity (%)
>
> 2. Complexity (%)
>
> 3. Conflicting goals (%)
>
> 4. Skill deficits (%)
>
> 5. Lack of resources (%)
>
> 6. Uncertainty (%)
>
> 7. Emotional distress (%)
>
> 8. Other obstacles (%)

Most of these obstacles can potentially act as general modifying factors that further activate clients' schemas of personal vulnerability in response to threat, for example, the greater the uncertainty and ambiguity of a threat situation the more vulnerable the client is likely to feel (Clark & Beck, 2010, pp. 48–49). Once the problem has been adequately defined, and goals identified, it may be worthwhile re-appraising whether the problem is still considered relevant and serious enough to be worth addressing, and screening out possible "pseudo-problems." If the problem is badly defined, particularly if it contains too many assumptions, cognitive distortions, or loaded, emotive terms, the client is more likely to end up on a "wild goose chase" trying to solve an unsolvable, badly-formulated or illusory problem (Nezu, Nezu & Perri, 1989, p. 73).

During the problem definition stage, the therapist should be on the lookout not only for unfounded assumptions but also for the other types of cognitive distortions documented in cognitive therapy (Beck, Rush, Shaw & Emery, 1979; Burns, 1980; Clark & Beck, 2010). The client should be helped to identify any distortions that may contribute to the problem or interfere with problem orientation or problem-solving. In developing a problem definition, important distortions may include unfounded assumptions (mind-reading, fortune-telling), selective attention for evidence of threat and against evidence of safety, and discounting evidence of coping ability, catastrophising ("What if?" thinking), etc. Likewise, based on Beck's revised cognitive therapy for anxiety, it may be helpful to encourage simple reappraisal of threat and vulnerability, where anxiety is part of the problem situation.

> **Quick reappraisal of threat & vulnerability**
>
> What is the problem situation?
>
> **Threat appraisal**
> What's the worst that could realistically happen? (Threat appraisal)
>
> **Coping appraisal**
> How would you cope even if that did happen? (Coping appraisal)
>
> **Reappraisal**
> What evidence is there that you're probably safe from serious harm?
>
> What evidence is there that you would probably be able to cope?

As noted above, in PST distressing feelings are usually taken as signs of another problem that needs to be resolved, that is, the client is encouraged to ask themselves what message is contained in their feelings. However, problem-solving can also be used to reduce distressing feelings, for example, being applied to exposure therapy for phobic anxiety, etc. An example problem definition for a specific phobia, with the emotion-focused goal of reducing anxiety, might be as follows:

> "When I try to face my fears by watching a video of a blood donation, my anxiety increases, I think I'm going to faint, and have to look away and stop watching. What can I do to help tolerate my discomfort and remain in the situation until the anxious feelings actually reduce sufficiently?"

Formulation of the problem in PST can be developed by helping the client to explore simple common sense factors, which make the problem into a problem, or by sharing a research-based conceptualisation model, such as Beck's generic model of anxiety (Clark & Beck, 2010).

Generation of alternative solutions (brainstorming)

An attempt is made to think creatively and exhaustively about the range of options available in problem-solving, that is, to "brainstorm" or draw up a comprehensive list of possible solutions. A wide range of varied, alternative solutions is often helpful, and increases the sense of having a broad and flexible repertoire of strategies, knowing which can itself help to reduce anxiety by enhancing appraisal of coping ability. It is therefore particularly important to list as many solutions as possible first before evaluating them, as this is a common reason for becoming "side-tracked" and failing to identify the full range of options available. People who fail at problem-solving often identify one or two possible solutions and become distracted by analysis or evaluation of them before identifying the full range of options available to them. The creativity expert Alex Osborn therefore defined the three key variables in successful brainstorming as quantity, deferment of judgement, and variety (Osborn, 1952). As with many other CBT interventions, the therapist is advised to prompt the client by asking "Anything else?" until they have exhausted all their ideas, or even to "take a moment to think a bit longer about it and see if you can come up with anything you haven't thought of yet." Sometimes the best ideas come out last. However, when the client feels she has "run out of ideas" or hit a creative block, there are a number of adjunctive strategies, which can be used to generate even more proposed solutions.

Brainstorming alternatives may have additional cognitive and emotional benefits (Nezu, Nezu & D'Zurilla, 2007, p. 58). Generating alternatives appears to counteract dichotomous ("black-and-white") thinking about a problem, by introducing a broad spectrum of different interpretations of the situation. It reduces the inclination to act on impulse by encouraging planning and contemplation of the situation. It may also broaden the focus of attention and range of information being processed, which runs counter to the narrowing of attention and interpretative bias associated with stress and anxiety responses. Thinking about things from different perspectives and looking at the bigger picture can, therefore, often reduce emotional distress, as well as increasing the probability of a good solution being identified. Generating "wild ideas" can help fuel creative thinking, even if they are not practical solutions. However, in some cases the "quantity breeds quality" principle may be counter-productive unless alternatives are perceived as sufficiently relevant to the process. In one study, students who generated a higher number of irrelevant solutions to interpersonal problems actually reported a subsequent *increase* in symptoms of depression (Wierzbicki, 1984). Care should be taken, therefore, that the rationale for generation of alternatives is understood by the client and that she perceives this task as relevant to her goals.

The first consideration when generating specific alternatives is usually that there are probably "standing items" worthy of inclusion on the list for further evaluation. It shouldn't be assumed that the client is only to evaluate "good" options, because considering the pros and cons of existing bad strategies can be very worthwhile, insofar as it fuels the generation of other alternatives, or clarifies the motivation for adopting new alternative solutions. The client should therefore normally include "do nothing" or "continue what you're already doing" (more of the same) as standing items on any list, although these may need to be broken down into specific tactics (see below), that is, "What does it mean to do nothing?", "What exactly are you currently doing to cope with this problem?" Actually, for some clients "doing nothing", especially if that means *abandoning* unhelpful behaviours ("response prevention") may be the best solution. Sometimes "less is more". However, this can be very difficult to achieve if there is a strong urge to perform maladaptive behavioural responses such as safety-seeking behaviours or subtle avoidance.

Distinguishing between "strategies" and "tactics" is often helpful at this stage (D'Zurilla & Nezu, 2007, p. 133). "Strategies" are general solutions, which can be broken down further into several more specific tactics. For example, a client who suffers from needle phobia might agree with her therapist that exposure therapy constitutes one general strategy that can be evaluated, whereas avoidance, cognitive restructuring, and hypnotic suggestion, provide others. Thinking in terms of these broad categories of solution is useful because clients often overlook whole strategies, that is, she may make assumptions about the best overall strategy and focus on different ways of putting it into practice (tactics) without considering whether there might be entirely different alternative strategies worth exploring. Therapists should be on the lookout for this common mistake, which is a kind of "tunnel vision". As the saying goes, "There's more than one way to skin a cat". There's more than one way (or "strategy") to solve a problem. Therapists should generally hold back on giving too much advice, and encourage clients instead to take responsibility for generating their own alternatives However, the therapist may sometimes need to prompt the client to consider broad solution strategies that are obviously being overlooked (Nezu, Nezu & Perri, 1989, p. 182). The client can then be encouraged to "fill in" the specific alternative tactics that might be used to implement new strategies. For example, the therapist might say, "You haven't mentioned anything about learning to fully accept your anxiety until it abates naturally, how does that sound as a strategy?" and "How specifically might you go about doing that?"

Of course, because strategies are broad in scope, they are also usually vague, and it's important to "get specific" in problem-solving, which leads to the generation of a range of individual tactics for each general strategy. The needle phobic may brainstorm different tactics for the general strategy of using exposure therapy to combat her problem, for example, using imaginal exposure on a memory or an anticipated event, observing a video clip of an injection taking place, handling a needle, having an actual injection, etc. Another important factor, which overlaps with decision-making, is the synthesis or merging of certain ideas produced during brainstorming. Different strategies or specific tactics may be combined, for example, the strategy of exposure therapy could be combined with using hypnotic suggestion—the two aren't necessarily mutually exclusive. Merging ideas can often trigger creativity and produce fresh suggestions, contributing to the process of generating alternatives. A final course of action, that should not be used prematurely, is for the client to seek advice or suggested solutions from other sources such as experts, books, or the internet (D'Zurilla & Nezu, 2007, p. 135). Depending too much on other people's solutions may hinder the development of problem-solving ability and self-confidence, however, so this is not an "elegant" way of generating alternatives.

A number of Socratic questioning strategies can contribute to the creative thinking process, mainly by encouraging the client to explore different perspectives on their problem. Meichenbaum particularly recommended beginning problem-solving simply by asking the client how they would advise someone else to deal with a similar problem (Meichenbaum, 1985, p. 68). This kind of technique aims to "distance" the client from their own emotions and limiting beliefs by encouraging them to adopt a different perspective. A similar method of generating alternatives by perspective-shifting is, for example, to ask how various other people might respond (or advise the client to respond) to the same situation. Clients can also imagine how they might deal with the situation if they possessed certain "strengths" or virtues, for example, "How would a wise person handle this?", "How about a courageous person?", "How would a patient person approach this problem?", "How would a creative person respond?", etc. Time projection can be used to change perspective, for example, asking "How have you (or would you have) coped with similar problems in the past?", or "In the future, when you've made progress, how do you think you'll cope with similar problems?", etc. It's important to use questioning to encourage clients to explore these perspectives in some detail rather than being satisfied with superficial answers, that is, to investigate specifically how they or others could cope with similar problems under different circumstances. A set of questions can be provided on a homework form, like the one below, to help the client learn typical perspective-shifting questions and other ways of creatively generating alternatives.

> **Some questions for creative solution-generation**
>
> 1. What specifically is the problem?
> 2. What specifically is your goal?
> 3. What have you done in the past to cope with similar problems?
> 4. What haven't you tried yet?
> 5. What would you advise someone you care about to do in a similar situation?
> 6. Think of someone you respect or admire. What would they do?
> 7. What do you think people you respect would advise you to do?
> 8. Who could you approach for help?
> 9. List all the other resources you can draw upon to cope?
> 10. What would a creative person do?
> 11. What would a wise person do?
> 12. What would a courageous person do?
> 13. What would be the easiest thing to do?
> 14. What would be the most effective solution possible? What's the ideal solution?
> 15. Overall, what do you think the best or most realistic solution would be?

As described below, hypnosis can be useful as a means of fostering creativity, for example, by the use of suggestion scripts to cultivate an attitude of creativity and to help clients imagine different perspectives on their problems, that is, through time projection of the kind employed in Melges' future autobiography technique, etc., an imagery technique we shall be examining shortly (Melges, 1982, p. 265).

Decision-making (evaluation of alternative solutions)

Decision-making essentially involves identifying the best solution. For some clients, it may be an effort to abandon their desire for a "perfect solution" and act pragmatically, upon the best option available, but they should normally be encouraged to do so. Each potential solution should normally be evaluated, perhaps after "rough screening out" of obviously unsuitable ideas. There are different ways of evaluating proposed solutions but they usually involve cost-benefit analysis, that is, consideration of the short and long-term consequences (pros and cons) of each option, and perhaps consideration both of the personal and social consequences, where relevant. Failure to predict the consequences of different options or to evaluate them adequately is a common error in problem-solving. However, a slightly different approach, which may better suit some clients, involves evaluating different solutions by rating how consistent they appear to be with the client's most important personal values (Hayes, Strosahl & Wilson, 2012). For example, a client who particularly values "integrity" might make a decision by considering which potential solution would be most consistent with her desire to act with integrity, if that's her priority.

Once a variety of solutions have been brainstormed, one of two main situations will tend to arise:

1. The client may be left with a series of *alternative* options to choose from, which may be mutually exclusive. The pros and cons of each option may be evaluated, before each alternative is rated for satisfactoriness. The client can then select the best option from those identified.
2. The client may be left with a series of solutions which can be synthesised or *merged* into a single "best" option. The emphasis falls upon the best way to combine solutions, rather than the best way to choose between them.

Sometimes certain options will be self-evidently unsatisfactory and may be rejected immediately ("rough screening") or others may be self-evidently preferable. Where appropriate the weighing-up of pros and cons can be dispensed with as superfluous in order to streamline the decision-making process. In other words, it's unhelpful to take too much time over decision-making and labour things unnecessarily. On the other hand, careful evaluation of consequences can be crucial in some cases.

It can be useful to rate potential solutions in a number of different ways, perhaps chosen collaboratively with the client. One of the simplest methods is to simply rate satisfaction with each proposed solution out of three, using stars or asterisks. A more elaborate method is to rate each proposed solution from 0–100 per cent in terms of three major criteria (D'Zurilla & Nezu, 2007, pp. 136–137).

1. The probability of the solution *working*, that is, achieving the stated goals (outcome expectancy).
2. The client's estimate of their *ability* to actually put the solution into practice (confidence, or self-efficacy).
3. The value of the solution in term of positive (pros) and negative (cons) *consequences*, including both short and long-term, and personal and social consequences.

Note that evaluating specific proposed solutions in terms of these criteria can modify the client's more general problem orientation, in the same way that restructuring automatic thoughts or appraisals in cognitive therapy can affect underlying beliefs and schemas. Rating the probability that solutions will work can help to modify the "outcome expectancy" part of clients' "perceive control", that is, their belief (optimism) that their problems are generally solvable in principle. Rating their estimate of their own ability to put the solution into practice can modify the "self-efficacy" part of perceived control, improving problem-solving confidence. Rating the likelihood of a solution working independently from the client's confidence about implementing it is important. It is often the case that an "ideal solution" is suggested, which would work extremely well in theory, but which the client feels unable to implement. There will also be "easy options" and "quick fixes", which the client is confident about trying but which are unlikely to satisfactorily resolve the main problem.

The developers of PST recommend employing a simplified rating scale for most problems, unless they are particularly complicated. This involves asking the following three or four questions for each solution and simply rating it minus one (negative), zero (neutral), or plus one (positive) (D'Zurilla & Nezu, 2007, pp. 137–138).

1. Will this solution actually solve the problem and help achieve my goal?
2. Will I be able to carry it out?
3. What are the personal consequences (both short and long-term)?
4. Where appropriate: What are the social consequences (both short and long-term)?

After rating different solutions in this way, the client can be asked to consider how advantages can be maximised and disadvantages minimised or prevented, or how solutions can be made more likely to solve the problem, or easier to implement, etc. Hence, rating solutions tends to actually provide an opportunity for further creative improvements to the range of suggestion, for example, the therapist might ask "You only rated your satisfaction with that proposed solution fifty per cent, but can you think of any ways to improve it and make it *more* satisfactory?"

An alternative approach involves dividing decision-making into two stages in which the client first chooses between different general strategies and then conducts a second level of brainstorming to determine what specific tactics would be best in order to apply the chosen strategy. For instance, a client whose problem involves bullying at work might choose between various general strategies such as doing nothing, making a complaint, avoiding the bully, confronting them assertively, etc. Assuming they chose to act assertively, they might then try to brainstorm and choose between specific tactics such as the broken record, three-step assertion methods, fixed-role therapy, etc. Mental imagery is also used sometimes in PST in the form of imaginal behavioural rehearsal, employed to explore the consequences of different proposed solutions (D'Zurilla & Nezu, 2007, pp. 138–139). Hypnotism can sometimes aid in decision-making by helping clients to better envisage the likely outcome of certain proposed solutions, for example, by using "time projection" in hypnosis to vividly picture the short, medium, and long-term consequences of one or more options in detail and evaluate them more carefully.

Solution implementation and verification

The final stage of problem-solving consists of developing an action plan, broken down into logical steps, putting it into practice, properly evaluating its effectiveness and reflecting on the outcome. This may start another cycle of problem-solving, if a plan isn't completely successful. People who procrastinate often find it difficult to complete this stage but no matter how good their plans are on paper they'll only really learn by testing them out in practice. The client may have to develop a "contingency plan" (Plan B) to cope with possible setbacks but that should be part of her preparation where necessary and the process of generating alternatives should already have provided suggestions for a backup plan.

The client is encouraged to adopt a "trial and error" or "experimental" attitude rather than expecting her plan to work perfectly first time, a common form of "all-or-nothing" thinking that frequently needs to be addressed. Complex solution plans may need to be broken down into more manageable sub-goals. Skills required can be rehearsed during sessions and emotions, such as anxiety about performing certain tasks, can be addressed with standard CBT interventions. Solution implementation and verification can be divided into four components:

1. *Performance*, that is, confronting the problem and applying the coping skills (solution-implementation proper, "doing").
2. *Self-monitoring*, that is, observation and recording of the actual performance and outcome
3. *Self-evaluation*, that is, reflection on the outcome, comparison against goal, and consolidation of learning.
4. *Self-reinforcement* and troubleshooting, that is, self-reward and self-praise and possibly recycling the problem-solving procedure.

Solution implementation can be compared to the notion of "behavioural experiments" in cognitive therapy, and it may be of value to explore the client's initial predictions about the outcome and to help them reflect on whether these are confirmed or disconfirmed by the actual outcome observed (Dobson & Dobson, 2009, p. 84). Whereas the emphasis in cognitive therapy is on forming hypotheses (predictions) and comparing them to the results of the experiment, problem-solving therapy, like earlier forms of behaviour therapy, is more focused on developing and reinforcing coping skills. Solution implementation is therefore also referred to as a form of coping performance (Nezu, Nezu & Perri, 1989, p. 29) and in Meichenbaum's stress-inoculation terminology it may be considered a form of confrontation with the stressor and application of the planned coping skills (Meichenbaum, 1985). Of course, solution implementation also frequently entails a form of *in vivo* exposure to feared situations, where PST is being used in the treatment of anxiety-related problems.

Where avoidance or procrastination are issues, especially where solution implementation involves facing a feared situation, it can be helpful to have clients undertake a "motivation review" by listing in detail the advantages of solving their problem and the disadvantages of inaction (D'Zurilla & Nezu, 2007, p. 142). These points can be written down, perhaps on a cue card, as reminders to the help the client boost her motivation outside of the consulting room. Sometimes clients may lack certain skills or experience anxiety about putting their plan into action, and this can lead to the use of other CBT techniques in preparation, such as behavioural rehearsal and cognitive restructuring, etc.

Meichenbaum proposed, based on his research, that Self-Instruction Training could be combined with problem-solving (1977) and this method is included in PST training manuals (D'Zurilla & Nezu, 2007, pp. 141–142; Nezu, Nezu & D'Zurilla, 2007, p. 34). For example, therapists might encourage clients to mentally rehearse their planned solution while talking to themselves aloud, and use Socratic questioning to help them modify their self-talk, gradually fading the speech. (See the chapter on cognitive therapy in this volume for a more detailed account of self-instruction training, in relation to hypnotherapy.) D'Zurilla & Nezu provide a detailed account of a "rapid problem-solving" protocol, which consists mainly of self-instructions (D'Zurilla & Nezu, 2007, pp. 145–146). Similar self-instructions can be incorporated in a self-hypnosis routine. Indeed, hypnosis can help with solution implementation in a number of other ways, most obviously in the use of mental rehearsal to build confidence and further refine the plan of action.

Solution implementation & verification

1. Which alternatives should you choose?
   (Try to incorporate your most highly-rated proposals in an action plan and describe the steps below.)

2. How satisfactory is your action plan (0–100%)? What could you do to improve it?

3. What obstacles might you encounter? How can you deal with them?

4. When are you going to begin putting your plan into action? What's the first step?

5. How will you evaluate the outcome? What will tell you that your plan has worked?

6. Now try it out! Rate your overall satisfaction with the outcome (0–100%):

7. What actually happened?
   (If appropriate, describe the personal, social, short-term and long-term consequences of your actions.)

8. What have you learned from the experience?

9. What do you plan to do next?

(Reward yourself for what you did well and consider going through the problem-solving steps again if necessary.)

Reflection on the overall process of problem-solving can be helpful, especially during training. It may also be helpful to ask clients to directly rate their satisfaction with their performance on the component skills, as in the form below.

> **Problem-solving self-evaluation questions**
>
> You should set time aside to reflect on things properly afterwards. After rating yourself on each item below, take time to write down what you learned and what you might do differently next time, if appropriate. Also consider where things went wrong in terms of which stage in problem-solving could have been done better.
>
> 1. Did you adopt a positive problem-solving attitude throughout? Rate yourself 0–100% ( )
>
> 2. Did you define your problem and goal specifically and accurately enough? Rate yourself 0–100% ( )
>
> 3. Did you brainstorm a wide enough variety of alternative solutions and consider different general strategies? Rate yourself 0–100% ( )
>
> 4. Did you predict and evaluate the possible consequences of your chosen solution adequately? Rate yourself 0–100% ( )
>
> 5. Did you plan and put your chosen solution into practice satisfactorily? Rate yourself 0–100% ( )
>
> This can form the basis of another problem definition, addressing residual problems in light of your experience. Problem-solving can be a circular process where feedback at the end of one cycle of problem-solving becomes the starting point for another cycle.

Example PSH treatment plan

The components of a problem-solving approach to *hypnotherapy* can be covered in any number of different ways, and should be tailored to the individual needs of the client. Some components may need considerable work, whereas others can sometimes be omitted entirely. However, an example of a generic plan of treatment, based on the template provided by D'Zurilla & Nezu (2007, p. 103) might look as follows:

1. Initial assessment, introduction, and socialisation to approach, including treatment rationale and definition of roles, assignment of initial self-monitoring homework.
2. Training in positive problem-orientation self-hypnosis skills training, and scripted self-hypnosis recording as homework to develop problem-solving attitude (this may require more than one session in some cases).
3. Training in problem definition and formulation, rehearsal of evocative imagery in hypnosis to define problem situation and identify thoughts, actions, feelings, etc., use of goal imagery or future autobiography in hypnosis to define concrete SMART goals and build motivation.
4. Training in generation of alternatives, use of hypnosis for relaxation, to manage emotional arousal, and suggestions of creative thinking, exploring alternative perspectives, etc.

5. Training in decision-making and prediction of consequences, using hypnotic time projection (age progression) to explore specific consequences of different courses of action (solutions).
6. Training in solution implementation, using repeated imaginal behavioural rehearsal in hypnosis to improve the action plan, rehearse skills, and reduce anxiety, to build motivation and confidence, etc., possible combination of self-instruction training and autosuggestion, or relaxation coping skills, for use during solution implementation between sessions.
7. Further training and guided practice in applying complete method to remaining (or hypothetical) problems to encourage generalisation and build resilience to future stressors.

A simple self-monitoring homework exercise can be used in the earlier stages of therapy, between sessions, whereby the client records the following information on a form in order to retrospectively self-monitor their daily (or weekly) coping with real-life problems (D'Zurilla & Nezu, 2007, p. 107; Nezu, Nezu & Perri, 1989, p. 128). Standard CBT self-monitoring forms can easily be adapted for this purpose, asking the clients to record, on a daily basis, the date and time of situations where they encountered a problem, and recording their thoughts, feelings, and actions (coping strategies), etc.

Brief record of problem-solving/coping attempts

What was the problem you encountered? (Date/Time)

What thoughts did you have before, during, and after the problem?

What feelings did you experience before, during, and after the problem?

What behaviours did you engage in to try to solve the problem or cope with it?

Rate your satisfaction with your coping 0–100%:

To this can be added, for example, ratings of belief (0–100 per cent) in thoughts, strength of emotions (0–100 per cent), and reflections on learning ("What would you do differently next time?"). In later sessions, a more detailed form can be introduced for planned (prospective) problem-solving, for example:

Brief problem-solving planning form

1. What specifically is the problem?

2. What specifically is your goal?

> 3. List and review your motives to change things.
>
> 4. Brainstorm as many alternative solutions as possible (deferring evaluation until the end). (Continue on another sheet of paper if necessary. When finished rate your satisfaction with each option from 0–100%)
>
> 5. Choose the best proposed solution or merge ideas and summarise your decision.
>
> 6. What are the pros (advantages) of your chosen solution?
>
> 7. What are the cons (disadvantages) of your chosen solution?
>
> 8. How can you maximise the pros and minimise or prevent the cons?
>
> 9. Plan and schedule the individual steps required to put the best solution into action.

Problem-solving, reflective-practice, and supervision

Problem-solving provides an eminent example of a therapeutic approach which can be applied *reflexively*, that is, to the therapist himself. There are some similarities between problem-solving methodologies in CBT and "reflective practice" models, hence therapists may choose to use problem-solving to help them cope with critical incidents arising during therapy sessions (Gibbs, 1988). Likewise, supervisors may find problem-solving methods useful as a methodology for helping supervisees handle difficulties they encounter in working with clients. Supervision may often take the form of reflecting on critical incidents during therapy and applying problem-solving methods to them.

Dobson & Dobson have pointed out that *all* CBT can be construed as entailing a form of problem-solving, although the therapist normally contributes more to the conceptualisation of the problem and selection of proposed solutions (treatment strategies) in other forms of CBT than he does in pure problem-solving therapy. Speaking of the PST methodology derived from D'Zurilla and Nezu, they write that:

> […] the problem-solving model is a metaphor for cognitive-behavioral therapy in general, and therapists are encouraged to also approach their clients' problems from a generic problem-solving orientation. When working with an individual client, though, we might or might not be explicit about the model itself. (Dobson & Dobson, 2009, p. 86).

Indeed, Beck's original cognitive therapy manual for anxiety was based upon a simplified problem-solving methodology, to be employed by the therapist in choosing treatment strategies and interventions (Beck, Emery & Greenberg, 2005, p. 181). Beck et al. described this in terms of four steps, which might be labelled as follows using the terminology familiar from PST in brackets:

1. Conceptualise the patient's problem, that is, develop a working hypothesis or problem formulation (Problem definition and formulation).
2. Choose a general treatment strategy based on the conceptualisation (Strategies).
3. Choose a specific treatment intervention (tactic) based on the strategy (Tactics).
4. Evaluate the outcome and repeat the cycle (Solution implementation and verification).

They don't explicitly mention generation or evaluation of *alternative* strategies and tactics, although consideration of different options does seem to be implied in their use of the word "choose."

Beck et al. note that whereas novice therapists tend to be more focused on the "toolbox" of techniques (tactics), more experienced therapists are more concerned with arriving at an accurate conceptualisation of the client's problem and deriving from it an overall treatment strategy and rationale. The process goals of CBT can be seen as "strategies": for example, reducing exaggerated appraisals of threat probability might be a strategy, which could be achieved by several tactics or techniques, such as questioning the evidence from past experience, comparing appraisals in the anxious and non-anxious modes, or carrying out a behavioural experiment to empirically test a specific hypothesis or prediction based on the threat appraisal, etc. Strategies and tactics should have a rationale based on the conceptualisation but there is always an acknowledged degree of "trial and error" or experimentation, and interventions that do not go as predicted should be viewed as providing feedback that can be used to re-evaluate the conceptualisation.

Problem-solving in hypnotherapy

Some possible ways in which hypnosis can be utilised in problem-solving therapy have been mentioned above. "Visualisation" is a core principle of PST and several mental imagery techniques are therefore used throughout the different stages, along with various "self-instruction" strategies, discussed above. These resemble the use of focused attention on mental imagery and verbal autosuggestions common in hypnotherapy. Hypnotherapy has seldom been explicitly combined with problem-solving therapy but doing so may be justified by the following considerations:

1. Both hypnotherapy and PST are brief interventions, typically delivered over about five or six sessions.
2. PST appears to be a relatively *generic* approach applicable to a wide range of presenting problems, including the kind dealt with in hypnotherapy.
3. PST is a simple technique, requiring minimal training, which makes it easier in practice to integrate it with other approaches.
4. PST emphasises simple therapeutic concepts, such as SMART goal-setting, which are familiar to many hypnotherapists from fields such as life coaching, and self-help literature.

Hypnotherapy techniques can be used in combination with problem-solving therapy in the following ways:

1. Hypnotherapy can be used, through relaxation and suggestion, to manage emotional arousal in a way that is believed to facilitate the different stages of problem-solving, for example, by reducing stress and anxiety during the procedures and enhancing positive emotions (D'Zurilla & Nezu, 2007, p. 56).
2. Hypnotherapy is well-suited to the development of cognitive sets ("mind-sets") by means of direct suggestion, especially in the form of self-hypnosis recordings, which could be used between sessions to enhance problem-solving orientation and confidence.
3. Hypnotherapy can be used to help problem definition and formulation by having clients imagine themselves in a problem situation, while describing in detail their thoughts, actions, and feelings—a form of "evocative imagery" not unlike regression hypnotherapy.
4. Hypnotherapy can be used to help "SMART" goal definition by having clients mentally rehearse their desired outcomes and elaborate in detail upon their thoughts, actions, feelings, etc.
5. Rehearsing goal imagery is already used in PST to increase motivation and this technique can easily be replicated and perhaps enhanced in hypnosis.
6. Hypnotherapy may facilitate the adoption of alternative perspectives and encourage creative thinking, which can facilitate the generation of alternative solutions.
7. Hypnotherapy may facilitate the use of mental rehearsal techniques, which allow clients to explore the consequences of proposed solutions using mental imagery, rehearse skills and develop confidence, in preparation for implementing their chosen solution and action plan.

There are three main ways in which traditional hypnotic interventions may be employed in support of PST, which can be loosely summarised in terms of the three systems (ABC) model.

1. *Affect* may be directly regulated by hypnotic relaxation techniques
2. *Behaviour* (solutions) may be rehearsed in hypnotic imagery
3. *Cognition* (orientation) may be directly modified by the use of self-instructions or hypnotic scripts and autosuggestions.

The developers of PST observed that relaxation training, using progressive muscle relaxation, breathing, meditation, imagery, etc., can serve a double purpose (Nezu, Nezu & Perri, 1989, p. 194). Relaxation may facilitate certain aspects of the problem-solving process, as discussed below. However, it is also a common coping strategy in its own right and, for example, is commonly employed in stress inoculation training and other "coping skills" approaches to therapy. The client therefore potentially learns a method that benefits her at two levels simultaneously, making it easier to engage in problem-solving but also providing part of the solution to some common problems.

Many different labels are attached to visualisation techniques employed in therapy. The specific term "cognitive rehearsal" is used to describe a variety of mental imagery techniques used in cognitive therapy. The use of cognitive rehearsal in problem-solving has been described as follows:

It refers to the detailed rehearsal in imagination of a particular task, including the details of the steps taken and the consequences. It is useful for helping a patient develop confidence in attempting a task, in identifying possible pitfalls that were not immediately obvious, and in establishing more clearly the likely consequences, including advantages and disadvantages, of a course of action. (Hawton & Kirk, 1989, pp. 421–422)

Of course, cognitive rehearsal can be employed in a state of heightened focused attention on the task, enhanced self-confidence, and with the use of autosuggestions, in hypnotherapy. When combining mental rehearsal with problem-solving, it's useful to make a distinction between two stages at which it functions in different ways.

1. *Generating alternatives.* By going through a series of events in their imagination the client can be helped to work through their thoughts and feelings and creatively generate alternative ways of coping. This often requires more interaction with the therapist than usual and may be better done prior to a formal hypnotic induction.
2. *Solution implementation.* Once a firm plan has been agreed, the client can rehearse it several times in her imagination, during hypnosis, to strengthen her motivation and resolve final details. Clients may still be making some modifications to their plan but if they are making too many changes, and still at the stage of generating alternatives, it may be better to approach the use of imagery in a different way, for example, without formal hypnosis.

We will consider some examples of hypnotic imagery and suggestion techniques in more detail.

Hypnotic problem orientation

Self-hypnosis is an ideal method for encouraging a positive problem-orientation because direct suggestions, such as ego-strengthening scripts, naturally lend themselves to the modification of attitudinal sets (Curwen, Palmer & Ruddell, 2000, pp. 140–142 ; Heap & Aravind, 2002, pp. 126–133). Dowd explicitly discusses the use of hypnosis to enhance problem-solving ability, with reference to his own research on the application of problem-solving to anxiety, in his book *Cognitive Hypnotherapy* (Dowd, 2000, pp. 190–195). After reviewing the components of PST, he concludes that problem orientation and problem definition seem particularly amenable to treatment by hypnosis and he provides examples of hypnotic scripts for enhancing both of these areas, incorporating typical ego-strengthening suggestions and confidence-building, etc.

A number of other hypnotists have provided example direct suggestion or mental imagery scripts designed to encourage creative problem-solving attitudes. For example, one published hypnotherapy script for problem-solving contains the following suggestions:

> In the coming days and weeks, your thoughts will often turn to the consideration of important decisions you have to make, and important problems for which you have as yet found no solution. Even when you are not consciously thinking about these topics, your mind will

> continue to deal with them so that, when your attention returns to them once more, you are going to be surprised and delighted at how many potentially useful ideas you are able to come up with [...] you are going to be surprised and pleased at how much more clearly and creatively you are going to be able to think, and at how much more confidently and effectively you will be able to deal with the issues and problems which lie before you. (Gibbons, quoted in Hammond, 1990, p. 130).

By listening to a generic problem-orientation script on a self-hypnosis recording each day, the client can help themselves to "get into the right mind-set" for problem-solving.

In PST, imagery techniques are specifically recommended as a means of improving problem-solving confidence and perceived control (D'Zurilla & Nezu, 2007, pp. 110–112). The client is asked to picture herself having *already* solved a significant problem. The rationale is that by visualising success the client experiences covert reinforcement, increases motivation, and begins to see herself as more competent (self-efficacious) and less helpless or vulnerable, and the problem as more solvable. The client is then asked questions such as, "How is your life different now the problem is solved?", "How are your feelings changed?", "What are you doing differently?", etc. (Nezu, Nezu & D'Zurilla, 2007, p. 29) This technique closely resembles *hypnotic* age progression and, in particular, the "future autobiography" technique of Melges, employed in Beck's cognitive therapy of anxiety (Beck, Emery & Greenberg, 2005; Melges, 1982, p. 265). The client's comments during this exercise can be recorded to be reviewed later. Melges emphasised that the use of hypnotic age progression in this way could help overcome the sense of uncertainty, intolerance of which frequently inhibits anxious clients from problem-solving.

> Future autobiography is another short-term [hypnotic] rehearsal technique that helps patients structure their plans of action according to their chosen goals. [...] In executing the future autobiography, it is important that the patient pretends it is one week ahead (or more) and looks back. This enhances a greater differentiation of what is likely to happen and also reduces the uncertainty of future events by making them seem as already accomplished facts. By contrast, if the patient talks about coming events of the week ahead by using the future tense, there are a host of ifs, ands, and buts. Thus the therapist has more to work on if he insists that the patient use the past tense to describe the one week ahead. If the patient describes a stultifying event, the therapist asks: "What did you do then, what options did you find? ... And when you did that, how did you feel inside? ... Which chosen-goal for yourself did you feel closer to?" (Melges, 1982, p. 265)

Where the client experiences difficulty imagining herself having overcome her problem, she is asked to begin imagining someone else (a role model) having overcome the problem first.

Likewise, two of the leading cognitive-behavioural theorists in the field of hypnosis, Lynn and Kirsch, describe an example hypnotic script involving imagery of a "wise inner advisor" and also describe the use of imaginal behavioural rehearsal and age progression during hypnosis to enhance problem-solving (Lynn & Kirsch, 2006, pp. 70–73). The form of hypnotic age progression they describe using for problem-solving, again, resembles the "future autobiography" method, which we shall shortly be discussing in relation to Beck's cognitive therapy (Beck, Emery & Greenberg, 2005; Melges, 1982).

> Imaginative rehearsal and finding exceptions to the problem can be done in the context of [hypnotic] age progression in which patients are asked to imagine a future time in which they have resolved their problems and take note of the steps taken to improve their lives. (Lynn & Kirsch, 2006, pp. 72–73)

As mentioned above, the developers of PST actually provide a full "visualisation script" in their self-help manual, *Solving Life's Problems*, which clearly resembles a *hypnotherapy* script, although they do not label it as such. They recommend using it by having a friend read it aloud or recording it on a tape and playing it back, which will be a familiar practice to hypnotherapists, who would prescribe self-hypnosis recordings for homework use in the same way. The subject is asked at the beginning to "Close your eyes and relax – let go of any tension in your body" and the script proceeds to describe a detailed metaphorical journey up a steep hill and through a dark forest, at the end of which the subject reviews her life in the future, focusing on her achievements (Nezu, Nezu & D'Zurilla, 2007, pp. 107–108). Again, this can be described as a form of time projection, similar to "hypnotic age progression", and Melges' hypnotic "future autobiography" technique. After reflecting on things from this perspective in the future, the subject finishes the exercise, returning to the "here and now", and writes down one or two ideas for major personal goals, which naturally leads on to problem definition.

Hypnotic problem definition and formulation

Imagery techniques similar to those used in other forms of CBT to assist conceptualisation can be used in the process of problem definition. When this is carried out in hypnosis, imagery may be made more vivid and realistic, as in hypnotic age regression or progression techniques. In PST clients are sometimes asked to close their eyes and describe a recent example of a problem situation, or sometimes an anticipated future problem (D'Zurilla & Nezu, 2007, p. 125; Nezu, Nezu & D'Zurilla, 2007, p. 45). This is initially done from a *first*-person perspective, as if the situation is happening now. The client is asked to describe her thoughts, actions, and feelings, as if she is currently experiencing them. In a second stage, the client is asked to shift perspective and review the same situation from a *third*-person (external) perspective, as though watching herself on a television set or in a movie clip, played in slow motion, while the she describes her thoughts, actions, and feelings as observed from the outside. This information should be noted down (externalised) and reviewed carefully in preparing a definition and formulation of the problem to be addressed. The technique can be further enhanced through direct suggestions of vividness and clarity, and combining time-expansion, or slow-motion, with suggestions of heightened awareness, particularly of low-intensity cues and relevant thoughts, actions, and feelings, etc. The "W" questions can, as always, be used to help the client identify relevant information.

Hypnotic generation of alternatives and decision-making

In PST, mental imagery is already used to enhance generation of alternatives. The client may be asked to repeatedly picture herself trying to cope with the problem situation, or to picture someone else, a role model, doing so (D'Zurilla & Nezu, 2007, p. 134; Nezu, Nezu & D'Zurilla, 2007, p. 63). Rehearsal of concrete imagery may generate new ideas about solving the problem. Of course, hypnosis can be used to facilitate vivid imagery and positive problem orientation, through suggestions of confidence in coping, creativity, etc.

Moreover, there are reasons to think that specific techniques of hypnotherapy may potentially be of benefit in facilitating both the creativity required for generation of alternatives and concreteness, which aids solution evaluation. In a recent article on hypnosis and cognitive-behavioural therapies for depression, Michael Yapko cites research suggesting that abstract, global thinking in depression tends to impair problem-solving.

> By stating a problem in global terms, no specific solution can be identified, thus there is no specific action to take. The result is a subjective sense of being "stuck," i.e., unable to move forward in a meaningful way. (Yapko, 2010, p. 189)

He provides scripted suggestions designed to address this issue directly by using hypnosis to encourage concrete thinking about problem-solving goals.

> […] the client with a global cognitive style is taught to recognize his or her overgeneral thinking, its negative effect on taking appropriate action, the importance of developing concrete and specific problem definitions, and the essential role of taking action with an effective problem-solving strategy. Following hypnosis, the client can be given a homework assignment to actively carry out in order to start building the skill of developing effective behavioral sequences. (Yapko, 2010, p. 191)

D'Zurilla & Nezu conclude from consideration of the research on stress and problem-solving that emotional arousal may sometimes have a facilitative effect but is more commonly a source of interference during all four stages of problem-solving, especially the generation of alternatives where stress or anxiety may narrow attention onto task-irrelevant cues and restrict decision-making to the most stereotypical and obvious solutions (D'Zurilla & Nezu, 2007, pp. 56–57). They recommend the use of Self-Instruction Training, progressive muscle relaxation, desensitisation, and imaginal rehearsal, which are obviously techniques that closely resemble the use of autosuggestion, relaxation, and mental rehearsal in hypnotherapy (D'Zurilla & Nezu, 2007, p. 59).

Beck also recognised that the natural adaptive tendency to "widen orientation", constructing and entertaining a range of perspectives on a situation, could be "foreclosed" by catastrophic anxiety-provoking thoughts, leaving the individual stuck in a narrow orientation to threat (Alford & Beck, 1997, pp. 21–22). In a similar vein, Borkovec has described how his research suggests relaxation can be used to facilitate the generation of alternative perspectives in cognitive-behavioural therapy for generalised anxiety disorder.

We often have clients generate a deeply relaxed state just prior to conducting CT [cognitive therapy], especially that portion of therapy involving the generation of alternative perspectives. Increased parasympathetic tone provides for more flexible attentional deployment, and reduction of anxious states via relaxation facilitates more flexible and more accurate thinking in general. A pilot data study supports this: After choosing their two most pressing worries, half of the participants relaxed via slow diaphragmatic breathing, whereas participants in the other half worried about one of their topics. They then wrote down as many possible outcomes to the second worry as they could think of. People who worried first generated mostly negative outcomes, whereas people who relaxed first listed mostly positive outcomes. (Borkovec & Sharpless, 2004, p. 228)

Clearly, the use of other relaxation techniques, such as those commonly employed in hypnotherapy, may potentially have similar benefits and the generation of alternative perspectives in cognitive therapy is a very similar process to generating alternative solutions during problems-solving. Again, the use of direct suggestions for developing a creative attitude used in combination with relaxation is likely to compound the potential benefits.

Evaluation of different solutions and decision-making is less well-suited to hypnotherapy. However, by having clients mentally rehearse several alternative strategies or tactics they can make a comparison between them more easily. Also, evaluating the longer-term consequences of a proposed solution can be made easier by using hypnotic time projection imagery. One common method involves asking the client to imagine two paths into the future, one that consists of following her current beliefs and behaviour, and another that involves adopting an alternative perspective and way of acting. The client can be asked to imagine this is as a fork in the road, the two paths diverging more and more over time. By surveying these two contrasting paths from above, the client can be brought into contact with the longer-term consequences of her behaviour and its wider impact, in contrast to an alternative future that consists of a different coping style. This imagery technique normally only allows the client to evaluate the consequences of two contrasting strategies; nevertheless, it does provide a powerful hypnotic tool for decision-making.

Hypnotic solution implementation and verification

It's relatively easy to see how hypnotic imagery and suggestion could facilitate solution implementation through covert (imaginal) rehearsal of the behaviour to be enacted, that is, the chosen solution. As in stress inoculation training, which emphasises the rehearsal of coping skills during imaginal exposure, the client can use hypnosis to practice coping in their imagination before putting their solution plan into action in the real world. Mental rehearsal at this stage often provides the following benefits:

1. Further clarification of the steps required for solution implementation.
2. Clarification of the possible consequences.
3. Anticipation of possible setbacks, and preparation of a backup plan.
4. Increasing relevant skills through rehearsal, for example, improving coping statements or assertiveness skills, etc.

5. Reduction of anxiety through repeated imaginal exposure and spontaneous cognitive restructuring.
6. Using direct suggestion or autosuggestion to enhance confidence and problem orientation while rehearsing the chosen solution.

In particular, if the client plans to use self-instruction as part of their action plan, this can easily be rehearsed in hypnosis, aloud at first, then internalised and faded, as in Meichenbaum's approach to Self-Instruction Training. (See the section in the chapter on cognitive therapy for more details.) As in conventional behaviour therapy, techniques such as instruction, coaching, prompting, modelling, shaping, feedback, and reinforcement can be used to develop coping skills and strategies and prepare the client for implementation of their chosen solution.

Problem-solving scripts

In cognitive therapy clients are often helped to develop "scripts", which may tell a story about certain situations or responses. For example, a client may write a cognitive therapy script in the form of a coping plan or story describing how they would think, act, and feel if they were coping better with a problem. Scripts can be developed to describe clients acting "as if" their core beliefs about themselves had improved. It is likewise possible to collaboratively develop problem-solving self-hypnosis scripts with clients, that is., asking them to write a story about how they would think, act, and feel if they were more proactive, confident, and optimistic about solving their problems in general and turning this into a self-hypnosis recording for cultivating positive problem-orientation. There's considerable overlap between positive problem-orientation and the traditional approach to "ego-strengthening" by suggestion in hypnotherapy (Heap & Aravind, 2002, p. 126). The components of positive and negative problem-orientation, discussed above, give hypnotists a clear template for developing suggestions, as do the components of rational problem-solving style. For example:

> "When you spot problems you now immediately start thinking of ways to solve them. You see them as challenges and feel confident and optimistic about taking constructive action. You see things in proportion and approach them at a sensible pace, open to learning from your experience. Problems are a normal part of everyday life and you've overcome countless things in the past. You already have the ability to become a skilled and confident problem-solver, and you approach life with a realistic and constructive attitude.
>
> "You get to the heart of the problem and clearly formulate it in terms that help you to look for practical solutions. You focus on your goals, and make these as clear and specific as possible. Once you've pinpointed the problem and set your goals, you creatively brainstorm a comprehensive list of solutions. You are a creative thinker, and ideas come easily to you as soon as you start to think about things, write them down, and explore new perspectives. You focus first of all on coming up with a full range of possible solutions, creativity comes first, analysis and evaluation later. You ask yourself questions like, 'What worked in the past?', 'What haven't I tried yet?', 'What would someone else do?' The more you think about it the more solutions come to your mind. When you're completely satisfied with your list of options

you set about choosing the best ones. You take time to think through the consequences of different courses of action. You can clearly picture what will happen if you choose one solution over another.

"Having worked out the best option, you put together a clear plan of action that you're confident about putting into practice. You plan things realistically, identify any help or resources you need, and prepare for different outcomes. When you're ready, you put your plans into action and observe what happens. You feel confident because you've planned things carefully and you always praise and reward yourself for your efforts, whatever the outcome. Plans don't have to work perfectly first time, and you are always ready to learn from your experience, and to develop new plans for the future. The most important outcome is that with every effort you make, you become more skilled and confident as a problem-solver in general, throughout all areas of your life."

Although the best long-term use of self-hypnosis scripts may be for positive problem-orientation, there are a number of possible applications of self-hypnosis recordings in PST worth considering:

1. Positive problem orientation.
2. Goal visualisation or age progression for motivation and increasing perceived control.
3. Relaxation and creativity for generation of alternative perspectives and behavioural strategies.
4. Imaginal behavioural rehearsal of solution implementation, picturing solutions being put into practice.

However, as in cognitive therapy generally, it is probably better if the client writes the script, with some prompting and coaching from the therapist, with perhaps the use of examples (models) to guide her. Clients should be encouraged to write a short script and then read it regularly, that is, every day, making revisions as they do so. When they're completely satisfied with the content they can record it for use in the future.

CHAPTER TEN

Cognition: cognitive hypnotherapy

How can standard cognitive therapy interventions be integrated with clinical hypnosis? Hypnotherapy historically shared more in common with early behaviour therapy than with the subsequent cognitive approaches of Ellis and Beck. However, modern cognitive therapy and hypnotherapy can easily be combined and a number of authors have already done so, by drawing on elements of Ellis' REBT or Beck's cognitive therapy (Alladin, 2008; Clarke & Jackson, 1983; Dowd, 2000; Golden, Dowd & Freidberg, 1987). Perhaps the main obstacle to integrating these approaches is the fact that direct verbal disputation of cognitions is usually better done *outside* of hypnosis. Nevertheless purely cognitive interventions can be enhanced by hypnosis in a number of ways, such as through the use of mental imagery techniques or coping statements combined with autosuggestion, etc. Moreover, the strategy of "distancing" from automatic negative thoughts in cognitive therapy (Beck A. T., 1976), which has been developed more extensively in recent mindfulness and acceptance-based approaches to CBT (Hayes, Follette & Linehan, 2004), can be conceptualised as a form of "dehypnosis", as we have seen.

This chapter particularly explores the integration of cognitive-behavioural hypnotherapy with Beck's cognitive therapy for anxiety. It begins by providing a simplified overview of Beck's revised cognitive therapy for anxiety disorders, interspersing comments about integrating hypnosis, and concludes with a detailed discussion of mental imagery techniques used in cognitive hypnotherapy, compatible with Beck's approach. Beck's first major book on cognitive therapy gave a very brief outline of his conceptualisation and treatment for anxiety (Beck A. T., 1976). Following the publication of his seminal treatment manual for depression (Beck, Rush, Shaw & Emery, 1979), a second manual, for anxiety disorders, adopting a broadly transdiagnostic approach, was published in 1985, and revised somewhat in 2005 (Beck, Emery & Greenberg,

2005). Beck's original account was considerably expanded, into a more technically eclectic approach, which actually assimilated several mental imagery techniques used in hypnotherapy (Melges, 1982). However, many other clinicians and researchers have contributed to the development of cognitive-behavioural therapy for anxiety since the 1990s, leading to increasing emphasis upon diagnosis-specific conceptualisation and treatment. Hence, Beck's original text on anxiety was effectively superseded by improvements to both the theory and practice of cognitive therapy described in careful detail in the recently-published *Cognitive Therapy of Anxiety Disorders* (Clark & Beck, 2010). A self-help version of the same approach has recently been published, entitled *The Anxiety & Worry Workbook* (Clark & Beck, 2012). This chapter draws primarily upon the current model of cognitive therapy, although it incorporates mental imagery techniques from Beck's earlier writings, and from other authors, which are particularly suitable for use in a cognitive-behavioural approach to hypnotherapy.

Cognitive interventions have been found particularly important in the treatment of panic disorder, social phobia, and generalised anxiety disorder, although less so in the more concrete and circumscribed fears characteristic of specific phobias, where behavioural exposure therapy of the kind described earlier in this volume is still the treatment of choice. Cognitive therapy for depression typically begins with a behavioural intervention, "activity scheduling", which is followed by cognitive interventions targeting automatic thoughts and underlying beliefs (Beck, Rush, Shaw & Emery, 1979). However, by contrast, in the cognitive therapy of anxiety this sequence is typically reversed and cognitive interventions are emphasised first, in preparation for subsequent exposure therapy and response prevention (Antony & Swinson, 2000, p. 240). In the treatment of specific phobias, cognitive interventions may help to facilitate exposure therapy but they do not appear to contribute very substantially to the outcome. Indeed, specific phobias are the only major anxiety disorder not represented in Beck's current treatment manual for anxiety.

In Beck's approach, the main goal of cognitive therapy for anxiety disorders is to correct exaggerated (faulty) appraisals of personal danger and vulnerability and replace these with a more rational and realistic reappraisal, which often means seeing threat levels as more trivial or acceptable and one's coping ability as good enough to get through things (Clark & Beck, 2010, pp. 181–182). Another key characteristic of cognitive therapy for anxiety is that because of the "double belief system" or difference between thoughts in the anxious and non-anxious modes, anxiety must generally be evoked in most treatment sessions in order to adequately identify or restructure relevant cognitions, for example, through evocative imagery or behavioural experiments conducted in the session (Beck, Emery & Greenberg, 2005, p. 192). One of the most obvious opportunities for using hypnosis in CBT is therefore to enhance the quality of imaginal exposure, activating schemas of threat and vulnerability in the consulting room in anticipation of real-world exposure, so that they can be better assessed and modified. As we've seen, Sarbin defined hypnosis as a form of "believed-in imagining" (Sarbin & Coe, 1972). This provides a good perspective from which to conceptualise the process of imaginal exposure, which should ideally entail activation of relevant anxiety-related schemas and beliefs. Hence, to the extent that beliefs about threat and vulnerability are activated in imagination, during hypnosis, they may be more readily modifiable through cognitive-behavioural treatment strategies.

Socratic questioning, the main technique of traditional cognitive therapy, may best be used in a session before or after inducing hypnosis, rather than *during* the procedure. For example, discussing the disputation of automatic negative thoughts, which they term "spontaneous negative self-suggestions", Lynn & Kirsch write:

> These can be challenged through Socratic questioning, either within or outside of hypnosis. Our experience suggests that this part of the process of cognitive restructuring can best be managed outside of hypnosis. Hypnosis can then be used again to reinforce the alternative positive self-suggestions that emerge from this process. (Lynn & Kirsch, 2006, pp. 125–126)

However, as we've seen, the use of very simple cognitive interventions such as self-instructions (coping statements) clearly resembles the role of "autosuggestions" in hypnotherapy, and combines well with traditional hypnosis and self-hypnosis techniques (Meichenbaum, 2007; Meichenbaum, 1977). Likewise, most of the "mental imagery" techniques used for cognitive restructuring can easily be adapted for use during hypnosis (Beck, Emery & Greenberg, 2005; Beck J. S., 1995). Hence, cognitive-behavioural hypnotherapy does typically involve the use of mental imagery techniques, and coping skills training, within the broader framework for cognitive therapy developed by Beck and others. We'll therefore begin by looking at cognitive therapy in general terms, linking aspects of it to the use of hypnosis, before proceeding to explore certain basic mental imagery techniques found in CBT in more detail, from the perspective of hypnotism.

Process aims of cognitive therapy

As noted earlier, cognitive therapy for anxiety is based on a cognitive conceptualisation of anxiety derived from Richard Lazarus' "transactional" model of stress (Beck A. T., 1976; Lazarus R. S., 1966). According to the transactional model, stress is due to an automatic "appraisal" of the extent by which the perceived threat of a situation, the possibility of impending harm, outweighs one's perceived ability to cope. Hence, Beck et al. described their early cognitive model of anxiety, in layman's terms, as follows:

> Anxious patients in the simplest terms believe, "Something bad is going to happen that I won't be able to handle." (Beck, Emery & Greenberg, 2005, p. 201)

To recap on what was said earlier about Beck's revised conceptualisation, it can be summed up as follows:

> The cognitive perspective views anxiety in terms of an information-processing system that exaggerates the probability and severity of threat, minimizes personal ability to cope, and fails to recognize aspects of safety. (Clark & Beck, 2010, p. 182)

Strictly speaking, "threat" refers to the possibility of future harm or loss, whether physical or social, etc. There are therefore four elements of appraisal that are targeted by cognitive therapy interventions, as a means of modifying the underlying schemas of threat and vulnerability central to anxiety disorders (Clark & Beck, 2010, p. 184).

1. *Probability*. Over-estimating the probability of some kind of harm actually occurring.
2. *Severity*. Over-estimating how "catastrophic" or harmful the threat's perceived consequences would be.
3. *Vulnerability*. Under-estimating one's coping ability, that is, experiencing a sense of personal helplessness, weakness and inability to cope.
4. *Safety*. Under-estimating *genuine* signs or evidence of safety, which are overlooked or undervalued due to a cognitive bias in favour of threat detection and also belief in the importance of engaging in maladaptive and unnecessary ("false") safety-seeking behaviours.

In addition to the general guidelines advanced in preceding chapters, the main process aims of cognitive therapy for anxiety have therefore been described as normalising the threat, socialising the client to the cognitive model, and modifying faulty schema-based appraisals of threat and vulnerability (Clark & Beck, 2010, p. 184). This typically also entails modifying behaviour, mainly by increasing approach and exposure to feared situations while reducing dependence upon "false" (maladaptive and unnecessary) safety-seeking behaviour, and thereby helping to disconfirm faulty appraisals through direct experience. False safety-seeking behaviours, that is, things people do *unnecessarily* to protect themselves in relation to perceived threats, such as taking ineffective herbal remedies or clinging to another person for security, prevent them from being able to notice genuine evidence of safety (Clark & Beck, 2010, pp. 184–185). They were, in many cases, *already* safe but didn't realise it and their way of trying to cope is unnecessary. It's therefore also integral to cognitive therapy for anxiety that unhelpful ways of trying to cope, through avoidance, safety-seeking, or thought-control, etc., are evaluated and removed, where necessary.

Normalisation and socialisation

An important initial component of cognitive therapy is the "normalisation" of anxiety, that is, making the threat seem more normal by highlighting the extent to which it may occur without evoking anxiety for other people, in the client's past, or in different situations or contexts, etc. Clark & Beck distinguish between three main forms of normalisation for threat content (Clark & Beck, 2010, pp. 186–187).

1. In relation to *other people's* experiences by asking: "Do these problems happen to other people as well? How do they cope? How do they think about them?"
2. In relation to *past experience* by asking: "Was there a time in the past where things like this didn't bother you as much or you coped better with them? Have you always worried as much about similar problems? How did you think differently?"
3. In relation to *other situations* by asking: "Do similar things occur in other contexts without causing you as much anxiety? Are there ever times or situations in which this doesn't bother you? What are you thinking then?"

Socialisation to the cognitive model can be described as a shift from the client asking "Why?" she is anxious (or "What?" she is anxious about) to asking "How?" she continues to make herself anxious. The basic answer that cognitive-behavioural therapy provides is that she does so by engaging in certain maladaptive cognitions (thoughts) and behaviours.

As noted earlier, in Beck's first book on cognitive therapy, he explained that although the cognitive model was innovative compared to previous psychotherapeutic approaches, its "philosophical underpinnings" went back to the ancient Stoic principle that men are not emotionally disturbed by events themselves but by their conceptions, or misconceptions, about events (Beck A. T., 1976, p. 3). In their later book on depression, Beck and his colleagues explained the cognitive model by employing a well-known quotation from the Stoic philosopher Epictetus, which was also used in Albert Ellis' rational-emotive behaviour therapy (REBT).

> Epictetus wrote in *The Enchiridion*: "Men are disturbed not by things but by the views which they take of them." [...] Control of most intense feelings may be achieved by changing one's ideas. (Beck, Rush, Shaw & Emery, 1979, p. 8)

One of the main objectives during the commencement of cognitive therapy is to turn the client's attention toward their cognitions as the main factor responsible for maintaining their anxiety (Clark & Beck, 2010, p. 182). Beck describes this as shifting the client's focus from threat "content" on to cognitive "appraisal" of threat, that is, from external events onto the client's internal appraisal of them. Another way of presenting the cognitive model of anxiety is to draw attention to the fact that other people, or the client at other times, may have the same automatic thought content, such as "I might make an idiot of myself", without becoming anxious as long as the threat is appraised as very improbable or trivial (not catastrophic) and their coping ability is appraised confidently (Clark & Beck, 2010, p. 183). To paraphrase Epictetus, "Men are made anxious not by events, or even the *content* of their fears, but by the *appraisals* that they make of threat probability and severity."

It is also important to help the client, from the outset, to identify a more "normal", or rational and realistic, perspective on threatening situations. Beck's self-help recommendations therefore place considerable emphasis on the client creating "normalisation cue-cards", early in therapy, which act as reminders of how they might think in a more normal and adaptive way about anxiety-provoking situations (Clark & Beck, 2012, p. 105). This typically consists of a paragraph or so describing the feared situation in terms of a more realistic appraisal of threat probability and severity, coping ability, and genuine signs of safety, etc. Clients are instructed to review these rational statements whenever the anxiety returns as a simple coping strategy, something that might be compared to certain ways of using *autosuggestion* in hypnotherapy. Another way of approaching this is simply to ask the client to compare anxious and non-anxious appraisals, describing what their estimation of the threat is when most anxious, as it would be in the midst of the problem situation, and to contrast this with a description of how they perceive the same situation when at a distance from it, and non-anxious. As Beck noted early in the development of cognitive therapy, appraisals of threatening situations tend to become more distorted and anxiety-provoking the closer the client is to them in space and time. For example, someone who has a fear of flying is likely to describe their appraisal of the threat of crashing in exaggerated terms during the most difficult part of a flight. However, in the safety of the consulting room, they will be more able to describe a more "normal" and realistic appraisal of the same situation, something Beck initially dubbed the "dual belief system" in anxiety, as we saw earlier.

Realistic appraisal of threat probability and severity

Hence, according to Beck, cognitive therapists should generally avoid trying to logically persuade the client that the threat content they perceive is not *possible*, that is, that it is "not going to happen", because there is usually always some possibility the client can cling to that their fears will come true. Put simply, the thought "Something bad *might* happen" cannot easily be disputed because it is essentially quite true. The primary source of anxiety, according to Beck's model, however, is the exaggerated appraisal of threat probability and severity.

> After all, any clever arguments that can be concocted by the therapist will be immediately dismissed by the client because mistakes do happen, people can become the victim of disease by contamination, and even the occasional young person dies from a heart attack. The reality is that threat can never be eliminated entirely. At best such persuasive debates will only amount to reassurance that provides temporary relief from anxiety and at worst the client's outright dismissal of the effectiveness of cognitive therapy. Thus it is critical to the success of cognitive therapy that therapy avoids a direct focus on the client's threat content. (Clark & Beck, 2010, p. 182)

Cognitive therapy, therefore, attempts to shift the client's focus of attention from the "content of threat" or the possibility of external events as a source of anxiety on to the role of (faulty or biased) cognitive appraisal in maintaining anxiety (Clark & Beck, 2010, p. 184).

This can be described as a way of encouraging the client to "own" their feelings, by taking responsibility for the role of their thoughts and behaviour in contributing to their emotions. Beck et al., in the original cognitive therapy manual for anxiety, recommend that clients are encouraged to employ the *active* rather than *passive* grammatical voice, saying "I make myself anxious about taking tests" rather than "Taking tests makes me anxious." In addition to increasing the sense of responsibility and encouraging thought-spotting, this also naturally leads on to the question: "How, specifically, do you make yourself anxious? What do you say to yourself or do that actually makes you feel that way?" A similar step may involve the concept of "verbification", where verbs ("doing" words) are used rather than nouns or adjectives. For example, saying "I'm *tensing* my body" (verb) rather than "I am tense" or "It makes me tense", emphasises that "tensing" is an activity being engaged in rather than a passive quality. Sometimes neologisms are created, such as the words "verbification" (or "verbing") itself. The most obvious example of this in the CBT literature is the neologism "catastrophising", which is intended to remind the client that she is actively making something into a catastrophe by her appraisal of it rather than it simply being inherently "catastrophic." Catastrophising is basically the central thinking error that underlies most anxiety disorders (Clark & Beck, 2012, pp. 23–24). However, in less severe forms of anxiety, and in ordinary stress management, appraisals of threat may be more within realistic bounds, although often still biased. With these issues, commonly dealt with using hypnotherapy, improving appraisals of coping ability and building self-confidence may be more important to the process of treatment. However, catastrophic thinking is normally the primary focus of cognitive therapy for anxiety because helping the client to cope better with an unrealistically inflated or illusory threat may simply constitute a "sticking plaster" approach if it doesn't address the underlying cognitive error.

Realistic appraisals of coping ability

People feel anxious when they estimate themselves as being highly vulnerable to immediate threat but feelings of anxiety are themselves interpreted by many people as signs of vulnerability and helplessness, in a vicious cycle. An interesting illustration of this is found in the tendency that many clients report, when anxious, to suddenly "feel like a little child" or even to spontaneously see an image themselves, in their mind's eye, as a small vulnerable child intimidated by an adult world (Beck, Emery & Greenberg, 2005, p. 214). Viewing oneself as vulnerable because feeling anxious is a form of "emotional reasoning", though. Feelings can often be an unreliable guide to the true level of risk in a situation.

The cognitive model of anxiety places considerable emphasis upon the activation of deep-seated schemas relating to personal "vulnerability" and appraisals of one's difficulty coping. Hence, Beck clearly emphasises that cognitive therapy for anxiety not only attempts to address faulty threat appraisals but also to modify beliefs about personal coping ability, such as perceived inability to cope, helplessness, or vulnerability in relation to anxious situations (Clark & Beck, 2010, p. 187). Clients' initial automatic thoughts may sometimes contain reference to their sense of helplessness but appraisal of coping usually comes slightly later in the sequence of events and their subsequent attempts to cope and worry also typically reveal concerns about personal helplessness. In fact, whereas individuals often struggle to identify or recall their *immediate* automatic thoughts about threat, they often find it easier to articulate the slower and more conscious thoughts about helplessness that follow. Beck therefore describes cognitive therapy as focusing throughout on building self-efficacy and a sense of mastery over the feared situation by seeking evidence for the client believing that they are stronger than they had previously realised (Clark & Beck, 2010, p. 187). For example, during the process of assessment it is common to identify the client's general strengths and assets, which can help increase confidence in their ability to cope. One of the first pieces of evidence worth highlighting is the fact that the client, unlike so many people with similar problems, has had the courage and resourcefulness to seek help from a therapist.

Bandura's influential theory of "self-efficacy" expectations as a key factor in psychological therapy was one of the developments that fuelled the increasing emphasis upon cognitive factors in behaviour therapy in the 1970s. Bandura distinguished *outcome* expectations from *self-efficacy* expectations, which he defined as follows: "An efficacy expectation is the conviction that one can successfully execute the behaviour required to produce the outcomes" (Bandura, 1977). Bandura's original conclusion, drawn from empirical research on the treatment of specific phobias and other studies, was that self-efficacy could be enhanced by a number of therapeutic approaches, listed in *descending* order of potency:

1. *Performance accomplishments*, that is, direct personal experience of behavioural mastery from *in vivo* exposure, etc.
2. *Vicarious experience*, that is, learning by observation of models either in imagination or live.
3. *Verbal persuasion*, that is, through persuasion, self-instruction, or certain cognitive interventions.
4. *Lowering of emotional arousal*, that is, through relaxation, systematic desensitisation, etc.

Hence, cognitive therapy "behavioural experiments", including graduated exposure, should provide an excellent opportunity for confidence-building and increasing expectations of self-efficacy. Cognitive therapy often involves obtaining initial predictions from the client of her ability to cope in a particular situation, which is re-evaluated by comparing them to the actual outcome (Clark & Beck, 2010, pp. 187–188). Clients may also identify evidence retrospectively, by reviewing and evaluating how well they actually coped with similar situations in the past. There may already be reasons for them to be more confident, that is, evidence that contradicts their appraisal of themselves as helpless and vulnerable. In *hypnotherapy*, greater emphasis is typically placed on improving the appraisal of coping ability by increasing self-confidence, within realistic bounds. Indeed, Braid made a famous quotation from the poet Virgil that encapsulates the power of self-efficacy the motto of his writings on hypnotism: "They can because they believe they can" (Braid, 2009).

Adopting a problem-solving attitude toward perceived threats and developing specific coping plans is another important way of increasing self-efficacy. Hence, some questions that can be asked about coping ability include:

1. How have you coped with similar situations in the past? Are there reasons to think you're more capable of handling this problem than you're giving yourself credit for?
2. How many alternative ways of coping with the problem can you identify? Can you identify the best option and develop it into a detailed and systematic coping plan? What if that doesn't work, do you need a backup plan ("Plan B")?
3. How well do you predict you'll cope with the situation now? Rate your confidence in your ability to cope 0–100 per cent.
4. Try it and see what happens. How did your prediction compare with how well you actually coped? What did you learn? How could you cope better with similar situations in future?

Indeed, the concept of positive problem-orientation, which includes self-efficacy along with other factors, and the methodology of problem-solving therapy (PST), provide a way of enhancing appraisals of coping ability. In other words, the cognitive therapist should normally place considerable emphasis upon the correction of poor self-efficacy in relation to anxiety, by drawing the client's attention to discrepancies between their anticipated helplessness and past experiences of more successful coping. In doing so, the therapist assumes a problem-solving orientation himself toward helping the client to develop a broad and flexible repertoire of more adaptive coping strategies and improving her skill and confidence in applying them through carefully constructed behavioural experiments, designed to progressively build self-efficacy (Clark & Beck, 2010, p. 189). This aspect of cognitive therapy potentially comes closer to "coping skills" approaches such as Meichenbaum's stress inoculation training and the coping skills approach to hypnotherapy described in the chapter on applied self-hypnosis earlier in the current volume.

Realistic appraisals of safety signs

Genuine evidence of safety is typically overlooked or discounted by people in an anxious mode of functioning, who exhibit an automatic bias toward the perception of signs of potential threat. In other words, signs of safety are automatically minimised in anxiety, whereas signs of threat are maximised. When a sense of safety is achieved it is often misattributed to irrelevant signs or procedures, safety-seeking behaviours, that become maladaptive ways of responding to the situation. Correction of faulty appraisals of safety has become an integral component in the cognitive therapy of anxiety (Clark & Beck, 2010, p. 189). The following three dimensions of faulty safety-cue processing have been identified in the current cognitive approach:

1. *Intolerance of risk and of uncertainty.* Is the client too intolerant of risk and uncertainty? Wha4nstitutes an acceptable level of risk? Is it realistic to try to eliminate risk? What are the costs of trying too hard to eliminate risk completely?
2. *Overlooking genuine signs of safety.* Are there reasons for the client to believe she's already safe? Is the client overlooking signs or evidence of genuine safety? The therapist should seek to compensate for the natural bias toward threat in anxiety by encouraging the client to reflect and elaborate in detail upon the possible signs of safety in the threat situation.
3. *Avoidance and safety-seeking behaviour.* Unhelpful safety-seeking strategies, such as tensing muscles, avoiding eye-contact, etc., need to be re-evaluated, which can only normally occur through response prevention, that is, by dropping the behaviour during exposure to the perceived threat.

As mentioned earlier, the problem of unhelpful safety-seeking behaviour, central to anxiety, can be illustrated by the joke about the man who carries a mouse around with him when he goes into town. One day someone asks him why he always has a mouse and he explains that it's a safety strategy, he's heard elephants are scared of mice and so carrying the mouse keeps him safe from being trampled by a herd of elephants. When it's pointed out that there are no elephants in the high street he replies: "Exactly, that just proves how well it works!" Of course the mouse is an *unnecessary* way of protecting himself against a completely *imaginary* threat but the only way he could ever discover this for certain would be by doing the very thing he fears most: going into town without a mouse. The cognitive therapist helps clients to drop their guard by abandoning maladaptive safety-seeking behaviours, in a safe and controlled manner, to help disconfirm faulty threat appraisals and the underlying schemas from which they derive.

Likewise, imagine an anthropologist discovering a primitive tribe who perform a ritual every night so that the sun will rise again in the morning. The ritual has been performed without fail for as long as their history records. They're terrified that anything might interfere with this practice because it could lead to a catastrophe by preventing the sun rising. All they know is that they perform the ritual every night and several hours later the sun rises, without fail. The only real way to test the effectiveness of their ritual would be to stop doing it, and see what happens, but this is something they refuse to contemplate because the perceived risk involved would be catastrophic. Fear has created a superstitious "closed system" out of this ritual behaviour where adaptation and learning have become impossible and genuine evidence of safety is obscured by the ritual itself. In reality, the ritual does nothing to *make* them safe because they are *already* safe; the sun would rise anyway, whether or not they performed the ritual.

The main difficulty that occurs in exposure-based therapy where the client clings on to some safety-behaviour is that they may discount evidence that would undermine faulty appraisals of threat by drawing the "yes ... but" conclusion: "Yes, nothing catastrophic happened when I faced my fears, but only because I did *xyz* to make sure I was safe." For example, agoraphobic clients may conclude: "Yes, I managed to walk along the street without fainting but only because I was trying to control my breathing and clinging on to my husband's arm for safety." *Genuine* evidence of safety, the non-occurrence of the feared catastrophe, is therefore effectively hidden by the presence of the safety-seeking response. Moreover, processing of safety cues in the environment tends to be more difficult and to require more conscious effort than responding to threat cues. For that reason, clients may be asked to carefully reflect upon and note down genuine evidence of safety, perhaps even developing a written "safety script", to encourage extended conscious processing of safety signals in the threatening environment.

Cognitive interventions/treatment plan

Beck's original cognitive therapy manual for anxiety followed a basic four-stage generic treatment plan, tailored for specific problems and different clients' needs (Beck, Emery & Greenberg, 2005, p. 179).

1. Initial relief of anxiety symptoms through "accepting the feelings, action strategies, self-observation, emotional review, and owning one's emotions" (Beck, Emery & Greenberg, 2005, p. 232).
2. Self-monitoring automatic thoughts and cognitive distortions, and developing the conceptualisation.
3. Restructuring automatic thoughts with questioning and empirical hypothesis-testing.
4. Modification of underlying cognitive structures, that is, more pervasive assumptions and core beliefs (schemas).

This is noteworthy because of the initial emphasis placed on "symptom relief" through self-observation, distancing from fearful cognitions (thereby "owning emotions") and acceptance of anxious feelings, processes that have assumed centre-stage in subsequent mindfulness and acceptance-based approaches to CBT (Hayes, Follette & Linehan, 2004). As we have seen, the

"AWARE" acronym was introduced by Beck in his 1985 manual to help define the client's role in similar terms, and this approach has returned in his most recent self-help manual (Clark & Beck, 2012, p. 142). Moreover, a specific mental imagery technique called "emotional review", derived from the early cognitive psychotherapy of Victor Raimy, was originally used in cognitive therapy for anxiety as a basic strategy of symptom reduction (Raimy, 1975). Raimy's technique of repeated emotional (or "cognitive") review forms a potential bridge between socialisation, initial symptom relief, and subsequent exposure therapy. However, it is probably of special interest to cognitive-behavioural *hypnotherapists* because this simple imagery technique happens to fit very neatly into a hypnotic approach to treatment. We shall therefore be describing it in more detail when we turn to the examination of mental imagery techniques in cognitive-behavioural hypnotherapy, later in this chapter.

By comparison, based on Beck's most recent account, the main categories of intervention in the current, revised cognitive therapy of anxiety are as follows (Clark & Beck, 2010):

1. Psycho-education and socialisation.
2. Self-monitoring.
3. Evidence-evaluation.
4. Cost-benefit analysis.
5. Identification of cognitive distortions.
6. Decatastrophising.
7. Generation of alternative cognitions.
8. Exposure-based behavioural experiments (empirical hypothesis-testing).

This approach makes less reference to initial symptom relief and there is greater emphasis on situation-specific appraisals than underlying schemas. Also, the habituation rationale for exposure appears to be more prominent, although, as we shall see, the benefits of exposure are thought to be improved by the inclusion of empirical hypothesis-testing of key cognitions. Psycho-education and self-monitoring, with which we will begin, are really precursors to "cognitive restructuring" *per se*.

Psycho-education and socialisation

Psycho-education

One of the first steps in treatment consists of educating the client ("psycho-education") about her problem and what to expect from treatment, etc. Education of the client should aim to be as Socratic as possible and to focus on relevant examples from her own experience. The main components of psycho-education are as follows:

1. Misconceptions about anxiety are extremely common and should be corrected by discussion of symptoms, including the positive "evolutionary" value of the fear response.
2. The cognitive model of anxiety and working hypothesis (conceptualisation) should be explained, focusing on the factors responsible for currently maintaining symptoms.

3. The rationale for the cognitive-behavioural hypnotherapy approach should be explained, especially the client's active role in treatment, the importance of homework, etc.

It is essential that the client comes to understand and accept things sufficiently to be able to fully participate in and benefit from therapy, that is, to be "socialised" to their role in treatment. The client's role in cognitive therapy primarily involves self-monitoring and other homework and the ability to adopt a problem-solving and thought-spotting orientation. However, the "AWARE" acronym, as discussed below, can also be seen as a kind of role-definition for the client in cognitive therapy for anxiety.

Regarding their symptoms of anxiety, clients should first of all be helped to appreciate the *evolutionary* basis of the primal threat response and the positive value of fear—several authors have noted the readiness with which clients are reassured by explanations of anxiety in terms of specific evolutionary-based responses such as automatic fight, flight, fainting, freezing, etc. As Beck puts it, they can be asked, "Has there ever been a time when anxiety may have saved your life?" (Clark & Beck, 2010, p. 192). A distinction can then be introduced between "rational and irrational" fears, or "adaptive" (helpful) and "maladaptive" (unhelpful) anxiety responses, etc. If necessary, this can be further elaborated upon by helping the client to evaluate the "pros and cons" of their anxiety to clarify the extent to which it is unhelpful. It is also worth observing, in some cases, that anxiety that was once helpful in the past, or in certain situations, may have become increasingly unhelpful over time. This helps to normalise anxiety, to reduce "anxiety about anxiety" and to pave the way for the next step in educating the client, discussion of the cognitive model of maladaptive anxiety. Discussion of the "pros" of anxiety may also help to minimise experiential avoidance to some extent, reducing over-sensitivity to anxiety by reframing it as something inherently normal and adaptive, although in some cases it may become excessive due to faulty appraisals, unhelpful coping, etc.

Beck explains the concept of schema-driven orientation to clients by using the metaphor of a photograph being taken of a situation, which simplifies three-dimensional reality by reducing it to a snapshot in two dimensions (Pretzer & Beck, 2007, p. 467). A lot of information is necessarily left out of the picture, as with one's immediate automatic thoughts. In other words, in stress or anxiety a series of "snapshot" thoughts are made of events, which may result from a narrow focus on signs of threat (selective attention) and therefore lead to a distorted appraisal of the whole situation, which exaggerates threat and overlooks evidence of safety or coping ability. Normally, we respond to automatic activation of threat schemas by quickly *reappraising* our initial snapshot thoughts, activating a rational and constructive mode of functioning in response to them, in light of our experience of the situation. However, when anxiety is particularly high or when worry and safety-seeking predominate, constructive reappraisal may be impaired and "thinking rationally" may appear virtually impossible.

Conceptualisation (working hypothesis)

Regarding the cognitive model, clients should be provided with an initial conceptualisation or "working hypothesis", ideally at the end of their initial assessment, that they are able to discuss and help develop and refine throughout treatment. (See the earlier chapter on conceptualisation.)

COGNITION: COGNITIVE HYPNOTHERAPY   367

Beck's revised generic cognitive model of anxiety can be presented in the form of a simplified diagram for this purpose (Clark & Beck, 2010, p. 193). This essentially consists of the following phases, presented below in an even more simplified "vicious circle" format:

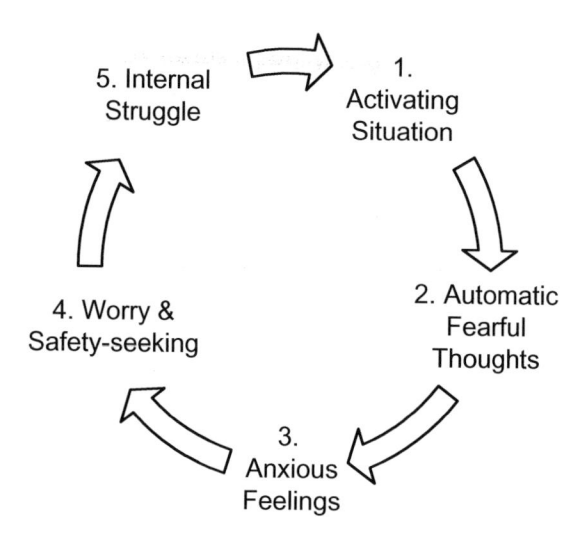

```
        5. Internal  ⟹  1. Activating
           Struggle         Situation
              ⬆                 ⬇
        4. Worry &        2. Automatic
        Safety-seeking     Fearful
              ⬉            Thoughts
                   3.       ⬋
                 Anxious
                 Feelings
```

The basic elements of the vicious cycle constitute a rough sequence of that can be summarised as follows:

1. An example of a specific situation or event (internal or external) that triggers the anxiety response, which the client may automatically perceive in a negative schema-biased manner from the outset.
2. The specific automatic apprehensive thoughts ("What do you fear will happen?")
3. The activation of the "anxiety mode", and associated symptoms, bodily sensations, and automatic inclinations and inhibitions.
4. Deliberate reappraisal and coping attempts.
    a. Escalating worry (continued thinking about possible catastrophes) and preoccupation with thoughts of helplessness.
    b. Safety-seeking, avoidance and escape behaviour.
5. Attempts to control or eliminate anxious thoughts and feelings (experiential avoidance).

The therapist should attempt to go through each of these components of the model and obtain examples of triggers, thoughts, feelings, and behaviours, etc. It's normal to complete a "draft" conceptualisation diagram at the beginning of treatment and assign the client the homework task of reviewing it and making any additions or modifications she feels are required or completing a fresh conceptualisation immediately following another anxiety episode (Clark & Beck, 2010, p. 192).

Attention should be drawn to the "vicious cycle" by which anxiety is maintained. That is, strategic responses, the main target of cognitive therapy, may "backfire" by simply fuelling further activation of the anxiety mode, preventing it from being "turned off" naturally. These constitute the latter part of the conceptualisation, that is, escape behaviour, subtle avoidance, safety-seeking, coping strategies, extended thinking (worry), and focus on anxiety symptoms, and maladaptive attempts to control anxious thoughts and feelings, etc. These strategic responses are potentially under the client's voluntary control and the point at which the "vicious cycle" can most easily be broken. Particular emphasis upon the counter-productive role of safety-seeking behaviours is often necessary with anxiety disorders. The client may benefit by being frequently brought back to the basic question: "How's that way of coping working out for you in the long-run?" Although not usually included on the conceptualisation diagram, it's important to also consider the wider negative impact of anxiety as this provides important contextual information and motivation for change. Typical questions include asking the client how her problem affects domains such as health, work, finances, family/close relationships, daily routine, leisure activity and socialising, etc. Beck refers to these costs as the "personal burden of anxiety" (Clark & Beck, 2010, p. 193).

Treatment rationale (tasks and goals)

Education regarding the treatment rationale, goals, and strategies should follow naturally from the conceptualisation of the problem. As noted above, the working alliance is built upon mutual trust but also a broad agreement on the goals and tasks of therapy. The basic message, put simply, is something like: "This is what seems to be wrong, this is what you want to achieve, and this is how we're planning to go about doing it." The client's expectations about the goal of treatment should be elicited and compared to the generic goal of cognitive therapy for anxiety which is as follows: To deactivate the anxiety mode by changing maladaptive cognitive and behavioural responses, responsible for maintaining it, at the strategic level (Clark & Beck, 2010, p. 195). Prevention of maladaptive strategic responses, however, presupposes a more "accepting" attitude toward automatic threat and anxiety reactions:

> [T]he objective of cognitive therapy is not to teach people more effective ways to "control their anxiety". Instead cognitive therapy focuses on helping individuals develop a more "accepting attitude" toward anxiety rather than a "combative (i.e., controlling) attitude." When thoughts like "I can't let these anxious feelings continue" are replaced with "I can allow myself to feel anxious because I know I'm exaggerating the threat and danger," then the intensity and persistence of anxiety are greatly diminished. (Clark & Beck, 2010, p. 195)

It may appear paradoxical to say that the best way to overcome or control anxiety is to accept it and abandon any attempts to control it. This emphasis upon acceptance has arguably been implicit in cognitive and behavioural therapies for a long time, although it has recently become the focus of the "third wave" approaches (Hayes, Follette & Linehan, 2004). As noted above, distancing from fearful thoughts and acceptance of anxious feelings were described as a typical part of the initial treatment phase in Beck's original 1985 cognitive therapy manual for anxiety (Beck, Emery & Greenberg, 2005). These basic strategies were also summed up in the "AWARE" acronym recommended for homework and self-help in Beck's original manual and in his recent self-help workbook (Clark & Beck, 2012, p. 142). As Beck implies above, the central problem is really the client's faulty appraisal of threat rather than her feelings of anxiety. Feelings of anxiety might be difficult to distinguish, for example, from physiological sensations of excitement, if it were not for the associated beliefs and thoughts about danger, etc.

In addition to discussion of the goals of cognitive therapy and the respective roles of the therapist and client, the client should be helped to understand the treatment plan and strategies employed, etc. This will normally have to be in layman's terms and broad strokes but the client should understand roughly how many sessions are being recommended, the format, frequency, and duration of the sessions, the importance placed on homework, and the main interventions planned. This should include educating the client about the role of self-monitoring thoughts, feelings and behaviour, changing anxious appraisals, engaging in behavioural experiments (particularly exposure tasks), and evaluating and preventing unhelpful coping responses such as safety-seeking behaviours, etc. (Clark & Beck, 2010, pp. 195–196).

In *hypnotherapy*, socialisation to the treatment approach is a common "sticking point" as clients have typically been exposed to misinformation about hypnosis through comedy "stage hypnosis" shows, popular psychology and self-help books, works of fiction, and the internet, etc. The main issue is arguably that clients in general must normally be prepared to adopt an active rather than passive role throughout treatment, to do homework, actively participate in sessions, etc. This conflicts with the preconception that many people have of hypnotherapy as a "quick fix" approach in which their role is to remain completely passive while the hypnotist "talks to their subconscious mind". Hence, we have explored the issue of socialisation to hypnotherapy and hypnotic skills training in some detail in an earlier chapter.

Finally, in these early therapy sessions, "mini-experiments" can be conducted in the session to help socialise the client and educate her regarding the process of therapy. It's common for clients who try to suppress negative thoughts to be asked to try "not to think of a white bear" or a "pink elephant" for a few minutes, and then to reflect upon and discuss the difficulty normally encountered in complying with this task. This can be used to illustrate the problem with "thought control", and the possibility of a "rebound" effect, that is, that attempts to suppress thoughts forcefully and directly can sometimes make them stronger and more frequent. In cognitive-behavioural approaches to hypnotherapy, it's a particularly good idea to introduce the client to self-hypnosis or autosuggestion at an early stage through simple experiments like the "mood induction" technique, ideally taking just a few minutes to illustrate an important point. The expression "mini experiment" should make hypnotists think immediately of "suggestion tests", such as eyelid closure or magnetic palms, which are ideal for this purpose, as discussed in the earlier chapter on socialisation and hypnotic skills training.

Distancing, acceptance, and repeated review

In his original book on cognitive therapy, Beck discusses the concepts of "distancing" and "decentring" as integral to treatment. These terms designate a basic shift in attitude toward cognitive events, described by Beck as a *"metacognitive"* process.

> Some patients who have learned to identify their automatic thoughts recognize their unreliable and maladaptive nature spontaneously. With successive observations of their thoughts, they became increasingly able to view these thoughts objectively. The process of regarding thoughts objectively is labelled distancing. (Beck A. T., 1976, pp. 242–243)

"Distancing" therefore refers to the client's ability to "examine automatic thoughts as psychological phenomena rather than as identical to reality." Beck also describes this as the tendency to regard automatic thoughts as "I believe ..." rather than "I know ...", that is, to treat them as hypotheses or as thoughts rather than facts. He later elaborated that "the notion of 'distancing' is equivalent to activation of the metacognitive level":

> Although the notion of "distancing" has been a central concept within cognitive clinical theory for some time, the relationship between this clinical construct and basic cognitive science has not previously been explicated. Distancing is an active, regulatory process that involves the activation of the metacognitive level of functioning. [...] Furthermore, the metacognitive level allows the person in cognitive therapy to report processing operations/errors (e.g., arbitrary inference, personalization) as well as cognitive content. (Alford & Beck, 1997, pp. 65–66)

Indeed, anxiety is typically compounded by second-order (metacognitive) feelings, that is, fear of anxiety and internal struggle against aversive thoughts and feelings. Moreover, because cognitive restructuring can take time, Beck's cognitive therapy for anxiety emphasised the use of five basic self-awareness strategies employed at the outset to help with immediate symptom relief (Beck, Emery & Greenberg, 2005, p. 232):

1. Accepting anxious feelings and other symptoms.
2. Action strategies, particularly acting "as if" non-anxious and scheduling positive activities.
3. Self-observation, of thoughts, in the present moment from a detached perspective ("distancing").
4. "Emotional review", Raimy's method of repeatedly imagining problematic situations and events.
5. Owning one's emotions by attributing them to one's thoughts and identifying key thinking errors.

Most of these strategies are combined in the "AWARE" acronym, taught to clients as part of the homework assigned in Beck's original cognitive therapy approach (Beck, Emery & Greenberg, 2005, pp. 232, 323–324) as well as his recent self-help manual for anxiety (Clark & Beck, 2012, p. 142). As noted earlier, this orientation, which constitutes a kind of definition of the client's initial role in therapy, and therefore part of the socialisation process, is summed up as follows:

A. Accept the anxiety, that is, don't battle with your feelings but actively allow yourself to experience anxiety, focus on the present (the "here and now") and remind yourself that anxiety is essentially normal, transient, and harmless.

W. Watch your thoughts and feelings, that is, view anxiety from a distance, with a non-judgemental and detached attitude, noticing as it comes and goes, from the perspective of a detached observer.
A. Act despite your anxiety, that is, continue to act "as if" anxiety is not a problem, act confidently, and face your fears until anxiety has abated, dropping "false" safety-seeking behaviours.
R. Repeat these steps, accepting your feelings, watching your thoughts from a distance, and acting independently of your anxiety, perhaps also using repeated "emotional review" imagery.
E. Expect that this will become easier over time, that is, adopt a realistic and optimistic attitude toward anxiety, anticipate its occasional return but realise that practicing these skills will help you cope.

We have already alluded to the possibility of conceptualising mindfulness and acceptance-based strategies, including "distancing", as forms of *dehypnosis*. Although, this concept has not been developed in detail in the existing literature of hypnotherapy, it is tempting to make a rough distinction between standard hypnosis and various meditation-like procedures, which lead to dehypnosis, as noted earlier.

This outline of foundational client skills in cognitive therapy of anxiety can be linked to Raimy's emotional review technique by having the client repeatedly review mental imagery of an anxious situation, while the therapist coaches her in mindful acceptance of anxiety, distancing, and replacing avoidance or safety-seeking with approach behaviour. Hence, using the "AWARE" acronym in combination with repeated emotional review imagery in the first few sessions can help socialise the client to basic meditation-like skills, conceptualised as dehypnosis. For example, by accepting anxious feelings, viewing old negative autosuggestions from a distance repeatedly, and imagining acting differently in response to them, the client may learn to reduce their "suggestive" quality and respond to them more indifferently. Probably the most convenient way to introduce this method in hypnotherapy is to begin by using imagery-based recall simply to have the client recount a typical recent example of her problem, for information gathering purposes. The therapist can then ask the client to review the same event several times, as if it were a video clip being replayed in the mind, while either allowing spontaneous change to happen or progressively coaching the client in the adoption of the (metacognitive) attitudinal set described in the "AWARE" acronym. For example:

> Now just go back to the beginning of that situation a few more times and imagine experiencing those events again, as if they were happening right now, but this time notice what happens if you take a step back and view your thoughts from a distance, as just words passing through your mind, or a script you're repeating to yourself, remaining aware of yourself as detached observer of your thoughts and feelings, and fully accepting and experiencing whatever feelings arise, without struggling against them in any way …

A full script for a similar imagery technique is described in the earlier chapter on applied self-hypnosis and coping skills.

Indeed, Barber's cognitive-behavioural theory of hypnosis was based on the analogy with other imaginative experiences such as reading a book or watching a movie, which can evoke emotions and other automatic reactions. Barber pointed out that the "spell" of imaginative involvement can be broken, however, by the subject reminding himself that the situation is not what it appears to be.

> At a movie, the person thinks with the communications from the screen. As he becomes engrossed or involved in the action, he does not have negative thoughts such as "These are only actors," "This is just a story that someone made up," or "This is just a series of lights playing upon a screen." Since he thinks and imagines with the communications, he feels, emotes, and experiences in line with the intentions of the writes of the screenplay—he may feel happy or sad and may empathize, laugh, weep, experience horror or shock, etc. (Barber, Spanos & Chaves, 1974, p. 12)

Hypnosis and fully engaging with a story both require that events are experienced "as if" they were real, through a willing suspension of disbelief, etc. However, this fact suggests a method for breaking or weakening the power of negative self-hypnosis, or negative automatic thoughts. To paraphrase from the quotation above, someone who said, "These are only thoughts", "This is just a story I tell myself", "These are just words and images in my mind", would be a poor hypnotic subject according to Barber. However, if those strategies are applied to negative automatic thoughts (autosuggestions), they can potentially be used to prevent them turning into negative self-hypnosis (NSH), and reduce subsequent emotional suffering and impact on functioning. Indeed, such strategies are widely used in modern cognitive therapy to undermine the emotional suffering caused by negative automatic thoughts and morbid extended-thinking processes like worry and rumination, etc. The symptom-reduction guidance found in the "AWARE" acronym and related dehypnosis strategies are therefore valuable topics to cover during the initial stage of treatment when employing cognitive therapy approaches in conjunction with hypnotherapy.

Identifying cognitions and other responses

In order to identify problematic cognitions reliably, the cognitive therapist gathers information in a number of ways, like a researcher "triangulating" data from multiple sources. In fact, there are *four* main strategies for eliciting problem cognitions:

1. *Direct open questions,* such as "What thoughts or images went through your mind automatically when you became anxious?" or "What did you fear was the worst that might happen when you were feeling anxious in that situation?", "What were your main concerns about that situation?", etc.
2. *Questionnaires and forms* such as the Dysfunctional Attitudes Scale (DAS), Beck Anxiety Inventory (BAI), etc., which provide more indirect information on threat-related schemas.
3. *Self-monitoring* by the client, recorded on logs such as the various automatic thought records used in cognitive therapy.

4. *Imagery-based recall* techniques such as the "evocative imagery" method, which asks the client to picture a recent event as if happening now and describe the thoughts that occurred while reliving them.

However, one of the first tasks in any form of CBT is simply to help the client to *distinguish* between thoughts, actions, and feelings, and examine their relationship with each other, etc. Clients tend to find it particularly difficult to distinguish between thoughts and feelings, and the expression "I feel" is often used to express thoughts about which the client experiences some conflict, for example, "I feel like nobody likes me but I know that's not true." In cognitive therapy, clients are sometimes helped to make this distinction by encouraging them to view their emotions in terms of three or four primary categories, or some commixture thereof: anger, anxiety, sadness, and the positive category of pleasure (Beck, Emery & Greenberg, 2005, pp. 168, 239; Beck A. T., 1976, pp. 73–74). Subsuming different "feelings" under these broad headings can constitute a form of "problem reduction", which often helps clients feel less overwhelmed by an apparent multitude of complex problems. Moreover, the tendency to express thoughts as feelings ("I feel like I'm going to make a fool of myself") can be seen as indicating a lack of meta-cognitive awareness or cognitive *distance* from thoughts. Hence, the basic initial task of learning to articulate thoughts as "I think" rather than "I feel" can contribute to mindfulness of them as mere hypotheses, or passing events in the mind, rather than facts about reality. In part, this may be because thoughts, unlike feelings, are typically viewed as being either true or false, and vulnerable to rational disputation or to disconfirmation by experience, the mere awareness of which may weaken their hold on the mind somewhat. Moreover, simply catching automatic thoughts and writing them down in the form of verbal statements can increase psychological distance from them in a way that contributes to therapy.

Self-monitoring of automatic thoughts has always been a characteristic feature of cognitive therapy and one of the things that distinguished it from earlier approaches such as rational-emotive behaviour therapy (REBT). Beck and his colleagues refer to recording automatic thoughts as gathering the "raw data" of cognitive therapy, from which inferences can be made about underlying cognitive structures such as beliefs and schemas (Beck, Emery & Greenberg, 2005, p. 175). This raw data consists of fleeting thoughts, or self-statements, and images, which pass through the "stream of consciousness" very rapidly and are easily taken for granted and overlooked, especially when anxiety is high or the demands of the situation distract one from self-observation. Ideally, the client will develop a habit of spotting her thoughts, especially at critical moments, and noticing how they function, in terms of influencing feelings and action. Over time, this habit should develop into a tendency to spontaneously "reality-check" automatic thoughts and images, and correct distortions and exaggerated appraisals, etc. Of course, as we've seen, from the perspective of *hypnotism*, this is essentially a process of spotting spontaneous negative autosuggestions and "dehypnotising" oneself by gaining psychological distance from them.

However, specific automatic thoughts can be very difficult to identify and not easily noticed or remembered. Moreover, the beliefs and schemas that thoughts are derived from may be difficult to recognise or may lie somewhat outside of conscious awareness. Also, in contrast to depression, some forms of anxiety may be so characterised by avoidance that the relevant schemas are rarely fully activated, meaning that clients lack the opportunity to properly observe their anxious thoughts (Beck A. T., 1976, p. 238). A highly avoidant agoraphobic who never leaves the house may lack insight into the specific thoughts and images that she *would* experience if she *did* expose herself to a relevant threatening situation. The anxious and non-anxious modes can seem like fundamentally different "states of mind", and thoughts which appear automatically in one may be difficult to recall in the other (Clark & Beck, 2010, p. 197). Moreover, as immediate threat appraisals ("Something bad is going to happen") are virtually instantaneous and often barely conscious, afterwards clients are more likely to remember their subsequent thoughts about helplessness and vulnerability (secondary appraisal of coping), such as "I can't handle this", "I need to get away", etc. (Clark & Beck, 2012, p. 34). For this reason, clients in cognitive therapy usually need some coaching and practice to learn the skill of catching their automatic thoughts and appraisals of threat (Clark & Beck, 2012, pp. 77–81).

Socratic questioning and guided discovery

According to Beck's model, anxiety is typically characterised by "What if?" thinking about feared outcomes or catastrophes (Clark & Beck, 2012, p. 23). The most basic and important technique for eliciting clients' anxious cognitions, their "core fear", is simply to ask them specific "open" questions either about actual past episodes of anxiety, anticipated future events, or possibly hypothetical situations. For example, "What do you think is the worst thing that might happen in this situation?" or "What are you afraid will happen?" (Antony & Swinson, 2000, p. 243).

Indeed, in contrast to cognitive therapy for depression, where more open questions are asked, anxious thoughts are better identified by asking about specific "appraisals" or predictions, that is, the client's estimate of the probability and severity of threat, etc.

> It is best to ask the client for specific fearful predictions, assumptions, and interpretations (e.g., "When you are feeling anxious at a party, what are you afraid will happen?") rather than asking for more general thoughts (e.g., "When you are feeling anxious at a party, what are your thoughts?"). General questions are more likely to elicit thoughts that do not lend themselves to restructuring (e.g., "I want to leave" and "I can cope with this situation") rather than specific anxious predictions (e.g., "People will think I am boring"). (Antony & Swinson, 2000, p. 243)

Likewise, rather than simply asking "what thoughts were going through your mind", Beck recommends questions such as the following (Clark & Beck, 2012, pp. 17, 78–79):

- "What were you thinking is the worst that could possibly happen in that situation?"
- "What consequences or outcome did you fear might happen?"
- "What is the catastrophe that you feared might happen?"
- "What was your 'what if?' thinking?"
- "What threat or danger is there in that situation?"
- "How were you thinking about the probability and severity of threat?"

It is also often a good idea to begin by having clients focus simply on recording situations that trigger anxiety and noting their overall level of distress (0–100 per cent), the frequency and duration of anxiety episodes, and any anxiety symptoms or bodily sensations and behavioural responses, as these are usually easier to identify than automatic thoughts (Clark & Beck, 2010, p. 197). Clients can then learn to record the core fear that they think was central to their anxiety each day.

Moreover, as anxious thoughts are less accessible when the client is not in the anxious mode, it is often preferable to evoke moderate anxiety during the session in order to have the client report on her thoughts and feelings. Information previously gathered on situations or events that trigger anxious feelings can be made use of in doing so. Obviously, techniques which evoke anxiety, even slightly, can potentially help to identify the actual thoughts, images, sensations, and behaviours that occur no matter how fleeting. These may include somehow engaging in feared activities, or replicating them through role-play or imaginal rehearsal techniques, etc. For example, a blood phobic might be asked to report her stream of thoughts, and other experiences, during the session in response to handling a syringe, role-playing a blood test with the therapist taking the part of the nurse, or while mentally rehearsing a previous blood test or even an anticipated one, with eyes open or closed.

Imagery-based recall (evocative imagery)

The use of mental imagery techniques to gather information and raise awareness of negative automatic thoughts will naturally be of special interest to cognitive-behavioural *hypnotherapists*. A variety of imagery techniques, known by different names, have been used in CBT to help clients carry out a functional cognitive-behavioural analysis of the interaction between affect, behaviour, cognition, and environment. The client is typically asked to mentally replay a recent event in order to describe the situation and their responses in detail. For example, Meichenbaum gives the following example of "imagery-based recall" during cognitive-behavioural assessment:

> Just settle back in the chair, close your eyes, and think about the experience. Take your time, there's no rush. Just replay the stressful event in your imagination as if you were rerunning a movie in slow motion. Begin at the point just before you felt distressed. [...] Just go through the whole experience and see what comes to mind. Describe anything you remember noticing, thinking, feeling, or doing. (Meichenbaum, 1985, p. 34)

It's particularly useful to have clients describe their thoughts, actions, and feelings at their peak level of anxiety and then go back to a point just before they noticed the first signs of distress and progress forward slowly through events, noticing other "early-warning signs" of anxiety, including additional negative automatic thoughts. Hence, imagery-based recall can be presented as a way of "reliving rather than simply recounting" events, turning a discussion into a more experiential process, by introducing mental imagery. Doing so also makes it possible, in many instances, to achieve additional habituation or to have the client rehearse mindfulness and acceptance skills, etc.

Beck and his colleagues likewise refer to the use of "evocative imagery", "fantasy induction" or "cognitive rehearsal" as similar means of identifying automatic thoughts and other responses (Beck, Emery & Greenberg, 2005, p. 212). From one point of view, this is merely an extension of the normal questioning method (Westbrook, Kennerley & Kirk, 2007, pp. 42–43). However, the client may be asked for a moment to close her eyes and revisit the event more fully in imagination to obtain a more complete account. She may also be asked to review the sequence of events before, during, and after the key incident, which usually takes a little more time to discuss. Of course, the more the client immerses herself in her imagination, the more this process may come to resemble certain forms of hypnotherapy. In particular, it has been noted that the use of cognitive rehearsal or evocative imagery in CBT superficially resembles certain forms of insight-oriented or regression hypnotherapy (Golden, Dowd & Freidberg, 1987, p. 40). Hypnotic regression is usually a more elaborate and prolonged technique. Moreover, from the cognitive-behavioural perspective there is no real reason why the target should be an early memory as it often is in regression hypnotherapy, which adopts a broadly psychodynamic set of assumptions about psychopathology. In cognitive-behavioural hypnotherapy, as in CBT, a *recent* memory is often chosen.

Nevertheless, the use of mental imagery to develop awareness and gather information fits very naturally into a hypnotherapeutic approach, which may be conceived in terms of three overlapping processes:

1. Reviewing imagery of a recent distressing event to gather information and develop awareness (imagery-based recall).
2. Repeatedly reviewing imagery of the event, for initial symptom relief, through spontaneous cognitive and emotional change and perhaps also to apply *distancing* and *acceptance* strategies (Raimy's repeated emotional review).
3. Rehearsing modified imagery involving deliberate cognitive and behavioural changes, including the use of coping statements, and coping skills such as relaxation or active acceptance, etc.

As we've seen, in Beck's original cognitive therapy manual for anxiety, treatment began with symptom relief using techniques such as Raimy's repeated "emotional review" method, which involved repeatedly reviewing distressing mental imagery and observing any spontaneous changes in one's cognitive, behavioural or emotional responses. We will return to this technique later because not only does it combine well with hypnotherapy but it also follows on naturally from imagery-based recall of recent distressing events. It also leads naturally into socialisation of the client to other hypnotic techniques, such as rehearsing changes to her cognition, introducing autosuggestions or coping statements, as in the hypnotic "mood induction" technique discussed earlier. Repeating imagery also naturally progresses into coaching in distancing and acceptance strategies, which may be presented as a form of *dehypnosis*.

Self-monitoring and awareness training

It is usually better if self-monitoring of automatic thoughts follows the use of evocative techniques during an early therapy session. This provides a perfect opportunity for the therapist to demonstrate how to complete a self-monitoring form by having the client record her experiences during the exercise as the first entry on the form being used. Self-monitoring, in some form, tends to continue throughout the course of treatment, although behavioural experiments and exposure will provide prescribed situations following which thoughts and other responses can be recorded. In addition to simply gathering "raw data" and increasing the client's self-awareness of their thoughts, etc., self-monitoring of automatic thoughts is also intended to help encourage spontaneous "reality checks". That is, self-monitoring facilitates the ongoing appraisal of whether anxious apprehension actually comes true or whether it consists of exaggerated estimations of the probability or severity of threat, etc. (Clark & Beck, 2010, p. 198). In other words, self-monitoring potentially acts as a record of whether catastrophic predictions were actually fulfilled or not, that is, whether the client is overly-focused on the worst-case scenario in response to threat. More fundamentally, this aids the primary goal of cognitive therapy in shifting focus away from the content of automatic thoughts and on to the underlying cognitive *appraisals* of threat, that is, over-estimates of probability and severity, etc.

Likewise, as we've seen, recording thoughts can facilitate psychological distance from them and may be presented as another tool of dehypnosis. By spotting automatic negative thoughts and writing them down, the client can learn to view them more objectively, in a detached manner, without reacting to them as if they were powerful, emotionally-evocative autosuggestions. Learning to pause, patiently write down thoughts on the form, and carefully put it away, in a way that deliberately creates a sense of psychological objectivity and distance can be an important initial skill in cognitive therapy.

Moreover, attitudes toward self-monitoring homework should be assessed, for example, by asking the client "Is there anything that might prevent you from completing the homework we've agreed?" or "How do you feel about doing that homework?", etc. Anxious clients are sometimes prone to avoid completing homework, including recording thoughts, because they think it might make them feel worse. The therapist should be on the lookout for beliefs that might be obstacles to completing homework and attempt to address them at the earliest opportunity as they may seriously interfere with the process of therapy. Homework should normally consist of written instructions, and ideally forms given to clients should be demonstrated during the session and contain brief instructions on how they are to be completed.

Likewise, in some cases it can be helpful, at the start of therapy, to simply ask clients to count how frequently they have certain thoughts (Beck, Emery & Greenberg, 2005, p. 195). For example, they might be given a "golf counter", which can be purchased cheaply, and asked to keep a tally of how many times they have self-critical thoughts each day. The task can be simplified further by confining it to a specific time period, such as during a meeting, or in the mornings, etc. It can also be applied to behaviours such as "compulsive apologising." Counting specific types of thoughts, cognitive distortions, or behaviours often reduces their frequency, and is a useful way of managing symptoms early in treatment. It often encourages the client to view her thoughts with psychological distance, without becoming too absorbed in them. Once this has been done for a week, it is usually much easier for clients to self-monitor and record more detailed information, such as the content of specific automatic thoughts, strength of belief, etc. It can also be very helpful to ask clients to keep a daily record of how much time (in hours and minutes) they spent worrying. Many clients respond to this by spontaneously coming to recognise their worry as excessive and wasteful of time, and reducing its duration quite substantially, often with little effort. This information probably helps to disconfirm underlying metacognitive beliefs about the value of worry, leading clients to say things like: "It just made me realise what a waste of time it was worrying so much about things."

The most typical homework task of cognitive therapy, however, is completion of an ongoing record of automatic negative thoughts between sessions. The original cognitive therapy for anxiety employed a modified version of the "dysfunctional thought record" or "daily record of automatic thoughts" used in the earlier treatment manual for depression (Beck, Rush, Shaw & Emery, 1979; Beck, Emery & Greenberg, 2005, pp. 204–205). This approach asked clients to record their automatic negative thoughts and rate their level of belief (0–100 per cent) in each one. However, this has been modified in Beck's revised approach, which places more explicit emphasis on monitoring and disputing threat appraisals (Clark & Beck, 2010). The client is now asked to initially self-monitor anxious thoughts by recording episodes on a simple log with columns headed as follows (Clark & Beck, 2012, p. 78):

1. Description of the anxiety episode, including the situation, symptoms and outcome.
2. The intensity level of anxiety, rated 0–100 per cent.
3. Automatic thoughts of threat, specifically feared outcomes.
4. Any feared catastrophes or the worst outcome that can be imagined in relation to the episode.

This is perhaps the most basic form of self-monitoring in cognitive therapy for anxiety. However, many other records and techniques can be used to gather detailed information on coping strategies, safety-seeking behaviour, bodily sensations, and other relevant factors, and numerous examples are provided by Beck and others (Clark & Beck, 2010). Moreover, basic thought records like the one described above are typically expanded to include columns relating to questions used in cognitive restructuring, such as "What's the evidence?", "What's an alternative view?", "What thinking errors does that thought contain?", "Even if the worst happened, what could you do?", etc. (Beck, Emery & Greenberg, 2005, pp. 204–205). We will look at these and other cognitive restructuring techniques in more detail in the following section.

Cognitive restructuring

The central technique of cognitive restructuring in anxiety is Socratic questioning, particularly repeated questioning about evidence for and against anxious appraisals. However, in his original manual, Beck describes the "three basic approaches" to Socratic questioning in cognitive therapy for anxiety as questioning the evidence, generating alternatives, and decatastrophising (Beck, Emery & Greenberg, 2005, p. 201). In his recent writings, evaluating the "pros and cons" of thoughts and actions is given greater emphasis (Clark & Beck, 2010). Hence, we can identify five key techniques of cognitive restructuring used in the treatment of anxiety as follows:

1. "What's the evidence for that appraisal?" (Questioning evidence).
2. "How's that way of thinking/behaving working out for you?" (Evaluating pros and cons).
3. "What thinking errors does that thought contain?" (Identifying cognitive distortions).

4. "So, what if the worst-case scenario does happen? How could you cope?" (Decatastrophising).
5. "What's an alternative way of looking at the whole situation?" (Generating alternative perspectives).

These strategies aim to verbally dispute and modify client's appraisals and underlying schemas of threat and vulnerability.

Clients often complain that they understand "intellectually" that their automatic thoughts are the problem but that they don't feel that way "emotionally" when in the threatening situation. In other words, when the threat and vulnerability schemas are activated, in the anxiety mode, the client adopts a different belief system and appraises situations differently, as noted in earlier chapters. Beck responds to this by noting that the evidence evaluated when non-anxious can, when combined with other methods, nevertheless be used to de-activate the anxiety mode once it has been aroused, or to prevent it from escalating (Clark & Beck, 2010, p. 201). It can also be explained that "normalisation cue-cards", coping statements, and other methods can be used as reminders in the anxious situation and that repeated restructuring will tend to weaken the underlying beliefs and schemas, especially when behavioural experiments are introduced during or between sessions. Moreover, through the use of behavioural experiments and imaginal exposure techniques, the therapist may evoke anxiety in the consulting room and activate the anxiety schemas, giving the client a chance to rehearse responding to them differently.

Threat appraisal versus thought content

The cardinal technique of traditional cognitive therapy is undoubtedly the Socratic question "Where's the evidence for that?" However, as we've seen, in Beck's revised cognitive therapy approach to anxiety the emphasis is upon questioning the evidence for faulty *appraisals* rather than the *content* of automatic thoughts. Because the future is inherently uncertain, cognitive disputation must shift the client's focus from "possibility to probability", that is, from their beliefs about the "content" or nature of possible threat on to the accuracy of their estimates concerning its likelihood and the seriousness of its consequences. For example, rather than questioning the evidence for the thought "I might lose my job", which refers to a possibility, the evidence is questioned for losing the job being highly probable and also for the consequences being catastrophic and one's coping ability being poor, etc., as these constitute the underlying appraisal or evaluation of the threat. The same thought, "I might lose my job", would be unlikely to cause anxiety if the threat were appraised as unlikely and trivial (non-catastrophic) or if one were confident about handling the consequences (coping ability).

> Thus therapeutic work may be directed toward modifying the conception of threat or challenge (primary appraisal) or toward the evaluation of coping resources (secondary appraisal). The validity of the primary and secondary appraisals is tested by subjecting them to a series of questions: What is the evidence of a threat? How serious is it? What coping resources are available? The individual can also reduce exaggerated threats through coping self-statements.
> (Pretzer & Beck, 2007)

This entails a shift from appraisal of threats in terms of their *possibility* ("It could happen") to estimation of their *probability* ("It's likely to happen").

> The central question is "Am I exaggerating the probability and severity of threat and underestimating my ability to cope?" and not whether a threat could happen or not. (Clark & Beck, 2010, p. 200)

As noted earlier, trying to convince someone that danger is impossible is a typically a losing argument because, strictly speaking, *anything* is possible. For example, if a client worries they will lose their job, cognitive restructuring should focus on the probability of this, its likelihood, etc., rather than upon the client's reasons for thinking that it is possible, that it *might* happen. Sometimes this distinction can be highlighted, where appropriate, by asking the client about a possibility they do *not* fear: "Is it possible you might be struck by lightning?" and "Is that something you think it's necessary to worry about or prepare yourself for?" The client should normally recognise that this threat is undeniably possible but not appraised by them as probable enough to be worth spending time worrying or feeling anxious about. This may lead on to discussion of how probable a threat has to be to justify feeling anxious about it and how probable the client's personal fears are in reality, as opposed to how probable they're falsely appraised as being when the anxiety mode is activated.

Evidence-evaluation

Beck describes evidence gathering as the *sine qua non*, the essence, of cognitive restructuring (Clark & Beck, 2010, p. 201). Hence, learning to question the evidence for their thoughts and beliefs, or to ask themselves the question "What's the evidence for that?", is typically characteristic of the clients' role in traditional cognitive therapy. This question is meant to be repeated, for example, by asking "Can you think of anything else?" to probe for further information until the client runs out of ideas. As in brainstorming exercises, the most useful responses clients give normally come after a chain of similar questions has encouraged them to reflect deeper than usual on a particular topic (Beck, Emery & Greenberg, 2005, p. 200).

However, as noted earlier, anxiety tends to be characterised by apprehensive thoughts about anticipated future threats. For that reason, the future typically being *uncertain*, anxious cognitions normally involve estimates ("appraisals") of the probability of the feared outcome and its consequences, etc. Beck emphasises that, in contrast to depression, cognitive therapy for anxiety focuses on evaluating the evidence for estimates of "high risk" and "serious outcome", that is, in terms of estimated probability and severity. Moreover, whereas cognitive therapy of depression typically rated the level of *belief* in automatic negative thoughts, in the cognitive therapy of anxiety, appraisals of threat are typically treated as predictions and rated in terms of their perceived level of *probability*. However, note that rating how strongly you believe in a prediction, like "I am going to faint", is quite similar to rating how probable you estimate it to be. However, there is a marked difference between the appraisal of probability and severity when in an anxious versus non-anxious state of mind. Anxious clients often report automatic thoughts that pose "What if?" questions that refer to what "might" happen, or their ability to cope with threats. As noted above, rather than the possibility of threat, it's typically "evidence for and against their belief that a threat is highly probable and will lead to severe consequences" that is gathered in cognitive restructuring of the appraisal (Clark & Beck, 2010, p. 201). Appraisal of coping ability is important but logically secondary to the primary appraisal of threat with which the client is trying to cope.

Trying to question the evidence for all elements of threat and coping appraisal can become verbally cumbersome. For example, in his current self-help workbook for anxiety, Beck frequently poses quite wordy questions such as the following:

> Keep asking yourself, "But what is the evidence that I am exaggerating the probability and severity of the situation and underestimating my ability to cope or that I'm ignoring the safety of the situation?" (Clark & Beck, 2012, p. 112)

These questions are often separated out on homework forms, etc. Hence, typical "Socratic" questions used to gather evidence for and against threat appraisals during the session, or on a homework form, might be as follows (Clark & Beck, 2010, pp. 201, 228).

1. "What is it that you fear might happen?" (Threat content).
2. "How likely do you feel that outcome is when you're anxious (0–100 per cent)?" (Probability appraisal).
3. "How severe does that outcome feel to you when you're anxious (0–100 per cent)?" (Severity appraisal).
4. "When you're most anxious, what's convincing you that something bad is *likely* to happen?" (Evidence for probability appraisal).
5. "What conflicting evidence is there that it's unlikely to happen?" (Evidence against probability appraisal).
6. "When you're anxious, what makes you believe that the outcome will be so serious?" (Evidence for severity appraisal).
7. "What conflicting evidence is there that it might not be as serious as you expect?" (Evidence against severity appraisal).
8. "Now, based on that evidence, how likely is that outcome in reality (0–100 per cent)?" (Re-rate probability).
9. "Now, based on that evidence, how severe would outcome actually be (0–100 per cent)? (Re-rate severity).

Beck also suggests asking, "What makes the evidence for your anxious thinking believable?" and, put very directly, "Do you think you might be exaggerating the probability and severity of the outcome?" (Clark & Beck, 2010, p. 201).

It is important to remember that the appraisal made *during* the anxiety mode is being evaluated, that is, during an anxiety episode or an anxiety-provoking experiment. The client's thoughts and appraisals when non-anxious may be completely different, and she should already be partially socialised to that distinction by this stage. To counteract the possible tendency toward selective attentional, interpretative, and recall bias for threat, the therapist will probably need to encourage the client to elaborate more on the evidence *against* the anxious appraisal. Often surprisingly simple points appear to be overlooked. For example, a client who rates the probability of fainting during a panic attack very highly might answer "never" to the question, "How many times have you actually fainted in the past?" This should be added to the list of evidence against the original threat appraisal, of course. It can also be helpful to ask clients whether the perceived evidence is really "good" evidence or whether there might be an alternative way of looking at each piece of evidence which doesn't contribute to the high estimation of threat.

Disputation and imagery

In order to help bridge the gap between evaluating evidence in the non-anxious mode, during sessions, and in the anxious mode, between sessions, the therapist may employ exposure-based experiments in session, including the use of mental imagery (Clark & Beck, 2010, p. 205). This can easily be presented as a self-hypnosis skill, with clients imagining themselves in the feared situation and reporting their thoughts, as in the basic imagery-based recall above, but proceeding to rehearse their cognitive disputation skills. Clients can also potentially be asked to imagine themselves pausing in the middle of an anxious situation, freezing the image, so that they can complete a cognitive therapy form of the kind being provided for homework. Of course, the therapist should prompt the client by reminding her of relevant questions, such as those above. This freezing the image to complete a restructuring exercise can be referred to as a "cognitive therapy time-out" during hypnotic imagery rehearsal.

> Okay just stop now and pause the image, freeze everything and everyone around you for a while, but you can still move around and do things. Now while things remain suspended around\ you, imagine putting your hand in your pocket and taking out the homework form that we looked at earlier in the session. I'm going to ask you some questions to prompt you and I want you to imagine you're there, in the situation, as if it's happening right now, but filling out the form with everything frozen around you, taking a cognitive therapy "time-out". Are you ready? Okay, first of all just imagine you're writing down the date and time as usual, and a brief description of the situation, then nod your head so I can see ... Good. How anxious do you feel, from 0–100 per cent? Write that down. Now what is it that you're afraid might be happening in that situation? Okay, right down your core fear. How likely do you feel that is to happen? Write down the percentage. How severe a problem do you feel that would be if it happened? Write down the percentage. Now pause to consider the evidence for and against. What evidence is there that the outcome will be as likely and as severe as you've said? Okay. Now what evidence is there that contradicts that and suggests things might be less likely or less severe than you initially felt they would be? Okay. Write that down on the form. Now considering that evidence, re-rate the actual probability and severity of the feared outcome. How likely do you think it is now? Okay. Write down the percentage. How severe do you think it would be now? Okay. Write down the percentage. Now, in a few words, what do you think would be a more helpful and realistic way of looking at the situation? Write that down. When you focus on that alternative appraisal of things, how anxious do you feel now, from 0–100

per cent? Write that down then, and slowly put the form back in your pocket. Okay, now just continue to focus on that way of looking at things and when you're ready to continue with the scene, nod your head so I can see ... Okay, now unfreeze things, and just continue imagining what happens, but with the evidence in mind, and focusing on your alternative way of looking at things ... What happens now? How do you feel? What difference does that make to the problem?

Once an anxious automatic thought or appraisal has been evaluated, an alternative interpretation is typically generated and evaluated, as in the script above. However, sometimes other strategies may be helpful in the reappraisal or cognitive restructuring of anxious thoughts.

Cost-benefit analysis

One of the most useful questions in therapy is: "How's that working out for you?" or "Where's that getting you?" Cost-benefit analysis, or weighing up "pros and cons" or "advantages and disadvantages", is a more elaborate version of these basic questions. This technique may be particularly well-suited to anxious clients, who are already quite focused upon the future and the consequences of things (Clark & Beck, 2010, p. 205). Cost-benefit analyses can be carried out upon either thoughts or actions:

1. *Cognition* can be evaluated by considering the advantages and disadvantages of holding a particular belief or way of thinking.
2. *Behaviour* can, likewise, be evaluated in terms of the pros and cons of a particular course of action or coping strategy.

However, rather than doing this by itself, in cognitive therapy cost-benefit analysis and questioning the evidence are often combined in the evaluation of key thoughts and beliefs, as part of the process of cognitive restructuring (Clark & Beck, 2012, p. 116).

The client will have been taught to consider the consequences of her thoughts and behaviour to some extent in developing the initial conceptualisation, at the beginning of therapy. One of the most basic questions in the cognitive therapy of anxiety is "What happens when you have that thought?" In other words, what are the *emotional* consequences of anxious apprehensive thoughts? An obvious "disadvantage" of most anxious appraisals is that they cause distressing anxious feelings, although the client must be somewhat socialised to the basic cognitive model to accept this view. The costs and benefits of anxiety itself are of interest, although the pros and cons of certain thoughts, beliefs, or behavioural strategies may be considered as well. The therapist might ask, "How does doing/thinking that *help* with your anxiety?" and "How might it be *unhelpful* in terms of your anxiety?" Sometimes this might be framed in terms of what the client judges to be "healthy" or "unhealthy" thoughts or behavioural strategies, in relation to her problem.

In the treatment of anxiety, as noted in an earlier chapter, one of the most common applications of cost-benefit analysis occurs during socialisation of the client to exposure therapy and response prevention. In order to overcome the urge to avoid feared situations, the therapist must usually help the client to reconsider the pros and cons of avoidance versus approach behaviour, particularly in relation to the goal of overcoming her anxiety. Subsequently, the client will probably have to consider the pros and cons of dropping her maladaptive defences, that is, her existing safety behaviours and cognitive and behavioural avoidance strategies, etc., in the same light. Perceived disadvantages of acting in a non-anxious way, by approaching feared situations, will often be based upon faulty threat and vulnerability appraisals and can therefore provide material for Socratic disputation.

It is usually important to distinguish between short-term (or immediate) and longer-term consequences. The long-term advantages of facing one's fears, such as therapeutic improvement, must be seen as outweighing the short-term disadvantages, such as discomfort and anxiety, etc. The initial assessment should have garnered information on the wider impact of the problem on different aspects of the client's functioning. This information can be used to enhance her sense of the advantages of therapy and her motivation to engage in exposure and endure the temporary discomfort it entails. Sometimes clients fail to identify any advantages to their existing ways of coping or thinking about things. This usually indicates a lack of insight into the function of the behaviour. Likewise, if the client cannot identify any *disadvantages* to modifying her behaviour or beliefs, and adopting an alternative, then it prompts the question: "Why haven't they *already* changed it?" For example, effort, discomfort, uncertainty, and potential risk are common disadvantages or costs of change that usually deserve to be properly considered. Other distinctions can be made between perceived benefits or disadvantages and real benefits or disadvantages, by asking the client to carefully consider "What's the evidence?" for some of the costs or benefits initially identified. For example, someone might list "prevents arguments" as an advantage of her "compulsive" apologising behaviour, but on close inspection this may be an illusory benefit.

Once the costs and benefits of a belief or behaviour have been evaluated and an alternative has been identified, it can also be evaluated in the same way. "What are the pros and cons of the new strategy you're proposing?"

1. "What is the negative belief or behaviour you want to evaluate?"
2. "What are the immediate or short-term costs and benefits of that way of thinking/acting?"
3. "What are the long-term costs and benefits of it?"
4. "Rate how helpful that belief/behaviour is (0–100 per cent)?"
5. "What would be a more helpful, alternative belief or behaviour?"
6. "What are the immediate or short-term costs and benefits of that way of thinking/acting?"
7. "What are the long-term costs and benefits of it?"
8. "Rate how helpful that alternative belief/behaviour would be (0–100 per cent)?".

Sometimes cost-benefit analysis can be abbreviated to simply remembering either the costs or benefits of a particular behaviour or belief. For example, a smoker might carry a cue card upon which he has written his "reasons for quitting", which he takes out and reads aloud whenever he is experiencing a craving. Likewise, Beck recommends that in some cases clients can practice shifting their focus from threat content onto the question, "Is this anxious thinking helpful or harmful?" (Clark & Beck, 2010, pp. 207–208). This is similar to the more general question: "How's that working out for you in the long-run?" As Beck notes, repeatedly turning one's attention to the costs and unhelpful nature of certain types of thoughts is a way of *distancing* oneself from immersion in them and reducing their strength and frequency. Likewise, taking a step back from automatic thoughts and noticing whether, right now, it's helpful to continue focusing on them can be seen as a basic strategy of *dehypnosis*. This can be particularly useful with worry and generalised anxiety, where perseverative anxious thinking may continue for long periods of time unless interrupted.

Cognitive distortions

Labelling thoughts as containing processing errors is a powerful, indirect way of weakening them. Clients can easily learn these concepts and labels and be on the lookout for their main thinking errors, for example, "I spotted myself catastrophising again", which can be treated as a cue for questioning the evidence or focusing on a rational response, etc. However, sometimes simply spotting and labelling the distortion is sufficient to weaken the thought.

David Burns published a widely-employed list of "thinking errors" or common cognitive distortions identified in the cognitive therapy of depression (Burns, 1980). Although this list remains useful, different cognitive distortions are emphasised by other authors, including Beck, with regard to anxiety. Some authors argue that lists like Burns' are too long and that several of the concepts overlap considerably, hence, they prefer to focus on teaching clients about a smaller set of distortions (Antony & Swinson, 2000, p. 246). Their list includes: arbitrary inference, selective abstraction, catastrophising, and all-or-nothing thinking. Beck's recently-revised manual contains these but adds "nearsightedness" and emotional reasoning (Clark & Beck, 2010, pp. 209–210).

A description of the most relevant thinking errors can often simply be given to clients on a written handout, as below, with instructions to self-monitor their automatic thoughts and to make a note on their thought record, for example, when they spot an distortion occurring.

Catastrophising ("What if?" thinking)

Catastrophising is defined as "focusing on the worst possible outcome in an anxious situation" (Clark & Beck, 2010, p. 169) or "exaggerating the probability and severity of bad outcomes" (Clark & Beck, 2012, p. 34). This can be described simply as "thinking the worst will happen" or interpreting relatively harmless events as signalling an impending catastrophe. This error is particularly apparent in most forms of anxiety, especially in relation to severe worry, which tends to involve prolonged verbal thinking that leads to a progressively more catastrophic appraisal of threat and a growing sense of helplessness or frustration. According to Beck, the core fear underlying most anxiety typically involves the error of catastrophising (Clark & Beck, 2012, p. 34).

Jumping to conclusions (arbitrary inference)

This is sometimes called "fortune telling" when it involves making unfounded assumptions about what will happen in the future, or "mind reading" when the assumptions made are about what other people might be thinking.

Selective abstraction (tunnel vision)

Anxiety tends to be associated with a tendency to notice and focus attention upon potential signs of danger ("attention bias" for threat) and to overlook, forget, or discount possible conflicting evidence or signs of safety. Tunnel vision also involves focusing on signs of vulnerability and weakness to the neglect of one's strengths and resources (Beck, Emery & Greenberg, 2005, p. 33).

All-or-nothing thinking (dichotomous thinking)

Things are viewed in "black-or-white" terms, for example, you are either totally safe or completely vulnerable, when there are usually shades of grey and acceptable levels of risk and uncertainty in life. The search for a "quick fix" in therapy and the desire to completely eliminate anxious thoughts and feelings may be important examples of all-or-nothing thinking.

Nearsightedness ("looming vulnerability")

This is the tendency to assume that danger is more imminent in time or physically near-at-hand than it actually is, that is, that things could rapidly go wrong at any moment, leading to a false sense of urgency and rapidly escalating perceived risk. Anxiety peaks as feared situations approach in either space or time, and anxious clients tend to over-estimate the proximity of danger (Beck, Emery & Greenberg, 2005, p. 34).

Emotional reasoning

This involves assuming that anxious feelings are evidence of real danger, that is, that there "must be something wrong" because that's what your feelings tell you, even though feelings can sometimes be just as mistaken as thoughts and are therefore simply false alarms.

Moreover, Beck notes that asking clients to explain in detail exactly how their inductive conclusions are drawn tends to highlight the presence of certain errors (Clark & Beck, 2010, p. 210). Hence, a related disputation strategy involves "questioning the mechanism" by which something could either lead to or prevent certain feared outcomes. For example, a client with generalised anxiety disorder who fears that worry will give her a stroke can be asked to explain in detail how one thing leads to the other, for example, "How exactly do you think worry would cause a stroke?", "How does that *actually* work?" Likewise, a client with social anxiety who avoids eye-contact can be asked, "How does that actually prevent people judging you negatively?"

Decatastrophising

Catastrophising is so fundamental to most anxiety disorders that the technique of directly countering it constitutes a core intervention in the cognitive therapy of anxiety. As noted above, catastrophising involves focusing upon feared outcomes that are either highly unlikely (probability appraisal) or "blowing things out of proportion" by exaggerating the seriousness (severity appraisal) of a problem or its consequences (Beck, Emery & Greenberg, 2005, p. 33; Clark & Beck, 2010, p. 207). Decatastrophising can be done through the use of normal Socratic questioning; however, Beck acknowledges that where possible "imagining the catastrophe is a more potent way to obtain the emotionally charged aspects of the worst possible outcome" (Clark & Beck, 2010, p. 208). Again, this obviously lends itself to integration with *hypnotic* imagery techniques, which we shall return to below.

There are several verbal strategies used for decatastrophising in cognitive therapy. In the original treatment manual for anxiety, Beck et al. defined it simply as asking "So what if it happens?" They also refer to the simple verbal technique of turning "What if?" questions into "So, what if?" ones, that is, "So, what if you do lose your job? Would that *literally* be the end of the world or would life go on? How would you cope?" Another approach involves "widening" the range of information being processed by the client in appraising the outcome of a feared situation, taking into account the failure of previous predictions of catastrophe to come true and "broadening his time perspective" to consider what would happen next if things did go wrong (Beck, Emery & Greenberg, 2005, p. 208). This is associated with developing "coping plans" to deal with potential feared outcomes, even if they did happen. However, Beck's current approach specifically defines "decatastrophising" as follows:

> Decatastrophising involves the identification of the "worst-case scenario" associated with an anxious concern, the evaluation of the likelihood of this scenario, and then the construction of a more likely moderately distressing outcome. Problem solving is used to develop a plan for dealing with the more probable negative outcome. (Clark & Beck, 2010, p. 209)

This is essentially a matter of "hypothetically", in imagination, confronting the worst-case scenario, the most feared outcome (Clark & Beck, 2010, p. 207). Indeed, as feared catastrophes are typically hypothetical, confrontation and exposure are bound to entail the use of the imagination in therapy, which often lends itself to hypnotic suggestion and mental imagery techniques. Confronting the worst-case scenario by exploring it in concrete terms and imagining what it would really be like if it happened, typically involves re-evaluating the severity of the feared catastrophe, that is, "Even if that really did happen, how bad would it actually be?"

Catastrophising is integral to "worry", which typically involves extended thinking about hypothetical worst-case scenarios. Worry has been conceptualised, paradoxically, as a form of cognitive avoidance, which substitutes extended thinking, abstract verbal processing, for more anxiety-provoking concrete mental images of feared catastrophes. In Beck's approach, the method consists primarily of obtaining a detailed verbal description of the worst-case scenario. This often involves a form of the "downward arrow" technique, repeatedly asking probing questions such as "What's the worst that could possibly happen?" and "What would be so awful about that?" This can be extended by probing questions about the wider impact of the catastrophe in different domains of life, that is, "How would that affect your life?", "How would it affect your relationships?", "What impact would it have on your work?", etc. Finally, the client should report their estimated ratings of the probability and severity of the catastrophe and their appraisal of their coping ability and any safety or rescue factors (Clark & Beck, 2010, p. 208). Initially, people typically report feeling "helpless" and "vulnerable" in relation to hypothetical catastrophes and "not knowing what to do or say", etc. This sense of a total inability to cope may be seen as indicative of stunted emotional and cognitive processing, which can often be modified by re-evaluating things in more concrete detail.

The final stage of decatastrophising often consists of adopting a problem-solving orientation toward the feared outcome (Clark & Beck, 2010, p. 208). A decision should be made as to whether planning to cope with the worst-case scenario or most likely outcome seems most appropriate, or in some cases both outcomes can be prepared for. The more severe and less probable the worst-case scenario is in reality, the less value there may be in planning how to cope with it. A "coping plan" can be developed collaboratively, often simply by the therapist chaining questions such as "So even if the worst happened, what would you actually do to cope?", "And then what would you do next?", etc. Indeed, where necessary most of the techniques employed in problem-solving therapy (PST) can be brought into play to help elaborate upon the coping plan being developed by the client. Elaborating upon the coping plan can be seen as a way of directly enhancing the client's rating of her coping ability or sense of master over the feared situation. The client can be assigned the homework task of reading the coping plan aloud three times whenever she begins to worry, and noting any improvements or modifications, to be reviewed in her next session with the therapist. When clients repeatedly review plans in this way they very quickly become more elaborate and satisfactory. It can be helpful for the client to rate her satisfaction with the plan (0–100 per cent) before and after reading and her perceived ability to cope with the feared outcome. Using hypnosis, or self-hypnosis recordings, the client may wish also to mentally rehearse her coping script.

Generation of alternative cognitions and behaviour ("alternative therapy")

In his earliest book on cognitive therapy, Beck refers to the client being helped to generate two types of "alternatives" – alternative cognitions and alternative behaviours. He refers to the generation of alternatives as "alternative therapy" (something of a play on words). Generation ("brainstorming") of alternative behaviours, strategies, or solutions to problems is a major component of problem-solving therapy (PST). Beck rightly compares this to the generation of alternative cognitions, thoughts, explanations, or interpretations of events in cognitive therapy.

In early approaches to cognitive therapy this was done by repeatedly asking clients to consider "What's another way of looking at it?" with regard to their anxious automatic thoughts (Beck, Emery & Greenberg, 2005, p. 203). It's worth bearing in mind that in practice, most, if not all, of the alternative interpretations or perspectives generated tend to be more realistic and balanced than the original automatic thought. Generating multiple alternative perspectives on a situation tends to reduce anxiety by encouraging cognitive flexibility. Clients can then be asked to evaluate which alternative viewpoint is most helpful and realistic and to rehearse reminding themselves of this in stressful situations, perhaps with the aid of cue-cards, coping statements, or cue-words as rapid reminders.

Anxiety tends to narrow attentional focus on to signs of potential danger and to make thinking and behaviour more rigid and stereotyped (Clark & Beck, 2010, p. 210). This makes it more difficult than normal to identify a range of alternative perspectives or interpretations of the situation. Clients will naturally tend to find generation of alternatives easier in the non-anxious mode, that is, in the consulting room, etc. Whereas extremes such as the worst-case and best-case (or "most desired") outcomes can usually be identified quite easily, clients tend to find it more effort to arrive at other, more balanced interpretations. This can be seen as an important example of "all-or-nothing" (dichotomous) thinking. However, the generation of more realistic, alternative interpretations or predictions that are substituted for faulty threat appraisals is integral to cognitive therapy for anxiety (Clark & Beck, 2010, p. 211). These should normally be more balanced and evidence-based perspectives.

Evidence-gathering can be used as part of a three-step process, to re-evaluate the probability of the worst-case scenario actually happening compared to the "likely-case", or most probable, scenario and, in some cases, the "best-case" or ideal outcome (Clark & Beck, 2012, p. 122). The saying goes that our greatest hopes and worst fears are seldom realised, so the most likely outcome will typically lie somewhere between the best and worst-case scenarios.

1. "What's the worst that could possibly happen?" (Worst-case scenario, catastrophising, or *negative* thinking)
    a. "What evidence do you have that's likely to happen?"
    b. "Rate how likely it is to happen (0–100 per cent)?"
2. "What's the best that you could hope would happen?" (Best-case scenario, "most desired" outcome, or *positive* thinking)
    a. "What evidence do you have that's likely to happen?"
    b. "Rate how likely it is to happen (0–100 per cent)?"
3. "What's most likely to actually happen in reality?" (Most-likely, alternative scenario, or rational and *realistic* thinking)
    a. "What evidence do you have that's likely to happen?"
    b. "Rate how likely it is to happen (0–100 per cent)?".

The generation of alternative perspectives alone can encourage clients to see their original viewpoint as just one of many, as a thought or hypothesis rather than a fact, and it therefore often leads to a sense of cognitive distance and flexibility that may itself be therapeutic. Moreover, the most-likely scenario will often constitute the most rational and adaptive way of viewing the situation and the client may rehearse reminding herself of that perspective and paying attention to it during stressful situations. Beck emphasises that the most realistic perspective should normally acknowledge that anxiety may be experienced, although it will probably be tolerable rather than catastrophic (Clark & Beck, 2012, p. 214). "I probably won't feel anxious", isn't usually a realistic alternative perspective, especially early in treatment.

Re-evaluation of relevant goals and values

The extent to which something is appraised as a threat or harm/loss logically depends upon a prior appraisal of the individual's vital interests or goals. In other words, if someone who is stressed or anxious changes his mind about whether a threatened goal is important to him or not, then the threat may cease to be relevant, and anxiety will be de-activated—he won't care anymore. For example, someone who is socially anxious may fear criticism from "authority figures", whose approval is highly prized, and yet be unafraid of criticism from people who are perceived as socially inferior, or from children, insofar as their opinions are not appraised as being so personally relevant or important. This aspect of appraisal is part of Lazarus' stress model but doesn't feature in most cognitive models of anxiety, apart from Beck's current model of generalised anxiety disorder (GAD). In Beck's cognitive therapy approach to stress, more emphasis is placed on evaluating the relevance of threatened goals in relation to one's more fundamental priorities (Pretzer & Beck, 2007, p. 489).

Stoic philosophy & cognitive-behavioural hypnotherapy

In addition to these common cognitive restructuring techniques, the author's earlier publications on Stoicism and CBT may have some relevance to the practice of cognitive-behavioural hypnotherapy (Robertson, 2005; Robertson, 2010). In particular, the appraisal of control, and distinction between which elements of a situation are under the individual's control and which are not, or only indirectly so, is similar to a number of established procedures in CBT, such as the "responsibility pie-chart" (Clark & Beck, 2012, p. 260). However, more careful and systematic appraisal of control may be of value to many clients across a variety of problems, and easily leads to an apparently lasting, generalisable skill. Indeed, this strategy was foundational to Graeco-Roman Stoicism, the philosophy which both Ellis and Beck repeatedly described as having provided the initial philosophical inspiration for REBT and cognitive therapy respectively (Robertson, 2010).

The "Stoic hypothesis", to coin a term, was that emotional disturbance and related problems were fundamentally maintained by the failure to clearly distinguish between things that are under one's direct control and things that are not. The Stoics sought to adopt a more accepting ("philosophical" in the modern *adjectival* sense) attitude toward things outside of their control while taking full ownership and responsibility for things under their control, and acting with virtue, in accord with their most important values. Of course, many situations are under our control indirectly, in a sense. Or rather it would be better to distinguish between "control" and "influence", for example, by saying that a person may positively influence how other people respond to her in some situations although she does not have direct control over other people's responses. It is only by doing certain things, directly under our control, that we influence our environment and other people. However, that influence is partly in the hands of fate, down to intervening variables beyond our control. It would be accurate therefore to say that although we may desire to influence other people or external events we can only do so by making changes under our *direct* control, hopeful that these "should probably" achieve our goals, fate permitting. In other words, we control our own actions but not their consequences, which we influence only to some degree and indirectly.

Clients can be helped to appraise control more accurately simply by drawing up a two-column form headed "directly controlled" and "not directly controlled" and brainstorming elements of their problems, placing them under one heading or the other. Only elements of a situation under direct personal control should be placed in the first column, although it's natural for this to lead to some reflective discussion.

Directly controlled	Not directly controlled
What I say to others	Other people's actions
The way I say things	Other people's opinions
What I physically do before, during, and after the situation	The consequences of my own actions, in terms of their success or failure
The way I do things	

This should be individualised to the client's problem. However, once completed, attention may be drawn to the fact that in a word, as the Stoics put it, the abbreviated appraisal of most situations is that we control our own thoughts and actions, to some extent, but that more or less everything else, particularly other people's thoughts and actions, and the outcome of events, is not directly under our personal control. In a sense, it is *definitional* to state that our own actions are under our control, because if they were not they would not really be accurately described as "our actions". Although some thoughts and behaviours may be involuntary, they are therefore perhaps best described as things that happen to us rather than things we actively do as agents.

A similar strategy involves asking clients to rate how much direct control they have over a situation, rated from 0–100 per cent. They can then be asked why it wasn't rated 0 per cent and why it wasn't rated 100 per cent, assuming the score was somewhere in-between. In other words, if they have partial or imperfect control over events, what specific aspects fall within their control and what aspects do not? Moreover, repeatedly appraising and re-appraising control across a variety of situations can improve the ability to do so more accurately and heighten awareness of one's "sphere of control" in general terms. This naturally helps the therapist set more realistic goals in therapy, especially where clients present problems involving other people, such as relationship issues. It may involve gently steering the client beyond (often) inappropriate goals defined too much in terms of other people or external events ("My problem is that my husband needs therapy!") and toward greater focus upon and responsibility for their own actions.

Simply introducing the two-column method above and other basic methods of control-appraisal, such as the use of percentage ratings, can shift the focus of therapy on to the client's actions in a valuable manner. Clients can be helped to adopt a more "experimental" and accepting attitude to the outcome of behaviour change, by realising that success or failure can never be guaranteed, in terms of external events. Cognitive-behavioural therapies, as the name implies, help clients to focus upon modifying their cognitions and behaviours, the aspects of any situation closest to the centre of their sphere of control. However, it's important in many cases to clarify that a rough distinction can be made between "automatic" and "strategic" (voluntary) thoughts and actions. Cognitive therapy typically begins by altering strategic cognitive and behavioural processes, under the client's control, in order to influence underlying schemas and thereby more automatic thoughts and actions, as well as feelings, over time.

Behavioural experiments and exposure

The concept of a "behavioural experiment" was introduced in Beck's original treatment manual for the cognitive therapy of depression (Beck, Rush, Shaw & Emery, 1979). It constitutes an important bridge between cognitive therapy and behaviour therapy, and forms part of the justification for the composite term "cognitive-behavioural therapy" (CBT).

> Behavioural experiments are planned experiential activities, based on experimentation or observation, which are undertaken by patients in or between therapy sessions. (Bennett-Levy, Butler, Fennell, Hackman, Mueller & Westbrook, 2004, p. 8)

Behavioural experiments can therefore take many different forms but in relation to anxiety disorders, in particular, they overlap considerably with the concept of exposure therapy. In other words, they present an alternative conceptualisation of exposure therapy, in terms of the cognitive model of anxiety rather than behavioural theories of habituation. In Beck's cognitive therapy for anxiety, "exposure-based hypothesis testing exercises", or behavioural experiments are introduced early in therapy and continue throughout the course of treatment, often constituting the central component of the treatment plan.

Experiments are usually derived from the case conceptualisation and designed to test and disconfirm thoughts and beliefs that maintain the client's problems. It is mainly through action and exposure in the real world that schemas of threat and vulnerability can be disconfirmed and that new ways of thinking and acting can be reinforced by personal experience (Meichenbaum, 1985, p. 9). Beck originally defined the procedure of "empirical hypothesis-testing" as follows (Beck, Rush, Shaw & Emery, 1979, p. 273):

1. Specify the problem.
2. Specify a hypothesis (an "operationalised belief") "about the cause of the problem" (that is, the maintaining factors).
3. Design an experiment to test the hypothesis.
4. Evaluate the results of the experiment.
5. Modify the hypothesis in light of the outcome.

Judith Beck adds that the client should plan how to respond if the negative belief is confirmed, which is similar to "contingency planning" or developing a "backup" coping plan (Beck J. S., 1995, p. 198). Although Beck mainly emphasises the "empirical hypothesis-testing" type, a common distinction is made between different classes of behavioural experiment (Rouf, Fennell, Westbrook, Cooper & Bennett-Levy, 2004, p. 24). For example, a basic distinction can be made between:

1. *Hypothesis-testing* experiments, which aim to disconfirm dysfunctional cognitions and strengthen new alternative cognitions.
2. *Discovery* experiments, which aim to gather data on automatic thoughts, etc., to develop the formulation, that is, to identify the major underlying beliefs (hypotheses) to be empirically tested.

A further distinction is possible between:

1. *Active* experiments, in which the client typically performs some behavioural task themselves, either *in vivo* or in role-play during sessions (or possibly even in imagination).
2. *Observation* experiments, where a model (such as the therapist) is directly observed, or surveys are conducted, or other information is collected by other means.

Experiments may also target different types of cognitions. In Beck's current cognitive therapy for anxiety, the focus is mainly on addressing catastrophic appraisals about specific situations, in order to progressively modify the underlying schemas upon which they are based. However, appraisals and schemas of personal helplessness or vulnerability may also be targeted, as discussed above, especially where the emphasis is upon experimenting with different coping strategies, as in assertiveness training, etc. In Beck's simplified self-help approach, the client is merely asked to record what the worst or most feared outcome of the exposure task might be and to treat that as the hypothesis to be empirically tested (Clark & Beck, 2012, p. 144). However, the more formal process of designing behavioural experiments in cognitive therapy for anxiety has been described in terms of the following sequence of "empirical hypothesis testing" steps (Clark & Beck, 2010, pp. 213–217):

1. The rationale
Just as the overall treatment plan should be based on a rationale derived from the case conceptualisation, the rationale for each individual experiment should also be based upon the client's conceptualisation.

2. Statement of threat appraisal and its alternative
The belief or thought to be tested needs to be clearly stated so that a specific testable hypothesis can be derived from it. For anxiety this will often take the form of a prediction about the feared outcome. This often relates to the generic cognitive formula for anxiety: "Something bad is bound to happen and I won't be able to handle it." In other words, the client's appraisal of threat and vulnerability will typically be the main targets. It's important that the client should rate her level of belief in the statement being tested (0–100 per cent) before and after the experiment. An alternative is identified that is distinct enough to be clearly distinguished when evaluating the results of the experiment.

3. Planning the experiment
The client and therapist should collaborate on deciding what would constitute a realistic and effective test of the belief under investigation. The client can simply be asked to consider, "What would be a good way of testing out that belief in practice?" Planning typically involves defining the experiment operationally and linking it to the conceptualisation before evaluating what resources might be required and anticipating any foreseeable problems or obstacles that might be encountered. The therapist needs to consider the possibility that in some cases the client's anxious thoughts or beliefs may be confirmed if an experiment doesn't go as hoped.

4. Hypothesis statement

The client can be asked to turn the initial belief or appraisal into a situation-specific hypothesis or prediction about the outcome of the planned experiment. Just like a hypothesis in a scientific experiment, this should take the form of one or more specific, unambiguous predictions, the accuracy of which can easily be confirmed or disconfirmed by the client's observations, that is, the results of the behavioural experiment.

5. Record the actual experiment and outcome

It's important that the predictions and results are accurately recorded. The client should record her predictions on a suitable form beforehand and note down the results immediately following the experiment, or as soon as possible. This information will be crucial when reviewing the experiment in the following therapy session.

6. Reflection and consolidation

At the start of the following therapy session the completed behavioural experiment form will normally be reviewed and the therapist will debrief the client with regard to his observations. Behavioural experiments provide a wealth of useful information but particular emphasis should be placed on the extent to which the specific hypothesis was confirmed or disconfirmed and the impact on the original cognition being investigated.

7. Findings and implications summarised

These reflections on the findings should be summarised in the form of a written statement, which the client can retain and use as a reminder. This is important to ensure that the information learned is not simply forgotten and to encourage further consolidation and cognitive modification over time.

A typical format for planning and recording the outcome of behavioural experiments might contain the following headings:

1. Core fear: "What is the feared outcome to be tested?"
2. Threat appraisal: "Rate your estimate of the probability and severity of threat in anticipation of the experiment (0–100 per cent)"
3. Rational alternative: "What is the alternative appraisal that you identified in cognitive therapy?"
4. Plan experiment: "How, specifically, is the experiment to be conducted?"
5. Specify predictions: "What specific hypothesis (prediction), derived from the threat appraisal above, is going to be tested?"
6. Carry out and note observations: "What results did you observe that relate to the hypothesis?"
7. Reappraise: "Now re-rate your estimate of the probability and severity of threat based on your observations (0–100 per cent)"
8. Record reflections: "What else did you learn in relation to your problem?"

Although *in vivo* exposure-based behavioural experiments are not central to traditional hypnotherapy they can easily be combined with imaginal exposure, which is part of the repertoire of mental imagery technique commonly used in hypnosis. For instance, it would be common in cognitive-behavioural *hypnotherapy* for the client to prepare for *in vivo* exposure and behavioural experiments between sessions by rehearsing similar situations in hypnosis using mental imagery.

Mental imagery in cognitive therapy

As we have seen, hypnotism was defined by Sarbin, one of the earliest cognitive-behavioural theorists, as "believed-in imagining" (Sarbin & Coe, 1972). The role of imagination in hypnosis is absolutely central. Indeed, Braid's original definition of hypnotism as "focused attention on an expectant, dominant idea", included absorption in mental imagery accompanied by a sense of expectation that corresponding responses were about to happen, something almost indistinguishable from believed-in imagining. Mental imagery techniques typically provide one of the most obvious avenues through which to combine CBT and hypnotherapy. Indeed, doing certain CBT mental imagery techniques with a mind-set of mental absorption, confidence, and favourable expectations, is so similar to hypnosis that clients themselves often ask: "Isn't this *hypnosis*?"

Although many CBT practitioners make little or no use of them, mental imagery techniques have always played an important role in both behaviour therapy and cognitive therapy. Wolpe's systematic desensitisation, the cardinal technique of early behaviour therapy for anxiety, was itself apparently derived from hypnotherapy and involved relaxation and repeated mental imagery (Wolpe, 1990). Likewise, from his earliest writings onward, Beck has emphasised the role of both spontaneous and induced mental imagery in anxiety. Indeed, he dedicated a whole paper to this specific topic in 1970 entitled "Role of Fantasies in Psychotherapy and Psychopathology" (Beck A. T., 1970). Beck reported that among a group of ten clients with "free floating" anxiety, "autonomous fantasies" or spontaneous (automatic) mental images of mental danger were found in each case, which seemed to explain the distress. When clients were taught to control them a "dramatic reduction" in anxiety levels was exhibited (Beck A. T., 1970, p. 3).

The more intense the anxiety, the more real these images typically appear, and they may easily be construed as a form of negative self-hypnosis. As Beck observed, the effectiveness of hypnotherapy and other techniques involving mental imagery may be due to the tendency for clients to become involved in imagination "as if" it were reality:

> In fact, the potency of induced fantasies, whether used in systematic desensitization, hypnotherapy, or other therapeutic operations may be related to the fact that the patient reacts, to some degree, to the fantasied event as though it were actually happening. (Beck A. T., 1970, p. 14)

Again, this way of looking at mental imagery in CBT resembles Sarbin's description of hypnosis as believed-in imagining. Proponents of hypnosis within the field of CBT have generally pointed to its apparent ability to evoke vivid and prolonged mental imagery as a key additive value, which is linked to the claim, supported by some recent research findings, that hypnosis may improve imaginal exposure in CBT.

> Hypnotic suggestions to engage in the imaginal or in vivo exposure, including suggestions to imagine the sensory, cognitive and emotional aspects of the experience in an intense manner, can enhance the exposure efficacy. It is for this reason that some commentators have argued that hypnotherapy is the treatment of choice for some anxiety disorders because it specifically breaches obstacles to accessing anxiety-producing images or memories. (Bryant R. A., 2008, pp. 538–539)

From the outset, Beck reported that *automatic* or spontaneous mental imagery was used to help clarify emotional problems and to pinpoint their underlying nature and that *deliberate* mental imagery strategies ("induced fantasies") were used in cognitive therapy for a wider range of purposes than in early behaviour therapy, *viz.*:

1. To help identify the precise nature of a current problem and the presence of cognitive distortions.
2. To facilitate more realistic appraisal of events.
3. To reduce anxiety and other distressing emotions through repeated review.
4. To modify the client's external (overt) behaviour through guided structured imagery, or imaginal (covert) behavioural rehearsal.

Based on his early observations regarding mental imagery in cognitive therapy, he concluded: "In general, the combination of the fantasy techniques with the more conventional interview procedures appeared to enhance therapeutic results" (Beck A. T., 1970, p. 16).

Indeed, Beck explicitly refers to the literature of hypnotherapy, and the use of mental imagery as a means of inducing hypnosis, in support of his argument that "induced fantasies" can have a "profound effect in inducing behavioural change" (Beck A. T., 1970, p. 4). In particular, he refers to the use of behaviour-rehearsal imagery in improving motor skills such as dart throwing, as indirect evidence of its potential efficacy in psychotherapy.

> Many people have discovered that they can reduce anxiety and can improve their performance in public speaking or in other stressful situations by repeatedly fantasizing the situation before it occurs ("rehearsal in fantasy"). These observations suggest that fantasies may contribute to achieving skills and overcoming anxiety in normal life situations as well as in cases of psychopathology. (Beck A. T., 1970, p. 5)

In his later writings, Beck claims that the use of mental imagery or fantasy allows more direct access to the preconscious "experiential" level of automatic thoughts.

> Clinical studies have shown that when reality distortions are incorporated into spontaneous fantasies, psychological disorder (e.g., anxiety) results. Moreover, structured or "guided" fantasies have been shown to modify (correct) patients' overt behaviour and to reduce maladaptive affect. Guided imagery theoretically serves two functions: (1) It activates metacognitive (rational) processing, and (2) it is employed clinically to communicate directly with the experiential (automatic system) "in its own medium, namely fantasy." (Alford & Beck, 1997, pp. 69–70)

Hence, although some forms of CBT make little or no use of mental imagery, Judith Beck dedicated a chapter to mental imagery techniques in her textbook on cognitive therapy, as did Aaron T. Beck and his colleagues in their original treatment manual for anxiety disorders (Beck J. S., 1995; Beck, Emery & Greenberg, 2005). Another useful resource is an old self-help book by Arnold Lazarus, *In the Mind's Eye* (1977), which contains many imagery techniques employed in early behaviour therapy and REBT, easily adapted for use in cognitive-behavioural hypnotherapy.

Spontaneous (automatic) mental imagery

Beck has always treated automatic thoughts as consisting of either words or images. Hence, the "raw" or "concrete data" of cognitive therapy consists partly in self-reported spontaneous images associated with emotional distress, especially in the treatment of anxiety. Automatic verbal thoughts and mental images are closely-related in terms of content, and appear to interact (Beck A. T., 1970, pp. 13,15). In particular, most anxious clients report mental images thematically-related to their automatic verbal thoughts, expressing distorted, unrealistic appraisals and underlying schemas of threat and vulnerability (Beck, Emery & Greenberg, 2005, p. 210). As with automatic verbal thoughts, the degree of belief that accompanies automatic imagery varies; some are appraised as absurd and unrealistic whereas others may, momentarily or persistently, be taken as realistic.

Like verbal statements, automatic or spontaneous mental images are unlikely to be reported by clients unless the therapist enquires about them and their retrospective accounts are seldom as accurate as self-monitoring records made at the time the images occurred (Beck A. T., 1970, p. 5). Spontaneous mental images frequently contain gross representations of reality, or of the anticipated outcome of a feared situation. Modification of spontaneous imagery, or helping the client to cope better with it, can often lead to almost immediate relief of certain symptoms (Beck A. T., 1970, pp. 12, 16). As Beck observed early-on, spontaneous negative imagery of a distorted kind often shows evidence of material intruding from childhood and recognising this fact can often help the client to spot the nature of her distortions and gain "distance" from them (Beck A. T., 1970, p. 12). In anxiety, images often intrude that appear to be derived from schemas of vulnerability, for example, images of oneself as a vulnerable child facing powerful adults, or images of helplessness and failure to cope with feared catastrophes in the future. As Beck noted, phobic clients often report vivid spontaneous images of harm occurring to them when exposed to feared situations (Beck A. T., 1970, p. 13).

Judith Beck described a number of mental imagery techniques that can be used to respond to automatic negative mental images, as well as more elaborate mental imagery strategies for use in the consulting room (Beck J. S., 1995). Although Judith Beck and others describe substituting alternative images, distraction techniques, and changing the content of imagery, these strategies are not included here because they do not lead to workable long-term therapeutic solutions in most cases. She likewise points out that interrupting images through thought-stopping or distraction does not provide as much opportunity for cognitive restructuring (Beck J. S., 1995, p. 241). These are all, essentially thought-control and experiential avoidance strategies that are increasingly considered problematic in modern CBT. Ideally, imagery should be confronted and held constant while habituation, distancing, acceptance, cognitive reappraisal or other adaptive ways of coping are either rehearsed deliberately or allowed to take place spontaneously.

Associated imagery/affect bridge regression

In the 1970s, the behaviour therapist Arnold Lazarus described a simple information-gathering technique he called "associated imagery", which resembles techniques long-used in hypnotherapy, particularly "affect bridge" techniques used in regression approaches (Lazarus A. A., 1977, pp. 12–19). As applied in therapy, the steps would appear as follows:

1. The client is to relax as much as possible before beginning.
2. She tries to imagine the negative feelings she wants to address, and makes them grow as much as possible by focusing on the associated thoughts, actions, and sensations.
3. She then tries to follow the emotion (affect) and notice what images come to mind in association with it.
4. Finally, she is to explore the associated image in as much detail as possible and notice any other images that come to mind as she does so.

Although this may resemble certain "free association" techniques used in psychodynamic therapy, it can easily be adapted to serve the needs of a cognitive-behavioural approach. The aim isn't to uncover "deep unconscious" associations, but simply to identify situations or feared catastrophes, etc., that the client consciously recognises as being linked to her distressing feelings. For instance, "If you allow yourself to fully experience your anxiety what images come to mind?"

Indeed, Beck et al. describes a similar technique in the cognitive therapy of anxiety in which the client is asked to close her eyes and try to recall the earliest memory she can think of that relates to her current distress (Beck, Emery & Greenberg, 2005, p. 290). Again, this obviously resembles hypnotic age regression. Once the client is reliving a past experience, she is asked to try to formulate in a single sentence the underlying belief she was experiencing at the time. Although the historical or autobiographical information gathered by such imaginative exercises must be treated with caution, particularly when hypnosis is involved, it can nevertheless still be viewed as a reflection of the client's current concerns and underlying assumptions about life.

Reality-testing the image/reducing the threat

In his original article on mental imagery, Beck also refers to clients being trained to "reality-test" spontaneous mental images and to identify the cognitive distortions in them (Beck A. T., 1970, p. 14). Whereas the other responses to spontaneous negative images described by Judith Beck involve countering them with modifications of the imagery itself, this approach constitutes a *verbal* response to the image. Reality-testing, in this sense, involves the fundamental strategy of cognitive therapy, questioning "Where is the evidence?", in response to negative automatic thoughts that take the form of mental imagery (Beck J. S., 1995, p. 240). However, following Beck's current treatment approach for anxiety, it should essentially be the probability of the imagined threat and the severity of its consequences that are reappraised (Clark & Beck, 2010). Although, in a sense, this is the most basic cognitive therapy intervention, Judith Beck observed that it typically seems more effective to respond to a negative mental image through other imagery techniques rather than verbal methods of cognitive restructuring.

She also refers to a type of reality-testing that involves picturing the scene in a way that represents the signs of threat and safety more realistically, encouraging greater attention to and elaborative processing of genuine safety cues in the environment.

> Pam, a patient who feared undergoing a Caesarean section, envisioned all the life-saving equipment in the delivery room and the caring faces of the nurses and doctor behind their masks. (Beck J. S., 1995, p. 247)

This particular use of imagery resembles the construction of "safety scripts", which may also be used in conjunction with mental imagery, for example, in self-hypnosis. Freezing the image (see below) and inserting cognitive restructuring strategies, for example, by asking the client to imagine time stopping while she completes a thought record and evaluates the evidence for appraisal, is another form of reality-testing that makes good use of mental imagery. However, where clients focus on worst-case scenarios, engaging in full-blown catastrophic thinking, various techniques of "decatastrophising" can be used to further reduce threat appraisals.

Decatastrophising imagery

Later, in his original manual for anxiety, Beck and his colleagues refer to "decatastrophising the image", which they describe as a method of progressively encouraging the client to envisage the "most extreme aspects" of her apprehensive imagery, that is, the worst-case scenario in order to help her re-appraise its likelihood and consequences (Beck, Emery & Greenberg, 2005, p. 219). They note that spontaneous images of feared outcomes tend to stop at the worst point and exaggerate the consequences, partly because there is no attempt to envisage "what happens next", which normally involves distress or pain abating and a process of recovery from setback, that is, coping with and surviving the feared "catastrophe".

Judith Beck, likewise, observed that many clients experience automatic mental imagery portraying a sequence of events that stops or freezes at the worst point without continuing to completion. The client is simply taught to continue picturing what comes next, a method called "following the image to completion." She recommends teaching this coping strategy first because she reports that it is "often the most helpful one" (Beck J. S., 1995, p. 233). This leads to one of two outcomes. Either the client will catastrophise, and picture the worst-case scenario happening next, or she will perform a spontaneous reality-check, and picture a more realistic outcome. If the client does picture a catastrophe this can be considered a way of uncovering feared outcomes, which can be addressed through cognitive therapy, including other imagery techniques. However, where the client follows an image to completion and the outcome is realistic and reduces anxiety, she has effectively discovered a simple way of coping with the original spontaneous image and restructuring her process of thinking in a way that is likely to have an impact over time on anxious beliefs and appraisals. The client can therefore be instructed to treat the automatic negative image as a cue or signal to immediately respond to by deliberately following it to completion, picturing "what happens next", in a realistic manner.

A more rigorous approach to decatastrophising is adopted in the treatment of worry, where it involves reversing the avoidance of mental imagery by elaborating upon feared catastrophes in greater detail than normal and enduring the associated anxiety until it abates before, in addition to this, developing and rehearsing a detailed coping plan. Decatastrophising for worry is therefore a form of imaginal exposure to hypothetical feared outcomes, which could often not be exposed to *in vivo* because of their improbable or extreme nature. As Beck et al. acknowledge, more or less the same decatastrophising technique was described by the philosopher Bertrand Russell in *The Conquest of Happiness*, a self-help book based on academic philosophy written in the 1930s. Speaking of individuals who suffer from worry and anxiety, which they are unwilling to face, Russell wrote:

> Probably all these people employ the wrong technique for dealing with their fear; whenever it comes into their mind, they try to think of something else; they distract their thoughts with amusement or work, or what not. Now every kind of fears grows worse by not being looked at. The effort of turning away one's thoughts is a tribute to the horribleness of the spectre from which one is averting one's gaze; the proper course with every kind of fear is to think about it rationally and calmly, but with great concentration, until it becomes completely familiar. In the end familiarity will blunt its terrors; the whole subject will become boring, and our thoughts will turn away from it, not, as formerly, by an effort of will, but through mere lack of interest in the topic. When you find yourself inclined to brood on anything, no matter what, the best plan always is to think about it even more than you naturally would until at last its morbid fascination is worn off. (Russell, 1930, p. 60)

He provides the following explanation of the technique itself:

> When some misfortune threatens, consider seriously and deliberately what is the very worst that could possibly happen. Having looked this possible misfortune in the face, give yourself sound reasons for thinking that after all it would be no such very terrible disaster. Such reasons always exist, since at the worst nothing that happens to oneself has any cosmic importance. When you have looked for some time steadily at the worst possibility and have said to yourself with real conviction, "Well, after all, that would not matter so very much", you will find that your worry diminishes to a quite extraordinary extent. It may be necessary to repeat the process a few times, but in the end, if you have shirked nothing in facing the worst possible issue, you will find that your worry disappears altogether, and is replaced by a kind of exhilaration. (Russell, 1930, pp. 59–60)

Decatastrophising, or imaginal exposure that involves thinking about the worst-case scenario, is something the client needs to be suitably prepared to do and is not usually introduced at the beginning of treatment. Imagining the scenario and elaborating on it in more specific detail usually encourages the client to engage in spontaneous "reality checking" and, with the help of the therapist, to re-evaluate probability, severity, coping ability, and evidence of safety. Strategies like those discussed in relation to problem-solving can be used to develop a detailed coping plan, where necessary, although often just asking "How would you actually cope if that happened?" is sufficient.

In their early text on cognitive-behavioural *hypnotherapy*, Clarke and Jackson describe a combination of hypnosis and stress-inoculation training, particularly employed in social phobia, which incorporates brief coping imagery for decatastrophising worst-case scenarios.

> After high levels of arousal and anxiety are evoked in the patient, while hypnotised, he is asked to silently repeat the appropriate and psychologically congruent adaptive self-instructions while the anxiety is maintained for another minute or so, and then reduced while the appropriate self-instruction is repeated. Finally, and again in hypnosis, a realistic depiction of an assertive scene is elicited and the realistic and reasonable self-verbalisation is used to terminate the scene. (Clarke & Jackson, 1983, p. 257)

The steps of their hypnotic decatastrophising technique can be broken down as follows:

1. Induce and deepen hypnosis
2. Expose to catastrophic (the worst-case scenario) imagery at moderately high levels of anxious arousal for a minute or so, while accepting and getting-used to the feelings
3. Repeat coping statements and self-instructions during anxiety, as congruent autosuggestions, while reducing the anxiety and relaxing
4. Conclude by shifting attention onto more realistic imagery (the most-likely scenario), while picturing coping (assertively) and repeating rational coping statements as autosuggestions in hypnosis.

Note that this involves patiently facing the worst-case scenario and preparing to cope with it before shifting attention to imagery of the most realistic scenario and how one would cope with that. This attempts to address excessive attention to unrealistic catastrophic fears by confronting them but also re-orienting attention to the most realistic picture of events, to correct faulty threat appraisals and catastrophising. It also involves rehearsal of coping strategies and statements to strengthen appraisal of coping ability.

However, in Beck's current cognitive therapy approach for anxiety, which places greater emphasis on prolonged imaginal exposure and habituation, prior to development of a detailed coping plan, decatastrophising through mental imagery typically involves the following steps:

1. Identify the feared catastrophe (worst-case scenario) that underlies anxiety
The way to get at the ultimate fear is often by repeatedly asking: "What's the worst that you fear might happen?" and "What's so bad about that?" When the ultimate feared outcome is made explicit, sometimes it will immediately seem less probable or less catastrophic than may have been assumed. However, usually the client needs to work systematically on her fear of the ultimate catastrophe to defuse or deflate it properly.

2. Develop a written catastrophising script

The client writes down a detailed description of exactly what would happen if her ultimate fear occurred, a "catastrophising script". How much actual harm would be done? How would it affect your life? What would be the wider impact? How would you have to cope? How long would it go on for? She should try to think through the immediate consequences and implications of the catastrophe, so that she can create a realistic picture in her mind's eye. With some problems the client may even find that the outcome is not as bad as she initially thought when she pictures it actually happening.

3. Practice repeated and prolonged imagination of the feared catastrophe

The client should spend at least thirty minutes reviewing her worst-case scenario, trying to imagine what it would actually be like to live through the catastrophe. Exposure to the mental image should be prolonged and involve as many senses as possible, "as if" it were really happening right now. The client should allow herself to "get used" to the image, and perhaps even grow bored with the experience. She may slowly read her script aloud, several times, and try to really imagine how she would feel. She should continue doing this every day until the anxiety caused by the image has at least halved from its original level, which might take anything from a few days to a few weeks, depending on the nature of the problem. This can also be done by listening to an audio recording of the catastrophising script, along with suggestions for mindfulness and dehypnosis (distancing), of the kind described in the chapter on applied self-hypnosis.

4. Develop a detailed coping plan or "decatastrophising script"

Next, the client should begin to develop a realistic and constructive coping plan that she could actually put into practice if her ultimate fear really did happen. She can write it down and make improvements until she's satisfied it's the best plan available to her. Helpful questions include:

- "How would you minimise the actual harm caused by the feared event?"
- "How long would it take you to move on in your life?"
- "How do you think other people might cope constructively with similar problems?"
- "What would you advise someone else to do in the same situation?"

5. Review the coping plan repeatedly

Finally, similar to the way she used her catastrophising script, the client should imagine this "decatastrophising script" repeatedly as if it were really happening and build her confidence in her coping ability. She should review her coping plan daily for about the next two weeks or so, spending up to half an hour imagining the steps involved and how things would turn out if she put her plan into action. In other words, picturing herself coping as best she can with the worst-case scenario, even if it did happen. She should keep doing this until her anxiety has reduced to roughly less than one-third of its original level and she's satisfied that she can imagine herself coping reasonably well with events. Improvements should be made along the way to the coping script as new ideas come up. Of course, the coping script, once developed, is ideal for use in *hypnosis* and can be turned into a self-hypnosis audio recording.

Jumping ahead in time (time projection)

"Time projection" in mental imagery has been used in many different ways by different cognitive-behavioural therapists, and involves going forward in time, often as another form of decatastrophising. The concept, and the term "time projection", seems to have been introduced to the field of CBT by Arnold Lazarus in the late 1960s. The similarity of Lazarus' approach to various hypnotherapy techniques has made it a natural choice for cognitive-behavioural hypnotherapists (Golden, Dowd & Freidberg, 1987, pp. 36–39). For example, Curwen et al. employ "time projection", based on Lazarus' approach, in hypnosis during brief CBT, stating, "Forward time projection imagery can be used to highlight that the client can stand current adverse situations and that events are seldom 'terrible' indefinitely'" (Curwen, Palmer & Ruddell, 2000, p. 136). However, Beck also incorporated it into his original 1970 article on mental imagery in cognitive therapy.

> When an individual is upset about a particular situation, it sometimes helps to have him imagine the situation 6 months, a year, or several years from the present time. When he is able to project himself into the future, he often gains greater detachment about the significance of the events his is currently disturbed about. (Beck A. T., 1970, p. 10)

Lazarus later wrote of using the method on himself, in a manner resembling self-hypnosis:

> Whenever I upset myself over various issues [...] I always picture myself looking back at the incident from about six months in the future. I instantly realize that a few months from now (or sometimes even a few days from now) it will make very little difference. This produces instant relief. I say "Tough luck!" and go about my business. (Lazarus A. A., 1977, pp. 133–134)

Beck has long recommended this technique for use in cognitive therapy, and describes it as a way of gaining greater perspective on current "traumatic" events:

> When he is upset about a current situation, the patient is instructed to visualise the situation at intervals in the future. When the problem is visualized from the perspective of the future, it often shrinks to appropriate proportions. (Beck A. T., 1976, p. 300)

Hence, Beck et al. describe "time projection" in terms of the client looking back on his current situation from a point in the distant future in order to gain detachment and perspective on problems (Beck, Emery & Greenberg, 2005, p. 217). As they note, Lazarus, in particular, made use of the method of projecting forward in time, which draws upon the truism "time heals" by asking clients to make an imaginative leap into the future, looking back on their current problems from a distance.

Judith Beck employs it as an extension of "following the image to completion", in which the client is advised to jump further ahead in time to the end of a situation or process (Beck J. S., 1995, p. 236). When an anxious image comes to mind, the client is instructed to practice picturing herself in the near future having achieved her goal and resolved the problem, and to explore that image in detail. She also refers to a variation of this technique called "distancing" imagery, employed during the therapy session (Beck J. S., 1995, p. 244). The client is helped to see time-limited problems from a broader perspective by picturing herself in the future looking back upon them "from a distance." This is often done progressively by asking the client to project herself, for example, six months from now, and to describe her situation, then a year, two years, ten years, etc. The same thing, of course, can easily be done in hypnosis and, in fact, hypnosis particularly lends itself to increasing the sense of identification with the new time-shifted perspective.

Future autobiography (age progression)

A technique similar to time projection involves exploring the future self's perspective in more detail. In their original manual for anxiety, Beck et al. refer several times to the incorporation of hypnotherapy techniques derived from an interesting, early book on hypnosis and cognitive therapy by Frederick Melges called *Time & the Inner Future* (Beck, Emery & Greenberg, 2005, pp. 227–230; Melges, 1982). In particular, Beck's early cognitive therapy for anxiety assimilated the hypnotic technique of "future autobiography", which Melges described as follows:

> In effect, the patient gives an autobiography of his future. The patient is asked to project himself ahead in time, usually one week ahead to the next appointment with the therapist. Both patient and therapist pretend it is actually that time ahead. The therapist then takes a detailed "history" of what supposedly "happened", and the patient describes how he coped with imagined situations in this future time span, now viewed as "past." In this way, the patient discovers options and rehearses plans of action that help him reach the goals he has chosen for himself. (Melges, 1982, p. 265)

As the name implies, future autobiography can be seen as a form of hypnotic "age progression", the opposite of "age regression", in which clients imagine themselves in the (hypothetical) future rather than reliving their past. This can be seen as a way of fostering a proactive attitude toward planning for the future and combines well with creative problem-solving methods. Although these techniques were used by Melges in conjunction with hypnosis, Beck and his colleagues felt this was unnecessary. However, cognitive hypnotherapists, who use hypnosis anyway, may wish to retain the use of a hypnotic induction, especially as Melges felt there were features of hypnosis that lent themselves particularly well to the use of such elaborate imaginative techniques.

The client first agrees a point in the future suitable for the exercise, that is, a time by which she hopes to have realistically achieved certain important goals or improvements. Melges typically set this point a week ahead, but sometimes it can be helpful to project several months or a year into the future. The client can then by hypnotised or simply asked to imagine herself in the future situation. As with age regression techniques, this is best facilitated by:

1. Preparing the client in advance by briefly discussing the scene to be envisaged
2. Counting from zero to ten with suggestions that the client is progressively travelling to the scene, which gives her time to get into the right frame of mind (orientation) for the exercise

3. Asking open questions that encourage the client to elaborate on the scene in the first person and present tense and drawing her attention to sensory details, etc., in order to keep her attention on it for a prolonged period and increase its vividness and detail
4. Having the client talk about her actual present situation and immediate future from the imagined future perspective, that is, in the past tense, as if certain future events have already happened.

In cognitive therapy for anxiety, the client is interviewed during age progression, and is encouraged to respond, in the present tense, as if she has already achieved her goals. The client may be asked, for example, to reflect on any obstacles she encountered on the road to success and how she overcame them. The therapist may ask about her accomplishments, how her attitude toward her problems has changed, how her beliefs have been modified, what strategies and resources she used to achieve her goals and her reflections on "how she got where she is today", all from her hypothetical future perspective, looking back on her current problems. Beck et al. recommend making an explicit distinction between "internal" and "external" goals and asking clients about how their circumstances have improved but also how they have changed as people, for example, in terms of their attitudes toward their self-concepts, life in general, and their problems in particular (Beck, Emery & Greenberg, 2005, p. 228). This imagery can be assigned as homework, with the client rehearsing every day how she imagines her life to be in the future, once her goals have been achieved.

Coping imagery/covert behaviour rehearsal

In their early cognitive-behavioural text on hypnotherapy, Clarke & Jackson observe the importance of behavioural responses to anxiety-provoking situations, which can be rehearsed in hypnosis.

> Clinical research [...] emphasises the relevance of the patient's (imaginal) behaviour in fear reduction. Specifically, patients improve more quickly if they are asked to interact with or engage in actions in the phobic situation, whereas patients given passive exposure procedures do not cope as well, and tend to experience more anxiety. (Clarke & Jackson, 1983, p. 226)

In his original article on mental imagery techniques, Beck also refers to the deliberate structuring of guided imagery to involve the rehearsal of more adaptive behaviour, that is, to imagine an alternative, more desirable, course of action (Beck A. T., 1970, p. 11). Beck et al. clearly state that "The rehearsal of a patient's desired goal is one of the most common uses of imagery in cognitive therapy" (Beck, Emery & Greenberg, 2005, p. 230). However, other than for its motivating effect and as a means of shifting perspective for cognitive restructuring, etc., goal visualisation (or "mastery imagery") is arguably less beneficial in therapy than the use of "coping imagery", in which the client progressively imagines herself overcoming problems and setbacks and dealing with distressing emotions, thereby acquiring skills and confidence. This is essentially a form of covert (imaginal) behavioural rehearsal. However, it's usually acknowledged that imagining coping (partial success), despite setbacks or distress, is more helpful to the majority of clients than imagery of "mastery", or having complete success in a situation. In particular, if "mastery" means the elimination of anxiety, this is seldom an appropriate short-term goal. Where "coping" means experiencing anxiety but learning to accept it and act more fearlessly anyway, this is typically a more adaptive response. Moreover, visualising goals does not make clients "magically" achieve them, although the technique is unfortunately sometimes presented in this way by hypnotherapists. Many people daydream about idealistic goals that they never make any progress toward, for example, people we might class as "daydreamers" and "fantasists" who contemplate their life goals in a passive or unrealistic way.

Judith Beck describes "coping in the image" as another response to spontaneous negative images; having the client deliberately imagine coping better with the problem, either "naturally" or by employing coping strategies learned in therapy (Beck J. S., 1995, p. 237). The client can be asked to repeat the image several times in the therapy session, trying to picture herself coping better each time, until a satisfactory response can be easily envisaged, and used as a response when the negative thought arises between sessions. This approach is also ideal as a way of rehearsing coping skills assigned for homework in order to anticipate possible setbacks and help the client acquire skill and confidence in using the chosen strategy. For example, the client may picture herself engaging in a planned *in vivo* self-exposure task, while reading aloud her coping statements from a cue card in order to manage her anxiety and prolong exposure sufficiently for improvement to take place. This also provides a way for clients to experiment with and evaluate several alternative coping strategies, which resembles a form of problem-solving. Beck et al. recommend the use of this coping skills approach, where the client mentally rehearses using strategies to overcome problems, along with self-instruction statements, as part of standard cognitive therapy for anxiety (Beck, Emery & Greenberg, 2005, p. 230).

Imaginal (covert) modelling

One way of rehearsing coping and improving the sense of mastery of a situation is by incorporating modelling strategies in hypnosis through the use of mental imagery. Beck et al. point out that "covert modelling" of coping can be used in cognitive therapy to have clients first envisage how *someone else* would cope with a similar problem (Beck, Emery & Greenberg, 2005, p. 225). This may also involve the client imagining coping with a problem while accompanied by another person, providing support, which may be the therapist in many cases or a personal hero or "role-model." Covert or imaginal approaches to modelling can be divided into various stages, as follows:

1. *Observing coping*. The client pictures someone like her (a role-model) *coping* with the same feared situation imperfectly, that is, struggling at first but persevering.
2. *Observing mastery*. The client pictures the role-model progressively approaching mastery of the situation.
3. *Participant modelling*. The client pictures herself coping with the situation, and progressively approaching mastery, with the role-model beside her offering guidance and support (participant modelling)

4. *Modelling coping.* The client pictures herself reducing ("fading") the presence of the role-model and coping with the same situation alone, without any support.
5. *Modelling mastery.* The client pictures herself progressively mastering the situation.

Likewise, Curwen et al. recommend the combination of "coping imagery" and ego-strengthening suggestions in the use of hypnosis as an adjunct to brief CBT for phobias or stressful situations such as giving presentations (Curwen, Palmer & Ruddell, 2000, p. 134; 136).

Slowing-down and freezing imagery

Where images consist of a sequence of events resembling a "movie clip", as is often the case, or where they can be turned into such a series, the speed of the imagery can easily be modified. Anxious clients tend to envisage threat approaching and overwhelming rapidly, at an exaggerated speed. For example, a spider phobic will typically report that when she thinks of spiders she sees them "darting" or jumping quickly toward her, etc. The speed of such imagery, it should be noted, tends to be *already* unrealistic. This is similar to the cognitive distortion some researchers have labelled "looming vulnerability". Having the client rehearse such imagery in slow motion allows her ample time to cognitively re-evaluate the situation, problem-solve, and practice new coping strategies. This can be referred to as "stopping the world", "pausing for thought", or "taking a time-out" in mental imagery, to allow more adaptive cognitive-behavioural responses to be introduced.

As a general coping strategy for managing the symptoms of anxiety early in cognitive therapy, Beck et al. recommend a similar technique drawn from Melges' use of hypnotic time distortion (Beck, Emery & Greenberg, 2005, pp. 248–249). The client is asked to imagine time being slowed down and stretched out, as though she has all the time in the world and things are moving very slowly around her. Likewise, Clarke and Jackson borrow the time expansion hypnotherapy techniques from Kroger & Fezler's seminal book on "imagery conditioning" techniques in behavioural hypnotherapy (Kroger & Fezler, 1976).

> Time-expansion imagery can be utilised to slow down the psychological clock in anxious and depressed patients, so that first it better matches the objective time and then slows still further. One achieved, the crucial scenes can be run through in very slow motion and the patients can "see" the problem as it begins to unfold. It may be helpful to "freeze the frame" and stop all of the participants in mid-motion and have the patients "insert" the correct self-instructions. (Clarke & Jackson, 1983, p. 259)

Clients can be encouraged to treat early signs of anxiety, etc., as signals to engage in their counter-acting coping responses. For example, these could be external triggers, like someone pulling a facial expression, or internal signs such as self-critical thoughts. These triggers and early symptoms are reframed as "warning lights" which the client is encouraged to treat as signals for the immediate use of self-help strategies. This concept can be augmented by asking clients to introduce imagery, for example, literally picturing flashing warning signs on other people's forehead's saying "Stop and think!" or "Breathe deeply!", etc., to encourage the client to pause, interrupt her habitual responses, and engage in her new strategies.

Alladin describes a similar strategy used for "cognitive restructuring" in his cognitive hypnotherapy for depression (Alladin, 2008, p. 49). The client is regressed to an upsetting past event and encouraged to carefully identify and "freeze" ("frame by frame, like a movie") the negative automatic thoughts and images occurring within the scene and systematically replace them with more helpful self-talk and images, while focusing upon the resulting change in feelings, etc. This process is repeated for each automatic negative thought or image until the whole scene has been restructured in this way.

Whereas speeding up perception often leads to more mistakes and dysfunctional responses, slowing things down often has the following advantages:

1. It seems to inherently reduce the sense of anxiety or "looming vulnerability"
2. It encourages greater awareness of the response chain, allowing the client to spot early warning signs and nip their reaction in the bud before it grows out of control
3. It allows room for creative thinking and spontaneous problem-solving, so that clients often report alternative ways of responding coming to mind during the process
4. It makes it easier for the client to "insert" and repeatedly rehearse alternative coping statements and skills, allowing time to "shape" increasing competency in using them
5. It allows the client to monitor and describe the sequence of events in more accurate detail to the therapist
6. It allows the client to become more aware of thoughts and feelings as internal experiences and to rehearse psychological "distancing" strategies.

Clarke and Jackson found that their anxious and depressed clients seemed to "run a fast clock" and when asked to close their eyes and gauge the passage of time, without counting or other aids, typically reported feeling as if thirty seconds of *subjective* time had elapsed when, in reality, only fifteen seconds of *clock* time had passed (Clarke & Jackson, 1983, p. 260).

Avoidance-reversal imagery

However, in some cases, it may also be beneficial to temporarily *increase* the speed of mental imagery somewhat to create a sense of unhesitant approach. For example, completing unpleasant tasks such as household chores very briskly in the imagination and dwelling on the sense of satisfaction that comes from contemplating them being finished, as a way of instilling a sense of motivation and enthusiasm for attempting them. Lazarus refers to a technique of "taking psychological risks", based on the observation that many clients exhibit avoidance and procrastination across a fairly wide range of everyday situations and tasks (Lazarus A. A., 1977, pp. 188–190). By deciding to "play it safe" and avoid emotional risks, clients narrow their sphere of activity and withdraw from many potentially rewarding experiences in life. These steps are modified from Lazarus' account of the technique:

1. Brainstorm a list of situations or tasks you have been avoiding, putting off, ignoring, etc.
2. Pick 4–5 different items from the list, beginning the mildly or moderately difficult ones

3. Picture yourself confidently and unhesitantly approaching each task and briskly completing it, three or four times in a row
4. Repeat this exercise twice per day, and try to cultivate a proactive and self-confident "mind-set" or attitude as you do so
5. In addition, make a strong and concerted effort to reverse avoidance and face the tasks you've been avoiding
6. Evaluate your achievements, then praise and reward yourself for the efforts you've made.

Some intrinsic self-reinforcement can be achieved by, after rapidly picturing the avoided task being completed, dwelling on the most pleasant aspects of the end result and fostering a sense of achievement.

Mood induction, rational-emotive imagery & emotional dial

"Rational-emotive imagery" is a broad term encompassing the main uses of imagery techniques in Albert Ellis' REBT that typically involve imaginal exposure to a problem situation, held constant, while the client first evokes and then reduces her distressing emotions, usually through self-talk and temporary modification of her attitude, which may facilitate more lasting change with practice. Curwen et al. recommend the use of this technique in hypnosis used as an adjunct to brief CBT, to help show the client that she can endure difficult situations (Curwen, Palmer & Ruddell, 2000, p. 136). We have already discussed a similar cognitive-behavioural hypnotherapy technique called "mood induction" in relation to socialisation. Rehearsing evoking a negative response, such as worry and anxiety, in response to an imagined problem situation and then rehearsing alternative, more adaptive ways of thinking and acting, is a very useful technique that can serve a socialisation function as well as being used as an ongoing homework exercise by clients.

A similar strategy involves asking clients simply to imagine that they have a dial, marked zero to ten, that controls their level of anxiety. After agreeing that it is initially set around the middle, at five, the client can be asked to place herself in an imaginary situation and slowly turn up the dial one number at a time, until it reaches or comes close to ten. This can be used to heighten awareness of the ingredients of anxiety and the stages of its development. If repeated, this often makes it easier to spot "early warning signs" and undermines the automatic quality of certain emotional reactions, improving psychological distance from the thoughts and feelings involved. It can also make it easier for clients to tolerate high levels of anxiety in a way that can reduce experiential avoidance and contribute to habituation.

Likewise, turning the dial slowly down to five and then all the way down to zero, allows clients to further develop their sense of control over the components of the anxiety reaction. "Turning the dial up and down" can be treated as a dehypnosis exercise, which is portable enough for the client to rehearse in a wide variety of real-world situations. This strategy also works well with feelings of anger. For example, a client was bumped into by someone on a busy train and noticed "early warning signs" in the form of initial angry thoughts ("You idiot!") and sudden feelings of physical tension. She responded by voluntarily imagining herself turning up her anger dial, slowly and patiently, with acceptance of the feelings experienced and a sense of psychological distance from her angry thoughts, pausing to observe her feelings at a high level in a detached way, before slowly turning the dial down as far as possible, voluntarily letting go of certain responses, while distancing herself from and accepting residual (automatic) thoughts and feelings.

Repeated cognitive review (Raimy)

In one of the earliest texts on cognitive psychotherapy, *Misunderstandings of the Self: Cognitive Psychotherapy and the Misconception Hypothesis* (Raimy, 1975), Victor Raimy forwarded the hypothesis that most forms of psychotherapy could be interpreted in terms of a common factor, which he termed "repeated cognitive review" or just "repeated review". Raimy had observed, since the early 1970s, that many different therapeutic approaches encourage clients to repeatedly expose themselves to distressing events, whether in the past, in anticipation of future problems, or even in fantasy. This is done by having clients physically expose themselves (*in vivo*) to tasks or situations that are distressing, by having them imagine things, repeatedly talk about them, or even write about them in journals or self-monitoring forms. It's possible that reviewing events in the presence of a therapist, in a safe environment, or in a manner that requires more focus of attention on the problem and one's responses (such as visualisation), tends to stimulate reflection in a way that can facilitate realistic and constructive reappraisal. Although this technique closely resembles imaginal exposure, it tends to be briefer and to place more emphasis upon repetition of the imagery, and the client verbally reviewing her responses, with attention to spontaneity at different levels, in terms of thoughts, actions or feelings. It is better suited for use initially with mild-moderate anxiety-provoking imagery than for more severely distressing scenes, which may benefit more from more prolonged imaginal exposure or cognitive decatastrophising techniques of the kind described above. Nevertheless, repeated review is a very simple and flexible mental imagery technique that can be easily integrated with cognitive-behavioural hypnotherapy and naturally lends itself to socialisation and early symptom-relief, thereby potentially helping to instil optimism in clients early in the treatment process.

Raimy's hypothesis was that the most important common factor was simply repeated exposure to the distressing experience, in one form or another. The fact that so many apparently quite different methods of doing this appear to achieve broadly similar results could be taken as an indication that a surprising amount of spontaneous change occurs during all of these approaches, that is, they may be different ways of evoking similar therapeutic processes in the client. Raimy, an early *cognitive* psychotherapist, believed that the main process catalysed by these different methods was cognitive restructuring. He concluded that the most effective way of engaging spontaneous cognitive restructuring was by involving the client as much as possible in repeated cognitive review of the distressing experience, asking them to visualise it about three or four times in a row, while describing aloud their changing thoughts and feelings. He described the process of repeated review for specific phobia as follows:

> Once the specific avoidance reaction has been isolated, I ask the individual to close his eyes and imagine himself in a concrete situation where he must interact in some fashion with what he fears or avoids. He is also asked to "describe what happens and tell me how you feel."

He proceeds at his own pace with little interference from the therapist unless he introduces conditions which would nullify the imaginary interaction. No training in relaxation is given, nor are the imaginary scenes hierarchically graded in terms of estimated threat. If a particular scene appears to be too threatening, the therapist can alter it instantly by changing or deleting some of the details. The client or patient is requested to open his eyes at the conclusion of each recital. If the avoidance reaction has not been satisfactorily dissipated in imagination, he is asked to repeat the task until the imagined avoidance disappears. (Raimy, 1975, p. 76)

To a surprising extent, clients, especially when adopting a positive orientation to the exercise, appear to report spontaneous "reality-testing" of their beliefs and changes in their internal dialogue, etc. As Raimy put it, "The repetition facilitates the individual's review of the evidence which supports his misconceptions" (Raimy, 1975, p. 77). Perhaps the closest analogy to Raimy's repeated review method is systematic desensitisation or imaginal exposure, but Raimy adopted a more generic stance and emphasised the spontaneous *cognitive* change rather than counter-conditioning or habituation. Hypnotherapy also typically involves repeated imaginal exposure to distressing events, in many different forms, perhaps most notably in "age regression", mental rehearsal, and a variety of related methods.

In his original article on mental imagery in psychotherapy, Beck referred to the technique of having the client repeatedly picture negative automatic images to encourage spontaneous reality-testing, which he reported was generally followed by lasting modification of underlying attitudes. He describes how successive repetitions in fantasy allowed the imagery to become more realistic and focused on more probable outcomes (Beck A. T., 1970, p. 7). He also noted that repeated imaginal exposure alone could often lead to reduction in anxiety, regardless of whether or not the image itself changed (Beck A. T., 1970, p. 9). Although, at this stage, Beck felt the technique did not lead to spontaneous change in most cases, others reported more consistent results.

As Beck later pointed out in his critical evaluation of behaviour therapy, Brown and Weitzman, having independently examined Wolpe's method of systematic desensitisation, which involves repeatedly presenting feared scenes in fantasy while remaining deeply relaxed, both found evidence of spontaneous problem-solving and cognitive restructuring, not accounted for in the behavioural theory of "reciprocal inhibition" (Beck A. T., 1976, p. 323). Interviews with clients strongly suggested that they had been experiencing more than just relaxation during the process of scene presentation in systematic desensitisation. Typically they described spontaneously modifying the content of imagery and their cognitive perspective on events in a more realistic and adaptive direction. Raimy's concept of repeated cognitive review better accounts, in some respects, for the subjective reports of these patients. Hence, Beck assimilated the notion of repeated fantasy into the earliest form of his cognitive therapy:

In some cases, the repeated imaging of a traumatic event may alleviate the associated distress. In other cases, expectations of future disaster may be reduced to realistic proportions by repeated visualization of the anticipated event. (Beck A. T., 1976, p. 300)

Beck and his colleagues describe Raimy's method as "emotional review", "imagery review", or repetition of a fantasy, in the early cognitive therapy of anxiety. This approach is discussed at length in Beck's original manual for the cognitive therapy of anxiety, where it is described as a common strategy used at the outset of treatment to facilitate initial symptom relief prior to cognitive restructuring (Beck, Emery & Greenberg, 2005, pp. 215–217, 249–253). First of all, this approach is applied to modifying the threat appraisals in specific automatic negative thoughts and images, which have occurred spontaneously. Beck et al. note that when cognitive therapy clients repeat in full a spontaneous fantasy or daydream that they have experienced, such as an image of some catastrophe befalling them, the content of the negative imagery tends to become progressively more realistic with repetition, which typically leads to a "persistent change of attitude", often constituting a form of "decatastrophising".

> With successive deliberate repetitions of a fantasy, its content often becomes more realistic. When concerned with anticipated events, a fantasy changes from having a less probable to a more probable outcome. While repeating the fantasy, the patient automatically tests the original fantasy and molds it into a more accurate reflection of reality. (Beck, Emery & Greenberg, 2005, p. 216)

The same method can be applied to any relevant image, however, not merely to ones occurring spontaneously, and is particularly applied to rehearsal of anticipated threat situations.

> This procedure works best when the patient closes his eyes and imagines the feared situation. This helps the person who is unable to simply talk about the feared situation. A combination is often used: the patient goes through the imagery once or twice and then discusses with the therapist some of his fears and possible reconceptualizations and then has another imagery review followed by a discussion. Usually after each review, the patient discovers new distortions in his structure of the situation. (Beck, Emery & Greenberg, 2005, p. 252)

Beck et al. noted the apparent paradox that *spontaneous* improvement only seems to occur as a result of *deliberate* repeated review of mental imagery, although this may take place during homework sessions, such as self-exposure, outside the consulting room and without the presence of a therapist. As Vygotsky observed long ago in relation to the development of childhood imagination, it's possible that the mere act of deliberately imagining something inherently activates different psychological resources, such as greater self-awareness; these differences may contribute to adaptive change in a way that is less likely to happen when imagery occurs automatically. The fact that imagery is being repeated in a different environment, the safety of the consulting room, and in the presence of the therapist, within the context of a favourable working alliance, may also help to explain why deliberately imagining problems in this way, several times in succession, often leads to a better outcome than might be expected under other circumstances. The technique is prescribed for homework sessions lasting fifteen to thirty minutes per day during which clients are advised to tape record the review or write it down, perhaps with the assistance of another person to aid objectivity, and possibly picturing the imagery in slow motion, before deciding whether any action could be taken differently as a result of the review (Beck, Emery & Greenberg, 2005, pp. 252–253). Judith Beck likewise described a basic technique called "repeating the image", which like Raimy's method simply involves having the client relive a specific distressing image three or four times while noticing what changes.

> The therapist suggests that the patient keep imaging the original image over and over again and pay attention to whether the image and her level of distress change. Some patients seem to do an automatic reality check and envision each succeeding image more realistically and with less dysphoria. (Beck J. S., 1995, p. 241)

Beck also acknowledged that sometimes anxiety would reduce with repeated imaginal exposure, even though the content of the image remained unchanged and there was no evidence of cognitive restructuring (Beck, Emery & Greenberg, 2005, p. 216). This is, of course, what behaviour therapists would predict, that is, habituation through repeated imaginal exposure. It's likely that cognitive (restructuring), affective (habituation), and also behavioural (problem-solving and skills acquisition) processes often occur roughly in parallel, varying between different individuals, and interact with each other in various ways. As Raimy notes, by simple "repetition in imagination of the individual's interaction with the object of his misconceptions", the client tends to desensitise anxiety, work out solutions to problems, and modify faulty thinking (Raimy, 1975, p. 77). He also emphasised the role of repeated review in flexibly expanding *attention*:

> The second recital of a specific scene is likely to be far more detailed than the first. This is in accord with the principle that as perceived threat diminishes, the perceptual field broadens and therefore more details are added. (Raimy, 1975, p. 77)

Indeed, the possible mechanisms of spontaneous change in simple repeated review of mental imagery include the following:

1. Affect
    a. Habituation of anxious responses and bodily sensations
    b. Relaxation and possibly "reciprocal inhibition" of anxiety
2. Behaviour
    a. Rehearsal and improvement of overt verbal and behavioural skills, for example, assertiveness
    b. Rehearsal of approach behaviour and reversal of avoidance
    c. Creative problem-solving and generation and evaluation of alternative strategies
    d. Rehearsal of coping strategies and anticipation of potential setbacks
3. Cognition
    a. Expansion of attention, making it more balanced and flexible, and less rigidly threat-biased
    b. Reality-testing and modification of the specific content of the imagery
    c. Reappraisal of estimates of probability and severity of feared events
    d. Reappraisal of coping ability, that is., increased self-efficacy
    e. Increased recognition and elaboration of genuine safety cues and rescue factors
    f. Increased sense of control of the content and appraisal of spontaneous imagery.

Providing the client with the opportunity to observe some of these processes happening spontaneously, as it were "organically", can help socialise the client to the cognitive-behavioural approach by providing personal evidence, from her own experience, of some of the key processes in action. Repeated review can therefore lead very naturally into training in coping skills training, problem-solving, more prolonged exposure (habituation), cognitive restructuring, behavioural experiments, etc. When a small initial change happens spontaneously during repeated imagery, it provides important "clues" for the therapist and client, suggesting that similar processes should be incorporated in the treatment plan.

Repeated review can be carried out very simply and informally or made into a slightly more elaborate procedure by preceding it with a hypnotic induction and deepening techniques. However, as described in the chapter on applied self-hypnosis and coping skills, it is perhaps best presented as a form of mindfulness and acceptance-based approach or as a dehypnosis strategy, perhaps following some basic scripted instructions for mindfulness and distancing, etc. This can easily be recorded for clients to listen to between sessions, which provides more opportunity for habituation, problem-solving, and cognitive reappraisal to take place in a lasting way. Varying the content of the imagery, to cover a number of different problems or situations, will also tend to improve the generalisation and durability of improvements experienced by the client. The permissive nature of the exercise, which allows change to happen organically with little interference from the therapist, also makes it a good choice early in therapy while the initial conceptualisation is still being developed and confirmed. The changes that clients actually report, in other words, can sometimes be slightly surprising and may contribute to key modifications of the conceptualisation. Repeated review of imagery in this way also helps the client to become more socialised to the use of imagery techniques in general and so it can act as a convenient gateway for the use of some of the other, more structured or prescriptive, imagery techniques described above.

CHAPTER ELEVEN

Conclusion and summary

This work has attempted to provide a detailed account of cognitive-behavioural hypnotherapy that integrates "nonstate" or "cognitive-behavioural" theories of hypnosis with techniques assimilated from hypnotherapy and CBT. The aim has been to do so in a more rigorous manner than previous books on the subject, and to draw on more contemporary research and clinical literature in the fields of hypnosis and CBT. A cornerstone of this integrative approach is the historical link between the parallel concepts of automatic negative thoughts in cognitive therapy and of morbid autosuggestion, or negative self-hypnosis (NSH), in hypnotherapy.

Based on the hypnosis research of Barber and others in the cognitive-behavioural tradition, a "problem-orientation" model of hypnosis has been proposed that identifies five elements of the hypnotic mind-set. This draws on the notion of the hypnotic subject as an active agent and a problem-solver, who selects strategies to help her enact hypnotic responses with a degree of perceived automaticity. To recap, the "hypnotic mind-set", or favourable cognitive set, has been defined in terms of the following beliefs and attitudes derived from cognitive-behavioural theories of problem-solving:

1. *Recognition* of the situation, induction, and suggestions as cues for hypnotic responses, from the outset, and selective attention to them and inattention to other thoughts and experiences (distractions).
2. *Attribution* of hypnotic responses, accurately, to one's own mind-set and agency, rather than to an external hypnotist or hypothetical constructs such as "the unconscious mind".
3. *Appraisal* of the hypnotic situation as an opportunity rather than a threat, and of suggestions as relevant to one's personal goals.

4. *Control* over one's ability to actively "think along with suggestions" and fulfil the role of a good hypnotic subject is appraised confidently ("self-efficacy") and hypnotic responses are expected to occur with a degree of automaticity ("response expectancy").
5. *Commitment* of appropriate time and effort is made by the hypnotic subject, insofar as she is motivated to patiently imagine the responses suggested, neither rushing things nor adopting an overly-passive "wait and see" attitude.

This model is inherently "metacognitive" insofar as the attitudes and expectations requisite to hypnotic responding primarily relate to certain cognitions themselves. Belief in the "power of hypnosis", or "power of suggestion", which becomes something of a self-fulfilling prophecy, involves the expectation that suggested ideas and autosuggestions (cognitions) are likely to evoke hypnotic responses in a relatively automatic manner. This is essentially what Braid appears to have meant by defining hypnotism as focused attention upon the dominant expectant idea, of some response being about to occur, which he termed the "mono-ideo-dynamic" model of hypnotism. Indeed, hypnotism might also be said to function by means of (metacognitive) belief in the ideo-dynamic response itself, and focused attention upon it.

Further research on the role of metacognition in cognitive-behavioural therapies is likely to shed additional light, indirectly, on the cognitive-behavioural theory of hypnosis. In particular, research on the role of metacognitive beliefs and processes in psychopathology is likely to contribute to the concept of negative self-hypnosis. It seems clear at present that "mindfulness and acceptance" strategies, particularly "distancing" or "defusion", play an important role in reducing the impact of these pathological processes and this lends support to the simple contention discussed earlier that hypnosis and dehypnosis should be viewed as two contrasting procedures in hypnotherapy, the latter being analogous to the practice of mindfulness meditation in key respects.

1. *Hypnosis*, which is essentially *self*-hypnosis, requires focused attention to ideas accompanied by the expectation of the responses they suggest occurring in a seemingly "automatic" manner.
2. *Dehypnosis*, by contrast, consists of doing the *opposite* and undermining (negative) self-hypnosis by "distancing" from autosuggestions, viewing them as mere words without the expectation of responses occurring automatically, and perhaps also expanding attention beyond them to include competing thoughts and experiences, rather than narrowly focusing upon them for a prolonged period.

Hypnosis and mindfulness meditation may therefore be seen as two opposite but essentially complementary therapeutic strategies.

The theory and practice of cognitive-behavioural hypnotherapy has been explored in some detail. The early chapters introduced the subject, provided an account of Braid's original theory and practice, and related this to modern cognitive-behavioural theories of hypnosis. An overview was provided of assessment, conceptualisation, and socialisation methods, including hypnotic skills training derived from the cognitive-behavioural research on hypnosis. Later chapters described a simplified "coping skills" approach to cognitive-behavioural hypnotherapy, incorporating elements of modern "mindfulness and acceptance-based" CBT, before elaborating in more detail upon important procedures such as exposure therapy, problem-solving, and cognitive restructuring interventions. The whole text has focused primarily upon the treatment of anxiety and stress, in generic (transdiagnostic) terms, because these are the most common symptoms addressed using hypnotherapy, particularly for subclinical cases. However, the approach described here can easily be adapted and integrated with other protocols for the treatment of a wide range of different problems in therapy, as well as for use in coaching with non-clinical populations.

Hypnotherapy is arguably the *oldest* psychological therapy, at least in the modern clinical context. Braid had the advantage of being able to define his approach in terms of what seemed to him the simplest, most obvious and "common sense" psychological factors of relevance to therapy: focused attention, expectation, and suggestion, etc. Today we know far more about psychological therapies. However, hypnosis is still very popular among therapists and the public, and peer-reviewed scientific research on hypnosis and suggestion continues to be published quite regularly. Whereas other therapeutic theories and techniques have come and gone over the past 170 years, since Braid first defined the concept, hypnotism has actually endured better than most. That is probably because, as a pioneer, he was able to stake his claim to the obvious. Phrenology and Mesmerism, both debunked by Braid, fell by the wayside long ago despite initially widespread enthusiasm for them as therapies. Freud's emphasis upon supposedly therapeutic processes such as emotional "catharsis" and, subsequently, the symbolic interpretation of dreams, jokes, and slips of the tongue is often seen as a mere historical curiosity today, along with other medical fads. However, no-one can reasonably deny the relevance of attention, expectation, and suggestion to psychological change. When other approaches, including CBT, attempt to adopt a similar emphasis, as in the use of certain mental imagery techniques, clients often remark: "Isn't this a bit like doing *hypnosis*?"—and it is quite astute of them to do so.

It seems unlikely that hypnosis will ever really "go away" completely or merely be superseded by alternative therapeutic approaches, such as CBT. The concept of "hypnotic trance" is not accepted by other therapeutic orientations, and has not been supported by research methods such as brain imaging studies. However, it was never an integral part of hypnotism anyway, and numerous cognitive-behavioural researchers in the field of hypnosis have shown that hypnotherapy can be just as effective, and probably more so, when reconceptualised in terms of the subject's attitudinal set and their use of simple cognitive and behavioural skills such as those taught in hypnotic skills training protocols. These draw upon principles and research from general psychology and so the future for hypnosis increasingly seems to be that it assumes a rightful place alongside other cognitive-behavioural therapies, as the therapeutic practice of "imaginative suggestion", within a broader integrative approach to "evidence-based psychological therapy" not confined by allegiance the traditional schools of thought or famous figures in the field of psychotherapy.

With the focus inevitably shifting on to the evidence, rather than the history or the "politics" of psychotherapy, we can perhaps be hopeful that hypnosis is now entering yet another period of popularity among clinicians and researchers. The history of hypnosis consists of recurring cycles of popularity but with each one some advances are made in our understanding of the subject and its therapeutic applications. Those advances, currently, are most likely to come from further integration with the leading evidence-based therapies of our time, particularly cognitive-behavioural therapy (CBT), and the preceding text has attempted somewhat to further this development, in its own way, by drawing together many of the relevant themes in a single volume on therapeutic practice. If this helps others to make better use of hypnosis, or to take a few steps forward in research or theory, then it will have eminently served its purpose. If it helps, in doing so, to restore even some small part of the recognition deserved by James Braid as a pioneer of hypnotism, and an important figure in the early history of psychological therapies, that will be a welcome bonus but his ideas shall stand or fall by their own merits. To date, it seems they have stood the test of time remarkably well.

REFERENCES

Alexander, J. (1928). *Thought Control in Everyday Life.* New York: Funk and Wagnalls.

Alford, B. A. & Beck, A. T. (1997). *The Integrative Power of Cognitive Therapy.* New York: Guilford.

Alladin, A. (2008). *Cognitive Hypnotherapy: An Integrated Approach to the Treatment of Emotional Disorders.* Chichester: John Wiley & Sons Ltd.

Alladin, A. & Alibhai, A. (2007). Cognitive-hypnotherapy for depression: An empirical investigation. *International Journal of Clinical & Experimental Hypnosis, 55*: 147–166.

Anonymous. (1841, December 11). Mr. Braid's Lectures on Animal Magnetism. *The Manchester Courier*, p. 5.

Antony, M. M. & Swinson, R. P. (2000). *Phobic Disorders & Panic in Adults: A Guide to Assessment and Treatment.* Washington, DC: American Psychological Association.

Antony, M. M., Orsillo, S. M. & Roemer, L. (2001). *Practitioner's Guide to Empirically Based Measures of Anxiety.* New York: Plenum.

Araoz, D. L. (1982). *Hypnosis and Sex Therapy.* New York: Brunner/Mazel.

Araoz, D. L. & Negley-Parker, E. (1988). *The New Hypnosis in Family Therapy.* New York: Brunner/Mazel.

Azrin, N. H. & Nunn, R. G. (1977). *Habit Control in a Day.* New York: Simon & Schuster.

Bandura, A. (1977). Self-efficacy: Toward a Unifying Theory of Behavioral Change. *Psychological Review, 84*(2), 191–215.

Banyai, E. I. & Hilgard, E. R. (1976). A comparison of active-alert hypnotic induction with traditional relaxation induction. *Journal of Abnormal Psychology, 85*: 218–224.

Barber, T. X. (1969). *Hypnosis: A Scientific Approach.* South Orange, NJ: Power Publishers.

Barber, T. X., Spanos, N. P. & Chaves, J. F. (1974). *Hypnotism, Imagination & Human Potentialities.* New York: Pergamon Press.

Barkham, M., Margison, F., Leach, C., Lucock, M., Mellor-Clark, J., Evans, C., et al. (2001). Service profiling and outcomes benchmarking using the CORE-OM: Toward practice-based evidence in the psychological therapies. *Journal of Consulting and Clinical Psychology, 69*: 184–196.

Barlow, D. H. (2002). *Anxiety and its Disorders: The Nature and Treatment of Anxiety and Panic* (Second ed.). New York: Guilford Press.

Bärmark, S. & Gaunitz, S. (1979). Transcendental Meditation and hetero-hypnosis as altered states of consciousness. *International Journal of Clinical and Experimental Hypnosis, 27*: 219–226.

Baudouin, C. (1920). *Suggestion & Autosuggestion*. London: George Allen and Unwin Ltd.

Beck, A. T. (1970). Role of Fantasies in Psychotherapy and Psychopathology. *The Journal of Nervous and Mental Disease, 150*: 3–17.

Beck, A. T. (1976). *Cognitive Therapy & Emotional Disorders*. New York: International University Press.

Beck, A. T. & Clark, D. A. (1997). An information processing model of anxiety: automatic and strategic processes. *Behaviour Research & Therapy, 35*: 49–58.

Beck, A. T., Emery, G. & Greenberg, R. (2005). *Anxiety Disorders and Phobias: A Cognitive Perspective* (20th Anniversary ed.). Cambridge, MA: Basic Books.

Beck, A. T., Rush, A. J., Shaw, B. F. & Emery, G. (1979). *Cognitive Therapy of Depression*. New York: Guilford Press.

Beck, J. S. (1995). *Cognitive Therapy: Basics & Beyond*. New York: Guilford Press.

Beecher, H. (1955). The Powerful Placebo. *JAMA, 159*: 1602–1606.

Bell, A. C. & D'Zurilla, T. J. (2009). Problem-Solving Therapy for Depression: A Meta-Analysis. *Clinical Psychology Review, 29*: 348–353.

Bennett-Levy, J., Butler, G., Fennell, M., Hackman, A., Mueller, M. & Westbrook, D. (2004). *Oxford Guide to Behavioural Experiments in Cognitive Therapy*. Oxford: Oxford University Press.

Benson, H. (1975). *The Relaxation Response*. New York: William Morrow.

Bernheim, H. (1887). *Suggestive Therapeutics: A Treatise on the Nature and Uses of Hypnotism*. New York: G. P. Putnam's Sons.

Bernheim, H. (1890). *New Studies in Hypnotism*. New York: International Universities Press.

Bernstein, D. A., Borkovec, T. D. & Hazlett-Stevens, H. (2000). *New Directions in Progressive Relaxation Training: A Guidebook for Helping Professionals*. Westport, CT: Praeger.

Bolton, R. (1979). *People Skills: How to Assert Yourself, Listen to Others, and Resolve Conflicts*. New Jersey: Prentice Hall.

Borckardt, J. J. & Nash, M. R. (2008). Making a contribution to the clinical literature: time-series designs. In: M. R. Nash & A. J. Barnier (Eds.), *The Oxford Handbook of Hypnosis: Theory, Research and Practice* (pp. 727–744). Oxford: Oxford University Press.

Bordin, E. S. (1979). The Generalizability of the Psychoanalytic Concept of the Working Alliance. *Psychotherapy: Theory, Research & Practice, 16*: 252–260.

Borkovec, T. & Sharpless, B. (2004). Generalized anxiety disorder: Bringing cognitive-behavioural therapy into the valued present. In: S. C. Hayes, V. M. Follette & M. M. Linehan (Eds.), *Mindfulness & Acceptance: Expanding the Cognitive-Behavioral Tradition* (pp. 209–242). New York: Guilford Press.

Braid, J. (1843). Neurypnology. In: J. Braid & D. J. Robertson (Ed.), *The Discovery of Hypnosis: The Complete Writings of James Braid, the Father of Hypnotherapy*. The National Council for Hypnotherapy (NCH).

Braid, J. (1844–1845). Magic, Mesmerism, Hypnotism, etc., Historically & Physiologically Considered. *The Medical Times, 11*: 203–204, 224–227, 270–273, 296–299, 399–400, 439–41.

Braid, J. (1846). On the Power of the Mind over the Body. In: J. Braid, *The Discovery of Hypnosis: The Complete Writings of James Braid.* London: The National Council for Hypnotherapy.

Braid, J. (1850). Observations on Trance or Human Hybernation. In: J. Braid, *The Discovery of Hypnosis: The Collected Writings of James Braid.* London: The National Council for Hypnotherapy.

Braid, J. (1851). Electro-Biological Phenomena Considered Physiologically & Psychologically. In: J. Braid, *The Discovery of Hypnosis: The Collected Writings of James Braid.* London: The National Council for Hypnotherapy.

Braid, J. (1851). Report of a Lecture on Electro-biology. In: J. Braid, *The Discovery of Hypnosis: The Complete Writings of James Braid.* London: The National Council for Hypnotherapy.

Braid, J. (1852). Magic, Witchcraft, Animal Magnetism, Hypnotism & Electro-biology. In: J. Braid & D. J. Robertson (Ed.), *The Discovery of Hypnosis: The Complete Writings of James Braid.* London: The National Council for Hypnotherapy.

Braid, J. (1853). Hypnotic Therapeutics. In: J. Braid, *The Discovery of Hypnosis: The Complete Writings of James Braid.* London: The National Council for Hypnotherapy.

Braid, J. (1855). The Physiology of Fascination & The Critics Criticised. In: J. Braid, *The Discovery of Hypnosis: The Complete Writings of James Braid.* London: The National Council for Hypnotherapy.

Braid, J. (1860). On Hypnotism. In: J. Braid & D. J. Robertson (Ed.), *The Discovery of Hypnosis: The Complete Writings of James Braid.* London: The National Council for Hypnotherapy.

Braid, J. (2009). "On Hypnotism" ("De L'Hypnotisme") (1860) (D. J. Robertson, Ed.). *The International Journal of Clinical & Experimental Hypnosis,* 57: 133–161.

Braid, J. (2009). *The Discovery of Hypnosis: The Complete Writings of James Braid, The Father of Hypnotherapy* (D. J. Robertson, Ed.). Studley: The National Council for Hypnotherapy (NCH).

Bramwell, J. M. (1896). James Braid: His Work & Writings. In: J. Braid, *The Discovery of Hypnosis: The Complete Writings of James Braid.* London: The National Council for Hypnotherapy.

Brown, T. A., Nardo, P. A. & Barolow, D. H. (1994). *Anxiety Disorders Interview Schedule for DSM-IV: Adult & Lifetime Version.* New York: Oxford University Press.

Bryant, R. A. (2008). Hypnosis and anxiety: Early interventions. In: M. R. Nash & A. J. Barnier (Eds.), *The Oxford Hanbdook of Hypnosis: Theory, Research and Practice* (pp. 535–547). Oxford: Oxford University Press.

Bryant, R., Moulds, M., Guthrie, R. & Nixon, R. (2005). The additive benefit of hypnosis and cognitive behavior therapy in treating acute stress disorder. *Journal of Consulting & Clinical Psychology,* 73: 334–340.

Burns, D. (1980). *Feeling Good: The New Mood Therapy.* New York: Avon Books.

Butler, G., Fennell, M. & Hackman, A. (2008). *Cognitive-Behavioural Therapy for Anxiety Disorders: Mastering Clinical Challenges.* New York: Guilford Press.

Chapman, R. A. (2006). Case conceptualisation model for integration of cognitive behavior therapy. In: R. A. Chapman (Ed.), *The Clinical Use of Hypnosis in Cognitive Behavior Therapy* (pp. 71–98). New York: Springer.

Chapman, R. A. (Ed.). (2006). *The Clinical Use of Hypnosis in Cognitive Behavior Therapy: A Practitioner's Casebook.* New York: Springer Publishing.

Clark, D. A. & Beck, A. T. (2010). *Cognitive Therapy of Anxiety Disorders: Science & Practice.* New York: Guilord Press.

Clark, D. A. & Beck, A. T. (2012). *The Anxiety & Worry Workbook: The Cognitive Behavioral Solution.* New York: Guilford Press.

Clarke, J. C. & Jackson, J. A. (1983). *Hypnosis & Behavior Therapy: The Treatment of Anxiety & Phobias.* New York: Springer Publishing.

Clarkin, J. F. & Levy, K. N. (2004). The influence of client variables on psychotherapy. In: M. J. Lambert (Ed.), *Bergin & Garfield's Handbook of Psychotherapy and Behavior Change* (Fifth edition) (pp. 194–226). New York: Wiley.

Coué, É. (1923). *My Method.* New York: Doubleday, Page.

Curwen, B., Palmer, S. & Ruddell, P. (2000). *Brief Cognitive Behaviour Therapy.* London: Sage.

Davey, G. C. (2006). The catastrophising interview. In: G. C. Davey & A. Wells (Eds.), *Worry and its Disorders: Theory, Assessment, and Treatment.* Chichester: Wiley.

Davis, M., Eshelman, E. R. & McKay, M. (1995). *The Relaxation and Stress Reduction Workbook.* New York: MJF Books.

Diamond, M. J. (1989). The cognitive skills model: An emerging paradigm for investigating hypnotic phenomena. In: N. P. Spanos & J. F. Chaves (Eds.), *Hypnosis: The Cognitive-Behavioural Perspective* (pp. 380–399). New York: Prometheus.

Dobson, D. & Dobson, K. S. (2009). *Evidence-Based Practice of Cognitive-Behavioral Therapy.* New York: Guilford Press.

Dobson, K. S. (Ed.). (2001). *Handbook of Cognitive-Behavioural Therapies* (Second Edition). New York: Guilford Press.

Dobson, K. S. & Dobson, D. J. (2001). Historical and philosophical bases of the cognitive-behavioral therapies. In: K. S. Dobson (Ed.), *Handbook of Cognitive-Behavioral Therapies* (Second edition) (pp. 3–39). New York: Guildford Press.

Dowd, T. E. (2000). *Cognitive Hypnotherapy.* New Jersey: Jason Aronson Inc.

D'Zurilla, T. J. & Nezu, A. M. (2001). Problem-solving therapies. In: K. S. Dobson (Ed.), *Handbook of Cognitive-Behavioral Therapies* (pp. 211–245). New York: Guilford.

D'Zurilla, T. J. & Nezu, A. M. (2007). *Problem-Solving Therapy: A Positive Approach to Clinical Intervention.* New York: Springer Publishing.

Edmonston, W. E. (1981). *Hypnosis & Relaxation: A Modern Verification of an Old Equation.* New York: Wiley.

Ellis, A. (1962). *Reason & Emotion in Psychotherapy.* New York: Lyle Stuart.

Ellis, A. (1979). A note on the treatment of agoraphobics with cognitive modification versus prolonged exposure in vivo. *Behavior Research & Therapy, 17:* 162–164.

Ellis, A. (2004). *The Road to Tolerance: The Philosophy of Rational Emotive Behavior Therapy.* New York: Prometheus Books.

Erickson, M. H. (1980). Explorations in hypnosis research. In: M. H. Erickson & E. L. Rossi (Ed.), *The Collected Papers of Milton H. Erickson* (Vol. II) (pp. 313–336). New York: Irvington.

Evans, D. (2004). *Placebo.* Oxford: Oxford University Press.

Eysenck, H. (1957). *Sense & Nonsense in Psychology.* London: Pelican.

Eysenck, H. J. (1947). *Dimensions of Personality.* London: Routledge & Kegan Paul.

Eysenck, H. J. (1977). *You and Neurosis.* London: Temple Smith.

Eysenck, H. J. & Martin, I. (Eds.). (1987). *Theoretical Foudnations of Behavior Therapy.* New York: Plenum Press.

Fennell, M. (1999). *Overcoming Low Self-Esteem: A Self-Help Guide Using Cognitive Behavioral Techniques.* London: Robinson.

Fish, J. M. (1973). *Placebo Therapy: A Practical Guide to Social Influence.* San Fransico, CA: Jossey-Bass.

Flammer, E. & Bongartz, W. (2003). On the efficacy of hypnosis: a meta-analytic study. *Contemporary Hypnosis, 20:* 179–197.

Folkman, S. & Moskowitz, J. T. (2004). Coping: Pitfalls and promise. *Annual Revue of Psychology,* 55: 745–774.

Frank, J. D. (1961). *Persuasion & Healing: A Comparative Study of Psychotherapy.* Baltimore: John Hopkins Press.

Fromm, E., Brown, D., Hurt, S., Oberlander, J., Boxer, A. & Pfeifer, G. (1981). The phenomena and characteristics of self-hypnosis. *The International Journal of Clinical & Experimental Hypnosis,* 29: 189–246.

Gibbs, G. (1988). *Learning by Doing: A Guide to Teaching and Learning Methods.* Oxford: Further Educational Unit, Oxford Polytechnic.

Golden, W. L., Dowd, E. T. & Freidberg, F. (1987). *Hypnotherapy: A Modern Approach.* New York: Pergamon Press.

Goldfried, M. R. & Davison, G. C. (1976). *Clinical Behaviour Therapy.* New York: Holt, Rinehart and Winston.

Goldfried, M. R. & D'Zurilla, T. J. (1971). Problem Solving and Behavior Modification. *Journal of Abnormal Psychology,* 78: 107–126.

Goldfried, M., Decenteceo, E. & Weinberg, L. (1974). Systematic rational restructuring as a self-control technique. *Behavior Therapy,* 5: 247–254.

Gorassini, D. R. & Spanos, N. P. (1999). The Carleton skill training program for modifying hypnotic suggestibility: Original version and variations. In: I. Kirsch, A. Capafons, E. Cardeña-Buelna & S. Amigó, *Clinical Hypnosis & Self-Regulation: Cognitive-Behavioural Perspectives* (pp. 141–177). Washington: American Psychological Association.

Graci, G. & Sexton-Radek, K. (2006). Treating sleep disorders using cognitive behavior therapy and hypnosis. In: R. A. Chapman (Ed.), *The Clinical use of Hypnosis in Cognitive Behavior Therapy.* New York: Springer Publishing.

Grant, A., Townend, M., Mills, J. & Cockx, A. (2008). *Assessment and Case Formulation in Cognitive Behavioural Therapy.* London: Sage.

Greenberger, D. & Padesky, C. A. (1995). *Mind Over Mood: Change How You Feel by Changing the Way You Think.* New York: Guilford Press.

Haaga, D. A. & Davison, G. C. (1991). Cognitive Change Methods. In: F. H. Kanfer & A. P. Goldstein (Eds.), *Helping People Change: A Textbook of Methods* (pp. 248–304). New York: Pergamon.

Hackmann, A., Bennett-Levy, J. & Holmes, E. A. (Eds.). (2011). *Oxford Guide to Imagery in Cognitive Therapy.* Oxford: Oxford University Press.

Hammond, D. C. (Ed.). (1990). *Handbook of Hypnotic Suggestions and Metaphors.* New York: American Society of Clinical Hypnosis.

Hawton, K. & Kirk, J. (1989). Problem-solving. In: K. Hawton, P. M. Salkovskis, J. Kirk & D. M. Clark (Eds.), *Cognitive Behavior Therapy for Psychiatric Problems: A Practical Guide.* Oxford: Oxford University Press.

Hayes, S. C., Follette, V. M. & Linehan, M. M. (Eds.). (2004). *Mindfulness and Acceptance: Expanding the Cognitive-Behavioral Tradition.* New York: Guildford Press.

Hayes, S. C., Strosahl, K. D. & Wilson, K. G. (1999). *Acceptance and Commitment Therapy: An Experiental Approach to Behavior Change.* New York: Guilford.

Hayes, S. C., Strosahl, K. D. & Wilson, K. G. (2012). *Acceptance and Commitment Therapy: The Process and Practice of Mindful Change* (Second ed.). New York: Guilford.

Heap, M. & Aravind, K. (2002). *Hartland's Medical & Dental Hypnosis* (Fourth ed.).

Herzberg, A. (1945). *Active Psychotherapy.* New York: Grune & Stratton.

Hilgard, E. R. (1977). *Divided Consciousness: Multiple Controls in Human Thought & Action.* New York: Wiley.

Horton, J. E. & Crawford, H. J. (2004). Neurophysiological and genetic determinants of high hypnotizability. In: M. Heap, R. J. Brown & D. A. Oakley (Eds.), *The Highly Hypnotizable Person: Theoretical, Experimental and Clinical Issues* (pp. 133–151). New York: Brunner-Routledge.

Hull, C. L. (1933). *Hypnosis & Suggestibility: An Experimental Approach.* Carmarthen: Crown House Publishing.

Jacobson, E. (1938). *Progressive Relaxation: A Physical and Clinical Investigation of Muscular States and Their Significance in Psychology and Medical Practice* (Second ed.). Chicago: University of Chicago Press.

Jacobson, E. (1977). *You Must Relax.* London: Unwin.

James, W. (1884). What is an emotion? *Mind, 9,* 188–205.

Jones, M. C. (1924a). A laboratory study of fear: The case of Peter. *The Pedagogical Seminary, 31:* 308–315.

Jones, M. C. (1924b). The elimination of children's fears. *Journal of Experimental Psychology, 7:* 382–390.

Kanter, J. W., Busch, A. M. & Rush, L. C. (2009). *Behavioral Activation.* New York: Routledge.

Kirk, J. (1989). Cognitive-behavioral assessment. In: K. Hawton, P. M. Salkovskis, J. Kirk & D. M. Clark (Eds.), *Cognitive Bejavior Therapy for Psychiatric Problems* (pp. 13–51). Oxford: Oxford Unviersity Press.

Kirsch, I. (1999). Clinical hypnosis as a nondeceptive placebo. In: I. Kirsch, A. Capafons, E. Cardeña-Buelna & S. Amigó, *Clinical Hypnosis & Self-Regulation: Cognitive-Behavioural Perspectives.* Washington: APA.

Kirsch, I. & Council, J. R. (1989). Response expectancy as a determinant of behavior. In: N. P. Spanos & J. F. Chaves (Eds.), *Hypnosis: The Cognitive-Behavioural Perspective.* New York: Prometheus Books.

Kirsch, I. & Lynn, S. J. (1999). Hypnotic involuntariness and the automaticity of everyday life. In: I. Kirsch, A. Capafons, E. Cardeña-Buelna & S. Amigó, *Clinical Hypnosis & Self-Regulation: Cognitive-Behavioural Perspectives.* Washington: APA.

Kirsch, I., Capafons, A., Cardeña-Buelna, E. & Amigó, S. (1999). *Clinical Hypnosis & Self-Regulation: Cognitive-Behavioural Perspectives.* Washington: American Psychological Association.

Kirsch, I., Montgomery, G. & Sapirstein, G. (1995). Hypnosis as an adjunct to cognitive-behavioral psychotherapy: A meta-analysis. *Journal of Consulting and Clinical Psychology, 63:* 214–220.

Koerner, N. & Dugas, M. J. (2006). A cognitive model of generalized anxiety disorder: The role of intolerance of uncertainty. In: G. C. Davey & A. Wells (Eds.), *Worry and Its Disorders: Theory, Assessment and Treatment.* Chichester: Wiley.

Kroger, W. S. & Fezler, W. D. (1976). *Hypnosis & Behavior Modificaiton: Imagery Conditioning.* Philadelphia: Lippincott.

Kuyken, W., Padesky, C. A. & Dudley, R. (2009). *Collaborative Case Conceptualization: Working Effectively with Clients in Cognitive-Behavioral Therapy.* New York: Guilford.

Lazarus, A. A. (1971). *Behavior Therapy & Beyond.* New Jersey: Jason Aronson.

Lazarus, A. A. (1977). *In the Mind's Eye: The Power of Imagery for Personal Enrichment.* New York: Guilford Press.

Lazarus, A. A. (1981). *The Practice of Multimodal Therapy.* Baltimore: John Hopkins University Press.

Lazarus, R. S. (1966). *Psychological Stress and the Coping Process.* New York: McGraw-Hill.

Lazarus, R. S. (1999). *Stress and Emotion: A New Synthesis.* New York: Springer Publishing.

Lazarus, R. S. & Folkman, S. (1984). *Stress Appraisal and Coping.* New York: Springer.

Leahy, R. L. (2005). *The Worry Cure: Stop Worrying & Start Living.* London: Piatkus.
Leahy, R. L. & Holland, S. J. (2000). *Treatment Plans & Interventions for Depression & Anxiety Disorders.* New York: Guilford Press.
Lewinsohn, P. M., Munoz, R. F., Youngren, M. A. & Zeiss, A. M. (1986). *Control Your Depression.* New York: Simon & Schuster.
Low, A. A. (1950). *Mental Health Through Will-Training: A System of Self-Help in Psychotherapy as Praciced by Recovery, Incorporated.* Winnetka: Willett.
Lynn, S. J. & Kirsch, I. (2006). *Essentials of Clinical Hypnosis: An Evidence-Based Approach.* Washington: APA.
Lynn, S. J. & O'Hagan, S. (2009). The Sociocognitive and Conditioning and Inhibition Theories of Hypnosis. *Contemporary Hypnosis, 26:* 121–125.
Lynn, S. J. & Sivec, H. (1992). The hypnotizable subject as creative problem-solving agent. In: E. Fromm & M. R. Nash (Eds.), *Contemporary Hypnosis Research* (pp. 292–333). New York: Guilford Press.
Lynn, S. J., Das, L. S., Hallquist, M. N. & Williams, J. C. (2006). Mindfulness, acceptance and hypnosis: cognitive and clinical perspectives. *International Journal of Clinical and Experimental Hypnosis, 54:* 143–166.
Lynn, S. J., Kirsch, I. & Hallquist, M. N. (2008). Social cognitive theories of hypnosis. In: M. R. Nash & A. J. Barnier (Eds.), *The Oxford Handbook of Hypnosis: Theory, Research & Practice* (pp. 111–139). Oxford: Oxford University Press.
Lynn, S. J., Kirsch, I., Neufeld, J. & Rhue, J. W. (1996). Clinical hypnosis: assessment, applications, and treatment considerations. In: S. J. Lynn, I. Kirsch & J. W. Rhue (Eds.), *Casebook of Clinical Hypnosis* (pp. 3–30). Washington, DC: American Psychological Association.
Lynn, S. J., Neufeld, V. & Maré, C. (1993). Direct versus indirect suggestions: a conceptual and methodological review. *International Journal for Clinical and Experimental Hypnosis, 41:* 124–152.
Macnish, R. (1830). *The Philosophy of Sleep.* Glasgow: E. McPhun.
Malouff, J. M., Thorsteinsson, E. B. & Schutte, N. S. (2007). The efficacy of problem-solving therapy in reducing mental and physical health problems: A meta-analysis. *Clinical Psychology Review, 27:* 46–57.
Marks, I. M. (1981). *Cure & Care of Neuroses: Theory & Practice of Behavioural Psychotherapy.* Washington: American Psychiatric Press.
Marks, I. M. (1986). *Behavioural Psychotherapy.* Bristol: Wright.
Marks, I. M. (2005). *Living with Fear: Understanding and Coping with Anxiety* (Second ed.). London: McGraw-Hill.
Marks, I., Gelder, M. & Edwards, G. (1968). Hypnosis and desensitisation for phobias: A controlled prospective trial. *British Journal of Psychiatry, 114:* 1263–1274.
Maydeu-Olivares, A. & D'Zurilla, T. (n.d.). The factor structure of the Problem-Solving Inventory. *European Journal of Psychological Assessment, 13:* 206–215.
Meichenbaum, D. (1977). *Cognitive-Behavior Modification: An Integrative Approach.* New York: Plenum Press.
Meichenbaum, D. (1985). *Stress Inoculation Training.* New York: Pergamon.
Meichenbaum, D. (2007). Stress Inoculation Training: A preventative and treatment approach. In: P. M. Lehrer, R. L. Woolfolk & W. E. Sime (Eds.), *Principles & Practice of Stress Management* (pp. 497–516). New York: Guilford.
Melges, F. (1982). *Time & the Inner Future.* New York: John Wiley.
Moll, A. (1889). *Hypnotism.* London: Walter Scott Ltd.

Mowrer, O. (1947). On the dual nature of learning: A reinterpretation of 'conditioning' and 'problem solving'. *Harvard Educational Review,* 17: 102–148.

Mynors-Wallis, L. M., Gath, D. H., Lloyd-Thomas, A. R. & Tomlinson, D. (1995). Randomised controlled trial comparing problem solving treatment with amitriptyline and placebo for major depression in primary care. *BMJ, 310*: 441–5.

Nezu, A. M., Nezu, C. M. & D'Zurilla, T. J. (2007). *Solving Life's Problems: A 5-Step Guide to Enhanced Well-Being.* New York: Springer.

Nezu, A. M., Nezu, C. M. & Perri, M. G. (1989). *Problem-Solving Therapy for Depression: Theory, Research and Clinical Guidelines.* New York: Wiley.

Nezu, A. M., Ronan, G. F., Meadows, E. A. & McClure, K. S. (2000). *Practitioner's Guide to Empirically Based Measures of Depression.* New York: Plenum.

Orne, M. T. (1965). Martin Orne's article 'Psychological factors maximizing resistance to stress with special reference to hypnosis. In: S. Klausner (Ed.), *The Quest for Self-Control.* New York: Free Press.

Orne, M. T. (1962). Psychological factors in maximizing self-control under stress with special reference to hypnosis and related states. Washington: Bureau Of Social Science Research Inc.

Orne, M. T. & Wender, P. H. (1968). Anticipatory socialization for psychotherapy: method and rationale. *American Journal of Psychiatry, 124*: 1202–1212.

Ornstein, R. (1977). *The Psychology of Consciousness.* New York: Harcourt Brace Jovanovich.

Osborn, A. (1952). *Wake up your Mind.* New York: Charles Scribner's Sons.

Öst, L. -G. (1987). Applied Relaxation: Description of a coping technique and review of controlled studies. *Behaviour Research & Therapy, 25*: 397–409.

Öst, L. -G., Sterner & Fellenius. (1989). Applied tension, applied relaxation, and the combination in the treatment of blood phobia. *Behaviour Research & Therapy, 27*: 109–121.

Park, L. C. & Covi, U. (1965). Nonblind placebo trial: An exploration of neurotic patients' responses to placebo when its inert content is disclosed. *The Archives of General Psychiatry, 12*: 336–345.

Persons, J. B. (2008). *The Case Formulation Approach to Cognitive-Behavior Therapy.* Guilford Press: New York.

Persons, J. B. & Davidson, J. (2001). Cognitive Behavioral Case Formulation. In: K. S. Dobson (Ed.), *Handbook of Cognitive-Behavioral Therapies* (Second ed.). New York: Guildford Press.

Pietsch, W. V. (1990). *The Serenity Prayer Book.* New York: Harper Collins.

Platonov, K. (1959). *The Word as a Physiological & Therapeutic Factor: The Theory & Practice of Psychotherapy According to I.P. Pavlov.* Moscow: Foreign Language Publishing House.

Powers, M. B., Vörding, M. B. & Emmelkamp, P. M. (2009). Acceptance and Commitment Therapy: A Meta-analytic Review. *Psychotherapy and Psychosomatics, 78*: 73–80.

Pretzer, J. L. & Beck, A. T. (2007). Cognitive approaches to stress and stress management. In: P. M. Lehrer, R. L. Woolfolk & W. E. Sime (Eds.), *Principles and Practice of Stress Management* (Third ed.) (pp. 465–496). New York: Guilford.

Prochaska, J. & DiClemente, C. (1983). Stages and process of self-change of smoking: Toward an integrative model of change. *Journal of Consulting and Clinical Psychology, 51*: 390–395.

Rachman, S. (2004). *Anxiety* (Second ed.). Hove: Psychology Press.

Rachman, S. & Wilson, G. (1980). *The Effects of Psychological Therapy* (Second ed.). New York: Pergamon.

Raimy, V. (1975). *Misunderstandings of the Self: Cognitive Psychotherapy and the Misconception Hypothesis.* San Francisco: Jossy-Bass Publishers.

Robertson, D. J. (2005, July). Stoicism: A lurking presence. *Counselling & Psychotherapy Journal (CPJ).*

Robertson, D. J. (2009). The discovery of hypnosis - Braid's lost manuscript, "On Hypnotism" (1860): A brief communication. *The International Journal of Clinical & Experimental Hypnosis, 57*: 127–132.

Robertson, D. J. (2010). *The Philosophy of Cognitive-Behavioural Therapy (CBT): Stoic Philosophy as Rational & Cognitive Psychotherapy.* London: Karnac.

Robichaud, M. & Dugas, M. J. (2006). A cognitive-behavioral treatment targeting intolerance of uncertainty. In: G. C. Davey & A. Wells (Eds.), *Worry and Its Disorders: Theory, Assessment and Treatment.* Chichester: Wiley.

Roemer, L. & Orsillo, S. M. (2009). *Mindfulness & Acceptance-Based Behavioural Therapies in Practice.* Guilford: New York.

Rokke, P. D. & Rehm, L. P. (2001). Self-management therapies. In: K. S. Dobson (Ed.), *Handbook of Cognitive-Behavioral Therapies* (Second ed) (pp. 173–211). New York: Guilford.

Rosqvist, J. (2005). *Exposure Treatments for Anxiety Disorders.* New York: Routledge.

Roth, A. & Fonagy, P. (2005). *What Works for Whom? A Critical Review of Psychotherapy Research* (Second ed.). New York: Guilford.

Rouf, K., Fennell, M., Westbrook, D., Cooper, M. & Bennett-Levy, J. (2004). Devising effective behavioural experiments. In: J. Bennett-Levy, G. Butler, M. Fennell, A. Hackman, M. Mueller & D. Westbrook (Eds.), *Oxford Guide to Behavioural Experiments in Cognitive Therapy* (pp. 21–58). Oxford: Oxford University Press.

Russell, B. (1930). *The Conquest of Happiness.* Padstow: Routledge.

Ryle, G. (1949). *The Concept of Mind.* Hutchinson's University Library.

Safran, J. D., Segal, Z. V., Vallis, T. M., Shaw, B. F. & Samstag, L. W. (1993). Assessing patient suitability for short-term cognitive therapy with an interpersonal focus. *Cognitive Therapy and Research, 17*: 23–38.

Salkovskis, P. (1991). The importance of behaviour in the maintenance of anxiety and panic: a cognitive account. *Behavioural Psychotherapy, 19*: 6–19.

Salovey, P. & Singer, J. A. (1991). Cognitive behavior modification. In: F. H. Kanfer & A. P. Goldstein (Eds.), *Helping People Change: A Textbook of Methods* (pp. 361–395). New York: Pergamon.

Salter, A. (1941). Three techniques of autohypnosis. *Journal of General Psychology, 24*: 423–428.

Salter, A. (1949). *Conditioned Reflex Therapy* (2002 Anniversary ed.). Gretna: Wellness Institute Ltd.

Sanders, D. & Wills, F. (2005). *Cognitive Therapy: An Introduction* (Second ed.). London: Sage.

Sarbin, T. R. (1950). Contributions to role-taking theory: I. Hypnotic behavior. *Psychological Review, 57*: 255–270.

Sarbin, T. R. (1989). The construction and reconstruction of hypnosis. In: N. P. Spanos & J. F. Chaves, *Hypnosis: The Cognitive-Behavioral Perspective.* New York: Prometheus.

Sarbin, T. R. & Coe, W. C. (1972). *Hypnosis: A Social Psychological Analysis of Influence Communication.* New York: Holt, Rinehart & Winston.

Saunders, T., Driskell, J. E., Johnston, J. H. & Salas, E. (1996). The effect of stress inoculation training on anxiety and performance. *Journal of Occupational Health Psychology, 1*: 170–186.

Schoenberger, N., Kirsch, I., Gearan, P., Montgomery, G. & Pastyrnak, S. (1997). Hypnotic enhancement of a cognitive-behavioural treatment for public speaking anxiety. *Behavior Therapy, 28*: 127–140.

Shapiro, F. (1997). *EMDR: The Breakthrough "Eye Movement" Therapy for Overcoming Anxiety, Stress, and Trauma.* New York: Basic Books.

Singer, J. L. (1974). *Imagery & Daydream Methods in Psychotherapy & Behaviour Modification.* New York: Academic Press.

Skinner, B. (1971). *Beyond Freedom & Dignity.* Cambridge, MA: Hacket.

Skinner, B. (1974). *About Behaviorism.* New York: Vintage Books.
Snaith, P. R. (1974). A method of psychiatry based on relaxation techniques. *British Journal of Psychiatry, 124:* 473–481.
Snaith, P. R. (1981). *Clinical Neurosis.* Oxford: Oxford Medical Publications.
Spanos, N. P. (1996). *Multiple Identities & False Memories: A Sociocognitive Perspective.* Washington, DC: American Psychological Association.
Spanos, N. P. & Chaves, J. F. (Eds.). (1989). *Hypnosis: The Cognitive-Behavioural Perspective.* New York: Prometheus Books.
Spiegel, H. & Spiegel, D. (1978). *Trance and Treatment: Clinical uses of Hypnosis.* New York: Basic Books.
Spinhoven, P., Van Dyck, R., Hoogduin, K. & Schaap, C. (1991). Differences in hypnotizability of Dutch psychiatric outpatients according to two different scales. *Australian Journal of Clinical and Experimental Hypnosis, 19:* 107–116.
Spivack, G., Platt, J. J. & Shure, M. B. (1976). *The Problem-Solving Approach to Adjustment.* San Francisco: Jossey-Bass.
Stanislavski, C. (1963). *An Actor's Handbook.* New York: Theatre Art Books.
Stern, R. & Drummond, L. (1991). *The Practice of Behavioural and Cognitive Psychotherapy.* Cambridge: Cambridge University Press.
Stewart, D. (1827). *Elements of the Philosophy of the Human Mind.*
Still, A. & Dryden, W. (1999). The Place of Rationality in Stoicism and REBT. *Journal of Rational-Emotive & Cognitive-Behavior Therapy, 17:* 143–164.
Straus, R. A. (1982). *Strategic Self-Hypnosis.* Lincoln: to Excel Press.
Sutcliffe, J. (1960). "Credulous" and "skeptical" views of hypnotic phenomena: A review of certain evidence and methodology. *International Journal of Clinical & Experimental Hypnosis, 8:* 73–101.
Tosi, D. J. & Baisden, B. S. (1984). Cognitive-experiential therapy and hypnosis. In: W. C. Wester & J. Alexander H. Smith (Eds.), *Clinical Hypnosis: A Multidisciplinary Approach* (pp. 155–178). Philadelphia: J.B. Lippincott.
Turk, D. C., Meichenbaum, D. & Genest, M. (1983). *Pain and Behavioral Medicine: A Cognitive-Behavioural Perspective.* New York: Guilford Press.
Ullmann, L. P. & Krasner, L. (1969). *A Psychological Approach to Abnormal Behavior.* New Jersey: Prentice Hall.
Vygotsky, L. S. (1978). *Mind in Society: The Development of Higher Psychological Processes.* Massachusetts: Harvard University Press.
Weitzenhoffer, A. M. (1972). Behavior Therapeutic Techniques & Hypnotherapeutic Methods. *The American Journal of Clinical Hypnosis, 15:* 71–82.
Weitzenhoffer, A. M. (2000). *The Practice of Hypnotism* (Second ed.). New York: John Wiley & Sons.
Weitzenhoffer, A. & Hilgard, E. (1962). *Stanford Hypnotic Susceptibility Scale: Form C.* Palo Alto, CA: Consulting Psychologists Press.
Wells, A. (2009). *Metacognitive Therapy for Anxiety and Depression.* New York: Guilford.
Westbrook, D., Kennerley, H. & Kirk, J. (2007). *An Introduction to Cognitive Behaviour Therapy: Skills and Applications.* London: Sage.
White, R. W. (1941). A preface to the theory of hypnotism. *Journal of Abnormal & Social Psychology, 24:* 477–505.
Wierzbicki, M. (1984). Social skills deficits and subsequent depressed mood in students. *Personality and Social Psychology Bulletin, 10:* 605–610.
Wolberg, L. R. (1948a). *Medical Hypnosis* (Vol. 1). New York: Grune & Stratton.

Wolberg, L. R. (1948b). *Medical Hypnosis* (Vol. 2). New York: Grune & Stratton.
Wolpe, J. (1954). Reciprocal inhibition as the main basis of psychotherapeutic effects. *Archives of Neurology & Psychiatry, 72*: 205–226.
Wolpe, J. (1958). *Psychotherapy by Reciprocal Inhibition.* Stanford, CA: Stanford University Press.
Wolpe, J. (1990). *The Practice of Behavior Therapy (Fourth Edition).* New York: Pergamon.
Wolpe, J. & Lazarus, A. A. (1966). *Behavior Therapy Techniques: A Guide to the Treatment of Neuroses.* Long Island City, NY: Pergamon.
Yapko, M. D. (2010). Hypnotically catalyzing experiential learning across treatments for depression: actions can speak louder than moods. *The International Journal for Clinical & Experimental Hypnosis, 58*: 186–201.
Zimmerman, M. (1994). *Interview Guide for Evaluating DSM-IV Psychiatric Disorders & the Mental State Examination.* East Greenwich, RI: Psych Products Press.

INDEX

abbreviated tension-release relaxation 259
ABC (affect, behaviour, cognition) 152–154, 181,
  185, 188, 259, 346
  activation-beliefs-consequences 156
  diagram 142, 156, 185
  distinction 153
  functional analysis 155
  model 259, 346
  thoughts/autosuggestions 75, 181
  three/four systems 152
  three-systems (ABC) conceptualisation 152
ABC conceptualisation diagram 12, 188
ABCDE model 154
acceptance and commitment therapy (ACT) 266
acting and muscular suggestion 91–92
activation-beliefs-consequences (ABC) model
  156–157
active experiments 393
Active Psychotherapy 277
active-alert hypnosis 96
active-positive
  responders 95
  responses 94
acute stress disorder (ASD) 16
ADAPT acronym 321
adaptive cognitive-behavioural responses 407

affect bridge regression 398
age progression 24, 312, 348–349, 353, 404–405
age regression 93, 349, 398, 404, 411
agreement on therapy
  goals 120
  tasks 120
Alladin, Assen 17, 23–24, 29, 143, 355, 408
all-or-nothing thinking (dichotomous thinking)
  340, 385–386, 389
altered state of consciousness 7–8, 17, 46, 81–85,
  103, 110, 113, 183, 188, 192, 208
alternative cognitions and behaviour
  ("alternative therapy") 388–389
anatomy of expression 67–68
animal magnetism 32, 34–41, 112
antecedents-behaviour-consequences (ABC)
  diagram, 155
anti-anxiety medication 178
anticipatory socialisation 181, 184
anti-depressive pathways 17
anxiety control training (ACT) 260
anxiety-management and exposure 297–298
anxiety-producing
  experiment 381
  imagery 250, 261, 305, 410
  images or memories 396

432   INDEX

  scene 152, 291
  situations 178, 280, 389, 405
anxious mind-set 11
application and generalisation 219
application (exposure) and generalisation phase 253–257
  maintenance of improvement 256–257
applied dehypnosis 257, 266, 271
  (mindfulness and acceptance) 266–273
applied dehypnosis script, example 271–273
applied hypnotic relaxation 257, 259–261, 264, 305
  overview of 259–261
applied hypnotic relaxation script
  example 264–266
applied mindfulness
  overview of 266
applied self-hypnosis (ASH) 215, 218, 220–224, 226, 228, 230–233, 235, 243–245, 247, 251, 253, 257, 305, 363, 402, 414
applied self-hypnosis process goals 222–224
appraisal of probability 181, 380
arm-levitation 104–105, 193, 196, 205, 278
  induction 278
Aroaz, Daniel 94
artificial somnambulism 35, 48, 52, 201
assess strengths & risks 144
assessment, conceptualisation, and hypnotic skills 117
assessment, conceptualisation, and socialisation 211, 218, 224–230, 416
associated imagery 398
attribution (causal conceptualisation) 116
automatic behavioural responses 172, 175–176
automatic fear response 171, 176, 181
automatic negative thoughts 14, 266, 355, 357, 377–378, 380, 412, 415
automatic physiological responses 174–175
automatic thoughts and images 173–174, 225, 307, 373, 408
automaticity 106–107, 237, 415–416
autonomous fantasies 395
autosuggestions 11–12, 25–27, 33, 54, 71, 75, 80, 115, 150, 174, 176, 181, 186–188, 198, 201, 207, 218, 221, 229, 233, 240, 242–245, 247, 249–253, 257, 260–261, 276, 345–347, 357, 371–373, 376–377, 401, 416

avoidance behaviour in anxiety 178
avoidance & safety-seeking 177–179
  behaviour 363
avoidance style (AS) 312
avoidance-reversal imagery 408–409
AWARE 233, 267, 282, 293, 297, 365–366, 368–372
  strategy 267, 293, 297

Bandura's influential theory of "self-efficacy" 361
Barber, T. X. 6–10, 17–18, 21, 23, 26, 40, 50, 68, 71, 82–83, 86, 92–96, 104, 107, 120–121, 190–191, 194, 206, 210, 250, 260, 325, 372, 415
  attitudes 10
  cognitive-behavioural theory 92–96
basic rationale for exposure 278–280
battle with mesmerism 38
Baudouin, Charles 152, 249
Beck, Aaron T. 5, 145, 215
  anxious "vulnerability" 169
  classic eye-fixation induction 205
  cognitive model of anxiety 159, 330
  cognitive model of depression 142
  cognitive reconceptualisation of behavioural treatment 299
  cognitive therapy 5, 26, 174, 216, 255, 280, 325, 349, 355
  cognitive therapy approach to stress 390
  cognitive therapy for anxiety 151, 267, 355
  cognitive therapy for anxiety 392
  cognitive therapy for depression 314
  cognitive therapy in conjunction with hypnosis 273
  "cognitive triad" model 169
  concept of automatic thoughts 159
  conceptualisation 169
  conceptualisation of anxiety or Lazarus' model of stress 319
  current cognitive therapy for anxiety 282, 393
  current treatment approach for anxiety 398
  dual belief system in anxiety 360
  early cognitive therapy for anxiety 404
  early writings on cognitive therapy 266
  generic models of anxiety and stress 225
  "metacognitive" process 369
  model of anxiety 161
  negative "automatic thoughts" 33

original cognitive model of anxiety 165–170, 317
original cognitive therapy manual for anxiety 246, 288, 344, 364, 376
original manual for anxiety 273
original manual for the cognitive therapy of anxiety 412
original treatment manual for the cognitive therapy of depression 392
revised cognitive model of anxiety 170–181, 325
revised cognitive therapy approach to anxiety 379
revised cognitive therapy for anxiety disorders 355
revised cognitive therapy for GAD 326
revised conceptualisation 357
revised generic cognitive model of anxiety 367
simplified self-help approach 393
Beck anxiety inventory (BAI) 128, 372
Beck depression inventory (BDI) 128, 147
Beck depression inventory-II (BDI-II) 128
Beck, Judith 24, 142, 146, 159, 392, 397–399, 403, 406, 412
Beckian model of anxiety 325
behaviour therapy 4–5, 7, 9, 13–14, 16, 20, 22–23, 25, 34, 62, 86, 109, 150–151, 156, 215–216, 234, 238, 241–243, 249–250, 257, 275–279, 284, 289, 294, 297–298, 303–305, 315, 340, 352, 355, 359, 361, 373, 392, 395–397, 411
behavioural analysis 155, 227, 375
behavioural avoidance 171, 173, 175, 236, 281, 293, 296, 384
  escape and safety-seeking 293–295
behavioural coping responses 164, 170, 317
behavioural experiments and exposure 377, 392–395
behavioural exposure therapy 276–277, 356
behavioural hypnotherapy, imagery conditioning techniques in 407
behavioural inclinations 176, 225
behavioural learning theory 234, 305
behavioural psychology 4, 62, 85, 155, 191, 216, 276–277
behavioural responses to anxiety-provoking situations 405

behaviour-rehearsal imagery 396
Benson, Herbert 76
blood-injection-injury type phobias 175, 285, 287
borderline personality structure 131
Braid, James 3, 31
  cognitive-behavioural return to 113
  father of hypnotherapy 36–38
  hypnotic induction 50
  hypnotic therapy 73–79
  model of reciprocal cognitive-behavioural (ideo-motor) interaction 72
  "monoideo-dynamic" account of hypnotism 65
  morbid dominant ideas 176
  "muscular suggestion" technique 92
  original definition of hypnotism 395
  original hypnotherapy 31
  original hypnotism 33
  original psychological conceptualisation of hypnosis 9
  original theory and practice of hypnotism 31
  original theory of hypnotism 29, 111
  positive definition of hypnotism 33
  psycho-physiological account 189
  "psycho-physiological" theory of hypnotism 107
  theory of "reciprocal interaction" 115
  theory of hypnotism 43–50, 58
  theory of suggestion 60
  yogic meditation 40–42
Braid's neuro-hypnotism, summary 79–80
bread pills 59, 100
Breuer's concept of therapeutic "abreaction" 35
British Medical Journal (BMJ) 38
bucket and balloon 197, 210
Burns, David 332–333, 385

Carleton skills training program (CSTP) 12, 55, 191–195
Carpenter, William B. 3, 33–34, 42, 62–64, 73, 90, 106, 199
  ideo-motor reflex 42
case-level formulation 143–159
catastrophising 333, 360, 385–387, 389, 401–402
  script 402
challenge suggestions 210

Chapman, R. A. 119, 129, 141, 143
Chaves, John 6–7, 17–18, 23, 26, 40, 50, 68, 71, 82, 86, 93, 95, 107, 121, 206, 372
Chevreul's pendulum 73, 134, 197–199
chronological conceptualisations 148
Clarke J. C. 5, 46–47, 97–98, 109, 242, 279, 303–304, 401, 405, 407–408
classic suggestion effect 206, 252
client expectancies 133
client life-history form 135–139
Clinical Outcomes in Routine Evaluation Outcome Measure (CORE-OM) 128–129
cognition 13, 23, 31, 34, 54, 62, 72–74, 79–80, 91, 104–105, 111, 114, 127, 147, 151–154, 165, 216, 223, 243, 252, 259, 273, 300, 302, 346, 355, 376, 383, 394, 413
    cognitive hypnotherapy 355
    identifying cognitions and other responses 372–378
cognitive and behavioural 210
    responses 170
    strategies 12, 115, 190, 192–193, 272, 297
    therapies 9, 22–24, 120, 368
cognitive and emotional avoidance (experiential avoidance) 295–296
cognitive avoidance 165, 175, 180, 304, 326, 387
cognitive distortions 29, 172, 174, 225, 327, 333, 364–365, 377–378, 385–386, 396, 398
cognitive experiential therapy (CET) 154
cognitive hierarchy and levels of conceptualisation 158–159
cognitive hypnotherapy 17, 23, 186, 188, 347, 355, 408
cognitive interventions/treatment plan 364–365
cognitive model
    of action 85
    of anxiety 104, 159, 165–166, 168, 170, 172, 222, 293, 317, 325, 330, 357, 359, 361, 365, 367, 392
Cognitive Psychotherapy and the Misconception Hypothesis 410
cognitive reconceptualisation of hypnosis 9
cognitive rehearsal 23, 346–347, 376
cognitive set (hypnotic mind-set) 194–195, 197
cognitive suggestions 192, 195, 210
cognitive therapy and exposure 298–302

Cognitive Therapy and the Emotional Disorders 266
cognitive therapy for anxiety 24–25, 123, 151, 181, 267, 269, 275–276, 282, 288, 294, 298–299, 325, 333, 355–358, 361, 365–366, 368, 370, 378, 380, 389, 392–393, 404–406
Cognitive Therapy of Anxiety Disorders 29, 170, 356
cognitive therapy of depression 380, 385
cognitive-behaviour
    modification 216, 324
    ("nonstate") theories of hypnosis 80
    "response set" theory 211
    analysis 227, 375
    approach 1, 6, 12, 14, 16, 21, 23, 29, 40, 49, 55, 86, 94, 102, 115, 121, 165, 243, 251, 283, 356, 369, 398, 414
    case conceptualization 12, 22, 119
    conceptualisation 12, 98, 142. 149, 191, 222
    hypnotherapists 73, 153, 305, 365, 375, 403
    literature on hypnotherapy 279
    methodology 220
    models 75, 191
    position, early history of 85–87
    processes 15
    reconceptualisation 3, 12, 18, 29
    reconceptualisation of hypnosis 3, 12, 18, 29
    researchers 6, 31, 46, 193, 208, 325, 417
    skills training in hypnotherapy 196–202
    strategies 7, 192–194, 244
    theories of hypnosis 5, 10, 12, 14, 17, 28, 41, 55, 81, 86, 113, 191, 415–416
    theories of hypnosis 5, 10, 12, 17, 28, 41, 55, 81, 86, 113, 191, 252, 415–416
    theorists 3, 6, 9, 17, 83–84, 97, 115, 348, 395
    theory & skills training 190–196
    therapies 142, 216, 244, 391, 416–417
    tradition in hypnosis 5–6, 64, 85
    treatment strategies 356
    viewpoint and terminology 87
cognitive-behavioural approach, 94
    collaborative and transparent 102
    introduction to 3
    to hypnosis 1

cognitive-behavioural conceptualisation 12
    of hypnosis 98
cognitive-behavioural hypnotherapy 3–4, 14–16,
    21–22, 24–25, 28–29, 46, 119, 125, 128, 132,
    134, 141, 143, 148, 152, 154, 157, 165, 172, 181,
    183–184, 186–187, 211, 215, 242–243, 257–258,
    303, 306, 309, 357, 365–366, 376, 390, 395, 401,
    409–410, 415–416
    assessment 119–125
    case formulation in 141
    clinical research on 15–17
    dehypnosis" strategies in 28
    integration with Beck's cognitive therapy
        for anxiety 355
    mental imagery in 24–25
    overview of 29
    rationale for 21–23
    socialisation to 184–186
    structure and agenda for initial assessment
        session 125
    suitability for 132–134
    technique 409
    theory and practice of 416
cognitive-behavioural therapy (CBT) 3–5, 7, 31,
    33, 43–44, 61, 71, 80–81, 142, 165, 215–216, 239,
    244, 278–279, 311, 313, 350, 356, 359, 392, 418
    acceptance-based approaches to 282
    cognitive-behavioural hypnotherapy 376
    cognitive rehearsal or evocative imagery in
        376
    conceptualisation 155
    coping skills methodologies in 215
    for generalised anxiety disorder (GAD) 316
    development of 24
    disaster script 305
    imaginal exposure in 395
    mental imagery in 395
    mindfulness-based 26, 28
    mindfulness and acceptance-based 106, 232,
        289, 417
    of hypnosis 6, 23, 98
    problem-solving methodologies in 344
    self-monitoring forms 343
    socialisation in 184
    suicide risk assessment in 131

cognitive-behavioural theories of hypnosis 5, 10,
    12, 17–18, 28, 41, 81, 86
    Kirsch's 54
cognitive conceptualisation 156, 159, 185, 223, 299,
    307, 312, 326, 357
    of anxiety (worksheet) 181
Cognitive Hypnotherapy 17, 23, 143, 188, 347, 355, 408
    for depression 408
    model 186
cognitive model of anxiety 104, 159, 165–166, 168,
    170, 172, 222, 293, 317, 325, 330, 357, 359, 361,
    365, 367, 392
    simplified 172
cognitive-physiological-behavioural responses 170
cognitive restructuring 16, 163, 165, 215, 221, 223,
    231, 236, 256, 272, 301, 303, 315, 318, 326, 335,
    341, 352, 357, 365, 370, 378–391, 397, 399, 405,
    408, 410–414, 417
    in anxiety is socratic questioning 378
    of appraisal 381
collaborative conceptualisation 181
collaborative empiricism 22, 141
common sense response 208
co-morbidity 132
compassionate trance-state 8
competing behavioural responses 297
comprehensive case conceptualisation 172
comprehensive cognitive-behavioural framework
    215
comprehensive distancing 266
compulsive apologising 146, 377, 384
concentrative meditation 27, 42, 59
conceptualisation 3, 9, 11–12, 14, 22, 29, 31, 42, 44,
    63–64, 75, 96, 98, 105, 107, 113, 115–117, 119–
    120, 122–128, 141–150, 152, 154–160, 165–181,
    184–186, 188, 191, 211, 218–219, 223–231, 234,
    246–248, 257, 259, 278, 280, 299, 308, 312–313,
    317, 319, 326, 334, 345, 349, 355–357, 364–368,
    383, 392–393, 414, 416
    diagrams 142, 188
    of problem 126
    of secondary reappraisal in anxiety 177
    model 178
    relational/problem-solving model of stress
        317–319

working hypothesis 366–368
conditioned reflex therapy 4
confronting and handling stressor 247
confusional inductions 205
conscious autosuggestion 96, 99, 249
constructive narrative perspective (CNP) 252
constructive problem-solving behaviour 326
contemplative meditation 27, 29, 42, 59
conversion hysteria 13, 74
coping imagery 135, 203, 220, 223, 234, 243–244, 252, 254–255, 261, 288, 305, 309, 401, 405, 407
coping imagery/covert behaviour rehearsal 405–406
cost-benefit analysis 296, 308, 365, 383–385
Coué, Émile 5, 13–14, 74, 96, 99, 249
Council, James R. 54, 103–104, 109–111
covert behaviour rehearsal 405–406
covert modelling 4, 406
creative melting pot 23
creative problem
   solver 9, 228, 313
   solving agent 113, 115, 324
creative problem-solving attitude 347
   generalised 324
creative solution-generation 337

decatastrophising 180, 232, 236, 242, 252, 304, 323, 365, 378–379, 386–388, 399–403, 410, 412
   for worry 400
   script 402
decatastrophising imagery 242, 399–403
decatastrophising script 402
decatastrophising worst-case scenarios 401
decision-making (evaluation of alternative solutions) 338–339
deep unconscious associations 398
defensive/protective behaviours 175–176
dehypnosis 22, 25–29, 71, 106, 115, 188, 207, 218–219, 228, 233, 236, 242, 253, 257, 261, 266, 268–269, 271, 372, 376–377, 385, 402, 409, 414, 416
   mindfulness and acceptance-based strategies 236
dehypnosis skills-acquisition script (repeated review)
   example 269

deliberate coping responses 182
deliberate safety-cue processing 232
depressive disorders and symptoms 128
descriptive conceptualisations 148, 159
diagnosis and medication 129–130
diagnosis-specific conceptualisations 29
dichotomous thinking 386, 389
differential relaxation training 260
direct-suggestion hypnotherapy 19
disaster script 305
disputation and imagery 382–383
dissociative disorders 134
distancing, acceptance, and repeated review 269, 369–372
dominant ideas 13, 26, 32, 54, 58–59, 74, 90, 104, 108, 110, 112, 176, 190, 211
"dramaturgical" model of hypnosis 61
dual belief system 150, 166, 168, 360
   in anxiety 360
Dubois, Paul
   "rational persuasion" 23, 314
Dugas, Michel 161, 286, 312, 316, 326–327
dysfunctional attitudes scale (DAS) 372
dysfunctional cognitions 12, 392
dysfunctional thought record 378

early warning signs 218–219, 222, 226, 229, 231, 245, 247, 256, 259, 261, 327, 375, 408–409
eating disorders 134
Edmonston, William E. 77, 79, 84
ego strength 133, 327, 347, 352, 407
ego-strengthening
   hypnosis script 133
   suggestions 347, 407
   type scripts 327, 347
elaborative reappraisal 171, 176
Elements of the Philosophy of the Human Mind 69
Elliotson, John 38, 42
Ellis, Albert 5, 13–14, 23, 74–75, 154, 156, 185, 215, 217–218, 243, 303, 355, 359, 390, 409
embedding emotive imagery 304
emotional
   crutch 266
   fainting response 175, 286
   imagery 269
   reasoning 361, 385–386

emotion-focused
   and problem-focused coping strategies 318
      coping 160, 163, 177, 228, 231, 235–236, 317–319, 329
      coping strategies 163, 318, 329
      goal of reducing anxiety 334
empirical hypothesis testing 255, 300, 325, 364–365, 392–393
empirically supported treatment (EST) 17
Erickson, Milton 5, 18–21, 45, 96, 102, 205–206, 209
Ericksonian
      hypnosis 18–19, 206
      hypnotherapy 19
      "indirect suggestion" 20
      tradition in hypnotism 21
evidence-evaluation 365, 380–382
evocative imagery method 373, 375–376
expanding spaced exposure schedule 289
expectancy modification procedures 102
expectancy-related cognition 111
expectation 53–54
      related cognition 104
experiential avoidance 127, 180, 182, 217, 228, 258–259, 261, 264–265, 292, 295–296, 309, 366–367, 397, 409
exposure
      and response prevention 292–298
      as behavioural experiment 300–301
      cognitive-behavioural hypnotherapy 306
      factors in 292
      frequency, duration and latency of 289–291
exposure and desensitization, origin of 276
exposure and response prevention (ERP) therapy 29, 292
exposure scripts 305–306
externalisation 322
eye-fixation induction 18, 44, 52, 67–68, 108–109, 197, 199, 205, 211
eye-fixation technique 32, 197, 204
eye-movement desensitisation and reprocessing therapy (EMDR) 290
Eysenck, Hans 4, 34, 277, 294

fading voluntary compliance 194
fail safe mechanism 175
fantasy induction 376

Faria, Abbé de 43
favourable motivation 87, 113
fear imagery script 305, 306
flexible coping repertoire 221
Fludd, Robert 34
Folkman, Susan 159, 162–163, 165, 226
formal diagnosis 141, 144
formulation models 148
Franklin, Benjamin 35
free association techniques 398
French Academy of Sciences 35, 103
Freud's psychoanalytic theory 14, 75
Freudian psychoanalysis 4–5, 82
Fromm, Erika 202
functional analysis (ABC model) 155–156
functional impairment 132
future autobiography 337, 342, 348–349
      age progression 404–405

generalisation of improvement 217, 222, 255–256
generalised anxiety disorder (GAD) 145, 160, 179, 258, 284, 303, 312, 316, 326, 350, 356, 386, 390
      cognitive conceptualisation of 326
      pervasive vulnerability in 326
general-purpose creative coping strategy 316
generation of alternative solutions 334–338, 346
goal definitions 146–147, 319
goal elaboration 147–148
goal-directed fantasies 6, 115, 250–252
goals and agenda-setting 123–125
Goldfried's coping skills 305
good hypnotic subject 9, 18, 27, 88, 113–114, 201, 235, 416
goodness of fit hypothesis 163
graded hierarchy construction 151–152
Graeco-Roman Stoicism 390

habit-reversal 296–297
habit-reversal therapy 297
hand heaviness 197
hand levitation 197
Herzberg, Alexander
      active psychotherapy 277
hetero-hypnosis 17, 49, 183, 191, 202–203
hetero-hypnotic induction 184, 202–204
hetero-suggestion 54, 184

hierarchical cognitive conceptualisation 159
hierarchy construction 150–152, 285
Hilgard, Ernest 23, 82, 97, 134
    "neodissociation" theory of hypnosis 82
Hull, Clark, L. 4, 5, 85, 120, 200
human hibernation 44
Hypnosis & Relaxation: A Modern Verification of an Old Equation 77
Hypnosis & Suggestibility: An Experimental Approach 5, 85
hypnotic coma 45
hypnotic conditioning therapy 4
    decatastrophising technique 401
    deepeners 206
    "deepening" techniques 204–207
    desensitisation 4, 28, 264, 278, 305
    desensitization 277–278, 302–309
    experiences and behaviours 86
    generation of alternatives and decision-making 350–351
    imaginal exposure 303–304
    induction profile (HIP) 134
    induction technique 4, 8, 18, 37, 194
    mind-set 9–11, 95–96, 113–115, 133, 183, 194–195, 197, 236, 269, 415
    monotone 70
    "mood induction" technique 376
    orientation questionnaire 115–116
    phenomena 5, 8, 34, 51, 83, 92–93, 98, 110, 112, 203
    problem definition and formulation 349
    problem orientation 347–349
    "rational persuasion" psychotherapy 313
    responses 5–10, 82–89, 93–96, 102, 104, 106–107, 110, 113–116, 189, 191–193, 415–416
    responsiveness 12, 16–17, 55, 88, 95, 192, 206
    skills training 4, 12, 55, 73, 134, 181, 183, 191–193, 196–197, 201, 211, 215, 235, 243, 313, 369, 416–417
    solution implementation and verification 351–352
    statement 394
    suggestions 5, 8–12, 16, 18–19, 22, 26, 46, 75, 89, 107, 113–114, 184, 195, 204, 208, 210, 251, 260, 277, 314, 396
    susceptibility (hypnotisability) 133–134
    termination 208
    Therapeutics 42, 90, 108
    trance 3, 6–11, 17–18, 23, 32, 44–46, 80–89, 94, 103, 111, 113, 183, 194, 205, 207–208, 417
    triggers and cues 68
hypnotic exposure therapy 302
    affect 275–309
hypnotic relaxation skills-acquisition script example 261–264
hypothesis testing 255, 300, 302, 325, 364–365, 392–393

ideo-dynamic
    formulation 64
    response 73–74, 199, 416
    theory of hypnosis 65
ideo-motor
    reflex response 42, 176, 198
    response (IMR) 63, 72, 105, 193, 199, 209
    suggestions 210
    theory 33, 64
ideo-motor reflex (IMR) 3, 18, 42, 62–63, 104, 107, 176, 189, 198
    Carpenter's conceptualisation 63
    theory 104, 107
imagery and expectation 104
imagery-based recall techniques 218, 261, 373, 375–376
imaginal (covert) modelling 406–407
imaginal absorption 9, 27, 93, 97–98, 269
imaginal exposure 16, 22, 28, 135, 180, 260, 264, 269, 276–277, 281, 283–284, 287, 289–291, 294, 303–309, 316, 336, 351–352, 356, 379, 394–395, 400–401, 409–411, 413
imagination as muted role-taking 89–90
imagination theory 71
imaginative suggestions 19–20
immediate fear response 173–174
    conceptualisation 173
impulsivity/carelessness style (ICS) 312
indirect suggestion therapy 19
induced fantasies 395–396
influential metacognitive theory 28
intensity of exposure 287
interoceptive exposure and panic attacks 301–302

interpersonal cognitive problem solving (ICPS) 315
Interview Guide for Evaluating DSM-IV Psychiatric Disorders 123
intolerance of risk and of uncertainty 363
involuntariness 20, 105
irrational autosuggestion 13
irritable bowel syndrome (IBS) 15

Jackson, J. A. 5, 46–47, 97–98, 242, 279, 303–304, 355, 404–405, 407–408
Jacobson, Edmund 89
    progressive muscle relaxation 231, 259
James-Lange theory of emotion 62, 66
James, William 66
    method of behaviourally acting 62
Jones, Mary Cover 276, 278
Journal of Clinical & Experimental Hypnosis 32
jumping ahead in time (time projection) 403–404
juxtaposing anxiety 276–277, 305

Keep it Sweet and Simple (KISS) 322
Kirsch, Irving 4–5, 7–9, 12, 16, 19–20, 23, 28–29, 31, 40, 46, 54, 83–86, 98–99, 102–111, 115, 123, 131, 133–134, 174, 189, 191, 193, 198–199, 202–203, 205, 208, 211, 348–349, 357
    response expectancy 189
    theory 104

law of sympathy and imitation 55, 69–70, 90, 109, 192, 195
Lazarus, Arnold 25, 129, 397–398, 403
Lazarus, Richard, 159, 227, 317, 325, 357
    influential "relational" (or "transactional") model) of stress 317
    primary and secondary appraisal 325
    "transactional" model of stress 159–165, 230, 357
learned resourcefulness 216, 228
Leahy, Robert 131, 146, 276, 284–285, 307, 328
    productive worry 328
Lewis, Wolberg 4, 277
Lind, Jenny 69–70
longitudinal conceptualisation 148, 157–158
looming vulnerability 386, 407–408

Lynn, Steven Jay 5, 7, 9, 12, 19–20, 28–29, 31, 40, 46, 81, 84–86, 102–107, 113, 115, 123, 131, 134, 174, 191, 193, 198–199, 202–203, 205, 208, 211, 269, 348–349, 357
    "response set" theory 115

magical thinking 21
magnetic palms 195, 197–198, 204, 369
maladaptive anxiety 169, 279, 366
maladaptive defensive responses 171
Marks, Isaac 217, 232, 246, 257–258, 275, 277–278, 280–283, 288, 290–291, 293–294, 304, 307, 309, 313
    golden rules 282
Medical Hypnosis 4, 277–278, 313
meditation as dehypnosis 25–28
Meichenbaum's
    application of the soviet developmental research 245
    "aspirin" of stress management 233
    coping skills 311
    generic SIT treatment manual 220
    guided self-dialogue 231
    "self-instruction training" 23, 220
    sense 244
    SIT guidelines 223
    stress inoculation training (SIT) approach 314
Melges, Frederick 337, 348–349, 356, 404, 407
    future autobiography technique 337
    Time & the Inner Future 404
mental abstraction 9, 33, 38, 41, 43, 46, 59, 64, 76, 97, 109, 112
    monoideism 43–44
mental concentration 43, 57, 67, 76, 91, 112
mental imagery 5, 8–9, 14–15, 22–25, 44, 46, 60, 104, 135, 148, 153, 180, 186, 189, 191, 193, 198, 205, 207, 221, 239, 243, 250, 254, 257, 269, 273, 276, 284, 288, 295, 303–304, 306, 312, 322, 326, 339, 345–347, 355–357, 365, 371, 375–376, 382, 387, 395–413, 417
    in cognitive therapy 395–410
    spontaneous (automatic) 397–398
    techniques 14, 339, 357, 376, 405
mental physiology 42
mental rehearsal of coping skills 223, 264, 288
mental state examination (MSE) 123, 127, 130–131

Mesmer, Franz 34–35, 37–38, 103
mesmeric crises 34
mesmeric sleep 76
mesmerism 3, 31–45, 48, 56–57, 69, 71, 77, 94, 103, 110–112, 114, 417
metacognitions 54, 80, 114
metacognitive beliefs 13, 27, 378, 416
metacognitive level 266, 370
metacognitive model of hypnosis 113
"metacognitive" theory 11
mild-to-moderate phobic anxiety clients 151
mind-body dualism 73
mindfulness and acceptance-based strategies 211, 223, 228, 231, 236, 329
mindfulness meditation 25, 27–28, 224, 271, 416
mindfulness-based cognitive therapy (MBCT), 271
mineral magnetism 34
mini coping-plan 246–247
Misunderstandings of the Self 410
model hypnotic subjects 55, 195
modelling coping 407
modelling mastery 196, 407
modern neuro-psychology 42
modern-day behaviour therapy 250
Moll, Albert 13, 109–110
mono-ideism 43, 59, 64
monoideo-dynamic 64–65
 model 31
 theory 31
mood induction 186, 188, 198, 369, 376, 409
motivation for exposure 282–283
muscular suggestion 62, 65–68, 72, 80, 90–92, 193, 210–211, 252

neutral hypnosis 76–77, 79, 201–202
 two modes of 77–79
naturally-occurring exposure 280–281, 289
nearsightedness 385–386
negative "autosuggestion" 12–14, 74, 222
negative automatic thoughts 12–14, 25–27, 73–75, 168, 186, 207, 218, 229, 233, 242, 245, 261, 267, 282, 293, 319, 372, 375, 398, 408
negative problem orientation (NPO) 312, 316, 320, 324, 326–328, 352
negative reinforcement 155, 293
negative responses 94, 166

negative self-hypnosis (NSH) 11–13, 25, 27–28, 44, 157, 181, 185, 207, 218, 222, 233, 372, 395, 415–416
neobraidism 29, 31, 113
neo-dissociationist theory 23
neo-Ericksonian hypnosis script 206
neuro-hypnotism 31, 38, 43, 47, 64, 79
neuro-psychological theory 63
Neurypnology 32, 38, 43, 49–50, 55, 79, 90–91, 97
Noble, Daniel 63–64
non-blind placebo trial 100–102
nondeceptive mega-placebo 102
non-deceptive placebos 101
nonstate Braid 109
normalisation and socialisation 358–360
normalisation cue-cards 359, 379
normalising self-hypnosis 188–190

observation experiments 393
observational learning and role-taking 54–55
Observations on Trance or Human Hybernation 44
observing coping 406
observing mastery 406
obsessive-compulsive disorder (OCD) 132, 180, 258, 284, 292, 294
Occam's Razor 39
ordinariness 6, 93
Orne, Martin 184, 216, 253
Öst, Lars-Goran 78, 236, 244, 259–260, 291, 305

"paradoxical" therapy techniques 20
participant modelling 276, 406
passive responses 94
Pavlov, Ivan 4, 199
Pavlov's physiological theory of hypnotism 77
Pavlovian hypnotic psychotherapy 5
Pavlovian laboratories 202
performance anxiety 98, 220
personality factors 132–133
Persons, Jacqueline 119, 142–144, 159
 case conceptualisation 143
philosophical origins 185
physical sensations, catastrophic misinterpretations 175
placebo deepeners 206
placebo effect and response expectancy 98–109

planful problem-solving 318
Pollyanna variety 188
positive
    attitude 9, 86, 93, 120–121
    expectancy 121
    motivation 121
    problem orientation (PPO) 312, 320–330, 342, 347, 350, 352–353, 362
    psychological functioning 190
    self-instruction 251
post-hypnotic suggestions 195, 210
    traditionally-worded 210
posttraumatic stress disorder (PTSD), 15–16, 28, 149–150, 258, 284, 302–303
Practitioner's Guide to Empirically Based Measures of Anxiety 128
primary cognitive appraisal 160
problem definition 120, 125, 222, 240, 321–322, 329–334, 342, 345–347, 349–350
problem definition and formulation 321, 330–334, 342, 345–346, 349
problem domains 136, 330
problem formulation questions 332–333
problem list 125, 143–145, 148–149, 330
problem orientation (PO) 9–10, 161, 312, 316, 320–330, 333, 339, 342, 347–348, 350, 352–353, 362, 415
problem orientation evaluation 327
problem reduction 145, 373
problem-domain analysis form 330
problem-focused coping 160, 177, 228, 231, 235, 317–318, 319, 329
problem-solving
    ability 312, 316, 326, 336, 347
    and thought-spotting orientation 366
    attitude 241, 312, 321, 324, 327, 342, 347, 362
    coping attempts 343
    deficits 312, 315
    in hypnotherapy 314, 345–347
    methodology 222, 273, 313, 316–319, 344
    planning form 343–344
    self-evaluation questions 342
    skills (PSS) 146, 312, 315, 323, 326–328
    therapy and cognitive therapy 164
    therapy for primary care (PST-PC) 312
problem-solving confidence 325, 339, 348

ability 327
problem-solving model 221, 317–318, 325, 344
    of hypnosis 325
problem-solving therapy (PST) 29, 161–162, 164–165, 227, 241, 311–316, 327, 332, 340, 344–346, 362, 388
    concept of developing a positive "problem orientation" 161
    methodology of 362
problem-solving hypnotherapy (PSH)
    behaviour 311, 313
    example treatment plan 342–344
progressive relaxation and autogenic training 89
pseudo-problems 333
psychiatric diagnoses 132, 143
psycho-education 128, 190, 218, 227, 234, 365–366
    and socialisation 365–372
    self-monitoring 365
psychological disorders 134, 396
psychological mindedness 133
Psychological Stress and the Coping Process 159
psychopathology 5, 12, 14, 21, 33, 73–75, 104, 110, 315–316, 376, 395–396, 416
psycho-physiological conceptualisation of hypnotism 31
psycho-physiology 31, 34, 36, 68, 71, 73, 91, 108
psycho-somatic problems 75
Psychotherapy by Reciprocal Inhibition 278

quasi-Freudian theories 32
quick reappraisal of threat & vulnerability 334

Raimy, Victor 236, 268–269, 288, 290, 295, 365, 370–371, 376, 410–413
    emotional review method 376, 411
    imagery review 411
    repeated cognitive review 410–414
randomised controlled trials (RCTs) 15, 19, 99, 133
rapid cue-controlled relaxation 222, 259–260
rate problem orientation 327
rational-emotive behaviour therapy (REBT) 13–14, 154, 156, 185, 217, 303, 355, 359, 373, 390, 397, 409
    Ellis' 217, 303, 355, 359, 409

rational problem solving (RPS) 247, 257, 312, 321, 323, 328, 331, 352
rational problem-solving style 321, 331, 352
rational reappraisal 180, 182
rational stage directed hypnotherapy (RSDH) 154
rational-emotive imagery& emotional dial 409–410
rational-emotive psychotherapy 13, 74
readiness to change 133
"realist" philosophy 36
realistic appraisal of threat probability and severity 359–361
realistic appraisals of coping ability 361–363
realistic appraisals of safety signs 363–364
reality-testing the image/reducing the threat 398–399
reappraisal of threat and coping 160, 177, 180–181
reciprocal inhibition of anxiety 413
reciprocal psycho-physiology 71
re-evaluation of relevant goals and values 389–390
regression hypnotherapy 35, 346, 376
relapse-prevention strategies 256
relaxation-based inductions and deepeners 206
relaxation response 76, 260
relaxation skills training 231, 233
relaxation techniques 152, 205, 218, 222, 233, 257–261, 346, 351
    criticisms of 257–259
repeated cognitive review (Raimy) 410–414
response "blocking" and habit-reversal 296–297
response expectancy 10, 27, 54–55, 98, 102–104, 107, 109, 111, 113, 116, 174, 189, 193, 205, 269, 416
    theory 102
response prevention 29, 236, 285, 292–298, 307, 323, 328, 335, 356, 363, 383
response sets 86, 106, 174
    social cognitive theory of preparatory 106
response systems 152
responsibility pie-chart 390
reviewing imagery 376
rigid arm-catalepsy 197
risk and contra-indications 131
risk-resources equation 159
role-involvement 6, 86, 88, 90–92, 97, 205, 238

role-modelling 61, 195–196, 241, 304
role-taking ability 87–89, 239
Rotter's social learning theory 102
Russell, Bertrand 400

safety, overlooking genuine signs 363
safety-seeking behaviours 156, 178–179, 217, 236, 280, 284, 287, 292, 294, 299, 309, 319, 335, 358, 363, 368–369, 371
safety-seeking strategies 288, 293, 363
Salter, Andrew 4
Sarbin's
    early socio-cognitive theory 11, 98
Sarbin, Theodore 85
    role-taking 87–92
    sense of intense role-involvement 88
scene-within-a-scene technique 304
schema of hypnosis 11
schema-related appraisals 225
Schultz, Johannes 89, 260–261
Scottish "Common Sense" 3, 36
secondary appraisal 155, 160–163, 167, 176, 225, 317, 325, 374, 379
secondary cognitive appraisal 160
selective abstraction 385–386
self-confidence 9, 44, 55, 74, 90, 114, 159, 169, 190, 223, 252–253, 325–326, 336, 347, 361–362
self-confirming expectancy disorders 174
self-efficacy scales 150
self-hypnosis
    and autosuggestion 49, 63, 257
    and coping skills 215, 305
    process goals 222–224
    training 73, 232, 244, 251, 253, 260
self-hypnotic
    desensitisation script 264
    relaxation routine 260
self-hypnotism 40–41, 56
    and meditation 55
self-hypnotising 6
self-instruction
    and autosuggestion 249–253
    training 23, 231, 236, 241, 242, 244–246, 250, 324, 341, 343, 350, 352
self-limiting nature of anxiety 280
self-magnetism 36, 40

self-monitoring and awareness training 261, 268–269, 376–378
self-monitoring record 226, 397
severity of symptoms 126, 132
sexual fantasy 189
sexual metaphor 190
silent willing 36, 55
simplification 145, 322–323
situational exposure 283–284, 287, 301–302
situation-specific cognitive responses 317
skills acquisition and rehearsal 218, 230–236
sleep-relaxation suggestions 79, 97
slowing-down and freezing imagery 407–408
SMART 144, 146, 331–332, 342
    goal-setting 345–346
social effectiveness 100
social problem-solving 311–312, 317–318
    inventory-revised (SPSI-R) 312
social problem-solving therapy 314
social role-taking model 87
socialisation and hypnotic skills training 183
socialisation to exposure-based therapy 280–283
socialisation to hypnotherapy, mood induction 186–190
socially-constructed role-definition 11
socio-cognitive theory 11
    of hypnosis 55
socio-demographic variables 132
Socratic irony 122
socratic questioning and guided discovery 374–375
solution implementation & verification 341
solution implementation and verification 321, 340–345, 351
solving life's problems 313, 349
Soviet psychotherapy 4
Spaghetti Junction 142
Spanos, Nicholas 6–8, 12, 17–18, 23, 26, 40, 50, 55, 68, 71, 82–83, 86, 93, 95, 104, 107, 121, 191–193, 196, 206, 215, 250, 372
    socio-cognitive approach to hypnotism 193
speech inhibition 201, 206
spontaneous autosuggestion and psychopathology 73–76
spontaneous negative self-suggestions 357

standard cognitive therapy
    for anxiety 325, 406
    strategies 267
Stanford Hypnotic Susceptibility Scale 97, 134
Stanislavski system 88
state versus nonstate argument 82–85, 191
Stewart, Dugald 36–37, 39, 69
sticking plaster 361
stimulus-response manner 93
stoic hypothesis 390
stoic philosophy & cognitive-behavioural hypnotherapy 390
Strasberg, Lee "method acting" 65, 88
strategic behavioural coping 177
Stress Appraisal and Coping 159
stress immunisation 217, 232
stressful and anxiety-provoking 223
stress-inoculation training (SIT) 29, 165, 215–221, 227, 233, 254, 261, 401
    essential ingredient of 230
    recent meta-analysis of 220
    research on 219–220
subjective rating of disturbance (SUD) 264, 291
subjective units of disturbance (SUD) scale 150
subsequent autosuggestions 260
subsequent sessions, typical agenda for 134
sucking a lemon (Pavlov's dogs) 199
suggestion-relevant imagery 191
suicidal ideation 131, 145
suitability for short-term cognitive therapy (SSCT) 132
SWOT analysis 144, 314
symptom-reduction strategy 288
symptom-relief strategies 267
systematic desensitisation 4, 23, 25, 86, 151, 216, 234, 244, 254, 257–259, 277–278, 283, 287, 290–291, 305, 309, 362, 395, 411
systematic exposure-based therapy 276

taking psychological risks 408
target internal cognitive 283
TEAM (trust, expectations, attitude, motivation) 121
tension-release training 260
The Anxiety & Worry Workbook 356
The Conquest of Happiness 400

The Discovery of Hypnosis 32
The Human Body 47
The Integrative Power of Cognitive Therapy 21
The Theory of Moral Sentiments 69
The Worry Cure 328
therapeutic relationship 120, 279
thinking errors 173–174, 370, 378, 385
thought suppression 165, 180, 292, 298, 329
thought-control, anxiety-management and exposure 297–298
threat and vulnerability schemas 168, 299, 305, 379
threat appraisal versus thought content 379–380
three deep breaths 197–198, 206, 247, 263–264
three/four systems (ABC model) 152–159
three-minute breathing space (3MBS) 271
three-stage model of anxiety 170–171, 325
three-systems (ABC) conceptualisation 152–155
time-expansion imagery 407
trance-induction hypothesis 17
transcendental mesmerism of the mesmerists 40
trans-diagnostic conceptualisation 170
treatment rationale (tasks and goals) 368–370
trial-and-error learning 12, 195
true hypnosis 84

unconscious mind 10, 21, 32, 96, 184, 206, 209, 250, 415
unconscious muscular movements 62, 104
unhelpful coping and safety-seeking 236
unproductive worry 326–329

verbal suggestion and voice tonality 70–71
Victorian
    autosuggestion concept 75
    "Common Sense" academic psychology, 112
    conceptualisation of hysteria 75
    hypnotherapy 13
    hypnotists' theory of "hysterical" autosuggestion 75
    nostrum remedies 34–36, 112
    philosophical psychology 3
    philosophy and psychology 62
    school of hypnotic psychotherapy 13
visualisation 22, 89, 239, 290, 312, 322, 326, 345–346, 349, 353, 405, 410

waking suggestion 85, 93, 97, 100, 102, 110, 112, 203
Watson, J. B. 276
Ways of Coping Questionnaire 164
Weitzenhoffer, Andre 4, 64–65, 86, 134
White, Robert W. 6, 53, 61, 85–86, 151, 335, 369, 386
Wilkinson, J. J. G. 47–48, 70, 76, 190
Wolberg, L. R. 4, 277–278, 305, 313–314
    earlier behavioural hypnotherapy technique 278
    "SWOT analysis" 314
Wolpe, Joseph 4, 14, 25, 69, 86, 151, 216, 234, 254, 257, 259, 277–278, 290–291, 303–305, 309, 395, 411
    passive stimulus-response approach 234
    systematic desensitisation 216, 254, 259, 277, 304
working alliance in psychotherapy 120, 146
working hypothesis 124, 128, 141, 143–144, 307, 345, 365–368
worry and thought-control 179–180
worry decision tree 329–330

Yapko, Michael 24, 350